CHRISTIAN DEMOCRACY A
OF EUROPEAN L

This is a major new study of the role of European Christian democratic parties in the making of the European Union. Based on extensive
archival research, it radically reconceptualises European integration in
long-term historical perspective as the outcome of partisan competition
of political ideologies and parties and their guiding ideas for the
future of Europe. Wolfram Kaiser takes a comparative approach to
political Catholicism in the nineteenth century, Catholic parties in
interwar Europe and Christian democratic parties in postwar Europe
and studies these parties' cross-border contacts and coordination of
policy-making. He shows how well-networked party elites, by intensifying their cross-border communication and coordinating their
political tactics and policy-making in government, ensured that the
origins of European Union were predominately Christian democratic,
with considerable long-term repercussions for the present-day EU.
This is a major contribution to the new transnational history of
Europe and to the history of European integration.

WOLFRAM KAISER is Professor of European Studies at the School of
Social, Historical and Literary Studies, University of Portsmouth.

NEW STUDIES IN EUROPEAN HISTORY

Edited by

PETER BALDWIN, University of California, Los Angeles
CHRISTOPHER CLARK, University of Cambridge
JAMES B. COLLINS, Georgetown University
MIA RODRÍGUEZ-SALGADO, London School of Economics
and Political Science
LYNDAL ROPER, University of Oxford

The aim of this series in early modern and modern European history is to publish outstanding works of research, addressed to important themes across a wide geographical range, from southern and central Europe, to Scandinavia and Russia, from the time of the Renaissance to the Second World War. As it develops the series will comprise focused works of wide contextual range and intellectual ambition.

For a full list of titles published in the series, please see the end of the book.

CHRISTIAN DEMOCRACY AND THE ORIGINS OF EUROPEAN UNION

WOLFRAM KAISER

University of Portsmouth

CAMBRIDGE UNIVERSITY PRESS
Cambridge, New York, Melbourne, Madrid, Cape Town, Singapore,
São Paulo, Delhi, Dubai, Tokyo, Mexico City

Cambridge University Press
The Edinburgh Building, Cambridge CB2 8RU, UK

Published in the United States of America by Cambridge University Press, New York

www.cambridge.org
Information on this title: www.cambridge.org/9780521173971

© Wolfram Kaiser 2007

First published 2007
Reprinted 2009
First paperback edition 2011

A catalogue record for this publication is available from the British Library

ISBN 978-0-521-88310-8 Hardback
ISBN 978-0-521-17397-1 Paperback

To Falk, Finja and Fleming

Contents

Acknowledgements

In the course of this project with its time-consuming research in some twenty-five archives in nine countries I have received generous support from many institutions and colleagues. I am especially grateful to the staff in all archives as well as to the British Arts and Humanities Research Council (BRL/AN10605/APN17931), the British Academy (SG-34679) and the Austrian Fonds zur Förderung der wissenschaftlichen Forschung (P12089-SOZ) for funding my research for this book at various stages. I would like to thank my CUP editor Michael Watson and copy-editor David Watson for excellent cooperation. I am indebted to colleagues too numerous to list in full, for stimulating discussions and insights, among them two anonymous referees and (in alphabetical order) John Boyer, Christopher Clark, Martin Conway, Anne Deighton, Jürgen Elvert, Robert Frank, Emiel Lamberts, Brigitte Leucht, Piers Ludlow, Geir Lundestad, Mikael af Malmborg (†), Alan S. Milward, Andrew Moravcsik, Guido Müller, Jürgen Osterhammel, Morten Rasmussen, Berthold Rittberger, Frank Schimmelfennig, Katja Seidel, Guido Thiemeyer, Antonio Varsori, Alex Warleigh and Pascaline Winand. My special thanks go to (also in alphabetical order) Heinz Duchardt, Richard J. Evans, Michael Gehler, Rainer Hudemann, Wilfried Loth, William Paterson, Georges-Henri Soutou and Helmut Wohnout for their additional contribution to ensuring at various points that I could continue to pursue my academic interests instead of having to earn my living as a taxi driver or gardener. I am particularly indebted to Werner Abelshauser for his surreal attempt at turning me into a gardener, thus stimulating my emigration at the most propitious point in time without negatively affecting my love of cultivating flowers and vegetables, which I enjoy immensely.
My wife Susanne may sometimes have been tempted to reduce me to the gardening role, combined with sole responsibility for our household. It would have made it so much easier for her to comply with her company's ridiculous expectation that its employees have an empty life of boundless

flexibility devoted to the death to increasing its shareholder value. I am not only grateful for her willingness to suppress this secret desire, but also for her enormous contribution, sometimes beyond the point of exhaustion, to sustaining our family. In these often strenuous conditions, I am, and always will be, grateful to our three wonderful children, Falk, Finja and Fleming, for reminding us with every one of their laughs and fits of rage what really counts in life. It is to them, who were born in the course of the research for this project, that I would like to dedicate this book.

Portsmouth, February 2007

Abbreviations

ACW/LNTC	Algemeen Christelijk Werkersverbond / Ligue Nationale des Travailleurs Chrétiens (Belgium)
ARP	Anti-Revolutionary Party (Netherlands)
BDI	Bundesverband der deutschen Industrie (Germany)
BVP	Bayerische Volkspartei / Bavarian People's Party (Germany)
CAP	Common Agricultural Policy
CD [Group]	Christian Democratic Group (in the European Parliament)
CDA	Christian Democratic Appeal (Netherlands)
CDU	Christlich-Demokratische Union / Christian Democratic Union (Germany)
CHN	Christliche Nothilfe (Switzerland)
CHU	Christian-Historical Union (Netherlands)
CIA	Central Intelligence Agency (United States)
CNPF	Conseil National du Patronat Français (France)
COPA	Committee of Professional Agricultural Organisations
CSU	Christlich-Soziale Union / Christian Social Union (Bavaria / Germany)
CSV	Christian Social People's Party (Luxembourg)
CVP/PSC	Christelijke Volkspartij / Parti Social Chrétien (Belgium)
CWI	Catholic Workers' International
DC	Democrazia Cristiana (Italy)
DDP	Deutsche Demokratische Partei / German Democratic Party
DFG	Deutsch-Französische Gesellschaft / German-French Society
DGB	Deutscher Gewerkschaftsbund / German Trade Union Congress

DNVP	Deutsch-Nationale Volkspartei / German National People's Party
DVP	Deutsche Volkspartei / German People's Party
EC	European Communities
ECJ	European Court of Justice
ECSC	European Coal and Steel Community
EDC	European Defence Community
EDU	European Democratic Union
EEC	European Economic Community
EFTA	European Free Trade Association
EP	European Parliament
EPC	European Political Community
EPP	European People's Party
EUCD	European Union of Christian Democrats
EU	European Union
FDP	Freie Demokratische Partei / Free Democratic Party (Germany)
FNC	Fédération Nationale Catholique (France)
ICDU	International Christian Democratic Union
ICHN	Internationale Christliche Nothilfe (Switzerland)
ICU	International Catholic Union
IFCTU	International Federation of Christian Trade Unions
IPU	International Parliamentary Union
ILO	International Labour Organisation
JR	Ligue de la Jeune République (France)
KVP	Katholieke Volkspartij / Catholic People's Party (Netherlands)
MEP	Member of the European Parliament
MRP	Mouvement Républicain Populaire / Popular Republican Party (France)
NATO	North Atlantic Treaty Organisation
NEF	Nouvelles Équipes Françaises (France)
NEI	Nouvelles Équipes Internationales
OEEC	Organisation for European Economic Cooperation
ÖVP	Österreichische Volkspartei / Austrian People's Party
PDP	Parti Démocrate Populaire / Popular Democratic Party (France)
PPI	Partito Popolare Italiano / Italian Popular Party
PSP	Partido Social Popular / Popular Social Party (Spain)
PvdA	Partij van der Arbeid / Labour Party (Netherlands)

RKSP	Rooms Katholieke Staats Partij / Roman Catholic State Party (Netherlands)
SEA	Single European Act
SFIO	Section Française de l'Internationale Ouvrière (France)
SI	Socialist International
SIPDIC	Sécretariat International des Partis Démocratiques d'Inspiration Chrétienne
SKVP	Schweizer Konservative Volkspartei / Swiss Conservative People's Party
SPD	Sozialdemokratische Partei Deutschlands / Social Democratic Party (Germany)
UN	United Nations
WEU	Western European Union

Introduction

Transnational political networks play a central role in shaping the political process within the present-day European Union (EU). This process is characterised above all by a high complexity of institutional procedures and policy issues. It involves national governments and supranational institutions like the European Commission and the European Parliament (EP), but also a large number of political and societal actors from political parties to socio-economic interest groups and non-governmental organisations that have developed from the new social movements of the 1970s. As scholars of public policy first observed in relation to national political systems in the late 1980s and early 1990s,[1] increasingly complex regulatory issues and growing domestic distributional conflicts have increased the importance of access to information, technical expertise and the ability to muster political support and create societal coalitions for policy options for influencing increasingly informal processes of coordination and decision-making. This informal coordination tends to marginalise parliaments as the traditional sites of deliberation and legislative decision-making. These conditions apply even more in the EU of twenty-seven member states, where no political actor or collective interest can easily dominate policy agendas. Indeed, national political actors and collective interests stand no realistic chance of influencing the policy-making process significantly unless they are well connected across borders in transnational political networks, from the more formalised cooperation of EU-level political parties with a general stake in EU politics to highly informal expert networks within a specific policy sector, or what Peter M. Haas first called an 'epistemic community'.[2]

[1] See by way of introduction, Karen Heard-Lauréote, 'Transnational Networks. Informal Governance in the European Political Space', in Wolfram Kaiser and Peter Starie (eds.), *Transnational European Union. Towards a Common Political Space* (London: Routledge, 2005), 36–60.
[2] Peter M. Haas, 'Introduction: Epistemic Communities and International Policy Co-ordination', *International Organization* 46 (1992), 1–35.

As Beate Kohler-Koch and others have argued,[3] the EU is and has no government in the sense of the exercise of clearly defined powers by state institutions in a hierarchical institutional system. Rather, it is a multi-level system of governance with supranational, national and subnational decision-making forums and actors in which political networks of one hue or another play a crucial role in vertically linking these different levels, and horizontally connecting member state governments, supranational institutions and non-governmental actors at the EU level. The term network governance seeks to capture the informality of the political process within the formal constitutional framework of the EU. Importantly, however, it also attempts to cover dimensions of governing Europe that extend beyond decision-making at the EU level, especially processes of socialisation and political transfer. Such processes are partially instigated and definitely facilitated by supranational integration as well as feeding back into this process, but they mainly take place in trans-governmental and transnational spaces. In short, transnational political networks play a crucial role in a European political space characterised by 'hollowed-out', more and more decentralised nation-states and fluid decision-making structures within a supranational political system.[4]

Defining governance as 'the practice of coordinating activities through networks, partnerships and deliberative forums', Paul Hirst has nonchalantly claimed with the historical innocence of a political scientist that this form of governance by networks has 'grown up on the ruins of the 1970s'.[5] In this perspective, the shift to governance in the present-day 'centre-less' European society occurred with the collapse of the unitary nation-states with state-centred government after the oil crisis of 1973, when economic growth across western Europe slowed down, unemployment rose massively, inflation went up and budget and state deficits soared. In the period of accelerated globalisation thereafter state institutions were less and less capable of securing lavish welfare state provisions, progressively losing their regulatory competence and legitimacy. Yet the first car-free day in 1973 was no more the zero hour of European governance

---

[3] For an overview see Beate Kohler-Koch and Berthold Rittberger, 'Review Article: The "Governance Turn" in EU Studies', *Journal of Common Market Studies* 44 (2006), 27–49.

[4] Cf. John C. Peterson, 'Policy Networks', in Antje Wiener and Thomas Diez (eds.), *European Integration Theory* (Oxford: OUP, 2003), 117–35. Still useful, Tanja Börzel, 'What's So Special about Policy Networks? An Exploration of the Concept and Its Usefulness in Studying European Governance', *European Integration online Papers* (EIoP) 1–16 (1997): http://eiop.or.at/eiop/texte/1997-016a.htm. Accessed 1 February 2007.

[5] Paul Hirst, 'Democracy and Governance', in Jon Pierre (ed.), *Debating Governance* (Oxford: Oxford University Press, 2000), 19.

signifying – from this often normative perspective – the end of the dark middle ages of centralised nation-state government than the German capitulation on 8 May 1945 marked a totally new beginning for the German and other western European democracies. After World War II the western European nation-states were not as hermetically sealed off from their international environment and their political systems and governments not nearly as autarchic, hierarchically structured and capable of stringent decision-making as Hirst's notion of their later 'ruins' would have us believe. In fact, national governments realised quickly after 1945 how interdependent the western European economies were. When Jean Monnet developed the plan for the European integration of the coal and steel sector in early 1950, it reflected in part his realisation that the French national modernisation plan for unilateral reconstruction had failed. The smaller Benelux economies depended even more on a German economic revival for their own welfare. At the same time, national political systems were also undergoing change. The neo-corporatist political structures of the Netherlands and Belgium were characterised by complex institutionalised coordination between state institutions and societal 'pillar' organisations. At the same time, the postwar political systems became more pluralistic with greater contestation of policy principles and ideas, especially in the larger western European countries – Germany,[6] Italy and France – which experienced sharp left–right political divides and confrontation over domestic and foreign policy. At the same time, political leaders had to manage at times fragile coalitions which also complicated decision-making, not least in foreign policy. This was no longer treated as the domain of small elites of diplomats defining and negotiating cohesive 'national interests'. Instead, European policy in particular was closely intertwined with domestic political party priorities and social group interests. These postwar circumstances were very propitious for the formation of cross-border links and political networks like transnational Christian democracy to influence especially the incipient integration process which started at the inter-governmental level with the creation – induced by the American Marshall Plan – of the Organisation for European Economic Cooperation (OEEC) in 1948.

The role of these early postwar transnational networks was discussed by neo-functionalists like Ernst B. Haas in his book *The Uniting of Europe*,

---

[6] Throughout this book the term Germany is used for the western zones of occupation and the Federal Republic of Germany from 1949 onwards.

published in 1958.[7] With their enthusiasm for the integration process and without access to sources other than those publicly available like policy statements and parliamentary debates, however, the neo-functionalists put too much emphasis on the formal institutionalisation of transnational cooperation. They also argued without much empirical evidence that the political collusion between especially transnational business and supranational institutions was driving the integration process forward, as both actors acquired a self-interest in upgrading policy-making to the new European level. They largely failed to capture the informality of the activities of transnational networks such as political parties. Instead, they basically treated them as nation-state type actors, only operating at the new supranational level, without bringing out the specificities of their transnational cooperation and integration. Focused on explaining supranational integration, moreover, the neo-functionalists also did not establish the crucial links between this new supranational level and the national levels of politics and policy-making.

Aside from misguided assumptions about semi-automatic functional 'spill-over' from one economic sector to another and from economic into political integration, however, neo-functionalist theory in its early days and its application to empirical case studies from the 1950s also operated on the assumption of a dichotomy between political forces interested in driving the integration process forward on the one hand and reticent nation-states and their governments on the other, who were fighting a lost battle. In this form, early neo-functionalism disintegrated with the Empty Chair crisis in the European Economic Community (EEC) in 1965–6, which seemed to demonstrate the resilience of the nation-state, and it was later even dropped altogether by one of its founders, Haas. Its deficiencies led to the discarding of the transnational dimension of integration by most later theories, especially the state-centric liberal inter-governmentalism of Andrew Moravcsik[8] developed from Stanley Hoffmann's earlier dissident realism.[9] Even political scientists, who have used the network concept for understanding present-day EU governance more recently, have not revisited the origins of European Union in the first two decades after World War II.

---

[7] Ernst B. Haas, *The Uniting of Europe. Political, Social, and Economic Forces 1950–57* (Notre Dame, Ind.: University of Notre Dame Press, 2004 [1958]).
[8] Andrew Moravcsik, *The Choice for Europe. Social Purpose and State Power from Messina to Maastricht* (London: UCL Press, 1998).
[9] Stanley Hoffmann, 'Obstinate or Obsolete? The Fate of the Nation State and the Case of Western Europe', *Daedalus* 95 (1966), 862–915.

The early historiography of European integration was similarly characterised by a strong normative overdrive. In a Hegelian perspective, European integration appeared as the linear ascendancy of federalist idealism over the nation-states and their internecine wars. Walter Lipgens – the first holder of the Chair in European Integration History at the European University Institute from 1976 to 1979 – founded this historiographical tradition.[10] A Catholic historian, who published critical essays about Bismarck's Prussian-dominated creation by stealth of the German Reich in the nineteenth century, and an active member of the European Movement and the German Christian Democratic Union (CDU), he fervently supported Chancellor Konrad Adenauer's policy of Western integration. To him, the formation of a geographically limited core Europe of the integrated European Coal and Steel Community (ECSC), founded in 1951–2, and the EEC, created in 1957–8, signified a morally superior attempt to overcome the nation-state. In a revealing passage in an article published in a German pedagogical history journal, Lipgens wrote that school teachers should discuss European integration as 'the most successful peace movement to date'. They would need to imprint on their pupils' minds that 'all deficiencies and weaknesses, the talk of Brussels bureaucrats and crises ... result almost without exception from areas where integration has not gone far enough'.[11] Lipgens was particularly fascinated by the contributions of the resistance movements and the European movements to the European 'idea'.[12] Crucially, however, he was not very concerned about, and failed to establish, causal links between these movements' ideas and proposals and the actual process of core Europe formation comprising France, Germany, Italy, the Netherlands, Belgium and Luxembourg. As a result, contemporary historians – like political scientists – subsequently also abandoned all attempts to trace transnational dimensions of European integration.

In view of this and similar cheerful narratives of the origins of European Union, Hans-Peter Schwarz predicted as early as 1983 that historians would in future deconstruct the idealist interpretation of integration 'with similar

[10] See in greater detail Wilfried Loth, 'Walter Lipgens (1925–1984)', in Heinz Duchardt *et al.* (eds.), *Europa-Historiker. Ein biographisches Handbuch*, vol. I (Göttingen: Vandenhoeck & Ruprecht, 2006), 317–36; Wolfram Kaiser, '"Überzeugter Katholik und CDU-Wähler": Zur Historiographie der Integrationsgeschichte am Beispiel Walter Lipgens', *Journal of European Integration History* 8 (2002), 119–28.

[11] Walter Lipgens, 'Der Zusammenschluß Westeuropas. Leitlinien für den historischen Unterricht', *Geschichte in Wissenschaft und Unterricht* 34 (1983), 345–72.

[12] See in particular, Walter Lipgens, *A History of European Integration*, vol. I: *1945–1947* (Oxford: Clarendon Press, 1982 [German 1977]).

cynical joy' as American revisionists in the 1960s writing about the alleged responsibility of US capitalist foreign policy for the start of the Cold War.[13] Shortly afterwards, without sharing the neo-Marxist assumptions of William Appleman Williams and other left-wing US historians of the Cold War, but with at times even greater cynicism, the British economic historian Alan S. Milward reconceptualised the origins of European integration as the result of the inter-state bargaining of 'national interests'. Milward replaced Lipgens' transnational movements with the nation-states as the only relevant and apparently cohesive actors, and ideas with material interests as the only motivating forces that have ever mattered in the integration process. In his first book,[14] Milward argued that the Schuman Plan of 1950 resulted from a search by western European governments for an economic peace settlement through integration to control Germany. In his second book, *The European Rescue of the Nation-State*,[15] he maintained much more provocatively that the core motive for European integration was not to overcome the nation-state, but to strengthen it. In this perspective, the formation of the ECSC and EEC stabilised the nation-states through the Europeanisation of welfare policies that no single state alone could have sustained in the longer run.

Bringing states back into the history of European integration, as Milward did, was crucial. After all, it was national governments that negotiated what Moravcsik has called the 'grand bargains' like the ECSC and EEC treaties. It is also important to consider the role of economic motives for integration in the analysis of the origins of European Union. After all, the integration process started with the creation of customs unions, first for coal and steel in the ECSC and then for all industrial and agricultural products in the EEC. Milward wrote transnational actors out of the history of integration altogether, however. Concentrating on the overriding importance in his view of material economic interests for national preference formation, moreover, he also confounded ideas and idealism, as in his superficial discussion of the European policies of leading politicians such as Robert Schuman, Konrad Adenauer and Paul-Henri Spaak.[16] Yet, as Markus Jachtenfuchs has argued in his study of the history of constitutional change in the EU, 'actors guided by ideas are not blue-eyed idealists who take decisions without considering their impact on

---

[13] Hans-Peter Schwarz, 'Die Europäische Integration als Aufgabe der Zeitgeschichtsforschung', *Vierteljahrshefte für Zeitgeschichte* 31 (1983), 566.
[14] Alan S. Milward, *The Reconstruction of Western Europe 1945–51* (London: Methuen, 1984).
[15] Alan S. Milward, *The European Rescue of the Nation-State* (London: Routledge, 1992).
[16] Ibid., chapter 6.

welfare and influence'.[17] Despite the emphasis on the economics of integration, Milward's analysis of what he has recently rephrased 'national
[integration] strategies'[18] still has profoundly realist connotations.
Although he has argued that 'the process of integration is not separable
from the evolution of domestic politics',[19] domestic politics mostly comes
alive in his books through the eyes of policy-makers in state institutions,
especially bureaucrats in ministries. Milward has not captured the nature of
the domestic politics of integration well enough, let alone the significance
of transnational networks for its contestation at domestic and European
level. Where Lipgens failed to show causal links between transnational
movements, their ideas and governmental decision-making, Milward –
juggling with economic statistics – has also largely failed to establish causal
links between shifts in trade or the musings of minor civil servants in
economic ministries about them and the integration policies of European
states.

At least, Lipgens and Milward have attempted to transgress the national
perspective in reconstructing the origins of European Union. Some
younger scholars are beginning to write about the history of the present-
day EU as the evolution of a political system with complex institutional
structures, multilateral bargaining by member-states, supranational institutions that were not easily controlled by governments and the growing
role of transnational political and societal actors in shaping the emerging
EEC policies.[20] For much of the last twenty years, however, most contemporary historians wrote about national policies 'towards Europe' based
on one set of government sources only.[21] This dominant approach has been
steeped in the most unreflected manner in 'realist' assumptions about the
autonomy of foreign policy-making elites in defining and negotiating
'national interests' of a mostly foreign and security policy type. European
integration appears as controlled by political leaders and foreign ministries
with fixed preferences. This 'Gaullist' historiography, in which unspecified

[17] Markus Jachtenfuchs, *Die Konstruktion Europas. Verfassungsideen und institutionelle Entwicklung* (Baden-Baden: Nomos, 2002), 261.
[18] Alan S. Milward, *The Rise and Fall of a National Strategy 1945–1963* (London: Frank Cass, 2002), 6.
[19] Alan S. Milward, 'Conclusion: the value of history', in Alan S. Milward *et al.*, *The Frontier of National Sovereignty. History and Theory 1945–1992* (London: Routledge, 1993), 187.
[20] See, for example, Piers Ludlow, *The European Community and the Crises of the 1960s. Negotiating the Gaullist Challenge* (London: Routledge, 2006). See also the contributions to Wolfram Kaiser, Brigitte Leucht and Morten Rasmussen (eds.), *Origins of a European Polity: Supranational and transnational Integration 1950–72* (forthcoming).
[21] For an overview see Wolfram Kaiser, 'From State to Society? The Historiography of European Integration', in Michelle Cini and Angela K. Bourne (eds.), *Palgrave Advances in European Union Studies* (Basingstoke: Palgrave, 2006), 190–208.

actors like 'France' (and other countries) sometimes appear capable of 'thinking' and 'feeling' (and probably making love, too), shockingly makes little difference in its analysis between the 'concert' of the Great Powers after the Congress of Vienna in 1814–15 and European policy-making by elected governments in pluralist democracies within the emerging highly institutionalised supranational and transnational political space.

The present-day EU penetrates its member-states and national societies and affects European citizens in such an all-pervasive way that it should be unacceptable to write about postwar (western) Europe without elaborate and intelligent reference to the integration process, as Tony Judt has largely done, for example.[22] Yet the historiography of European integration has been so conceptually underdeveloped and, for the most part, boring to read that it has remained marginal in research on contemporary European history – and this exactly at a time when modern European history even of the nineteenth century, which was treated for too long as a period only of national integration and conflict, has been reconceptualised as the over-lapping and 'networked' history[23] of socio-economic, cultural and political phenomena transcending, and of individuals and social groups linked across, national boundaries. It is vital therefore to move decisively beyond nation-state-centric approaches to understanding the increasingly inte-grated western Europe after 1945 and to connect it for the first time with the political and societal history of (western) Europe more generally. One important path towards such better integration, and the approach of this book, is the study of transnational networks of political and social groups that engaged with, and influenced, European integration while remaining embedded in national political and cultural contexts. Rejecting Lipgens' and more recent normative assumptions about the superior democratic quality *per se* of the involvement of 'civil society' actors in European policy-making, moreover, this new focus needs to target the most relevant net-works. They were not the resistance and European movements, but, at least in the early postwar period, political parties and party leaders. Only they could use various channels to translate transnationally deliberated and negotiated ideas and policies into national governmental policy-making and European-level decision-making, while providing the crucial link with

---

[22] Tony Judt, *Postwar. A History of Europe since 1945* (London: Heinemann, 2005).
[23] Cf. Michael Werner and Bénédicte Zimmermann, 'Vergleich, Transfer, Verflechtung: der Ansatz der histoire croisée und die Herausforderung des Transnationalen', *Geschichte und Gesellschaft* 28 (2002), 607–36.

national polities to guarantee the ratification of treaties and enhance the democratic legitimacy of integration. Of these party networks, transnational Christian democracy was hegemonic in western Europe in the first twenty years after World War II. It dominated the formation of the ECSC/EEC core Europe with fundamental long-term repercussions for the present-day EU.

Transnational Christian democracy was not limited to the national parties or the European-level predecessors of the present-day European People's Party (EPP). Their congresses were forums for intensive communication and exchange of ideas, but their resolutions had a more declamatory character. Christian democratic leaders also met informally in many different contexts, most importantly in the so-called Geneva Circle, however, and when they engaged in inter-state cooperation and negotiating, they never made a clear-cut distinction between their political party and governmental roles either. Transnational Christian democracy was thus an only partly formalised and institutionalised web of multilateral and bilateral contacts and communication. This network fulfilled multiple functions, not least creating political trust, deliberating policy, especially on European integration, marginalising internal dissent within the national parties, socialising new members into an existing policy consensus, coordinating governmental policy-making and facilitating parliamentary ratification of integration treaties. These and other functions together provided crucial guarantees for the exercise of what political scientists have called entrepreneurial leadership by politicians like Robert Schuman and Konrad Adenauer, for example, by limiting their domestic political risks in a decisive way to facilitate bold and at times extremely controversial policy choices.

For reconstructing transnational Christian democracy as a political network, it is paramount to overcome the prevalent national fragmentation and introspectiveness of most research on political Catholicism and Catholic and Christian democratic parties as they developed from about the mid-nineteenth century. Recent collaborative comparative research has underlined once more the national, and even regional and local, specificities of their development.[24] More often than not the impression of national difference fades out in European comparisons of this kind the

---

[24] Michael Gehler and Wolfram Kaiser (eds.), *Christian Democracy in Europe since 1945* (London: Routledge, 2004); Wolfram Kaiser and Helmut Wohnout (eds.), *Political Catholicism in Europe 1918–1945* (London: Routledge, 2004); Emiel Lamberts (ed.), *Christian Democracy in the European Union [1945/1995]* (Leuven: Leuven University Press, 1997); Tom Buchanan and Martin Conway (eds.), *Political Catholicism in Europe, 1918–1965* (Oxford: Clarendon Press, 1996).

extreme heterogeneity of the national parties themselves. A fresh look at Christian democracy from a transnational network perspective suggests, however, that particular sections of these confessional or people's parties often had more in common with similar groups in other national parties than with their favourite enemies within their own party. This in turn impacted on the evolution of the Christian democratic network with indirect consequences for the way European integration developed after 1945. Whereas their initial cooperation after 1918 was controlled by left-Catholics with a primary interest in national welfare state policies, their intensified postwar networking was dominated by middle-class liberal-conservative elites with a common project for creating an integrated Europe based on a curious mélange of traditional confessional notions of occidental culture and anti-communism and broadly liberal economic ideas. These elites initially were not even in the majority within some national parties, let alone in domestic politics and parliaments. By utilising their transnational cooperation effectively, however, they succeeded to a very large extent at implanting their core ideas in supranational European integration.

With this much more comprehensive concept of transnational Christian democracy, which transcends the national fragmentation, this book will also take a fresh look at the role of particular values and guiding ideas for European integration, which were deeply embedded in the collective historical experience, societal structures and political interests of Christian democracy. Just as historical and sociological institutionalists have rightly argued that the politics of the present-day EU cannot be understood without reference to its historical development since 1945, this book demonstrates that any explanation of the origins of European Union after World War II needs to address the long-term continuities and change from the nineteenth century through to the postwar period to understand the formation and evolution of the ECSC/EEC core Europe. The roots of transnational Christian democracy's broad constitutional ideas and preferences for European integration were embedded in their largely shared collective experience of the overbearing centralised liberal nation-state, their regional political anchoring and identity, their preferences for societal – and political – organisation in line with the principle of subsidiarity derived from Catholic social teaching and federalist thought as it largely developed inside the intellectual tradition of personalism – and this combined with the borrowing of essentially liberal interwar ideas about functional market integration as a suitable mechanism for eventually bringing about political integration as well. At the same time, the experience of the failed transnational cooperation by left-Catholic minorities within the Catholic parties in interwar Europe and of Catholic-conservative collaboration with fascist and clerical regimes also helps to explain why and how transnational Christian democracy managed to agree a set of cohesive preferences for western European reconstruction after 1945, which were to have such enormous long-term impact.

By bringing transnationally connected people and ideas back into the history of European integration as a core dimension of postwar (western) Europe, this book will hopefully contribute to an improved understanding of the present-day EU, too, which appears enveloped in a crisis of legitimacy after the two failed constitutional referendums in France and the Netherlands of 2005, and is trying at the same time to adjust to the pressures of globalisation and demands for greater transparency of policy-making and democratic participation. Despite such recurring crises, which now frequently also affect democratic institutions and political parties in many member-states, the EU has proved – surprisingly for some – a durable legal-institutional supranational framework for the peaceful regulation of conflicts and decision-making on common policies. That its history should not attract the same attention as Hitler and Stalin owes much to the fact that it has not left the same deep tracks of blood across twentieth-century Europe.

CHAPTER I

All paths to Rome? Transnational Catholicism in the nineteenth century

In the beginning was Pope Pius IX (1846–78). This would appear to be at least as true in relation to the origins of the transnationalisation of Catholicism in the nineteenth century as Richard Evans's assertion in his recent study of national socialist Germany that in the beginning really was Otto von Bismarck,[1] the chancellor who initiated – with strong liberal support – the repression of the Catholic Church in the *Kulturkampf* in the newly created Protestant-dominated *kleindeutsch* Empire in the 1870s. Yet the process of transnationalisation was largely limited to Catholicism and the more centralised Catholic Church. It partially extended to ideological preferences and notions of societal and political conflict in an age of rapid industrialisation, nationalism and democratisation – preferences and notions that transgressed borders uniting Catholics across Europe who shared similar political beliefs and fears of a modern liberal-capitalist and secular world. Crucially, however, this process did not encompass incipient Catholic political parties who by and large accepted the quintessentially liberal terms of parliamentary politics in increasingly nationally delineated polities with the primary objective of defending Catholic interests against liberal-secular national legislation. Nonetheless, the transnationalisation of Catholicism and the common experience of the European culture wars in the second half of the nineteenth century produced the foundation for incipient transnational party cooperation after World War I, not least by creating a set of common ideas and facilitating networking across borders on an initially informal level.

Responding in part to expectations of the Catholic faithful in an era of marked religious revival and pressures from liberal and anticlerical elites, Pope Pius IX played a crucial role in three main respects in the trans-nationalisation of Catholicism and the Europeanisation of the Catholic Church. Under his direction, the previously much more heterogeneous

[1] Richard Evans, *The Coming of the Third Reich* (London: Allen Lane 2003).

Church first of all transformed itself into what John Boyer has termed a 'transnational matrix of power based on formal rationality and hierarchical leadership',[2] making it capable of exercising influence at a continental level. Secondly, Pius IX and his successors contributed significantly to the mobilisation of Catholics. They encouraged their political and social engagement with, in some cases, strong transnational dimensions and the cultural transfer across borders of religious practices, forms of social organisation and political demands. Finally, with the support of conservative Catholic aristocrats from across Europe, Pius IX even attempted, albeit with only limited success, to transform the Church into a European political force challenging liberalism and anticlericalism outright in a coordinated fashion in the conflict over its temporal powers lost in 1870 and, more importantly, in the battles of the culture wars in different states over hotly contested political issues from civil marriage to schooling.

The increasing homogeneity of Catholicism did not result exclusively from initiatives originating in Rome. The Catholic revival, which started in the first half of the nineteenth century, created popular demand for more emotive extra-sacerdotal forms of worship and experience such as pilgrimages and rosarial devotions, for example.[3] Many forms of revitalised popular piety had a cross-border dimension such as regional pilgrimages between Baden and the French Alsace and between the Prussian Rhineland and the southern Belgian and Dutch provinces of Limburg. Some social historians have interpreted the new forms of popular piety as resulting from collusion between conservative Catholic priests and state authorities attempting to channel social discontent into politically harmless collective expressions of religious belief. The argument about the essentially manipulative character of Church policy was put forward by Wolfgang Schieder, for example, in his study of the 1844 Trier pilgrimage that mobilised 500,000 Catholics.[4] More recently, it has become clear, however, to what extent the Catholic revival was spurred by local initiatives to develop new devotional cultures, which were often lay-driven, strongly supported by women and at times actually bypassed sceptical local clergy and the Church hierarchy. This is true, for example, of the May venerations of the Virgin Mary that became popular

[2] John W. Boyer, 'Catholics, Christians and the Challenges of Democracy: The Heritage of the Nineteenth Century', in Kaiser and Wohnout (eds.), *Political Catholicism*, 22.

[3] See, for example, Ruth Harris, *Lourdes. Body and Spirit in the Secular Age* (London: Allen Lane, 1999); David Blackbourn, *Marpingen. Apparitions of the Virgin Mary in Bismarckian Germany* (Oxford: Clarendon Press, 1993).

[4] Wolfgang Schieder, 'Kirche und Revolution. Sozialgeschichtliche Aspekte der Trierer Wallfahrt von 1844', *Archiv für Sozialgeschichte* 14 (1974), 419–54.

among Catholic believers between the 1820s and the 1850s. As Christopher Clark has pointed out, new forms of devotion and religious practice during the Catholic revival in fact resulted from 'a potent convergence of clerical activism at many levels with a revitalised popular piety',[5] not the simple imposition of clerical control.

Nonetheless, Pope Pius IX seized upon the opportunities offered by the Catholic revival to foster the increasingly ultramontane Roman orientation of the lower clergy and many Catholic believers, to impose a greater homogeneity of religious practice and to develop a centralised doctrinal policy implemented across Europe by a more and more bureaucratised hierarchy increasingly controlled from Rome.[6] Also contributing to this process of centralisation were the 'papalist' religious orders, especially the Jesuits, who played an important role in spreading new and more uniform religious practices such as the May devotions and the cult of the Sacred Heart of Jesus. Pius IX took the first major step towards doctrinal centralisation with the definition in 1854 of the Immaculate Conception of Mary as a Catholic doctrine after a careful analysis of the popular cult as it had developed until then. He then expanded the scope of his growing doctrinal control very significantly with the encyclical *Quanta cura* and the accompanying *Syllabus errorum*, the Syllabus of Errors, of 1864, in which he attempted to decree an ideological position opposed to capitalism, liberalism, socialism and other supposed evils of modern society. His position reflected manifold anxieties about a de-Christianisation of European society, the loss of traditional and often institutionalised Church rights and of social influence in an age of national integration and beginning secularisation, and the threat of Italian nationalism to the Pope's remaining temporal powers. The climax of doctrinal centralisation finally came with the Vatican Council of 1869–70 and the highly contested declaration of papal infallibility.[7]

The resulting new 'bureaucratic-hierarchical system', as Michael Ebertz has called it,[8] of clerical authority was directed as much against liberal Catholicism intent on negotiated accommodation of Church interests

---

[5] Christopher Clark, 'The New Catholicism and the European Culture Wars', in Christopher Clark and Wolfram Kaiser (eds.), *Culture Wars. Secular-Catholic Conflict in Nineteenth-Century Europe* (Cambridge: Cambridge University Press, 2003), 17.

[6] For the role of Pope Pius IX in the centralisation of the Catholic Church see also Owen Chadwick, *A History of the Popes, 1830–1914* (Oxford: Clarendon Press, 1998).

[7] On the Vatican Council see in particular Klaus Schatz, *Vaticanum I, 1869–1870*, 2 vols. (Paderborn: Schöningh, 1992); Giacomo Martina, *Pio IX*, vol. III: *1867–1878* (Rome: University Gregoriana, 1990).

[8] Michael N. Ebertz, 'Herrschaft in der Kirche. Hierarchie, Tradition und Charisma im 19. Jahrhundert', in Kurt Gabriel and Franz-Xaver Kaufmann (eds.), *Zur Soziologie des Katholizismus* (Mainz: Matthias-Grünewald-Verlag, 1980), 105.

within the integrating nation-states as against more traditional forms of national Catholicism such as Gallicanism in France. In his policy of organisational and doctrinal integration the Pope was supported by ultramontanes who constituted a 'broad church',[9] ranging from reactionary integralists, whose world-view was absolutist and theocratic, to lay and clerical progressives who supported the emancipation of a 'supranational' Church from national state control and increasingly began to advocate social reformist ideas. Pius IX's policy of centralisation had the potential to mobilise Catholics for the transnational defence of Church interests as defined by him and, more particularly, for the cause of the Papal States and his own, as pontiff. Systematically encouraged by the Church leadership, ultramontanes throughout Europe increasingly saw and supported the Pope as the symbolic incarnation of Catholic virtues and suffering, especially after the occupation of Rome by Italian troops in 1870 and his 'imprisonment' in the Vatican. Thus, under Pius IX's leadership until 1878, the Catholic Church became a much more centralised and unified 'supranational' religious and political force and the Pope himself the focal point of Catholic resistance in the culture wars throughout Europe from the Prussian *Kulturkampf* in the 1870s to the French republican policy of progressive secularisation and the eventual separation of Church and state in 1905.

The transnationalisation of Catholicism and its increasing Roman orientation started within the Catholic Church. Yet this process was strengthened by the increasing pressures exerted by liberal and anticlerical political forces in national and European politics. As I have shown elsewhere,[10] their programme, ranging from moderate to wholesale secularisation, had a pronounced European dimension too. Although the political battles were primarily fought in national politics, liberals and anticlericals also had transnational networks facilitating their cross-border communication within a partially Europeanised political space. These networks permitted the intensive exchange and adaptation of foreign models and, although less often, concerted transnational political action. The repeated attacks on the Church as an unenlightened hierarchical institution manipulating the uneducated masses and opposing the necessary economic, societal and political modernisation were a core element in a conflict of the two Europes – not just the two Frances or the two Spains – characterised by

---

[9] Clark, 'The New Catholicism', 21.
[10] Wolfram Kaiser, '"Clericalism – That Is Our Enemy!" European Anticlericalism and the Culture Wars', in Clark and Kaiser (eds.), *Culture Wars*, 47–76.

an almost binary divide between two fundamentally opposed world-views. Both were supported by partially transnationally constituted alliances of societal forces that were in fact more heterogeneous than the sharp rhetoric of the culture wars made them seem, both within nation-states and at the European level. Nonetheless, the attacks on the Church and the policies of secularisation strengthened the sense among European Catholics of belonging to what Sudhir Hazareesingh (in discussing the case of French Catholics) has called a 'transnational community whose widely acknowledged source of authority was based in Rome',[11] committing them to a 'communion transcending [the] particularities' of nations.[12] In fact, John Boyer has even proposed to understand transnational European Catholicism in the second half of the nineteenth century as 'a civilization ... as a whole way of life involving many different folk communities, each having its own physical identity but bound together by a higher order ... of shared legal and moral norms, sacred cultural rites and performances, overlapping forms'.[13] The anticlerical attacks and his counterattacks also allowed the Pope to stigmatise deviant behaviour within the Church and impose drastic sanctions against it such as in the case of the liberal Catholic professor of theology Ignaz Döllinger who was excommunicated by the Archbishop of Munich for his continued opposition to papal infallibility in 1870.

The contribution of Pius IX to the transnationalisation of Catholicism in the nineteenth century was not limited to the organisational and doctrinal centralisation of the Church, however. The increasingly ultramontane and Romanised Church also encouraged the mobilisation and political engagement of Catholics for the defence of established Church rights and influence and later also for social reforms. This mobilisation facilitated transnational grassroots activities and resulting cultural transfer. The annexation of the northern Papal States by the Kingdom of Piedmont/Italy had already outraged many Catholics across Europe. They sent numerous addresses of public support to the Pope, gathering more than five and a half million signatures.[14] Catholics across the continent also

---

[11] Sudhir Hazareesingh, *Political Traditions in Modern France* (Oxford: Oxford University Press, 1994), 103.
[12] Adrian Hastings, *The Construction of Nationhood. Ethnicity, Religion and Nationalism* (Cambridge: Cambridge University Press, 1997), 203.
[13] John W. Boyer, 'Catholics, Christians', 20.
[14] Cf. Vincent Viaene, 'The Roman Question. Catholic Mobilisation and Papal Diplomacy during the Pontificate of Pius IX (1846–1878)', in Emiel Lamberts (ed.), *The Black International / L'Internationale noire 1870–1878* (Leuven: Leuven University Press, 2002), 143.

collected money as a contribution to the costs of the military defence of the Papal States during the 1860s. The 'Peter's Pence' movement, which revived a medieval levy on a voluntary basis, appears to have started in London in 1859, but it quickly spread to other parts of Europe.[15] Moreover, Catholic volunteers from all over Europe were recruited for the Zouave army and engaged in fighting with anticlericals, including those from their own countries, who supported Guiseppe Garibaldi's militia. Paul Luykx has shown, for example, how the 'extensive cult of the Papacy which was current in Catholic circles' motivated many Dutch Catholics to fight for the Pope in Italy at the price of losing their citizenship, or even their life.[16] Other volunteers came from Austria and Ireland, for example. Thus the conflict between the new Italian state and the irregular nationalist forces on one side and the Pope defending his temporal powers against the claims of the Italian *risorgimento* on the other foreshadowed comparable transnational conflicts in the twentieth century, especially the Spanish Civil War of 1936–9, which was also to involve numerous volunteers from across Europe on both sides.

More importantly, Pope Pius IX collaborated with ultramontanes across Europe in the mobilisation of Catholics for the defence of Church rights and influence where they were under threat nationally from liberals and anticlericals, their political rhetoric and their secularising legislation. Several accounts of Catholic mobilisation during the European culture wars in the left-liberal tradition have characterised it as a form of conservative hegemony. It aimed essentially at the restoration of hierarchically structured societies controlled by unquestioned authorities, especially the Church, and opposed to all forms of economic liberalisation and political reform and democratisation.[17] In contrast, Thomas Nipperdey first emphasised the democratic emancipatory implications of Catholic mass popular mobilisation.[18] In this perspective, their political mobilisation ultimately assisted Catholics in becoming more independent from the Church hierarchy, defining their religious, social and political interests, developing effective forms of political campaigning and eventually achieving

[15] Ibid., 143; Hartmut Benz, 'Der Peterspfennig im Pontifikat Pius IX. Initiativen zur Unterstützung des Papsttums (1859–1878)', *Römische Quartalschrift* 90 (1995), 90–109.
[16] Paul Luykx, 'The Netherlands', in Buchanan and Conway (eds.), *Political Catholicism*, 243.
[17] See, for example, Olaf Blaschke, *Religion im Kaiserreich. Milieus, Mentalitäten, Krisen* (Gütersloh: Kaiser, 1996); Christoph Weber, 'Ultramontanismus als katholischer Fundamentalismus', in Wilfried Loth (ed.), *Deutscher Katholizismus im Umbruch zur Moderne* (Stuttgart: Kohlhammer, 1991), 20–45.
[18] Thomas Nipperdey, *Religion im Umbruch* (Munich: Beck, 1988), 45.

their integration in the emerging democratising polities. Margaret Anderson, too, has made the case for a close link between ultramontanism and democracy, as Catholic popular participation 'shook the deference' that had characterised their predominant social attitudes – not only in Germany – for a long time. She goes too far, however, in ascribing ultramontanism a liberating influence that instilled in German Catholics (and, presumably, Catholics throughout Europe) 'civic courage, the gumption . . . to stand up for one's rights, human and civil, against authority'[19] – this at a time when they were in fact following the lead of another such authority, Pope Pius IX, who ruled autocratically and systematically suppressed all internal opposition against the Romanisation of the Church and his anti-modern political world-view.

Be this as it may, Catholic mobilisation in the culture wars certainly facilitated the adoption and development of modern forms of political organisation and campaigning, even if the political content may have been anti-modern. This is true, first of all, of the increasingly dense Catholic associational cultures which structured the everyday lives of most Catholics. In countries like Belgium and the Netherlands, they even developed organised societal 'pillars', which were separate from liberal, Protestant and, later, socialist milieus of national societies. Catholics also developed highly effective forms of political communication including public demonstrations, symbolic politics and media campaigns. Across Europe, Catholics easily surpassed the middle-class dominated liberals and alone succeeded in competing effectively with the expanding socialism when it came to organising and mobilising their supporters and retaining their allegiance and personal commitment to common political causes. Moreover, the emergence of tightly organised associational cultures at least potentially allowed the transformation of existing transnational networks from a level of more sporadic links between individuals to more organised or even institutionalised forms of cross-border cooperation. Catholic mass mobilisation in the culture wars also encouraged the formation and strengthening of Catholic political parties. Although the political-party organisation of Catholics in some European countries started in a more rudimentary form much earlier, with a Catholic faction sitting in the centre of the Paulskirche parliament at Frankfurt in 1848–9, for example, it really took off in

---

[19] Margaret L. Anderson, 'Voter, Junker, *Landrat*, Priest. The Old Authorities and the New Franchise in Imperial Germany', *American Historical Review* 98 (1993), 1466.

opposition to liberal and anticlerical forces and their increasingly more combative political agendas of anti-Catholicism and secularisation.[20]

Towards the end of the nineteenth century, finally, the Catholic Church under the leadership of Pope Leo XIII (1878–1903), who favoured accommodation with liberal regimes, strongly encouraged Catholic interest in, and commitment to, addressing the social question, as it was commonly called at the time. This in turn had important organisational repercussions and increased the potential for transnational links. The encyclical *Rerum novarum* of 1891 marked a doctrinal watershed. Although Leo XIII criticised the excesses of liberal capitalism, he primarily responded to the rise of organised socialism, its strongly anticlerical and even largely atheist orientation and its potential for attracting also Catholic workers with its social programme and promises. The exact ideological and political implications of the encyclical's demand for a just wage, for example, remained unclear. Yet Leo XIII gave a ringing endorsement of the emerging Catholic workers' associations and trade unions, even at the expense of Catholic political engagement in representative state institutions. The Volksverein in Mönchengladbach founded in 1890, which had 800,000 members on the eve of World War I, offered German social-reformist and democratic left-wing Catholicism an 'institutional home'.[21] It also attracted participants from neighbouring countries for its various social and educational activities, providing a model for left-Catholicism in the Netherlands and elsewhere. Other forums for transnational communication among European Catholics about religious, social and political issues included the French *Semaines sociales* for the debate of social reform, an idea that was transferred to other European countries,[22] and the national and regional *Katholikentage* for lay Catholics in German-speaking Europe.[23] Although

---

[20] For a comparative introduction to Catholic party formation in nineteenth-century Europe see Ellen L. Evans, *The Cross and the Ballot: Catholic Political Parties in Germany, Switzerland, Austria, Belgium and the Netherlands, 1785–1985* (Boston, Mass.: Humanities Press, 1999); Stathis N. Kalyvas, *The Rise of Christian Democracy in Europe* (Ithaca, N.Y.: Cornell University Press, 1996).

[21] Jürgen Elvert, 'A Microcosm of Society or the Key to a Majority in the Reichstag? The Centre Party in Germany,' in Kaiser and Wohnout (eds.), *Political Catholicism*, 53. On the Volksverein, see also Horstwalter Heitzer, *Der Volksverein für das katholische Deutschland im Kaiserreich 1890–1918* (Mainz: Matthias-Grünewald-Verlag, 1979).

[22] See in national and European perspective, Jean-Dominique Durand (ed.), *Les Semaines sociales de France. Cent ans d'engagement social des catholiques français 1904–2004* (Paris: Parole et Silence, 2006).

[23] See Marie-Emmanuelle Reytier, 'L'Allemagne: les *Katholikentage*', in Durand (ed.), *Les Semaines*, 359–75, and in greater detail Heinz Hürten, *Spiegel der Kirche – Spiegel der Gesellschaft? Katholikentage im Wandel der Welt* (Paderborn: Schöningh, 1998); Ulrich von Hehl and Friedrich Kronenberg (eds.), *Zeitzeichen: 150 Jahre Deutsche Katholikentage 1848–1998* (Paderborn: Schöningh, 1999).

Rerum novarum aimed at avoiding class conflict and socialist revolution, the social question had an obvious international dimension in a rapidly growing world economy. Moreover, it was a 'supranational' institution – the Church – that addressed the issue, so that Dutch workers' leaders actually encouraged their comrades to take part in the Catholic social movement with the slogan 'Catholic workers of the world unite: Rerum novarum!'[24]

Pius IX not only contributed to the transnationalisation of European Catholicism through the formation of a more centralised and Romanised Church and the mobilisation of Catholics for Church interests and influence, however. Temporarily he even attempted to develop the Church into a more coherent European political actor with a coordinated public relations and press policy with the aim of influencing national politics. For this purpose the Vatican established close links with a group of eminent Catholic laymen who were outraged by the annexation of the Papal States by the Kingdom of Italy and could be relied upon to support the Pope's ultramontane agenda. Many were aristocrats, with a preponderance of Catholics from Central Europe, especially Austria and Germany. Already in October 1870, Cardinal Gaspard Mermillod invited some thirty Catholic laymen to Geneva to discuss a European response to the annexation of the Papal States and other issues in the early days of the culture wars in different countries. At the following meeting in the Benedictine abbey of Einsiedeln, also in neutral Switzerland, in September 1871, the group created the Comité de Genève, or Geneva Committee, to coordinate their policies.[25] Most importantly, from the end of 1870 through to the end of 1873 the Geneva Committee published the *Correspondance de Genève* in French, which also came out in a German version, *Genfer Korrespondenz*.[26] It was a Catholic press service with opinion articles, which was sent to selected influential politicians and 300 Catholic newspapers and journals, encouraging them to reprint the material that was known in essence to reflect papal policy. Although the press service was not officially supported by the Vatican, Cardinal Wladimir Czacki, in the name of Pope Pius IX, exercised tight control over the contents. It sometimes included articles

[24] Jan Roes, 'A Historical Detour: The Roman Catholic State Party in the Netherlands', in Kaiser and Wohnout (eds.), *Political Catholicism*, 87.
[25] Emiel Lamberts, 'L'Internationale noire. Une organisation secrète au service du Sainte-Siège', in Lamberts (ed.), *The Black International*, 15–101.
[26] Cf. Vincent Viaene, 'A Brilliant Failure. Wladimir Czacki, the Legacy of the Geneva Committee and the Origins of Vatican Press Policy from Pius IX to Leo XIII', in Lamberts (ed.), *The Black International*, 231–56.

taken from the influential and strongly intransigent Jesuit newspaper *Civiltà Cattolica*, which had previously prepared the ground for the declaration of papal infallibility from 1867 onwards.

As Emiel Lamberts and his team of researchers have demonstrated in some detail,[27] Vatican control over the activities of the Geneva Committee and the editorial content of the *Correspondance de Genève* was actually much tighter than hitherto thought. Initially, Pope Pius IX appears to have believed that this kind of coordinated European propaganda could actually help him regain his temporal powers. Throughout 1871, the press service increased its attacks on Bismarck for the German failure to support the Pope in his conflict with the Italian State. It also propagated the ultramontane agenda more generally, to boost intransigent, militant organisations within European Catholicism and to strengthen them in competition with their liberal and anticlerical political competitors. The Geneva Committee's radically intransigent agenda did not meet with enthusiasm everywhere in European Catholicism, however. Liberal Catholic leaders in Germany around Bishop Wilhelm von Ketteler and the directorate of the German *Katholikentag* were keen to avoid an open confrontation with the Protestant-dominated and liberal-influenced state authorities in the heated political atmosphere after the creation of the Empire. They distanced themselves from the Committee and its press service in 1871. Likewise, many liberal Catholic bishops in Eastern Austria and Bohemia also opposed the radically intransigent agenda. By 1872, moreover, it was clear that the campaign had failed to realise some of its main aims such as the legitimist restoration of the monarchy in France and the regaining of the Pope's temporal powers. The German *Kulturkampf* seemed to demand greater caution to avoid putting the minority Catholics into a totally intolerable position. At the end of 1873, therefore, the Vatican decided to stop the publication of the press service. It was replaced with a more informal network involving Catholic publications throughout Europe that were prepared to print papal guidelines on major religious and political issues.

With the death of Cardinal Giacomo Antonelli, the influential Vatican state secretary, in December 1876, the Pope discontinued his support for the Geneva Committee, which was finally disbanded two years later, in 1878. A more informal transnational network largely remained intact, however, and Catholic aristocrats eventually created the Union de Fribourg in 1884, which lasted until 1891. This, too, was a closed elite

---

[27] See the contributions in Lamberts (ed.), *The Black International*.

network, again encouraged by Mermillod, which essentially brought together conservative legitimists. As Lamberts has pointed out, these activists were 'unconditionally opposed to [what they saw as] the individualism, anticlericalism and etatism of liberalism'.[28] Most of them rejected the parliamentary system, striving for the restoration of Christian monarchies or governments, especially in France, Austria, Italy and Spain. They loathed democracy, which appeared to be in the ascendancy. The crash of the Viennese stock market in 1873 and the resulting economic slowdown in Europe encouraged some interest among these conservative legitimists in the social question, but this was generally in the form of support for corporatist dreams of a restoration of the medieval guild system within a hierarchically structured paternalist society. Even by contemporary standards, their political ideology was anachronistic and had very little appeal for developing political Catholicism. It was more and more dominated by an educated middle class of professional lawyers, businessmen, teachers and others who provided a new lay leadership, with the increasingly self-confident involvement of Catholic workers through their organisations in countries like Germany, Belgium and the Netherlands.

Up to a point, it is therefore true that in the beginning of the transnationalisation of European Catholicism was Pius IX. For thirty-two years, the longest-serving Pope in the history of Catholicism advanced the organisational and doctrinal centralisation of the Church; his exposed political role in the culture wars helped Catholic believers to overcome their prevailing deference, mobilising and energising them into becoming politically and socially more active and to formulate collective demands; and finally, Pius IX also encouraged the adoption of modern forms of political communication with the aim of transforming the Catholic Church into a much more coherent political actor capable of taking on the liberal and anticlerical challenge effectively. In a more general sense, Pius IX strengthened the Church, personified by himself, as a 'supranational' institution and even – as Martin Conway has aptly put it – a (seemingly) 'supernatural fortress'[29] and focus of Catholic religious, but also political, orientation and allegiance. Thus, as Adrian Hastings has pointed out,[30] the Church with its 'supranational' organisation and doctrine (like socialism with its internationalist ideology) could be a bulwark

---

[28] Emiel Lamberts, 'Conclusion. The Black International and Its Influence on European Catholicism (1870–1878)', in Lamberts (ed.), *The Black International*, 471.
[29] Martin Conway, 'Introduction', in Buchanan and Conway (eds.), *Political Catholicism*, 13.
[30] Hastings, *The Construction*, 203.

against aggressive nationalism which increasingly seemed to be on the rise in Europe. It had at least the potential to encourage the formation of informal or more formalised transnational networks extending beyond the immediate confines of the Church and religious activities. Nevertheless, such formalised transnational networks going beyond personal contacts between individuals hardly developed in a significant form within political Catholicism before World War I, and especially not among Catholic parties. At the European level it was actually the way in which Pius IX and his successors promoted the transnationalisation of European Catholicism which impeded the transnational organisation of political Catholicism and Catholic parties in a number of different ways.

To begin with, Pope Pius IX had his own political agenda, which focused for some time after 1870 on the illusory objective of regaining his temporal powers over the Papal States. Many Catholics certainly sympathised with this agenda, but it was also far removed from their daily concerns such as the protection of Church-controlled schooling from secularist intrusions by liberal and anticlerical governments. Ultimately, these and other contested issues during the culture wars were played out in national politics and decided by national legislation. The battles were not only fought by political elites in national capitals, however. Catholics as well as liberals and anticlericals were involved in running battles over schools, religious processions and public festivities within localities. The Pope's self-declared 'imprisonment' in the Vatican certainly aroused much sympathy and support among the Catholic faithful. Yet whether or not he could re-establish Church rule over marshland northeast of Rome had no influence whatsoever on whether the children of Catholics throughout Europe were taught the biblical version of the creation of mankind by Catholic priests and Jesuits or Darwinist ideas of biological evolution by liberal or socialist teachers in state schools. Moreover, many German Catholics had in fact supported the *kleindeutsch* unification of Germany once their preferred *grossdeutsch* option including Catholic Austria was clearly out of the question. It was not immediately clear to them why they should not sympathise with Italian national unification, too. If anything, the Church's refusal to formally recognise the legitimacy of the Italian state erected (in Pius IX's words) by the 'subalpine usurpers' – a policy that it only gave up with the signing of the Lateran Treaties with fascist Italy in 1929 – impeded the potentially transnational political organisation of Catholics. This was obviously the case in Italy, where the encyclical *Non expedit* of 1874 actually forbade Catholics to participate in politics at all.

Pope Pius IX's policy also proved detrimental to the political organisation of European Catholics for another reason. His radically intransigent policies aimed at the homogenisation of the Church as a hierarchically structured ultramontane institution. He thrived on the prospect of open battle with the evil forces of modernity that he had identified in the *Syllabus errorum*. Within the Church and in the culture wars, Pius IX more so than his successors deliberately followed a policy of massive polarisation. His ultramontane doctrinal policy stigmatised and marginalised liberal Catholics and actually succeeded in forcing members of middle-class Catholic elites in particular into religious exile in 'Old Catholic' communities. However, if Catholic parties wanted to be effective parliamentary and extra-parliamentary political forces, they desperately needed to integrate all social classes and all religious orientations under the banner of the defence of Church interests and influence. This interest in part explains, for example, the critical attitude of von Ketteler and others in Germany toward confrontational papal policies after 1870. At the same time, the Pope's territorial claims, his often violently anti-modernist rhetoric as well as his apparent unwillingness to compromise with liberal governments trapped Catholic politicians between their allegiance to the pontiff and their growing desire to play a full role in domestic politics. The latter, however, clearly required adjustment to parliamentary politics and, most importantly, the willingness in principle to cooperate with other political groups, and to compromise. Paradoxically, the Pope's 'supranational' ultramontane policies forced Catholic politicians to concentrate even more on national conflict and compromise than would otherwise have been necessary. Although Pius IX's successors followed more conciliatory policies, which also facilitated the end of the German *Kulturkampf* after 1878, the years of confrontation actually encouraged national introspection and set narrow limits to possible transnational cooperation and action.

Finally, papal policy on the organisation of Catholics in political parties was from the beginning – and remained until World War I and thereafter – highly ambivalent. While political parties seemed to be necessary for the organisation of political Catholicism as an effective force under the conditions of liberal-imposed parliamentary systems, they also had a strong subversive potential. Parliamentary politics offered incentives for cooperation and compromise, which might well lure Catholic politicians away from following the more intransigent policies and positions decreed in Rome. Moreover, it could contribute to the formation of a new elite of lay middle-class politicians with less direct links with the Church hierarchy than the priests turned politicians who initially played an important role in

Catholic parties. In any case, political parties were separate and independent entities that would perhaps be under the influence, but not the direct control of, the Church hierarchy. This is in fact how the Catholic parties evolved over time as they developed their organisations and policy-making functions. On top of this ambivalence came the encyclical *Non expedit.* The interdiction of political participation in Italian elections was only modified from 1905 on when the Vatican allowed the conditional participation of Catholics in local politics and the electoral support of liberal candidates against socialist opposition in national elections.[31]

Even more importantly, the encyclical *Rerum novarum* actually commanded Catholics to prioritise social action over political participation.[32] Committing themselves to the social and educational advancement of Catholic workers, making them immune against the temptations of socialism, now appeared to be much more urgent for safeguarding the interests of the Church and the existing social order than petty battles with moderate liberals. By the turn of the century, they were not only the lesser evil compared to radical democrats, socialists and communists, but almost natural allies in the fight against socialist revolution. With its one-sided emphasis on social justice, the Church's strong support for Catholic associationalism and social action failed to grasp, however, that social issues were highly politicised and necessarily contested and decided by political parties in the political and legislative process. The encyclical's *de facto* conceptual separation of societies into a social and a political sphere was artificial and did nothing to strengthen overall Catholic influence. It successfully encouraged many Catholics to concentrate on social action, creating incentives to develop initially informal transnational contacts among Catholic workers' organisations, but not political parties.

In fact, the Christian trade unions were the first to formalise existing transnational contacts when they founded the International Secretariat of Christian Trade Unions at their first congress in Zurich in August 1908. It had its secretariat in Cologne, under the leadership of Adam Stegerwald, the secretary of the German Christian trade unions, which had been founded in 1899. Catholic trade unionism demonstrated the extent to which papal policy since *Rerum novarum* was primarily directed at supporting Catholic associations and protecting them from state intrusion.

---

[31] Cf. Sidney Pollard, 'Italy', in Buchanan and Conway (eds.), *Political Catholicism*, 70.
[32] See, for example, John Molony, *The Worker Question: A New Historical Perspective on Rerum Novarum* (Dublin: Gill and Macmillan, 1991); Helmut Sorgenfrei, *Die geistesgeschichtlichen Hintergründe der Sozialenzyklika 'Rerum Novarum'* (Heidelberg: Kerle, 1970).

Apart from that, the Vatican was not very clear about the objectives and desired organisational forms of social action. During the so-called *Gewerkschaftsstreit* in Germany, which opposed a Rhenish wing in favour of inter-confessional Christian unions and a Berlin-centred confessional Catholic union tradition, Pope Pius X (1903–14) stopped short of condemning the predominant inter-confessional tendency in 1912. He merely tolerated it, outraging union leaders like Stegerwald and Heinrich Brauns, who were to become leading politicians in the Zentrum – the Centre Party – in the Weimar Republic. Effectively, therefore, the international inter-confessional organisation of Christian trade unions was created against the Pope's preference for Catholic unions and union cooperation, and thus received no Church support.

In 1910, the Pope actually condemned the French Sillon, a social reform movement founded by Marc Sangnier in 1894 which was also developing pacifist tendencies with the potential for transnational cooperation at a time of growing nationalist tensions[33] – a European agenda that Sangnier pushed strongly after World War I. The Vatican continued to support the virulently nationalistic Action Française founded at the time of the Dreyfus affair and headed by Charles Maurras.[34] It was – from the Roman perspective – at least strongly monarchical and anti-republican and seemed to be a more effective fighting force against the radically secularising separation laws of 1905.[35] This Vatican policy led to even more confusion among European Catholics, not just ecclesiastical leaders, over 'who was authorized to accomplish what on the front of social justice'[36] – or, indeed, in national and European politics.

In addition to the impact of Vatican policy, the prevailing structures of domestic party competition during and after the culture wars and the framing of dominant political issues also impeded transnational cooperation of Catholic parties before World War I. Most importantly, liberal and anticlerical political forces essentially determined the main issues of national politics and when and how they were contested domestically. Their ideological hegemony contributed to the extremely defensive introspective character of Catholic politics and policy-making as a major barrier to transnational cooperation, with different dimensions. One of these was the way in which liberalism shaped the process of the creation and

---

[33] See also Jeanne Caron, *Le Sillon et la démocratie chrétienne, 1894–1910* (Paris: Plon, 1967).

[34] On the Action Française see Eugen Weber, *Action Française. Royalism and Reaction in Twentieth-Century France* (Stanford, Calif.: Stanford University Press, 1962).

[35] See also Giorgio Vecchio, *La democrazia cristiana in Europa (1891–1963)* (Milan: Marsia, 1979), 271.

[36] Boyer, 'Catholics, Christians', 26.

integration of 'closed' nation-states. In Germany and Italy, liberals were the driving force behind the process of nation-state formation, which created grave problems for political Catholicism in both countries. The *kleindeutsch* option traditionally had Protestant-Prussian connotations. When it came about in 1870–1, it led to the confessional marginalising of Catholics, who only constituted approximately one-third of the population of the new Empire. Importantly, the Pope's radically ultramontane policies stigmatised liberal Catholicism within the Church and inflamed the latent anti-Catholicism among liberal and conservative Protestantism. In conjunction with the rhetoric of nationalist anti-Catholic protestants and its subsequent exploitation by Bismarck in his *Kulturkampf* policies, this prevented the more organic integration of Catholics in Empire politics.[37] In Italy, the Pope and the Italian state actually developed habits of accommodation from the mid-1870s which contained the practical consequences of the often equally violent political rhetoric of the Pope and his supporters as well as anticlerical liberals and socialists. Nonetheless, the Pope's support for the Habsburg Empire and other Catholic-inspired minor states such as the Kingdom of Naples as protectors of the Church and its interests and social influence had stood in the way of national integration. His insistence on the recreation of the Papal States remained a source of insecurity for the Italian state after 1870. Elsewhere in Europe, national integration was also achieved against Catholic opposition. In Switzerland, Protestant liberals imposed the new constitution creating a federal state with a somewhat stronger centre than before in the *Sonderbund* war against Catholic cantons in 1847–8. Although the Catholics largely managed to regain political control over the administration of most Catholic cantons by the 1870s, they remained marginalised in Swiss national politics.[38] Dutch Catholics, too, were a confessional minority of slightly over one-third in a state that was dominated by Calvinism. They were still known among Protestants for a long time as the 'Spanish-Roman party' implying national unreliability resulting from their allegiance to a 'supranational' institution.

In Austria, the Christian Socials were under attack from a variety of nationalisms within the multi-ethnic Empire.[39] For the German

---

[37] See in particular Wilfried Loth, *Katholiken im Kaiserreich. Der politische Katholizismus in der Krise des wilhelminischen Deutschlands* (Düsseldorf: Droste, 1984).

[38] Urs Altermatt, *Katholizismus und Moderne. Zur Sozial- und Mentalitätsgeschichte der Schweizer Katholiken im 19. und 20. Jahrhundert* (Zurich: Benzinger, 1989). See also, by the same author, *Der Weg der Schweizer Katholiken ins Ghetto. Die Entstehungsgeschichte der nationalen Volksorganisationen im Schweizer Katholizismus 1848–1919* (Zurich: Benzinger, 1972).

[39] Cf. John Boyer, *Culture and Political Crisis in Vienna. Christian Socialism in Power, 1897–1918* (Chicago Ill.: Chicago University Press, 1995).

nationalists and even many German-speaking socialists they were not sufficiently German-minded and supportive of some kind of *grossdeutsch* solution. For other ethnic nationalists they were not sufficiently federalist and in favour of far-reaching autonomy of the constituent parts of the Empire. This was because they strongly supported the two central imperial institutions, the monarchy and the Church, which fully justifies Helmut Wohnout's description of the Christian Socials as the 'secular arm of the Catholic Church'.[40] In France, the national reliability of Catholic conservatives was hardly in doubt in that they in fact propagated the most aggressive revanchist policy vis-à-vis Germany after the lost war of 1870–1. However, their traditional advocacy of a France of the regions and their refusal to integrate themselves fully into the emerging republican consensus of the Third Republic made them vulnerable to other accusations of a lack of national 'reliability'. This was especially the case after their political behaviour during the Dreyfus affair thoroughly discredited Catholic-conservative chauvinism and anti-Semitism. In Belgium, however, the Catholics' national credentials were not doubted. Together with the liberals, they had supported national independence from the predominately Protestant Netherlands in 1830, and also the liberal constitution of 1831. Towards the end of the century, however, the ethnic fragmentation of Belgium and the social and political claims of the people of Flanders, where the Catholics were particularly strong, began to preoccupy Catholic politicians at the expense of possible transnational contacts and cooperation.

Elsewhere in Europe, Catholic politics was either fragmented, disorganised and largely disconnected from mainstream European political Catholicism as in Spain and Portugal;[41] had only a limited ability to articulate Catholic interests and views and to develop external links as in the case of Polish Catholics in Austria and also in Prussia, where their ethnicity, Catholicism and national aspirations combined to make them seem natural 'enemies of the Empire', as Bismarck first called the organised Catholics; or in fact became so intimately linked with dissident nationalism as happened in the Irish case before World War I that the achievement of national 'home rule' or full independence became almost its sole preoccupation. All that mattered (apart from papal policy originating in Rome) was the Westminster parliament, not continental European Catholic politics.

---

[40] Helmut Wohnout, 'Middle-class Governmental Party and Secular Arm of the Catholic Church: The Christian Socials in Austria', in Kaiser and Wohnout (eds.), *Political Catholicism*, 172–94.

[41] By way of introduction see Mary Vincent, 'Spain', in Buchanan and Conway (eds.), *Political Catholicism*, 97–128; Tom Gallagher, 'Portugal', in ibid., 129–55.

Ultimately, the nationalist pressures combined with the prevailing structural conditions for party cooperation – especially the minority status of Catholicism in Germany, the Netherlands and Switzerland and the enforced self-exclusion of Catholics from political activities in Italy – were so dominant before World War I that they easily cancelled out all incentives for a transnationalisation of political Catholicism and Catholic parties as opposed to Catholicism as a religion and the Church as an institution. Papal policy on nation-state formation and national integration had a lasting impact on political Catholicism. If, as a 'pariah nation' within the state – a term originally coined by Michael Geyer to characterise the situation of the German Catholics in the Empire[42] – they desired their full integration in national politics and a leading political role for themselves, Catholic parties henceforth had to demonstrate that their national 'reliability' was beyond doubt. The German Centre Party did so, for example, by voting for Admiral Alfred von Tirpitz's Naval Law of 1898, which turned out to be an important step in the accelerating European arms race.[43] This is turn helped to create the psychological conditions in which a great war could be contemplated, although it was by no means inevitable, in 1914. It became imaginable also for the vast majority of European Catholics. By then, their national 'reliability' was not doubted (from a nationalist perspective) nearly as much as that of socialists with their Second Socialist International (SI), and even they took up arms in the end.

The extremely defensive character of Catholic politics before World War I, which contributed to the predominately introspective domestic orientation of Catholic parties, also resulted from the imposition of the agenda of moderate to wholesale secularisation by liberals, republicans, democrats and socialists throughout Europe. The battles over such issues as state support for Church schools or the introduction of compulsory civil marriage certainly had the potential to allow social learning across borders in terms of national legislation and its administration – not only for liberals and anticlericals, but also for Catholics. Ultimately, however, the political battles were fought in national politics, by national parties and in national parliaments and media. These were clearly domestic societal issues without even a distant prospect of European regulation. Indeed, to date, the current EU possesses practically no competences in these policy areas. There were

---

[42] Michael Geyer, 'Germany, or, The Twentieth Century as History', *South Atlantic Quarterly* 96 (1997), 675–6.
[43] On German Catholicism and nationalism see also Karl Rohe, *Wahlen und Wählertraditionen in Deutschland. Kulturelle Grundlagen deutscher Parteien und Parteiensysteme im 19. und 20. Jahrhundert* (Frankfurt/Main: Suhrkamp, 1992), 157.

therefore no institutional incentives for transnational party cooperation. Domestically, moreover, Catholic political parties totally focused on securing their internal unity in the face of the political challenge from liberalism and anticlericalism, and on the defence of Church rights and influence, which left very little room for foreign contacts and cooperation.

The defensive character of Catholic politics also resulted, at least initially, in a political programme and policies that were almost exclusively directed at the protection of Church rights and interests, not at shaping domestic economic and social policies, for example. When social Catholicism developed a distinctive political agenda of social reform in the wake of *Rerum novarum*,[44] it once more led to the search for intra-party mediation, consensus and unity. This despite the obvious transnational dimension of the social question at a time of a rapidly expanding world economy with growing European and international competition which in turn had repercussions for national economic performance, wages, unemployment and migration patterns, for example. One of the greatest strengths of Catholic parties, namely their ability to integrate Catholics from all social classes, also required the conciliation of increasingly conflicting socio-economic interests and views. The search for internal compromise was given great attention and also distracted from possible greater transnational links and cooperation. The parties acquired a 'catch-all nature'.[45] Bismarck was not far off the mark when he characterised the Centre Party as 'encompassing seven intellectual directions reflecting all the colours of the political rainbow, from the extreme Right to the most radical Left'.[46] Political Catholicism clearly had no ready-made internationalist ideology like socialism, which evidently required a certain degree of international organisation and rhetoric, although it turned out to have limited consequences for socialist party politics in practice.[47]

If this was the case despite the 'supranational', but ephemeral, allegiance to the Pope, Catholic parties in Europe needed other incentives to cooperate. Principally, they could have derived from the desire to

---

[44] As a comparative introduction to social Catholicism see Paul Misner, *Social Catholicism in Europe. From the Onset of Industrialization to the First World War* (New York: Crossroad, 1991).

[45] Kalyvas, *The Rise*, 263.

[46] Heinrich von Poschinger (ed.), *Fürst Bismarck und die Parlamentarier*, vol. III: *1879–1890* (Breslau: Trewendt, 1896), 231.

[47] Moira Donald, 'Workers of the World Unite? Exploring the Enigma of the Second International', in Martin H. Geyer and Johannes Paulmann (eds.), *The Mechanics of Internationalism* (Oxford: Oxford University Press, 2001), 177–203, for an attempt to map transnational socialism as a network. See still James Joll, *The Second International, 1889–1914*, 2nd edn (London: Routledge, 1974); Julius Braunthal, *Geschichte der Internationale*, 2 vols. (Hanover: Dietz, 1961–3).

coordinate their foreign policies, as happened after World War I and World War II. Until 1914–18, however, Catholic parties were too preoccupied with rebutting the accusation that they were always looking with one eye to Rome. In view of the legacy of the papal policies on nation-state formation, national integration and the culture wars, Catholic politicians feared that their transnational cooperation could, and would, be portrayed by their political opponents as the creation of a 'black international' that was just as 'unpatriotic' and dangerous as the 'red international' of socialists. In fact, this is how Bismarck first tried to stigmatise the Catholic Church. Subsequently, the long-term effects of his rhetorical strategy for Catholic transnational political relations were aggravated by the fact that the ultramontane network of the Geneva Committee took up the term. Its activists proudly called themselves 'black internationalists' in revolt against the modern liberal state.[48] Through its association with an intransigent Church the term 'black international' actually remained a red rag for Catholic politicians until well after World War II, as they feared domestic nationalist attacks on them.

It is also true, moreover, that Catholics had no particular foreign policy concept which was clearly distinctive from that of other parties – this at a time when foreign policy was still formulated by small political and military elites and foreign ministries dominated in most countries by a relatively cohesive social group of aristocrats. The influence of nongovernmental organisations on foreign policy-making was still limited. In view of the increasingly nationalistic climate before World War I, moreover, the more internationalist voices of transnational organisations like the International Parliamentary Union (IPU) or the SI – both founded in 1889 – were marginal compared to national racist and imperialist far-right pressure groups.

Even if Catholic parties had developed distinctive and compatible European and foreign policy goals, moreover, three structural factors in European politics would still have mitigated against cooperation. The first was the established neutrality policy of the Netherlands, Belgium and Switzerland, all of which had strong Catholic parties. Their leaderships feared that any transnational engagements could compromise government policy – even where they actually decided it as in the case of Belgium. The second problem originated in the adverse consequences for European politics of the Franco-German war of 1870–1. This war turned Franco-German

---

[48] *Correspondance de Genève*, 30 November 1871, cited in Lamberts, 'Introduction', in Lamberts (ed.), *The Black International*, 7.

relations into the core issue of European politics, but no political force on either side of the border had the will or ability to advance a long-term solution for it before World War I. This certainly holds true for political Catholicism, which was virulently nationalistic and anti-German in France, and in Germany was increasingly characterised by a compensatory nationalism, which did not initially come naturally to the Centre Party, but helped it to become more fully integrated in the new Empire. Finally, the time before World War I was dominated by great power politics and alliances and included as important actors Britain and Russia, both of which only had Catholic minorities that were not even organised as such in political parties and had no influence on foreign policy.

Despite the transnationalisation of Catholicism as a religion and of the centralisation of the Catholic Church as an institution, Catholic political parties thus remained quite nationally introspective until World War I. This was so despite important general similarities in the process of their formation, which has been interpreted in different and competing ways. From a historical sociological perspective, Seymour Lipset and Stein Rokkan have discussed Catholic parties as creations of the Catholic Church in the face of the rise of anticlericalism and mass politics. According to them, the intense conflict between liberal state-building elites and the Church produced new political cleavages which in turn led to the mass organisation of Catholics in political parties.[49] Other authors have emphasised the influence of traditional conservative elites in appropriating religion to build Catholic-conservative mass parties as a bulwark against socialism as a fundamental threat to the existing social order, emphasising the essentially conservative nature of political Catholicism in the nineteenth century. Maurice Duverger characterised the Catholic parties in Austria, Belgium and the Netherlands as in essence conservative parties that changed name.[50] More recently, Kalyvas has rejected both views, analysing Catholic party formation as 'the unplanned, unintended, and unwanted by-product of the strategic steps taken by the Catholic church in response to Liberal anticlerical attacks'.[51] Kalyvas has argued that the liberal and anticlerical attacks provoked Catholic mobilisation fostered by the Church. This in turn created a distinctive Catholic political identity, which had not existed before. This process facilitated party formation, which had not in fact been foreseen by the Church hierarchy, and was not really supported by it.

---

[49] Seymour Lipset and Stein Rokkan, *Party Systems and Voter Alignment: Cross-national Perspectives* (New York: Free Press, 1967), 103.
[50] Maurice Duverger, *Les Partis politiques*, 5th edn (Paris: Colin, 1964).   [51] Kalyvas, *The Rise*, 6.

Although the Church was extremely influential in binding Catholic voters to Catholic parties until well after World War II, the reduced emphasis on the Church and conservative elites as prime movers behind Catholic party formation is also corroborated by recent research on the culture wars.[52] This has clearly brought out the grassroots dimension of Catholic mobilisation, which did not begin with the *Syllabus errorum* and the Vatican Council or, for that matter, the acute perception of socialism as a significant political threat by conservative aristocrats. Major political events like the revolutions of 1830 and 1848–9 had already contributed to greater Catholic political awareness. Catholic associational cultures across Europe quickly expanded from the 1850s onwards, creating a suitable societal basis for political party formation and action. It is also true, moreover, that party elites quickly became dominated by an educated Catholic middle class, not Catholic conservative aristocrats. These elites also emancipated themselves from informal Church control, de-emphasising the Church link in order to broaden the parties' electoral appeal. At the same time, Kalyvas exaggerates the importance of actors and their (rational) political choices. He also underestimates the extent to which successful party formation depended on the prior existence of individual and collective religious and social identities, which had in fact developed over a long time in relation to historical cleavages created by the reformation and the French Revolution of 1789, for example. Successful party formation also depended on pre-existing functioning societal networks. Catholic identity was not created by the culture wars. Rather, it was strengthened, transformed and more strongly politicised at a time of mass politics. It became more geared towards political action and, to some extent, emancipation from the established authorities of the Catholic Church and the conservative aristocracy.

Another, related, controversy about the formation and subsequent evolution of Catholic parties concerns their 'Christian democratic' character. In contrast to Duverger and others, who have emphasised the parties' conservative orientation, some Catholic authors have recently written rather too cheerful histories of political Catholicism as 'progressive' Christian democracy. In one version of what John Boyer has termed the 'imaginary Catholic ... vision of the Whig theory of history',[53] Jean-Dominique Durand, a historian at the Lateran University in Rome, has reconstructed the history of political Catholicism as the unstoppable rise of

---

[52] See, for example, various contributions in Clark and Kaiser (eds.), *Culture Wars*.
[53] Boyer, 'Catholics, Christians', 9.

social reform-oriented Christian democracy, which was always fully committed to democracy.[54] At a time in the early twenty-first century when even left-wing politicians and contemporary historians recognise the generally benign influence of Christian democracy in western Europe after 1945 on the containment of right-wing nationalism and extremism and the process of European integration, few historians have bothered to engage in a critical way with Durand's thesis. Amongst others, Martin Conway has cautioned against this type of teleological interpretation of Christian democracy, however, which exaggerates the degree of continuity from the nineteenth century through to Christian democratic hegemony in western Europe after 1945.[55]

As I have argued elsewhere,[56] Durand constructs a history of long-term democratic continuity of Christian democracy by concentrating exclusively on democratic Catholic thinkers like the Italian Luigi Sturzo, the founder of the short-lived Partito Popolare Italiano (PPI), the Italian Popular Party, in 1918. Yet these thinkers were politically marginal before 1914 and in interwar Europe. Moreover, even within the narrow framework of such a history of ideas, which is not embedded in a social and political history of Catholic parties, Durand's thesis hinges on the arbitrary selection of a few Catholic thinkers. When it comes to the inclusion of neo-Thomists like Jacques Maritain, even this arbitrary selection does not support the continuity thesis. Maritain originally had a strongly communitarian conception of society, which idealised institutionalised cooperation of, and consensual decision-making by, professional bodies with the aim of creating and fostering social harmony. His societal vision had pronounced anti-pluralist connotations inclusive of the usual criticism of representative government and modern political parties which was commonplace among Catholic intellectuals at the time.[57] Maritain only became fully converted to (parliamentary) democracy in opposition to the growing threat from totalitarian ideologies and states in the 1930s and during his exile in the United States.

Within and beyond Catholic parties, moreover, the term 'Christian democracy' was used in a variety of different and often conflicting ways around the turn of the century, which also contradicts the continuity thesis.

---

[54] Jean-Dominique Durand, *L'Europe de la démocratie chrétienne* (Paris: Editions Complexe, 1995).
[55] Conway, 'Introduction', 10.
[56] Wolfram Kaiser, 'Christian Democracy in Twentieth-century Europe', *Journal of Contemporary History* 39 (2004), 131–2.
[57] Thomas Keller, *Deutsch-französische Dritte-Weg-Diskurse. Personalistische Intellektuellendebatten in der Zwischenkriegszeit* (Munich: Fink, 2001), 234–7.

Some self-styled Christian democrats supported social reform within the existing capitalist system, but many others wanted to replace it with a paternalist corporatist consensus society. As Ellen L. Evans has aptly put it,[58] 'its very impracticability served to keep [corporatism] ever fresh and attractive as a theory, in the 1930s as in the 1830s'. This is especially true of many Christian democratic social reformers inside Catholic parties who often remained hostile to the market economy. The same ambivalence also characterised Christian democratic attitudes to modern political systems and forms of decision-making. With the partial exception of the Belgian and Dutch, Catholic parties including many Christian democrats initially remained sceptical about parliamentary government and, even more so, mass democracy, even in its short European honeymoon after World War I. In a more general sense, Christoph Weber has argued that many Catholics (including many Christian democrats) still greatly feared the all-pervasive consequences of socio-economic and political modernity around 1900, suffering from 'a feeling of loss and of catastrophe'.[59] The fragmented character also of the incipient Christian democratic movement is particularly relevant as left-Catholics with Christian democratic leanings actually initiated the institutionalised cooperation of Catholic parties in 1925. With notable individual exceptions like Sturzo, however, their project was not directed at the transnational defence of democracy.

Despite these broad similarities in the evolution of political Catholicism and the incipient Christian democracy before 1914, however, the development of Catholic parties was also characterised by strong national variations and structural incompatibilities. These constitute a third set of factors impeding Catholic party cooperation before World War I. The first and most obvious structural problem concerned the uneven organisation and representation of political Catholicism. In those countries where Catholics formed a confessional minority, Catholic parties were particularly successful at organising the majority of them. In the 1874 Reichstag elections, the German Centre Party succeeded in securing 83 per cent of the Catholic vote, gaining almost 28 per cent nationally, and a quarter of the seats.[60] Wilfried Loth has made a robust argument that, subsequently, the Centre Party suffered increasingly from the great socio-economic diversity of its electoral constituency. It encompassed a growing Catholic proletariat

[58] Evans, *The Cross*, 283.
[59] Weber, 'Ultramontanismus', 34. With a less polemical tinge, Ronald J. Ross, 'Catholic Plight in the Kaiserreich: A Reappraisal', in Jack R. Dukes and Joachim Remak (eds.), *Another Germany. A Reconsideration of the Imperial Era* (Boulder, Colo.: Westview Press, 1988), 73–94.
[60] Karl-Egon Lönne, 'Germany', in Buchanan and Conway (eds.), *Political Catholicism*, 157.

becoming more assertive in its political demands, an agrarian and urban middle class which on the whole was fearful of change, and a new Catholic bourgeoisie intent on exploiting the opportunities of industrialisation and capitalism.[61] The Centre Party continued to use Catholic associationalism, confessional interests and the idea of social compromise for the electoral integration of Catholics. By 1912, however, it had only managed to secure 16 per cent of the vote, or 55 per cent of the Catholic vote. At this time, between 80 and 90 per cent of Dutch Catholics still voted Catholic, however.[62] Swiss political Catholicism also remained highly successful in organising the Catholic vote, although more so in the traditional Catholic cantons than among Catholic migrants in the growing Protestant-dominated industrial centres.

Of the predominately Catholic countries, Belgium had by far the strongest Catholic party. In contrast, due to Vatican policy there was not even a Catholic party in Italy before 1918. More importantly, France had parties and political groups supported by Catholic believers, but no Catholic party. The core political cleavage resulted from attitudes to the Revolution of 1789 and support for monarchical or republican government. Both main political camps were internally fragmented, with the political Right historically encompassing legitimists, liberal Orleanists and Bonapartists as supporters of the various monarchical regimes in eighteenth- and nineteenth-century France. Crucially, however, all of these conservative tendencies of one hue or another were anti-republican and in favour of a strong role for Catholicism and the Catholic Church as the basis of a traditional society and political system. Catholics had no incentive in the prevailing circumstances to organise themselves politically as Catholics, as their interests were catered for by traditional pro-Catholic conservative political forces. Moreover, there were also no external incentives in the form of attractive foreign models. Jean-Marie Mayeur has described the model character of the German Centre Party before 1914 as 'Germania docet' in political Catholicism in Europe.[63] Nowhere were the cultural barriers higher to the possible political transfer of such a model, or aspects of it, from Germany of all countries than among the virulently nationalistic political Catholicism in France after the lost war of 1870–1. Only the left-wing and pro-republican social-reform Catholicism led by Sangnier was an exception to the rule of conservative Catholic political

[61] Loth, *Katholiken im Kaiserreich.*   [62] Roes, 'A Historical Detour', 83.
[63] Jean-Marie Mayeur, *Des partis catholiques à la démocratie chrétienne XIXe–XXe siècles* (Paris: Colin, 1980), 98.

representation, but it did not initially organise itself in the form of a political party. When Sangnier created the Ligue de la Jeune République, or simply Jeune République (JR), in 1912 following the dissolution of Sillon two years previously, he conceived it to be a broad societal movement, not a party.

Even the successful Catholic parties did not in all cases have comparable internal structures and political constituencies represented in the party leadership who shared broadly similar transnational interests and political concepts. In this respect, the most important division with long-term consequences after World War I was between those parties that depended up to a point on strong support among Catholic workers, who increasingly organised themselves within the parties to influence their programmes and policies, and others who already before World War I had had very little residual social and electoral control over Catholic workers in the growing industrial centres. The German, Dutch and Belgian parties had such well-organised left-Catholic workers' sections, with a high degree of institutional and personal overlap with the trade unions, who started their transnational cooperation in 1908. These party sections began to develop a stronger interest in transnational networking arising initially from their concern with socio-economic issues and social reform, where strong incentives existed to use transnational contacts for the partial transfer of policy ideas across borders adjusted to local circumstances. At the other end of the spectrum, the Austrian Christian Socials formally founded as a party in 1896 were dominated in terms of their electoral support by lower-middle-class and agrarian interests.[64] By then, many Catholic workers had already deserted the more traditional conservatives for the rising socialists in Vienna and industrial centres in the German-speaking parts of the Austrian half of the Empire. The Swiss Catholics had a comparable lower middle-class and agrarian character, which also limited their interest in transnational contacts and cooperation.

On top of these important structural differences came the fact that Catholic parties in Europe operated under different political systems. Belgium and the Netherlands already had fully fledged parliamentary government. The Belgian Catholics ruled with absolute majorities between 1884 and 1917 when they created a government of national unity. The Dutch Catholics formed a coalition with the Protestants for the first time in 1888 over the divisive question of state support for confessional schools,

---

[64] On these structural problems see also Jürgen Hartmann, 'Strukturprobleme christdemokratischer Parteien in Europa', *Zeitschrift für Politik* 25 (1978), 177.

sending the Liberals into opposition. These parties therefore determined government policy. In Germany, the Centre Party was a core element of the parliamentary support for subsequent national governments from the mid-1890s, with the exception of the bourgeois Bülow bloc of 1907–9. While the German political system progressively acquired quasi-parliamentary features before World War I, however, it did not have parliamentary government. Ultimately, national governments depended on the goodwill of the Emperor, and their composition was highly person-alised, with no direct control or influence by the political parties. However, a party like the Centre Party that could not at least potentially acquire a direct stake in government and policy-making neither had the same incentives for cross-border contacts to facilitate policy transfer or coordi-nate foreign policy nor the same political capital to be attractive as a partner for sister parties abroad.

Besides, the nature of the emerging political parties and of national politics in the second half of the nineteenth century was not inimical to formalised transnational cooperation either. In their attempt to integrate if possible all Catholic believers from all social classes, Catholic parties began to develop a mass membership, putting some of them in a position to compete even with socialist parties on this account. Yet they largely retained for a long time the organisational model of early liberal parties whereby a small circle of leading clerical and middle-class politicians made policy at the national as well as the local level, co-opting younger members wherever possible in a quasi-corporatist, non-competitive manner designed to limit dissent and retain control over decision-making. These mecha-nisms were only undermined with the rise of Catholic trade unionism and challenged more directly in some countries after World War I. The local and national network character of Catholic politics and policy-making in the second half of the nineteenth century meant, however, that a strong organisational centre was dispensable, if not actually undesirable, as it could formalise power relations within the parties, facilitating a central-isation of decision-making. More than anything else, however, formalised transnational cooperation extending beyond personal contacts between some individuals, which of course existed before World War I, would have required a greater organisational strength and cohesion at the level of the participating parties, if not necessarily at the European level. The parties would have needed resources for the efficient exchange of informa-tion and the organisation of meetings as well as possibly more formalised policy-making mechanisms that could have allowed some degree of inter-national exchange of ideas and concepts. Yet most Catholic parties were not sufficiently integrated at the national level before World War I to guarantee these functions. In fact, even after 1918, the degree of their organisational integration and efficiency at the national level remained quite low.

It is therefore a combination of different factors that help to explain the absence of organised cooperation between Catholic parties before World War I, despite the transnationalisation of Catholicism and the centralisation of the Catholic Church.[65] One set of factors actually relates to papal policy as the 'supranational' framework for Catholic political activism, which in effect forced Catholic parties – for the reasons outlined above – into a defensive and nationally introspective mode. Another concerns domestic party competition and the framing of the dominant political issues. These were largely imposed upon Catholic parties by liberal and anticlerical forces, preventing the possible evolution of a less defensive and more constructive programme and policies with a stronger European dimension, which could in turn have provided a catalyst for transnational party cooperation. A third set of factors, finally, consists of the strong national variations in party development, which *inter alia* depended on historical experience, societal structures, existing cleavages and contemporary political circumstances, and the resulting structural incompatibilities which would have made party cooperation even more difficult than it actually was after 1925.

In these prevailing circumstances, it is not surprising that individual Catholic politicians started the only significant initiative for transnational Catholic political cooperation under the exceptional conditions of World War I. For Catholics in the countries participating in the war, it was initially a great temptation. They could prove their national credentials beyond doubt, even with the sacrifice of their lives. Thus, many Catholics were not less enthusiastic at the beginning of the war than other sections of national societies. When the war did not end quickly, as many had anticipated, but instead descended into the stalemate of trench warfare, it increasingly appeared in a different light, however – as a 'useless massacre', as Pope Benedict XV (1914–22) called it,[66] with terrible dehumanising effects; in short, as a catastrophe. In fact, the Pope condemned the war

---

[65] On transnational party cooperation before World War I see also in comparative perspective, with special emphasis on the socialist parties, Jürgen Mittag and Helga Grebing, 'Im Spannungsfeld von nationalstaatlicher Politik und internationaler Weltanschauung. Annäherung an die europäische Parteienkooperation vor dem Ersten Weltkrieg', in Jürgen Mittag (ed.), *Politische Parteien und europäische Integration. Entwicklung und Perspektiven transnationaler Parteienkooperation in Europa* (Essen: Klartext, 2006) 165–95.

[66] Cited in Francis Latour, 'La Voix de Benoît XV contre le "suicide de l'Europe" pendant la Grande Guerre', in Gérard Cholvy (ed.), *L'Europe: ses dimensions religieuses* (Montpellier: Carrefour, 1998), 31.

from his first public interventions in September 1914. From the 'supranational' Roman perspective, it appeared as a family feud that had miserably got out of hand, was now threatening to bring down European (Catholic) civilisation and had to be stopped as soon as possible.[67] During 1914–15 the Pope started several initiatives to keep the Italian government, which was formally allied to the Central Powers, but tempted by Entente promises of substantial territorial gains, from entering the war, albeit without success. The Pope was concerned about the allegiance of Italian Catholics to the Church, but also about the threat that the war posed to the external security and internal cohesion of the Habsburg Empire. The Vatican traditionally regarded the 'supranational' monarchy as the guarantor of Catholic rights and influence in Central Europe. It also hoped that the monarchy and the Church could keep a lid on the virulent nationalist claims and conflicts, which might actually get much worse after the Empire's possible collapse as a consequence of the war.

Encouraged by the strong papal guidance on the desirability of bringing an end to the war, Catholics from Germany, Austria-Hungary, Italy and France met in Switzerland in February 1917 under the banner of the International Catholic Union (ICU). The initiative for this first meeting came from Italian Catholics, who on the whole had been uneasy about Italian entry into the war in 1915 in view of the strong papal preference against it. They encouraged Catholics from neutral Switzerland to convene the first congress. Matthias Erzberger, the leader of the Centre Party, who was later German finance minister from 1919–20 before he was assassinated by two members of the radically nationalist Consul organisation in August 1921, regarded the ICU as an 'instrument for creating durable world peace'.[68] Other participants included Heinrich Held, who was later a leading politician in the regionalist Bayerische Volkspartei (BVP), the Bavarian People's Party, after it split off from the Centre Party in January 1920, and became Bavarian minister-president in 1924.[69] The German and Austrian politicians were not at this stage unequivocally supported by their Catholic parties, however, and the Italian and French participants completely lacked a suitable party basis and societal support. Moreover, all that the participants could agree on at the congress was their desire to bring an end to the war, but not the question of guilt, the

---

[67] For papal policy during World War I see in detail Francis Latour, *La Papauté et les problèmes de la paix pendant la Première Guerre Mondiale* (Paris: L'Harmattan, 1996).
[68] Matthias Erzberger, *Erlebnisse im Weltkrieg* (Stuttgart, Berlin: DVA, 1920), 17.
[69] Cf. Richard Keßler, *Heinrich Held als Parlamentarier. Eine Teilbiographie 1868–1924* (Berlin: Duncker & Humblot, 1971), 311–13.

legitimacy of the respective national war aims or, indeed, the conditions under which the war should stop.

On 1 August 1917, Pope Benedict XV attempted to instil new life into the peace movement with his peace appeal to all European powers engaged in the war. Some Catholic politicians and intellectuals like Erzberger and Sangnier supported him publicly.[70] Catholic nationalists in France, however, saw it as an initiative which probably had its origins in Berlin. Indeed, in the previous month the majority of the German Reichstag, on the initiative of Erzberger, had passed a resolution which called for a peace without annexations. In France, the Pope was now frequently denounced as the 'pape boche', or 'German pope',[71] at a time when the fortunes of war were slowly appearing to shift in France's favour after the entry of the United States into the war in April 1917. Consequently, when the ICU convened a second congress in January 1918 to follow up the papal initiative, it only included representatives of the Central Powers including the Austrian Christian Social Ignaz Seipel, who participated in consultation with Emperor Karl I.[72] The war was fought to the point of complete exhaustion and the collapse of the Habsburg and German monarchies in the autumn of 1918.

---

[70] Cf. Ilde Gorguet, *Les Mouvements pacifistes et la réconciliation franco-allemande dans les années vingt (1919–1931)* (Bern: Lang, 1999), 70.
[71] Latour, 'La Voix', 29.
[72] Klemens von Klemperer, *Ignaz Seipel. Christian Statesman in a Time of Crisis* (Princeton, N.J.: Princeton University Press, 1972), 78.

CHAPTER 2

Under siege: Catholic parties in interwar Europe

World War I was indeed a useless massacre. Its end in 1918 initially brought exciting new opportunities for political Catholicism across Europe, however. New Catholic parties were created in Italy, Spain, France and the successor states of the Habsburg Empire. Existing Catholic parties successfully continued to integrate large sections of (practising) Catholics. Although with 37 per cent of the vote the Belgian Catholics only narrowly remained the strongest party in the first postwar elections, they continued to play a dominant role in government formation.[1] While electoral support for the German Centre Party declined somewhat from 13.6 per cent in 1920 to 11.9 per cent in the last free elections in November 1932, it was the core political force in all parliamentary governments in the Weimar Republic until 1930, with nine of twenty chancellors until 1932 coming from its ranks. Catholics throughout Europe became more eager to participate in political life, not just through Catholic parties, but also through newly created youth organisations and the publication of a large number of periodicals. Some of these – such as the German *Abendland* and *Hochland*, the Belgian *La Cité chrétienne*, the French *Politique* and *L'Aube* – acquired excellent intellectual reputations and were read throughout Europe and also outside of Catholic circles. Even more importantly, Catholic politics became much less introspective in concentrating on the defence of Church rights and influence. It increasingly began to engage with general socio-economic and political issues of society as a whole, developing a new programmatic vitality. In largely shedding its much more defensive attitudes and policies from the prewar period, political Catholicism, as Martin Conway has put it, developed in the 1920s a 'Europe-wide sense of shared purpose and common identity'.[2]

---

[1] See Martin Conway, 'Belgium', in Buchanan and Conway (eds.), *Political Catholicism*, 193.
[2] Martin Conway, *Catholic Politics in Europe 1918–1945* (London: Routledge, 1997), 3.

At least temporarily, the new opportunities also resulted in significantly improved structural conditions for Catholic party cooperation. This concerned, first of all, the attitudes of the Vatican to Catholic political parties and their activities. After World War I, the Catholic Church ceased open combat with political liberalism and 'silently began to tolerate modern democracy'.[3] It became clear after Benito Mussolini's fascist usurpation of power in Italy in October 1922 that this was still conditional tolerance within narrow limits, an attitude and policy that could be modified at any time in the interests of the Church as defined by the Vatican. Nevertheless, for Catholic parties it marked a clear improvement compared to the earlier ultramontane-motivated rejection of liberal parliamentary politics and democratisation. It encouraged the Catholic laity to play a much more active role in Catholic politics and parties. Despite the continued influence of individual clerical figureheads like Sturzo in Italy, Ludwig Kaas in Germany, Seipel in Austria, Josef Tiso in Slovakia and others, Catholic parties increasingly emancipated themselves from the residual clerical supervision. Culture war type conflicts flared up from time to time in different European countries, but the Catholic Church was more careful not to radicalise them unnecessarily, instead seeking compromise solutions. The broader trend of secularisation also touched the Catholic parties. They began to de-emphasise the salience of religion and the remaining culture war issues to avoid alienating those voters who felt increasingly less bound to the Catholic Church as an institution or their political partners in coalition governments. As a consequence, some newly created parties actually preferred the political label 'of Christian inspiration' to a more explicitly 'Catholic' denomination.

As a consequence of this shift in Church policy, Pope Benedict XV also allowed the formation of a Catholic party in Italy after World War I at a time when the 'Roman Question' – including the territorial dispute with the Italian state – was not yet formally closed. The PPI, as it was called, was founded in January 1919. In the national elections in the same year, it became the second-largest party behind the Socialists, gaining 20 per cent of the vote and 100 of the 508 seats in parliament. It played a leading role in all coalition governments in the period 1919–22. Initially, it also participated informally in the first Mussolini government, which two conservative PPI members entered as ministers in a personal capacity.[4] The Popolari, as they were called, drew support from right-wing Catholics sceptical of parliamentary democracy, but also from more left-wing

[3] Kalyvas, 'The Rise', 260.   [4] As a concise introduction see Pollard, 'Italy'.

Christian democratic groups led by Sturzo and including the Catholic trade union organisation Confederazione Italiana Lavoratori. It had a significant mass membership comparable to the German Christian unions. Social reform Catholicism developed in Italy around the turn of the century and was strongly influenced by the German model, as Sturzo himself emphasised in the 1920s.[5] In its party programme, the PPI propagated *inter alia* 'communalism' – a strengthening of local government and the devolution of the highly centralised liberal nation-state – social reform (as opposed to 'state socialism') to benefit industrial and agrarian workers and opposition to extreme nationalism. Although conservative Catholics would have preferred a clearer confessional label, the PPI described itself as a 'non-confessional' people's party. From the viewpoint of Cardinal Pietro Gasparri, the Vatican state secretary, the PPI was only the least bad of all Italian parties, however.[6] The Vatican stopped short of publicly endorsing it to avoid domestic political problems for the PPI, but also to keep a free hand for alternative political strategies.

The threat of socialism, as the Vatican saw it, was perhaps the most potent factor behind its greater support for Catholic parties as a bulwark against revolutionary upheaval. In view of the decline of liberalism in many parts of Europe, and its more moderate political agenda, which became more geared towards stabilising the societal status quo instead of political reform, socialism was the new ideological and political arch-enemy against which the Catholic Church and Catholic parties increasingly defined themselves. This had two important dimensions.[7] The first concerned the domestic contest with socialist parties. Unlike in Britain, where the Catholic Church reluctantly tolerated political support for the Labour Party as a non-revolutionary party from the mid-1920s,[8] the Vatican and Church hierarchy still judged continental socialist parties as absolutely unelectable. They continued to regard coalitions with them, as in the case of the German Centre Party after the war and again during 1928–30, as undesirable and a policy of last resort only. Even more importantly, however, the Russian revolution of 1917 and the short-lived communist government under Béla Kun in Hungary in 1919 raised the spectre of

[5] Luigi Sturzo, 'Vorgeschichte und Programm der italienischen Volkspartei', *Abendland. Deutsche Monatshefte für europäische Kultur, Politik und Wirtschaft* 1 (1926), 240.

[6] Pollard, 'Italy', 77.

[7] See also Martin Conway, 'Catholic Politics or Christian Democracy? The Evolution of Inter-War Political Catholicism', in Kaiser and Wohnout (eds.), *Political Catholicism*, 235–51.

[8] Cf. Joan Keating, 'The British Experience: Christian Democrats without a Party', in David Hanley (ed.), *Christian Democracy in Europe. A Comparative Perspective* (London: Pinter, 1994), 169; Tom Buchanan, 'Great Britain', in Buchanan and Conway (eds.), *Political Catholicism*, 263–4.

bolshevist world revolution and the total destruction of all existing social structures including religion and Christian churches. Although the existence of such an enemy assisted the Catholic Church and Catholic parties in keeping their flock together, their extreme anti-bolshevism was not merely political rhetoric. It reflected widespread existential fears about the future of Christian European civilisation as it had been shaped not least by the Catholic Church for hundreds of years.[9] The apocalyptic visions also explain why the continued Vatican emphasis on social reform, especially in the papal encyclical *Quadragesimo anno* of 1931, was no longer disassociated from Catholic political activism including work for Catholic parties that played an essential role in the Church's anti-communist grand strategy in parliamentary regimes. It is true that Pius XI (1922–39) was – in the words of James McMillan – 'the Pope of Catholic Action'[10] and much more sceptical about Catholic party politics than his predecessor. Nevertheless, he did not as a matter of principle discourage political activism during this new high phase of the centrality of the Papacy for European Catholicism. Exclusive emphasis was placed on Catholic social action only when other political forces in non-democratic political systems promised to be a more effective bulwark against socialism and bolshevism than Catholic political parties, as well as guaranteeing essential Church rights and social influence, as the PPI and Sturzo were to find out as early as 1923–4.

Nevertheless, the Vatican's changed priorities and strategy compared to those in the prewar period, including its strong support for Franco-German reconciliation, gave Catholic parties a much freer hand in developing a less defensive and introspective vision of national and European politics. This also reduced the barriers to transnational contacts and cooperation. In addition, the structures of domestic party competition and the contestation of the dominant domestic and foreign policy issues also changed after 1918. Territorial disputes remained important, of course, such as over Alsace-Lorraine, which returned to France, and Eupen-Malmedy, which Germany had to cede to Belgium in accordance with the Versailles Treaty. The potential for long-term political strife was much greater in east-central Europe, however, where most newly created borders were highly contested. This concerned the German-Polish border, especially the question of the so-called Polish Corridor, which gave Poland access to the Baltic Sea west of Danzig (Gdansk), but also all borders

---

[9] See also Conway, *Catholic Politics*, 69–70.
[10] James F. McMillan, 'France', in Buchanan and Conway (eds.), *Political Catholicism*, 41.

between the successor states of the Habsburg Empire after the multi-national state was replaced with smaller multi-national states that claimed to be nation-states.

Within western Europe, however, national integration was much less contested domestically than before World War I. In particular, Catholics everywhere had proven their national(ist) credentials in the European slaughter of 1914–18. This assured them of a legitimate role in political reconstruction both in Italy and in Germany after 1918–19, where the Centre Party initially formed a government with the Social Democrats and the left-liberal Deutsche Demokratische Partei (DDP), the German Democratic Party. In Austria, the Christian Socials initially pleaded – like the Socialists – for national unification of what they regarded as their rump-Austria, with the German Empire, before replacing this objective – in view of the *Anschluss* prohibition of the peace treaties – with a Catholic-inspired *Reichsromantik* of emotional attachment to the old German Empire prior to 1806.[11] In Belgium, the Catholics had been in power during the war and formed a government of national unity in 1917. In France, finally, the war temporarily unified the vast majority of the people in the defence not only of their country, but also of the Republic. After World War I, the republican regime was more accepted by the conservative Right, which also acquired a greater stake in it as it in fact ruled France in different coalitions for most of the 1920s and 1930s. In these various ways, World War I assisted the national integration of Catholic parties. Catholics remained vulnerable to the accusation of a lack of national 'reliability' as the preferred rhetorical device of the nationalist Right. This influenced their transnational party cooperation, but it was no longer a principal barrier to it.

Not only did papal policy and the less contested nature of national integration in western Europe constitute a more favourable environment that was more inimical to transnational contacts and cooperation after World War I than before; the increased Catholic engagement with general political issues and the resulting greater programmatic orientation of Catholic parties also led to a growing interest in transnational networks that could provide the parties, or at least sections within those parties, with greater non-material resources. These resources potentially included improved access to nationally formulated programmatic ideas and policies from abroad, a strengthened ideological profile and the easier transfer of ideas and policies across borders adjusted to the respective national

---

[11] Cf. Wohnout, 'Middle-class Governmental Party'.

circumstances. In a long-term perspective, the greater non-material resources could also potentially encompass policy coordination at a societal level, between parties, in order to influence inter-state relations in Europe.

Structurally, the greater programmatic vitality resulted from the decreased salience of culture war issues and reduced emphasis on the defence of Church rights and influence in national politics. It was also informed by the greater competition, especially for the votes of Catholic workers, from socialist parties and the resulting electoral pressures to adjust their agendas. As class parties, socialist parties had more consistent and formalised programmes with promises for workers of material gains allegedly resulting from socialist revolution or reform. Despite continuing strong national variations, they also had an explicit internationalist dimension and appeal. In these circumstances, as Jean-Marie Mayeur has pointed out,[12] the new Catholic combination of anti-socialist opposition to class-based politics with a certain social reform orientation (as in Germany and Italy, for example) proved attractive for some time after the war. Due to the severe budgetary constraints during the 1920s, competing socio-economic interests within Catholic parties and the need to compromise in coalitions, however, the programmatic social reform orientation did not necessarily translate into extensive Catholic social reform policies in government. This was especially true during the world economic crisis, when Catholic parties (and even socialist parties as in Britain during 1929–31) generally preferred traditional economic austerity measures to balance budgets to new Keynesian-type policies of deficit spending, which were only slowly becoming more prominent in economic policy discourses at the time.

The greater social reform programmatic profile of Catholic parties did not only result from structural pressures external to political Catholicism, however. It also reflected the greater political voice of Catholic workers strengthened by the introduction of universal manhood suffrage and their more effective organisation than before World War I. Within some parties, Catholic workers' associations and trade unions began to play a much greater and more independent role. In Italy, the Catholic unions were an important source of support for Sturzo's pro-democratic social reform orientation after the war. In Germany, trade union leaders like Stegerwald propagated social reform and advocated breaking out of the confessional ghetto through the creation of a truly inter-confessional people's party in line with the Christian union organisation and the original conception of Ludwig Windthorst, the first leader of the Centre

---

[12] Mayeur, *Des partis*, 104.

Party.[13] This issue was already debated in the *Zentrumsstreit* of 1906. Stegerwald and others continued to advocate the inter-confessional approach during the 1920s, although it only gained majority support after World War II.[14] Unlike Stegerwald, the Catholic *Arbeitervereine* – the workers' associations – led by Joseph Joos, clung to the confessional organisational principle, but they, too, played an influential role in Centre Party politics. In fact, Joos and Stegerwald stood for the party leadership in 1928, after the resignation of Wilhelm Marx. Both were defeated in a curiously disorganised contest following sharp intra-party frictions at the party congress, but by Prelate Kaas as a clerical compromise candidate, not by a middle-class candidate.[15] The self-confidence and political independence of the Belgian Algemeen Christelijk Werkersverbond/ Ligue Nationale des Travailleurs Chrétiens, or National League of Christian Workers (ACW/LNTC) within the extremely heterogeneous Catholic Party, which institutionalised interest representation under its corporatist party constitution of 1921, was even more pronounced. Organised in a separate Christian democratic group in the Chamber of Deputies, the ACW actually supported the socialist-led 'democratic government' of Prime Minister Émile Vandervelde during 1925–6, against the opposition of the other Catholic deputies, resulting in an enduring legacy of internal strife.[16]

The Catholic unions and workers' associations played a crucial role in the attempt to bind Catholic workers to Catholic parties. Where they were sufficiently strong, they also had a major influence on the evolution of Catholic parties into centre parties with moderate reform programmes and alternative coalition options, as in Germany and Belgium, although not in Austria, for example, which had a much more highly polarised party system. Crucially, the unions and workers' associations provided a social and ideological bridge to moderate socialist and left-liberal parties, preventing an otherwise possible exclusive orientation of Catholic parties towards cooperation with conservative liberals, nationalists and, later, fascists. Importantly, the unions and workers' associations also supported

---

[13] On Windthorst's conception of Catholic political organisation see also Margaret L. Anderson, *Windthorst. A Political Biography* (Oxford: Clarendon Press, 1981).

[14] See also John K. Zeender, 'German Catholics and the Concept of an Inter-confessional Party 1900–1922', *Journal of Central European Affairs* 23 (1964), 425–39.

[15] See in greater detail Karsten Ruppert, *Im Dienst am Staat von Weimar. Das Zentrum als regierende Partei in der Weimarer Demokratie 1923–1930* (Düsseldorf: Droste, 1992).

[16] Cf. Conway, 'Belgium', 194; Emmanuel Gerard, 'Religion, Class and Language: The Catholic Party in Belgium', in: Kaiser and Wohnout (eds.), *Political Catholicism*, 94–115.

a greater institutionalisation of Catholic party structures and decision-making, as well as improved organisation and recruitment of members, to counteract middle-class and clerical control over the older network system of party governance. The growing professionalism of Catholic party organisation in turn constituted an important precondition for the subsequent investment of party resources in transnational contacts and cooperation.

Unlike before World War I, transnational policy coordination potentially also encompassed foreign policy. Catholic leaders of unions and workers' associations were not *per se* advocates of European policy coordination, or even integration, as the example of Stegerwald, a pronounced nationalist, illustrates.[17] Due to the social basis and ideological orientation of left-Catholicism, however, they were generally more predisposed towards countenancing new forms of European politics than most conservative Catholics. After their experience of World War I as a catastrophe, moreover, they were even less inclined than before to believe in the superiority of foreign policy-making by small political elites and professional diplomats in foreign ministries dominated by conservative aristocrats. This was a secluded community that had been encouraged in its nationalist policies in countries like France and Germany by even more nationalistic domestic imperialist pressure groups dominated by middle-class members. In retrospect these groups seemed to have advocated war as a kind of national pastime at the expense of workers and their social and political advancement. In this changed postwar perspective, the more left-wing, pro-democratic Catholics in particular began to search for a suitable basis for a more durable peace within an institutionalised international order. Although the League of Nations was initially seen in Germany and Austria and, up to a point, also in many neutral countries as a treaty instrument of the victorious powers to cement their hegemony, leaders of Catholic unions and workers' associations began to realise its potential to help establish such an order in the context of the Locarno Treaty of 1925. This prospect provided another incentive for cross-border party cooperation with the aim of influencing European policy-making and embedding the emerging new order in stable transnational societal links. Also facilitating party cooperation was the way in which the German invasion of neutral Belgium in 1914 had at least called into question the sustainability of neutrality, although not necessarily the policy principle as such. The

[17] Bernhard Forster, *Adam Stegerwald (1874–1945). Christlich-nationaler Gewerkschafter, Zentrumspolitiker, Mitbegründer der Unionsparteien* (Düsseldorf: Droste, 2003).

Dutch and Swiss Catholic parties even more so than any of the others still shrank from making binding transnational policy commitments.[18] The leadership of the Schweizer Konservative Volkspartei (SKVP), or Swiss Conservative People's Party, even rejected by four votes to two in December 1929 that the 1930 congress of the Sécretariat International des Partis Démocratiques d'Inspiration Chrétienne (SIPDIC) could take place in Switzerland as proposed by its own observer at the previous congress in 's-Hertogenbosch.[19] Nevertheless, these parties at least began to see the advantages of transnational cooperation in contributing to a less hostile international environment for national politics and policy-making in neutral countries.

Before World War I, the third set of barriers against transnational party cooperation–alongside papal and international policy and a lack of pro-grammatic and policy incentives–consisted in the strong national varia-tions in party traditions and development and important structural incompatibilities. These barriers, too, were at least temporarily lower after 1918. Alongside the relatively 'closed [political] Catholicism'[20] of the German, Dutch, Belgian, Luxembourg, Swiss and Austrian Catholic par-ties, which had their main roots in the nineteenth century culture wars, new parties were founded in other European countries within the larger Catholic community. They were less confessional and more pluralistic. They did not use the label 'Catholic' and instead opted for the 'popolar-ismo' propagated by Sturzo: a broadly based reform-minded people's party 'of Christian [Catholic] inspiration'. The PPI was initially the most sig-nificant exponent of this new tendency. Leading Popolari also played a crucial role in establishing bilateral party contacts shortly after the war.

Even more importantly, as a prerequisite for any meaningful Catholic party cooperation in interwar Europe, the formation of the Parti Démocrate Populaire (PDP), the Popular Democratic Party, in November 1924 for the first time created a serious interlocutor at the party level in France.[21] It had something of a predecessor in the Popular Liberal Action of 1902 led by Albert de Mun. It had already attempted to integrate a moderate political

---

[18] Cf. Roes, 'A Historical Detour'; Markus Hodel, *Die Schweizerische Konservative Volkspartei 1918–1929. Die goldenen Jahre des politischen Katholizismus* (Fribourg: Universitätsverlag, 1994).

[19] Cf. Roberto Papini, *Le Courage de la démocratie* (Paris: Desclée de Brouwer, 2003 [Italian 1995]), 167, footnote 49.

[20] John H. Whyte, *Catholics in Western Democracies. A Study in Political Behaviour* (Dublin: Gill and Macmillan, 1981), 118.

[21] For the formation of the PDP see Jean-Claude Delbreil, *Centrisme et démocratie-chrétienne en France. Le Parti Démocrate Populaire des origines au M.R.P. (1919–1944)* (Paris: Publications de la Sorbonne, 1990).

Catholicism into the republican regime. Unable to reconcile the residual clerical monarchism of many Catholics with conservative republicanism, however, it did miserably in the parliamentary elections of 1906, and subsequently disintegrated.[22] At the same time, Sangnier always conceived of Sillon and JR as social movements, not parties. In 1919, he refused to head the small and heterogeneous group of Christian democrats in the Chamber of Deputies, which he feared would be too right-wing. Instead, he concentrated his energies on the formation of a European transnational pacifist movement. His followers eventually transformed the JR into a political party in 1932, but it was far too far to the left for the taste of the vast majority of French Catholics.

In contrast, with the formation of the PDP, Christian democrats like Robert Cornilleau, Ernest Pezet and Jean Raymond-Laurent aimed at creating a popular party on the model of the Italian PPI which could provide a bridge to conservative republicans in the centre of French politics. The PDP was not a Catholic party, but certainly 'a party of Catholics', and 'of Catholics inspired by Catholic social teaching and committed to the ideals of Christian democracy'.[23] Although located more in the centre-right of French politics, it distanced itself from the social conservatism of the Fédération Républicaine as the main party on the Right. It also had an uneasy relationship with the Fédération Nationale Catholique (FNC), formed as a powerful Catholic lobby group in 1924 in response to the creation of the left-wing *Cartel des gauches* government. While some Popular Democrats like Pezet and Henri Teitgen pleaded in favour of close relations with the FNC, and Teitgen even spoke at FNC rallies, others were more hostile, in particular to its extreme nationalism under its leader General Edouard Castelnau, who was a die-hard Germanophobe. In the extremely polarised party system, the PDP's position was uncomfortable. Due to their social reform orientation and increasingly moderate nationalism, the Popular Democrats, rather bizarrely, were at times denounced by the Right, and especially the extremely nationalist Action Française, as 'Christian Reds'.[24] At the same time, many left-Catholic supporters of Sangnier and the JR regarded them as too wedded to traditional Catholic conservatism. Sandwiched between the small Catholic and very much larger anticlerical Left and the Catholic

---

[22] Cf. Benjamin F. Martin, *Count Albert de Mun. Paladin of the Third Republic* (Chapel Hill, N.C.: University of North Carolina Press, 1978); Benjamin F. Martin, 'The Creation of the Action Libérale Populaire. An Example of Party Formation in Third Republic France', *French Historical Studies* 9 (1975–6), 660–89.
[23] McMillan, 'France', 44.   [24] Ibid., 45.

Right, the PDP, which had regional strongholds mainly in Alsace-Lorraine and Brittany, never gained more than 3 per cent of the vote in national elections, with its parliamentary representation shrinking from seventeen deputies elected in 1928 to only thirteen in 1936. By then, the continued fragmentation and electoral weakness of the pro-democratic Catholic political forces led to attempts to reorganise the 'Christian-inspired' political centre, including the left-Catholicism of Sangnier and the JR, and to the creation in 1938 of the Nouvelles Équipes Françaises (NEF). The search for a stronger centre in a polarised political system was fostered, among others, by the journal *L'Aube* created in 1932, and its editor Georges Bidault. Bidault strongly opposed – against Catholic majority opinion – the Italian invasion of Ethiopia in 1935 and the Munich Agreement of 1938, which forced Czechoslovakia to cede the so-called Sudeten territory, which was predominately inhabited by German-speakers, to the German Empire.[25]

Despite its weaknesses compared to other Catholic or 'popular' parties, the formation of the PDP was an indispensable precondition for transnational Catholic party cooperation which had to include French and German partners to be meaningful. Moreover, there was a prospect of further geographical expansion of Catholic parties and party cooperation. Also based on the PPI model, the Spanish Partido Social Popular (PSP) was created in 1922, although the dictatorship of José Antonio Primo de Rivera established in 1923 quickly put an end to its activities.[26] In Spain, political Catholicism was intimately linked with monarchical carlism and its aim of a pre-Napoleonic Habsburg restoration. Although the party remained strongly clerical and anti-republican, the creation of the PSP at least marked a conditional opening toward democracy and social reform with the aim of connecting Spanish political Catholicism with mainstream European Catholic and 'popular' party development since the mid-nineteenth century. The PPI also had a certain model function after the war for the newly created Polish, Lithuanian, Czech, Slovak and Hungarian Catholic and Christian democratic parties.[27] New regionalist

[25] Mayeur, *Des partis*, 121–2.   [26] Cf. Vincent, 'Spain'.

[27] See Leszek Kuk, 'A Powerful Catholic Church, Unstable State and Authoritarian Political Regime: The Christian Democratic Party in Poland', in Kaiser and Wohnout (eds.), *Political Catholicism*, 150–71; Csaba Fazekas, 'Collaborating with Horthy: Political Catholicism and Christian Political Organizations in Hungary', in ibid., 195–216; Arnold Suppan, 'Catholic People's Parties in East Central Europe: The Bohemian Lands and Slovakia', in ibid., 217–34; Miloš Trapl, *Political Catholicism and the Czechoslovak People's Party in Czechoslovakia 1918–1938* (Boulder/Colo.: Social Science Monographs, 1995); more in the form of an autobiographical account, Algirdas J. Kasulaitis, *Lithuanian Christian Democracy* (Chicago: Leo XIII Fund, 1976).

Catholic parties like the Bavarian BVP in Germany, the Christian Social People's Party of German speakers in Czechoslovakia, who entered the newly formed bourgeois bloc government in October 1926 together with other German parties, broadening its ethnic basis, and the Slovenská ljudska stranka, the Slovene People's Party in Yugoslavia were also potential participants in the party cooperation of political Catholicism, which was for the first time in the early 1920s a truly European political force.

Also improving the structural conditions for Catholic party cooperation was the more efficient organisation and greater influence of the Catholic unions and workers' associations in several parties, with their stronger interest in the additional programmatic resources from party cooperation, and in possible policy coordination. The French PDP was largely middle-class and rural in terms of its membership of 13,000 and its electoral support. The relatively small Christian trade unions were not organisationally bound to it, as a party. Crucially, however, the PDP nevertheless developed a social reform agenda that was broadly compatible with that of left-Catholicism elsewhere. In its socio-economic programme of 1924, the PDP demanded 'bold reform', not through confrontation and violence, but through 'the sincere cooperation of all the different groups involved in the production process'.[28] It proposed the formation and self-organisation of permanent joint committees of employers and trade unions to coordinate labour relations below the level of representative government. It also recommended schemes to allow workers to participate in profit-sharing and to encourage worker and trade union share-ownership.

Catholic unions and workers' associations also had their own organisational resources. These allowed the Belgian ACW to participate in Catholic party cooperation after 1925, although the Catholic Union as a whole did not. More generally, most Catholic and 'popular' parties strengthened their previously rudimentary national headquarters after World War I. As a result, the PDP's secretariat was in a position to take responsibility for the organisation of party cooperation when it started in 1925. Secretary-generals from other important parties, like Heinrich Vockel from the Centre Party, also played a leading role. Their participation at least created the organisational potential for the diffusion of the programmatic and policy content of party cooperation within national parties. They did so, finally, in democratic constitutional states which, unlike in the case of

---

[28] Jean-Claude Delbreil, 'Christian Democracy and Centrism: The Popular Democratic Party in France', in Kaiser and Wohnout (eds.), *Political Catholicism*, 123.

Germany in the prewar period, gave all parties potentially a direct stake in governmental policy-making including foreign relations.

These improved conditions temporarily created a window of opportunity for transnational party cooperation shortly after World War I. This window of opportunity was never more than half-open, however. While some important conditions were still improving, others had already begun to deteriorate again. This concerned not least the conditional character of papal tolerance of democracy and support for Catholic parties. In July 1923, the Vatican mobbed Sturzo into stepping down as PPI leader, effectively forcing him into exile in October 1924, because of his refusal to cooperate with the fascists.[29] Pope Pius XI now regarded Mussolini, supported by conservative Catholics and liberals, as a better guarantee against social turmoil and revolution. He encouraged the conservative philo-fascist Conservatori Nazionali to split off from the still pro-democratic majority of the PPI in 1924, which continued with an interregnum solution, and then under the leadership of Alcide De Gasperi from 1924 until November 1926, when all opposition parties were finally dissolved. In Catholic majority opinion throughout Europe, the legitimacy of the fascist state increased even more when the Vatican signed the Lateran Treaties in 1929, which finally closed the contentious 'Roman Question'. Even Konrad Adenauer, at that time a leading liberal-conservative democratic Catholic in the Centre Party and mayor of Cologne, was full of praise for Mussolini for making peace with the Church.[30] Similarly, the Vatican strongly supported the Centre Party leader Kaas and the clear majority of its Reichstag members in their appeal of March 1933 for unified Catholic support for Adolf Hitler's so-called Enabling Law, swiftly leading to the party's dissolution in July 1933 and the signing of another Concordat, this time with national socialist Germany.

Throughout the interwar period, Vatican policy – as in the Italian and German cases – prioritised the protection of Church rights over that of democratic governance and Catholic parties. Its apocalyptic fears of socialist-bolshevist revolution led it to support any right-wing anti-communist authoritarian regime from Miklós Horthy in Hungary to Francisco Franco in Spain. Moreover, the muddled advocacy of the desirable role of *ordines*, or professional bodies, in some form of corporatist governance as propagated in

---

[29] For Sturzo within the Italian anti-fascist exile generally, see Charles F. Delzell, *Mussolini's Enemies. The Italian Anti-Fascist Resistance* (Princeton, N.J.: Princeton University Press, 1961), 48.
[30] Jutta Bohn, *Das Verhältnis zwischen katholischer Kirche und faschistischem Staat in Italien und die Rezeption in deutschen Zentrumskreisen* (Frankfurt/Main: Lang, 1992), 147.

the encyclical *Quadragesimo anno* in fact encouraged Catholic discourses about political corporatism aimed at replacing parliamentary democracy with professional chambers or bodies, instead of subordinating them to existing representative democratic structures, as Sturzo and other Catholic democrats demanded. Even some moderate Catholics like Karl Romme, the leader of the Dutch Rooms Katholieke Staats Partij (RKSP), the Roman Catholic State Party, officially founded in 1926, actually supported such political corporatism until shortly after World War II.[31] More often than not, however, political or state corporatism was advocated by extreme right-wing and nationalist movements intent on winning over Catholic opinion for some form of authoritarian government. This is true, for example, of the Rexist movement in Wallonia, which gained 11.5 per cent of the vote in the Belgian elections of 1936,[32] or of the Austrian *Heimwehren*, which contributed to the rightward drift of the Christian Socials during the last years of the First Republic. Many Catholics throughout Europe increasingly saw authoritarian corporatist regimes as 'a Catholic alternative to fascism'.[33] This also explains their often enthusiastic support for the corporatist constitution *Estado Novo* established by Antonio Oliviera Salazar in Portugal in 1933 or the equally authoritarian Austrian *Ständestaat* created by the leading Christian Social politician Engelbert Dollfuss. Dollfuss dissolved parliament in March 1933 and suppressed an uprising of Austrian Social Democrats at the beginning of 1934, before he was killed later in the same year by national socialist assassins and replaced with Kurt Schuschnigg.

The authoritarian trend in European political Catholicism in part reflected a generational change in the 1930s. Younger Catholics, who were confronted with the extreme socio-economic insecurity of the depression years, increasingly opposed the capitalist economic system, which was failing them, and the parliamentary system with it. Instead, they called for a new 'system' with emphasis on social harmony and order, as a new form of 'community' transcending social classes. They were drawn towards 'movements' that claimed to represent and fight for such values, not parties. They increasingly saw parties as corrupt and dangerous in their representation of sectoral economic and social interests, which allegedly came at the expense of the common good of society. Such attitudes were partly informed by new Catholic intellectual trends. In France, but with a larger impact

---

[31] Luykx, 'The Netherlands', 232. On Romme, see also Jac Bosmans, *Romme: biografie 1896–1946* (Utrecht: Uitgev. Het Spectrum, 1991).
[32] See Martin Conway, *Collaboration in Belgium. Léon Degrelle and the Rexist Movement 1940–1944* (New Haven, Conn.: Yale University Press, 1991).
[33] Conway, *Catholic Politics*, 56.

extending beyond it, they included the Christian personalism of the *Esprit* group, which emphasised individual values in advocating its 'community' concept, rejecting the nationalist or biological community myths that were propagated by fascism and national socialism, and the so-called federalist personalism of the much more right-wing L'Ordre Nouveau group.[34] Personalism supported the idea of 'natural living communities' and stressed the importance of regions in the older French tradition of clerical and royalist opposition to centralisation. It also went beyond it in its criticism of the nation-state as 'oppressive within [and] imperialist without', however, developing a political concept of 'subsidiarity' which potentially included the cession of national sovereignty in favour of supranational political forms, in an analogy with the Catholic Church.[35] Personalism also developed various forms of corporatist concepts. Without advocating concrete economic policy ideas, Emmanuel Mounier, as the most influential thinker of (Christian) personalism, nevertheless opposed the 'Americanisation' of Europe and what he believed were American values of individualism and greed, instead propagating some kind of diffuse corporatist 'middle way'.[36]

In the deepening crisis of European civilisation, as many Catholics saw it, Catholic politics was highly contentious. Only in a very general sense were Catholic parties in interwar Europe agents of the Church, as their domestic political opponents alleged. Catholic parties defended the interests of the Church, but the Church did not defend the Catholic parties – at least not when it came to the crunch during severe crises of democratic governance. Catholic party leaders – even including some clerics like Sturzo – acted quite independently of Church guidance. Many of their voters were still guided by the Church, however, which enjoyed almost unquestioned legitimacy and unconditional support among most practising Catholics. Under these conditions, the Vatican's initial support for the fascist Italian state and its toleration of national socialism as well as its pronounced support for Catholic-influenced authoritarian corporatist dictatorships as in Portugal and Austria very much undermined the legitimacy and effectiveness of pro-democratic Catholic parties everywhere in Europe even before 1933, with negative repercussions for their transnational

---

[34] As an excellent introduction to these intellectual trends see Thomas Keller, 'Katholische Europakonzeptionen in den deutsch-französischen Beziehungen', in Hans Manfred Bock, Reinhart Meyer-Kalkus and Michel Trebitsch (eds.), *Entre Locarno et Vichy. Les relations culturelles franco-allemandes dans les années 1930*, vol. I (Paris: CNRS Editions, 1993), 219–39.

[35] John Loughlin, 'French Personalist and Federalist Movements in the Interwar Period', in: Peter M. R. Stirk (ed.), *European Unity in Context. The Interwar Period* (London: Pinter, 1989), 189–92.

[36] Ibid.

party cooperation. As Michael Burgess has emphasised, progressive democratic Catholics comprising intellectuals, some middle-class groups and trade unionists continued to cling 'tenaciously to their democratic and reformist beliefs' and often ended up in exile or the resistance, but, on the whole, they were a minority.[37] Sturzo bitterly wrote retrospectively in 1939 that conservative Catholics in Italy, Germany and elsewhere had 'betrayed' Catholic democrats. For Sturzo, Franz von Papen, who helped bring down the technocratic government led by the Centre Party politician Heinrich Brüning in 1932 to become Chancellor, and then Vice-Chancellor in Hitler's government from January 1933, was the German Stefano Cavazzoni, a leading conservative Catholic in the PPI, who joined Mussolini's first government in a personal capacity, as minister of labour and social security, in 1922.[38]

In some countries less than in others, the conversion of Catholics to democracy and their integration into parliamentary politics after World War I was superficial and fragile, so that it could easily be reversed in unfavourable circumstances. Support for the PPI evaporated and then collapsed quickly, as many Catholic conservatives started to support fascism or at least accommodated themselves within the new regime.[39] In Germany, Catholic enthusiasm for the abolition of the monarchy and the introduction of full parliamentary democracy was limited from the beginning to the strongly pro-republican wing of the Centre Party around Joseph Wirth, chancellor from 1921 to 1922, who declared after the assassination of Foreign Minister Walter Rathenau, 'The enemy stands on the Right'.[40] The party as a whole avoided formally committing itself to the defence of the Weimar Republic's constitution, fearing that this might alienate many of its traditional monarchical voters. Large sections of the party only reluctantly supported the last fully democratic Social Democrat-led government during 1928–30, which ruled with a parliamentary majority. The party then began to propagate the bizarre concept of 'authoritarian democracy' from 1930, and endorsed the Brüning government's rule by executive decree during 1930–2. The rightward drift in the late 1920s also reflected the loss of voters, including to the radical

---

[37] Michael Burgess, 'Political Catholicism, European Unity and the Rise of Christian Democracy', in M. L. Stirk and Peter M. R. Stirk (eds.), *Making the New Europe. European Unity and the Second World War* (London: Pinter, 1990), 149.

[38] Luigi Sturzo, *Miscellanea Londinese. Volume quarto (anni 1937–1940)* (Bologna: Zanichelli, 1974), 239. See also Luigi Sturzo, *Scritti storico-politici (1929–1949)* (Rome: Zanichelli, 1984), 73–85.

[39] Lönne, 'Germany', 258.

[40] Quoted in Rudolf Morsey, *Die Deutsche Zentrumspartei 1917–1923* (Düsseldorf: Droste, 1966), 459, who adds with a view to the Centre Party as a whole 'but only for Wirth'.

right-wing Deutsch-Nationale Volkspartei (DNVP), the German National People's Party, and the extremist National Socialists. These voters were placated with a more nationalist foreign policy rhetoric precisely at a time when there still seemed to be room for the settlement of outstanding European political questions like disarmament.

Historically motivated predispositions, ethnic and nationalist conflicts and the breakdown of democratic structures also constituted unfavourable conditions for democratic Catholicism in other countries. The Austrian Christian Socials, for example, had strongly supported the Habsburg monarchy and never fully accepted the First Republic as 'their' state. Many leading Christian Socials supported Dollfuss in the establishment of the *Ständestaat* in 1933–4.[41] Other Catholic parties increasingly identi-fied with militant nationalism as in Slovakia, where the Catholic priest Tiso eventually established a collaborationist clerical dictatorship after the final destruction of Czechoslovakia by Hitler in March 1939, or they were challenged by extreme nationalist movements such as the Vlaams Nationaal Verbond, which gained 13.5 per cent in Flanders in the national elections in Belgium in 1936, mostly at the expense of the Catholics.[42] Other parties had to operate under difficult pseudo-parliamentary con-ditions. The Polish Chadecja, or Christian Democracy, gained 10 per cent in the national elections of 1922, and had between forty-three and forty-four deputies until 1928. After the successful *coup d'état* by Marshall Józef Piłsudski in May 1926, however, the governing National Democrats with their totalitarian ambitions marginalised the opposition. They manipulated the fake elections of 1928 and 1930 and persecuted individual politicians like the Christian Democratic Party leader Wojciech Korfanty, the Polish leader in the Polish–German conflict over the future of Upper Silesia after 1918 and a participant in transnational party cooperation, who was arrested in 1930 and expelled from Poland in 1935. As in Italy, the Church did not support the Christian Democrats, but instead concen-trated exclusively on Catholic Action.[43] In Lithuania, where the Christian Democrats formed a single-party government from 1922 to 1926, the Nationalists ousted the newly installed left-wing government in a military *coup d'état* in December 1926. They sought the cooperation of the Catholics, who initially entered the new government, but then left it in

---

[41] See Helmut Wohnout, *Regierungsdiktatur oder Ständeparlament? Gesetzgebung im autoritären Österreich* (Vienna: Böhlau, 1993); more generally, Ernst Hanisch, *Der lange Schatten des Staates. Österreichische Gesellschaftsgeschichte im 20. Jahrhundert* (Vienna: Ueberreuter, 1994).
[42] Conway, 'Belgium', 198.   [43] Cf. Kuk, 'A Powerful Catholic Church'.

May 1927 because of the Nationalists' anti-democratic and anti-Christian orientation. In Yugoslavia, the *coup d'état* by King Alexander I succeeded in January 1929, leading on to the dissolution of parliament and political parties, including the Slovene People's Party. In Hungary, finally, the vice-regent Horthy named his friend Gyula Gömbös – an exponent of the nationalistic middle-class – prime minister, establishing a semi-dictatorial regime there, which left little room for independent political action by the various Christian democratic groups.

In view of the sharply deteriorating conditions for democratic Catholic politics in Europe as a whole during the 1920s, the importance of the economic depression following upon the crash of the New York stock market in October 1929 for halting and reversing the integration of political Catholicism in parliamentary politics should not be overrated. Nonetheless, it created severe socio-economic tensions, which also deepened intra-party frictions. Arguably, the middle classes were most affected by the economic depression at a time when their dominance in Catholic party politics was increasingly challenged by unions and workers' associations, fostering a very defensive attitude. More importantly, as Martin Conway has argued,[44] the economic depression aggravated the existing urban–rural tensions and strengthened anti-democratic tendencies in the countryside. Catholic middle classes and farmers were important constituencies of Catholic parties, however. They were increasingly tempted to desert 'their' parties for nationalist and fascist political formations that were beginning to trump each other with promises of simplistic economic policy cures and the vision of 'organic' national unity. In doing so, they very effectively played on the latent anti-modernist and anti-pluralist dispositions of many Catholics which had originally developed in ultramontane opposition to economic modernity and liberal parliamentary politics in the nineteenth century.

During the economic depression and the ever-greater political radicalisation throughout Europe in the 1930s, the traditional centrist politics and policies of most Catholic parties geared towards moderation and compromise promised few electoral rewards. Political Catholicism saw itself increasingly engulfed by the battles of totalitarian ideologies and regimes for European supremacy. Opposing communism on one side and fascism and national socialism on the other, these battles not only took place in parliamentary politics as in Italy before 1922–3 and in Germany before 1933, but also in the streets. Elsewhere, National Socialists also gained 8 per cent

---

[44] Conway, 'Catholic Politics'.

in the Dutch elections in 1935, although the Catholic Church there sharply condemned it, in the light of the Catholic experience in neighbouring Germany since 1933.[45] In France, the formation of the Radical-socialist Popular Front government tolerated by the communists during 1936–8 at the same time seemed to reflect and deepen the ever greater Left–Right polarisation. Elsewhere, the struggle was already taking place on the battlefield. More than anything else, the Spanish Civil War of 1936–9, opposing the elected republican government, which was also supported by communists and anarchists and received military aid from the Soviet Union, and Franco's nationalist insurgents, who fought with substantial support from regular German and Italian military units disguised as 'volunteers', appeared to symbolise a larger struggle that was increasingly engulfing almost all of Europe. In this struggle, many Catholics deserted their previous centrist positions, which seemed to be more and more indefensible and politically irrelevant. In view of their political socialisation and prevailing norms and values, and as this increasingly seemed to be the relevant choice, they opted against socialist revolution, and for non-democratic right-wing ideologies and regimes. For European Catholics the authoritarian right-wing temptation was not primarily the result of specific national circumstances, but of their spiritual and political predispositions.

Not all was yet lost for democratic Catholic politics and party cooperation after World War I, however. The war experience initially stimulated the search for a durable societal basis for a new, more peaceful European order. The 1920s – especially before and after the Locarno Treaty of 1925 – were a first boom period for organised transnational relations in Europe, including even at the bilateral level between France and Germany. Cross-border links between intellectuals, industrialists, trade unionists, politicians and others had of course existed before the war. They had mostly been of an informal character, however, and were quite fragile. In the 1920s, more cross-border networks were established, and they became increasingly more formalised to guarantee their institutional stability independent of the personal interest and commitment of some activists. For politicians with an interest in European politics, these institutionalised and partly overlapping networks presented many new opportunities for personal contacts and the exchange of information and views in different, more or less politicised contexts, within their own political party family and across party divides. The growing societal networks also gave greater *prima facie* legitimacy to formalised party cooperation.

---

[45] Luykx, 'The Netherlands', 229.

After World War I, such formalised party cooperation was no longer limited to the socialists. In 1919, they refounded the SI, which had never completely ceased its activities during the war. Subsequently, in 1923, it was transformed to reinclude the social democrats from the Central Powers.[46] Significantly, the formation of a separate international organisation of communist parties under the direction of the Soviet communists and the progressive integration of social democratic parties into parliamentary politics made socialist internationalism appear less threatening for Catholics than before – not so much as an ideology, but as a form of organisation. More importantly, the democratic and left-liberal parties also created their own international organisation at a meeting in Geneva in August 1924.[47] Democrats developed informal transnational links during the nineteenth century, mainly during the revolutions and in exile. Now, under the leadership of the French Radical Socialists and Radical Republicans, they formed the Entente Internationale des Partis Radicaux et des Partis Démocratiques Similaire, which held its first congress in the context of the twentieth party congress of the French Radicals in October 1924. European agrarian parties also created an international office for information exchange in 1923, and organised two congresses in 1928–9.[48] Before World War I, party 'internationalism' was widely denounced as a specifically socialist and 'unpatriotic' phenomenon. Now it increasingly appeared natural for democratic parties to establish transnational links. Indeed, it even seemed necessary if they did not want to be perceived as ideologically isolated, providing an additional incentive of party competition for Catholic parties in Europe. Thus, the French Christian democratic newspaper *Petit Démocrate* characterised the newly founded 'popular' international SIPDIC as necessary for counter-balancing the socialist and democratic internationals.[49]

When Catholic party cooperation began, the network overlapped with other increasingly institutionalised Catholic or at least Catholic-dominated networks of a primarily political character. Some limited overlap existed with Sangnier's organisation Internationale Démocratique, founded in

[46] Cf. Stefan Berger, 'Internationalismus als Lippenbekenntnis? Überlegungen zur Kooperation sozialdemokratischer Parteien in der Zwischenkriegszeit', in Mittag (ed.), *Politische Parteien*, 197–214; Donald Sassoon, *One Hundred Years of Socialism. The West European Left in the Twentieth Century* (London, New York: I. B. Tauris, 1996), chapter 2.

[47] Alwin Hanschmidt, 'Anläufe zu internationaler Kooperation radikaler und liberaler Parteien Europas 1919–1923', *Francia* 16 (1989), 35–48.

[48] Cf. Horst Haushefer, 'Die internationale Organisation der Bauernparteien', in Heinz Gollwitzer (ed.), *Europäische Bauernparteien im 20. Jahrhundert* (Stuttgart: Fischer, 1977), 668–90.

[49] *Le Petit Démocrate*, 4 March 1926.

1921, which was heavily dominated by left-wing Catholic peace activists. It was especially marked in the case of transnational cooperation of Christian trade unions and Catholic workers' associations. Sangnier, who was elected to the Chamber of Deputies in 1919, developed his transnational initiative out of the JR movement. He opposed the rigidly nationalist anti-German policy of the *Bloc national* governments, adopting Aristide Briand's idea of the two Germanies: one under the militarist Prussian influence, the other pro-democratic and republican and represented in essence by the three political parties of the Weimar coalition, which France had a moral duty to support in their attempt to establish parliamentary democracy and to follow a moderate foreign policy.[50] In 1922, Sangnier sharply attacked Prime Minister Raymond Poincaré for his intransigent policy, which resulted in the occupation of the Ruhr area in January 1923. The Internationale Démocratique organised a first congress in Paris in December 1921, which was not yet attended by representatives from the Central Powers,[51] and a second in Vienna in 1922. The third, in the university town of Freiburg in south-west Germany in August 1923, at the height of the Ruhr conflict, attracted some 1,500 German and 130 French participants.[52] After two more congresses, in London in 1924 and Luxembourg in 1925, the organisation's greatest success was the congress of August–September 1926, which took place during one full month in Sangnier's privately owned palace in Bierville in France. Although the participants came from all over Europe, the French and German delegations were by far the largest.

It was mainly left-wing Catholics and liberal democrats who participated in the activities of the Internationale Démocratique. They included, on the German side, members of the Centre Party and the DDP. The driving force was clearly the Friedensbund Deutscher Katholiken, an organisation of Catholic pacifists created in 1920 which had 49,000 members by 1931.[53] Once founded, it quickly established contacts with Sangnier's JR, which was greatly facilitated by its moderate and increasingly pacifist stance. In fact, Sangnier even called into question Germany's

[50] Gorguet, *Les Mouvements*, 77; Hermann Hagspiel, *Verständigung zwischen Deutschland und Frankreich. Die deutsch-französische Außenpolitik der zwanziger Jahre im innenpolitischen Kräftefeld beider Länder* (Bonn: Ludwig Röhrscheid, 1987), 241.
[51] Giorgio Vecchio, *Alla ricerca del partito. Cultura politica ed esperienze dei cattolici italiani nel primo Novecento* (Brescia: Morcelliana, 1987), 293.
[52] Rudolf Lambrecht, *Deutsche und französische Katholiken, 1914–1933. Auseinandersetzungen, Standpunkte, Meinungen, Kontakte*, PhD (Münster: Westfälische Wilhelms-Universität, 1967), 104.
[53] Beate Höfling, *Katholische Friedensbewegung zwischen zwei Weltkriegen. Der 'Friedensbund Deutscher Katholiken' 1917–1933* (Waldkirch: Waldkircher Verlagsgesellschaft, 1979), 162ff.

sole war guilt, which the German delegation had been forced to sign up to in the Versailles Treaty, with very negative repercussions for the legitimacy of the pro-democratic Weimar coalition in German politics. He also favoured substantial revisions of the treaty to create a more durable basis for better Franco-German relations in the future.[54] In view of these policies, the nationalist Action Française regularly denounced Sangnier in the 1920s as 'le boche', the German.[55] The PDP, which had tense relations with the much more left-wing JR, also distanced itself from his foreign policy.

On the other hand, it was precisely his moderate approach which initially made Sangnier attractive as a partner for transnational cooperation. Already in 1920–2, Sturzo and other PPI politicians approached him with the idea of creating a cross-border alliance of 'popular' parties, and Sturzo participated in the fourth congress in London in 1924. Some left-wing members of the German Centre Party also took part in Sangnier's activities.[56] Joos, who had already built up private contacts with Swiss, Dutch, Belgian and French politicians,[57] led the German delegation at Freiburg in 1923.[58] This congress agreed a compromise resolution condemning the French occupation of the Ruhr, but also asserting the legitimacy in principle of French reparation demands and demanding a role for the League of Nations in the regulation of the Ruhr conflict.[59] Other German participants included Christine Teusch, who – like Joos – also was to participate regularly in Catholic party cooperation. Yet Sturzo and Joos were mainly interested in politically meaningful party cooperation, whereas Sangnier conceived of his organisation more as a non-partisan democratic European youth movement working for a non-Marxist, anti-capitalist transformation of European industrial society and for some kind of new world order. As such, however, the Internationale Démocratique transformed itself more and more into a movement of radical pacifists, ultimately with no potential for effective links with transnational party politics.

In contrast, the overlap between Christian trade union and Catholic party cooperation was more pronounced. After all, the trade unions had

[54] Jean-Claude Delbreil, *Les Catholiques français et les tentatives de rapprochement franco-allemand (1920–1933)* (Metz: S. M. E. I., 1972), 218–21.

[55] As recalled by Sturzo in his report of the Franco-German meeting of leading Catholics in 1929, in 'Le conversazioni di Berlino' [Italian translation], *El Matì* [Barcelona], 16 January 1930, printed in Luigi Sturzo, *Miscellanea Londinese. Volume primo (anni 1925–1930)* (Bologna: Zanichelli, 1965), 229.

[56] Cf. Delbreil, *Centrisme*, 260.

[57] Oswald Wachtling, *Joseph Joos: Journalist, Arbeiterführer, Zentrumspolitiker. Politische Biographie 1878–1933* (Mainz: Matthias-Grünewald-Verlag, 1974), 75.

[58] Delbreil, *Les Catholiques*, 26.   [59] Gorguet, *Les Mouvements*, 83.

already institutionalised their cross-border links in 1908. The war under-mined the German leadership role, however. In 1919, the trade unions from western Europe and the Central Powers organised two separate congresses. In February 1920, a joint meeting took place in Rotterdam in the Netherlands, leading to the formation of the International Federation of Christian Trade Unions (IFCTU) in June 1920 with a secretariat in Utrecht, in the neutral Netherlands.[60] To minimise national conflicts after the war experience, the leading positions were initially allocated to two representatives of trade unions from neutral states. The Swiss Joseph Scherrer was the first president of the new organisation from 1920 to 1928, when he was succeeded by the German Bernhard Otte. After the dissolu-tion of the Italian Catholic trade unions, he represented by far the largest national organisation, with some 720,000 members. Throughout the interwar period, the IFCTU's secretary-general was the Dutchman P. J. S. Serrarens, who was also a board member of the Dutch Catholic trade unions.

The IFCTU organised seven major congresses until the start of World War II. Its own activities were supplemented by the cross-border cooper-ation of sectoral Christian trade unions.[61] Cooperation proved difficult after the war experience, however. Stegerwald strongly resented the loss of the leading role of the German unions. As Serrarens later recalled, Stegerwald frequently tried to use the IFCTU as a 'political instrument'[62] for propagating revisions of the Versailles Treaty and for isolating the French delegation, which succeeded, for example, at the IFCTU congress in Innsbruck in 1922 over the thorny question of reparations.[63] At the same time, the French delegations found it difficult to acknowledge the longer tradition as well as the greater organisational power and efficiency of the German trade unions, and their leading role in starting cooperation before the war. In some cases, personal experiences and resulting inhibi-tions also played a role. This is true of Jules Zirnheld, for example, the main French representative who became IFCTU president in 1933, after the dissolution of the German unions. Zirnheld came from the Alsace region, which belonged to Germany during 1871–1918, but he opted to fight on

[60] On the cooperation of Christian trade unions see in greater detail Patrick Pasture, *Histoire du syndicalisme chrétien international: la difficile recherche d'une troisième voie* (Paris: L'Harmattan, 1999).
[61] Jules Verstraelen, 'Die internationale christliche Arbeiterbewegung', in S. Herman Scholl (ed.), *Katholische Arbeiterbewegung in Westeuropa* (Bonn: Eichholz-Verlag, 1966), 425.
[62] P. J. S. Serrarens, *25 Jahre Christliche Gewerkschafts-Internationale* (Utrecht: Huis van den Arbeid, 1946), 18.
[63] Delbreil, *Les Catholiques*, 63.

the French side as a pilot in World War I. When he was shot down and captured, he was condemned to death for desertion by a German war tribunal. He was eventually pardoned, but had to spend one and a half years in a single prison cell during the rest of the war.[64]

Several of the regular participants in IFCTU activities also played an important role in Catholic party cooperation. This is true of Serrarens, for example. Other active trade unionists, who regularly attended SIPDIC meetings, included Georges Rutten from the Belgian ACW and Gaston Tessier from the French PDP. Similar overlap in participating national representatives existed between SIPDIC and the Catholic workers' organisations with their well-established transnational links that were only institutionalised in 1928, however. In that year, 350 representatives attended the founding congress of the Catholic Workers' International (CWI) in Cologne. One of the main speakers at the congress was Carl Sonnenschein, the *enfant terrible* of German Catholic workers' education and self-help initiatives, who had strong Italian connections and helped Sturzo establish contacts with the Centre Party leadership in 1921. Joos, who represented the Centre Party at every SIPDIC congress between 1925 and 1932 with the single exception of 1931, which the Germans boycotted, became president of the new organisation. Adenauer, the mayor of Cologne, supported the CWI as well as SIPDIC, without being an active participant, and gave a reception for the delegations of the CWI founding congress.[65] Other leading CWI activists, who also regularly attended SIPDIC events, included Hendrik Heyman and Paul W. Segers from Belgium, for example.

The 1920s also saw the growth of other transnational networks that did not have the same overtly political character, but nonetheless created important connections between Catholic party cooperation and lay religious and publishing activities. Many Catholic politicians, who played an important role, or at least took a keen interest in, party cooperation were also regular participants in Europe-wide activities of Pax Romana, founded in 1921, for example. They included from Germany, among others, Joos, Wirth and Julius Stocky, the editor of the influential Catholic newspaper *Kölnische Volkszeitung* in Cologne, and from France, Auguste Champetier de Ribes, Louis-Alfred Pagès, Tessier and Bidault, as well as Catholic

---

[64] Verstraelen, 'Die internationale christliche Arbeiterbewegung', 423.
[65] Ibid., 438–40. See also Joseph Joos, *Am Räderwerk der Zeit. Erinnerungen aus der katholischen und sozialen Bewegung und Politik* (Augsburg: Verlag Winfried-Werk, 1951), 75ff.

politicians with connections with the trade unions like Stegerwald, or with Catholic conservative networks like von Papen.[66] The editors of important Catholic newspapers and journals also had cross-border links and, on the initiative of Stocky, created a permanent secretariat for the exchange of information and articles in Cologne in June 1928. These newspapers included *inter alia* the *Kölnische Volkszeitung*, *El Matí* from Barcelona, *La Croix* from Paris, *La Libre Belgique* from Brussels, *De Maasbode* from Rotterdam, *Luxemburger Wort* from Luxembourg, *Vaterland* from Luzerne, *Reichspost* from Vienna and *Katholische Korrespondenz* from Münster, a German Catholic news agency with international connections directed by Friedrich Muckermann. Several editors like Stocky or journalists working for these and other newspapers also participated in SIPDIC activities, or at least kept in close touch, to develop editorial guidelines compatible with the priorities of party cooperation, and to facilitate the publishing activities in several languages of leading Catholic politicians like Sturzo from his exile in London.[67]

Other European non-partisan organisations outside the Catholic milieu also provided opportunities for contacts. Thus, Sturzo originally envisaged the creation of a European 'popular' party organisation to take place in the context of the first postwar IPU congress in Stockholm in 1921.[68] Many politicians, who participated in SIPDIC activities like Teusch, were also engaged in the IPU as an international inter-party forum for parliamentarians. The incipient European movements created cross-party thematic networks directed at some form of closer European cooperation or integration.[69] The Paneuropean Union, formed in 1923–4 by Count Richard Coudenhove-Kalergi, an Austrian Catholic conservative, had a strongly continental European and anti-bolshevist agenda. It organised two major congresses, one in Vienna in 1926 and the other in Berlin in 1930.[70] The Committee for European Cooperation, on the other hand, favoured cooperation with Britain and the Soviet Union to create a new European order. It was originally founded in Germany in 1924 by the liberal DDP

---

[66] Papini, *Le Courage*, 176.   [67] Ibid., 175–6.

[68] On the IPU after World War I see Ralph Uhlig, 'Internationalismus in den zwanziger Jahren. Die Interparlamentarische Union', *Historische Mitteilungen der Ranke-Gesellschaft* 4 (1991), 89–100.

[69] As an introduction to the history of the European movements and the European 'idea' in interwar Europe see Carl H. Pegg, *Evolution of the European Idea, 1914–1932* (Chapel Hill: University of North Carolina Press, 1983).

[70] Drawing in part upon previously inaccessible sources see Anita Ziegerhofer-Prettenthaler, *Botschafter Europas. Richard Nikolaus Coudenhove-Kalergi und die Paneuropa-Bewegung in den zwanziger und dreißiger Jahren* (Vienna: Böhlau, 2004).

politician Wilhelm Heile, who was also one of the vice-presidents of the European organisation of democratic parties. Subsequently, it was extended to other countries, with a first European congress in September 1926.[71] Both organisations had national committees, however, limiting transnational communication outside of the major congresses; their aims remained quite vague, and their penetration of political parties and parliamentary politics was low. In fact, the adhesion of individual members often appears to have depended more on personal contacts than ideological predispositions. Thus, Wirth, although a left-wing republican in favour of cooperation with the Soviet Union, who had been responsible, as chancellor, for the 1922 German-Russian Treaty of Rapallo, joined the relatively small German section of the Paneuropean Union and gave a speech at its congress in Berlin.[72] On the other hand, the more strongly anti-communist Catholic conservatives Kaas and Marx, without becoming engaged, officially supported the competing organisation formed by Heile.[73] The national sections of both organisations were in part funded by the Auswärtiges Amt, the German foreign ministry. It regarded them as a potentially useful back-up for its policy of peaceful revision under the leadership of the national-liberal foreign minister, Gustav Stresemann, from November 1923 until his death in October 1929, and for a short while thereafter.[74] The Quai d'Orsay, the French foreign ministry, also had relations with all European groups, but was suspicious of Coudenhove, who they believed was too germanophile.[75]

After World War II, the Christian democratic Nouvelles Équipes Internationales (NEI) were actually formally part of the European Movement and thus, participated in its congress at The Hague in May 1948. In contrast, the overlap between Catholic party cooperation and European movements was very limited in interwar Europe. This was even more true of some other 'pro-European' institutionalised networks such as the Franco-German Committee for Documentation and Information founded in 1926 by Emile Mayrisch, the owner of the

---

[71] Cf. Karl Holl, 'Europapolitik im Vorfeld der deutschen Regierungspolitik. Zur Tätigkeit proeuropäischer Organisationen in der Weimarer Republik', *Historische Zeitschrift* 219 (1974), 33–94.
[72] Pegg, *Evolution*, 106 and 144. On Wirth see in greater detail Ulrike Hörster-Philipps, *Joseph Wirth 1879–1956. Eine politische Biographie* (Paderborn: Schöningh, 1998); Heinrich Küppers, *Joseph Wirth. Parlamentarier, Minister und Kanzler der Weimarer Republik* (Stuttgart: Franz Steiner, 1997).
[73] Holl, 'Europapolitik', 62.   [74] Ibid., 75.
[75] Laurence Badel, 'Le Quai d'Orsay, les associations privées et l'Europe (1925–1932)', in René Girault and Gérard Bossuat (eds.), *Europe brisée, Europe retrouvée. Nouvelles réflexions sur l'unité européenne au XXe siècle* (Paris: Publications de la Sorbonne, 1994), 122.

ARBED steel empire in Luxembourg.[76] It had offices in Luxembourg, Paris and Berlin and mainly involved company executives and civil servants. It supported the creation of the International Steel Cartel in September 1926 and pushed for the Franco-German commercial treaty, which was concluded in July 1927.[77] It explicitly excluded active politicians from participation, however, for fear of importing national conflicts into its organisation and activities. Although some Catholic politicians like von Papen had contacts with members of the Mayrisch Committee, its activities did not overlap with party cooperation. Similarly, the International Committee for a European Customs Union was also only very loosely connected with political circles. The Fédération des Unions Intellectuelles, created in 1922–4 by Prince Karl Anton Rohan, also tried to avoid politicised topics. It mainly involved conservative Catholic intellectuals. Although some contacts existed with Catholic politicians like Seipel, they were sporadic and provided no basis for meaningful interaction with party cooperation. Moreover, whereas Catholic party cooperation was dominated by left-Catholic politicians with close links to the Christian trade unions and Catholic workers' associations, some of these other organisations mainly involved Catholic conservatives, philo-fascists and even fascists like Hermann Göring, Alfred Rosenberg and other national socialists who attended meetings of the Paneuropean Union.

At the more strictly bilateral and regional level, other openings for transnational links were more important. This is especially true of the two Franco-German Catholic congresses in Paris in 1928 and in Berlin in 1929. They included pro-democratic SIPDIC activists like Pezet from the PDP and – from the Centre Party – Joos, who was well versed in the art of mediation and conducted the debates in 1929, Teusch and Heinrich Krone, its deputy secretary-general during 1927–33, as well as Wirth and

---

[76] For these other organisations see – as a short introduction – Guido Müller, 'France and Germany after the Great War. Business Men, Intellectuals and Artists in Non-Governmental European Networks', in Jessica C. E. Gienow-Hecht and Frank Schumacher (eds.), *Culture and International History* (New York: Berghahn, 2003), 97–114; in much greater detail Guido Müller, *Europäische Gesellschaftsbeziehungen nach dem Ersten Weltkrieg. Das Deutsch-Französische Studienkomitee und der Europäische Kulturbund* (Munich: Oldenbourg, 2005).

[77] On the role of transnational societal (economic) actors in the preparation of the international steel cartel see Clemens Wurm, 'Deutsche Frankreichpolitik und deutsch-französische Beziehungen in der Weimarer Republik 1923/24–1929: Politik, Kultur, Wirtschaft', in Klaus Schwabe and Francesca Schinzinger (eds.), *Deutschland und der Westen im 19. und 20. Jahrhundert*, vol. II: *Deutschland und Westeuropa* (Stuttgart: Franz Steiner, 1994), 137–57. On the steel cartel as part of the corporatist organisation of capitalism in interwar Europe, see also Charles S. Maier, *Recasting Bourgeois Europe: Stabilization in France, Germany and Italy in the Decade after World War I* (Princeton, N.J.: Princeton University Press, 1975), 516–45.

Stegerwald, for example. Crucially, these congresses made an attempt to extend Franco-German cooperation to Catholic conservatives from France, like Frédéric François Marsal, who was prime minister for a short period in 1924, and others from the more nationalist political camp of André Tardieu and Louis Marin, as well as Catholic conservative intellectuals like Count Vladimir d'Ormesson, and, in Germany, to more conservative Centre Party politicians like Marx, Brüning, von Papen and others.[78] The exchanges at the two congresses were tense and dominated by nationalist claims and counter-claims, however. The Centre Party politician, member of the Reichstag and priest Karl Ulitzka, from Upper Silesia, made a particularly controversial speech in which he expressed disappointment with political developments since the Locarno Treaty and demanded *inter alia* the return of the south-eastern part of Upper Silesia and of the Polish Corridor to Germany. His remarks were deliberately leaked and caused uproar in the right-wing press in France, forcing the PDP newspaper *Petit Démocrate* to play down the political character of the meeting.[79] The Berlin congress ended with a very general and meaningless resolution emphasising the need for a better Franco-German mutual 'understanding' and the particular 'obligation' of Catholics to contribute towards it. It clearly demonstrated the extremely narrow limits of rapprochement in networks including Catholic conservatives and nationalists.

In these prevailing circumstances, societal networks could only have a limited influence on the bilateral relations between Catholics of different political orientation and, in the French case, party allegiance. This is true, for example, for the non-confessional Deutsch-Französische Gesellschaft (DFG), founded in 1928 by the art historian Otto Grautoff, who saw himself as a 'mediator in bilateral cultural and societal relations'.[80] Its Berlin office held forty-two public events on political and economic topics during 1928–33, also utilising the existing left-Catholic networks when it organised speeches by Joos on 'What Germany expects of France' and by

---

[78] Cf. Lambrecht, *Deutsche und französische Katholiken*, 180–3; Höfling, *Katholische Friedensbewegung*, 190–1.

[79] *Le Petit Démocrate*, 5 January 1930.

[80] Ina Belitz, *Befreundung mit dem Fremden: Die Deutsch-Französische Gesellschaft in den deutsch-französischen Kultur- und Gesellschaftsbeziehungen der Locarno-Ära. Programme und Protagonisten der transnationalen Verständigung zwischen Pragmatismus und Idealismus* (Frankfurt/Main: Lang, 1997), 3. See also Hans-Manfred Bock, 'Kulturelle Eliten in den deutsch-französischen Gesellschaftsbeziehungen der Zwischenkriegszeit', in Rainer Hudemann and Georges-Henri Soutou (eds.), *Eliten in Deutschland und Frankreich im 19. und 20. Jahrhundert. Strukturen und Beziehungen*, vol. I (Munich: Oldenbourg, 1994), 82ff.

Pezet on 'The French parties before the elections'. Funded by the German foreign ministry, it also published the journals *Revue d'Allemagne* and *Deutsch-Französische Rundschau*. In August 1930 the DFG organised the Sohlberg camp for German and French youths, with representatives from the PDP, JR and the Centre Party, among others. As Ina Belitz has emphasised, however, these events were already overshadowed in the early 1930s by the world economic crisis and the sharp deterioration in the bilateral governmental relations between both countries, and its 'appeals for reconciliation were very general and devoid of meaningful content'.[81] By this time, the Lake Constance conferences, a more regional forum for Catholic cooperation during 1921–6, had already ceased, as they hinged on the personal initiative of Hugo Baur, a Catholic supporter of the Sangnier movement, who fell seriously ill in 1926. They initially brought together Catholic politicians from Germany, Austria and Switzerland, and in their final years also from other countries like Belgium, including Joos, Heyman and other SIPDIC activists.[82]

This boom in cross-border institutionalised societal networks in Europe after World War I was significant in that it also gave greater legitimacy to Catholic party cooperation. It now appeared to be part of a larger trend of European transnationalisation. In fact, to underline the difference from socialists, who allegedly felt greater allegiance to their ideology than their country, Pagès wrote about SIPDIC in *Petit Démocrate* in July 1927, 'we are absolutely not internationalists, in the sense in which this term is normally used. Another term appears much more appropriate ... we are transnationalists.'[83] The wider process of transnationalisation was largely limited to small socio-cultural elites, however, especially from the churches, worker organisations, and the peace and youth movements. Their efforts remained quite isolated from society at large.[84] Even within their specific contexts, the success of the growing networks was contingent on favourable international circumstances. When these sharply deteriorated in the late 1920s and early 1930s, their activities declined and their

---

[81] Belitz, *Befreundung*, 377.

[82] Georg Schreiber, *Deutschland und Österreich. Deutsche Begegnungen mit Österreichs Wissenschaft und Kultur. Erinnerungen aus den letzten Jahrzehnten* (Cologne, Graz: Böhlau, 1956), 70–8. See also the personal recollection in Hugo Baur, *Mein politischer Lebenslauf* (Konstanz: Oberbadische Verlagsanstalt, 1929).

[83] L. A. Pagès, 'La Conférence internationale de Cologne', *Petit Démocrate*, 25 July 1927.

[84] Michel Trebitsch and Hans Manfred Bock, 'L'Image du voisin: opinion et rencontres', in Robert Frank, Laurent Gerrereau and Hans Joachim Neyer (eds.), *La Course au moderne. France et Allemagne dans l'Europe des années vingt, 1919–1933* (Paris: Musée d'histoire contemporaine de la Bibliothèque de documentation internationale contemporaine, 1992), 30.

relevance diminished further. Moreover, as Clemens Wurm has rightly emphasised, the growth of transnational contacts as such did not necessarily result in better relations at governmental level, the more so as the two spheres remained quite distinct, with almost no overlap.[85] Catholic party cooperation was only very partially embedded in the various transnational links. It was mainly supported by the networks of Christian trade unions and Catholic workers' associations and, up to a point, the Catholic peace movement. It did not extend to Catholic conservatives and nationalists, who – when they met as in 1928–9 – found no sufficient common ground for more than a superficial exchange of nationalist demands. Even within a SIPDIC dominated by left-Catholics, with the principal will to discuss and regulate national conflicts peacefully, however, the cultural and political barriers to effective cooperation were still very high.

[85] Wurm, 'Deutsche Frankreichpolitik', 150.

CHAPTER 3

After Versailles: left-Catholic cooperation

Among the Catholic parties in Europe, the Italian PPI was the only one to quickly develop a keen interest in foreign policy shortly after the end of World War I. Organised transnational cooperation of Catholic parties played an important role in their concept of a more peaceful European order. Already at the party congress in Bologna in June 1919, Achille Grandi proposed that the PPI should initiate such transnational contacts, although it appears that he was still thinking more in terms of trade union cooperation.[1] One month after the national elections, in which the PPI came second to the Socialists, the party executive resolved to establish bilateral contacts with other Catholic and 'popular' parties with the aim of creating a 'popular international'.[2] Subsequently, in May 1920, the PPI congress passed a motion calling for such formalised transnational party cooperation.[3] Sturzo strongly pushed for the establishment of foreign links, together with other leading Popolari. They included, *inter alia*, Cavazzoni, the conservative leader of the PPI parliamentary party 1919–22, and Livio Tovini, vice-president of the newly elected parliament. Also interested in transnational party cooperation were De Gasperi, parliamentary party leader 1922–4, party leader 1924–6 and Italian prime minister after World War II, and Rufo Ruffo della Scaletta, who presided over the PPI foreign policy committee and was elected to the party executive in November 1921. Like Sturzo, these last two Popolari had closer contacts with the German-speaking world. De Gasperi was a member of the Austrian *Reichrat* parliament from 1911 to 1918.

Why this enthusiasm for transnational cooperation of the Popolari leadership at a time when other Catholic parties were still almost wholly

---

[1] Vecchio, *Alla ricerca*, 277.   [2] Ibid.
[3] Stefano Trinchese, 'L'internazionale democratico-cristiana attraverso la corrispondenza di F. L. Ferrari', in *Universalità e cultura nel pensiero dei Luigi Sturzo. Atti del Convegno Internazionale di Studio Roma, Istituto Luigi Sturzo 28, 29, 30 ottobre 1999* (Soveria Mannelli: Rubbettino, 2001), 339.

preoccupied with domestic socio-economic and political concerns so shortly after the war? In his biography of Ruffo della Scaletta, Gabriele De Rosa has emphasised the ambivalent Italian identity after World War I, which induced the Popolari to seek a mediating role for themselves in European party cooperation and foreign policy. Italy won the war by default. 'Spiritually and economically, [Italians] felt like a vanquished nation', however.[4] The Popolari shared this widespread sentiment, the more so as most of them had been more sceptical in the first place about Italy's entry into the war in 1915 against Vatican opposition. Militarily, without massive Allied support Italy would have succumbed to the onslaught of the Central Powers in 1918. Economically, it depended on their assistance after 1918. Politically, it did not secure the large territorial gains, especially in the Adriatic, which the French and British had dangled as a carrot in front of the Italian government in 1914–15 to lure it into the war. At the same time, the annexation of the very predominantly German-speaking South Tyrol could be reversed and was still a surmountable barrier to the normalisation of relations with Austria and Germany.[5]

The majority of the PPI leadership, including Sturzo, began to advocate a constructive policy towards Germany shortly after the war. They saw the Versailles Treaty as an unreasonable punishment of an entire nation and its economic clauses as a barrier to the reconstruction in Europe as a whole, which was of great importance for Italy. At the same time, its political clauses undermined the stability of the new German democracy, which was crucial for a durable European peace order. De Gasperi believed that the German question was the key to the pacification of Europe, and that the German Centre Party had to play a crucial role in this process.[6] At the PPI congress in Turin in 1923, Ruffo della Scaletta strongly opposed French reparation demands, which in his view hung like the sword of Damocles 'not only over Germany, but over Europe as a whole'.[7] Opposition to what appeared, from the perspective of many Popolari, as a 'French policy of retribution'[8] became so strong during the occupation of the Ruhr that, in 1923, the previously more francophile PPI newspaper *Corriere d'Italia* also moved towards a much more pro-German reporting of European politics.

---

[4] Gabriele De Rosa, *Rufo Ruffo della Scaletta e Luigi Sturzo (con lettere e documenti inediti tratti dall'archivio Ruffo della Scaletta)* (Rome: Edizioni di Storia e Letteratura, 1961), 17.
[5] For PPI foreign policy see also Giorgio Gualerzi, *La politica estera dei popolari* (Rome: Cinque lune, 1959).
[6] Francesco Malgeri, 'Alle origini del Partito Popolare Europeo', *Storia e Politica* 18 (1979), 296.
[7] Ibid.
[8] Maddalena Guiotto, 'Luigi Sturzo e il mondo politico e intellettuale della Germania di Weimar', in *Universalità*, 446.

By then, the PPI demanded a thorough revision of the Versailles Treaty inclusive of territorial changes to Germany's advantage.

PPI policy on Germany, which aimed at quickly integrating the Weimar Republic as a fully equal partner into the new Europe, was also informed by the traditional admiration for German political Catholicism. Left-Catholics like Sturzo were primarily impressed with the German tradition of Catholic trade unionism and worker associationalism including self-help organisations and adult education. More generally, as Maddalena Guiotto has pointed out, Sturzo and other Popolari had always regarded the Centre Party as a shining example of a non-clerical people's party attracting voters from all social classes, although in the confessionally mixed country, it remained limited to the Catholic population.[9] They were also impressed by the progress of the early Weimar Republic. At one point in 1921, the pro-democratic Catholic republican Wirth was chancellor, the political position that the conservative Protestant aristocrat Bismarck had occupied when he started the *Kulturkampf* against German Catholics fifty years previously. At the same time, the Catholic trade unionist Stegerwald presided over the *Staatsrat*, the government of the largest German state of Prussia, allegedly the incarnation of German militarism. Germany appeared to transform itself from a Prussian-Protestant dominated militaristic great power to a constitutional civilian power under strong Catholic democratic influence at the heart of Europe.

In these favourable circumstances, the interests of the Centre Party and the revisionist national cause were very effectively pushed by the German embassy to the Vatican. This was now largely under the political influence of the Centre Party and developed close relations with the PPI. In July 1920, the embassy began to supply the PPI leadership with information material on the Centre Party and its policies, and with German arguments for the revision of the Versailles Treaty.[10] When the influential Centre Party newspaper *Germania* published an article shortly afterwards, which was somewhat critical of Sturzo for his strongly left-Catholic views, the embassy immediately contacted the German party leadership via the foreign ministry, and advised them that Sturzo deserved to be supported for his pro-German attitudes.[11] The embassy also had direct links with influential Centre Party politicians like Marx, party leader 1922–8 and chancellor 1923–4, 1926 and 1927–8, who narrowly lost the 1925 presidential

[9] Ibid., 444.   [10] Ibid., 446.
[11] Deutsche Botschaft Vatikan an Auswärtiges Amt, 4 August 1920, PA AA Rom-Vatikan, 1062, cited in ibid., 447.

elections to Paul von Hindenburg, the conservative war hero.[12] It continued to inform them about its close contacts with Popolari like Sturzo and Ruffo della Scaletta,[13] and it also helped with the organisation of visits to Germany by PPI politicians.

With the ultimate aim of creating a 'popular' international, which could foster their foreign policy goals, several Popolari were involved in establishing a network of contacts during 1920–21. In May 1920, Cavazzoni went to Paris. In the absence of a mainstream Catholic party there, he mainly talked to French trade unionists, however. In June, he participated in the IFCTU founding congress in The Hague. He also travelled to Belgium and Germany. In Berlin he met with the Centre Party politician Karl Trimborn, the party leader, Konstantin Fehrenbach, who at that time was chancellor, Heinrich Brauns, minister of labour 1920–28, as well as Wirth, who all appeared to be open-minded about the creation of a transnational organisation for devising a common policy against the rise of communism and for some form of European policy coordination.[14] Giulio De Rossi activated his contacts in France. De Rossi directed PPI press policy. He was close to Sturzo and had a large personal network dating from his previous role in the international student movement.[15] In Belgium, the ACW showed great interest in the PPI and, on 10 October 1920, its leaders discussed the Popolari initiative with Dutch and Italian representatives.[16] Subsequently, Tovini set out for a European tour of Catholic parties in early 1921. He visited Switzerland, France (where he coordinated the meetings with his French interlocutors with Cavazzoni), Belgium, Germany, Poland, Austria, Czechoslovakia and Hungary.[17] Tovini returned from his journey with the distinct impression that the prevailing 'postwar psychological state of mind'[18] for the time being made the creation of a party international impossible. Moreover, the leaders of some more traditional Catholic parties, as in the Netherlands and Belgium, were sceptical, whether Catholic parties should form an

---

[12] On Marx's central role in the Centre Party in the 1920s see in more detail Ulrich von Hehl, *Wilhelm Marx 1863–1946. Eine politische Biographie* (Mainz: Matthias-Grünewald-Verlag, 1987).

[13] See, for example, Klee to Marx, 6 April 1923, Historisches Archiv der Stadt Köln (henceforth: HAStK), NL 1070; Rieth to Marx, 10 April 1923, ibid.

[14] *Germania*, 18 July 1920 and 27 July 1920. See also Vecchio, *Alla ricerca*, 279; Papini, *Le Courage*, 117. The bilateral contacts were also reported in the Centre Party parliamentary party. Report Dr Herschel, 5 November 1920, printed in *Die Protokolle der Reichstagsfraktion der Deutschen Zentrumspartei 1920–1925* (Mainz: Matthias-Grünewald-Verlag, 1981), 105.

[15] Carl Sonnenschein, 'Italienisches Reisetagebuch', *Hochland* 18 (1921), 547; Vecchio, *Alla ricerca*, 280.

[16] Emmanuel Gerard, 'Uit de voorgeschiedenis van het ACW: het einde van de Volksbond en de oprichting van het Democratisch Blok (1918–1921)', *De Gids op Maatschappelijk Gebied* 69 (1978), 514.

[17] Cf. Malgeri, 'Alle origini', 292; Papini, *Le Courage*, 119.   [18] Vecchio, *Alla ricerca*, 283.

international when – in the words of Roberto Papini – 'the Church is the Catholic International par excellence'.[19] Indeed, when the Popolari approached Cardinal Gasparri, the Vatican state secretary, later on in 1921 to elucidate the likely papal reaction to the formation of a 'popular' international, he argued in the same vein that it could be seen as competing with the Church for the legitimate international representation of Catholic interests. The question would, therefore, be, 'What is the advantage of creating a new organisation, which will only lead to confusion?'[20]

In these circumstances, Tovini suggested adopting a more modest project for an 'inter-parliamentary union' of Catholic deputies to the PPI executive in March 1921.[21] In line with his recommendation, on 1 August 1921, Cavazzoni wrote to the leaders of Catholic parties in Europe with the proposal for such a Catholic inter-parliamentary union.[22] In his letter he emphasised that the new organisation would be geared towards parties and policy coordination. As such, it would be distinct from other forms of transnational Catholic cooperation like the trade union organisation IFCTU. Its overriding aim would be to 'increasingly develop an international political consciousness, which is informed by our principles' as Catholic parties.[23] Cavazzoni included the proposed draft statutes. They envisaged the creation of a secretariat with a secretary-general, the annual organisation of conferences of Catholic parliamentarians, the regular publication of a bulletin, the exchange of information on national policies and law-making, as well as contacts with other Catholic transnational societal organisations. To counter concerns about national sovereignty – especially, but not only in the neutral countries – Cavazzoni emphasised that all member parties would retain 'complete national liberty' to pursue their own policies. He suggested that the PPI proposal should be discussed later in the same month, in the context of the first postwar IPU congress in Stockholm. PPI representatives did talk to German and Austrian politicians in Stockholm.[24] Due to their presence, however, the French and Belgians boycotted the congress.[25] Moreover, several Catholic parties did

[19] Papini, *Le Courage*, 58.
[20] Cited in Pietro Scoppola, *La Chiesa e il fascismo. Documenti e interpretazioni* (Bari: Laterza, 1971), 49.
[21] Alwin Hanschmidt, 'Eine christlich-demokratische "Internationale" zwischen den Weltkriegen. Das "Secrétariat International des Partis Démocratiques d'Inspiration Chrétienne" in Paris', in Winfried Becker and Rudolf Morsey (eds.), *Christliche Demokratie in Europa. Grundlagen und Entwicklungen seit dem 19. Jahrhundert* (Cologne, Vienna: Böhlau, 1988), 155.
[22] Cavazzoni to Nolens, 1 August 1921, Katholiek Documentatie Centrum (henceforth: KDC), Archief W. H. Nolens, 483/485.
[23] Ibid.   [24] See Guiotto, 'Luigi Sturzo', 450.   [25] Cf. Uhlig, 'Internationalismus'.

not receive the Italian proposal in time, had no delegates at the IPU congress, or did not provide them with instructions.

Thus, the Popolari first concentrated on strengthening their bilateral contacts with the Centre Party to create a basis for possible later party cooperation on a multilateral level. During his journey to Italy in May 1921, Carl Sonnenschein worked with Sturzo to reactivate the contacts dating from the previous visits to Germany by Cavazzoni and Tovini.[26] Sonnenschein is an excellent example of an intercultural mediator in Catholic politics in interwar Europe.[27] He studied at the Collegium Germanicum Hungaricum in Rome, and then at the papal University Gregoriana. After finishing his doctoral studies, he became a priest in 1900. In 1901 he first visited Sturzo in Caltagirone in Sicily, to study and discuss his extensive social work. They later met several times in Milan and Rome.[28] Sonnenschein began to work for the Catholic Volksverein in Mönchengladbach. His many social and educational activities included work with Italian migrant workers in the mines in the Neandertal valley between Düsseldorf and Wuppertal. After World War I, Sonnenschein also cared for Italian workers and exchange students in Berlin.[29] Together with De Rossi, 'an old friend from international student congresses',[30] Sonnenschein coordinated a telegram from Sturzo to Wirth of 20 May 1921 proposing closer relations between the PPI and the Centre Party with the ultimate aim of forming a party international to 'work together for the creation of a Christian Europe'.[31] Wirth responded positively five days later, declaring his interest in closer links, which created a favourable impression among Popolari leaders, and especially Sturzo.[32]

Following upon this initiative, and despite the failure to organise a larger meeting in Stockholm for mid-September, a high-level PPI delegation visited Germany in late September 1921. It comprised Sturzo, De Gasperi, Ruffo della Scaletta, Stefano Jacini and Francesco Bianco. Sonnenschein travelled with the group and acted as interpreter. They mainly visited Munich, where they held talks with BVP politicians, Berlin and Cologne including meetings with Wirth, Stegerwald, Brauns, Johannes Giesberts, the minister for postal affairs, and Adenauer. In the

---

[26] Sonnenschein, 'Italienisches Reisetagebuch', 547–55.
[27] For the only biography of Sonnenschein see Ernst Thrasolt, *Dr. Carl Sonnenschein. Der Mensch und sein Werk* (Munich: Verlag Jos. Kösel & Friedr. Pustet, 1930).
[28] Ibid., 52.
[29] Werner Krebber (ed.), *Den Menschen Recht verschaffen. Carl Sonnenschein: Person und Werk* (Würzburg: Echter, 1996), 13–17.
[30] Sonnenschein, 'Italienisches Reisetagebuch', 547.   [31] Ibid.   [32] Ibid., 555.

consultations, Sturzo strongly supported the left-Catholic preference for continued collaboration of the Centre Party with the social democrats as opposed to the alternative of a centre-right majority including Stresemann's national-liberal Deutsche Volkspartei (DVP), the German People's Party, and possibly even, the conservative-nationalist DNVP. The Popolari once more set out their plan for an inter-parliamentary union. Its guiding idea was not, Sturzo argued, to replace the nation-state, but to overcome the 'egoistic structure of a pagan character' of international relations, which in his view was characterised, especially in the age of nationalism, by attempts by the great powers to achieve hegemonic control over other states and peoples.[33] The new 'Christian' European order should be equally opposed to liberal cosmopolitanism and the SI's idea of class unity. It would be in complete harmony with Wilson's original programme for a postwar peace order, providing for the full economic reconstruction of Germany and the successor states of the Habsburg Monarchy.[34] Sturzo also reiterated that Italians – and the Popolari in the context of party cooperation – were in his view ideally placed due to their peculiar war experience, to mediate between France and Germany.

The PPI consultations with the Centre Party were widely reported in the European press. The Dutch *De Maasbode* wrote, for example, that the Italian and German Catholics were in basic agreement, and that Sturzo wanted to call a first meeting of Catholic parties as soon as February 1922.[35] With the exception of Sangnier and the JR, however, French Catholics reacted very negatively to the intensification of contacts between the PPI and the Centre Party. They regarded Sturzo as much too germanophile and were strictly opposed to any revisions of the Versailles Treaty, which the PPI leader contemplated. To counteract allegations in the anticlerical press throughout Europe that the Catholics were preparing a 'black international', and also to keep a free hand politically, the Vatican also explicitly distanced itself from Sturzo's initiative. In a semi-official statement in the *L'Osservatore Romano*, it emphasised that the Church had nothing to do with the preparatory talks in Germany, and that Sturzo's plans were for parties only and did not involve Church organisations in any way.[36]

Sturzo returned from Germany with the impression that he had won the leading Centre Party politicians over for his plan. De Gasperi was more

---

[33] 'Il significato dell'Internazionale Popolare', *Il Popolo nuovo*, 2 October 1921. See also Malgeri, 'Alle origini', 295.
[34] Papini, *Le Courage*, 113–5.   [35] *De Maasbode*, 28 September 1921.
[36] 'L'Internazionale popolare', *L'Osservatore Romano*, 26–7 September 1921.

sceptical, however, as it could be difficult domestically for the Germans to agree to formalised party contacts without the prior assurance that they would indeed result in some kind of support for their revisionist foreign policy goals. Within the PPI, Sturzo continued to argue for the creation of a 'popular' international, linking this increasingly to the long-term goal of creating a political federation in Europe.[37] During 1922–3, however, the Popolari became more and more preoccupied with the deteriorating domestic political situation, and with clarifying their policy towards Mussolini. The PPI congress in Turin in April 1923 finally concluded that the time was not yet ripe for creating a 'popular' international, and that the plans had to be put on ice.[38] During these years, the idea continued to be discussed informally, for example between Sturzo, Sangnier, Wirth and others on the margins of the Genoa Conference in April 1922,[39] during the first postwar conference of Catholic workers' associations in Konstanz in January 1923, which was attended by Joos from Germany, Heyman from Belgium and W. H. Nolens from the Netherlands, among others,[40] and in the context of Sangnier's congress in Freiburg later in the same year. The core problem remained, however, that the Catholic parties lacked a serious mainstream partner in France – a French Catholic or 'popular' party, moreover, that would have been willing to cooperate with German Catholics on an equal footing.

The first postwar years were characterised by the heated nationalist atmosphere of what Michel Trebitsch and Hans Manfred Bock have called a 'cold war', especially in Franco-German relations.[41] Negative mutual images had developed since 1870–1, if not actually since the Napoleonic wars. The great power rivalry was reflected in, and reinforced by, stereo-typical juxtapositions of alleged national character traits and identity, of German culture and French civilisation. By neatly delineating sharp cultural borders, as Michael Jeismann has pointed out,[42] the enemy image was an important constitutive element in nation-building for elites in both countries: in Germany, for national integration, and in France, for the political consolidation of the Third Republic after the lost war of 1870–1. The experience of World War I and its immediate aftermath

---

[37] As reported in *De Maasbode*, 2 May 1922.
[38] Hanschmidt, 'Eine christlich-demokratische', 162.   [39] Vecchio, *Alla ricerca*, 286.
[40] As recalled in Joseph Joos, 'Offener Brief an Marc Sangnier, Abgeordneter in Paris', *Westdeutsche Arbeiter-Zeitung*, 8 September 1923.
[41] Trebitsch and Bock, 'L'Image', 28.
[42] Michael Jeismann, *Das Vaterland der Feinde: Studien zum nationalen Feindbegriff und Selbstverständnis in Deutschland und Frankreich 1792–1918* (Stuttgart: Klett-Cotta 1992).

reinforced the negative mutual images: the physical devastation of north-eastern France and German war crimes, which were blown out of proportion by the Entente war propaganda,[43] in the case of France, and the in some respects draconic measures of the Versailles Treaty in the case of Germany. These measures largely resulted from a strong French desire to replace the dominant role of Germany in continental Europe before 1914 with a new French hegemony, which would guarantee its national security once and for all. Even more than before World War I, the Franco-German antagonism appeared like an eternal characteristic of European politics – or, as Jean Fabry, who was later defence minister in 1934 and 1935–6, claimed in the Chamber of Deputies in 1924, 'There will never be at the same time a strong Germany and a strong France or a weak Germany and a weak France. One will be strong, and the other will be weak. We cannot escape this basic fact of life.'[44]

As Georges-Henri Soutou has pointed out, the Versailles Treaty was novel compared to earlier international peace treaties in that – not least due to strong disagreements among the Western Allies – it left many important points open for later decision.[45] The reparations and the mode of their payment originally were to be fixed in 1921. In the same year, a referendum would decide the fate of Upper Silesia. The population of the Saar region, which was occupied by France, would have to wait until 1935 before it could opt for its possible reintegration into the German Empire. Moreover, if Germany did not fulfil its treaty obligations, the Allies could extend their occupation of the Rhineland. This was a particularly thorny issue for the Centre Party, as it traditionally had one of its main electoral strongholds there. In fact, Prime Minister Georges Clemenceau (1917–20) expected that Germany would default on its obligations, leading to the extended occupation of the Rhineland and its eventual annexation by France[46] – a long-standing goal of French nationalists, who had argued for a long time that the Rhine was the 'natural' border between the two countries.

The nationalist fervour in France after the war extended well into the centre of French politics, encompassing influential Radicals like

---

[43] For a sophisticated introduction to the realities and myths of German war crimes see John N. Horne and Alan Kramer, *German Atrocities, 1914: A History of Denial* (New Haven, Conn.: Yale University Press, 2001).

[44] Cited in Wurm, 'Deutsche Frankreichpolitik', 139.

[45] Georges-Henri Soutou, 'Deutschland, Frankreich und das System von Versailles. Strategien und Winkelzüge der Nachkriegs-Diplomatie', in Franz Knipping and Ernst Weisenfeld (eds.), *Eine ungewöhnliche Geschichte. Deutschland – Frankreich seit 1870* (Bonn: Europa Union Verlag, 1988), 73.

[46] Cf. Jean-Jacques Becker and Serge Berstein, *Victoire et frustrations 1914–1929* (Paris: Éditions du Seuil, 1990), 211.

Clemenceau and conservative republicans like Poincaré.[47] The centre-right *Bloc National* governments continued until 1924, and until 1923 they were supported by sections of the Radicals and independent socialists. It was never entirely clear, however, whether these governments primarily aimed at securing French interests through cooperation with the United States and Britain. This element in their strategy was undermined early on after the war when the US Congress failed to ratify the Versailles Treaty including US membership in the League of Nations, both countries refused to ratify a military guarantee treaty with France, and American and British negotiators increasingly favoured the economic reconstruction of Germany. Or, alternatively, whether the *Bloc National* governments would rely more on independent action to force the Weimar Republic, if necessary, to comply with the Versailles Treaty and French economic and security demands.[48]

On the question of German reparations in particular, Jacques Becker and Serge Berstein have argued that there were in fact 'two French policies'.[49] Depending on the economic and political interests of policy-makers, and changes in their preferences over time, they were applied simultaneously, resulting in a muddled policy, which contributed to the increasing international isolation of France. One policy aimed at the full payment of German reparations for use in the economic reconstruction of France and debt repayment to its Western Allies. The other policy was targeted at achieving territorial gains beyond the reintegration of Alsace-Lorraine into France. Such gains could better be achieved with German non-payment legitimising further military occupation as a first step to annexation. In fact, when the Berlin government refused to fulfil the provisional French reparation demands in 1920, French troops first occupied the cities of Frankfurt and Darmstadt on the Main, and then, in 1921, Düsseldorf, Duisburg and Ruhrort on the eastern bank of the Rhine. When, on 6 January 1923, Germany marginally defaulted on its temporary reparation obligations agreed in 1922, French and Belgian troops occupied the Ruhr area in the face of American and British hostility. The Germans started a policy of passive resistance to the occupation, which was only stopped on

---

[47] Cf. Danièle Zéraffa-Dray, *Histoire de la France: d'une République à l'autre 1918–1958* (Paris: Hachette, 1992), 52.
[48] For the international context see Anthony Adamthwaite, *Grandeur and Misery: France's Bid for Power in Europe 1914–1940* (London: Arnold, 1995).
[49] Becker and Berstein, *Victoire*, 212.

26 September 1923 on the initiative of the national-liberal Stresemann, who had become chancellor one month previously.[50]

The experience of the Ruhr conflict actually promoted the search on both sides for a way out of the cul-de-sac of bilateral confrontation. In Germany, Stresemann, foreign minister 1923–9, began to propagate a policy of reconciliation and peaceful revision. Some authors like Peter Krüger have argued that his policy aimed at the long-term stabilisation of European politics, had real potential for achieving solutions to the remaining conflicts, and essentially prefigured the politics of Western integration after 1945.[51] Others, like Jacques Bariéty and Hermann Hagspiel, are more sceptical. They have argued that it was only German (and French) foreign policy *methods*, but not their main goals, which changed between 1923–5 and 1929. They see Stresemann's policy, which was fully supported by the Centre Party, as preparing the ground for a much more active policy of revisionism, especially concerning Germany's eastern borders.[52] In this perspective, Stresemann stood for what Clemens Wurm has called 'an economic variant of German great power policy'[53] prioritising Germany's full economic reconstruction and regaining of its dominant role in the European economy as a precondition for renewed great power status and influence and later political revisions.

The shift in German policy during 1923–5 certainly resulted in an atmospheric change, which also facilitated the slow reorientation of French policy. In many ways, as Jean-Baptiste Duroselle has pointed out,[54] the occupation strategy proved to be 'a costly policy' – not only in material terms, as France had to support its large army, draining resources from economic reconstruction and debt repayment, but also psychologically. The French efforts appeared increasingly useless, as some kind of economic restoration of Germany was becoming inevitable under American and British pressure and the nationalist territorial ambitions more and more unrealistic. They lacked international support, and attempts by the French occupation

[50] For domestic German and international aspects of the Ruhr occupation see Gerd Krumeich and Joachim Schröder (eds.), *Der Schatten des Weltkriegs. Die Ruhrbesetzung 1923* (Essen: Klartext, 2004).

[51] Peter Krüger, *Die Außenpolitik der Republik von Weimar* (Darmstadt: Wissenschaftliche Buchgesellschaft, 1985), 136 and, by the same author, 'Briand, Stresemann und der Völkerbund. Männer, Mächte, Institutionen – und das Schicksal', in Knipping and Weisenfeld (eds.), *Eine ungewöhnliche Geschichte*, 85–100.

[52] Hagspiel, *Verständigung*; Jacques Bariéty, *Les Relations franco-allemandes après la première guerre mondiale* (Paris: Pedone, 1977).

[53] Wurm, 'Deutsche Frankreichpolitik', 143.

[54] Jean-Baptiste Duroselle, *Les Relations franco-allemandes de 1918 à 1950*, vol. II (Paris: Centre de Documentation Universitaire, 1967), 36.

administration to foster a movement in the Rhineland for autonomy within Germany, or even integration into France, met with little success. As Duroselle has put it, 'French opinion was tired'[55] at the end of German passive resistance to the Ruhr occupation and, on the whole, willing to contemplate a policy change.

This change came with the election in 1924 of the *Cartels des gauches* government of Radicals and socialists led by the Radical prime minister Edouard Herriot, which gained a parliamentary majority on a minority of the votes cast. As foreign minister in changing governments during 1925–31, Aristide Briand, who had already propagated this option internally, as prime minister, in January 1922, prioritised the achievement of a long-term solution to the reparation question. The French and German governments finally agreed to the Dawes Plan, which was a provisional reparation agreement for five years, at the London conference in July–August 1924. The reparations were no longer to be taken out of production, but would mainly come from increased state revenue, so that the recipients of reparation payments from then on had an in-built interest in German economic recovery. At the same time, France agreed to the withdrawal of its troops from the Ruhr area and the occupied cities by mid-August 1925. On 27 December 1924, a conference of Allied ambassadors, arguing that Germany was not fully in compliance with the demilitarisation regulations of the Versailles Treaty, postponed the withdrawal from the first (Cologne) zone of the Rhineland, which was scheduled for 1 January 1925. In the end, the French and Belgian troops withdrew from the Ruhr area and the cities on the eastern bank of the Rhine in August 1925, and from the Rhenish zone of Cologne at the beginning of 1926.

This dual solution to the reparation and occupation issues did not, by some magic, totally transform the Franco-German relationship and result in durable reconciliation. In fact, Duroselle has argued that the Franco-Belgian occupation of the Ruhr 'destroyed the Franco-German relationship for one whole generation', with its negative psychological effects extending far beyond the actual occupation period.[56] In Germany, the government bought DNVP support for the Dawes Plan with a public renunciation by Stresemann of the idea of sole German war guilt as laid down in the Versailles Treaty, which caused uproar in France.[57] Nevertheless, the agreement on the Dawes Plan largely put an end to what Guido Müller has called (to adopt a phrase of Robert Musil) Germany's

---

[55] Ibid.   [56] Ibid., 29.   [57] Hagspiel, *Verständigung*, 220.

post-World War I 'foreign policy without qualities',[58] with its half-hearted attempts, as in the Treaty of Rapallo with the Soviet Union of 1922, to develop some kind of Eastern policy to counteract French hegemony. The agreement led on to the German security pact initiative in two memoranda submitted to the British government on 20 January 1925 and the French on 9 February 1925, which proposed Germany's recognition of its western borders and the conclusion of arbitration treaties.

European prime ministers and foreign ministers eventually convened in Switzerland in October 1925, and concluded the Locarno Treaty.[59] In this treaty, Germany recognised the Franco-German and Belgian-German postwar borders, which was seen as a major diplomatic gain in France. For the Centre Party, the permanent loss of Alsace-Lorraine was difficult to swallow because of the Catholic population there. Yet it recognised the legitimacy of the predominately pro-French attitudes of the population in these two regions, for which it held the nationalist Prussian-Protestant policies during 1871–1918 responsible.[60] Germany also concluded arbitration treaties with France, Poland and Czechoslovakia, but left the question of its eastern borders open. They were supplemented with Franco-Czechoslovak and Franco-Polish alliance treaties to reassure these two countries of French military support in the event that Germany should break its obligations under the arbitration treaties and attack them. Germany would enter the League of Nations, which – importantly, for the democratic parties there – symbolised its full reintegration into European politics. Moreover, the German government, and with it the Centre Party, hoped that this would be followed up with further concessions such as the quick withdrawal of Allied troops from the remaining two Rhenish occupation zones.

In this period of détente in Franco-German relations, the newly created PDP quickly moved towards support for Briand's foreign policy. It broke ranks with the Right and, instead of merely abstaining, voted for the ratification of the Locarno Treaty after endorsing it at its party congress in November 1925.[61] As Hermann Hagspiel has emphasised,[62] however, the PDP was prepared to accept the full inclusion of Germany in European

---

[58] Guido Müller, '"Außenpolitik ohne Eigenschaften?" Der russische Faktor in der deutsch-französischen Annäherung 1922/23–1932', in: Ilja Mieck and Pierre Guillen (eds.), *Deutschland – Frankreich – Russland. Begegnungen und Konfrontationen* (Munich: Oldenbourg, 2000), 181–213.

[59] For a recent analysis see Gaynor Johnson (ed.), *Locarno Revisited. European Diplomacy 1920–1929* (London: Routledge, 2004).

[60] Hagspiel, *Verständigung*, 284.   [61] Delbreil, *Centrisme*, 265; Delbreil, *Les Catholiques*, 112.

[62] Hagspiel, *Verständigung*, 122.

and international politics on the basis of equality, but it opposed changes to existing treaties. Concessions to Germany could be made, but only outside of the Versailles Treaty, as a kind of 'pedagogical tool' to reward German compliance.[63] For the Popular Democrats – unlike for Sangnier and the JR, or the Italian Popolari – revisions of the Versailles Treaty were and would remain out of the question. As Jean-Claude Delbreil has put it, the PDP's foreign policy concept was 'resolutely French but at the same time definitely in favour of measures aimed at international reconciliation'.[64] This is also why the PDP leaders were concerned about the increasing isolation of France in European politics, and of French political Catholicism from incipient transnational contacts and cooperation. This presented Sturzo with an opportunity to revive his project for a 'popular' international. Although he had been in exile in London since October 1924, he retained contacts with Italian Catholics in Paris, such as the journalist Domenico Russo, and with several Catholic intellectuals, who became members of the newly founded PDP, such as Maurice Vaussard, Francisque Gay and Marcel Prélot. Apparently on the suggestion of Russo,[65] Sturzo came to Paris to give a lecture on fascism on 30 March 1925,[66] in which he outlined the main ideas of a book on the same theme published in the following year.[67] On 4 April, he met with PDP executive members to explain his project, which they endorsed in a general way.[68] After informal preliminary soundings with Rutten from Belgium and Heinrich Mataja, the Austrian foreign minister 1924–6, among others,[69] it led on to another meeting on 20 July which decided who should be invited to a first multilateral conference.[70]

The PDP secretary-general, Raymond-Laurent, sent out an invitation to this conference on 7 August 1925.[71] Referring to preliminary consultations with 'our friends from Italy, Belgium and Austria', he announced a 'limited meeting ... of a strictly private character' with not more than forty participants, which would discuss and decide the future form of party cooperation. Originally planned for late October, the conference was eventually put back to 12–13 December 1925, after the PDP party congress.[72] In his letter, Raymond-Laurent included two draft statutes for the future

[63] Ibid.   [64] Delbreil, 'Christian Democracy', 127.   [65] Papini, *Le Courage*, 101.   [66] Ibid., 72.
[67] Luigi Sturzo, *Italy and Fascism* (London: Faber and Gnyer, 1926).   [68] Vecchio, *Alla ricerca*, 303.
[69] *Le Petit Démocrate*, 5 July 1925. See also Giuseppe Rossini, *Il movimento cattolico nel periodo fascista (momenti e problemi)* (Rome: Cinque lune, 1966), 215.
[70] Cf. Papini, *Le Courage*, 135.
[71] Raymond-Laurent to Nolens, 7 August 1925, KDC, Archief W. H. Nolens, 485; Raymond-Laurent to Marx, 7 August 1925, HAStK, NL 1070.
[72] Raymond-Laurent to Nolens, 14 November 1925, KDC, Archief W. H. Nolens, 485.

organisation.[73] One of the two was Sturzo's proposal for an inter-parliamentary union in the toned-down version first suggested by Tovini three years earlier. Still, it envisaged the creation of a fairly integrated organisation with an annual assembly, a president and a secretary-general, with one vote per national delegation. Although member parties would remain free to follow their own policies, Sturzo at least foresaw the debate and possible coordination of potentially contentious international policy issues, especially concerning the work of the League of Nations and the International Labour Organisation (ILO) in Geneva. The secretariat would primarily act as an information broker between the parties. It would also coordinate the organisation's media activities. Although it was quite similar in its institutional design, the alternative, more modest PDP plan for an 'international bureau' of Christian democratic parties avoided mentioning the aim of international policy coordination. Fearful of attacks from the nationalist Right, moreover, the Popular Democrats also conceived of future party cooperation exclusively as the confidential exchange of views without any publicity for advancing common political causes. Both plans envisaged the creation of the new organisation for one year in the first place, as a trial phase.

Representatives from only five parties attended the first meeting in Paris in December 1925: the PDP itself, with fifteen of its leading politicians; the Belgian ACW with Heyman and Rutten; the Polish Christian democrats with Wacław Bitner, deputy leader of its parliamentary party 1922–35, and Aleksander Wóycicki, a leading social Catholic thinker, professor at the University of Wilno (Vilnius) 1924–39 and Polish government representative at international congresses including the ILO; the German Centre Party with Joos, Vockel, Helene Weber, a Reichstag deputy, and Richard Kuenzer, the editor of *Germania*; and, finally, the PPI with Sturzo and Russo. De Gasperi, Ruffo della Scaletta and Jacini also wanted to travel to Paris, but Mussolini refused to issue them with passports.[74] The party representatives resolved to create SIPDIC (with a provisional secretariat in Paris) as a 'permanent alliance (*entente*), in a form to be determined, between the parties and their parliamentary parties'.[75] The institutional

[73] Raymond-Laurent to Nolens, 7 August 1925, KDC, Archief W. H. Nolens, 485; Raymond-Laurent to Marx, 7 August 1925, HAStK, NL 1070. The Italian proposal is also printed in Rossini, *Il movimento*, 212–14.

[74] Ibid., 206.

[75] Francesco Luigi Ferrari, 'L'Organisation internationale de la démocratie populaire', *Politique* 5 (1931), 320. See also the slightly different reports by Heinrich Vockel, Bericht über eine Zusammenkunft christlicher Volksparteien verschiedener Länder am 12. und 13. Dezember 1925 in Paris, n. d., HAStK, NL 1070 and in Archiv für christlich-demokratische Politik (henceforth: ACDP), 01-396–004/3.

structure and procedural rules were only fixed at the second congress in Brussels on 22–3 May 1926.[76] The parties decided to create a central committee with one official representative from each associated party. The secretariat in the PDP offices was declared permanent, and was initially directed by Raymond-Laurent, then by Philippe de Las Cases. As the internal SIPDIC bulletin first published in 1928 recalled in its second edition, the Brussels congress decided that the new organisation 'does not aim for the time being at constituting an international federation of the represented parties'. Rather, its main aim was to foster communication between them. The report cites one participant: 'Before we can think of common action, we first have to get to know each other.'[77]

The first meeting in December 1925 already highlighted some of the major fault-lines within the new organisation. Vockel, secretary-general of the Centre Party, discussed them in his report which was circulated to the party leader Marx and other prominent politicians with an interest in European matters.[78] These fault-lines concerned especially the bilateral relationship between the French and German and the Polish and German party representatives. In some respects, the Franco-German discussions were a dialogue of the deaf from the beginning. Joos made a powerful argument at the meeting that the Locarno Treaty sufficiently provided for French security. It should therefore be followed up as a 'natural consequence' with the quick withdrawal of French troops from the two remaining Rhenish zones of occupation and the Saar region, to support the Weimar Republic in its new foreign policy. As Vockel noted, his demand met with 'icy silence' on the part of the Popular Democrats.[79] They in turn were still unsure how whole-heartedly the Centre Party supported the substance of the Locarno Treaty, especially on the border issue, and whether it would actually be ratified in the Reichstag. The critical questions to this effect asked by the Belgians Heyman and Rutten also reflected French concerns. Despite continuing mutual suspicions and the obvious limits to possible French concessions, Vockel concluded that it would be important to continue the exchange with the PDP, although it played a marginal role

---

[76] Compte rendu de la réunion de Bruxelles, Paris, July 1926, printed in Francesco Luigi Ferrari, *Lettere e documenti inediti*, vol. II (Rome: Edizioni S. I. A. S., 1986), 755–69. See also Hanschmidt, 'Eine christlich-demokratische', 171–3.

[77] *Bulletin du Secrétariat International des Partis Démocratiques d'Inspiration Chrétienne* 2 (1929), 37. This PDP version of the formation of SIPDIC completely ignores the important role of Sturzo in initiating party cooperation, however.

[78] Heinrich Vockel, Bericht über eine Zusammenkunft christlicher Volksparteien verschiedener Länder am 12. und 13. Dezember 1925 in Paris, n.d., HAStK, NL 1070.

[79] Ibid.

in French politics, because 'with the exception of Marc Sangnier's move-ment it is currently the only group within French Catholicism which at least seeks an exchange of views with German Catholics'.[80]

On the margins of the meeting, Polish-German conflicts, which were to deepen at the end of the 1920s, also became evident. As a preventive measure to counteract possible German demands, Woycicki strongly emphasised the larger significance of the newly created Polish state as 'an advance West European bulwark against bolshevism'. Joos proclaimed his party's support for an independent Polish state within western Europe as a future 'common bloc in world politics'. He also indirectly reminded the participants of German demands for revisions of the border, however, by expressing his hope that bilateral border issues could be resolved 'in a friendly manner'.[81] The meeting also revealed sharp differences over the desirability of internal debates and – even more so – joint public statements about ideological issues with strong foreign policy connotations when Sturzo suggested to pass a resolution against fascism. For fear of compro-mising French policy towards Italy, the Popular Democrats even prevented a discussion of the proposal, let alone a decision on it.[82] The German representatives would in fact have been 'split down the middle' over whether or not to support such a resolution.[83] Sturzo also proposed to send a telegram to Briand to express SIPDIC support for his foreign policy of reconciliation. This, too, went too far for the PDP politicians who supported the Locarno process, but opposed the *Cartel des gauches* govern-ment domestically, mainly on the grounds of their socio-economic poli-cies. In fact, according to one of the two German summaries of the meeting, the Popular Democrats, who were obsessed with the fear of attacks from the nationalist Right, 'anxiously tried to avoid that any information on the meeting at all would become known to the public'.[84]

The institutional arrangements for SIPDIC as they were confirmed in 1926, actually looked more comprehensive and binding than they were in practice. Only thirteen representatives of only four parties participated in the second congress in Brussels. Vockel from the Centre Party, Paul Simon from the PDP, Heyman from the ACW and Rossi from the PPI

[80] Ibid.   [81] Ibid.
[82] For French Catholic attitudes to fascist Italy see in greater detail Jean-Luc Pouthier, *Les Catholiques sociaux et les democrates chrétiens français devant l'Italie fasciste, 1922–1935*, PhD (Paris: Institut d'Études Politiques, 1981).
[83] Heinrich Vockel, Bericht über eine Zusammenkunft christlicher Volksparteien verschiedener Länder am 12. und 13. Dezember 1925 in Paris, n.d., HAStK, NL 1070.
[84] Heinrich Vockel, Bericht über eine Zusammenkunft christlicher Volksparteien verschiedener Länder am 12. und 13. Dezember 1925 in Paris, n.d., ACDP, 01-396-004/3.

were named as national party representatives on the central committee,[85] but this body existed in name only and did not perform any functions outside of the annual congresses. Moreover, the SIPDIC secretariat was effectively an appendix of the PDP secretariat. The PDP initially covered all costs, but was unable to invest significant human resources in the transnational activities. It mainly organised the annual congress and sent circular letters on an irregular basis with information on national party developments, which it received from the member parties. As Franco-German tensions continued to ease somewhat with the ratification of the Locarno Treaty and the Weimar Republic's accession to the League of Nations in 1926, these arrangements no longer seemed sufficient even to the PDP leadership. The newly appointed SIPDIC secretary-general, Henri Simondet, concluded in 1928 that SIPDIC had 'a central organisation which is too weak; the relations between the secretariat and the member parties are so far not very stable and too irregular'.[86] The Italian exiles saw this as a chance to revive their plan for a party international, which they propagated internally in 1928, and again in 1931.

At the fourth congress in 's-Hertogenbosch in the Netherlands in July 1928 the parties decided on a moderate reform of the SIPDIC structures. The central committee was renamed the executive committee and from then onwards met twice annually, in conjunction with the congress and at the beginning of each year. The parties also appointed a secretary-general for SIPDIC only. They chose Simondet, a member of the PDP executive, who could act as a cultural broker between the French and the Germans in SIPDIC. Simondet was professor of German at the Institut d'Études Politiques and the Institut Catholique in Paris.[87] He had published extensively on German grammar and translated several books from German into French such as, for example, a biography of Albert Ballin, the shipping magnate from Hamburg.[88] Moreover, the member parties were obliged for the first time to make small regular financial contributions to the SIPDIC budget. They also named 'correspondents' who were responsible for providing Simondet with information on national party developments and policies on issues of common interest for inclusion in the new confidential

[85] Compte rendu de la réunion de Bruxelles, Paris, July 1926, in Ferrari, *Lettere e documenti inediti*, vol. II, 768.
[86] *Bulletin du SIPDIC* 1 (1928), 12.
[87] Simondet's son also recalled later that his father's core qualification for the position was his knowledge of Germany and the German language. See Papini, *Le Courage*, 205, footnote 41.
[88] Cf. Ernest Pezet, *Chrétiens au service de la Cité: de Léon XIII au Sillon et au M. R. P. 1891–1965* (Paris: Nouvelles Éditions Latines, 1965), 229.

bulletin, which replaced the irregular circular letters and was published three times annually from 1928 to 1931 before the system reverted to letters once more. The print-run averaged 160, with one-third being used by the PDP and two-thirds sent abroad for circulation among the member parties.[89] The delegates also discussed the publicity question again. Serrarens from the Dutch RKSP insisted that 'our meetings and congresses have the sole aim of getting to know each other better and exchanging information, so that we do not need any publicity'.[90] Joos agreed that 'our bulletin and our congresses are purely internal affairs and confidential. We cannot therefore have any publicity except if all parties agree.' In his view, any publicity could compromise eminent national politicians who would refuse to participate in meetings.[91] Raymond-Laurent and Pezet agreed, but preferred a short general communiqué to be issued by SIPDIC or the member parties for use by the party newspapers in order to prevent any speculation in the nationalist press.[92] In fact, party newspapers like *Petit Démocrate*, *Kölnische Volkszeitung* and *Luxemburger Wort* usually published reports on the annual congresses, but they never touched upon sensitive political issues discussed in the meetings.

In the period 1928–31, Simondet tried to extend the scope of SIPDIC. Referring to the initiative of Heyman and others at the annual congress in 1929 to increase the thematic debate of policy issues like the role of professional bodies in modern economic governance or family policy, he wrote in the bulletin that 'We now know each other, and have confidence in each other . . . We desire to work together to study the great problems of our time and to develop together directives which we follow and solutions which we will try to implement.'[93] In the executive committee on 5 January 1931, Francesco Luigi Ferrari, who replaced Sturzo in SIPDIC after the conclusion of the Lateran Treaties forbidding Italian priests any political activity, once more pushed the Italian preference for a strengthened committee which would be capable of providing SIPDIC with greater political direction. He proposed that the parties 'establish something which is similar to the international organisation of social democracy', with the aim of 'common directives and decisions'.[94] Frans Teulings, the Dutch RKSP secretary-general, suggested the election of a SIPDIC president who would be solely responsible for coordinating party cooperation.[95] In his experience, upon returning from SIPDIC meetings, the party representatives became totally reimmersed in intra-party and domestic political

[89] *Bulletin du SIPDIC* 4 (1929), 81–5.   [90] *Bulletin du SIPDIC* 1 (1928), 14.   [91] Ibid.   [92] Ibid., 15.
[93] *Bulletin du SIPDIC* 6 (1930), 158.   [94] *Bulletin du SIPDIC* 8 (1931), 216.   [95] Ibid., 219.

problems. As a result, they did not have enough time and energy to sustain continuous contacts. In the end, the parties could only agree on a minor reform, however, which allowed the secretary-general to call special meetings of the executive committee outside of the regular schedule.[96] C. M. J. F. Goseling, the RKSP party leader, who was more concerned than his own secretary-general about politically binding SIPDIC structures and decisions, argued that technically better cooperation was desirable, but no further deepening of the organisation.[97] The French, German and Belgian representatives also agreed that practical progress was more important than institutional reform. As for Teulings' idea of an elected SIPDIC president, the Popular Democrat Simon emphasised the danger that such a personality would find it difficult to follow a common European line, and that he could always be accused of a 'lack of impartiality'.[98] His remark once more reflected the strong predominance of national over transnational ideological conceptions of SIPDIC cooperation.

Roberto Papini has characterised the period from 1928 through to 1932 as a 'consolidation phase' for SIPDIC after the initial period with 'minimalist structures'.[99] This only holds true from an institutionalist perspective that emphasises the degree of formal integration within the organisation. In reality, the internal frictions became much more pronounced after the end of constitutional government in Germany in March 1930 and the sensational success of the National Socialists in the German elections in September of that year. For SIPDIC, the period from 1930 through to the demise of the Weimar Republic and, with it, the Centre Party in 1933 were years of increasingly severe crisis. In contrast, the earlier period (despite the lack of greater institutionalisation until 1928) was one of relative stability which resulted from the favourable international climate temporarily created by the Locarno Treaty and the relative cohesion of the core group of participants from Italy, France, Germany, Belgium, the Netherlands and Luxembourg in this period. Party representatives from the first four countries were already present in 1925. The RKSP and the Rechtspartei from Luxembourg initially sent observers and formally joined SIPDIC in 1928.[100] Unlike the parties from east-central Europe, which in most cases began to take part later and more sporadically, all six western European parties were regularly represented in the first seven years at SIPDIC congresses and executive committee meetings.

---

[96] Ibid., 219. No such special meeting was ever called until the demise of SIPDIC in 1938–9, however.
[97] Ibid., 216.　[98] Ibid., 219.　[99] Papini, *Le Courage*, 181.　[100] *Bulletin du SIPDIC* 1 (1928), 32.

The German SIPDIC group is an excellent example of self-selection within a socially and ideologically very heterogeneous party like the Centre Party, of the participants in transnational cooperation, and of the operation of incipient 'European' micro networks within the member parties. At the centre of the German group, and its informal speaker, was Joos. He was born in the Alsace region in 1878, after its annexation by the German Empire.[101] The family spoke the Alsatian German dialect, but his mother still wrote in French.[102] The Alsace had a strong regional culture of its own, but, as Joos grew up, he was confronted with conflicting demands for national allegiance. As he recalled after World War II, he felt more drawn towards German than French culture through the Catholic social movement which expanded into Alsace-Lorraine from the Rhineland.[103] After vocational training and work as a journalist for the German-language *Oberelsässische Landeszeitung*, a local newspaper in Mülhausen, the present-day Mulhouse,[104] Joos was invited in 1904 to participate in an adult educational course in economics at the Volksverein in Mönchengladbach, the centre of Rhenish and German social Catholicism.[105] From there, Brauns recruited him as a journalist for the *Westdeutsche Arbeiter-Zeitung*, a newspaper for Catholic workers with a large circulation of 200,000, where he first worked under the direction of the editor-in-chief Giesberts before he later succeeded him. Both Brauns and Giesberts became ministers in the Weimar Republic, participated in the talks with Sturzo and other Popolari in 1920–1, and supported Joos's rise in the Centre Party.

Joos at first enthusiastically supported the war in 1914, but he quickly became disillusioned, turned his mind to domestic socio-economic topics, which he discussed in his newspaper, and supported Erzberger's peace initiative in 1917. Joos was not originally a republican, but when the Empire collapsed and William II fled to the Netherlands, he supported collaboration with the mainstream social democrats in the creation of the Weimar Republic.[106] While continuing his journalistic work, he was a

---

[101] Cf. Wachtling, *Joseph Joos*.

[102] Joseph Joos, *So sah ich sie: Menschen und Geschehnisse* (Augsburg: Verlag Winfried-Werk, 1958), 140.

[103] Radio interview with Rudolf Morsey, 'Die von unten kommen. Joseph Joos erzählt an seinem 85. Geburtstag aus seinem Leben', *Westdeutscher Rundfunk*, 13 November 1963, 9–10 p.m., transcript in Archiv der Kommission für Zeitgeschichte (henceforth: AKZG), Nachlasssplitter Joseph Joos, Karton 2.

[104] Wilhelm Spael, *Das katholische Deutschland im 20. Jahrhundert. Seine Pionier- und Krisenzeiten 1890–1945* (Würzburg: Echter, 1964), 32.

[105] Radio interview with Rudolf Morsey, AKZG, Nachlasssplitter Joseph Joos, Karton 2; Spael, *Das katholische Deutschland*, 32, gives the year 1903.

[106] Radio interview with Rudolf Morsey, AKZG, Nachlasssplitter Joseph Joos, Karton 2.

member of the Reichstag throughout the Weimar Republic and deputy leader of the Centre Party 1928–33. He also created a nationwide organisation of Catholic workers' associations and, in 1928, became president of their new international organisation.[107] As Brüning recalled in his memoirs, Joos was known in the party as a 'left-winger'[108] who was close to Wirth and regularly exposed himself for the republican order. After the assassination of Rathenau, Joos strongly supported Wirth's so-called Laws for the Protection of the Republic, acted as a lay judge in the new court, the Staatsgerichtshof zum Schutze der Republik, entered the pro-republican inter-party Reichsbanner organisation and was a member of its executive from 1926 to 1932. Towards the end of the Weimar Republic, Joos became more conservative. He even supported the informal talks with the National Socialists in the autumn of 1932 with a view to binding them into a new broadly based constitutional government with parliamentary support. He hoped that this could provoke their electoral decline, which in fact started in the national elections in November of the same year.[109] After the failure of these talks, however, he once again strongly rejected any form of collaboration with the National Socialists.

Joos shared most of the revisionist aims of German foreign policy (and the Centre Party), which largely remained geared towards re-establishing German hegemony over central Europe.[110] He had a keen interest in Franco-German reconciliation, however, and established many contacts in France. Even at the height of the Ruhr conflict in 1923, he distanced himself in his articles for the *Westdeutsche Arbeiter-Zeitung* from the prevailing extreme nationalist fervour, denouncing nationalism as 'a sin against the Holy Ghost' in the German version of his contribution to the Europe-wide critical enquiry into nationalism, which the Catholic intellectual and journalist Vaussard put together for the French journal *Les Lettres*.[111] Instead, he propagated the application of the 'federalist principle' to Europe's future political organisation.[112] This guiding idea – shared also by Adenauer, for example – reflected the traditional preference of

---

[107] Wachtling, *Joseph Joos*, 246.
[108] Heinrich Brüning, *Memoiren 1918–1934* (Stuttgart: DVA, 1970), 667.
[109] For these talks see in greater detail Rudolf Morsey, *Der Untergang des politischen Katholizismus. Die Zentrumspartei zwischen christlichem Selbstverständnis und 'Nationaler Erhebung' 1932/33* (Stuttgart, Zurich: Belser, 1977); Detlef Junker, *Die Deutsche Zentrumspartei und Hitler 1932/33. Ein Beitrag zur Problematik des politischen Katholizismus in Deutschland* (Stuttgart: Ernst Klett, 1969).
[110] In a more long-term perspective, Jürgen Elvert, *Mitteleuropa! Deutsche Pläne zur europäischen Neuordnung (1918–1945)* (Stuttgart: Steiner, 1999).
[111] Joseph Joos, 'Ungeistiger Nationalismus', *Westdeutsche Arbeiter-Zeitung*, 23 June 1926.
[112] Ibid. See also Joseph Joos, 'Unser Ruf ins Leere', *Westdeutsche Arbeiter-Zeitung*, 2 June 1923.

Rhenish-Westfalian Catholicism for a more federal organisation of Germany with the aim of overcoming Prussian-Protestant hegemony.[113] In the case of Joos, it also derived from the preference of Catholic social teaching for the application of the principle of subsidiarity in all social relations including the organisation of the state and international affairs.

Throughout the Weimar Republic, Joos sought contacts with French Catholics in European organisations like Sangnier's Internationale Démocratique, SIPDIC and the CWI, as well as in bilateral forums like the Franco-German Catholic congresses of 1928 and 1929. More than once, Joos was caught between the fronts. He later recalled that when he and a few close collaborators were first in touch with Sangnier, and then the PDP, many of his colleagues in the Centre Party 'laughed at us'.[114] In his own assessment, his French connection was one reason among others for his failure to become Centre Party leader in 1928 because many of the most influential left-wing trade unionists like Stegerwald and Jacob Kaiser were much more nationalist.[115] In Germany, he was regularly denounced as a pacifist traitor by the nationalist Right, especially in the press of the DNVP after the election of its new extreme right-wing leader, Alfred Hugenberg, in 1928, and of the National Socialists. In France, nationalist newspapers like *L'Ami du peuple* – often drawing upon reports in the German nationalist press – attacked Joos's insistence on a great power role for Germany and revisions of the Versailles Treaty couched in the language of Franco-German reconciliation as a particularly devious form of German nationalism coming, moreover, from an Alsatian traitor who had failed to opt for France in 1918. Centrist Catholic publications on both sides defended Joos and other Catholic political brokers in vain. In April 1931, for example, *Politique* denounced vicious attacks on Joos after he had attended a public meeting of the Comité National d'Études Politiques et Sociales in Paris. Perhaps Joos was making opportunist rhetorical concessions to the more heated nationalist climate in Germany, the journal argued, but his interest in Franco-German reconciliation was sincere, and he deserved to be supported.[116] In Germany, the *Allgemeine Rundschau*, for example, similarly defended Joos against attacks from the German and French nationalist Right after he had participated in a demonstration for disarmament in the Trocadéro Palace in Paris later in the same year.[117]

[113] Keller, 'Katholische Europakonzeptionen', 232.
[114] Radio interview with Rudolf Morsey, AKZG, Nachlasssplitter Joseph Joos, Karton 2.
[115] Ibid.   [116] 'L'Affaire Joos', *Politique*, 14 April 1931, 369–71.
[117] *Allgemeine Rundschau. Wochenschrift für Politik und Kultur*, 5 December 1931.

For his French contacts, Joos assembled a small team of like-minded Centre Party politicians. The group included Helene Weber from the Rhineland. She was a member of the Weimar National Assembly in 1919, then of the Prussian Landtag parliament 1921–4 and of the Reichstag 1924–33, where she became a member of the parliamentary party executive in 1927.[118] Like Joos, Weber, whose mother came from Dutch Friesland, was brought up with – as Rudolf Morsey has put it – 'a sense of European belonging'.[119] She studied history and French at the universities of Bonn and Grenoble and came to admire French culture. Her first contact with Joos dated from 1906 and their joint interest in Catholic social teaching and social work.[120] While investing a substantial amount of time in her parliamentary work during the Weimar Republic, Weber mainly worked as a senior civil servant in the Prussian Ministry of Welfare, where she played an influential role in the preparation of social security legislation. This is also how she developed a close relationship with Christine Teusch, another left-Catholic Rhenish member of the Weimar National Assembly in 1919 and of the Reichstag 1920–33, with close relations with Joos and Wirth, whose primary political interest was also social policy.[121] Teusch was a teacher by profession and became a school director in 1913, but in 1918 she founded and directed (until 1920) the women's department in the Christian trade unions. Joos, Weber and Teusch recruited another social reformer, Helene Wessel, a member of the Prussian Landtag 1928–33, to participate in the 1931 SIPDIC congress. The German delegation ended up boycotting this, however.[122] Several other German SIPDIC participants also had a background in social Catholicism and combined this with functional roles that were important for transnational party cooperation. They included, from the Centre Party secretariat, Vockel and Krone, the spokesperson of the youth organisation Windthorstbund and a member of the Reichstag 1925–33, as well as Catholic journalists like Joos and Johannes

---

[118] For a brief biographical sketch see Rudolf Morsey, 'Helene Weber (1881–1962)', in Rudolf Morsey (ed.), *Zeitgeschichte in Lebensbildern. Aus dem deutschen Katholizismus des 19. und 20. Jahrhunderts*, vol. III (Mainz: Matthias-Grünewald-Verlag, 1979), 223–4.

[119] Ibid., 223.

[120] See also Elisabeth Prégardier, *Engagiert. Drei Frauen aus dem Ruhrgebiet* (Annweiler: Plöger, 2003); Elisabeth Prégardier and Anne Mohr (eds.), *Helene Weber (1881–1962). Ernte eines Lebens, Weg einer Politikerin*, Annweiler: Plöger, 1991.

[121] For a brief introduction see J. Dominica Ballof, 'Christine Teusch (1888–1968)', in Morsey (ed.), *Zeitgeschichte in Lebensbildern*, vol. II, 202–13.

[122] Elisabeth Friese, *Helene Wessel (1898–1969). Von der Zentrumspartei zur Sozialdemokratie* (Essen: Klartext Verlag, 1993), 25. Wessel joined the refounded Centre Party after 1945 and then created the Gesamtdeutsche Volkspartei with Gustav Heinemann before ending up (like Heinemann) in the Social Democratic Party.

Hofmann. The young Hofmann met Joos for the first time at Sangnier's congress in Bierville in 1926. At the time, he was working for the regional newspaper *Osnabrücker Volkszeitung* before later joining the *Kölnische Volkszeitung* in 1929. He subsequently participated in the SIPDIC congresses in Paris in 1929 and Antwerp in 1930.[123]

The German SIPDIC group shared a general willingness to work for Franco-German reconciliation, but some were more nationalist than others. Weber actually belonged to the small group of Centre Party deputies who voted against the Versailles Treaty in 1919. Unlike Joos, she also supported the highly controversial demand from the Reichswehr Ministry in December 1927 for a first slice of funding for a *Panzerkreuzer* battleship. The plan was formally compatible with the Versailles Treaty, but could not easily be reconciled with Stresemann's policy of reconciliation and disarmament. It also came at the expense of social expenditure.[124] In his autobiography, Hofmann recollects how shocked he was when Weber, whilst visiting the empty debating chamber of the French parliament during the SIPDIC congress in Paris in 1929, entered the podium and half-jokingly, quietly said that 'Alsace-Lorraine will become German again after all'.[125]

The German group were united in their anti-totalitarian attitudes, however. Joos, Weber, Teusch and Krone belonged to the minority of between twelve and fifteen Reichstag members from the Centre Party who opted against supporting Hitler's so-called Enabling Law in a test vote in a meeting of the parliamentary party on 23 March 1933, alongside some more nationalist politicians like Wirth, Stegerwald, Kaiser and the much more conservative Brüning, who were also resolutely opposed to national socialism.[126] In the end, though, they succumbed to Kaas's argument that the Catholics had to present a united front, and voted in favour in the Reichstag. While Brüning and Wirth, who had always kept in close touch with the German group, although he never participated in SIPDIC activities, went into exile, Joos stayed in Germany. He was arrested in 1939 and survived four and a half years as a political prisoner in the concentration camp at Dachau.[127] Weber and Teusch initially stayed in Berlin, continuing their social work. They escaped the rounding-up of democratic

---

[123] Josef Hofmann, *Journalist in Republik, Diktatur und Besatzungszeit. Erinnerungen 1916–1947* (Mainz: Matthias-Grünewald-Verlag, 1977), 34 and 57.

[124] Radio interview with Rudolf Morsey, AKZG, Nachlasssplitter Joseph Joos, Karton 2. For the debate on this issue in the Centre Party at large, see Ruppert, *Im Dienst*, 362.

[125] Hofmann, *Journalist*, 57.

[126] No written records exist, but later recollections by participants are compatible. See, for example, Morsey, *Der Untergang*; Forster, *Adam Stegerwald*, 595–6.

[127] Cf. Joos, *So sah ich sie*.

politicians after the attempted assassination of Hitler on 20 July 1944, whereas Krone was interned in the concentration camp at Sachsenhausen, but – like Joos – survived.

The experiences of other western European SIPDIC participants were broadly similar. Although the majority of the remaining PDP politicians voted for special powers for Marshal Philippe Pétain after the German troops overran France in 1940, those who opposed the new authoritarian regime – Champetier de Ribes, Simon and Pierre Trémintin – had regularly participated in SIPDIC activities. Other SIPDIC activists such as Pezet, who voted in favour, nevertheless joined the resistance in the course of World War II. The RKSP leader Goseling (1930–7), who participated in the SIPDIC congresses during 1930–2 (giving a speech in Luxembourg in 1931)[128] and many executive committee meetings during the 1930s, actually died in the concentration camp at Buchenwald in 1941.[129] Others, such as his left-Catholic RKSP party colleague J. A. Veraart, who took part in several SIPDIC meetings including the annual congresses in 1927 and 1928, followed Sturzo into exile. Conservative Catholics from western Europe at best played a marginal role in SIPDIC. Robert Schuman, who was so influential in the early stages of European integration after World War II, was one such conservative Catholic. His family came from the Lorraine region, but was pro-French. He studied law in Germany before practising as a lawyer in Metz. Unlike Joos, he opted for France in 1918–19 and was elected to the French parliament in 1919. Schuman at first belonged to a regional group of parliamentarians in the period 1919–24, before joining Marin's right-wing Union Républicaine. Although he agreed with much of its political programme, he ultimately found it too nationalistic and anti-German, and joined the PDP in 1932, before leaving it again in early 1939 because it was not in his view strongly enough pro-Franco in the Spanish Civil War. Schuman was almost unique amongst more conservative French Catholics in his preference for Franco-German reconciliation, however, which can only be explained by his regional background and immersion over so many years in German culture.[130] On the German side, von Papen, who had connections with French conservative Catholics through the Mayrisch Committee, was a

---

[128] Discours du Président de la délégation du R. K. Staatspartij de Hollande Mr. Goseling, SIPDIC, Congrès de Luxembourg, 23 July 1931, KDC, Archief C. M. J. F. Goseling, 158.

[129] Cf. Roes, 'A Historical Detour'.

[130] For Schuman's upbringing and early political career in the Third Republic see also François Roth, 'Robert Schuman: du catholique lorrain à l'homme d'état européen, 1886–1963', in: Gérard Cholvy (ed.), *L'Europe*, 113–35.

partial exception. He asked to be invited to the SIPDIC congresses in 1931 and 1932, but in the end attended neither because of the German boycott in 1931 and his final break with the Centre Party over the bringing down of Brüning as chancellor in July 1932.

Despite the national fault-lines, this relative ideological cohesion of the western European core group of SIPDIC allowed constructive internal debate and some attempts at formulating common positions in the early years of transnational party cooperation. At the congresses and executive committee meetings, the representatives usually spent much time exchanging information on internal party and national political developments, to be followed by more thematic debates. These debates increasingly extended to domestic policy issues including the exchange of information on recent policy initiatives by member parties, and national legislation. After a discussion about the relationship with socialist parties in Cologne in 1927 and on the future of the League of Nations in 's-Hertogenbosch in 1928, the congresses in Paris in 1929 and Antwerp in 1930 were mainly devoted to corporatism and the role of professional organisations in society, for example. The 'conclusions' agreed at the end of the congress advocated 'an organic conception of the popular state' understood here as 'a state in which the intermediate and institutionalised bodies work together harmoniously and hierarchically, for the common good, under the control and the directives of the organs of democratic government'.[131] Serrarens in particular argued for an institutionalised role for trade unions within state institutions. However, most party representatives led by the French and Germans were still committed to corporatism as the organisation of social forces subordinated to representative democracy, not (even partially) replacing it. They emphasised in the conclusions that 'the last word – sovereignty – lies with the political institutions'. At the following congress in Luxembourg in 1931, the theme was family policy. The Belgians had strongly pushed for it since mid-1929,[132] largely reflecting their own domestic preoccupations. As Emmanuel Gerard has emphasised, it was the one topic in the field of social policy 'that rallied Catholics'.[133] In fact, an important national law on allocations for families was passed in 1930. It was partly inspired by the idea that, ideally, women should not work

---

[131] *Bulletin du SIPDIC* 7 (1931), 204.
[132] At the annual congress in 's-Hertogenbosch in 1929: *Bulletin du SIPDIC* 4 (1929), 102; at the executive committee of 4 January 1930: *Bulletin du SIPDIC* 5 (1930), 127; again at the congress in Antwerp and the executive meeting of 5 January 1931: *Bulletin du SIPDIC* 8 (1931), 220.
[133] Gerard, 'Religion, Class, and Language', 103.

outside the household, a policy that the ACW representatives also propagated in the SIPDIC context.

In the early stages of their cooperation, the SIPDIC parties even managed to agree a common line on the challenge of fascism and bolshevism. At the second SIPDIC congress in Brussels in May 1926, Sturzo once more brought up the subject after his initial failure in December 1925 to get agreement for a joint resolution.[134] According to him, the middle classes in Italy had largely gone over to Mussolini, but the PPI still had support among the 'popular masses'. Fascism appeared to seek good relations with the Vatican. If the Vatican was seen to support fascism, however, this might well strengthen anticlerical attitudes among the opponents of the dictatorship, with catastrophic long-term effects for Catholicism in Italy and beyond. Joos supported Sturzo in his outright rejection of fascism on political and moral grounds. Fascism, he argued, was a protest movement against some evident weaknesses of democratic systems and pro-democratic movements and parties, and therefore had to be opposed with 'a positive programme of democracy'.[135] Even the Dominican father Rutten from the traditionally more clerical Belgian Catholic Union did not oppose Sturzo on this occasion. While the Vatican might tolerate different political systems (including fascism), parliamentary democracy had the great advantage that no majority or minority could permanently exercise all power.[136]

In these favourable circumstances of a small congress with only thirteen participants and sufficient support for his initiative, Sturzo submitted a resolution which was passed in a slightly toned-down version. It was largely in line with the main arguments of his book on fascism published in several European languages in the same year. In it, Sturzo sharply criticised fascism, but also the widespread exaggerated fear of bolshevism – a 'disease like the influenza' – which in his view helped to explain the support for Mussolini within Italy as well as outside it, not least in France and Britain.[137] In his foreword to Sturzo's book, Gilbert Murray warned that 'outside Italy, Mussolini is largely regarded as a theatrical performer, and Fascism . . . as a subject for jests. But the farce is a desperately dangerous, as well as a cruel one.'[138] To make it more palatable for the more

---

[134] Compte-rendu de la réunion de Bruxelles, 22–23 May 1926, KDC, Archief W. H. Nolens, 485; also printed in Ferrari, *Lettere e documenti inediti*, vol. II, 755–69. See also the brief summary in *Bulletin du SIPDIC* 2 (1929), 36.

[135] Ibid.   [136] Ibid.

[137] Cited from the German translation: Luigi Sturzo, *Italien und der Faschismus* (Cologne: Im Gilde-Verlag, 1926 [English 1926]), 237.

[138] Sturzo, *Italy and Fascism*, viii.

clerical-inclined party representatives, the SIPDIC resolution was simultaneously directed against fascism and bolshevism. It stipulated that Catholic and 'popular' parties had to reject both as dictatorships aimed at centralising all powers and functions of the state and suppressing individual liberties.[139] Both ideologies and political systems should be opposed with 'organic democracy' based on 'moral forces, liberty and an absolute respect for the human personality' – a characterisation of democracy which owed much already to the influence of personalism. Linked to this resolution, the congress also passed a second one for peace 'through arbitration or obligatory mediation'. While acknowledging the right of self-defence, it denounced 'national hegemonies'. Instead, against the background of German membership agreed in the Locarno Treaty, it advocated conflict resolution through the League of Nations, which should also have a major role in coordinating disarmament and European economic reconstruction.[140]

Subsequently, the Italian exiles repeatedly sought to rally SIPDIC against fascist Italy, but without the same success as in 1926. At the annual congress in Cologne in 1927, Sturzo tried to organise support for a resolution protesting against the dissolution of the PPI by Mussolini in late 1926. As Sturzo recollected in a letter to Ferrari in 1929 with a briefing on the previous congresses,[141] the Germans would probably have been prepared to support him. The Popular Democrats were at best lukewarm, however, and did not want to compromise the bilateral relationship with Italy, while the Belgians and Dutch were strictly opposed in view of the fact that the Vatican had evidently dropped the PPI.[142] In fact, if it had not been for Adenauer's mediation, the Popolari in exile might even have lost their official representation and right to vote in SIPDIC at this stage. One year later, at 's-Hertogenbosch in 1928, Sturzo again failed to win sufficient support for a resolution (evidently directed at Italy) expressing sympathy with people in countries where 'liberty is suppressed', which was rejected by several

---

[139] According to Papini, *Le Courage*, 196, Sturzo's original draft even spoke of fascism as 'a bolshevism of the Right and bolshevism as a fascism of the Left' to underline the similiarities between the totalitarian systems.

[140] Compte-rendu de la réunion de Bruxelles, 22–23 May 1926, KDC, Archief W. H. Nolens, 485.

[141] Sturzo to Ferrari, 14 May 1929, cited in Gabriele De Rosa, *Luigi Sturzo* (Turin: Unione Tipografico – Editrice Torinese, 1977), 301.

[142] See also Francesco Malgeri, 'Il popolarismo e la crisi della democrazia italiana: gli anni dell'esilio', in Giorgio Campanini (ed.), *Francesco Luigi Ferrari a cinquant' anni dalla morte* (Rome: Edizioni di Storia e Letteratura, 1983), 126.

delegations.[143] Depressed by the clear preference of many of his SIPDIC colleagues for good diplomatic relations with fascist Italy, which was still on good terms with the Vatican, Sturzo wrote to Ferrari about the two congresses that they had 'no vitality, [and showed] not a bit of determination'.[144]

Having replaced Sturzo, Ferrari continued the increasingly futile attempt at rallying SIPDIC against fascist Italy, and dictatorships more generally. At the congress in Paris in 1929, he used the debate about the political situation in Poland to suggest the renewal of the resolution from 1926.[145] Although he was opposed to it, Michał Kwiatkowski, the Polish representative, half-heartedly defended Piłsudski's regime. He was fiercely nationalist and primarily concerned about defending Polish statehood. Thus, he argued that relations between the government and parliament were 'not normal', but the constitution was still formally intact despite the blatantly anti-democratic changes of 1926. Ferrari strongly opposed the blurring between legitimate democratic and illegitimate non-democratic systems, however: 'We are democrats. If the Church accepts all sorts of forms of government, we condemn dictatorships.' Reflecting the growing accommodation with authoritarian forms of government even in some left-Catholic circles, Rutten laconically remarked, however, that 'it seems difficult to have an absolutely clear-cut doctrinaire position on this'. The Popular Democrat Champetier de Ribes discarded Ferrari's initiative with the argument that SIPDIC policy remained unchanged, so there was really nothing to discuss or agree on.[146] The Italian exiles did not give up, however. With the help of Sturzo, Ferrari prepared a critical report on the domestic situation in Italy for the SIPDIC executive committee in January 1931.[147] Arguing that the fascist state (described here as 'a kind of synthesis between the reactionary conservatism of the Habsburgs, the adventurous spirit of the Hohenzollern, and the brutality of the Romanoffs') was in a deep internal crisis, they warned that it would revert more and more to revisionist foreign policy demands to secure popular support. While some of these demands might actually be legitimate in

[143] *Bulletin du SIPDIC* 1 (1928), 30. See also the recollections of the French participant Maurice Lemesle in his autobiographical account published as Maurice Germain [Maurice Lemesle], *Les Chrétiens à la recherche de l'Europe. Essai romancé. Préface de M. Champetier de Ribes* (Paris: Editions Spes, 1931), 71.
[144] Sturzo to Ferrari, 14 May 1929, cited in De Rosa, *Luigi Sturzo*, 301. See also Rossini, *Il movimento*, 205.
[145] *Bulletin du SIPDIC* 4 (1929), 92.   [146] Ibid.
[147] La situation italienne. Rapport présenté par le secrétariat du parti populaire italien à la réunion de la Commission exécutive de l'Internationale démocrate-populaire, Paris, 5 January 1931, Österreichisches Staatsarchiv (henceforth: ÖstA), Allgemeines Verwaltungsarchiv (henceforth: AVA), NL Richard Schmitz E/1786.246.

principle – also in the eyes of the Popolari – Ferrari and Sturzo insisted that the democratic states should make no concessions to Mussolini: 'To assure peace, we have first of all to eliminate the fascist dictatorship ... Do not support the fascist regime if you really desire peace. Not one favour, not one sou: this is the approach which the European democracies have to adopt towards fascism.'

Once more, this Italian initiative came to nothing. At this stage, Ferrari was not surprised, however. He had enough personal experience with the narrow limits of Catholic support for the Popolari exiles. Having fled to Belgium in November 1926, he passed the viva for his doctoral thesis, *The Fascist Regime*, at the Catholic University of Louvain in July 1928, in the presence of Sturzo and Count Carlo Sforza, the liberal Italian foreign minister 1921–2 and ambassador to France in 1922, who was also in exile.[148] Ferrari applied to become a professor at Louvain, but the Italian embassy intervened, and he was rejected. He also failed to secure another position at the Free University of Brussels, which, however, had a strong socialist and anticlerical tradition and did not as a general rule employ Catholic academics. Ferrari then earned a living as a journalist. While in Belgium, he also failed in his attempt to motivate leading Catholic politicians to support a committee for assistance to refugees from Italy after comparable organisations had been formed in France, where it was headed by Sangnier, and in Britain, where the Italian Refugees Relief Committee was initiated by Sturzo. Ferrari complained to Sturzo that neither Rutten nor Heyman from the ACW, who were after all regular participants in SIPDIC, could be bothered to reply to his letters as they obviously did not want (because of Vatican policy) to expose themselves in opposition to fascist Italy.[149]

Instead of discussing Ferrari's report on the fascist regime, and adopting a common position against it, the executive committee, on 5 January 1931, debated the proposal for a public peace declaration. Under the impression of the sensational election result for the National Socialists in September 1930, Simondet first suggested such a declaration in a circular letter in October.[150] By December, he had mobilised sufficient support for it in principle to remind the member parties of the special importance of the executive committee in January 1931,[151] which was attended *inter alia* by

[148] Cf. Anne Morelli, 'Francesco Luigi Ferrari au sein du monde universitaire, journalistique et politique belge', in Campanini (ed.), *Francesco Luigi Ferrari*, 451–70.
[149] Ibid., 464–7.
[150] SIPDIC, Circulaire no. 11, Bundesarchiv (henceforth: BAR), CVP-Archiv JII.181, 2658.
[151] SIPDIC, Circulaire no. 12, ibid.

Julius Stocky from Germany, Champetier de Ribes, Simon, Pezet and Raymond-Laurent from France, Heyman and Philip Van Isacker from Belgium, Sturzo, Ferrari and Russo from Italy, Goseling and Teulings from the Netherlands, Kwiatkowski and Bitner from Poland, and some others.[152] At the meeting, Simondet justified the PDP initiative with the need to 'manifest publicly our existence and create an element of calmness and confidence in relating to nervous public opinion in different countries that we ... are unanimous and sincerely devoted to do everything to avoid renewed recourse to the force of weapons'.[153]

Despite the very general nature of the proposed declaration, a joint public statement went too far for some. Thus, the Swiss SKVP leadership discussed the draft resolution internally and found nothing wrong with its substance. However, it did not want to be associated with it for fear of compromising its domestic political position, and Swiss neutrality, so that it decided to send no observer to this particular executive committee meeting.[154] For the Dutch RKSP, Goseling insisted that the draft declaration was too strongly worded in some respects. In any case, he was not authorised by the RKSP executive to sign a public declaration.[155] In contrast, Stocky wanted to strengthen its ideological dimension by emphasising (in an interesting adaptation of historical materialist theory) the need to oppose fascism 'as a prelude to a bolshevist evolution' and the overriding aim 'to bar the route to all revolutionary movements'. He also suggested referring to the world economic crisis as a potent factor behind the recent political radicalisation in Germany and elsewhere, and the need to revise the Versailles Treaty, although this idea was deliberately phrased in an unclear way.[156] For their part, the Popular Democrats argued against the background of French politics that the 'popular' parties should not leave it to the socialists and Radicals to be seen as working for peace in Europe. Heyman, too, insisted that such a public declaration was necessary to avoid the impression that only the Left was for peace. In the end, Simondet suggested integrating a reference to the world economic crisis and a strengthened formula for the fight against 'the extremists', but not of course the revisionist dimension, from Stocky's alternative draft, and the

---

[152] For the list of participants see ÖstA, AVA, NL Richard Schmitz E/1786.246.
[153] *Bulletin du SIPDIC* 8 (1931), 209.
[154] Wager [?] an die Herren Mitglieder des Leitenden Ausschusses der SKVP, 4 November 1930, BAR, CVP-Archiv J II.181, 2658. For the background see also Lukas Rölli-Alkemper, 'Catholics between Emancipation and Integration: The Conservative People's Party in Switzerland', in: Kaiser and Wohnout (eds.), *Political Catholicism*, 65–79.
[155] *Bulletin du SIPDIC* 8 (1931), 210 and 215.   [156] *Bulletin du SIPDIC* 8 (1931), 211–2.

declaration was finally passed and signed by representatives of eight SIPDIC parties.[157] It emphasised the need to maintain peace in Europe and for all states to adhere to the principles of the League of Nations, including peaceful conflict resolution, but its wording was vague. The declaration was made public, but mainly printed in the Catholic press throughout Europe.[158] It did not have any significant impact beyond the Catholic and 'popular' parties and ultimately, mainly served to reassure their own supporters.

As the issue of Italian fascism and the peace declaration demonstrated, the SIPDIC parties increasingly had great difficulty agreeing on a common line on more highly politicised issues of European politics. This also holds true for the Briand Plan. The French foreign minister first informally launched the idea of a European federation in July 1929.[159] Soon thereafter, at the conference in The Hague in August 1929, the Young Plan was agreed on, which provided for a permanent settlement of the thorny issue of German reparations with payments until 1988. It was linked politically to the withdrawal of French troops from the Rhineland by 30 June 1930. The resolution of these two issues seemed to create a window of opportunity for more far-reaching plans. In Germany, the social democrats and the remaining left-liberal democrats supported the Briand Plan. The reaction of the left-Catholic *Kölnische Volkszeitung*, which was intimately involved in Catholic party cooperation through Stocky, its editor, who had close links with Adenauer,[160] was also positive.[161] Yet, German nationalists aggressively fought the plan as an attempt to enshrine French hegemony in new regional institutions and to prevent the integration of Austria with the German Empire. Their parallel agitation against the Young Plan reached new noise levels when Hugenberg, Hitler and Paul Seldte, the leader of the paramilitary Stahlhelm organisation, warned against 'the enslavement of the German people' at their meeting on 11 September 1929.[162]

---

[157] 'Manifestes de Paix', *Politique*, 5 January 1931, 184–6. The authorised German version in ÖstA, AVA, NL Richard Schmitz E/1786.246.

[158] See, for example, *Kölnische Volkszeitung*, 10 January 1931. For a list of some (although presumably, not all) of the European newspapers and journals that published the peace declaration, see Papini, *Le Courage*, 220, footnote 71.

[159] Cf. Pegg, *Evolution*, 112. See also Peter Krüger, *Das unberechenbare Europa. Epochen des Integrationsprozesses vom späten 18. Jahrhundert bis zur Europäischen Union* (Stuttgart: Kohlhammer, 2006), 160–5.

[160] Cf. Ekkhard Häussermann, 'Konrad Adenauer und die Presse vor 1933', in Hugo Stehkämper (ed.), *Konrad Adenauer. Oberbürgermeister von Köln* (Cologne: Rheinland-Verlag, 1976), 207–47.

[161] Pegg, *Evolution*, 112–4.   [162] Ibid., 128.

The Popular Democrats strongly supported the Briand Plan. In their manifesto *Our Foreign Policy*, published in 1930, they advocated an 'organised Europe' to create greater regional stability within the League of Nations. One year later, *Politique* launched an 'investigation into European Union', albeit only with contributions from French writers like François de Menthon. Finally, in 1931, the PDP annual conference declared that 'European union has never been more essential'.[163] The Popular Democrats tried several times to get the Briand Plan on the SIPDIC agenda. Immediately following its launch, Marcel Prélot (supported by Ferrari) first proposed it in the name of the PDP executive in late July 1929 at the congress in Paris, as the theme for the next congress in Antwerp in 1930.[164] At the executive meeting on 4 January 1930, Ferrari once more suggested concentrating on debating plans for the 'United States of Europe'.[165] The Dutch and Belgians were opposed to this, however. Heyman made the point that in his view, it was not for the political parties to discuss this question, as 'the governments are currently addressing the extreme difficulties which this question poses. Would it not be better to discuss this in small circles with a view to eliminating existing difficulties?'[166] Together with the Dutch representatives, he successfully argued for the continued debate of corporatism within SIPDIC.

By the time Briand formally submitted his plan in a government memorandum of 17 May 1930, however, the European political situation had deteriorated. The Belgian and Dutch Catholics, who played a leading role in their national governments, were at best lukewarm. They were only interested in plans for European cooperation with a strong economic dimension. The Briand Plan, which was in any case extremely general and contained no specific proposals, largely lacked such a dimension. As Michel Dumoulin has shown, it had 'no significant immediate impact' on Belgian politics and foreign policy.[167] At the same time, and in the vain hope of safeguarding free trade, the Dutch government concentrated on international economic issues, particularly the Tariff Truce Conference of February 1930, which produced minimal results that were only ratified by

---

[163] Cf. Delbreil, 'Christian Democracy', 128.   [164] *Bulletin du SIPDIC* 4 (1929), 102.
[165] *Bulletin du SIPDIC* 5 (1930), 130.   [166] Ibid.
[167] Michel Dumoulin, 'La Belgique et le Plan Briand: l'annonce de réformes de structures au plan européen', in Antoine Fleury and Lubor Jílek (eds.), *Le Plan Briand d'Union fédérale européenne. Perspectives nationales et transnationales, avec documents* (Bern: Lang, 1998), 101.

106 Christian Democracy and the Origins of European Union

few countries. The government in The Hague was also concerned about the implications of the Briand Plan for Dutch neutrality.[168] More importantly, however, despite some sympathy for the plan among left-Catholics, the official German reaction was negative.[169] By May 1930, Brüning ruled by executive decree. In line with his personal preferences, but also to enhance the legitimacy of his government, his foreign policy differed markedly from that of Stresemann. Under Brüning, Germany 'turned decisively towards a nationalist policy', as Peter Krüger has put it.[170] Like the nationalist Right, the Auswärtiges Amt saw the Briand Plan as a French device to prevent any revision of the Versailles Treaty and permanently to secure French hegemony in Europe.[171] As a result, the German government, in its formal reply to the French memorandum, demanded changes to the postwar settlement as a precondition for its participation in any talks.[172] At best, Brüning was interested in economic cooperation, but this was difficult to achieve at a time during the world economic crisis when national trade policies were becoming increasingly protectionist. In the end, the Briand Plan was sidelined, discussed from 1930 to 1932 in the Commission of Inquiry for European Union in the League of Nations, and came to nothing.

In fact, the failure of the Briand Plan, which many Catholic politicians regarded as too vague, lacking strategic direction and mainly designed to serve specific French interests, created new opportunities for the discussion of 'Europe' in SIPDIC. At the executive committee on 5 January 1931, Stocky first suggested making the world economic crisis the main theme of the next congress in Luxembourg.[173] It ended up being family policy, but the parties prepared reports on national economic policy which provided the basis for a larger integrated report on this theme at Luxembourg. Subsequently, the parties decided to devote the annual congress in Cologne in October 1932 to the theme of European economic cooperation, with proposals prepared in advance by a small commission from the member

168 Hein A. M. Klemann, 'The Dutch Reaction to the Briand Plan', in Fleury and Jílek (eds.), Le Plan Briand, 161.
169 See also Franz Knipping, Deutschland, Frankreich und das Ende der Locarno-Ära 1928–1931 (Munich: Oldenbourg, 1987), 141–57.
170 Peter Krüger, 'Der abgebrochene Dialog: die deutschen Reaktionen auf die Europavorstellungen Briands 1929', in Fleury and Jílek (eds.), Le Plan Briand, 289.
171 Cf. Martin Vogt, 'Die deutsche Haltung zum Briand-Plan im Sommer 1930: Hintergründe und politisches Umfeld der Europapolitik des Kabinetts Brüning', in Fleury and Jílek (eds.), Le Plan Briand, 316.
172 Pegg, Evolution, 140.   173 Bulletin du SIPDIC 8 (1931), 220.

parties.[174] The Centre Party initially planned to be represented by a large number of their leading politicians. In the end, however, only Joos, Stocky, Adenauer and some others actually attended because of the demands of the ongoing election campaign. Other national delegations came with prominent members, such as the Belgians with Hyman, Van Isacker, Rutten, Segers and Gaston Eyskens, or the French with Champetier de Ribes, Simon, Pezet, Trémintin, Schuman, Raymond-Laurent and Jean Lerolle.[175] In the end, they agreed a resolution demanding the creation of a European 'common market' for the production and trade of goods.[176] National governments should 'give up the current trade policy' and liberalise their economic policies with the aim of a 'freer exchange of goods, capital and people' in Europe. The resolution also addressed the agricultural crisis and demanded Europe-wide measures to stabilise the income of farmers, who were especially prone to opt for right-wing extremist parties.

The 1932 SIPDIC resolution outlined European integration with its emphasis on market integration and support for farmers as it actually happened under Christian democratic influence after World War II. It largely borrowed liberal concepts for European economic integration developed originally in the second half of the 1920s – not by Catholics but by liberals and liberal economic pressure groups like the International Committee for a European Customs Union. Crucially, the left-Catholics who dominated SIPDIC did not have a major ideological or socioeconomic stake in this particular form of integration. It seemed to be much more designed for the industrial middle class and, possibly, farmers. In contrast, the left-Catholics were still much more concerned with national social policies to improve the lot of workers under the rapidly deteriorating circumstances of the world economic crisis. Moreover, the Cologne resolution coincided with an extreme crisis in European politics, and especially in the Franco-German relationship, so that it had no consequences at the time. Within SIPDIC, Franco-German relations already began to deteriorate from 1928–9 onward, and especially after 1930. From the beginning, the Centre Party group expected that SIPDIC would advance German revisionist aims, if not over reversing some of the territorial changes made

[174] According to Ferrari to Sturzo, 27 July 1931, printed in Ferrari, *Lettere e documenti inediti*, vol. II, 566, the congress in Luxembourg in July 1931 resolved to create a special commission for the study of European economic problems which was scheduled to meet for the first time in Brussels on 28 September 1931. Unfortunately, no minutes of any meetings of this committee have been preserved.

[175] See also Alfred Pierrey, 'Après la conférence de Cologne', *Le Petit Démocrate*, 30 October 1932.

[176] *Luxemburger Wort*, 11 October 1932; *Kölnische Volkszeitung*, 10 October 1932, reprinted in *UMDC Informations*, 5 July 1982.

in the Versailles Treaty, then at least concerning the occupation of the Rhineland and the Saar region and perhaps the integration of Austria into the German Empire. The informal meeting between Stresemann and Briand at Thoiry in September 1926, which was leaked to the press, strengthened the expectations that the Locarno Treaty and German accession to the League of Nations would bring about rapid changes.[177] In return for a German contribution toward the stabilisation of the French budget and currency, Briand suggested that Germany might be allowed to buy back Eupen-Malmédy from Belgium and the Saar coal mines from France, that the Rhineland could be evacuated within one year and the Saar region returned to Germany. Poincaré's stabilisation policy and the domestic protest within France pulled the rug from underneath Briand's far-reaching ideas. From Thoiry onward, however, German politics measured French European policy by the standards of these informal proposals, and this is also true for the bilateral contacts in SIPDIC.

The Franco-German tensions became only too obvious during the debate about the Young Plan at the congress in Paris in 1929.[178] Joos predicted a majority for it in the Reichstag, but added: 'I have to admit honestly that this is a majority which simply says, we will try. Will we succeed at executing the plan? You will find nobody in Germany who would be prepared to say so.' Stocky added that the Young Plan alone, with its reparation payments for sixty years, was not exactly attractive for the Germans, and that 'one has to add a little bit of sugar'. The French and Belgian representatives reacted very critically to this, however. Auguste Bastianelli, the director of the PDP study centre, emphasised that non-fulfilment by Germany would be a catastrophe for the Popular Democrats in domestic politics, and 'the peace policy and European reconciliation will be gravely compromised'. The German reparations, he argued, did not even cover all French debt repayments and expenditure for reconstruction. Heyman made the same point about Belgium, adding that 'ministers everywhere have to add some sugar' to make the consequences of the war more palatable for their citizens. Champetier de Ribes also emphasised that the Young Plan had to be fulfilled 100 per cent. When Weber brought up the Saar question (as possible sugar for the Germans), he simply replied that the Popular Democrats were not prepared to discuss the issue, as it was a matter for governments.

---

[177] Cf. Wurm, 'Deutsche Frankreichpolitik', 141. See also Ruppert, *Im Dienst*, 172–8.
[178] For the following see *Bulletin du SIPDIC* 4 (1929), 75–92.

When the evacuation of the Rhineland finally happened in 1930, it no longer 'caused any excitement among the Catholics' in Germany, according to Hermann Hagspiel.[179] In fact, Kaas and Brüning initially argued at the beginning of 1929 that Germany had a legal right to the evacuation of the Rhineland in accordance with the Versailles Treaty, and, on this basis, rejected the issue linkage with the Young Plan. They only advocated parliamentary support for it after the Centre Party re-entered the social democrat-led government in April 1929.[180] From 1928 onward, Kaas – the party's conservative foreign policy spokesman – was busy developing a set of far-reaching revisionist demands, which were also reflected in the party's foreign policy programme of 1930.[181] They included *inter alia* revisions of the eastern borders, the immediate return of the Saar region and the *Anschluss* of Austria which was fully in line with the traditional Catholic *grossdeutsch* preference.[182] Kaas also favoured a foreign policy of closer cooperation with fascist Italy as a counterbalance to France.[183]

The Popular Democrats were hardly reassured by the growing nationalist tide in Germany and within the Centre Party. At Antwerp in 1930, the debate continued.[184] Bastianelli insisted that France had in fact made many concessions from reducing its original reparation demands to evacuating the third Rhenish zone early, adding, 'what makes me nervous is that the Centre Party, which is very much stronger than we are, nevertheless does not have the same positive influence on the Right'. Lerolle, a PDP deputy, argued that the example of Italian fascism demonstrated how ever-greater foreign policy demands could eventually lead to a situation where the government is no longer in control of its people, and that this might well happen in Germany. Pezet added that it was possible in theory to imagine specific revisions of the Versailles Treaty. Even if small adjustments could be agreed on, however, Germany would then call everything into question, leading to the breakdown of the postwar order, so that the PDP had no leeway. At the same time, Joos pleaded that it was extremely difficult for the Germans in the deteriorating economic circumstances to envisage the payment of approximately two billion Reichsmark annually over a period of sixty years. With the same argument, Weber defended Brüning, who

[179] Hagspiel, *Verständigung*, 443. This is also reflected in Joos's lecture at the Deutsch-Französische Gesellschaft in Berlin on 16 October, when he spoke of 'what Germany expected [rather than expects] of France'. See Joseph Joos, 'Was erwartet Deutschland von Frankreich', *Deutsch-Französische Rundschau* 3 (1930), 985.
[180] Ruppert, *Im Dienst*, 377.   [181] Cf. Jürgen Elvert, 'A Microcosm of Society', 57–8.
[182] See also Hagspiel, *Verständigung*, 80–1.   [183] Ibid., 397 and 424.
[184] For the following see *Bulletin du SIPDIC* 7 (1931), 175–99.

had publicly called into question that the Young Plan was indeed the last word on the reparation issue. Ferrari supported the German group, arguing that 'treaties are never eternal', and that it would be better to make appropriate concessions now, or the conflicts could 'lead once more fatally to war'.[185] Stocky aptly described the basic Franco-German misunderstanding: 'When we speak of the new Europe, you speak of stabilisation, we speak of revision. You say to us Germans: our doubts will disappear only if you prove that you merit our confidence. But we say that confidence is impossible without revision.'

The Franco-German quarrels continued in 1931. The signing of the German-Austrian customs union project on 14 March 1931, which only became known in Paris six days later, caused uproar in France. In a meeting of the Centre Party parliamentary party shortly afterwards, on 26 March, Brüning supported continued contacts with the PDP, although he also said that 'we have not so far got ahead one step' through transnational party cooperation.[186] Together with some leading PDP politicians, Brüning later participated in a peace mass in Notre-Dame-des-Victoires in Paris.[187] Nonetheless, the German group boycotted the Luxembourg congress in July 1931 at short notice.[188] Joos in fact assured Simondet of his participation two days before it was scheduled to begin, so that it is almost certain that he acted on the initiative of Brüning and the Auswärtiges Amt. Brüning was annoyed about the strict French opposition to the customs union project and concerned that in the aftermath of the collapse of the Viennese Creditanstalt bank, France would try to establish a hegemony in south-eastern Europe and to make Germany economically dependent on it.[189] According to Ferrari, the German-Austrian customs union project was undiplomatically defended at Luxembourg by Richard Schmitz, the Austrian Christian Social representative.[190] This, and the German boycott, strengthened the growing disillusionment among the Popular Democrats with the Centre Party, and they started to revise their policy on Germany in the period 1931–2, before the collapse of the Weimar Republic.

---

[185] See also Trinchese, 'L'internazionale', 348.

[186] Parliamentary party meeting, 26 March 1931, *Die Protokolle der Reichstagsfraktion und des Fraktionsvorstands der Deutschen Zentrumspartei 1926–1933* (Mainz: Matthias-Grünewald-Verlag, 1969), 527.

[187] Delbreil, *Les Catholiques*, 225.   [188] *Bulletin du SIPDIC* 9–10 (1931), 236.

[189] See Brüning's comments in the Centre Party parliamentary party on 14 June 1931: *Die Protokolle 1926–1933*, 531.

[190] Ferrari to Sturzo, 27 July 1931, printed in Ferrari, *Lettere e documenti inediti*, vol. II, 564.

Once Hitler was in power and the Centre Party dissolved, SIPDIC lacked its main rationale, which was to foster European reconciliation – especially between France and Germany – through the transnational cooperation of Catholic and 'popular' parties. After some debate, the remaining parties decided to continue their cooperation, but – as Goseling put it in an internal discussion in the RKSP executive – in 'a more modest form',[191] without the annual congresses and with more limited policy discussions in the executive committee. Thus, SIPDIC continued to exist until the last executive committee meeting in January 1939,[192] but it became increasingly irrelevant. Summarising an executive committee meeting in 1935, Pezet described its main task as sustaining a 'spiritual Commonwealth' and organising some residual contacts for the exchange of information and views on current political issues.[193] In fact, the PDP tried to transform SIPDIC into something more than that: an instrument for the support of French alliance policy against Germany, adjusting the original rationale to avoid the international isolation of French political Catholicism and to seek allies through party cooperation. Pezet played the leading role in this strategy. He was a member of the foreign policy committee of the French parliament, and rapporteur for Central Europe. Already in the period 1925–32 he established many contacts there, especially in Czechoslovakia, Poland and Austria. He made a particular effort to draw Catholic politicians from these countries into SIPDIC. From 1933 onward, Pezet and the Popular Democrats subordinated everything in SIPDIC and beyond to the overriding aim of isolating Germany.

The Popular Democrats motivated the Polish representatives to participate more regularly. As opposed to the Polish foreign minister, Józef Beck, who followed a relatively pro-German policy during the 1930s, they were strongly pro-French. Pezet also intensified the contacts with the Československá strana lidová, the Czech People's Party led by Jan Šrámek. Until 1933, their representatives only participated sporadically in SIPDIC activities as observers, but then became more active, with the party formally joining in 1934. They also saw the organisation as a useful

[191] Dagelijks Bestuur van de R. K. Staatspartij, 's-Gravenhage, 9 June 1933, KDC, Archief van de R. K. Staatspartij, 1.3, 19. See already Dagelijks Bestuur van de R. K. Staatspartij, Amsterdam, 8 May 1933, ibid.

[192] Cf. Dagelijks Bestuur van de R. K. Staatspartij, 's-Gravenhage, 30 December 1938, KDC, Archief van de R. K. Staatspartij, 1.3, 20. The following meeting scheduled for July 1939 was put back and then did not take place due to the outbreak of World War II. Cf. Sturzo to Crawford, 15 September 1940, Nationaal Archief [henceforth: NA], Collectie J. A. Veraart, 216.

[193] Ernest Pezet, 'Une rencontre internationale. Des hommes politiques à la recherche de l'Europe', *Petit Démocrate*, 11 August 1935.

societal forum for strengthening the Little Entente alliance. Most spectacularly, however, Pezet succeeded in transforming the SIPDIC relationship with leading representatives of the Christian Socials who supported the Austrian *Ständestaat* after 1933–4. The Christian Socials only formally joined SIPDIC in 1931, after prior consultation with the Centre Party secretariat.[194] Schmitz, who was close to the ageing Seipel, became their official representative.[195] Opposed to national socialism, but inclined towards political corporatism, he turned from being an ardent supporter of the *Anschluss* at the SIPDIC congress in Luxembourg in 1931 into an anti-national socialist protagonist of Austrian nationalism as it was propagated by the *Ständestaat* regime. On 6 April 1934, he was appointed mayor of Vienna, which had been ruled by the socialists before their suppression earlier in the same year. With the Christian Socials dissolved as a party, Schmitz began to act in SIPDIC as the personal representative of the dictator Schuschnigg. Before and at the executive committee in January 1938, Pezet and Schmitz coordinated the last meaningful SIPDIC initiative:[196] an appeal to the Pope, to be transmitted via Cardinal Jean Verdier, the Archbishop of Paris, to launch a peace initiative with the aim of preventing the possible annexation of Austria by the German Empire and a general European war.[197]

With the aim of containing Germany, the Popular Democrats also continued their lenient attitude to Italian fascism after 1933. They did not openly condemn Italy's invasion of Ethiopia in 1935 and the terrible atrocities committed by Italian troops there. Despite their strong anticommunism, moreover, the Popular Democrats even supported the Franco-Soviet Pact of the same year.[198] In the deteriorating international circumstances of the late 1930s, including the new alliance between Hitler and Mussolini, some Popular Democrats like Champetier de Ribes and Bidault were increasingly prepared to contemplate war, but the majority supported the Appeasement policy of the government of Edouard Daladier

---

[194] Vockel to Schmitz, 2 January 1931, ÖStA, AVA, Nachlass Richard Schmitz.

[195] Simondet to Schmitz, 10 February 1931, as well as some other documents in ÖStA, AVA, Nachlass Richard Schmitz including Bericht über die Pariser internationale Konferenz der christlichen Volksparteien, erstattet von Richard Schmitz, 20 January 1931. See also *Bulletin of SIPDIC* 8 (1931), 227.

[196] Archives d'histoire contemporaine (henceforth: AHC), Fonds Ernest Pezet, P. E. 8, Dossier 8: Autriche, and Pezet's recollections in Pezet, *Chrétiens*, 115.

[197] Note sur la situation internationale remise au Cardinal Verdier par Champetier de Ribes, Ernest Pezet et Georges Bidault au nom de SIPDIC, appel à l'intervention du Saint-Siège en faveur de la paix, janvier 1938, AHC, Fonds Ernest Pezet, P. E. 3, Dossier 4. Whether this appeal actually reached the Pope and was considered by the Vatican could not be verified.

[198] Cf. Delbreil, 'Christian Democracy', 126–30.

beyond the Munich Agreement of October 1938.[199] Some like Pezet were now prepared to discuss major revisions of the Versailles Treaty with Hitler, which they had categorically excluded in their SIPDIC relations with the Centre Party before 1933. The new PDP foreign policy was thus marked by a full return to traditional great power politics. Although this reorientation was mainly motivated by the fear of national socialist Germany, the collective security approach with moralist overtures of the period 1925–32 had always been half-hearted and ambivalent, especially in relation to Germany.

The Popolari continued to fight for their original conception of SIPDIC as an organisation of democratic 'popular' parties. Sturzo also tried for many years to bring British Catholic politicians from the Labour Party into SIPDIC.[200] He also protested loudly, although without success, against the participation of Schmitz.[201] At the executive committee in June 1934, Schmitz defended Dollfuss's *coup d'état*. Sturzo understood very well that Mussolini had colluded with Dollfuss in the suppression of the Austrian socialists combined with the desired Italian security guarantee for the *Ständestaat*. At the SIPDIC meeting, he insisted that Schmitz represented no regular member party and should only be allowed to participate as an observer. When Pezet accorded Schmitz the full rights of a national party representative, Sturzo left the meeting in protest.[202] Replacing the PPI founder at another executive meeting, Russo wrote to Sturzo in 1935 that it was hardly possible to speak of an organisation of 'democratic' parties any longer. The PDP still qualified as such a party, but the Belgian Catholics were already more clerical than 'popular'. In Russo's view, several other parties no longer qualified as fully democratic. With support from the liberals, the Catholics in Luxembourg under their leader, Prime Minister Joseph Bech, had just expelled the democratically elected communist deputy Zénon Bernard from parliament, arguing that the communist programme was incompatible 'under the constitution' with democratic

---

[199] Delbreil, *Centrisme*, 392–402.

[200] *Bulletin du SIPDIC* 4 (1929), 87; *Bulletin du SIPDIC* 9–10 (1931), 233.

[201] For a comparable controversy about the Austrian participation in the ILO in Geneva, where Serrarens protested against the presence of the Austrian delegate after the abolition of independent unions, see Maurice Bouladoux, 'Chronique syndicale', *L'Aube*, 16 July 1935.

[202] See the account in De Rosa, *Luigi Sturzo*, 329–32. On Sturzo's attitude to corporatist dictatorships in the 1930s see also Francesco Malgeri, *Chiesa, cattolici e democrazia. Da Sturzo a De Gasperi* (Brescia: Morcelliana, 1990), 194. Other Popolari in opposition to Mussolini were not nearly as resolutely opposed to the *Ständestaat* model as Sturzo, however. This is especially true of De Gasperi, who saw it as 'an important experimental laboratory for social Catholics'. See Gabriele De Rosa, *Da Luigi Sturzo ad Aldo Moro* (Brescia: Morcelliana, 1988), 108.

political representation. Russo also lamented that the Slovene Catholics now favoured accommodation with the monarchical regime following the assassination of King Alexander I by Croatian nationalists in October 1934, after their leader, Anton Korosec, had previously been interned in 1933 following the publication of a memorandum critical of the regime.[203] More obviously, Schmitz was even the personal representative of a clerical dictator.

Sturzo continued for some time to upset the cosy semi-democratic, pro-French SIPDIC circle. In a letter to Simondet of 4 October 1935 he complained that neither the Centre Party nor any other SIPDIC party had protested against the anti-Semitic persecutions in Germany in 1933 and thereafter.[204] In reality, the universal silence on this point was not only motivated by fear of national socialism, of course, but by a widespread lack of concern for the fate of the Jews, if not outright anti-Semitism, among many Catholic politicians. For the Austrian Christian Socials, Catholic anti-Judaism turned secular anti-Semitism was a constitutive element of their party ideology.[205] Of the Christian Social politicians with SIPDIC contacts, Mataja was a notorious anti-Semite, and Schmitz proudly wrote in his explanatory notes on the Christian Social Party programme in 1932 that anti-Semitism 'since the origins of the movement, has been a part of the Christian social character'.[206] As Leszek Kuk has pointed out, the same was essentially the case for the nationalistic Polish Christian democracy.[207] Anti-Semitism was also widespread amongst Catholics in France and Germany, although Olaf Blaschke has clearly exaggerated its influence on the Centre Party.[208]

Sturzo and Russo made one final attempt to reinvigorate SIPDIC with a memorandum that they circulated to the parties via Simondet in 1935,[209] proposing to transform it into an organisation for the 'defence of Christian

---

[203] In this case, Russo was only partially correct, as the formation of a new Serb-Slovene-Muslim coalition in May–June 1935 actually started a degree of liberalisation of the regime. See also Arnold Suppan, *Jugoslawien und Österreich 1918–1938. Bilaterale Außenpolitik im europäischen Umfeld* (Vienna, Munich: Verlag für Geschichte und Politik, 1996).

[204] Sturzo to Simondet, 4 October 1935, Archivio Storico Istituto Luigi Sturzo (henceforth: ASILS), Fondo Luigi Sturzo, fasc. 10A. See also Malgeri, *Chiesa*, 91.

[205] See Wohnout, 'Middle-Class Governmental Party,' and, in greater detail, Bruce F. Pauley, *From Prejudice to Persecution: A History of Austrian Antisemitism* (Chapel Hill: University of North Carolina Press, 1992).

[206] *Das christlichsoziale Programm*, Vienna, 1932, 67, cited in Wohnout, 'Middle-Class Governmental Party', endnote 17.

[207] Cf. Kuk, 'A Powerful Catholic Church', 152.

[208] Olaf Blaschke, *Katholizismus und Antisemitismus im deutschen Kaiserreich* (Göttingen: Vandenhoeck & Ruprecht, 1997).

[209] Sturzo to Simondet, 21 August 1935, ASILS, Fondo Luigi Sturzo, fasc. CS 489 (SIPDIC).

civilisation'.[210] They brought out very clearly the basic fault-line in SIPDIC between those parties intent on defending representative democracy and those in favour of taking 'a holiday from legality' including curtailed individual liberties. These disparate parties could do no more than to exchange information, and certainly not agree on common action. Instead, the new organisation with a strengthened secretariat with at least five members would concentrate on publicly defending basic moral values everywhere. It appears that the executive committee at least discussed Sturzo's initiative. It was quickly discarded by Simondet and Pezet, however, and came to nothing. The Popular Democrats were much more preoccupied with saving France than saving democracy, and they hoped that the one could be achieved without the other.

Against this background it is not surprising that the Belgian Van Isacker concluded in his memoirs that SIPDIC never achieved 'what, with our initial enthusiasm, we had expected'.[211] For one, the network was small. Its relatively strong left-Catholic ideological cohesion in the early years came at the expense of greater influence within the Catholic and 'popular' parties as a whole, and in domestic politics. The Popular Democrats were marginal in French politics, had no significant influence on French foreign policy and were too afraid of the nationalist Right to develop a bolder policy towards the integration of Germany into new European political structures. They were prepared to make concessions to Hitler under the threat of military force which they had refused to make to the Germans in SIPDIC, who were in favour of Franco-German reconciliation. At the same time, the German group led by Joos and representing the nationally moderate Left of the Centre Party totally failed to socialise the more nationalist Left around Stegerwald and – even more importantly – the conservative-nationalist Right into transnational party cooperation and new forms of European politics.[212] Ultimately, Centre Party foreign policy was decided by the likes of Kaas and Brüning. They tolerated the SIPDIC activities as potentially useful for their increasingly far-reaching revisionist programme. As Joos recalled later, however, these and other conservative Catholics in Germany as in France were still deeply influenced by the fixed idea of a Franco-German antagonism and saw SIPDIC as an 'emotionally insincere attempt at making contact' that was of necessity

---

[210] Sturzo, Pour la défense de la civilisation, ibid.
[211] Philip van Isacker, *Tussen Staat en Volk. Nagelaten Memoires* (Antwerp: Uitgeverij Sheed & Ward N. V., 1953), 70.
[212] See also Hanschmidt, 'Eine christlich-demokratische', 182–3.

bordering on the 'betrayal of national interests'.[213] Yet even the Joos group as well as the moderate Popular Democrats and representatives even in the early years of SIPDIC were far from immune against 'the virus of nationalism'. As Sturzo wrote retrospectively in 1941, it was this virus that 'paralysed the activity of the secretariat from the start'.[214]

In contrast, Roberto Papini has suggested two other reasons for the failure of SIPDIC which are not, however, corroborated in a long-term comparative perspective. According to Papini, they were the Catholic parties' lack of a social foundation and a common ideology, such as the socialist class myth, and the absence of a supranational institutional framework that could have induced greater transnational party integration.[215] Yet, the SIPDIC group was actually more internally cohesive ideologically in the early years than the Catholic parties as a whole, or, indeed, compared to the Christian democrats after 1945, who nevertheless managed to coordinate their policies much better and to dominate European policy-making. Moreover, although the socialist parties (despite great ideological and social variations) had the class myth, they also failed in the interwar years to develop effective transnational political action. At the same time, supranational institutionalisation may provide for strong incentives for transnational organisations to gain access to resources such as funding, and to decision-making, but it is clearly not a precondition for effective party cooperation. In fact, Christian democratic party cooperation after World War II was most intense and effective at a time when it attempted to bring about supranational integration, only to decline somewhat when the new institutions, and the national governments directed by Christian democrats, appeared to guarantee the implementation of their core strategic objectives.

Instead, the main problem of the Catholic and 'popular' parties in interwar Europe was that they could not agree on these core strategic objectives. This concerned both the functional role of party cooperation and its policy content. The French Popular Democrats in particular were still fixated with using SIPDIC to prevent the international isolation of French political Catholicism and, beyond that, to foster alliances against any revisions of the Versailles Treaty and, in essence, against the German Centre Party and the German Empire.[216] Transposing an

[213] Joos, *Am Räderwerk*, 125.
[214] Luigi Sturzo, 'The White International', *People & Freedom* 22 (1941), 1.
[215] Papini, *Le Courage*, 165.
[216] Delbreil, *Centrisme*, 269 has also pointed to the 'contradiction' between these aims.

intergovernmental great power mode of interaction onto party cooperation failed to generate sufficient trust between the SIPDIC parties, however, which in turn would have been a necessary precondition for better inter-personal and inter-party relations and policy coordination. The parties also failed to agree on their core policy objectives. They succeeded in discussing different concepts of corporatism and aspects of family policy. Yet the comparative discussion of such domestic policy issues and the potential cross-border transfer of policy concepts were totally overshadowed by the highly contested future of the Versailles Treaty, with French and Belgian demands for 'stability' in European politics and German counter-demands for 'revision' of the status quo, which were wholly incompatible.

The structural conditions for party cooperation temporarily improved after World War I compared to the period before 1914, but they deteriorated again quickly from the late 1920s onward. In these difficult circumstances, although failing to influence European politics in any significant way, SIPDIC nevertheless had long-term significance. Firstly, it managed at least partially to overcome the stigmatising of transnational party cooperation as essentially a socialist phenomenon, and the idea that its extension to Catholic and 'popular' parties could call into question the authority of the Catholic Church as the sole legitimate international representation of Catholic interests and ideas. Thus, the incipient party cooperation fostered the secularisation of Catholic politics in an international context, which was an important precondition for Christian democratic integration policies after 1945. Secondly, SIPDIC also facilitated a collective learning process. In particular, it showed to all involved that party cooperation could only be effective if it combined strictly pro-democratic parties with a shared value system and was extended to democratic liberal and conservative Catholics to broaden its basis and strengthen its potential influence – and that it required some shared core strategic policy objectives. Thirdly, concerning these strategic objectives, the Catholic and 'popular' parties also found out towards the end of their regular activities in 1932 that the only way forward in European politics was probably what would later be called the 'functionalist' approach starting with economic integration. While there is no direct line from the SIPDIC congress in Cologne through to postwar integration, the resolution nevertheless reflected a growing realisation that political divisions could be more easily overcome with shared socio-economic objectives with long-term potential for political cooperation or integration. Actually, some Catholic politicians like Adenauer and Schuman, who were later to adopt this approach after World War II, were present at this congress and already supported this approach then, while many left-Catholics like Sturzo were concerned that economic integration could lack sufficient moral and democratic legitimacy.[217]

Nevertheless, as Martin Conway has rightly pointed out, Catholic politics in interwar Europe was still predominantly shaped nationally, 'seeking to achieve its goals within rather than across national frontiers'.[218] The left-Catholics in SIPDIC in its early years were something of a transnational avant-garde. For their methods of transnational cooperation and general aims such as Franco-German reconciliation to have any real impact clearly required significant changes in the structural conditions under which they operated, and which only came about as a result of the experience of totalitarianism and occupation and collaboration during World War II. In the period 1925–33, the SIPDIC group were still, as Guido Müller has put it, 'a minority with a European disposition in a continent torn by increasing nationalism'.[219] From this perspective, SIPDIC increasingly looked like 'anticipated exile'.[220]

---

[217] Cf. Malgeri, 'Alle origini', 303.   [218] Conway, 'Catholic Politics', 237.

[219] Guido Müller, 'Anticipated Exile of Catholic Democrats: The Secrétariat International des Partis Démocratiques d'Inspiration Chrétienne', in Kaiser and Wohnout (eds.), *Political Catholicism*, 255.

[220] Ibid., 262.

CHAPTER 4

In the shadow of dictatorship: contacts in exile

Those Catholic politicians who actually went into exile before the start of World War II usually felt even more isolated abroad than refugees of a different political persuasion. The Catholic exile community was small. Compared to the communists and social democrats, few Catholic politicians went into exile while Mussolini was consolidating his power in Italy during 1922–6, after Hitler destroyed the remnants of legality in Germany in 1933 and after the annexation of Austria by Germany in March 1938. In Italy, many conservative Catholics deserted the PPI for the fascists after 1922–4. Many more Catholic politicians there, as well as in Germany and in Austria, preferred internal emigration to exile. De Gasperi, the last PPI leader, worked in the Vatican library.[1] Adenauer, who was sacked by the National Socialists as mayor of Cologne in 1933, retired to a house in Rhöndorf near Bonn. He later refused to establish close contact with the German resistance for fear of reprisals against his family, but apparently also because he saw the total collapse of the regime as a precondition for successful postwar reconstruction and democratisation.[2]

At the same time, many younger, socially 'progressive' Catholic democrats joined the resistance. This is true of Josef Müller, the first postwar leader of the Bavarian Christlich-Soziale Union (CSU), the Christian Social Union. Müller knew Pope Pius XII from his time as papal nuntius in Munich. He established contacts with the Vatican for the German resistance in the *Abwehr*, the defence secret service, early on in the war in the hope that the Pope could mediate a negotiated peace

---

[1] Malgeri, *Chiesa*, 100; Daniela Preda, *Alcide De Gasperi federalista europeo* (Bologna: il Mulino, 2004), 113–20. See also Piero Craveri, *De Gasperi* (Bologna: il Mulino, 2006).

[2] On Adenauer and the German resistance see the annotated documentation *Adenauer im Dritten Reich* (Berlin: Siedler Verlag, 1991).

with Britain after the possible overthrow of Hitler.[3] He was later interned in the concentration camp at Dachau and freed by US troops in Austria. An example from Austria is Felix Hurdes, the first secretary-general of the Österreichische Volkspartei (ÖVP), the Austrian People's Party, after 1945, who was also interned at Dachau. Both Christian democratic politicians played a leading role in the NEI after the war. On the whole, the resistance experience was much more significant for Christian democrats in Italy and especially in France, however, in circles which had formed around *L'Aube* and the NEF shortly before the war. They included Georges Bidault, the editor of *L'Aube*, who succeeded Jean Moulin as leader of the Conseil National de la Résistance (CNR) after his arrest in 1943, Pierre-Henri Teitgen, the son of the PDP politician Henri Teitgen, the brothers Paul and Alfred Coste-Floret, as well as de Menthon.[4] All of them became engaged in transnational party cooperation after the war, with Bidault playing a key role in the informal Geneva Circle and Alfred Coste-Floret acting as NEI secretary-general from 1955 to 1960.

The Catholic exiles were not only small in number, they were also very dispersed. While many communists fled to the Soviet Union, where the German Communist Party established its headquarters, for example, many social democrats went to Britain. They had a natural partner in the Labour Party there, and could draw on long-standing contacts, not least through the SI, although the relationship between the approximately 160 German social democrats in London with the Labour Party was nonetheless tense, as Anthony Glees has shown.[5] The concentration of refugees with the same political orientation from different parts of Europe in one country at least facilitated their transnational networking, however. Compared to the communists and social democrats, this was more difficult for the much smaller group of Catholic refugees. Nevertheless, it was still easier for them to forge links in exile, and to formalise them in some rudimentary way, than for the Christian democrats engaged in the resistance.

---

[3] Friedrich Hermann Hettler, *Josef Müller ('Ochsensepp')*. *Mann des Widerstandes und erster CSU-Vorsitzender* (Munich: Kommissionsverlag UNI-Druck, 1991), 71–80; Ulrich Schlie, *Kein Friede mit Deutschland. Die geheimen Gespräche im Zweiten Weltkrieg 1939–1941* (Munich, Berlin: Langen Müller, 1994), 139ff.

[4] On the French Christian democratic resistance and the formation of the MRP see Maurice Vaussard, *Histoire de la démocratie chrétienne*, vol. I: *France – Belgique – Italie* (Paris: Éditions du Seuil, 1956), 102–8; Pezet, *Chrétiens*, 128.

[5] Anthony Glees, 'Das deutsche politische Exil in London 1939–1945', in Gerhard Hirschfeld (ed.), *Exil in Großbritannien. Zur Emigration aus dem nationalsozialistischen Deutschland* (Stuttgart: Klett-Cotta, 1983), 62.

Among the small group of Italian refugees, Sturzo went to London, not Paris, in 1924. In their biography of the PPI founder, Francesco Piva and Francesco Malgeri have explained this choice with his desire, as a Catholic priest, to escape Vatican control as much as possible in predominantly Protestant Britain.[6] Aside from his leading role in the formation of SIPDIC, and his continued involvement in it, Sturzo published extensively in European newspapers and journals. Together with British anti-fascist sympathisers like Henry Wickham Steed, who assisted him in establishing contacts with British editors and journalists,[7] he also initiated the formation of some inter-confessional, cross-party single issue pressure groups such as the British Committee for Civil and Religious Peace in Spain, which was linked to the French organisation of the same name headed by Maritain. Supported by the Anglican Archbishop of Canterbury, among others, this committee advocated 'peace by conciliation' in the Spanish Civil War in an attempt to counteract the strongly pro-Franco mood among Catholics and conservatives in Britain.[8] Although he only visited Spain once, Sturzo was very sensitive to the similarities between the Catholic experience in Italy and Spain, and the strength of Catholic clericalism and authoritarian temptations there. In 1934, in a letter to Alfredo Mendizábal, a professor at the University of Oviedo, who later went into exile in the United States, Sturzo demanded that Spanish Catholics should support the Republic wholeheartedly.[9] Because of the atrocities against Catholic priests at the start of the war and Vatican support for Franco, Sturzo could not bring himself to come out in favour of the republican government. Yet he was deeply distressed by the failure of the Vatican at least to castigate military brutality such as the first aerial saturation bombing of the small Basque town of Guernica by German fighter planes on 26 April 1937, which Pablo Picasso encapsulated in his famous painting for the world exhibition in Paris in the same year.[10] In his publications, for example in *L'Aube*, Sturzo also strongly defended the Basque Catholic desire for autonomy

---

[6] Francesco Piva and Francesco Malgeri, *Vita di Luigi Sturzo* (Rome: Cinque lune, 1972), 295.
[7] De Rosa, *Luigi Sturzo*, 267.
[8] See also the recollections by Barbara Barclay Carter, *Italy Speaks, with a Preface by Luigi Sturzo* (London: Victor Gollancz, 1947), 43.
[9] Sturzo to Mendizábal, 13 March 1934, quoted in Piva and Malgeri, *Vita*, 360. On Sturzo and Spain see also Francesco Malgeri, 'Sturzo e la Spagna negli anni Trenta', in *Universalità*, 403–23.
[10] Specifically on Sturzo and the Spanish Civil War see Anne Morelli, 'Don Sturzo face à la guerre d'Espagne et spécialement au problème de la Catalogne et du Pays Basque', *Sociologia* 24 (1990), 15–37.

within Spain, which he compared with the Irish experience, and their resulting support for the Republic.[11]

Sturzo was quite isolated from mainstream British politics during the 1930s, however. While Brüning had access to British government circles in this period, they did not accept the much more left-wing Sturzo, who was also staunchly opposed to the policy of Appeasement, as an interlocutor.[12] Sturzo's limited political contacts were mostly with Labour Party members and sympathisers in the People and Freedom Group and a few others like Sidney Webb, the Labour MP and co-founder of the Fabian Society.[13] After Italy's entry into the war, Sturzo left Britain for the United States in September 1940 to avoid his possible internment as an 'enemy alien', which most German and Austrian political refugees had suffered in the previous spring.[14] He spent much time in a hospital in Jacksonville in Florida, where Brüning visited him in May 1941 and found him isolated and lonely,[15] and largely kept up his extensive personal network through writing letters and publishing in Catholic journals, before moving to New York in April 1944. In the United States, his Italian contacts extended to politicians of a different political persuasion like Sforza and Gaetano Salvemini,[16] and artists such as the conductor Arturo Toscanini.[17] Although Sturzo kept in touch with other refugees from the PPI, they mostly settled in Paris and Brussels like Ferrari, who edited the journal *Res Publica* from 1931 until his death in 1933.[18]

The German Catholic refugees were also 'scattered and isolated individuals who had no organization behind them'.[19] Günter Buchstab has calculated that Centre Party politicians only made up 5 per cent of those

[11] Luigi Sturzo, 'La causa del popolo basco', *L'Aube*, 15 May 1937, and printed in this Italian version in *Miscellanea Londinese. Volume quarto*, 43–6.
[12] Cf. Joan Keating, *Roman Catholics, Christian Democracy and the British Labour Movement 1910–1960*, PhD (Manchester: University of Manchester, 1992), 92.
[13] De Rosa, *Luigi Sturzo*, 266.
[14] Francesco Malgeri, *Luigi Sturzo* (Milan: Edizioni Paoline, 1993), 239. On the British internment policy see Peter and Leni Gillman, *Collar the lot! How Britain Interned and Expelled Its Wartime Refugees* (London: Quartet Books, 1980); Michael Seyfert, ' "His Majesty's Most Loyal Internees": Die Internierung und Deportation deutscher und österreichischer Flüchtlinge als "enemy aliens". Historische, kulturelle und literarische Aspekte', in Hirschfeld (ed.), *Exil in Großbritannien*, 155–82.
[15] Heinrich Brüning, *Briefe und Gespräche 1934–1945*, ed. Claire Nix (Stuttgart: DVA, 1974), 358.
[16] Ariane Landuyt, 'Ideas of Italian Exiles on the Postwar Order in Europe', in Walter Lipgens (ed.), *Documents on the History of European Integration*, vol. II: *Plans for European Union in Great Britain and in Exile 1939–1945* (Berlin, New York: Walter de Gruyter, 1986), 492.
[17] Malgeri, *Chiesa*, 187–8.   [18] Delzell, *Mussolini's Enemies*, 55.
[19] Klaus Voigt, 'Ideas of German Exiles on the Postwar Order in Europe', in Lipgens (ed.), *Plans for European Union*, 561.

Germans in exile who were politically active.[20] Brüning, their most prominent representative, left Germany in 1934. At first, he lived in the Netherlands and Britain, where he had contacts with Ramsay MacDonald and Winston Churchill, amongst others, before settling in the United States. He became professor of public law and administration at Harvard University in 1937. As in one of his letters to the Duchess of Atholl – one of the few British Conservative MPs opposed to the Appeasement policy –[21] Brüning supported work by British (and American) activists to alert the general public to the need for 'moderate democracy, freedom of conscience and equality before the law' in Germany. He refused to be drawn into activities, however, which he thought could be interpreted as directed against Germany, not just the National Socialists – a fine distinction that was increasingly difficult to sustain. As Joachim Radkau has suggested in his study of the German political emigration to the United States, Brüning, as the last chancellor with some parliamentary legitimacy, might have been expected to lead the Centre Party politicians in exile, if not the German democratic exiles as a whole.[22] Yet, resulting from his belief that the failure of the Weimar Republic, and of his government in 1932, was mainly due to the Versailles Treaty and the refusal by the Western Allies to concede major revisions to it, Brüning was too embittered. He showed 'an aversion to refugee politics'[23] and never played a prominent public role in the German exile.

Moreover, Brüning had difficult relations with some other Catholic refugees in the United States like Muckermann, who had directed the Catholic press network from Münster and came from the Netherlands,[24] but especially Hubertus Friedrich Prinz zu Löwenstein. During the Weimar Republic, Löwenstein was one of the few prominent Centre Party politicians in the republican Reichsbanner organisation. He temporarily had sympathies for a philo-fascist conception of the Empire led by a strong *Führer*, or leader, however, which Brüning did not share. Löwenstein attained a certain prominence as secretary-general of the American Guild for German Cultural Freedom from 1936. He continued to show a romantic admiration of Germany even after German troops overran Poland, and despite the German war crimes. This eventually led to the resignation from the organisation of Thomas Mann, the writer and Nobel Prize laureate.[25]

---

[20] Günter Buchstab (ed.), *Christliche Demokraten gegen Hitler. Aus Verfolgung und Widerstand zur Union* (Freiburg: Herder, 2004), 77.
[21] Brüning to Duchess of Atholl, 23 September 1936, printed in Brüning, *Briefe*, 129.
[22] Joachim Radkau, *Die deutsche Emigration in den USA. Ihr Einfluß auf die amerikanische Europapolitik 1933–1945* (Düsseldorf: Bertelsmann, 1971), 185.
[23] Ibid., 184.   [24] Spael, *Das katholische Deutschland*, 283.   [25] Ibid., 185–90.

Other Centre Party refugees included Carl Spiecker, who first went to France and, from there, to Britain. A journalist by training, Spiecker – like Joos – was a member of the Reichsbanner leadership and exposed himself as special Empire representative for the fight against national socialism in the Interior Ministry from 1930 to 1931, under the direction of Wirth. In Paris, he edited the *Freiheitsbriefe*, which were smuggled into Germany. In London, he worked for the BBC radio programme *Hier spricht Deutschland* from 1940 to 1941, which was mainly directed at middle-class conservative Germans, before he fell seriously ill and left for Canada in 1941.[26] Spiecker played a leading role in the re-founded Rhenish Centre Party after the war. Other Catholic politicians moved to Austria, then Switzerland, such as Wirth, for example.

The Austrian Christian social group was even smaller. Schuschnigg, who refused to go into exile, was arrested after the annexation of Austria. In his highly tendentious study of the Austrian exile, which prefers the attachment of leading representatives of the authoritarian *Ständestaat* to Austrian national identity and independence over support for democratic governance in a united *grossdeutsch* Germany, which initially remained the position of most Austrian socialists abroad after 1933–4, Franz Goldner has argued that Schuschnigg's decision robbed the Catholic refugees of their only internationally prominent figurehead.[27] The Association of Austrian Christian Socialists in Britain, founded in the autumn of 1941 with only fifteen members, was the smallest Austrian political organisation there.[28] More Catholics, including intellectuals and priests, went to North America, such as the former ministers Hans Rott from the left wing of the old Christian Social Party and Guido Zernatto, who fled to Canada and the United States respectively.[29] They were not sufficiently well known, however, and were marginalised by the hyperactive conservative legitimists around Otto and Robert von Habsburg. They aimed at the restoration of the Monarchy after the war, which Schuschnigg also supported, and attempted after 1938 to gain British and US support for the creation and official recognition of an Austrian government in exile. Although the British and Americans contemplated for some time Danubian concepts

---

[26] For the marginal influence of German political refugees in Britain in the 1930s see also Lothar Kettenacker, 'Der Einfluß der deutschen Emigranten auf die britische Kriegszielpolitik', in Hirschfeld (ed.), *Exil in Großbritannien*, 80–105.

[27] Franz Goldner, *Die österreichische Emigration 1938–1945* (Vienna, Munich: Herold, 1972), 225.

[28] Helene Maimann, *Politik im Wartesaal. Österreichische Exilpolitik in Großbritannien 1938–1945* (Vienna, Cologne, Graz: Böhlau, 1975), 101.

[29] Goldner, *Die österreichische Emigration*, 20 and 65.

for postwar reconstruction in central Europe, they were opposed to the restoration of the Habsburg Monarchy, and refused to support these initiatives.[30]

The political refugees from Italy, Germany and Austria experienced a kind of exile within their exile. One of their main problems was whether and on what basis to develop cooperation with the non-Catholic democratic political refugees, and especially with the socialists. When the much more numerous Italian socialists and republicans in exile founded the Anti-Fascist Concentration in 1927, they excluded the Popolari because of the Vatican's support for Mussolini, which reinvigorated older culture wars cleavages.[31] In Britain, the Free Italy association was also dominated by socialists and had some links with the Labour Party.[32] It was only after a brief and (for the socialists) disillusioning period of Popular Front collaboration after 1935 that Sturzo developed a close personal rapport with Sforza and other liberal as well as socialist refugees. He refused to join the Mazzini Society of Italians in exile founded in 1939 and named after the leading liberal thinker and activist of the *risorgimento*, though, which he regarded with some justification as an anticlerical organisation.[33] The German social democrats, who alone voted against Hitler's so-called Enabling Law in March 1933, were also sceptical about cooperation with the few Catholic refugees. The tensions between Austrian Christian socials and socialists were much greater, however. Many Catholic refugees clung to the model of the *Ständestaat*, which had after all suppressed parliamentary democracy and the Socialist Party in 1933–4, for much longer than most Catholics in the Austrian resistance. This precluded closer contacts with the socialists. Moreover, while the Danubian Club in London facilitated transnational contacts of political refugees from central Europe, it was also dominated by socialists.[34]

Catholic refugees from countries occupied by Germany in 1939–40 did not have the same problems, although – as the Belgian example demonstrates – their relationship with socialists and liberals could be tense, too. When German troops overran Belgium in May 1940, the government fled to France. King Leopold III stayed in Belgium, however, signed an armistice and declared the war over, aiming at the restoration of national

---

[30] Maimann, *Politik im Wartesaal*, 631.
[31] Guiseppe Ignesti, 'Momenti del popolarismo in esilio', in Pietro Scoppola and Francesco Traniello (eds.), *I cattolici tra fascismo e democrazia* (Bologna: il Mulino, 1975), 101.
[32] Landuyt, 'Ideas of Italian Exiles', 494.   [33] De Rosa, *Luigi Sturzo*, 409; Malgeri, *Chiesa*, 189.
[34] Feliks Gross, 'Views of East European Transnational Groups on the Postwar Order in Europe', in Lipgens (ed.), *Plans for European Union*, 755.

sovereignty within a new regime based on corporatist principles.[35] At first, only four ministers fled to Britain to establish a government in exile. Many leading politicians, especially from the Catholic Party, remained loyal to the King, initially stayed in Belgium or Vichy France and only went to Britain or the US later during the war. Thus, the Catholic politicians Antoine Delfosse and August-Edmond de Schryver, 'the most royalist minister' according to Godfried Kwanten,[36] and later NEI president 1949–59, only arrived in London in the summer of 1942. After acrimonious debate, de Schryver was first sent to New York as a government representative in December 1942 before he was co-opted into the government in May 1943, as interior minister.[37] Other leading Catholic politicians in exile included the former Catholic prime ministers Frans Van Cauwelaert, Paul Van Zeeland and Georges Theunis in the United States.

During World War II, the Belgian refugee community in London numbered between 15,000 and 20,000. At 30,000, only the Dutch refugee community was larger, although, as G. M. V. Mans has rightly emphasised, 'only a very small minority were interested in politics'.[38] Whereas the Belgian Catholics in Britain did not organise themselves separately, Veraart founded a Dutch group within the International Christian Democratic Union (ICDU) in April 1942 which comprised some 56 RKSP members and sympathisers and met quite regularly.[39] French Christian democrats in London also had separate political activities. From the summer of 1941 they published the monthly journal *Volontaire pour la Cité Chrétienne*. It was initially edited by the first postwar leader of the Mouvement Républicain Populaire (MRP), the Popular Republicans, Maurice Schumann, at that time the spokesperson of Charles De Gaulle, the leader of the Free French, and then by François-Louis Clason after the

---

[35] See Conway, 'Belgium', 204. On the role of King Leopold III see also Jan Velaers and Herman Van Goethem, *Leopold III. De koning, het land, de oorlog* (Tielt: Lannoo, 1994).

[36] Godfried Kwanten, *August-Edmond De Schryver 1898–1991. Politieke biografie van een gentleman-staatsman* (Leuven: Leuven University Press, 2001), 259.

[37] Theo Luykx, 'De rol van August De Schryver in het politieke leven tot en met de Tweede Wereldoorlog', in *Veertig jaar Belgische politiek. Liber amicorum aangeboden aan Minister van Staat A. E. De Schryver ter gelegenheid van zijn 70ste verjaardag* (Antwerp, Utrecht: Standaard, 1968), 199–203. See also de Schryver's autobiographical account in August de Schryver, *Oorlogsdagboeken 1940–1942* (Tielt: Lannoo, 1998).

[38] G. M. V. Mans, 'Ideas of Netherlands Exiles on the Postwar International Order', in Lipgens (ed.), *Plans for European Union*, 452.

[39] Veraart to Carter, 1 March 1944, NA, Collectie J. A. Veraart, 216. Louis de Jong, *Het Koninkrijk der Nederlanden in de Tweede Wereldoorlog*, vol. IX/2: *Londen* (The Hague: Martinus Nijhoff, 1979), 1445. See also 'International Christian Democratic Union', *People & Freedom* 48 (1943), 5.

government's (and Schumann's) move to Algiers in 1943.[40] In the United
States, French political refugees, together with American citizens of French
descent, founded the inter-party organisation France Forever with some
200,000 members. It published a journal with the same title and had close
links with the École Libre des Hautes Études in New York founded in
November 1941 where Maritain was vice-president.[41]

For Catholic politicians from these and other countries such as Poland
and Czechoslovakia occupied during 1939–40, their primary national focus
during the war was strengthened by their work for their governments in
exile and planning for postwar reconstruction, especially from 1943–4.[42]
Their cooperation often took place at the inter-governmental level, such as
in the context of the bilateral talks leading up to the Polish-Czechoslovak
treaty of confederation of January 1942[43] and of the negotiations between
the Netherlands and Belgium about the creation of a customs union
including Luxembourg.[44] The establishment of reasonably stable transnational contacts at party level was also complicated by the fluctuation in the
personnel of the governments in exile as in the case of de Schryver and
Schumann. Both participated in ICDU meetings, but their presence in
London overlapped for only six months in two periods during 1942 and
1943. Moreover, the social life of political refugees was also shaped by the
predominantly national cultural setting in which they lived in London and
New York, like so many writers, journalists, businessmen and others. As
Luc Schepens has shown, for example, the social life of Belgian refugees in
London was largely structured by their national clubs and some 105
national professional associations.[45] Like other national groups, French
refugees mainly met in French cafés and restaurants, like Le Coq d'or and

[40] Pierre Guillen, 'Plans by Exiles from France', in Lipgens (ed.), *Plans for European Union*, 280. On
the relocation of the Free French government to Algiers see also, by way of introduction, Henri
Michel, *Histoire de la France libre*, 3rd edn (Paris: Presses Universitaire de France, 1972), 92–108.
[41] Guillen, 'Plans by Exiles', 281.
[42] On the governments in exile see also, from an all-European perspective, Martin Conway, 'Legacies
of Exile: The Exile Governments in London during World War II and the Politics of Postwar
Europe', in Martin Conway and José Gotovitch (eds.), *Europe in Exile. European Refugee
Communities in Britain 1939–1945* (Oxford, New York: Berghahn Books, 2001), 255–74.
[43] 'Vertrag über eine polnisch-tschechoslowakische Konföderation', in Walter Lipgens (ed.), *Europa-
Föderationspläne der Widerstandsbewegungen 1940–1945* (Munich: Oldenbourg, 1968). 451–533; see
also Gross, 'Views of East European Transnational Groups'; Detlef Brandes, 'Confederation Plans
in Eastern Europe during World War II', in Michel Dumoulin (ed.), *Wartime Plans for Postwar
Europe 1940–1947* (Brussels: Bruylant, 1995), 83–94.
[44] Pierre-Henri Laurent, 'Reality not Rhetoric: Belgian-Dutch Diplomacy in Wartime London,
1940–44', in Stirk and Stirk (eds.), *Making the New Europe*, 133–41.
[45] Luc Schepens, *De Belgen in Groot-Brittannië 1940–1944. Feiten en Getuigenissen* (Nijmegen:
Uitgeverij B. Gottmer, 1980), 71–112.

L'Escargot in London.[46] When the refugees left their national circles, they often first sought closer contacts with British and American citizens and groups, for example in the Anglo-Belgian Union in London, rather than with refugees from other European countries – and when they did, it was sometimes by chance, as in the case of Schumann, who lived in the same hotel as Joseph Bech, the Christian democratic foreign minister from Luxembourg.

At the level of political parties, however, the Catholic politicians in exile had no natural partners in either Britain or the United States due to these countries' secular, non-confessional party traditions and the resulting absence of comparable Catholic or 'popular' parties. Unlike on the European continent – with the notable exceptions of Germany, the Netherlands and Switzerland – Catholicism formed minority cultures in Britain and the United States. In both countries, Protestantism and anti-Catholicism were important constitutive elements of the predominant national identity. This tradition reached back to the reformation and the wars against the Catholic powers Spain, France and the Stuarts in the case of England and to the first waves of Anglo-Saxon and other Protestant settlers from German states and Scandinavia in the case of the United States, where these groups were still socio-economically and politically hegemonic. In these circumstances, the Catholic minorities were politically entrenched for confessional, social and cultural reasons, not least because they were at least partially identified in both countries with recent waves of immigration.

In Britain, Catholics made up only about 5 per cent of the population during the 1920s.[47] In absolute numbers, according to Tom Buchanan,[48] there were 1.9 million Catholics in England and Wales in 1918, rising to 2.4 million in 1945. A small minority of them were quite affluent upper-class 'old Catholics' who would have voted for the Tories in the nineteenth century. A growing number were recent, mostly middle-class, converts, as 750,000 British citizens joined the Catholic Church between 1900 and 1960. By far the largest group was made up of Irish immigrants, however, who mostly still worked in British industry as unskilled labourers. The majority of those who had the vote supported the Liberals in the nineteenth century, as they were for Home Rule for Ireland and began around the turn of the century to develop social-liberal policies. By the 1920s,

---

[46] Michèle Cointet, *La France à Londres: renaissance d'un état (1940–1943)* (Brussels: Éditions Complexes, 1980), 73.
[47] Keating, 'The British Experience', 169.   [48] Buchanan, 'Great Britain', 249.

they – together with the clear majority of the working class – mostly voted for the Labour Party – a choice that the Church hierarchy publicly condoned in 1924–5, referring to its lack of anticlericalism and its reform tradition, declaring it not to be socialist in the continental sense.[49] At the same time, a hugely disproportionate number of Catholics supported the relatively small British Union of Fascists. Although its leader Oswald Mosley was Protestant, it has been estimated that 50 per cent of the members were Catholic, that is, ten times the percentage of Catholics in the population at large. Moreover, leading Catholic intellectuals also espoused philo-fascist views. Although he regarded fascism as not suitable for England, the writer T. S. Eliot, for example, advocated it for Italy.[50]

In the United States, between 20 and 30 per cent of the population was Catholic in the 1930s.[51] Ethnic background and social status had an important influence on their political views. Although some German immigrants were Catholic, many more had come from Ireland, especially following the potato famine of 1846–50. Later waves of immigration from the 1880s included large numbers of Catholic Italians and Poles. Although in the spheres of work and politics, Protestants and Catholics were fairly integrated in cities like Chicago by 1918, their ethnicity and religion continued to set Catholic immigrant groups apart from Protestant Americans, who still tended to regard the Catholic church as a 'Church of foreigners'.[52] Many Protestant Americans had existential fears that Catholic European (as well as Asian) immigration would undermine the existing social fabric and American national identity, as well as their dominant societal status and influence. In the 1920s, and strengthened by the economic crisis after 1929, Anglo-Saxonism and anti-Catholicism were widespread once more. In their most extreme form they were espoused by the racist Ku Klux Klan. When the Democratic Party candidate Al Smith, who was Catholic, was crushed by Herbert Hoover in the presidential elections of 1928, it only strengthened the Catholic fortress mentality, as Charles A. Morris has pointed out.[53] The American Catholic Church, which had always looked to Rome and supported Pius IX's agenda of

---

[49] Ibid., 253 and 263–4. [50] Keating, *Roman Catholics*, 81–3.
[51] In the United States, religious questions cannot be asked of individuals in a census, so that no reliable figures are available. The existing estimates are mostly based on regional Church data. For more detail, see Roger Finke and Rodney Stark, *The Churching of America, 1776–1990: The Winners and Losers in our Religious Economy* (New Brunswick, N.J.: Rutgers University Press, 1992).
[52] Jay P. Dolan, *In Search of an American Catholicism. A History of Religion and Culture in Tension* (Oxford: Oxford University Press, 2002), 128.
[53] Charles R. Morris, *American Catholic. The Saints and Sinners Who Built America's Most Powerful Church* (New York: Times Books, 1997), 159.

centralisation in the nineteenth century, became even more Romanised as a consequence, with repercussions for the way in which American Catholics perceived European politics in the 1930s.

Around the turn of the century, many Catholic immigrants were attracted by progressivism, which opposed the power of industrial trusts and made social promises geared towards a redistribution of wealth. As they were continuing to 'battle for bread rather than for culture' after World War I, as William A. Halsey has put it,[54] Catholics became closely associated with the Democratic Party in American politics. They overwhelmingly supported Franklin D. Roosevelt in the presidential elections of 1932. Once elected, Roosevelt gave a speech at the Convention of the National Conference of Catholic Charities in New York in 1933, which reflected the electoral alliance.[55] Most Catholics were also behind the New Deal economic policy, although this was much more informed by technocratic policy-making ideas than Catholic corporatism.[56] Yet the modest success of Roosevelt's programme in his first term in office also strengthened once more the search for a 'third way', and support for a third political party. In December 1934, Father Charles Coughlin, a Catholic priest with his own radio channel, founded the National Union for Social Justice with a political programme broadly based on the papal encyclicals *Rerum novarum* and *Quadragesimo anno*. This programme was directed against 'vested interests' of 'property owners and international bankers' who allegedly exercised invisible control over the capitalist economy at the expense of (not least, Catholic immigrant) workers.[57] Coughlin advocated banking and monetary reform, a bonus for war veterans and a federal public works programme.[58] As Alan Brinkley has pointed out, his movement, like fascism in Europe, was 'the product of similar social and economic crises and drew from similar political traditions'.[59] Coughlin's

---

[54] William M. Halsey, *The Survival of American Innocence: Catholicism in an Era of Disillusionment, 1920–1940* (Notre Dame, Ind.: University of Notre Dame Press, 1980), 94.

[55] Dorothy M. Brown and Elizabeth McKeown, *The Poor Belong to Us. Catholic Charities and American Welfare* (Cambridge, Mass: Harvard University Press, 1997), 151.

[56] Morris, *American Catholic*, 152. In the 1930s, Catholic social reformers like John Ryan from the Catholic University in Washington, who was also director of the National Catholic Welfare Conference, played an important role in transferring Catholic social teaching and corporatist ideas from Europe to America. For the New Deal see, for example, the relevant chapters in William H. Chafe (ed.), *The Achievement of American Liberalism: The New Deal and Its Legacies* (New York: Columbia University Press, 2003).

[57] Cf. Sheldon Marcus, *Father Coughlin. The Tumultuous Life of the Priest of the Little Flower* (Boston, Toronto: Little, Brown and Company, 1973), 71–6.

[58] Morris, *American Catholic*, 148.

[59] Alan Brinkley, *Voices of Protest. Huey Long, Father Coughlin, and the Great Depression* (New York: Alfred Knopf, 1982), 279.

ideology favoured the idea of the traditional rooted community, was strongly anti-modernist, and influenced by British right-wing thinkers like Hilaire Belloc and Mosley. In 1935, Coughlin entered into an alliance with Senator Huey Long, who proposed 'Share-the-wealth' policies. Roosevelt regarded him as a credible and dangerous challenger for the presidency in 1936. Long was assassinated in September 1935, however, and his replacement as 'Union Party' candidate, Congressman William Lemke from North Dakota, gained fewer than one million votes in 1936, with many coming from Catholics, however.[60]

Catholic political refugees from continental Europe made the profoundly disturbing experience during the 1930s that they were often not only quite isolated among their own compatriots of a different political persuasion, as in the case of Sturzo, for example, but also from these Catholic host communities in Britain and the United States. Among them, support for Mussolini and Franco was widespread, and they were also the most ardent supporters of the policies of Appeasement and isolationism. When he arrived in Britain in 1924, Sturzo was struck by the extent to which the perception of fascist Italy – not only among British Catholics – appeared to be formed by the *Daily Mail* and the Rothermere press.[61] From this perspective, Mussolini was the first Italian politician to have established an 'orderly' society in which trains ran on time. He was also staunchly anti-communist, a preference that largely united working-class Catholic socialists, who tended to be on the Right of the party, and middle- and upper-class Protestant conservatives.

Sympathy for Mussolini (as well as for Franco in the 1930s) among Catholics in Britain was strengthened by three additional factors, however. First, due to the minority status of Catholicism in Britain, the Catholic hierarchy, as in the United States, tended to look to Rome for leadership and was thus particularly impressed by the initially strong Vatican support for Mussolini and, later, for Franco. Secondly, Mussolini and Franco seemed to guarantee the rights of the Church against a staunchly anticlerical political Left in Italy and Spain. Thirdly, fascism and authoritarian dictatorships as in Portugal, Austria and Franco's Spain advocated and implemented concepts of a new social order that seemed to be broadly compatible with Catholic social teaching, despite the muted criticism of

[60] Ronald H. Carpenter, *Father Charles E. Coughlin. Surrogate Spokesman for the Disaffected* (Westport, Conn.: Greenwood Press, 1998), 62–5.
[61] David Forgacs, 'Sturzo e la cultura politica inglese', in Gabriele De Rosa (ed.), *Luigi Sturzo e la democrazia europea* (Rome: Editori Laterza, 1990), 343.

fascist 'state corporatism' in *Quadragesimo anno*.[62] These factors also influenced the preferences of many American Catholics. On top of such general considerations, however, their ethnicity still played a role and was behind the continued allegiance in many cases to their country of origin. Support for Mussolini was particularly marked among the Italian immigrants, for example.

These cleavages were highlighted by the heated domestic debates in Britain and the United States about the Spanish Civil War. As James Flint has pointed out, the Catholic press in Britain was initially sceptical about Franco's insurrection as it might lead to a personal dictatorship or, alternatively, a Soviet-type political system resulting from the radicalisation of the pro-republican side.[63] The atrocities by pro-republicans at the beginning of the war, in which almost 7,000 Catholic bishops, priests and members of religious orders died, swiftly united most Catholic opinion leaders behind Franco, however. The Church hierarchy deemed Franco on a crusade to save the Catholic Church and strongly desired a Nationalist victory. Cardinal Arthur Hinsley, the Archbishop of Westminster, who later became famous for his resistance during the Battle of Britain, refused to condemn Nationalist atrocities such as the bombing of Guernica.[64] He then congratulated Franco in March 1939 upon winning the war, praising him in a personal letter as 'the great defender of the true Spain, the country of Catholic principles where Catholic social justice and charity will be applied for the common good under a firm and peace-loving government.'[65] The leading Catholic newspaper *The Tablet* concluded as early as 1 August 1936 that 'all those Spaniards who wish to see the Church survive in Spain will have had to side with the insurgents.'[66] Well-known Catholic intellectuals like the writers Belloc and Evelyn Waugh also supported Franco. Belloc even exalted at the end of the war in 1939 that Franco's victory marked not only the 'salvation of Spain', but of Europe, from the terrible danger of communism.[67] Only very few Catholic publications like the Dominican monthly *Blackfriars* were more critical of the Nationalists.

[62] See in greater detail Keating, *Roman Catholics*, chapter 3.
[63] James Flint, ' "Must God go Fascist?" English Catholic Opinion and the Spanish Civil War', *Church History* 56 (1987), 367.
[64] Ibid., 369.
[65] Hinsley to Franco, 28 March 1939, Westminster Diocesan Archives, Hinsley Papers, HI 2/217.
[66] *The Tablet*, 1 August 1936.
[67] Hilaire Belloc, 'The Salvation of Spain', *The Tablet*, 25 February 1939.

The battle-lines in the Spanish Civil War were of course never as clearly drawn as the pro-Franco opinion leaders wanted to make the Catholic faithful believe. Franco used Muslim troops, for example, against Basque regionalists, who were strongly supported by the local Catholic clergy and fought with the Republic to safeguard Basque autonomy. Republican atrocities against the Catholic Church also ceased after the early stages of the war, as the Duchess of Atholl, Ellen Wilkinson, Eleanor Rathborne and Rachel Crowdie testified after their inter-party fact-finding visit to Spain in April 1937. In June 1938, Katharine Atholl, who (although Protestant herself) had close links with the small People and Freedom Group of British middle-class Catholics around Sturzo, published *Searchlight on Spain*.[68] This book provided an alternative perspective on the war, effectively siding with the Republic, and sold 100,000 copies in the first week alone.[69] As her female colleagues from other political parties, Atholl – aside from her growing preoccupation with the threat posed by Hitler – was mainly concerned about the humanitarian plight of the civil population in Spain, especially children. She worked as chairman of the All-Party Committee for Spanish Relief and even became involved in the organisation International Brigade Dependents and Wounded Aid Committee.[70] As S. J. Hetherington has pointed out in her biography of Atholl, however, 'a great many Conservatives regarded [her participation in this committee] as perfidy'.[71] Even anti-Appeasement MPs like Churchill, Harold Macmillan and Robert Boothby were against confronting Hitler and Mussolini by siding with the Spanish Republic, and only one conservative MP, Jack Hills, supported Atholl.[72]

In the absence of opinion polls, it is not entirely clear how the allegiances of British working-class Catholics were divided in the face of overwhelming support for Franco from Catholic opinion leaders, especially the Church hierarchy. Although the precise degree of support for Franco among them is disputed, it is clear that the religious cleavage largely overshadowed the class cleavage. As Tom Buchanan has emphasised, 'the most striking feature of the Catholic response to the Civil War was the degree to which it united the socially disparate Catholic community in

---

[68] Katharine Atholl, *Searchlight on Spain* (London: Allen Lane, 1938).

[69] According to Katharine Atholl, *Working Partnership. Being the Lives of John George, 8th Duke of Atholl and of His Wife Katharine Marjory Ramsay* (London: Arthur Barker, 1958), 213.

[70] Angela Jackson, *British Women and the Spanish Civil War* (London, New York, Routledge, 2002), 247.

[71] S. J. Hetherington, *Katharine Atholl 1874–1960. Against the Tide* (Aberdeen: Aberdeen University Press, 1989), 187.

[72] Atholl, *Working Partnership*, 219.

Britain – in defence, at least, of the Spanish Church, if not necessarily in support of Franco's regime.'[73] The overwhelming support among British Catholics for the Nationalists, and their strong opposition to changing the British and French policy of non-intervention, is also indirectly reflected in Labour Party policy on the Civil War. Only very few leading socialists like Clement Attlee were for direct British support for the Republicans. Many others had misgivings about what they saw – with some justification – as the strong tradition of anticlerical violence among the Spanish Left, or they wanted to gain time for a likely war with Germany. As Buchanan has demonstrated in his study of the British Labour movement and the Spanish Civil War, however, the lack of stronger support for the Republic also reflected the tactical consideration that such a policy would alienate Catholic working-class voters, who were an important political constituency.[74]

Catholic opinion also helps to explain the neutral policy of the Roosevelt administration on the Spanish Civil War. In the United States, a Gallup poll found in 1938 that 83 per cent of Protestants were for the Republicans, but 58 per cent of Catholics for the Nationalists.[75] Although the religious divide on this issue was very marked, the poll also showed strong minority support among Catholics for the Republic, but it was not organised or very articulate. As in Britain, Catholic opinion leaders were almost unanimously behind Franco. This is true of the Catholic hierarchy and of almost all Catholic publications. Even Dorothy Day, the charismatic liberal Catholic social reformer, did not come out in favour of the Republic. While her newspaper, the *Catholic Worker*, did not endorse the Nationalists, it was strongly pacifist and favoured the government policy of non-intervention.[76] In the high-quality *Commonweal*, with its circulation of 15,000, George N. Shuster, its managing editor with close contacts with Brüning, Sturzo and other Catholic refugees, published his 'Reflections on Spain' in April 1937, which were critical of Franco. Like Sturzo, Shuster pleaded for Catholic neutrality in the conflict. As Thomas E. Blantz has shown in his biography of Shuster, the journal subscriptions immediately plummeted by 25 per cent, and the managing director was sharply attacked for his stance, especially by the Catholic establishment in

[73] Tom Buchanan, *Britain and the Spanish Civil War* (Cambridge: Cambridge University Press, 1997), 117.
[74] Tom Buchanan, *The Spanish Civil War and the British Labour Movement* (Cambridge: Cambridge University Press, 1991), 222–6.
[75] Morris, *American Catholic*, 234.   [76] Ibid., 141–5.

New York.[77] Michael Williams, the journal editor, upheld the pro-Nationalist line and actually participated in a pro-Franco rally in the Madison Square. Shuster had to resign from his post. In his study of the *Commonweal*, Rodger Van Allen cites Shuster as recollecting later, 'It now dawned on me that for Catholic New York the world around the United States was either Communist or Fascist and that therefore they had opted for fascism.'[78]

According to Shuster, American Catholics in the 1930s still suffered from a 'minority-itis' which made them 'susceptible to the irrational appeals of anti-Semites, pro-Nazis and Fascists'.[79] Among them were the appeals by Coughlin, whose movement became more and more radicalised during 1936–8. Coughlin began to speak of the 'Jewish question', using translated excerpts from speeches by Joseph Goebbels, Hitler's propaganda minister,[80] and he established contacts with American fascists. In 1938, he founded the so-called Christian Front, which identified Roosevelt, Jews and communists as 'enemies' of America.[81] Coughlin actually defended the anti-Jewish pogrom in Germany of 9 November 1938 as a 'necessary defence mechanism against [the spread of] communism'.[82] This was too much even for the Vatican, which finally distanced itself from him publicly. Although Coughlin's popularity declined somewhat with the increasing radicalisation of his movement, he still had up to 15 million mostly Catholic listeners for his radio broadcasts in 1938–9.[83] Coughlin's movement was very isolationist. On the question of American policy towards the Spanish Civil War, he played a leading role in organising the highly effective lobbying group Keep the Spanish Embargo Committee. As Leo V. Kanawada has demonstrated in his study of religious and ethnic influences on Roosevelt's foreign policy, Coughlin's stance on Spain, which was strongly supported by the Catholic Church and press, played an important role in keeping the president, who needed Catholic electoral backing, from supporting the Republic, which he, as well as his wife Eleanor, were privately inclined to do.[84]

[77] Thomas E. Blantz, *George N. Shuster: On the Side of Truth* (Notre Dame, Ind.: University of Notre Dame Press, 1993), 84–7; Morris, *American Catholic*, 234.
[78] Rodger Van Allen, *The Commonweal and American Catholicism. The Magazine, the Movement, the Meaning* (Philadelphia: Fortress Press, 1974), 64. See also George N. Shuster, *The Ground I Walked on. Reflections of a College President* (Notre Dame, Ind.: Notre Dame University Press, 1961), 169.
[79] Cited in Halsey, *The Survival*, 98.   [80] Carpenter, *Father Charles E. Coughlin*, 122.
[81] Cf. Brinkley, *Voices of Protest*, 216–80; Marcus, *Father Coughlin*, 82, 126 and 155.   [82] Ibid., 160.
[83] Carpenter, *Father Charles E. Coughlin*, 77. After the United States' entry into World War II, Coughlin's radio broadcasts were finally suppressed. Ibid., 122.
[84] Leo V. Kanawada, *Franklin D. Roosevelt's Diplomacy and American Catholics, Italians and Jews* (Epping: Bowker, 1982), 49–70. See also Morris, *American Catholic*, 233.

On the whole, Catholics in Britain and the United States were the most ardent supporters of the foreign policies of Appeasement and isolationism. It is indicative of the strength of pro-Appeasement feeling among Catholics in Britain that they often caused the greatest trouble for opponents of Appeasement at the grassroots level. Thus, when Katharine Atholl came out in support of the Spanish Republic, the staunchest opposition to her within her Scottish constituency party came – as her husband observed in a private letter – from 'very hot RC[s] [Roman Catholics]'.[85] They even denounced her as the 'Red Duchess' for her viewpoint (also put in a letter to Prime Minister Stanley Baldwin in May 1936) that Hitler – and not Stalin – 'is the only serious danger to peace in Europe',[86] especially after she dared to participate together with left-wing politicians in a public rally for the Spanish Republic in Glasgow. Atholl resigned the Conservative whip in a public exchange of letters with the new prime minister, Joseph Chamberlain, in April 1938 in protest against the continued Appeasement policy. One month later, she was deselected by her constituency party as candidate for the next elections. She then resigned her seat in the House of Commons to provoke a by-election fought on the Appeasement issue, which (despite support from the Liberals) she narrowly lost against the official Conservative candidate in December 1938.[87]

Having already experienced the strong preference for the Appeasement policy among the vast majority of British Catholics at least until the British declaration of war in September 1939, Sturzo arrived in the United States in 1940 to encounter broadly comparable attitudes among the Catholic minority there. According to Francesco Malgeri, his 'greatest disillusionment' was that, in his assessment, 90 per cent of American Catholics were strongly against the United States' entry into the war.[88] In a retrospective analysis after the Japanese attack on Pearl Harbor in December 1941, Sturzo

[85] Duke of Atholl to G. Mickel, 31 May 1937, Blair Castle Archives, Atholl MSS 22/6, cited in Stuart Ball, 'The Politics of Appeasement: The Fall of the Duchess of Atholl and the Kinross and West Perth By-election, December 1938', *The Scottish Historical Review* 64 (1990), 58.
[86] Duchess of Atholl to Baldwin, 19 May 1936, Blair Castle Archives, Atholl MSS 22/4, cited in Ball, 'The Politics of Appeasement', 56. See also her letter to the editor in the *Daily Telegraph*, 25 July 1936 and other newspaper articles, for example the *Morning Post*, 30 July 1936 and *Manchester Guardian*, 13 November 1936.
[87] See in greater detail Ball, 'The Politics of Appeasement' and, by the same author, *The Conservative Party and British Politics 1902–1951* (Harlow: Longman, 1995), 94; Atholl to Spears, 20 January 1939, Churchill Archives Centre (henceforth: CAC), Private Papers of Sir Edward Louis Spears, 1/18. On Atholl and her later links with Catholic democrats of the People and Freedom Group and her brief role as British representative in the NEI in 1947 see the short comments in Hetherington, *Katharine Atholl*, 251.
[88] Malgeri, *Luigi Sturzo*, 249.

wrote that, previously, 'many Catholic papers [in the United States] were anti-British, and hence gave their sympathies to the Vichy Government [in France, which collaborated with Germany] – as well as to Franco and even to Mussolini'. According to Sturzo, American Catholics generally placed 'their own democracy above discussion'. When it came to Europe, however, 'anti-democratic and pseudo-religious feelings and resentments' led them to see 'a Mussolini, a Hitler, and their imitators [as] protectors and defenders of the church'.[89] Moreover, their ethnic origin often strengthened their preference for non-intervention. Thus, the anti-British attitudes, which Sturzo observed, were particularly marked among immigrants of Irish descent, who played an influential role in the Catholic Church hierarchy. Their collective memory was dominated by the experience of British colonial rule over their country of origin, and they strongly resented the division of Ireland after World War I. Their support for non-intervention was also strengthened by the official neutrality of the Republic of Ireland during World War II.

In these adverse circumstances, small groups of articulate, but hardly representative, liberal Catholics in Britain and the United States tried to provide an alternative intellectual and political focus and to create a friendlier environment for Catholic politicians in exile. In Britain, the Catholic democratic and social reform tradition was established and upheld mainly by the Catholic Social Guild, founded in 1909, which had some 4,000 members in 1938.[90] Some Catholics, who mostly supported the Labour Party and the Liberals, founded the People and Freedom Group in November 1936. According to one member, Anthony Moore, the group allowed progressive Catholic democrats for the first time 'to show an English Catholic contribution to political thought, to show too that Catholics did not necessarily support reaction'.[91] In the United States, liberal Catholics organised themselves against Coughlin's Christian Front and founded the Committee of Catholics for Human Rights with the support, among others, of John Ryan and Charles Miltner from the Catholic universities of Washington and Notre Dame.[92] Shuster, who became president of the Catholic Hunter College in New York after his resignation from the *Commonweal*, was also very active in assisting

---

[89] Luigi Sturzo, 'Anglo-American Catholics and Vichy', *People & Freedom* 36 (1942), 3.
[90] Cf. Joan Keating, 'Looking to Europe: Roman Catholicism and Christian Democracy in 1930s Britain', *European History Quarterly* 26 (1996), 64.
[91] 'General Meeting', *People & Freedom* 4 (1939), 4.   [92] Marcus, *Father Couglin*, 158.

Catholic politicians in exile. Later on, partly on the initiative of Sturzo, the British People and Freedom Group expanded across the Atlantic.

The People and Freedom Group was founded in 1936 and consisted exclusively of Catholics, although some non-Catholics were linked to the group as 'friends'. Most members were middle-class converts. Unlike the Catholic trade unionists, who had a tradition of close relations with the German Christian trade unions, many members of the People and Freedom Group had strong links with France, Belgium and Italy. Many women with a high degree of personal and financial independence and a strong commitment to refugee and other social work played a leading role in the group even before the war. According to the group's constitution, its general purpose was 'to promote a sound grasp of political and social problems, and to further the application of Christian principles to national and international life'.[93] Sturzo later said of the group at a meeting of the New York branch in August 1944 that

it is not a political party, but it concerns itself with politics. It is not a Catholic Action Group, but it maintains that politics must be moral or fail in their purpose. It is not a mouthpiece of the Church, but it considers that there can be no sound politics without the application of the Church's social teaching. It is not a study circle, but a circle for practical action; there can, however, be no effective action without a study of the political, social and economic problems of each state and those of an international character.[94]

The group regularly organised speeches and passed resolutions. These were printed in the newssheet *People & Freedom*, which appeared from 1938 and was published monthly during the war. They were also diffused through letters to the editor and reports in Catholic publications, but also in the *Manchester Guardian*, *The Times* and other daily newspapers. The group never had more than 150 members. Its newssheet had a circulation of approximately 900. It was distributed to members, 'friends' and selected institutions including fifty in the United States. It was also available at selected news-stalls.[95] Members of the group regularly complained, however, that their newssheet was not sold and read widely enough. On the other hand, it was read not only in Britain, but also by American Catholics, who were inspired to

[93] 'People & Freedom', *People & Freedom* 1 (1938), 1–2.
[94] 'US People & Freedom. The New York Group', *People & Freedom* 63 (1944), 4.
[95] 'Monthly Report', *People & Freedom* 9 (1940), 4; 'Annual Report', *People & Freedom* 10 (1940).

form a similar group in the United States, and even by De Gasperi in the Vatican library.[96]

The People and Freedom Group's chairman from 1936 to 1944 was Virginia Crawford. As a young woman, Crawford had been implicated in the most notorious divorce case of Victorian England. It resulted from a love affair which she claimed to have had with the MP Charles Dilke. At the time, Dilke was regarded as a possible successor to William Gladstone as Liberal Party leader and prime minister who might have avoided the splitting off of the Unionists around Joseph Chamberlain, who formed an alliance with the Conservatives over the Irish Home Rule issue.[97] Crawford converted to Catholicism in 1889. She developed many contacts with Catholic politicians and social reformers on the European continent, especially in France and Belgium. She published extensively on Christian democracy with the explicit aim of transferring recent ideas and policies from continental Europe to England to overcome what she later described in a report on the Catholic Social Guild as 'the peculiar ignorance, even among educated Catholics, concerning contemporary religious developments on the Continent'.[98] Crawford's articles and pamphlets dealt with very diverse issues ranging from 'Feminism in France' and 'Aspects of Charity in Vienna' to 'Catholic Women in Italy Today' and 'Unemployment and Education: a Lesson from Switzerland'.[99] Most of them concerned continental European Catholic thinkers and social questions in which Crawford also became involved as an activist. She was a co-founder of the Catholic Social Guild in 1909 and a Labour Party borough councillor in Marylebone in London for fourteen years. Crawford also played a leading role in the St Joan's Alliance, the Catholic women's suffrage society founded in 1911 and renamed in 1923, which she headed as chairman from 1925 to 1926.[100] She came in contact with Sturzo early on and was the editor of the anti-fascist journal *Italy Today*,

---

[96] Cf. 'From the Christian Democrats of Italy' [Alcide De Gasperi to Conrad Bonacina], *People & Freedom* 68 (1945), 2; see already Veraart to De Gasperi, 1 September 1944, NA, Collectie J. A. Veraart, 216.

[97] Virginia Crawford publicly claimed to have had a love affair with Charles Dilke, MP. As a result, she was divorced from her husband, another Liberal MP. Dilke's political career was effectively destroyed when he unsuccessfully tried to refute Crawford's claim in a second court case. Cf. Notes on a talk [among relatives of Crawford and Dilke] about Virginia Crawford and the case of Crawford v. Crawford & Dilke (1886) held on Wednesday 8 July 1973, CAC, Dilke – Crawford – Roskill Collection, 13/1.

[98] Virginia M. Crawford, 'The Coming of Age of the Catholic Social Guild', *Studies* (September 1930), 457, CAC, Dilke – Crawford – Roskill Collection, 12/11/2.

[99] Many of her publications are collected in CAC, Dilke – Crawford – Roskill Collection, 12/11/1–3.

[100] For more information on these Catholic organisations and their role within British Catholicism see also Buchanan, 'Great Britain'.

which was published by the group Friends of Italian Freedom from 1929 to 1932.[101]

The People and Freedom Group's honorary secretary with responsibility for day-to-day administration was Barbara Barclay Carter from 1936 up until 1948, when she joined the United Nations (UN) in Geneva.[102] Carter was born in the United States as the daughter of an American father and an Irish mother. She grew up in England and, after her mother's death, developed a great enthusiasm for Gaelic and Sinn Fein, the Irish nationalist movement. Like Crawford, she converted to Catholicism in 1921 and studied medieval history and literature at the Sorbonne in Paris, where she became an expert on Dante Aligheri. Carter met Sturzo in 1924, when he gave a lecture to the St Joan's Alliance. Biographers of Sturzo have on the whole portrayed her as a willing secretary and translator. As Giovanna Farrell-Vinay has recently shown in some detail, however,[103] Carter played an extremely important role not only by creating a stable social network for Sturzo in what he once called 'my little family', but also through establishing contacts with publishers, journalists and 'progressive' Catholic democrats in Britain. On her initiative, Sturzo moved in together with her and Cicely Mary Marshall, her friend. From 1933, they lived in a large semi-detached house in Notting Hill Gate which became a meeting place for Catholic refugees. Carter translated Sturzo's articles and books. She also played a key coordinating role from the beginning in his social and political activities like the Italian Refugees Relief Committee.

Although the People and Freedom Group had no eminent British politicians as members, some of their Protestant 'friends' were quite influential and assisted the Catholic democrats in establishing indirect links with Labour and Conservative opponents of Appeasement such as Churchill. Wickham Steed, for example, was at that time lecturer in central European history at King's College in London and one of the most eminent academic-journalistic experts of continental European politics. He studied in Jena and Berlin, but later became 'a bitter opponent of Germany'.[104] He was foreign correspondent of *The Times* in Berlin (1896), Rome (1897–1902) and Vienna (1902–13). In 1913, he published his book

---

[101] See the copies in CAC, Dilke – Crawford – Roskill Collection, 12/12. On Crawford, see also the obituary by Barbara Barclay Carter, 'Virginia Crawford', *People & Freedom* 108 (1948), 1.

[102] See also the obituary by Conrad Bonacina, 'Obituary – Barbara Barclay Carter', *People & Freedom* (1951), 1–3.

[103] Giovanna Farrell-Vinay, 'Sturzo e l'Inghilterra', in *Universalità*, 181–223.

[104] Peter Schuster, *Henry Wickham Steed und die Habsburgermonarchie* (Vienna, Cologne, Weimar: Böhlau, 1970), 11.

The Hapsburg Monarchy.[105] In it, he essentially portrayed the state as a *Völkerkerker*, or prison of peoples, as Slav nationalists saw it, and wholly dependent on the German Empire. Copies of the book were confiscated by the Austrian authorities, and he was expelled from the country, becoming the foreign editor of *The Times* in London. Wickham Steed possibly knew Sturzo already from his time in Italy or met him shortly after his arrival in England. He became active in the Italian Refugees Relief Committee, the British Committee for Civil and Religious Peace and – as a 'friend' – the People and Freedom Group.

Katharine Atholl was another 'friend'. She was not initially interested in foreign policy. When she had the unabridged German version of Hitler's *Mein Kampf* personally translated for her in 1935, however, she became a vociferous opponent of the Appeasement policy.[106] She later refuted the absurd allegation that she had philo-communist views, when, on the initiative of the Polish government in exile, she published *The Tragedy of Warsaw and Its Documentation*[107] in late 1944. In it, without political restraint, she attacked Britain's war ally, the Soviet Union, for deliberately allowing the Polish national resistance to be annihilated by German troops during the Warsaw Uprising. Atholl also established a link for the People and Freedom Group with Edward Louis Spears, another anti-Appeasement Conservative MP with close relations with Churchill. In 1940 Spears became the new prime minister's personal representative with de Gaulle.

Up to a point, the People and Freedom Group became integrated in the transnational political network of Catholic democrats in the last years before World War II. The group had close links with *L'Aube*. Carter took part in the first conference of Les Amis de L'Aube in Paris in November 1937 and gave a speech at the closing banquet. She regarded this France-centred international group as 'a really vital and inspiring movement which could really claim to stand for Christian Democracy'.[108] She also represented the British group in the following year, when the NEF were founded.[109] Foreign refugees and visitors also regularly gave speeches and participated in discussions at meetings of the People and Freedom group in London.

---

[105] Henry Wickham Steed, *The Hapsburg Monarchy* (London: Constable and Company, 1913).
[106] Atholl, *Working Partnership*, 200.
[107] Katharine Atholl, *The Tragedy of Warsaw and Its Documentation* (London: J. Murray, 1944).
[108] The People & Freedom Group, Monthly Report, 27 November 1937, CAC, Dilke – Crawford – Roskill Collection, 12/4. See also 'People & Freedom', *People & Freedom* 1 (1938), 1–2.
[109] D. W., 'L'Aube and the Nef', *People & Freedom* 3 (1939), 3. On the international policies propagated by *L'Aube*, and its isolation within French Catholicism, see also McMillan, 'France', 50–3; Conway, *Catholic Politics*, 72.

They included, for example, the priest Emanuel Reichenberger from the Christian Social People's Party (of German speakers) in Czechoslovakia,[110] Mendizábal from Oviedo, whom Sturzo had first met in 1934, and Javier Landaburu, a former deputy of the Spanish Cortes who was later the Basque representative in the NEI.[111] The group did not keep a record of those who attended the meetings. It is known, however, that after his arrival in London, de Schryver went to several lectures,[112] and other Catholic refugees may well have done the same. The group's role in facilitating transnational contacts among Catholic refugees from different countries during the war is also underlined by the fact that Crawford, Carter and Sturzo conceived of the idea of a successor organisation to SIPDIC, and that the formation of the ICDU was prepared at a meeting of the People and Freedom Group in the Sesame Club on 21 November 1940.[113]

Although the group could not agree to come out in favour of the Spanish Republic and instead argued for a negotiated settlement, it was generally far ahead of public opinion in Britain, and most certainly of the Catholic community and the national government. It supported an appeal 'for the Basque People' published in *L'Aube*, *Le Temps* and other French newspapers, but at the same time encouraged the Basque government to repeal the death sentence against three captured German Luftwaffe pilots.[114] After the end of the Spanish Civil War, the group also demanded a joint Western effort to restrain Franco, and a wide amnesty for Republicans.[115] In reaction to the anti-Jewish pogrom on 9 November 1938 and inspired by a similar manifesto of the newly founded French NEF in the same month,[116] they passed a strongly worded resolution against anti-Semitism and the persecution of Jews in Germany at the beginning of 1939.[117] In view of the

[110] Cf. 'January to April', *People & Freedom* 4 (1939), 4. Reichenberger, who was born and studied in Bavaria, opposed national socialism and supported the autonomy of German Bohemia within the Czechoslovak state. He emigrated to Britain in 1939 and to the United States in 1940 where he co-founded the foreign representation of the Christian Social People's Party in Czechoslovakia. He returned to Austria in 1952 and moved to West Germany in 1962. After World War II he became a nationalist right-winger and worked for the *Deutsche National-Zeitung*. Cf. Ferdinand Seibt, Hans Lemberg and Helmut Slapnicka (eds.), *Biographisches Lexikon zur Geschichte der Böhmischen Länder*, vol. III (Munich: Oldenbourg, 1991), 406.
[111] *People & Freedom* 1 (1938), 1–2.
[112] Philippe Chenaux, 'Bijdrage tot de internationale christen-democratie', in Wilfried Dewachter *et al.* (eds.), *Tussen staat en maatschapsij 1945–1995. Christen-democratie in België* (Tielt: Lannoo, 1995), 253.
[113] 'Reception for Leading Christian Democrats', *People & Freedom* 18 (1940), 4.
[114] The People and Freedom Group, Report of Meeting, 26 May [1937], CAC, Dilke – Crawford – Roskill Collection, 12/4.
[115] 'General Meeting', *People & Freedom* 4 (1939), 4.
[116] D. W., 'L'Aube and the Nef', *People & Freedom* 3 (1939), 3.
[117] '"White War"', *People & Freedom* 5 (1939), 1.

widespread habitual anti-Semitism, especially among the British upper
class and the official silence on the part of the government, this was already
more controversial than their appeal to Franco. One of the group's members, James Langdale, wrote in *People & Freedom* that 'in face of this
persecution the apathy and indifference of many Christians is both dis-
tressing and inexplicable ... To be silent at the present moment would be
nothing less than criminal.'[118] The People and Freedom Group also congratulated Anthony Eden in February 1938 on his principled resignation as
foreign secretary as a protest against the Appeasement policy.[119] After the
Munich Agreement later in the same year, they wrote in their newssheet
that the world 'awoke to ugly realities. Hitler's concessions were slight ...
The price paid for peace was surrender to naked threats.'[120] After the
British declaration of war in September 1939, Crawford told Sturzo how
relieved she was that the government had kept its word.[121] The group
immediately demanded the inclusion of the leading Conservative dissi-
dents Churchill, Eden, Duff Cooper and Lord Cranborne in a new and
'truly National Government',[122] which only happened after the military
disaster at Dunkirk in May 1940, however. These were only resolutions, of
course, directed mainly at the Catholic community in Britain and without
any significant effect on British politics.

Nonetheless, the British example inspired several American Catholics to
create similar groups, also named People and Freedom, often seeking
Sturzo's advice.[123] Groups were established in New York, where Shuster
acted as chairman; in Boston, where some of its twenty-five members were
associated with the Catholic Association for International Peace; in Notre
Dame in Indiana, where the university professor Willis D. Nutting was
chairman; in Philadelphia, where the group was headed by a certain
Godfrey Schmidt; in Los Angeles and possibly in a few more American
cities. There is much less information on the American groups, but it seems
clear that they were even more marginal within the wider Catholic community in the United States compared to the British group. When in April
1942, for example, Michael J. Ready of the National Catholic Welfare
Conference in Washington attempted to get information on the Los

---

[118] James Langdale, 'The Jews and Us', *People & Freedom* 5 (1939), 3.
[119] The People and Freedom Group, March Report [1938], CAC, Dilke – Crawford – Roskill
Collection, 12/4.
[120] 'The Czech Tragedy', *People & Freedom* 2 (1938), 1.
[121] Crawford to Sturzo, 5 September 1939, ASILS, Fondo Luigi Sturzo, fasc. DS 548.
[122] ' "White War" ', *People & Freedom* 5 (1939), 1.
[123] See, for example, Sturzo to Reilly, 14 January 1941, published in Luigi Sturzo, *Scritti inediti*, vol. III:
1940–1946, ed. Francesco Malgeri (Rome: Cinque lune, 1976), document 10.

Angeles branch, the local bishop, Joseph T. McGucken, made 'investigations through the Intelligence Association and various other sources', but could not locate the group.[124] In his letter, Ready had already advised the bishop that his was 'one of our lower forms of request'.[125]

On the other hand, the American People and Freedom groups were not the only forum for fostering transnational contacts among Catholic politicians in exile. The Hunter College in New York organised many meetings and guest lectures, for example by Brüning and Maritain.[126] The small, but very active French École Libre des Hautes Études within the New York School of Social Sciences also organised events and publications. At the same time, opportunities for transnational contacts were slightly less important to Catholic politicians in exile in the United States, especially in New York, as they also had contacts with the non-philo-fascist sections of the respective immigrant communities. This was true, for example, of the People and Liberty group under the chairmanship of Antony P. Ullo, which attempted to bring together Italian Americans and Italian refugees like Sturzo,[127] and of the inter-party organisation France Forever.[128]

In the first place, the People and Freedom Group was for British and American Catholics who wanted to uphold and develop the Christian democratic tradition. It also facilitated transnational contacts among Catholic politicians in exile. Sturzo and Alberto de Onaindía, a Basque refugee, and others felt, however, that this was insufficient. In a letter to Crawford, Sturzo wrote in September 1940 after consulting de Onaindía, whom he recommended as 'a man of ideas, courage and initiative':[129] 'It seems to me opportune that a centre of supporters of democratic parties or groups of Christian inspiration should be created in London; whether or not they have government responsibility, they can gather support for our political and social ideals.'[130] He suggested the creation of 'a centre for an exchange of ideas and a contact', adding that 'I should see with keen pleasure what would thus be a rebirth of one of my old initiatives, which

---

[124] Joseph T. McGucken to Michael J. Ready, 4 May 1942, Archives of the Catholic University of America (henceforth: ACUA), National Catholic Welfare Conference (NCWC/USCC), Executive Department, 18-A Church: Hierarchy: Mitty, John J., ABP.1942.

[125] Michael J. Ready to Joseph T. McGucken, 13 April 1942, ibid.   [126] Shuster, *The Ground*, 146.

[127] Malgeri, *Chiesa*, 196–8.   [128] Guillen, 'Plans by Exiles', 281.

[129] After Sturzo's departure for the United States, de Onaindía played a leading role in setting up the ICDU in collaboration with the People and Freedom Group secretariat and Carter. Cf. 'International Christian Democratic Union', *People & Freedom* 20 (1941), 4; Alberto de Onaindía, *Capitulos de mi vida II: Experiencias del exilio* (Buenos Aires: Editorial Vasca Ekin S.R.L., 1974), 216–18.

[130] Sturzo to Crawford, 15 September 1940, NA, Collectie J. A. Veraart, 216.

in my dream of 1920, was to be of a far higher political bearing than the Secretariat that was established in Paris.'[131] Using Sturzo's SIPDIC materials, Carter then located Catholic refugees, who had already participated in SIPDIC congresses and executive committee meetings, like the Dutch RKSP politician Veraart and others, 'to see if it would be possible to reconstitute a Christian Democratic centre [on the lines of SIPDIC]'.[132] The participants at the first preparatory meeting on 21 November 1940 included Veraart; de la Souchère, the female head of the foreign propaganda section in de Gaulle's government; Eugène de Waha-Baillonville, the Chairman of the Belgian Red Cross; Onaindía and Manuel Irujo, Acting President of the Basques; Józef Haller, Chairman of the Supreme Council of the Polish Party of Labour and Minister of Education in the Polish government in exile; and František Hala, Secretary-General of the Czech People's Party. Schumann, Jan Šrámek, the Czechoslovak Prime Minister, and several others sent messages of support.[133]

The inaugural meeting of the ICDU took place on 28 January 1941. It included a lecture by Veraart on 'Some Principles of Democracy'.[134] The discussions about the statutes of the new organisation, which were based on a first draft by Onaindía, went on for three more months, however. In the early stages, Carter intervened several times to secure core British conditions. In particular, she insisted on the use of the term 'parliamentary democracy' rather than 'organic democracy', which was too open to corporatist interpretations.[135] Carter also made certain that the new organisation was non-confessional by rephrasing Onaindía's references to political Catholicism.[136] In talking to Veraart, she explained Onaindía's confessional approach with the lack of integration of the Basque Catholics in the interwar SIPDIC cooperation and discourses. Carter, who like her colleagues from the People and Freedom Group was afraid of a repetition of the Versailles Treaty after World War II, also inserted a clause in the statutes that the ICDU would contribute to postwar planning for a Peace Conference 'to ensure the respect of those principles for which the Union stands'.[137] The British initially also proposed the inclusion of German and Italian representatives on the basis of equality. The French,

---

[131] Ibid.   [132] Carter to Veraart, 18 November 1940, NA, Collectie J. A. Veraart, 216.
[133] Confidential – Private conference of leading Christian Democrats, 21 November 1940, NA, Collectie J. A. Veraart, 216; 'Reception for Leading Christian Democrats', *People & Freedom* 18 (1940), 4.
[134] 'International Christian Democratic Union', *People & Freedom* 19 (1941), 4.
[135] Carter to Veraart, 21 December 1940, NA, Collectie J. A. Veraart, 216; Carter to Veraart, 10 January 1941, ibid.
[136] Ibid.   [137] Carter to Veraart, 21 December 1940, NA, Collectie J. A. Veraart, 216.

Czech, Polish and Basque refugees in particular strongly protested against this idea, however. They insisted that they should only be allowed to participate as observers, in a personal capacity, and it was thus decided.[138]

According to its statutes, the ICDU's main aim was to create 'permanent bonds of solidarity between the Christian democratic movements in the various nations' and to organise them against 'the forces of materialism and totalitarian oppression, and for the triumph of organic and parliamentary democracy'.[139] The ICDU had the political backing of leading Catholic politicians like Šrámek and Haller, who, together with Sturzo, formed the ICDU's Committee of Honour. They did not, however, play an active personal role in it. Compared to the interwar SIPDIC, moreover, Catholic refugees from parties from east-central Europe[140] and from peripheral regions like the Basque country[141] were clearly over-represented. It was mostly the ICDU members from these countries, who had important functions within their parties and governments in exile, like Hála from the Czech People's Party and Kwiatkowski, spokesman of the Polish Party of Labour and a member of the Polish National Council, who had already taken part in SIPDIC activities.

It was indicative of the relatively low importance attached to the ICDU by leading politicians from western Europe that its chairmanship was given to Veraart, a professor at the University of Delft. Although he had participated in SIPDIC activities, which was regarded as an asset, his Dutch party colleagues considered him as an outsider, even a maverick. In the early 1930s, he was very critical of capitalism and parliamentary government, which at that time gave him a latently philo-fascist and anti-democratic following.[142] He left the RKSP in 1933 to found his own party, the Catholic Democratic League/Party, but rejoined it in 1939. As a result, Veraart was

---

[138] De la Souchère to Veraart, no date, NA, Collectie J. A. Veraart, 216; [Basque] Amendments to the Statutes of the International Christian Democratic Union, ibid. See also the British comments in Carter to Veraart, 2 March 1941, ibid.

[139] 'International Christian Democratic Union', *People & Freedom* 22 (1941), 2.

[140] For more detail on the Polish exile see Jan E. Zamojski, 'The Social History of Polish Exile (1939–1945). The Exile State and the Clandestine State: Society, Problems and Reflections', in Conway and Gotovitch (eds.), *Europe in Exile*, 183–211 and John Coutouvidis and Jaime Reynolds, *Poland 1939–1947* (Leicester: Leicester University Press, 1986). For the Czech exile see Peter Heumos, *Die Emigration aus der Tschechoslowakei nach Westeuropa und dem Nahen Osten 1938–1945* (Munich: Oldenbourg, 1989).

[141] The Basque exile is treated in the context of Spanish opposition to Franco after 1939 in Sergio Vilar, *Historia del anti-franquismo 1939–1975* (Barcelona: Plaza & Janes, 1984).

[142] Sjef Schmiermann, 'Prof. Dr. J. A. Veraart (1886–1955). Een recalcitrant katholiek democraat', *Jaarboek van het Katholiek Documentatie Centrum* 20 (1990), 130. See also in more detail by the same author, *Prof. Dr. J. A. Veraart (1886–1955). Aspecten van het politieke leven van een recalcitrant katholiek democraat*, PhD (Nijmegen: University of Nijmegen, 1988).

not surprised to find the Dutch government in exile somewhat anxious when he arrived in London in May 1940. He recollected after the war that even some of his party colleagues seemed to think 'now we have got that man here again'.[143] Veraart was first given a job in the Dutch Ministry of Justice and then became personal economic adviser to the Calvinist prime minister P. S. Gerbrandy in May 1942. Dutch support for his chairmanship of the ICDU, for which he was very enthusiastic, thus amounted to a promotion sideways to keep a politically controversial figure with a difficult personality out of Dutch consociational, consensus-based exile politics.[144]

As ICDU chairman, Veraart organised regular meetings with guest speakers who lectured on different national party traditions and on themes of common interest, such as economic and social reform and the German question. Veraart himself gave several such lectures, mostly on economic and social policy.[145] These meetings appear to have been well attended. From 1943, however, and especially after the Allied invasion of France in 1944, when concrete postwar planning became more urgent, they increasingly seemed 'too great a tax on [the ICDU members'] time',[146] and no longer took place on a monthly basis. Thus, the ICDU developed into a transnational forum for debate on postwar Europe, but it was a more modest affair than Sturzo, Onaindía and Veraart had originally envisaged in 1940–1. The idea of turning the ICDU into a successor organisation of SIPDIC was clearly wishful thinking, as national political party organisation was only rudimentary in exile and postwar planning still focused on national reconstruction, with the partial exception of plans for regional integration which were discussed and negotiated by the governments in exile, however. With the exception of the Dutch,[147] the individual ICDU members also failed to form larger organised national groups. The ICDU, which had no secretariat and whose administrative work was done by Carter, its honorary secretary until 1944, also did not succeed in establishing a credible information service. According to initial plans, such a service would have provided the Catholic parties with economic and political facts

---

[143] Quoted in Schmiermann, 'Prof. Dr. J. A. Veraart', 134.
[144] For Gerbrandy's support see also Onaindía, *Capítulos*, 216–18. On Veraart's isolation among the Dutch politicians in exile see also de Jong, *Het koninkrijk*, vol. IX/2, 1445–6.
[145] NA, Collectie J. A. Veraart, 217 for his ICDU speeches.
[146] 'International Christian Democratic Union', *People & Freedom* 48 (1943), 5.
[147] Some additional information on the Dutch group can be gleaned from Veraart's own recollections in J. A. Veraart, 'Internationaal werk in Londen. Fragmenten uit mijn dagboek, 1940–1945', *Katholiek Cultureel Tijdschrift* 3 (1946–7), 58–9.

and information on other parties' history and policies.[148] In fact, some member parties even had difficulty paying their small membership fee regularly. By early 1944, Carter was so exasperated that she wrote to Veraart that 'in Hitler's words, "my patience is exhausted!" '[149]

Three main themes dominated the lectures and debates at the meetings of both the People and Freedom Group and the ICDU and the publications by Catholic politicians in exile in Britain and the United States: economic and social reform and the relationship between corporatism and liberal democracy; plans for a world organisation in succession to the League of Nations and the related question of closer European cooperation; and possible solutions to the German question. Their experience of exile in functioning non-Catholic liberal democracies first of all led Catholic politicians to reconceptualise and downgrade corporatist concepts, as it provided them with an alternative perspective on Anglo-Saxon political traditions. Compared to their compatriots in the resistance or internal emigration, they also put greater emphasis on creating a modern world organisation including Britain and the United States. 'Europe' played a major role only for a brief period at the time of the symbolic offer of an Anglo-French 'union' by Churchill in June 1940. Finally, while the Catholic refugees were in basic agreement about the need for some form of economic recovery of Germany after the war as necessary for European reconstruction, they still differed fundamentally over its political future and territorial issues.

When the Catholic political refugees arrived in Britain and the United States, their thinking on economic and social reform had been influenced for a long time by the discourse about the contribution corporatist institutions could make to better economic management and greater social equality and cohesion. They often regarded such institutions as the key to a European 'third way' between, as they saw it, the laissez-faire capitalism of the United States and the centrally planned state economy of the Soviet Union. The reform rhetoric of the more left-wing Catholics was often quite violently anti-capitalist, and it remained so in exile. In his speech at the inaugural meeting of the ICDU in January 1941, for example, Veraart spoke of capitalism as a 'monster'.[150] Later in the same year, he attacked in

---

[148] In 1941–2, for example, the ICDU spent the small sum of £10 on paper, stamps etc., and until May 1943 it had only dealt with three requests for information from 'semi-official circles'. Cf. 'Annual General Meeting [1942]', *People & Freedom* 36 (1942), 4; 'International Christian Democratic Union', *People & Freedom* 48 (1943), 5.

[149] Carter to Veraart, 1 February 1944, NA, Collectie J. A. Veraart, 216.

[150] 'Some Principles of Democracy, by Prof. Veraart (Address Given at the Inaugural Meeting of the International Christian Democratic Union, on January 28, 1941)', *People & Freedom* 20 (1941), 2.

language that was effectively (although unintentionally, as Veraart strongly denounced German anti-Semitism) not too dissimilar from anti-Semitic national socialist rhetoric, the 'parasitic finance that [is] strangling the finest enterprises'[151]. In another speech he demanded that 'the empire of the money market over human life must be shattered'[152]. Sturzo, too, frequently attacked the liberal capitalist order, and especially its American version with its 'secret monopolies' and 'capitalist speculation at the expense of the community'.[153]

Catholic politicians in exile continued to hold very different views on the most desirable socio-economic institutions. Their common expectation was, however, that as a result of the world economic crisis, the totalitarian challenge and the war, the capitalist system would collapse and have to be replaced with a more efficient and socially just, non-socialist alternative. Any enthusiasm for political corporatism had already declined during the 1930s, however. This was the result of the experience of actual corporatist solutions that were imposed from above by fascist and authoritarian states and combined with the abolition of free trade unions and political rights. This experience led to a greater emphasis on the need for the growth from below of *voluntary* corporatist institutions as intermediate authorities between private enterprises and the state with a much more limited scope. As the French Catholic democrat Louis Terrenoire put it in his essay for a joint European publication of the People and Freedom Group in 1939, the crucial question was how to make corporatism 'reconcilable with the political regime founded on liberty'.[154] Sturzo wrote in his contribution to the same book that corporatist institutions absolutely had to conform with political democracy in 'the endeavour to realize the combination of Authority and Liberty in an order, in which ... all adult citizens ... participate'.[155]

Equally, Catholic refugees in America, including Sturzo, Maritain, Van Zeeland, Theunis and the Basque President José Antonio de Aguirre, emphasised in their manifesto *Devant la Crise Mondiale*, published by the Maison Française in 1942, that 'the organic elements of the social order – the family, vocational associations, regions, cultural groups' should

---

[151] 'Veraart, Christian Democracy: Economic and Social Programme', *People & Freedom* 28 (1941), 3.
[152] 'International Christian Democratic Union', *People & Freedom* 40 (1942), 4.
[153] 'Luigi Sturzo, "The Bolshevist Peril" ', *People & Freedom* 37 (1942), 1.
[154] Louis Terrenoire, 'Corporatism and Democracy', in People and Freedom Group (ed.), *For Democracy* (London: Burns Oates, 1939), 186.
[155] Luigi Sturzo, 'Democracy, Authority, and Liberty', in ibid., 105. On Sturzo's views on corporatism, see also Nicola di Antonetti, 'Sturzo e il modello della rappresentanza organica', in De Rosa (ed.), *Luigi Sturzo e la democrazia europea*, 202–20.

in future play a central role in the European economy and society. But they strongly rejected the 'corporatist and paternalist state'. They argued that a clear distinction was needed between 'the political structure of the state and the economic organization of society'.[156] Thus, as Ellen L. Evans has also emphasised,[157] the experience of fascism, national socialism and corporatist dictatorial regimes as in Austria led to a marked shift in Catholic democratic thinking to less authority and more liberty and also towards a new emphasis on participation of workers in economic decision-making independent of its precise institutional form. In the case of the Catholic political refugees, especially in Britain, the relative shift from authority to liberty and – in the terminology of the ICDU constitution – from 'organic' to 'parliamentary' democracy was strengthened further by the experience of exile in a liberal parliamentary democracy they came to respect and, sometimes, to admire. This experience could be quite emotional. For example, Albert Masoin, a Belgian Catholic who came to Britain from Vichy France in the winter of 1943–4, wrote in *People & Freedom* that 'when one arrives in war-time England; when one feels a welcome of quite, sincere sympathy, so delicate and discreet; when one begins to live again, there is in reality no more exile ... In plain truth, the fatherland is also there where there is the breath of freedom.'[158]

Joan Keating has rightly pointed out that, originally, the thinking of Sturzo and other Catholic refugees was informed by 'a long tradition of Catholic social thought which opposed political individualism, seeing it as the product of religious individualism, that is, Protestantism'.[159] Importantly, however, it became significantly more individualistic and, in that sense only, more 'Protestant' in exile. The refugees were impressed by the relative stability of their host countries' political institutions and by the sheer tenacity with which especially the British defended their liberty. Even before the war, Sturzo in almost Whiggish terms praised the British political tradition and its parliament, which 'never remains the same, but evolves with the times, in an historical continuity stretching through seven centuries, and with an admirable capacity for adaptation'.[160] He valued what he saw as the pragmatism of the British, the non-ideological character of their social institutions and their tradition of international solidarity, as

[156] *Devant la crise mondiale. Manifeste de catholiques européens séjournant en Amérique* (New York: Éditions de la Maison française, 1942). See also the report 'Catholic Principles for the New Order', *People & Freedom* 39 (1942), 1 and 4.
[157] Evans, *The Cross*, 284.
[158] Albert Masoin, 'Home-Coming to Liberty', *People & Freedom* 57 (1944), 1.
[159] Keating, 'Looking to Europe', 76.   [160] Sturzo, 'Democracy', 107.

reflected in their cooperative movement and their comparatively liberal refugee policy, for example.[161]

Sturzo criticised what he saw as the lack of working-class integration in the British economic and political system. Nonetheless, he and most other Catholic political refugees came back from Britain and the United States with a changed normative hierarchy in which individual liberty was, relative to the sometimes conflicting aim of social cohesion, more important than before, thus pointing the way intellectually towards the more liberal Christian democracy of postwar western Europe. This shift was also reflected in the changing theological conceptions and discourses of influential Catholic thinkers like Maritain. In view of the widespread disposition of Catholics to support authoritarian dictatorships in continental Europe, and of their experience of 'Protestant' political traditions in exile, they increasingly discarded the mysticism with its peculiar notion of 'community', which was so widespread in European Catholicism in the late 1920s and the 1930s, in favour of greater emphasis on the individual person. As the publicist Waldemar Gurian, who fled Germany in 1934 and eventually became a professor at the Catholic University of Notre Dame in Indiana in 1937, aptly put it in 1941: 'If St. Thomas lived today he would be for Franco, for Tizo, for Pétain.'[162]

Their exile in Britain and the United States also contributed to a more Atlanticist view of postwar Europe among Catholic political refugees. Federalist ideas applied to Europe only played a significant role in their debates and publications in the period 1939–41. In a report for the ICDU on 'Italy of Tomorrow', for example, Sturzo took up key ideas of the SIPDIC resolution of 1932 advocating a European federation, the lowering of customs barriers and equal access to raw materials.[163] British members and 'friends' of the People and Freedom Group shared his ideas. In an article for *People & Freedom* published in January 1940, for example, Crawford spoke of the need to establish a 'supranational authority' with 'political and judicial functions'.[164] Wickham Steed also advocated a

---

[161] The People and Freedom Group, Monthly Report, 27 November 1937, CAC, Dilke – Crawford – Roskill Collection, 12/4; Forgacs, 'Sturzo e la cultura politica inglese', 346.

[162] Cited in John T. McGreevy, *Catholicism and American Freedom. A History* (New York: W. W. Norton & Company, 2003), 198.

[163] Luigi Sturzo, Report to the Committee of the ICDU in London on Italy of Tomorrow, n.d., NA, Collectie J. A. Veraart, 218. For Sturzo's thinking on postwar Europe see also Landuyt, 'Ideas of Italian Exiles', 494–8.

[164] Virginia Crawford, 'For a Christian Order', *People & Freedom* 7 (1940), 1. See also 'Beginnings of Federation', ibid.; Virginia Crawford, 'Where We Stand', *People & Freedom* 6 (1939), 1; Virginia Crawford, 'For a New Europe', *People & Freedom* 19 (1941), 1.

'federal union' which could include Germany after the signing of a peace treaty, or 'this war would prove to be merely another episode in a series of attempts to decide whether men and peoples are worthy and capable of peace.'[165] Wickham Steed also had contacts with Federal Union founded in 1938, and he spoke at their conference in London in July 1939.[166] Other members of the People and Freedom Group and Catholic refugees perhaps had loose contacts with this organisation, and some intellectual cross-fertilisation may have taken place. Yet only one ICDU member, Irujo from the Basque country, was represented on the European Committee of Federal Union.[167]

After the fall of France, most Catholic politicians in exile supported regional projects for cooperation or integration, such as between Belgium and the Netherlands, Poland and Czechoslovakia or for the Danube region – for economic reasons, but also as an insurance policy against a resurgent Germany. In contrast, they mostly thought that a larger European federation was either unrealistic or even dangerous. Bech from Luxembourg, who later played an important role in the formation of the ECSC and the EEC, believed, for example, that a wider 'European economic union' was 'for the time being, impossible'. In his speech at the Belgian Institute in London in February 1943 he suggested instead a regional customs union, such as the future Benelux, that could be extended to other states bordering on the Atlantic, principally France, but – he implied – not Germany or Italy.[168] The inclusion of Germany in any new organisation, whether federal, inter-governmental or with a mixed institutional structure, was excluded more explicitly by Van Cauwelaert, president of the Belgian Chamber of Deputies, in a speech in Washington in April 1942. Such a larger integrated Europe, Van Cauwelaert argued, would inevitably be dominated by Germany, and it was therefore crucial for the United States and Britain to play a leading role in the reconstruction of Europe and in any new organisations.[169]

---

[165] Henry Wickham Steed, 'Foreground and Background', *Fortnightly Review* 146 (1939), 369–70. See also Philip M. H. Bell, 'British Plans for European Union 1939–45. II: Other Contributions 1939–41', in Lipgens (ed.), *Plans for European Union*, 156–204.

[166] Richard Mayne and John Pinder, *Federal Union: The Pioneers. A History of Federal Union* (Basingstoke: Macmillan, 1990), 11. See also John Pinder, 'Federalism in Britain and Italy: Radicals and the English Liberal Tradition', in: Stirk (ed.), *European Unity*, 208.

[167] For a list of the committee members see Walter Lipgens, 'Plans of other Transnational Groups for European Union', in Lipgens (ed.), *Plans for European Union*, 802, footnote 3.

[168] Quoted in Lipgens (ed.), *Europa-Föderationspläne*, 471–2.

[169] Frans Van Cauwelaert, 'Dangers of a European Federation', 2 April 1942, reprinted in *Washington Post*, 10 May 1942. See also José Gotovitch, 'Views of Belgian Exiles on the Postwar Order in Europe', in Lipgens (ed.), *Plans for European Union*, 414–50; Laurent, 'Reality'.

When Catholic politicians in exile did advocate federalism after 1940–1, they applied the concept in a rather loose way to an imagined Atlantic community or even to the world. As Maritain argued in a speech at a public meeting of France Forever in Shuster's Hunter College on 14 July 1943, what was required was a 'collective vision and inspiration ... The nations must choose between the prospect of aggravated, irremediable chaos and a strenuous effort at cooperation, working with patience and perseverance towards a progressive organisation *of the world* [my emphasis] in a supranational community.'[170]

Not surprisingly, therefore, the Catholic refugees greeted the Atlantic Charter of 1941 and its promise of a better world order with enthusiasm. The Anglo-American initiative appeared to take up demands of the late 1930s, also made by *L'Aube*, NEF, the People and Freedom Group and Catholic refugees, for a more effective League of Nations or, as the ICDU put it in a resolution in April 1943, a new 'Commonwealth of democratic nations'.[171] The members of the People and Freedom Group and of the ICDU spent much time after 1941 debating the best political and institutional formula for such a world organisation. From mid-1943 onwards, however, they became disillusioned with Allied great power politics and the fact that the new organisation would be neither democratic nor based on the principle of equality which alone would guarantee the continental European countries a real voice in future world affairs. The inclusion of the Soviet Union and the veto envisaged for the great powers was incompatible with the lessons the Catholic refugees had drawn from the experience of the interwar period. Principally, this was that a world organisation should only consist of democratic states that fully supported its principles, and that it should mainly be concerned with protecting its smaller members against any hegemonic threat.[172] In contrast, a 'hegemony of the Big Three', as the People and Freedom Group argued, would make the continental European countries mere 'client states' of the new world powers.[173] Their disillusionment was complete when Churchill publicly exempted the so-called enemy states and colonies from the Charter's guarantees. In March 1944, the People and Freedom Group protested vehemently that

[170] Quoted in Pierre Guillen, 'Plans by Exiles', 303. Maritain taught at Columbia University, New York, and at the Pontifical Institute, Toronto. For his wartime thinking see also Jacques Maritain, *Messages 1941–1944* (Paris: P. Hartmann, 1944).

[171] 'A New League of Nations Now. Proposal Endorsed by International Christian Democratic Union', *People & Freedom* 46 (1943), 3.

[172] This general view among Catholic refugees was expressed most coherently after the war by Luigi Sturzo, *Nationalism and Internationalism* (New York: Roy Publishers, 1946).

[173] 'The Voice of Europe', *People & Freedom* 53 (1943), 3.

his redefinition of the Charter, as they saw it, 'knocks away the already frail foundations of a new international order'.[174] Sturzo wrote sarcastically one month later that, if Turkey inconveniently remained neutral, 'sooner or later we shall have a declaration that "neutrals" without belligerent quali-fications cannot enjoy the Atlantic Charter'. The Charter, he concluded, 'after so many torpedos, is well and truly sunk'.[175]

The idea of a new world organisation had appeared so attractive not least because it could have acted as an arbiter with respect to the postwar settlement. As such, it would not only have had a better claim to greater political legitimacy than the Allies at Versailles and Trianon; crucially, it might also have found solutions to the problems the Catholic refugees themselves could not agree upon, especially territorial issues. Instead, Churchill's public surrender of the universality of the Atlantic Charter made it absolutely clear that each nation would be able to secure its objectives only through direct lobbying of the great powers. As a result, also the Catholic politicians in exile spent much of the last two war years exercising such limited influence as they had in Britain and the United States through their exile governments or – especially in the case of the Italians and Austrians – through the media. It is indicative of this general trend that Sturzo became totally preoccupied towards the end of the war with defending what he regarded as Italian interests, especially its territorial integrity. Sturzo gave much space in his publications to analysing and condemning national socialism, and he conceded that some German loss of territory in the east was clearly inevitable. In contrast, he mentioned fascism only in passing. It now almost seemed a historical accident. Sturzo argued that, especially in view of French collaboration in Vichy France, the Badoglio government deserved the same treatment as the Free French government. As if this did not apply to Germany, he also insisted that it was of central importance for Europe that the new Italian democracy should not be burdened with any loss of territory, be it the Trentino, South Tyrol or Istria.[176] South Tyrol and Istria, of course, had large non-Italian majorities. Thus, Sturzo's argument illustrates very well how much easier it was also for Catholic democrats to accept the Charter's principles – in this

[174] 'Downward Steps', *People & Freedom* 57 (1944), 1.
[175] 'Sturzo, The Shade of Wilson and the Atlantic Charter', *People & Freedom* 58 (1944) 1.
[176] See especially Luigi Sturzo, 'Italy after Mussolini', *Foreign Affairs* 21 (1943), 412–26. Sturzo's preoccupation towards the end of the war with narrow Italian interests is also reflected in his autobiography, *La mia battaglia da New York* (Milan: Garzanti, 1949). After the war, Carter defended the Italian case against the peace treaty in the somewhat one-sided book, published in English and Italian, *Italy Speaks*.

particular case the right to self-determination – than their actual application to concrete controversial issues.

Thus, plans for a new world organisation temporarily took precedence over geographically more narrowly conceived concepts for (continental) European cooperation in debates about the future of the international system during World War II.[177] For the Catholic refugees, this mainly holds true until it became clear that the Soviet Union would be included in the future United Nations and that the five member-states of its Security Council would have a veto power. Moreover, the importance attached to the inclusion of Britain and the United States in new structures and organisations varied considerably. The transnational activities and debates in the ICDU confirm the findings of several national case studies that the transatlantic and global orientation was much more pronounced among politicians in exile than those engaged in the resistance or in internal emigration in continental Europe. As a general rule, and despite variations, this was true for socialists and liberals as much as for Catholics. For the French case, for example, Pierre Guillen has found that 'the themes of European ideology were developed in circles that were somewhat detached from the more or less official organization of Free France'.[178] They included the resistance group Combat with the Christian democrats de Menthon, Teitgen and Coste-Floret, which developed 'the objective of integrating Germany into a West European bloc under French leadership, so as to eliminate the nightmare of a German threat once and for all'.[179] Similarly, G. M. V. Mans has argued for the Netherlands, where the elites on the whole had the most transatlantic orientation across party divides after the war, that Catholic (and other) politicians in the resistance or internal emigration were much more open towards continental European integration options than their compatriots in exile.[180] In a more global perspective, Walter Lipgens has rightly argued that the non-communist resistance movements were increasingly more interested in European than worldwide solutions, although he fails to distinguish according to political ideology and party allegiance and to demonstrate a causal link between these ideas formed in the resistance and postwar European politics.[181]

Securing short-term territorial and other interests, as most Catholic politicians in exile tried in the final stages of the war, was in many cases

---

[177] See also Rolf Hellmut Foerster, *Die Idee Europa 1300–1946* (Munich: dtv, 1963), 253.
[178] Guillen, 'Plans by Exiles', 279.   [179] Ibid., 285.
[180] Mans, 'Ideas', 453 makes this point comparing the Dutch exile and resistance without, however, distinguishing according to party allegiance.
[181] Lipgens (ed.), *Europa-Föderationspläne*.

linked to the German question. Among the Catholic refugees in the ICDU and beyond, a minimum consensus existed that – in the words of Paul Tschoffen, a Belgian councillor of state – 'there must be no economic war against a defeated Germany, first because it would not be Christian, and secondly because it would be fruitless'[182]; and thirdly, it should be added, because such a policy would be disadvantageous for countries such as Belgium whose economies were highly interdependent with the German economy. As Veraart summarised it, 'contrary to Versailles Germany must not be destroyed economically'.[183] Beyond such generalities, however, the Catholic politicians in exile were deeply divided as to the causes of national socialism and their war aims.

The simplistic view of a German collective guilt was still widely held. For Tschoffen, for example, 'Germany as a whole was behind Hitler and guilty with him'.[184] Veraart – well known for his strongly anti-German views before the war – believed that national socialism 'responded to something in the souls of the German people'[185]. Such views were often linked to anti-Prussian sentiments that were also prevalent among other political groups at the time. In Sturzo's view, for example, the greatest danger was 'the Prussian mentality, as forged by the Teutonic Knights, the Brandenburgs, the Hohenzollerns and Bismarks [sic!] . . . of whom Nazism is the heir'[186]. Before the Germans might one day be reintegrated into the community of democratic states, Sturzo argued, they were in need of 'a real moral and psychological purification'.[187] Others believed strongly in political securities which they did not yet see in some kind of European construction. Instead, many ICDU members wanted to go beyond the imposition, if necessary, of fully fledged federalism and saw the only real solution in the dismemberment of Germany. This country, Veraart argued in a speech on the future of Germany in March 1943, was an 'artificially big unit' and had to be divided into at least five different states. Veraart's statement was followed by an animated discussion in which the German

---

[182] 'International Christian Democratic Union. Annual General Meeting', *People & Freedom* 61 (1944), 4.
[183] 'International Christian Democratic Union. "How to Deal with Germany and the Germans"', *People & Freedom* 58 (1944), 3.
[184] 'International Christian Democratic Union. Annual General Meeting', *People & Freedom* 61 (1944), 4.
[185] 'International Christian Democratic Union. "How to Deal with Germany and the Germans"', *People & Freedom* 58 (1944), 3.
[186] 'Sturzo, A New Germany', *People & Freedom* 9 (1940), 3. Carl Spiecker, a Catholic from Prussian Westfalia, put forward a more differentiated view of Prussia's role in his book *Germany – from Defeat to Defeat*, with a Preface by Professor R. W. Seton-Watson (London: MacDonald & Co., 1945).
[187] 'Sturzo, A New Germany', *People & Freedom* 9 (1940), 3.

political refugees Karl Meyer[188] and Franz Xaver Aenderl[189] argued strongly in favour of federalism, but warned against an imposed division of Germany.[190] Carter also insisted that 'lasting peace must rest on assent'. On the whole, however, many ICDU members were quite sympathetic to Veraart's propositions.[191]

Concerning changes in Germany's external borders, most Catholic politicians in exile were quite happy to go beyond the restoration of the pre-1938 situation. Among the more lenient suggestions for German cession of territory in the east were those Sturzo made, with the Italian situation in mind. He advocated some adjustments in Silesia and elsewhere, but categorically rejected the idea of giving the very predominantly German East Prussia to Poland. 'Mass deportation,' he argued, 'would be a crime that the Allies cannot and must not commit.' Sturzo also insisted that 'those who think of the annexation of the Rhine valley are but unconscious warmongers'.[192] On the other hand, the Polish ICDU representatives made the most far-reaching territorial demands even before the Soviet occupation and annexation of eastern Poland. Responding to a letter to the editor in *People & Freedom*, Kwiatkowski (who was strongly supported on this point by Veraart, for example)[193] defended Polish demands for the annexation of East Prussia, 'the sword of Damocles' hanging over Poland. In his view, the 'expulsion of a few hundred thousand of Prussian Junkers who amply share the responsibility for all the crimes committed both in the first and the present world war' was easily justified.[194] As Jan E. Zamojski has shown in his concise introduction to the social history of the Polish exile in London, Kwiatkowski's demands were fully in line with the official policy of the Party of Work.[195] Like the Nationalists, they were committed before

---

[188] *Biographisches Handbuch der deutschsprachigen Emigration nach 1933*, 2 vols. (Munich, New York: K. G. Saur, 1980) has no entry under Karl Meyer.

[189] Aenderl had in fact been a social democratic member of the Bavarian Landtag during 1928–32. During the war he worked as a journalist in London and prepared Catholic BBC broadcasts for Bavaria. After the war he joined the staunchly regionalist Bavaria Party. Cf. Werner Röder, *Die deutschen sozialistischen Exilgruppen in Großbritannien. Ein Beitrag zur Geschichte des Widerstandes gegen den Nationalsozialismus*, 2nd edn (Bonn-Bad Godesberg: Verlag Neue Gesellschaft, 1973).

[190] See also Meyer's speech on German political Catholicism: 'German Catholics Yesterday and Tomorrow', *People & Freedom* 36 (1942), 4.

[191] 'International Christian Democratic Union. "How to Deal with Germany and the Germans" ', *People & Freedom* 58 (1944), 3.

[192] 'Sturzo, What to Do with Germany', *People & Freedom* 63 (1944), 1.

[193] J. A. Veraart, How to Deal with Germany and the Germans after the War, ICDU, 4 March 1944, NA, Collectie J. A. Veraart, 217. Veraart believed that the integration of eastern Prussia into Poland was an 'obvious' result of the war.

[194] Michał Kwiatkowski, 'Poland and East Prussia', *People & Freedom* 57 (1944), 3.

[195] Zamojski, 'The Social History', 202.

the war to the enforced polonisation of national minorities and the 'emigration' of Jews from Poland. During the war, they made far-reaching demands for territorial gains in East Prussia, Pomerania and Silesia. In fact, Kwiatkowski, who was near to the Polish prime minister General Władysław Sikorski until his death in a plane crash in July 1943, was especially rabidly anti-German.[196] He was born in the Prussian Gnesen (Gniezno) near Posen (Poznan) in 1883, where he became involved in the nationalist movement, opposed Prussian attempts to impose the use of the German language in schools and was briefly imprisoned at the fortress in Danzig (Gdansk) in 1902. He worked in the Ruhr area from 1903 and then studied at Münster in Westphalia before he later played a leading role in Polish propaganda in Upper Silesia in the run-up to the plebiscite there after World War I. Opposed to Piłsudski, he left Poland for France in 1927 or 1928, where he published the influential Polish newspaper *Narodowiec*, before he fled to Britain in 1940.

Whereas the Catholic politicians in exile still differed widely by 1945 over the future of Germany, the British People and Freedom Group took a very consistent view of this issue throughout the war. They were, of course, comparatively detached from the conflicts of the continent. Unlike many others, they had no direct stake in the peace settlement. Crawford warned in her first published comment after the British declaration of war that 'we must resolutely cherish our sanity of judgement, our mental balance, our sense of moral values, our faith in all our Christian traditions of justice and charity even towards our enemies. Ultimately, we must work for a just and not a revengeful peace.'[197] Just as they had strongly protested after the destruction of Guernica, the People and Freedom Group also expressed their opposition to the indiscriminate aerial saturation bombing of German cities during the war.[198] Towards the end of the war, they strongly opposed the cession of territory very predominantly inhabited by Germans, such as East Prussia. In reply to Kwiatkowski's demands, the Group's Committee took the unprecedented step of publishing a formal resolution together with his letter to the editor to the effect that such large-scale annexations as he was envisaging 'would be disastrous ... Arguments founded on racial origin, the brutalities of mediaeval colonisation ... or feudal suzerainty seem to us supremely irrelevant.

[196] I am grateful to Leszek Kuk for providing me with biographical information on Kwiatkowski.
[197] 'Crawford, Where We Stand', *People & Freedom* 6 (1939), 1.
[198] See, for example, 'Downward Steps', *People & Freedom* 57 (1944), 1.

Prussia is an integral part of Germany, and its forced incorporation in Poland would weaken Poland herself and make the general pacification of Europe impossible.'[199]

At a meeting of the People and Freedom Group in January 1945, Conrad Bonacina, Crawford's successor as chairman, insisted that 'a Carthaginian peace would be no peace' and that any major territorial changes would mean either 'huge transfers, with terrible human misery, or the incorporation of some millions of hostile people in the Polish State'.[200] Subsequently, in March 1945, the People and Freedom Group protested against the Polish border changes which reflected 'a preoccupation with States rather than peoples – or, more basically, simply people – [which] implies an impenitent pursuance of the process that has made modern history a series of wars of ever more destructive range'.[201] The People and Freedom Group also protested against the intellectual justification of Allied policy towards Germany. In an article about American re-education plans for their journal published in 1942, Sturzo insisted that the Germans 'are neither a superior Aryan Race nor a race of inferior brutes'.[202] The Group's Committee emphasised that the idea of the Germans as a 'guilty people' was 'a myth'. It made national socialism seem like 'no tyranny, rooted in terrorism, but as resting on general consent, as though subject to the control of free opinion. In that delusion, the necessary discrimination between guilty and innocent vanishes ... In these last months, the truth that was our strength has been distorted. History has been fantastically twisted to prove the Germans a people of aggressors throughout the ages, creating an atmosphere of falsehood in which even Mr. Churchill's historical sense succumbs.'[203] And in response to a letter to the editor from Robert Vansittart, who was notorious for his hatred of Germany and the Germans, the Committee published a statement in the summer of 1945 that 'the idea of "national crimes" for which whole peoples must acknowledge guilt could come only in a generation that has lost the sense of sin in its real implications, sin that is always individual'.[204]

Their views on the future of Germany were consistent with their general belief system, and they thought that they were Christian, ethically right and

---

[199] 'Statement by the People and Freedom Group Committee', *People & Freedom* 57 (1944), 3.
[200] 'Principles of Peace', *People & Freedom* 68 (1945), 4.
[201] 'States or Peoples', *People & Freedom* 69 (1945), 1.
[202] Luigi Sturzo, 'PostWar Germany', *People & Freedom* 37 (1942), 1.
[203] 'Victory and After', *People & Freedom* 71 (1945), 1; see also 'Points from our Programme', ibid.
[204] 'Our Answer', *People & Freedom* 73 (1945), 2–4.

morally superior. They were, of course, highly unpopular with the vast majority of the British people, who had a mental image of the destruction of Coventry or real experience with German V1 or V2 rockets. They were also incompatible with the majority view among the Catholic politicians in exile. Thus, it must have taken even the financially and personally independent middle-class members of the People and Freedom Group considerable social courage to pronounce and publish them so consistently during the war. Of course, their pronouncements and resolutions had absolutely no effect on the wartime reality, as historians have come to know it. When they protested against aerial saturation bombing, Churchill was about to consider the indiscriminate use of poison gas against German cities in the hope that this would shorten the war. When they opposed far-reaching territorial changes in east-central Europe, Stalin had already decided, with implicit British and American consent, to annex eastern Poland. When, finally, the Group spoke out against large-scale resettlements, the expulsion of millions of Poles from eastern Poland and of many more millions of Germans from eastern Germany was already in full swing.

With their social background and these views on the war and the postwar European order, the People and Freedom Group was – as Tom Buchanan has argued for the British case – 'a small group of articulate, but hardly representative Catholics':[205] a minority within the Catholic minorities in Britain and the US. Nevertheless, the Group provided an alternative intellectual focus for Catholic refugees. It also initiated and supported transnational contacts among them, especially in Britain, and thus contributed to the greater formalisation of their cooperation in the ICDU. This transnational cooperation in exile was much less systematic and effective than Veraart and others originally hoped, however. The ICDU fostered contacts among individual Catholic politicians, not formal party cooperation. The majority of its members, including its chairman, did not play leading roles in their own parties. It cannot be verified whether more influential Catholic politicians like Hubert Pierlot, the Belgian prime minister, Šrámek and Haller attended meetings of the People and Freedom Group or the ICDU, but they certainly gave no speeches. De Schryver, who became the first leader of the postwar Belgian Christelijke Volkspartij / Parti Social Chrétien (CVP/PSC), did participate several times, and Schumann was even the official French representative from 1942–3,[206] although – as Carter recalled later – he only took part once

---

[205] Buchanan, *Britain*, 181.   [206] 'Annual General Meeting', *People & Freedom* 36 (1942), 3.

to give a speech.[207] It is not surprising, therefore, that Onaindía concluded at the annual meeting in 1944 that the organisation '[has] served a valuable purpose in enabling Christian Democrats of various nationalities to get to know one another . . . but it must be admitted that it [has] not attained the influence or development that might have been hoped'. He believed that one reason for this failure to make a difference was that so few prominent politicians became engaged in the ICDU activities, not least because of the growing workload in their respective governments in exile.[208]

The ICDU activities had little effect, if any on the postwar planning in exile for national and European reconstruction. Sturzo even arrived at the depressing conclusion that none of his political activism in exile since 1924 ever had any effect at all in terms of strengthening the values of freedom against the totalitarian threat or promoting a new international order based on equality.[209] Moreover, there is no direct continuity, institutionally or politically, from the rudimentary transnationalism in exile to Christian democratic party cooperation in the NEI and the Geneva Circle after 1945–7. Carter travelled to continental Europe in 1946 and helped to establish new transnational contacts including Christian democrats from the resistance and internal emigration. In as much as they saw their new activities embedded in a particular institutional tradition, it was the democratic SIPDIC period in the 1920s, however, not the ICDU, which was marked by internal strife especially among the Polish and Czech members over future relations with the Soviet Union, and everyone over the future of Germany. In fact, when Bidault, who as editor of *L'Aube* was a corresponding member of the British People and Freedom Group before the war, met Sturzo in New York in October 1944, they agreed to promote 'a regional, western-European conference' of Christian democratic parties after the war in order to exclude the Catholic parties from east-central Europe and to retain a free hand over policy towards the Soviet Union.[210] With the end of World War II, moreover, British influence came to an abrupt end.

The experience of working together with the People and Freedom Group and in the ICDU may well have made de Schryver, Schumann and a few other Catholic refugees, who had a high political profile in western Europe after 1945, value transnational party cooperation more highly. On the whole, however, Catholic refugees only played a marginal

---

[207] Carter to Sturzo, 30 June 1945, ASILS, fasc. 201A. For this speech see also 'Annual General Meeting', *People & Freedom* 36 (1942), 3. According to Onaindía, Schumann participated twice. Cf. Onaindía, *Capítulos*, 217.

[208] 'International Christian Democratic Union, Annual General Meeting', *People & Freedom* 61 (1944), 4.

[209] Cited in De Rosa, *Luigi Sturzo*, 407–8.   [210] Cf. 'Georges Bidault', *People & Freedom* 63 (1944), 1.

role in most national parties as well as within the NEI, especially in the case of France, West Germany, Italy and Austria, where the new party leaderships were clearly dominated by Christian democrats who had preferred the resistance or internal emigration over exile. Most of the prominent interwar Catholic leaders in exile retired from politics, like Sturzo and Brüning, or when they tried to re-enter national politics, they were marginalised, like Wirth, who developed very left-wing, pro-Soviet views.

Moreover, it is clear from the analysis of the speeches and debates at the meetings of both the People and Freedom Group and the ICDU that there is also no political continuity from the thinking of Catholic politicians in exile on such crucial issues as the future role of Britain in Europe or policy towards Germany, to postwar European reconstruction. The Catholic refugees were united in their much clearer rejection of political corporatism, but so were those Catholic politicians who had stayed on the continent during the war. They gave absolute preference to the creation of a new world organisation of democratic states. They quickly became disillusioned with Allied policy long before the creation of the United Nations in 1945, but failed to advance alternative concepts. Finally, the experience of exile generally led the Catholic refugees to develop a strongly Atlanticist vision of postwar Europe which excluded the possibility of any continental European solution to the German question. With the notable exception of the German Catholics in exile, who almost universally regarded the 'European vocation', as Spiecker called it,[211] as their salvation from national socialism and a precondition for the reintegration of Germany into the international system, the debates in exile clearly did not anticipate the later fundamental solution of the German question through integration in the ECSC and the EEC. On the whole, therefore, transnational cooperation in exile had only a marginal effect on the development of both the new Christian democratic parties and their transnational cooperation and of western Europe after the war. As Martin Conway has argued, postwar Europe was not made in the British (or, for that matter, US) exile[212] – nor, more specifically, by the Catholics in exile.

[211] Spiecker, *Germany*, 153.   [212] Conway, 'Legacies of Exile', 255.

CHAPTER 5

Hegemony by default: Christian democracy in postwar Europe

It appeared unlikely that Christian democracy would emerge victorious from World War II. Conservative political Catholicism was discredited. Its interwar economic policies seemed to have aggravated the effects of the world economic crisis, contributing to the breakdown of democratic regimes everywhere. Many conservative Catholics subsequently supported clerical dictatorships and fascism. Moreover, most Catholics who opted for resistance against the German occupation were democratic left-Catholics – a minority within the Catholic political camp in interwar Europe. At the same time, the Catholic Church hierarchy was morally compromised. The Vatican had strongly supported clerical dictatorships out of fear of communist revolution in Europe. It had also failed to take a strong stance against the extermination of Jews.

To many, the future seemed to belong to socialism. It offered voters an innovative economic policy of nationalisation, state intervention and planning, which promised to cure the ills of industrial capitalism and to homogenise internally fragmented national societies. As such it appeared to be the only credible democratic alternative to revolutionary communism that would lead Europe straight into the emerging Soviet camp. Socialism also had a proud tradition of resistance to national socialism, fascism and militant clericalism. Moreover, at the core of its political belief system was a kind of internationalism that seemed to fit ideally with the agenda of the newly founded United Nations. The sensational Labour Party landslide victory over the Conservative wartime prime minister, Winston Churchill, in the British general elections of 5 July 1945 appeared to herald the breakthrough of democratic socialism in Europe. Continental European socialists were also encouraged by the strong moral and material support from the newly elected British government as well as from American Democrats in the Truman Administration and voluntary institutions like the Ford Foundation. They aimed at reconstructing democratic socialism as the main bulwark against revolutionary communism.

It was not to be, however. Instead of democratic socialism, Christian democratic parties became the hegemonic political force in continental western Europe in the first twenty years after World War II. In the Low Countries the three refounded and renamed Catholic parties were the strongest political forces and dominated government formation. The Dutch Katholieke Volkspartij (KVP), or Catholic People's Party, continued to represent 80–90 per cent of Catholic voters, winning 30.8 per cent in the elections for the Second Chamber in 1946 as against 28.3 per cent for the Social Democrats, with whom they formed coalitions until 1958.[1] In Belgium, the CVP/PSC easily became the largest party in 1946, when it obtained 42.5 per cent of the vote in the national elections. In 1950, it increased its support to 47.7 per cent. It was excluded from government by Socialist–Liberal coalitions until 1950 and once more during 1954–8.[2] This resulted from the domestic confrontation over the King Question, the future of Leopold III who had accepted the German occupation and not left the country in 1940, and residual culture war issues, especially the question of public funding for Catholic schools. In Luxembourg, finally, the Christian Social People's Party (CSV) continued its interwar dominance and controlled postwar coalition governments.

Christian democracy's electoral success was most spectacular in Italy and Germany, however. Under the leadership of Alcide De Gasperi, the Italian Democrazia Cristiana (DC) won 48.5 per cent in the hotly contested national elections of 1948, easily outpacing the unified list of communists and socialists, which gained 31 per cent.[3] DC support fell to under 40 per cent for the first time only in 1963. Government instability in Italy mainly resulted from conflicts within and between the different DC wings, or *corrente*, while the party continued to control government formation until its collapse in the early 1990s. In western Germany, the newly formed interconfessional CDU, together with the CSU, established itself in regional elections in 1946 as the main rival of the Sozialdemokratische Partei Deutschlands (SPD), the Social Democratic Party. In the first elections after the creation of the Federal Republic of Germany on 14 August 1949, the

[1] Cf. Jac Bosmans, 'The Primacy of Domestic Politics: Christian Democracy in the Netherlands', in Gehler and Kaiser (eds.), *Christian Democracy*, 54–66. See in greater detail Johannes A. Bornewasser, *Katholieke Volkspartij, 1945–1980*, vol. I: *Herkomst en groei (tot 1963)* (Nijmegen: Valkhof Pers, 1995).

[2] Emiel Lamberts, 'The Zenith of Christian Democracy: The Christelijke Volkspartij / Parti Social Chrétien in Belgium', in Gehler and Kaiser (eds.), *Christian Democracy*, 67–84. See in greater detail Wouter Beke, *De Christelijke Volkspartij tussen 1945 en 1968: breuklijnen en pacificatiemechanismen in een catch-allpartij* (Leuven: Leuven University Press, 2004).

[3] Pollard, 'Italy', 69–96. See in greater detail Agostino Giovagnoli, *Il partito italiano: la democrazia cristiana dal 1942 al 1994* (Rome: Laterza, 1996).

CDU/CSU won 31 per cent of the vote – 1.8 per cent more than the SPD. Against internal opposition from rival leaders who favoured a grand coalition with the SPD, Konrad Adenauer succeeded in constructing a centre-right government including the liberal Free Democrats, the Freie Demokratische Partei (FDP), the and some smaller fringe parties. Facilitated by a new electoral law – the 5 per cent threshold for representation in the Bundestag – the CDU/CSU subsequently absorbed these fringe parties. In 1957, it won an absolute majority, and Adenauer remained chancellor until 1963.[4]

In France, where the PDP had hovered around 3 per cent of the vote in interwar elections, the newly founded MRP achieved a breakthrough with 28.2 per cent of the vote in the national elections of June 1946. Its support declined marginally to 25.9 per cent in November 1946, although it won more seats than six months earlier.[5] Until the creation of a rival Gaullist party in 1947, the MRP profited greatly from its image as the effective parliamentary representation of Charles de Gaulle, the Free French leader and president until his resignation in 1946. In the face of Gaullist electoral competition, MRP support collapsed to 12.6 per cent in 1951. The nationalist competition strengthened the MRP's European orientation, however, and the party continued to play a crucial role in the political centre of the Fourth Republic. For 83 per cent of the period from 1945 to 1957, the MRP participated in government, first in centre-left 'Third Force' coalitions with the socialist Section Française de l'Internationale Ouvrière (SFIO), then in centre-right coalitions.[6] Crucially for transnational Christian democratic party cooperation, moreover, Bidault, Schuman and again Bidault continuously controlled the French foreign ministry, the Quai d'Orsay, from 1945 to 1953, giving the MRP party leadership a strong influence over French European and foreign policy.

Although Switzerland and Austria did not take part in the creation of the ECSC and the EEC for different reasons, the SKVP and the ÖVP initially played an important role in establishing transnational Christian democratic party contacts after 1945. As Urs Altermatt has shown, the electoral support for the confessional SKVP was characterised by an 'extraordinary

[4] Cf. Frank Bösch, *Die Adenauer-CDU. Gründung, Aufstieg und Krise einer Erfolgspartei 1945–1969* (Stuttgart, Munich: DVA, 2001); Hans-Otto Kleinmann, *Geschichte der CDU 1945–1982* (Stuttgart: DVA, 1993).

[5] McMillan, 'France', 60; see also Pierre Letamendia, *Le Mouvement Républicain Populaire. Histoire d'un grand parti français* (Paris: Beauchesne, 1995).

[6] Émile-François Callot, *Le Mouvement Républicain Populaire. Origine, structure, doctrine, programme et action politique* (Paris: Marcel Rivière, 1978), 248.

stability'.[7] Similar to the Catholic KVP in the Netherlands, it continued to integrate a large majority of Swiss Catholics, winning 21.2 per cent of the vote in 1947. It achieved its best postwar result with 23.4 per cent in 1963. In occupied Austria, finally, the centre-right ÖVP performed better than the socialists in all national elections until 1970 and formed a grand coalition with them until 1966, when it succeeded in establishing a single party government for four years.[8]

This phenomenal success was a crucial precondition for the translation of Christian democratic ideas and policies for 'Europe' into effective coordination and decision-making at the party and governmental level. It came about partly by default. The continental European socialist parties remained largely confined to the class ghetto. Despite attempts to imitate the British socialists, they failed to attract middle-class and rural voters to the extent the Labour Party achieved in 1945.[9] The internal structures, programmes and electoral strategies of some socialist parties were so engrained in a traditional class-based politics that they did not even make a sustained attempt to win over voters from traditionally non-socialist sections of society. Although it supported parliamentary democracy and moderate state interventionism in the economy, it was not until the party congress at Bad Godesberg in 1959 that the German SPD abandoned its antiquated Marxist programme. The Italian socialists put off Catholic middle-class and rural voters with their plans for the introduction of a state economy and their Popular Front-type collaboration with the much stronger communists. In 1947–8, the party's right wing under the leadership of Giuseppe Saragat split off and began to cooperate with the DC. Even in the Netherlands, where the reformed Partij van der Arbeid (PvdA) more closely resembled the British Labour Party, the social democrats failed to make the substantial inroads into the Catholic vote that the KVP and the Catholic Church hierarchy originally feared. At the same time, the Christian democrats profited from the continued decline of liberal parties. Their societal basis had been further eroded by the economic crisis of the 1930s and World War II. Moreover, their political credo of

---

[7] Urs Altermatt, 'Die Christlichdemokratische Volkspartei der Schweiz 1945–1999', in Hans-Joachim Veen (ed.), *Christlich-demokratische und konservative Parteien in Westeuropa*, vol. V (Paderborn: Schöningh, 2000), 47.

[8] Cf. Robert Kriechbaumer (ed.), *Anspruch und Realität: zur Geschichte der ÖVP seit 1945* (Vienna, Cologne, Weimar: Böhlau, 1995).

[9] For a comparative overview see Sassoon, *One Hundred Years*. On the important role of the Labour Party for continental socialism immediately after 1945 see also William I. Hitchcock, *The Struggle for Europe. A History of the Continent since 1945* (London: Profile Books, 2003), chapter 2.

individual freedom and economic liberalisation was ill-suited to the more collectivist climate of national reconstruction shortly after 1945.

That the Christian democrats were so successful in warding off the socialist challenge was due in large measure to the extreme domestic polarising impact of communism on the postwar political landscape. Communist parties performed strongly in the first elections. Until 1947, they were included in national unity governments in France, Italy, Belgium and Luxembourg. Even in the Netherlands, the communists received 10.6 per cent of the vote in 1946. In Italy, they became the main challengers of the DC, culminating in the apparent threat of a communist coup in 1948. In France, the communists marginally replaced the MRP as the strongest single party in the national elections of November 1946, supporting the violent labour unrest in the winter of 1947–8. Although the western German communists only just managed to gain representation in the first Bundestag, the forced merger with the SPD in the Soviet zone in 1946 and the progressive introduction of a Soviet-type regime there deterred voters in the West also from democratic left-wing political experiments. Against this background, and in the absence of electoral competition from the discredited nationalist, clerical or fascist Right, the Christian democrats with their traditional strong anti-communism appeared to be the only safe haven for middle-class and rural voters as well as confessionally oriented workers. The DC rallied Catholics against the alleged threat of a communist coup. The MRP under Prime Minister Schuman upheld government policies and state control in the face of protests from the communist unions in 1947–8. In western Germany, Adenauer established the CDU/CSU as the forward defence against the forces of what he repeatedly called 'Asia on the river Elbe'. By the time the Cold War reached its height in 1948–9, all Christian democratic parties had effectively given up the idea of Europe as a 'third force' positioned between the superpowers. Instead, they strongly advocated cooperation with the United States in Western integration as the only credible foreign policy response to the Soviet threat. Without Stalin's assistance, it would have been much more difficult for the Christian democrats to establish political hegemony over the extended continental western core Europe after World War II.

The Christian democrats not only succeeded in the early Cold War at sharpening the ideological conflict; the parties were also intrinsically more attractive to a larger electorate than their Catholic predecessors in interwar Europe. Their success cannot be attributed solely to the favourable structural circumstances of the incipient Cold War. Recently, Martin Conway has made a powerful argument for a high degree of continuity in political

Catholicism from 1918 through to the mid-1960s. According to him, it was only in the transition years of the 1960s, when the Christian democratic parties experienced structural problems and electoral decline, that the Second Vatican Council of 1962–5 brought about more profound change including a more sincere and complete acceptance of democracy, pluralism and societal change. In contrast, Catholic resistance during World War II was an ephemeral phenomenon without significant effect on the internal constitution of political Catholicism and the religious and political attitudes of the Catholic masses during the first twenty years after the war. According to Conway, European Catholicism remained essentially 'intransigent, hierarchical, and dismissive of the values of other denominations and political traditions'.[10] It retained its 'fortress mentality' until the death of Pope Pius XII in 1958 and beyond.

Other recent research appears to corroborate Conway's heavy emphasis on the stability in political Catholicism across World War II. In her analysis of the political beliefs of those western German Catholic cultural elites that were not compromised by support for national socialism, Doris Brelie-Lewien has found a 'great continuity' from the 1920s through to the postwar period concerning their existential fears of bolshevism, their continued cultural ambivalence, if not outright hostility towards the societal model of the United States, and conceptions of a Catholic-inspired 'Abendland' as a superior Christian cultural space, for example.[11] This emphasis on continuity in political Catholicism is part of a larger historiographical trend to debunk the postwar foundation myth of the end of the war as a 'break' and a 'new beginning' in western European history. The continuity thesis has tended to obscure the significant changes that did occur in the first two decades after the war, however. This also applies to Christian democratic party politics, especially at the elite level, which is where transnational contacts mainly occurred and the policy of European integration was devised and implemented. Arguably, it was precisely the attempted reconciliation of tradition and innovation which allowed the Christian democrats to be so successful in elections after 1945: the

---

[10] Martin Conway, 'The Age of Christian Democracy. The Frontiers of Success and Failure', in Thomas Kselman and Joseph A. Buttigieg (eds.), *European Christian Democracy. Historical Legacies and Comparative Perspectives* (Notre Dame, Ind.: University of Notre Dame Press, 2003), 47.

[11] Doris von der Brelie-Lewien, 'Abendland und Sozialismus. Zur Kontinuität politisch-kultureller Denkhaltungen im Katholizismus von der Weimarer Republik zur frühen Nachkriegszeit', in Detlef Lehnert and Klaus Megerle (eds.), *Politische Teilkulturen zwischen Integration und Polarisierung. Zur politischen Kultur der Weimarer Republik* (Opladen: Westdeutscher Verlag, 1990), 196. See also Axel Schildt, *Zwischen Abendland und Amerika. Studien zur westdeutschen Ideenlandschaft der 50er Jahre* (Munich: Oldenbourg, 1999).

promise of continuity of many core Catholic values, beliefs and preferences combined with new economic opportunities, more effective, but relatively non-intrusive government and new welfare state policies in a pacified western Europe.

The continuity thesis has yielded important insights into European Catholicism from the 1920s to the 1960s. It is true, for example, that the Pope's support for democracy in his Christmas message of 1944 was still more motivated by his extreme anti-communism than anything else.[12] Moreover, large sections of the Christian democratic electorate were initially not fully reconciled to parliamentary democracy after 1945. In the absence of an organised Catholic Right, many former supporters of clerical and fascist regimes as well as collaborators with the German occupation voted for the Christian democrats. With some justification the French communists alleged, for example, that the MRP – whatever the personal background of its leaders in the national resistance or the Free French government – was effectively the party of former Vichy supporters. The German CDU/CSU offered many former Catholic as well as Protestant sympathisers with Hitler's dictatorship a new political home. They included Hans Globke, a close adviser to Adenauer in the Federal Chancellery and former legal commentator of the Nuremberg Race Laws of 1935, and Kurt-Georg Kiesinger, a NSDAP member during 1933–45, minister-president of Baden-Württemberg during 1958–66 and then chancellor until 1969.[13] The Christian democrats' deliberately inclusive electoral appeal was not just motivated by opportunistic seeking of votes, although it was that in part. It also has to be seen in the light of the Catholic conception of reconciliation and judgement of individual sin by God, not humans. Thus, the Christian democratic parties succeeded in integrating members and voters with very different, even diametrically opposed experiences and prior political beliefs and behaviour. In this way, they contributed to the societal stability of postwar western Europe before the consensus about priority for national and European reconstruction eroded, giving way to a more open climate of much greater public contestation of the past from the 1960s.

---

[12] For the origins of his apocalyptic fear of bolshevism and for his initially friendly attitude towards the National Socialists in Germany see also Gerhard Besier and Francesca Piombo, *Der Heilige Stuhl und Hitler-Deutschland: die Faszination des Totalitären* (Munich: DVA, 2004). In relation to the postwar period, see also R. E. M. Irving, *The Christian Democratic Parties of Western Europe* (London: George Allen & Unwin, 1979), 239.

[13] On Kiesinger – but without reference to his role in transnational Christian democratic party cooperation – see in greater detail Philipp Gassert, *Kurt Georg Kiesinger 1904–1988. Kanzler zwischen den Zeiten* (Munich: DVA, 2006).

Crucially, however, the Christian democratic party leaderships were fully committed to parliamentary democracy after 1945. The party elites in core Europe no longer contemplated alternatives to it. This was of paramount importance both for their transnational party cooperation and for European integration. After their isolation from the violent destruction of old Europe during the war, some Swiss Catholics initially believed in business as usual after 1945. Reporting back to SKVP secretary-general Martin Rosenberg from a discussion with DC representatives in October 1946 about a possible first meeting of European Christian democrats, prelate Josef Meier from the Catholic *Volksverein* expressed his astonishment that the Italians 'stated categorically that they were strictly opposed to the participation of any delegates from Franco's Spain. They insisted that democracy was the sole political system compatible with Christian beliefs.' He added that 'we were surprised by this exclusive valuation of the democratic system'.[14] Unlike in the interwar SIPDIC, the Christian democrats no longer tolerated non-democratic political Catholicism in their transnational cooperation, however, nor was the full membership in the ECSC and EEC of authoritarian states like Spain ever seriously advocated by Christian democrats from core Europe. While they mostly saw economic and political cooperation with Spain under Franco and Portugal under Salazar as essential in the confrontation with the Soviet Union during the Cold War, the Christian democratic parties nonetheless were to include persecuted exiles from these countries as from communist eastern Europe in their transnational organisations after 1945.

At the same time – and not surprisingly in view of the long tradition of corporatist concepts in Catholic political thought – the parliamentary democracy of the Christian democratic elites was not that of the competitive liberal Anglo-American model. Instead, they emphasised the role of natural communities, subsidiarity to protect these communities from excessive state intrusion and consociational relations to structure society as well as the parties themselves. In the Low Countries, the Christian democrats continued to protect societal pillarisation against socialist projects for centralisation. In the Netherlands, the KVP was behind the 1950 law for the public regulation of company statues and the introduction of a tripartite Social-Economic Council with representatives from employers, unions and the state to coordinate economic policy making with the aim of harmonising social group interests.[15] In Austria, the ÖVP invented the system

[14] Meier to Rosenberg, 29 October 1946, BAR, CVP-Archiv JII.181, 2659.
[15] Bosmans, 'The Primacy', 59.

of social partnership of state-funded institutionalised representation of social group interests with a major influence on governmental decision-making of the grand coalition.[16] Even in Germany, where direct state intervention to structure societal relations remained limited, the policies of the CDU/CSU as an emerging people's party were directed at harmonising conflicting societal interests through welfare state policies. They included agricultural subsidies and extended social security benefits, especially increased pension rights. The prevailing ideology of social compromise and societal harmony was mirrored in the complex internal organisation of Christian democratic parties. In the extreme case of Austria, ÖVP membership could only be obtained through association with one of its so-called Bünde representing farmers or civil servants, for example.[17] Other parties institutionalised the internal representation of the interests of Christian workers, young members, women and other social groups to channel their demands for policy change or representation in the party leadership and government, whereas the Italian DC operated the more informal *corrente* system.

These consociational patterns of intra-party and national decision-making were mainly geared towards interest mediation and harmonisation, facilitating compromise between different social groups and also across party divides. They did not aim at transparent antagonistic democratic competition within a more fully pluralistic society. Christian democratic policy was primarily oriented towards achieving an electorally attractive 'output'. In the political lyric of the Christian democratic German Chancellor Helmut Kohl, 'what matters is what comes out at the back'.[18] Importantly, these were also going to be essential characteristics of the Christian democratic approach to integrating western Europe through common welfare state policies developed and administered by a complex consociational semi-supranational institutional system with formal and more informal input from social groups, especially employers and unions – not, however, with the aim to 'rescue the nation-state', as Alan S. Milward has claimed.[19] Instead, the Christian democrats transposed domestic experiences and preferences to the European level with the overriding political aims of strengthening Europe's competitiveness, guaranteeing peace within western Europe and securing a more independent role for it in the joint struggle with the United States against the Soviet Union.

---

[16] Cf. Dieter A. Binder, '"Rescuing the Christian Occident" and "Europe in Us": The People's Party in Austria', in: Gehler and Kaiser (eds.), *Christian Democracy*, 139–54.
[17] Ibid., 140. [18] Quoted in *Der Spiegel*, 3 September 1984. [19] Milward, *The European Rescue*.

Appropriately, the consociational patterns of governance were combined with a deliberately conservative, dull form of political representation and decision-making by 'indistinguishable "men in suits"'[20] – the precise opposite of the flamboyant dictatorial style of the likes of Hitler and Mussolini. The more dull it was, the more reassuring it was, shortly after World War II, however. This was true not only of national reconstruction, but also of the strategy of Christian democratic leaders like Adenauer, Schuman and De Gasperi of boring core Europe into supranational integration, to parody Barbara Castle's later judgement of the half-hearted attempt by Harold Wilson, the Labour prime minister, to apply for British EEC membership in 1967. For the Christian democratic elites, creating an integrated core Europe did not promise the dawn of a new millennium. Rather, it seemed the only sensible politics of what Max Weber once described as the continuous drilling of thick boards, using the tools of transnational cooperation and reconciliation.

In terms of their internal structures and political behaviour, the Christian democratic parties after 1945 differed from their Catholic predecessors also in another important respect. Some were mass membership parties. The Belgian CVP/PSC managed to organise approximately 10 per cent of its voters.[21] The Italian DC had a similarly high organisational density. The ÖVP even achieved an indirect mass membership through its *Bünde* of 30 per cent of its voters. Other Christian democratic parties initially had low membership figures, such as the German CDU/CSU and the MRP. Compared to the interwar Centre Party and the PDP, however, they were characterised by much greater organisational cohesion and in some ways the most modern and effective campaigning – something the secretary-generals of the Christian democratic parties began to discuss between 1953 and 1954 with the aim of facilitating the exchange of experiences and the transfer of campaigning strategies and methods. Importantly for their transnational cooperation, moreover, all parties – especially the CDU/CSU and the MRP – had highly centralised informal decision-making structures with a prominent role for leaders like Adenauer and Bidault. Unlike in interwar Europe, these leaders also exercised a strong influence on national European policy-making, which in turn was crucial for coordinating party contacts with intergovernmental initiatives and negotiations.

---

[20] Martin Conway, 'The Rise and Fall of Western Europe's Democratic Age 1945–1973', *Contemporary European History* 13 (2004), 71.

[21] Paul Lucardie, 'From Family Father to DJ: Christian Democratic Parties and Civil Society in Western Europe', in Lamberts (ed.), *Christian Democracy*, 211.

The Christian democratic party elites were not only fully reconciled to parliamentary democracy and, compared to interwar Europe, more capable of operating effectively in this institutional environment; they also succeeded in creating a moderately more secular, non-confessional or inter-confessional party image to broaden their electoral basis without alienating traditional voters from the Catholic milieu. Their support remained crucial for the Christian democrats' electoral success. In the French elections of 1946, 75 per cent of practising Catholics voted MRP. By the early 1950s, this figure was still 54 per cent despite strong additional competition from the Gaullists for the Catholic vote.[22] In Germany, some 60 per cent of all Catholics voted CDU/CSU until the late 1960s.[23] This degree of Catholic mobilisation was actually significantly higher than what the confessional Centre Party managed during the Weimar Republic. In Italy, Catholic Action played an important role in the mobilisation of Catholic voters for the DC.[24] Everywhere in the extended core Europe, moreover, Catholic priests still advised their flock to vote for 'Christian' parties. Not surprisingly, therefore, competing socialist and liberal parties continued to attack the Christian democrats as confessional Catholic parties in disguise. At the start of the Adenauer era in Germany, the Lutheran pastor Martin Niemöller, who had been interned in a concentration camp by the National Socialists, denounced the newly created Federal Republic as a 'Catholic state ... begotten in the Vatican and born in Washington'.[25] Even within the CDU/CSU, Protestants were very concerned about the overrepresentation of Catholics in the leadership and among its members and voters. Frank Bösch has demonstrated how much time the party leadership, especially Adenauer, spent in the first decade after the war, refuting the allegation that the CDU/CSU was inter-confessional in name only, producing elaborate statistics about intra-party confessional representation and intervening at the regional level with a view to increasing the number of Protestants in leading positions.[26]

While Catholic confessional support remained crucial for all Christian democratic parties, however, the party elites' politics, and not just their rhetoric, became more secular in a number of ways after the war. Importantly, clerics no longer played a role in Christian democratic party politics as they had still done in interwar Europe. Christian democratic party leaders like Adenauer, De Gasperi and Bidault were typically middle-class liberal-conservative Catholics. The transformation from interwar to

---

[22] McMillan, 'France', 67.　　[23] Lönne, 'Germany', 184.　　[24] Pollard, 'Italy', 87.
[25] Quoted in Bösch, *Die Adenauer-CDU*, 109.　　[26] Ibid., chapter 3.

postwar Europe is particularly striking in the case of Germany. Whereas prelate Kaas, the Centre Party leader during 1928–33, was a nationalist right-wing cleric with close links to the Vatican, Adenauer was a liberal Rhenish Catholic. He insisted that his religious beliefs were part of his private life, not to be abused for legitimising his political ideas and strategy.[27] Moreover, direct intervention by the Church hierarchy in Christian democratic party politics was much less frequent after the war. This was in line with the expectations of party leaders. It also avoided compromising the parties in domestic and European politics. Even in Italy, where the Vatican initially worked hard to strengthen the Catholic Right within the DC to prevent what later came to be known as the 'opening to the Left' in terms of both its party programme and coalition options,[28] the Church refrained more and more from direct political interventions after the death of Pius XII in 1958.[29]

Although the Christian democratic parties continued to defend Catholic interests in residual culture war issues like divorce in Italy and public funding of Catholic schools in Belgium, they were largely overshadowed by questions which had no clear-cut confessional connotations, especially national reconstruction, new welfare policies and European cooperation. Against this background, the choice of party names like MRP and ÖVP without any confessional content or, alternatively, the replacement of the traditional 'Catholic' with 'Christian' as in CVP/PSC reflected the intention of opening the parties up towards broader sections of society and transforming them into what political scientists have called people's or catch-all parties. True, the social reality of Christian democratic politics did not fully match the rhetoric of de-confessionalisation. From the perspective of 1945, however, the success of some of these parties in broadening their appeal was actually spectacular. Whereas the PPI had only won some 20 per cent of the vote after World War I, the DC did become the Italian *partito nazionale*, as De Gasperi demanded at the party congress in 1947.[30] Despite the legacy of confessional conflict and Bismarck's *Kulturkampf*, the CDU/CSU was in fact very successful in the long term at integrating Protestant liberals and conservatives into a more broadly

---

[27] Anselm Doering-Manteuffel, 'Rheinischer Katholik im Kalten Krieg. Das "christliche Europa" in der Weltsicht Konrad Adenauers', in Martin Greschat and Wilfried Loth (eds.), *Die Christen und die Entstehung der Europäischen Gemeinschaft* (Stuttgart: Kohlhammer, 1994), 237.

[28] On the 'opening to the Left' see in greater detail Manlio Di Lalla, *Storia della Democrazia Cristiana*, vol. II (Turin: Marietti, 1981).

[29] Cf. Carlo Masala, 'Born for Government: The Democrazia Cristiana in Italy', in Gehler and Kaiser (eds.), *Christian Democracy*, 101–17.

[30] Cited in ibid., 105.

based centre-right party and giving them access to leading positions within the party. This was the case with Ludwig Erhard, economics minister 1949–63 and chancellor 1963–6, and Gerhard Schröder, foreign minister 1961–6, who was also president of the Evangelischer Arbeitskreis, the institutionalised committee of Protestants within the CDU/CSU, 1955–78.

The moderate de-confessionalisation of the early postwar years was significant not only for national politics, but also for European integration. It allowed the parties to occupy a role in the centre or centre-right of national politics with different coalition options. These included the socialists and social democrats in countries such as France and the Netherlands. This in turn was a crucial precondition for constructing larger domestic and transnational coalitions for Christian democratic policies for 'Europe'. The horror scenario of a 'Vatican Europe' run by the Pope drew upon and utilised deeply engrained collective fears of organised Catholicism going back to the culture wars and beyond, to the French Revolution and the reformation. This scenario appeared more and more antiquated and had much less appeal in the changing circumstances of postwar Europe, however, especially as the Vatican strictly stayed out of Christian democratic policy-making on Europe.

A factor that also strengthened the electoral appeal of the Christian democrats after World War II was their conversion to moderate welfare state interventionism. Their socio-economic political programme responded to the growing expectations of many citizens in relation to the state's managerial and redistributional capabilities. Parodying the words of John F. Kennedy, Martin Conway has emphasised that, after World War II, many citizens 'tended to ask not what they could do for their rulers, but what their rulers could do for them'.[31] The strongly left-wing Christian socialist orientation of the early postwar party programmes reflected this trend. Jean-Marie Mayeur has characterised the MRP's socio-economic policy orientation after 1945 as the dream of 'travaillisme': the creation of a French Labour Party with a strong Christian identity.[32] Bidault himself described the MRP's strategy as governing 'in the centre with right-wing methods to attain left-wing ends'.[33] Despite the party's strong middle-class and rural voter base, its socio-economic policies were sufficiently left-wing to prevent the successful integration of more liberal-conservative voters

---

[31] Conway, 'The Rise and Fall', 76.
[32] Jean-Marie Mayeur, 'La Démocratie d'inspiration chrétienne en France', in Lamberts (ed.), *Christian Democracy*, 92.
[33] Quoted in Russell B. Capelle, *The MRP and French Foreign Policy* (New York: Frederick A. Praeger, 1963), 106.

within an ideologically more broadly based people's party, as in the case of the CDU/CSU, for example.

Similarly, other parties also went through what Anton Pelinka has called – in relation to the Austrian ÖVP – the 'French phase' of postwar Christian democracy.[34] Thus, the 1947 *Ahlener Programm* of the CDU in the British zone of occupation was a detailed critique of 'unlimited domination of private capitalism', advocating a 'third way' combining the nationalisation of the coal and steel industries with other ideas for greater state intervention in the economy.[35] The refounded Centre Party competed with the CDU/CSU on the Left with an even more explicitly Christian socialist programme. Its leader during 1948–9, Spiecker, told Adenauer in March 1946 that he wanted to establish the party as a political 'force of the centre' reaching from the right wing of the SPD to the left wing of the CDU.[36] In the electoral campaign in 1945, the ÖVP actually called itself 'Austria's Labour Party' in an attempt to discredit the SPÖ as an unreformed Marxist party.[37] In Luxembourg, as Michael Schroen has pointed out, the renaming of the interwar Rechtspartei as the Christian Social People's Party was intended to symbolise the conversion to welfare state ideas and principles and to appeal to the party's working-class supporters in the industrial South.[38] In Belgium, the left-Catholic Union Démocratique Belge, which developed out of the Resistance with the aim of overcoming the traditional Catholic confessional orientation, only obtained 2.2 per cent of the vote in the elections in February 1946.[39] It nevertheless induced the CVP/PSC to strengthen its own social policy profile as a centrist party on socio-economic policy issues – between the socialists and liberals. In Italy, finally, the *linea Einaudi* combined a more conservative fiscal and economic policy with the creation in 1950 of the Cassa per il Mezzogiorno, a well-funded body with the strategic objective of promoting the development of southern Italy. The more left-wing 'French phase' of Christian democracy was also reflected in the choice of socio-economic issues as the theme for the first conference of the Nouvelles Équipes Internationales

---

[34] Binder, '"Rescuing the Christian Occident"', 140.
[35] Cf. Lönne, 'Germany', 182. See in greater detail Rudolf Uertz, *Christentum und Sozialismus in der frühen CDU. Grundlage und Wirkungen der christlich-sozialen Ideen 1945–1949* (Stuttgart: DVA, 1981).
[36] *Adenauer. Briefe 1945–1947* (Berlin: Siedler, 1983), 200. Cf. Also Horstwalter Heitzer, *Die CDU in der britischen Zone 1945–1949. Gründung, Organisation, Programm und Politik* (Düsseldorf: Droste, 1988), 643–9.
[37] Binder, '"Rescuing the Christian Occident"', 139–40.
[38] Michael Schroen, 'Die Christlich-Soziale Volkspartei Luxemburgs (CSV)', in Veen (ed.), *Christlich-demokratische und konservative Parteien*, 346.
[39] See Conway, 'Belgium', 207–8.

(NEI) in Liège in May 1947 with all reports characterised by strongly interventionist overtures.[40]

The Christian socialist rhetoric soon gave way to more traditional market-oriented economic policy making with limited state interventionism and moderate social reforms. The shift was especially marked in the case of the German CDU, whose new *Düsseldorfer Leitsätze* – under the strong influence of Erhard – developed the idea of the 'social market economy' with strong liberal connotations and limited state interventionism. Similarly, the ÖVP entered what Kurt Skalnik has called the second, 'German', phase of its policy development after the war.[41] The other Christian democratic parties in core Europe retained a more centrist position on socio-economic policy issues. In part, the toning down of Christian socialist demands reflected the widely felt need to delineate the Christian democratic approach from socialism and to offer a more strongly anti-communist alternative in the Cold War confrontation with communist parties and the Soviet Union. It also reflected the decreased intra-party influence of Christian trade unions, however. The MRP links with the CFTC/CFDT were close, but not exclusive. In western Germany – as in Austria – unified trade unions were created after 1945, which reduced the organisational cohesion and influence of left-Catholicism within the much more broadly based CDU/CSU compared to the interwar Centre Party.

Nonetheless, the Christian democrats' search for a 'third way' in economic and social policy between capitalism and socialism continued. It was reflected in their transnational debates as well as in their policies for European integration at a time when they had long since given up the idea of Europe as a 'third force' in world politics. The divergences between more market-oriented and more interventionist socio-economic orientations remained a cause for strife within the national parties and also in their transnational cooperation. They were to play a major role in the 1970s in the hotly contested debate about the possible extension of party cooperation to include traditional conservative parties – in particular the British Tories – as advocated by the CDU/CSU. Despite these internal fault-lines, however, all Christian democratic parties were united in their support for a mixed economy and their opposition to socialist centralisation. Their

---

[40] NEI, Conférence Internationale de Liège mai 1947, Editions du Centre International de Documentation Politique 1947, Katholiek Documentatie- en Oderzoeckscentrum (henceforth: KADOC), Archief August E. de Schryver, 7.2.4.1. See also Procès-verbal de la Conférence politique internationale de Lucerne, 27.2.–2.3.1947, SKVP, Generalsekretariat, Bern, 22 March 1947, BAR, CVP-Archiv JII.181, 2372.

[41] Cited in Binder, '"Rescuing the Christian Occident"', 141.

promise of new economic opportunities and greater welfare benefits at a time of economic expansion in the 1950s, combined with limited state intrusion in the prevailing postwar climate of a retreat into the private sphere, proved electorally successful. It also had major repercussions for their European policies.

The Christian democratic parties in the extended core Europe not only managed to establish political hegemony after 1945, the conditions for their transnational cooperation were also much more propitious than in inter-war Europe. This concerned, first of all, the structural changes in the international system. The Cold War created a clear ideological battle-ground which fostered transnational Christian democratic solidarity and cohesion in the face of bolshevism as the common enemy. The division of Germany and of Europe, moreover, externalised those east-central European national conflicts and border issues which had overshadowed all SIPDIC activities. For the German Christian democrats, the trans-national party contacts would not have been a suitable vehicle for territorial demands. Unlike Joos in SIPDIC, Adenauer never even raised the topic in his transnational contacts. When others from his own party like Jacob Kaiser did, Adenauer used the opportunity to discredit and exclude them from all European forums. At the same time, in the absence of political parties from east-central Europe, the French representatives no longer had the choice of extending the Little Entente mentality to their transnational contacts, of isolating Germany through a peripheral alliance against it. At the end of the war, the position of France in European and international relations had changed almost as profoundly as that of the now divided Germany. Contrary to what the French deputy Jean Fabry had predicted in 1924, both countries were now weak – a fundamental precondition for a new French approach to the 'German problem'.

Moreover, the exclusion of any political parties from east-central Europe as a result of the Cold War also marginalised Catholic traditions which on the whole were more influenced by, and attached to, nationalism and authoritarian concepts. The participation of Catholic exiles without a political mandate was an ephemeral phenomenon of Christian demo-cratic contacts in postwar core Europe compared to the role of Catholics from east-central Europe during the 1930s. Finally, World War II and the Cold War also reduced former reservations about fuller involvement in transnational contacts. Dutch membership of the North Atlantic Treaty Organisation (NATO) founded in 1949 allowed the KVP to play a much greater role in party cooperation. The Swiss Catholics, who even refused to hold a SIPDIC congress for fear of compromising Swiss neutrality, actually played a leading role in bringing together Christian democrats from core Europe after 1945.

Other important structural changes occurred after World War II in the form of much stronger institutional incentives for closer party cooperation. The first set of incentives resulted from the changed role of the Christian democratic parties as natural parties of government. Their new political hegemony in the extended core Europe encouraged closer transnational party cooperation to give their foreign and European policies in government and intergovernmental relations a sense of purpose and direction. Although the Centre Party was already a natural party of government in the Weimar Republic, it never developed a distinct foreign policy nor did it – as a party – exercise any influence over German foreign policy, which was still largely controlled by a small nationalist foreign policy-making elite. The PDP was a minor force in some coalition governments, but without any influence over French foreign policy. The situation in 1945–9 was fundamentally different. The CDU/CSU – and especially Adenauer – dominated German foreign and European policy after the creation of the Federal Republic, and the MRP as a leading party in French centrist and centre-right coalition governments controlled the foreign ministry during 1945–53. For the Christian democrats in core Europe the early postwar years provided a window of opportunity for the first time to develop and implement – with cross-party support where necessary – their own concept for European cooperation and integration.

A second set of institutional incentives derived from the incipient process of European institutionalisation. Initially, this process did not result in supranational decision-making, but it facilitated additional transnational contacts and brought about opportunities to develop new political initiatives together. Although the geographically larger Council of Europe created in 1949 did not lead to deeper economic or political integration, as many hoped, the debates of its Consultative Assembly became an important forum for transnational exchanges and allowed political parties to practise informal transnational organisation and cooperation. Membership in the Consultative Assembly and Christian democratic party links overlapped to a great extent. For example, all eight Assembly members from the MRP participated regularly in transnational party activities.[42] The same was even more true of the Common Assembly of the ECSC from 1952. For example, Heinrich von Brentano, the leader of the CDU/CSU

---

[42] Robert Bichet, *La Démocratie chrétienne en France. Le Mouvement Républicain Populaire* (Besançon: Jacques et Demontrond 1980), 305.

parliamentary party in the Bundestag, and Pierre-Henri Teitgen, at that time MRP party leader, played a crucial role in devising the constitution for the European Political Community (EPC) in the ECSC's Ad hoc Assembly in 1953. They were already very well acquainted with each other through their transnational party contacts in the NEI and the Geneva Circle since 1948 and in the two parliamentary assemblies.

A further structural change facilitating closer transnational party coop-eration occurred in the form of the Vatican's changed attitude to the Christian democratic parties as well as their transnational cooperation and European policies after 1945. In October 1946 the Swiss SKVP initially suggested that the Vatican might want to send an observer to the first meeting of European Christian democrats. A close advisor to the Pope, Giovanni Battista Montini – the future Pope Paul VI – rejected the idea, however.[43] According to him, Pope Pius XII supported international meetings of Christian politicians with a view to opposing the emerging 'communist front'. Whereas Sturzo had to develop his interwar initiative as an outcast and against the clear Vatican preference to keep an entirely free hand in its domestic Italian and foreign policy, this new moral support from the Church hierarchy gave added legitimacy to transnational party cooperation. At the same time, however, the Vatican never attempted to influence transnational political consultations. Montini already insisted that the Pope would not even intervene in transnational Christian demo-cratic policy-making 'if they took decisions which were not in line with the preferences of the Church'. If the Vatican were to send an observer, it could lead to 'misunderstandings' and would be used by 'the enemies of the Church' to discredit Christian democratic political action.[44] Subsequently, Pius XII's only intervention in Christian democratic cooperation was to grant the participants of the NEI congress in Arezzo in 1957 an audience – something that could hardly frighten the 'enemies of the Church' even at a time when sports champions and pop stars were not yet received by the Pope.

Even if the Christian democratic parties were not as non-confessional or inter-confessional as they claimed, their transnational cooperation and European policy-making was fully secular. Broad Church support for core Europe integration helped to legitimise the policy of Franco-German reconciliation in particular. In June 1950, the French cardinals

---

[43] Rosenberg to Meier, 11 October 1946; Meier to Rosenberg, 29 October 1946, BAR, CVP-Archiv JII.181, 2659.
[44] Ibid.

and bishops called upon all Catholics to interest themselves in, and work for, European integration.[45] For the pious Catholic Schuman, Church support for his policies was definitely reassuring.[46] Bidault – a Gallican Catholic in favour of national autonomy from Rome within a more federal Church –[47] nevertheless argued in the Geneva Circle that 'the positive reception of the European idea by the Vatican should encourage Christian civilisation'.[48] Philippe Chenaux has suggested that Pius XII's general support for core Europe integration also helped to rally German Catholics behind Adenauer's effective preference for European integration over German unification.[49] The origins of the Christian democratic policies for core Europe integration were not in the Vatican, however. Pius XII only called upon the 'great nations of the continent' to form a 'larger political association' in February 1948, after the shock of the imprisonment of the Hungarian cardinal József Mindszenty.[50] Thereafter, he supported the creation of a core Europe without Britain. Otherwise, however, his idea of Europe and Christian democratic preferences differed fundamentally. Unlike the Christian democratic parties, Pius XII was still more interested in the defence of Catholicism than of democracy. He would have preferred the full participation of Catholic Spain under Franco in a continental European political arrangement. Moreover, the Pope had a much more conservative spiritual concept of Europe. He certainly had no sympathy for the chosen policy instruments of market liberalisation and supranational technocratic institutions. Accordingly, even the left-Catholic French Senator Léo Hamon – the most prominent of the few internal critics of the federalist MRP party line, who voted against the European Defence Community (EDC) Treaty in 1954 and was subsequently expelled from the party – has argued that the Christian democrats perhaps constructed a 'Lotharingian Europe', but certainly not a 'Vatican Europe', after 1945.[51]

The Catholic Church mattered for Christian democratic party cooperation in a more general sense, however, as an agency for the transnational

---

[45] Capelle, *The MRP*, 37.
[46] Cf. Grégoire Eldin *et al.*, *L'Europe de Robert Schuman* (Paris: Presses de l'Université de Paris-Sorbonne, 2001), 28.
[47] Capelle, *The MRP*, 18.
[48] Geneva Circle, 22 December 1948, Archives Nationales (henceforth: AN) 519, AP 10.
[49] Philippe Chenaux, 'Der Vatikan und die Entstehung der Europäischen Gemeinschaft', in Greschat and Loth (eds.), *Die Christen*, 97–124.
[50] Ibid., 104–12.
[51] Cited in Jean-Claude Delbreil, 'Le MRP et la construction européenne: résultats, interprétation et conclusion d'une enquête écrite et orale', in Serge Berstein, Jean-Marie Mayeur and Pierre Milza (eds.), *Le MRP et la construction européenne* (Paris: Editions Complexe, 1993), 359.

socialisation of future politicians. The French senator during 1946–8 and 1952–96, interim President in 1969 and 1974 and leader of the Christian democratic (CD) Group in the EP during 1958–66 Alain Poher, for example, has recalled in his memoirs that his participation in activities of Pax Romana in interwar Europe provided him with many transnational contacts especially with Germans, which made it easier for him to opt for a policy of reconciliation after 1945.[52] Jean-Claude Delbreil has found through a questionnaire and interviews with French eyewitnesses that many MRP politicians like Robert Bichet – NEI secretary-general from 1949–55 – and Philippe Farine, for example, were similarly influenced and motivated by transnational contacts through Church organisations.[53] These cross-border societal contacts were also strengthened by new secular initiatives, especially in the bilateral Franco-German context, which were no longer closely linked to the peace movement as had been the case in interwar Europe. For example, Poher and Pierre Pflimlin – *inter alia* mayor of Strasbourg 1959–83, minister of agriculture 1947–51, prime minister in 1958 and EP president 1984–87 – regularly took part in meetings of the Mont-Pèlerin Union of mayors from France and Germany. Other initiatives included the Comité d'Échanges avec l'Allemagne Nouvelle initiated by Alfred Grosser, a French journalist of German-Jewish origin, and the Deutsch-Französisches Institut in Ludwigsburg founded in 1948. These and other societal organisations played an important role in what Gesa Bluhm has called Franco-German (and European) 'Vertrauensarbeit'.[54] These networking activities to build trust across borders facilitated Christian democratic political initiatives. They helped to transform public opinion, which progressively became more positive about Franco-German reconciliation and European integration before this could bring any material benefits. They also allowed economic, political and cultural elites in the national societies of core Europe to develop a stake in the incipient integration progress.

In contrast, there was less overlap between some other important transnational networks in postwar western Europe and Christian democratic party cooperation. This is true, first of all, of the various European movements. The NEI gave no institutional support to the European Parliamentary Union created by the veteran of the European idea

[52] Cf. Alain Poher, *Trois fois président. Mémoires* (Paris: Plon, 1993), 33 and 43.
[53] Delbreil, 'Le MRP'; see also Capelle, *The MRP*, 37–8.
[54] Gesa Bluhm, 'Vertrauensarbeit. Deutsch-französische Beziehungen nach 1945', in Ute Frevert (ed.), *Vertrauen. Historische Annäherungen* (Göttingen: Vandenhoeck & Ruprecht, 2003), 386.

Coudenhove-Kalergi. His image was tainted by his close contact with Rudolf and Otto von Habsburg during his exile in the United States, when he toyed with the idea of a restoration of the Habsburg Empire. At the same time, the more left-wing Christian democrats – especially those from France – did not want the NEI to become associated with the work of the Ligue Européenne de Coopération Économique founded in 1946. This organisation was actually headed by a Belgian Christian democrat, the former prime minister in the 1930s and foreign minister during 1949–54, Paul Van Zeeland. For many Christian democrats from France, Italy and the Low Countries, however, this organisation was too exclusively focused on the primary goal of liberal market integration and too much under the influence of Americans in the State Department and the Ford Foundation who inspired and co-funded it.[55] While Coudenhove seemed too conservative and Van Zeeland too economically liberal to many western European Christian democrats, the Churchill-inspired United Europe Movement was both too British-influenced and – as a result – too intergovernmentalist in its approach to European cooperation. In April 1947, Albert Gortais, MRP deputy secretary-general, concluded that his party could only cooperate with the European Federalist Union under the leadership of the Dutch socialist and first rector of the College of Europe, Hendrik Brugmans, founded in December 1946.[56]

The different pro-European groups agreed to unite under the roof of the European Movement in 1947–8, with the NEI's formal representation as a member organisation. Nevertheless, the Christian democratic elites continued to regard the link as somewhat problematic. Leading Christian democrats attended the European Movement's congress at The Hague in May 1948. Some committed federalists like de Menthon actually invested significant resources in supporting the Movement. He submitted the first draft constitution for a 'United States of Europe' for the European Parliamentary Union in June 1948.[57] Yet most Christian democrats were fairly agnostic about the precise constitutional form of integration. They were under the impression that the European Movement was too

---

[55] Cf. Michel Dumoulin and Anne-Myriam Dutrieue, *La Ligue Européenne de Coopération Économique (1946–1981). Un groupe d'étude et de pression dans la construction européenne* (Bern: Lang, 1993).

[56] Nicole Bacharan-Gressel, 'Les Organisations et les associations pro-européennes', in Berstein, Mayeur and Milza (eds.), *Le MRP*, 42.

[57] Wilfried Loth, *Entwürfe einer Europäischen Verfassung. Eine historische Bilanz* (Bonn: Europa Union Verlag, 2002), 9. On de Menthon see also Laurent Ducerf, 'François de Menthon, un démocrate chrétien au service de l'Europe (1948–1958)', in *La Savoie dans l'Europe* (Moûtiers-Tarentaise: Mémoires et documents de l'Académie de la Val d'Isère, 2002), 295–316.

dominated by socialists and liberals who were using it for their ideological and political party purposes. In April 1949, for example, Bichet reported to the NEI executive committee that he failed to prevent the election of the two socialists Léon Jouhaux – founder of the Confédération Générale du Travail-Force Ouvrière trade union in 1947–8 – and André Philip as president and delegate general of the French section of the European Movement. Philip was 'a practising Protestant', Bichet hastened to add, which was at least better than an atheist socialist.[58] In January 1955, when they discussed the possible nomination of Schuman as the next president of the European Movement in the Geneva Circle, the Christian democrats were unified in their violent opposition to another potential French candidate, the Liberal Paul Ramadier. Bidault reactivated images from the nineteenth century culture wars denouncing Ramadier as 'a free mason who has voted for 15 years to abandon the French embassy to the Vatican'.[59] Otto Lenz pledged CDU/CSU support for Schuman, who was duly elected in June 1955, as the European Movement was clearly 'in danger of falling into the hands of the Liberals'.[60] The issue of cooperation with the European Movement only became less politicised as a result of Schuman's election, the greater socialisation of continental socialists and liberals into the Christian democratic-inspired core Europe consensus during the creation of the EEC, and the further institutionalisation and bureaucratisation of European policy-making.

Moreover, few points of contact existed between Christian democratic party networks and the growing transatlantic networks after 1945. Two structural factors largely account for this. The first is the traditionally ethnically circumscribed, conservative and extremely ultramontane character of American diaspora Catholicism. It was very marginal in the European-dominated global Catholic Church, and it had never contributed much intellectually to its evolution or internal reform. At the time of the First Vatican Council in 1870–1, for example, liberal European Catholics regarded North American Catholicism as closed and uninspiring and American bishops as mere voting sheep brought to Rome to rubber-stamp the centralising policies of Pope Pius IX. Major developments within the wider Catholic community since then – especially the evolution of social reform Catholicism – also owed nothing to the American

---

[58] NEI, Political Commission, 8 April 1949; Executive Committee, 9–10 April 1949, Institut für Zeitgeschichte (henceforth: IfZG Innsbruck), Karl Gruber Archiv, Karton 6.
[59] Geneva Circle, 31 January 1955, ACDP, 01-172-31.   [60] Ibid.

experience. When cultural transfers did take place, they were from Europe to the United States, not vice-versa. In short, nothing inspired European Christian democrats – as Catholics – to look to the United States for guidance in what might be coined the spiritual reconstruction of western Europe after 1945. The greater de-confessionalisation of the West German CDU/CSU and growing role of Protestant politicians like Kai-Uwe von Hassel in the Christian democratic party network, as well as the merger of the Dutch Catholic and Protestant parties, facilitated a certain cultural opening towards American politics and political culture, but only in the 1960s and 1970s – after the formative years of European integration – when the US model was fast losing its postwar attractiveness.

The second structural factor was the secular character of the American political parties. As a presidential political system and very heterogeneous federal state, the US did not even have a developed party system as in Europe, where political parties played a much greater role in policy formulation and decision-making. Not only was there no party with a substantial Catholic influence, let alone a Catholic or Christian democratic party in the US, but European Catholic refugees experienced the disparate political Catholicism that did exist as overwhelmingly conservative and philo-fascist during their time in exile. On the whole, European Christian democrats had little knowledge of, or cultural contacts with, the United States, and no organised contacts at the political party level. Crucially, their policies for European reconstruction were informed by European traditions and experience, not some kind of US 'model' of democracy, federalism or capitalist market economy.

At the same time, US assistance for Christian democratic parties was marginal, too. The Central Intelligence Agency (CIA) supported the DC in the crucial 1948 election campaign. As the German finance minister Fritz Schäffer complained in the Geneva Circle in February 1950, however, many American policy-makers took European Christian democrats for reactionary conservatives, preferring instead to support almost any group calling itself 'anti-fascist' and 'democratic'.[61] As Richard Aldrich, Volker Berghahn and Michael Hochgeschwender have shown, US funding channelled through the CIA, the American Committee for United Europe founded by Allen Dulles in 1948, the Ford Foundation, the Congress for Cultural Freedom and other cultural institutions was in fact heavily concentrated on the European Movement, democratic socialism and

---

[61] Geneva Circle, 13 February 1950, AN 457, AP 59.

left-liberals.[62] At the political party level, the US strongly supported reform-ist, 'pro-European' social democrats such as, for example, Giuseppe Saragat in Italy, whose group split off from the Socialist Party over the issue of cooperation with the communists. In Germany, support was targeted at reform-minded social democrats like Willy Brandt and Carlo Schmid. These moderate European social democrats in fact had much more in common with liberal American Democrats than Catholic Christian democrats. In contrast, the networking of Christian democrats within and across national borders was not US-funded. Rudolf Jungnickel – a journalist and aggressive opponent of Adenauer's policy of Western integration in the 1950s – has alleged – without any supportive evidence – that the CIA had links with the informal Geneva Circle.[63] It is clear, however, that its small secretariat in Geneva and the informal meetings were initially sponsored by Johann Jacob Kindt-Kiefer – a German refugee from national socialist Germany – and then with financial profits from a dubious allegedly charitable enterprise concerned with sending Swiss Care-type parcels to the western zones of occupation. The Quai d'Orsay, and possibly the French secret service, also appear to have supported the network financially, but not the CIA or other US institutions.

The internal structure of the Christian democratic network was also very different from the interwar SIPDIC cooperation. Few SIPDIC delegates, who were still politically active, played a role in the transnational network after 1945. Bidault used the cultural competence of Pezet, who feared that Germany would become 'a Soviet protectorate',[64] to prepare his initial contacts with German Christian democrats. Other SIPDIC activists still worked for Franco-German reconciliation and European cooperation, but outside of the party network. They included, from the German SIPDIC

---

[62] Cf. Richard Aldrich, *The Hidden Hand. Britain, America and the Cold War Intelligence* (London: John Murray, 2001); Volker Berghahn, *America and the Intellectual Cold Wars in Europe. Shepard Stone between Philanthropy, Academy, and Diplomacy* (Princeton, N.J.: Princeton University Press, 2002); Michael Hochgeschwender, *Freiheit in der Offensive? Der Kongreß für Kulturelle Freiheit und die Deutschen* (Munich: Oldenbourg, 1998). On the CIA's role in organising and funding the Congress for Cultural Freedom, whose activities were primarily directed at intellectuals, however, see also Frances Stonor Saunders, *Who Paid the Piper? The CIA and the Cultural Cold War* (London: Granta Books, 1999).

[63] Rudolf Jungnickel, *Kabale am Rhein. Der Kanzler und sein Monsignore* (Weimar: Wartburg Verlag, 1994), 333 and 341.

[64] Gérard Bossuat, *L'Europe des français 1943–1959. La IVe République aux sources de l'Europe commu-nautaire* (Paris: Publications de la Sorbonne, 1996), 25. See also François-Georges Dreyfus, 'Les Réticences du MRP face à l'Europe 1944–1948', in Berstein, Mayeur and Milza (eds.), *Le MRP*, 115–30.

delegation, Teusch, who was Northrhine-Westphalian minister of cultural affairs 1947–54 and one of the co-founders of the College of Europe, and Weber, member of the Bundestag 1949–61, co-founder of the European organisation of Christian democratic women, member of the Council of Europe Assembly and chairwoman of the German delegation from 1957. Some other Christian democrats with links to the Catholic workers' organisations and Christian trade unions did participate in the NEI and the Geneva Circle, most notably P. J. S. Serrarens, member of the Dutch Second Chamber 1937–52 and secretary-general of the European Christian trade unions 1920–52. They were a small minority there as well as in the European assemblies, however. In the ECSC Consultative Assembly, for example, only 4 of 36 Christian democrats had union links.[65]

The degree of continuity from SIPDIC to the emerging postwar Christian democratic party network reflected in the role of politicians like Pezet and Serrarens was thus minimal. World War II marked the end of the control of transnational party cooperation by left-Catholics with links to the Catholic workers' organisations and Christian trade unions. The NEI and the Geneva Circle were instead heavily dominated by predominately middle-class liberal and conservative Catholics. Moderate left-Catholics continued to form an intra-party reservoir of general support for European cooperation and integration. This is true, for example, of the left-Catholic Rhenish wing of the CDU under the leadership of the Christian socialist Karl Arnold, co-founder of the unified trade union congress Deutscher Gewerkschaftsbund (DGB) in the Rhineland in 1945 and CDU minister-president of Northrhine-Westphalia 1947–56. Although Arnold was at loggerheads with Adenauer over the CDU's socio-economic policies and his own preference for a grand coalition with the SPD, he strongly advocated Franco-German reconciliation and specifically, cooperation in the coal and steel sector as early as 1948.[66] Characteristically, however, Arnold was not active in the Christian democratic party network – although he had his own transnational contacts, for example with Poher, the Christian democratic general

---

[65] Patrick Pasture, 'The Fist of the Dwarf. Formation, Organisation and Representation of the Christian Trade Unions as a European Pressure Group (1945–1958)', *Journal of European Integration History* 1 (1995), 20.

[66] Cf. Kurt Düwell, 'Karl Arnold. Überzeugter Föderalist zwischen gesamtdeutschen Zielen und europäischen Visionen', in Präsident des Landtags Nordrhein-Westfalen (ed.), *Karl Arnold: Nordrhein-Westfalens Ministerpräsident 1947–1956* (Düsseldorf: Landtag Nordrhein-Westfalen, 2001), 91–112.

commissioner for German and Austrian Affairs 1948–50, and in the Quai d'Orsay.[67]

The domination of the new party network by middle-class liberal-conservative elites reflects what Martin Conway has called the dominant influence of the 'farmer-bourgeois alliance' in postwar Christian democracy.[68] Christian trade unionists, who held their first international postwar conference in St Gallen in Switzerland in January 1947, had growing difficulties asserting their own social reform agenda within their national parties, and they invested few resources in influencing party cooperation. Their organisational density and power decreased compared to that in interwar Europe, not least as the result of the formation of unified trade unions in countries like Germany and Austria. These trade unions were theoretically non-partisan, but effectively became more and more allied to the social democratic parties. The diminishing role of left-Catholicism also resulted from the adoption by middle-class party elites of more interventionist welfare state policies within a mixed economy which helped to neutralise more far-reaching demands of socialisation. More generally, the declining influence of organised Christian workers – not necessarily of the left wing, which temporarily gained influence in the DC, for example – was in line with 'a broader marginalization of the industrial working class from power'[69] – a phenomenon that was later accelerated by the transition to an economy increasingly dominated by the service sector, not industry, and lower rates of unionisation from the 1970s.

Linked to the middle-class liberal-conservative domination of the Christian democratic party network were a particular concept of, and policies for, 'Europe'. The more universalist-pacifist SIPDIC ideas and the primary interest of left-Catholics in national social reform policies in comparative perspective were replaced by the new networking elites with a more concrete concept of functional economic integration with liberal connotations, although with European-level welfare dimensions to legitimise market liberalisation and ease possible socio-economic adjustment problems. 'Europe' became upgraded in the course of Christian democratic party networking and intergovernmental decision-making in the first decade after World War II to their main collective policy instrument. In the face of the external Soviet and domestic communist challenge in the

---

[67] Werner Bührer, *Ruhrstahl und Europa. Die Wirtschaftsvereinigung Eisen- und Stahlindustrie und die Anfänge der europäischen Integration 1945–1952* (Munich: Oldenbourg, 1986), 115 and 122; Bossuat, *L'Europe des français*, 125–6; Raymond Poidevin, *Robert Schuman, homme d'État 1886–1963* (Paris: Imprimerie nationale, 1986), 209.
[68] Conway, 'The Age', 54.   [69] Ibid., 54.

Cold War, their evolving European policy was designed to simultaneously overcome the legacy of nationalism and national conflict and find common European-level solutions to domestic socio-economic issues. 'Europe' thus became a core element of the Christian democratic parties' postwar identities, contributing in a major way to their distinctiveness in domestic party competition. As Étienne Borne claimed for the MRP at the national party congress at Lille in 1954, 'We are the party of Europe. Europe is our form of refusing a return to the past.'[70]

Three important traditions of political Catholicism facilitated this new European vocation. They became more influential once more after 1945 in a collective reaction to the combined experience of the two world wars and against what Peter Pulzer has called 'the hypertrophied, pagan, racially based and aggressive nation-state' of national socialist Germany and its lesser fascist and clerical-dictatorial relatives.[71] The first tradition was the quintessentially continental European, not global, orientation of political Catholicism as opposed to the ideologically and organisationally pan-European and internationalist socialism. When the Christian democrats began to develop first transnational links beyond continental western Europe in the second half of the 1950s, they were initially limited to the emerging more left-wing Christian democracy in the Catholic majority cultures of Latin America. The second tradition was the unifying mistrust of the centralised almighty nation-state – a mistrust rooted in the collective European Catholic experience of liberal-dominated national integration and the culture wars in the nineteenth century and accentuated by the shared fear of the Stalinist version of centralisation. The third, closely linked, tradition was the strong regional anchoring and identity of political Catholicism – from the south-eastern provinces of Limburg and North Brabant in the case of the KVP, Flanders in the case of the CVP, the Rhineland and Bavaria in the case of the CDU and CSU, Alsace-Lorraine, Britanny and Savoy in the case of the MRP, and Trento, Lombardy and Sicily in the case of the DC. The MRP actually debated in 1950 to what extent its own political traditions – despite its post-revolutionary republican programme – had roots in Burgundian clericalism and provincialism going back to the eleventh century.[72]

---

[70] Cited in Pierre Gerbet, 'Les Partis politiques et les Communautés europénnes sous la Quatrième République', in Joël Rideau *et al.* (eds.), *La France et les Communautés europénnes* (Paris: Fondations Nationale de Sciences Politiques, 1975), 79.

[71] Peter Pulzer, 'Nationalism and Internationalism in European Christian Democracy', in Gehler and Kaiser (eds.), *Christian Democracy*, 21.

[72] Capelle, *The MRP*, 16.

The overlapping Catholic and strong regional identity and – in the case of many leading Christian democrats like Schuman and De Gasperi – experience of cross-border contacts between the different 'petite patrie', as Schuman called his Lorraine region,[73] largely account for the interest in some kind of supranational solution for continental western Europe as a guarantee of subnational regional identity and autonomy. In contrast – with the partial exception of the Benelux and French parties – European socialists were initially committed to the national road to socialism in one country. As Donald Sassoon has emphasised, 'The idea that postwar reconstruction would require a growing economic and political interdependence expressed through . . . a 'common market' could not have come from the Left.'[74]

---

[73] Rudolf Mittendorfer, *Robert Schuman – Architekt des neuen Europa* (Hildesheim, Zurich, New York: Georg Olms, 1983), 16.
[74] Sassoon, *One Hundred Years*, 170.

CHAPTER 6

Creating core Europe: the rise of the party network

In the immediate aftermath of World War II, the first priority of all Catholics coming back into politics from exile, the resistance or internal emigration was national reconstruction. Infrastructure had to be rebuilt, businesses restarted, elections held and colonies occupied once more as in the case of Dutch Indonesia, for example. In 1944–6, forging institutional links with Christian democrats in other countries would at best have seemed like an esoteric pastime. As the transport infrastructure was largely destroyed, European conferences would also have been very time consuming. At the same time, systematic contacts with German Christian democrats were impossible while they were not permitted to travel abroad. Despite the rudimentary cooperation in exile, moreover, the Christian democrats faced the predicament that the interwar network had collapsed. As the Swiss SKVP President Joseph Escher bemoaned at the first informal European meeting in Switzerland in early 1947, World War II put an end 'to the links between Catholics of all European countries. ... Relations between countries and between individuals have been interrupted, organisations destroyed, and many who used to work as brokers between the peoples, are dead. The younger generation no longer know each other.'[1]

In this postwar vacuum, individual Catholics from different countries took the initiative to forge new links and establish a new network. Having assisted the Catholic refugees in exile in Britain, members of the People & Freedom Group enthusiastically planned to help reconstruct party links at the end of World War II. At first, Barbara Barclay Carter aimed at continuing the ICDU activities for a limited period of time in the form of an International Information Service as a forum of exchange for the

---

[1] Joseph Escher, Eröffnungsansprache, 28.2.1947, Convenium christlicher Politiker Europas, Luzern, 27 February to 2 March 1947, BAR, CVP-Archiv JII.1981, 2372.

newly formed Christian democratic parties.[2] In the early spring of 1946 she went on an exploratory tour of continental Europe with the aim of reviving the interwar SIPDIC cooperation. Carter travelled to the Netherlands, where she met with Serrarens as well as Veraart, the former ICDU president, who was back at the University of Utrecht. She also held consultations with politicians from Belgium, Luxembourg, Switzerland and France as well as attending the National Congress of the Italian DC in late April 1946. Before leaving London, she wrote to Veraart, 'It would be such an opportunity to get things moving for the new international.'[3]

Continental western European Christian democracy in 1945–6 was very different from the Catholic Europe in exile in London during World War II, however. Carter found the new party elites decidedly unenthusiastic about any cooperation initiated by an unelected middle-class lady from England with charitable intentions. When Veraart reproached her later for not having succeeded in establishing an institutional link between the ICDU and postwar party cooperation, she wrote back in January 1948 about her experience at the first NEI meetings, where she represented the tiny, politically heterogenous British NEI équipe that eventually dissolved in 1952:[4]

I found myself in a difficult position, as the only person present with no real political status, while among the more important delegations (in particular the MRP) there was a deliberate purpose to cut any links with the past. I sought in vain to get some recognition for our International Information Service, which could have helped to make a bridge between the two organisations, but I had to face the fact that some people there were determined to eliminate us . . . Any recall of past initiatives was practically taboo.'[5]

The Christian democrats wanted a fresh start in party cooperation for a number of reasons. In spite of Sturzo's original intentions, SIPDIC was tainted with the cooperation of democratic parties with more clerical parties and individual anti-democratic representatives like the Austrian Schmitz, who was close to Schuschnigg. It did not succeed in controlling nationalist conflicts, let alone in making a signficant contribution to overcoming them. Despite their original sincere interest in Franco-German reconciliation at the outset, the French and Germans ended up instrumentalising SIPDIC for advancing their nationalist and revisionist claims for Europe.

[2] Der erste Schritt zur Errichtung einer Christlich-Demokratischen Internationale, no date [1946?], BAR, CVP-Archiv JII.181, 2659.
[3] Barclay Carter to Veraart, 10 March 1946 and 11 April 1946, NA, Collectie J. A. Veraart, 216.
[4] Cf. Philip M. Coupland, *Britannia, Europa and Christendom. British Christians and European Integration* (Basingstoke: Palgrave, 2006), 116–18.
[5] Barclay Carter to Veraart, 2 January 1948, NA, Collectie J. A. Veraart, 216.

Ultimately, SIPDIC also failed to operate completely independently of Church influence, as became clear over its failure to condemn fascism, especially after Mussolini and the Vatican concluded the Lateran Treaties. Against this background, De Gasperi – when he met with Bichet from the MRP in Rome in 1946 – warned against creating 'a black international'[6] – an even greater red rag for Christian democrats intent on avoiding a clerical image in domestic politics after 1945 than it had been after 1918.

Continental Christian democrats were also not keen on Carter's arbitration as they had already begun to develop new links among themselves. At a meeting with Sturzo in New York in October 1944, Bidault – then leader of the French Resistance – agreed to promote 'a regional, western-European conference' of Christian democratic parties.[7] Shortly after the end of the war, Bichet – at that time MRP secretary-general and close to Bidault – met with the Belgian CVP/PSC politicians Désirée Lamalle and Étienne de la Vallée Poussin as well as Jules Soyeur, a Catholic Belgian businessman in Paris.[8] Bichet also invited delegations from the Italian, Belgian, Dutch, Luxembourg and Austrian sister parties to attend the MRP party congress in Paris in December 1945, two months after its surprise election victory.[9] In early 1946 he travelled to Belgium, Austria and Italy for meetings with Van Zeeland, Felix Hurdes, De Gasperi, Attilio Piccioni and Sturzo to discuss party cooperation.[10] At that stage, however, the MRP executive concluded that it was too early to create a European organisation of parties.[11]

In the Bavarian Catholic Josef Müller, the MRP also identified at least one western German interlocutor early on. Having been liberated by American troops after his internment in the Dachau concentration camp, Müller was taken by US secret service agents to the Italian island of Capri for questioning. Before returning to Munich in May 1945 he had a private audience with the Pope and also met with De Gasperi, who probably recommended him to the MRP.[12] Müller subsequently became a leading CSU politician with Christian social leanings and a strong Western orientation. He was invited to the MRP party congress in 1946 as the only German observer. It was there that he saw Bidault and Schuman.[13] As

---

[6] Bichet, *La Démocratie chrétienne*, 244.
[7] Barclay Carter to Veraart, 30 October 1944, NA, Collectie J. A. Veraart, 216.
[8] Bacharan-Gressel, 'Les organisations', 45; Bichet, *La Démocratie chrétienne*, 243.
[9] Bichet, *La Démocratie chrétienne*, 100–1.   [10] Ibid., 244.
[11] Ibid., 243.   [12] Hettler, *Josef Müller*, 200.
[13] Josef Müller, *Bis zur letzten Konsequenz. Ein Leben für Frieden und Freiheit* (Munich: Süddeutscher Verlag, 1975), 360.

Rudolf Lewandowski – an Austrian student, journalist and informal ÖVP representative in Paris from 1946 – recalled later, some MRP politicians were still hoping at that time to use Müller to strengthen Bavarian separatism, as he had expressed some sympathy for the creation of a Bavarian-Austrian southern German state in the case of Germany's dismemberment.[14]

Austrian ÖVP politicians also developed contacts in western Europe independently. Having attended the MRP party congress in December 1945, Hurdes – ÖVP secretary-general 1945–52 – worked with Lewandowski to keep in touch with the MRP, which he regarded as a model for his own party. Hurdes also initiated contacts with Italian Christian democrats, not least with the bilateral objective of coming to an understanding with the DC over the thorny South Tyrol issue.[15] After another meeting with Swiss Catholics, the Strategic Services Unit in the US War Department observed that Hurdes 'intends to form a Catholic international, and has already done much work to this end'.[16] East-central European politicians also tried to foster networking under the increasingly difficult circumstances of progressive Sovietisation. Konrad Sieniewicz – the Polish Labour Party's secretary-general 1945–90 – fled from Poland in 1945. On his way into exile in London, he met with PSC and MRP politicians in Brussels and Paris, and suggested restarting party cooperation in a reformed SIPDIC.[17]

It was the Swiss SKVP, however, which took the initiative that led to the first meeting to discuss party cooperation after World War II. When Serrarens contacted the Swiss in the summer of 1946 to suggest holding such a meeting in the context of the first postwar congress of the Interparliamentary Union in Sankt Moritz in late August 1946, the SKVP executive had already agreed to propose a European meeting.[18] SKVP Secretary-General

---

[14] Rudolf Lewandowski, 'Das Europa der christlichen Demokratie', in Andreas Khol, Robert Prantner and Alfred Stirnemann (eds.), *Um Parlament und Partei. Alfred Maleta zum 70. Geburtstag* (Graz, Vienna, Cologne: Styria, 1976), 348; Rudolf Lewandowski, 'Der Traum von Europa. Die Christlich-Demokratische Internationale: Ihr Ursprung und ihre Entwicklung', in EVP-Fraktion des Europäischen Parlaments (ed.), *Zur Geschichte der christlich-demokratischen Bewegung in Europa* (Melle: Ernst Knoth, 1990), 68.

[15] Cf. Michael Gehler, '"Politisch unabhängig", aber "ideologisch eindeutig europäisch". Die ÖVP, die Vereinigung christlicher Volksparteien (NEI) und die Anfänge der europäischen Integration 1947–1960', in Michael Gehler and Rolf Steininger (eds.), *Österreich und die europäische Integration 1945–1993. Aspekte einer wechselvollen Entwicklung* (Vienna, Cologne, Weimar: Böhlau, 1993), 291–326; Binder, '"Rescuing the Christian Occident"'.

[16] Hurdes Interest in Formation of Catholic International, Austria, Strategic Services Unit, War Department, 13 August 1946, National Archives (henceforth: NA USA), RG 263, Box 184.

[17] Konrad Sieniewicz, 'Die Beteiligung der Christlichen Demokraten aus Mitteleuropa', in EVP-Fraktion (ed.), *Zur Geschichte*, 42–3.

[18] Rosenberg to Serrarens, 13 July 1946, BAR, CVP-Archiv JII.181, 2659.

Martin Rosenberg, who had studied at Fribourg, Leuven and the Sorbonne in Paris and was keen to integrate his party better in transnational networks after World War II, had already come up with the plan in May 1946.[19] When Rosenberg met with the ÖVP member of the Austrian Nationalrat Hans Pernter in Bern on 20 July 1946, they agreed that the separate organisation of such a meeting would be preferable to combining it with the inter-party IPU occasion.[20] The Swiss plan was delayed twice, however,[21] before the European Christian democrats eventually met in Lucerne from 27 February to 2 March 1947.

At Lucerne, the options for the organisational form of party cooperation were limited from the start as both the MRP and the CVP/PSC executives agreed minimalist positions in advance. Bichet and other Christian democrats within the MRP including Bidault supported organic links with sister parties. Yet the party's left wing in particular was strongly opposed to such a commitment. It feared that the association with what it saw as more conservative and even clerical right-wing parties elsewhere in Europe would undermine its attempt to finally integrate French political Catholicism with a more left-wing policy agenda wholesale into the republican consensus without any reservations. Georges Lebrun Kéris, who took part in the Lucerne meeting, recalled later that the MRP leadership was afraid of 'colonisation by the Belgians' who were at that time adopting – from the French perspective – 'reactionary and aggressively confessional' positions in domestic Belgian politics.[22] Thus, the MRP sent a delegation to Lucerne, but only as observers.

At the same time, the CVP/PSC also refused to create a more integrated party international. Its leaders were concerned about the danger of diluting the party's new left-of-centre socio-economic policy profile, which under the Belgian conditions of tripartite party competition with the socialists on the left and liberals on the right, was easily compatible with the more confessional approach to domestic issues such as public funding for Catholic schools. As Carter noticed at Lucerne, moreover, some Belgians – in particular its leader from 1945 to 1949, August de Schryver – were also still concerned that a Christian democratic party international 'would not

---

[19] Cf. Schürmann to Rosenberg, 21 May 1946, BAR, CVP-Archiv JII.181, 2659.
[20] E. Hänggi, Rapport über eine Besprechung zwischen Herrn Dr. Pernter und dem Generalsekretariat der Schweizer Konservativen Volkspartei vom 20.7.1946 im Hotel Bristol, Bern, BAR, CVP-Archiv JII.181, 2659.
[21] Cf. SKVP, Generalsekretariat, Vorschläge für die Durchführung eines Conveniums führender Vertreter der christlichen Parteien, 25 September 1946, BAR, CVP-Archiv JII.181, 2659.
[22] Mayeur, *Des partis*, 229. See also Bacharan-Gressel, 'Les Organisations', 47.

be understood in England, on whose cooperation they set especial store'.[23] In fact, the CVP/PSC executive decided as early as 11 April 1946 against entering into official party links.[24] De Schryver met with Soyeur, who shared his approach, for the first time in Paris in October 1946.[25] The CVP/ PSC leader informed Lamalle that he had the best impression of the Belgian businessman, who he felt could play a useful role for the party in more informal networks.[26] Soyeur subsequently submitted a short outline for the future organisation of such a network in late 1946, early 1947, proposing 'a connection between movements and individual politicians of a Christian and democratic tendency ... in total independence from the Church', based on non-official, 'personal contacts'.[27] The CVP/PSC executive approved Soyeur's plan on 16 January 1947.[28] It sent a delegation to Lucerne with the objective of getting this Belgian blueprint adopted for future party cooperation.

Opposing the Franco-Belgian thesis at Lucerne were the Austrians and Italians, with Swiss support.[29] Hurdes and Piccioni aggressively advocated the creation of a Christian democratic party international. Piccioni submitted a draft resolution which called for the creation of a committee of party representatives to draft a statute for the 'formation of an international association of parties of Christian orientation'. This new organisation would have the main objective of creating 'a peaceful and democratic Europe'. Moreover, the member parties would sign up to common 'principles' as a shared ideological basis.[30] Yet the Dutch and Luxembourg representatives, who had close links with the Belgian sister party which were formalised in 1948, were more inclined towards the modest Franco-Belgian scheme. In fact, Piccioni and Hurdes were even accused of advocating a more integrated organisation mainly with the aim of using it to advance specific national interests. In the case of Italy, this was an implicit reference to the contested issue of the future of Trieste, for which the DC-led Italian government needed French support. In the Austrian case,

---

[23] 'Christian-Democrats and Industrial Democracy. A New International Body', *People & Freedom* 94 (1947), 1.
[24] Kwanten, *August-Edmond De Schryver*, 478.   [25] See also Chenaux, 'Bijdrage', 251.
[26] De Schryver to Lamalle, 4 October 1946, KADOC, Archief August E. de Schryver, 7.2.1.
[27] NEI, Secrétariat Général, Jules Soyeur, Notes Préliminaires, no date [January 1947], KADOC, Archief August E. de Schryver, 7.2.1.
[28] PSC, Rapport de la réunion du Comité National du Jeudi 16 janvier 1947, KADOC, Archief August E. de Schryver, 7.2.1.
[29] See also the retrospective analysis in PSC, La conférence de Lucerne, no date, ibid.
[30] Procès-verbal de la Conférence politique internationale de Lucerne, 27.3.-2.3.1947, SKVP, Generalsekretariat, Bern, 22 March 1947, BAR, CVP-Archiv JII.181, 2372.

it might have been the interest in securing a quick end to the four-power occupation, full national independence and, possibly, Italian concessions over South Tyrol.

The MRP observers insisted that the creation of a party international was out of the question for them. Robert Wirth – one of the personal advisors to Foreign Minister Bidault – explained that the MRP was ' a new force' and did not want to be associated with anything that could look like, or be attacked as, a 'black international'. 'The papal encyclicals,' he emphasised, 'can inspire a doctrine, but we must not forget that they are not directly applicable to politics.'[31] The French were also concerned about the possible use of the term 'Christian democratic' which they had studiously avoided for their own party. Reporting on the Lucerne meeting, Carter sensed a strong fear among the MRP observers that their association with a 'Christian democratic' organisation 'would lay them open to a charge of clericalism and took no account of the number of non-believers and even, in North Africa, of Moslems among their adherents'.[32] Perhaps most important was another concern that remained implicit. The MRP was not yet prepared to enter into binding commitments that could limit the freedom of manœuvre of Foreign Minister Bidault in the ongoing negotiations with the US, Britain and the Soviet Union concerning the future of Germany in particular. At this early stage after World War II, neither Bidault nor the MRP as a party were fully committed yet to a constructive policy on the German question.

When it seemed, after tedious negotiations during a night session, that a compromise had at last been struck, including the creation of a temporary secretariat until the next meeting, Lamalle suddenly pulled a rabbit out of the hat. As the suggested solution still included a reference to political parties, the CVP/PSC could not accept it. In any case, individual Belgian Christian democrats were already cooperating with a new group, the NEI, organised by Soyeur, which comprised politicians as well as trade unionists and intellectuals of a Christian democratic orientation. This NEI was going to hold a first meeting at the end of the month. The question was therefore whether other participants wanted to adhere to this new group, too.[33] No organisation to speak of existed at this stage. It was a Franco-Belgian plot to minimise the network's organisational integration and to

[31] Ibid.
[32] 'Christian-Democrats and Industrial Democracy. A New International Body', *People & Freedom* 94 (1947), 1.
[33] Procès-verbal de la Conférence politique internationale de Lucerne, 27.3.-2.3.1947, SKVP, Generalsekretariat, Bern, 22 March 1947, BAR, CVP-Archiv JII.181, 2372.

control key posts and its future development. Bichet needed to create conditions that would at least allow individual MRP politicians to play a role in the network.[34] The name NEI, which was ideologically neutral, was Bichet's brainchild.[35] At best, it was meaningful in the French political context, referring back to the NEF founded by Francisque Gay and Bidault in 1937–8 with the aim of creating a new centrist political force in a polarised political system. As Christian democratic party cooperation would have been ineffectual without French and Belgian participation, the other delegations had no real choice. At least they managed to secure the small concession that the NEI's national 'équipes' could de facto consist of political parties. The agreed resolution simply asked the Belgians to make the necessary preparations for 'planned and useful cooperation' including the organisation of a first congress, which took place in Liège in May 1947.

Although the Christian democratic parties continued to diverge over the desirable degree of institutionalisation, they did agree on the rationale for closer transnational links and cooperation. One crucial incentive for them was the potential effect on domestic and transnational party competition. 'When the political Right and Left organise themselves across borders, the Christian parties must not be left behind,' argued Josef Escher – the SKVP president – in his opening speech.[36] At that time, the liberal parties were in the process of coming together, leading to the formation of the Liberal International in April 1947. The socialists were also beginning to meet again, although the Socialist International was only officially resurrected in Frankfurt in 1951. They received substantial material and ideational support from the British Labour government and American Democrats. Against the background of the early stages of the Cold War, this international support added legitimacy to their claim to reconstitute the nation-states and western Europe as a whole in the democratic socialist image. Although it was anxious not to be lumped together with reactionary clericals, even the MRP needed transnational contacts in these circumstances. For others like the DC and the ÖVP and even more so, the CDU/CSU, their inclusion in transnational party cooperation was crucial. It

---

[34] Cf. the internal deliberations within the CVP/PSC documented in PSC, Rapport de la réunion du Comité National du jeudi 16 janvier 1947, KADOC, Archief August E. de Schryver, 7.2.1. Cf. also Jürgen Hollstein, 'Zur Geschichte christlich-demokratischer Zusammenarbeit in Europa: Die "Nouvelles Equipes Internationales" (NEI)', *Libertas* 23 (1989), 85–7.

[35] Bichet, *La Démocratie chrétienne*, 246.

[36] Procès-verbal de la Conférence politique internationale de Lucerne, 27.3.-2.3.1947, SKVP, Generalsekretariat, Bern, 22 March 1947, BAR, CVP-Archiv JII.181, 2372.

helped them to demonstrate their acceptance, equality and influence within western Europe and to show that they could be trusted to advance particular economic and political interests internationally and reap rewards for that in government. In this respect, the situation after 1945 was fundamentally different from the 1920s, when small minorities within the Catholic parties saw transnational links as necessary, but extremely hazardous in their party and country because of the latent accusation that they were selling out 'national interests'.

The Marshall Plan, the creation of the Organisation for European Economic Cooperation (OEEC) and the incipient institutionalisation of initially inter-governmental European policy-making added a second very important structural incentive: to enhance the ability to influence actual policy-making in cooperation with like-minded parties under the structural conditions of an international system that was undergoing fundamental change. The interwar system with its weak inter-governmental League of Nations was multi-polar and fragmented. In contrast, the emerging Cold War system was bi-polar, with a western Europe that depended on the continued engagement of the United States for its prosperity and external security. These systemic changes narrowed down the options for unilateral policies as the French governments soon discovered in relation to the issue of the future of Germany. Instead, the changed structural conditions encouraged and demanded cooperation and cohesion with the overriding common objective of enhancing western Europe's security. As the Dutch KVP politician Emmanuel Sassen drastically put it at Lucerne, in view of the Soviet danger 'Europe must overcome its state of egoistic Balkanisation' to avoid 'the genocide of Europeans'.[37] Importantly, security was no longer defined in purely military terms. Western Europeans had to respond to the ideological challenge of communism with its boundless promises of human welfare and its apparent technological and socio-economic advances. They needed to join forces to redefine their own societal model of parliamentary democracy and market economy to strengthen its internal stability and external attraction.

Unlike after World War I, moreover, the Christian democrats were confronted with a very clear policy priority for transnational cooperation and intergovernmental bargaining: how to sort out the 'German question' in a way that was compatible with the security interests of Germany's neighbours, especially France, but would nevertheless contribute to strengthening the region's welfare and external security. The Christian

---

[37] Ibid.

democrats' preoccupation during the first years of their transnational cooperation with the Europeanisation of the German question also provided a strong incentive for developing contacts with western German politicians who shared their normative assumptions, especially about the priority of freedom and Western integration of the western zones of occupation over German reunification, and related strategic objectives.

At Lucerne, the Christian democrats held a private meeting with Wirth, the former Reich chancellor, whom the French occupation authorities were still not allowing to return to his home town in Germany. He clung to the confessional party model and later advocated a conciliatory policy towards the Soviet Union to restore a unified Germany, opposing Adenauer on both counts.[38] At Lucerne, Wirth recommended that the Christian democrats invite representatives of the CDU/CSU and the reconstituted Centre Party to participate in future NEI events.[39] The Centre Party was only partially successful in local and regional elections in 1946, especially in Northrhine-Westphalia, where Rudolf Amelunxen was minister-president of a coalition with social democrats and Christian democrats from 1946 to 1947. Its left-wing Christian socialist programme temporarily made it a more attractive partner for the MRP than the CDU, however. Thus, the NEI invited Spiecker to its second congress in Luxembourg in early February 1948, alongside Adenauer and other politicians from the CDU/CSU.[40] As he did not want to clash with Adenauer at the congress, Spiecker sent the 23-year-old journalist Rainer Barzel instead.[41] In March 1948, the NEI issued an invitation to Adenauer to form a German NEI équipe including representatives from the Centre Party.[42] Adenauer mentioned this invitation at a meeting of the CDU executive in the British zone, which he chaired, in the context of a report on the congress of the European

---

[38] On Wirth after 1945 see also the relevant chapters in Hörster-Philipps, *Joseph Wirth*; Küppers, *Joseph Wirth*.

[39] Procès-verbal de la Conférence politique internationale de Lucerne, 27.3.-2.3.1947, SKVP, Generalsekretariat, Bern, 22 March 1947, BAR, CVP-Archiv JII.181, 2372. See also Philippe Chenaux, *Une Europe Vaticane? Entre le Plan Marshall et les Traités de Rome* (Brussels: Éditions Ciaco, 1990), 125.

[40] Adenauer apparently sought an invitation to the NEI congress with the assistance of Josef Löns, the secretary-general of the CDU in the British zone 1946-8, who probably got in touch with Hurdes from the Austrian ÖVP. Cf. Paul Weymar, *Konrad Adenauer. Die autorisierte Biographie* (Munich: Kindler Verlag, 1955); Gehler, '"Politisch unabhängig"', 293.

[41] Spiecker to Bichet, 6 March 1948, ACDP, 09-002-005/1; Barzel to Bichet, 2 February 1948, ACDP, 09-002-011/2; Rainer Barzel, *Ein gewagtes Leben. Erinnerungen* (Stuttgart, Leipzig, Hohenheim, 2001), 86 and, by the same author, 'Deutschland – ein europäisches Problem', *Rhein-Ruhr-Zeitung*, 16 February 1948.

[42] Procès-verbal de la réunion du 21 mars 1948 du Comité Exécutif des N. E. I., ACDP, 09-002-002.

Movement at The Hague. He did nothing, however.[43] Increasingly exasperated with Adenauer's delaying tactics, the NEI tried to involve Müller, who appeared to be 'more flexible',[44] but to no avail. Adenauer successfully established personal control over his party's transnational contacts and the inclusion of politicians who fully shared his policy objectives. The issue of the Centre Party, which he intended to absorb into the CDU, finally disappeared in 1949, when Spiecker was deselected as its leader over his attempts to prepare a merger, and joined the CDU, as did Barzel, who was CDU/CSU parliamentary party leader from 1964 to 1973 and CDU party leader from 1971 to 1973.

The eventual formal inclusion of the CDU/CSU in the NEI strengthened those who were keen on greater integration of party cooperation. The initial NEI formula was based on the lowest common denominator because at this stage – so shortly after the war – the French effectively had an informal veto. A slightly greater degree of formalisation quickly proved inevitable, however. An executive committee was created which was headed by the NEI president. Alongside the president, it comprised four vice-presidents. Whereas the president had oversight functions, the secretary-general, initially working from the MRP offices in Paris, was responsible for day-to-day business. The NEI also instituted committees for political, cultural and socio-economic matters as well as for parliamentary affairs when the Council of Europe was formed in 1949. At its meeting in Liège in June 1948, moreover, the NEI executive also decided that the national équipes could in fact use the subtitle Union of European Christian Democrats[45] – a title that most parties soon began to use exclusively as only it allowed the domestic recognition of their transnational cooperation.

The somewhat greater institutionalisation came at a price for the DC, ÖVP and CDU/CSU, however, as the MRP and the CVP/PSC claimed both important NEI posts for themselves and succeeded in filling them until 1965. First, Bichet was president and Soyeur secretary-general. In April 1949, however, Soyeur demanded that the NEI cease its involvement in the European Movement on the grounds that the interests of workers were not sufficiently represented and its socio-economic policy proposals

---

[43] Zonenausschuß CDU britische Zone, Bad Meinberg, 19–20 May 1948, *Konrad Adenauer und die CDU der britischen Besatzungszone 1946–1949. Dokumente zur Gründungsgeschichte der CDU Deutschlands* (Bonn: Eichholz-Verlag, 1975), 496.

[44] Hurdes to Gruber, 25 June 1948, Bericht über die Exekutivausschuss-Sitzung der Nouvelles Equipes Internationales (Vereinigung der christlich-demokratischen Volksparteien), 21.6.1948, Lüttich, Institut für Zeitgeschichte Vienna (henceforth: IfZG Vienna), NL 48, DO 365.

[45] NEI, Procès-verbal de la réunion du Comité Exécutif, 21 June 1948, Liège, ACDP, 09-002-002.

were too conservative. As the Political Commission did not approve his proposal at its meeting on 8 April and instead recommended that Bichet as the NEI representative become more active with the aim of influencing the European Movement in a Christian democratic direction, Soyeur resigned abruptly.[46] Hurdes believed that the real reason had to do with the NEI's financial difficulties.[47] In any case, by 1949 Soyeur was not sufficiently integrated in the CVP/PSC to be able to play a more political role within the NEI. He was a relic of the early contact phase after World War II. Bichet tried to fill the political vacuum created by Soyeur's resignation with a proposal for an apparently modest reform. In future the NEI would be represented by a president elected for one year only, instead of up to three, this with the obvious aim of strengthening the role of the secretary-general.[48] Bichet formally proposed the outgoing CVP/PSC leader de Schryver, who remained influential in Belgian politics throughout the 1950s,[49] as the new president at the helm of the NEI in November 1949. He offered to become secretary-general instead as part of a package deal agreed between the MRP and the CVP/PSC.[50] Hurdes protested that such a solution would only be acceptable if the four vice-presidents came from other parties. The Belgian Lamalle withdrew his candidature and Hurdes, Rosenberg, Sassen and Paolo Emilio Taviani – a close collaborator of De Gasperi – were duly elected. Sassen then opposed the reduction of the president's term in office to one year, and was supported by everyone. The proposed constitutional change was rejected, but the Italians, Austrians, Swiss and Dutch accepted the continued domination of the NEI by the two parties most reluctant to construct a formal party alliance: the French MRP and the Belgian CVP/PSC.

The representatives of the MRP and CVP/PSC already repeatedly came under pressure in the early phase of cooperation to get their national leaderships to agree to the parties' formal integration with the national équipes and thus, the *de jure*, not merely *de facto*, transformation of the

---

[46] Soyeur to Bichet, 26 March 1949, Archiv für christlich-soziale Politik (henceforth: ACSP), Nachlass Josef Müller; Jules Soyeur, Erläuterungen für die Mitglieder des NEI-Exekutivausschusses [regarding his resignation as NEI secretary-general], 6 April 1949, ibid. See also the documentation in BAR, CVP-Archiv JII.181, 2352.

[47] Politische Kommission, Paris, 8 April 1949, Exekutivausschuss, Paris, 9–10 April 1949, Niederschrift Felix Hurdes, IfZG Innsbruck, Karl Gruber Archiv, Karton 6. See also the official protocol in ACDP, 09-002-002.

[48] Cf. Rosenberg to Tosi, 7 July 1949, BAR, CVP-Archiv JII.181, 2348.

[49] For the perspective of the Dutch KVP member responsible for party relations, see Karl Josef Hahn, *Standplaats Europa. Memoires van een christen-democraat* (Weesp: De Haan, 1984), 158.

[50] Executive Committee, Paris, 18–19 November 1949, ACDP, 09-002-002.

NEI into a party alliance. The DC, ÖVP, CDU/CSU and, increasingly, internationally networked KVP politicians were keen to strengthen ideological as well as institutional cohesion. They anticipated some progress towards a parliamentarisation of western European politics resulting from the creation of the Consultative Assembly of the Council of Europe, in which the Christian democrats sat together in a group and wanted to be in a position to formulate joint proposals backed up and publicised by their parties. They increasingly regarded the French insistence on treating the NEI officially as primarily a section of the European Movement to diffuse opposition within the MRP to formal party cooperation as ridiculous. In fact, the NEI's name was so meaningless, and its ideological profile sufficiently diffuse, that in spring 1949 the Catholic section of the Dutch Labour Party applied for membership.[51] Although the KVP formed a coalition government with it, its leaders as well as the Church hierarchy saw the Catholics who had joined the PvdA with the aim of creating a broadly based non-confessional Labour Party on the British model as the greatest threat to Catholic unity and the established pillarisation of Dutch society along confessional and ideological lines. The domestic inter-party competition clearly demanded not only a rejection of the application from the Catholic social democrats, but a strengthening of the NEI's profile as a Christian democratic party organisation.

At a meeting in Hofgastein in Austria in mid-July 1949, the majority of NEI representatives demanded that the MRP and CVP/PSC leaderships be formally asked to adhere to the NEI. Bichet agreed to send letters, but there was never any chance that the two parties would cave in at this stage. The MRP executive had actually decided at a meeting in mid-February that it would not do so.[52] In mid-November 1949, Bichet reported back that de Schryver and Bidault, who was in fact more enthusiastic about MRP membership in the NEI than Schuman and de Menthon, for example, had signalled informally that they were still unwilling to risk deep intra-party divisions over this issue.[53] In Sorrent in April 1950, Hurdes once more brought up the question, insisting that, for him, the organisation of a future NEI congress in France was out of the question as long as the MRP was refusing to join as a party.[54] The question was also on the agenda of a

---

[51] Executive Committee, Hofgastein, 15–16 July 1949, ACDP, 09-002-002.
[52] Bacharan-Gressel, 'Les Organisations', 47.
[53] Executive Committee, Paris, 18–19 November 1949, ACDP, 09-002-002. See also Elisabeth Du Réau, 'Le MRP et la naissance du Conseil de l'Europe', in Berstein, Mayeur and Milza (eds.), *Le MRP*, 79.
[54] Executive Committee, Sorrent, 12–13 April 1950, ACDP, 09-002-002.

meeting of party leaders and their representatives in early July 1950, which de Schryver and Bichet actually attended, officially as NEI observers.[55] From his own internal knowledge as NEI president, de Schryver now admitted that it was 'necessary to strengthen the existing bonds'. He also insisted, however, that 'we need to be more careful than the socialists' lest the NEI be portrayed 'as a black organisation under Roman control'.[56] During the sharp domestic confrontation over the future of the Belgian monarchy, the CVP/PSC, as probably the most clerical of all parties, was most afraid of this label being used by the socialists and liberals to denounce it.

The Swiss, Austrians and Italians were so annoyed about the French and Belgian delaying tactics over the membership issue because they were also convinced that the NEI were managed inefficiently. In April 1949, Rosenberg reported back to Escher from the NEI executive meeting that 'upon our arrival, the NEI secretariat in Paris was in a terrible state. There was no light or heating. On the whole we got the impression of a secretariat in liquidation.'[57] After the departure of Soyeur, the NEI's problem of under-funding was resolved by the introduction of a system of national budgetary contributions.[58] However, the secretariat's communication and publicity activities were also too focused on Francophone Europe. The NEI were not visible enough outside of France and Belgium. Hurdes argued that it was high time 'that the parties of Central Europe exercise a decisive influence on the NEI's future'.[59] He even contemplated threatening Bichet with the relocation of the secretariat from Paris to Switzerland to achieve fundamental reforms. The time seemed ripe for such a move, as the exiled East European representatives were beginning to detach themselves from French protection.[60] Ultimately, however, the SKVP leadership was anxious about how such a move might be perceived in the light of Swiss neutrality. At the same time, the ÖVP leadership was concerned about not exposing itself too much during the ongoing negotiations about the so-called State Treaty and the withdrawal of foreign troops from Austria. Crucially, Adenauer had no intention of upsetting his French partners. He was much more interested in smooth informal contacts

[55] Meeting of NEI party leaders, Brussels, 3 July 1950, KADOC, Archief CEPESS, 3.1.11.
[56] Ibid.   [57] Rosenberg to Escher, 13 April 1949, BAR, CVP-Archiv JII.181, 2348.
[58] See Politische Kommission, Paris, 8 April 1949, Executive Committee, Paris, 9–10 April 1949, Niederschrift Felix Hurdes, IfZG Innsbruck, Karl Gruber Archiv, Karton 6 as well as the following meetings of the NEI's executive committee.
[59] Cited in Rosenberg to Escher, 13 April 1949, BAR, CVP-Archiv JII.181, 2348.   [60] Ibid.

than formalised organisation – especially before the creation of the Federal Republic and his own election as Chancellor on 15 September 1949.

It was with the aim of establishing such informal contacts with suitable German partners that Bidault initiated the secret meetings in the so-called Geneva Circle that took place from November 1947 to 1955. Despite its organisational limitations, the NEI could fulfil particular functions including facilitating networking across borders, the formulation of major shared policy objectives and the socialisation of future leaders in the slowly emerging integrationist consensus. NEI congresses and meetings were not yet suitable for giving Christian democratic governmental action strategic direction, however. This was mainly due to the inclusion of eastern European exiles and the continued strong aversion of French public opinion to reconciliation and cooperation with Germany so shortly after World War II. According to one opinion poll after the end of the war, 78 per cent of the French initially demanded the annexation by France of the entire Rhineland, and 73 per cent the organisation of rump-Germany into a decentralised confederation.[61] Bidault was keen to compensate for the initial lack of public support with informal exchanges about developing and future policy issues which would not be influenced by considerations of intra-party faultlines or domestic public opinion. As he insisted in the Geneva Circle at one point, 'the masses have no imagination'.[62] It was the task of political leaders to drive cooperation forward informally without getting too far ahead of public opinion.

Exploiting what Dietmar Hüser has called the 'institutional chaos' in official French foreign policy-making,[63] Bidault utilised private contacts to develop links with prominent German Christian democrats as early as the beginning of July 1947. At this time, he was not only far ahead of French public opinion, but also of his own official Gaullist policy as foreign minister: a policy that aimed at the extreme decentralisation, if not dismemberment, of Germany and the annexation of the Saar region. This policy was fast becoming redundant under the impact of East–West confrontation, however: the Sovietisation of eastern Europe, the American Truman doctrine and Marshall Plan, as well as American and British

[61] Gérard Bossuat, *Les Fondateurs de l'Europe* (Paris: Éditions Belin, 1994), 97. See also Pierre Melandri and Maurice Vaïsse, 'France: from Powerlessness to the Search of Influence', in Josef Becker and Franz Knipping (eds.), *Power in Europe? Great Britain, France, Italy and Germany in a Postwar World, 1945–1950* (Berlin, New York: Walter de Gruyter, 1986), 467.
[62] Geneva Circle, 10 June 1949, ACDP 01-009-017.
[63] Dietmar Hüser, *Frankreichs 'doppelte Deutschlandpolitik'. Dynamik aus der Defensive – Planen, Entscheiden, Umsetzen in gesellschaftlichen und wirtschaftlichen, innen- und außenpolitischen Krisenzeiten 1944–1950* (Berlin: Duncker & Humblot, 1996), 715.

collusion over the merger and reconstruction of their German zones of occupation and their ever stricter opposition to deals with Stalin. The traditional nationalist objectives also came under attack domestically. The socialist SFIO first demanded a more constructive policy on Germany in the internationalist Briandist tradition.[64] Bidault's own party was also rapidly distancing itself from the Gaullist agenda. Already in January 1946, Barthélémy Ott – a professor of German and expert on the history of German political ideas in the 1930s and now an MRP deputy close to Bidault – suggested that the annexation of the German-speaking Rhineland and Saar regions by France would only lead to further conflict, and that it would be more appropriate 'to use the language of Briand than that of Poincaré' – this at a time when the MRP leader, Maurice Schumann, still publicly demanded the Rhine as the 'natural' frontier between France and a dismembered Germany.[65] At the MRP national congress in March 1947, the majority of its foreign policy commission already pleaded for a positive policy on Germany. This majority included Ott, Marc Schérer, another MRP deputy, and Senator Pezet.[66] The next national congress in May 1948 merely formalised the new MRP policy of German decentralisation within an integrated Europe, quietly dropping the far-reaching territorial demands.[67] At the same time, the exclusion of the Communists from the coalition government in November 1947 created new domestic political opportunities for a reorientation of French policy on Germany and Europe.

Bidault's advance guard consisted of the French and German citizens Victor Koutzine and Johann Jakob Kindt-Kiefer.[68] Koutzine, who headed the small informal secretariat of the Geneva Circle, knew Bidault from interwar Paris.[69] Born in Tsarist Russia in 1910, he first worked as a lawyer, then as a journalist, obtaining a degree in literature in 1937. In 1935, he married Henriette Nemanoff, the daughter of a Russian journalist who fled to Geneva and reported on the League of Nations for various press agencies

---

[64] On SFIO's European policy formation see in detail Wilfried Loth, *Sozialismus und Internationalismus. Die französischen Sozialisten und die Nachkriegsordnung Europas 1940–1950* (Stuttgart: DVA, 1977).

[65] Cited in Reinhard Schreiner, *Bidault, der MRP und die französische Deutschlandpolitik, 1944–1948* (Frankfurt/Main: Lang, 1985), 111 and 123.

[66] Ibid, 132.   [67] Ibid., 161–5.

[68] On Koutzine and Kindt-Kiefer see also in greater detail Michael Gehler and Wolfram Kaiser (eds.), *Transnationale Parteienkooperation der europäischen Christdemokraten. Dokumente 1945–1965 / Coopération transnationale des démocrates-chrétiens en Europe. Documents 1945–1965* (Munich: K. G. Saur, 2004), 53–7.

[69] Cf. Jacques Dalloz, *Georges Bidault. Biographie Politique* (Paris: L'Harmattan, 1992), 295.

and newspapers. Koutzine became a German prisoner of war in 1940. He was released in June 1941 and began to work for the press office of the Turkish embassy in Vichy France.[70] In December 1942, he and his wife fled to Switzerland, where they were rounded up by the Swiss foreigner police, with Koutzine being interned in a work-camp near Zurich. When his wife first applied for a period of leave to work on a dissertation on Byzantine art in Geneva, where her parents lived, the responsible Swiss civil servant noted that in view of the forthcoming 'agricultural battle' (to secure Swiss food supplies) he could see no justification for her release 'or she must gobble up her Byzantine essay next winter'.[71]

The Koutzine and Nemanoff families were repatriated to France in November 1944. In April 1945, however, Koutzine returned to Geneva as cultural attaché in the French consulate general. In the following years, while writing for various mostly Christian democratic journals including *Combat, L'Aube, France intérieure* and *La Nation belge*, he also worked more informally, but apparently with financial support from the French foreign ministry, for Bidault as a consultant and informer. Rosenberg recounted later that he and other participants in the Geneva Circle actually thought that Koutzine also had links with the French secret service.[72] In the spring of 1947, Koutzine accompanied Bidault to the conference of foreign ministers in Moscow. The Swiss authorities all the while regarded him with intense suspicion. In 1951, the foreigner police concluded that he was a 'dangerous foreign subject' suspected 'of illegal activities'.[73] The ill-informed Swiss bureaucrats actually believed that he was a Soviet spy, but as they had no proof, they failed to prevent the extension of Koutzine's residence permit.

Koutzine and Kindt-Kiefer, who was from the Saar region, appear to have met for the first time in January 1946.[74] Kindt-Kiefer studied in Berlin and at the Sorbonne in the 1930s. It is possible, but not certain, that he also came in contact with Bidault during his time in Paris. Kindt-Kiefer was married to the daughter of a wealthy Swiss businessman, which made him financially independent and able to pursue his literary and political interests during and after World War II. He supported Wirth in exile in Lucerne. He also worked together with Wirth in organising the small

---

[70] Declaration, 12 November 1942 (Polizeiabteilung); Curriculum Vitae (1943), BAR, E 4264, 620; Dossier Victor Koutzine (224'443), Département de l'intérieur, de l'environnement et des affaires régionales, Archives d'État, République et Canton de Genève, Archives de la Police des Étrangers.
[71] Bericht gemäß beiliegendem Schreiben, Dr. Simmen, BAR, E 4264, 620.
[72] Rosenberg to Heck, 14 May 1966, ACDP, 01-022-101/22.
[73] Police Federale des Étrangers, 5 January 1951, BAR, E 4320 (B), 102.
[74] Jungnickel, *Kabale am Rhein*, 11. Jungnickel claims to be in the possession of Kindt-Kiefer's private archives, but has refused to make this material accessible to researchers.

Catholic and inter-party political exile in Switzerland.[75] Together with the former Reich chancellor and Aloys Stegerwald – the son of the interwar Centre Party politician – he also founded the Christliche Nothilfe (CHN) on 1 May 1946 – a charity with the objective of supporting the German zones of occupation with food parcels bought by Swiss citizens, organised by the CHN and distributed in Germany by the Catholic Caritas network.[76]

As the CHN's managing director, Kindt-Kiefer soon began to use the organisation for his and Koutzine's initiative to establish high-level secret contacts between French and German Christian democrats.[77] Illegally under Swiss law, he employed himself on a monthly salary of 1,300 Swiss francs.[78] He also funded the early meetings of the Geneva Circle under the pretext of CHN activities including meetings of its board. In the spring of 1947, the Swiss socialists first initiated a parliamentary enquiry into the CHN activities. In 1948, the Zurich cantonal police searched the CHN's offices and withdrew work permits from all German collaborators on the grounds that the organisation had misused funding for 'political purposes'. The CHN moved from Zurich to Zug, was subsequently liquidated and its budget and activities transferred to the newly created Internationale Christliche Nothilfe (ICHN).[79] Kindt-Kiefer continued as representative on the ICHN board of the German CHN. The latter had been founded to provide him with a legal platform for continuing his role in the Geneva Circle, before the ICHN was eventually closed down in July 1950. Kindt-Kiefer estimated the value of the content of the remaining undistributed parcels at 1.5 million Swiss francs – a huge sum largely transferred to Germany with the help of tax exemptions granted by Werner Hilpert, the CDU finance minister of Hesse, where the party was the junior partner in a coalition with the social democrats. The sum was channelled into a new and similarly dubious enterprise directed by Stegerwald – a building programme in Adenauer's home town of Cologne.[80]

---

[75] Cf. Küppers, *Joseph Wirth*, 303. See also the impressions of the former social-democratic Prussian minister-president Otto Braun cited in Hagen Schulze, *Otto Braun oder Preußens demokratische Sendung* (Frankfurt, Berlin, Vienna: Propyläen, 1981), 834.

[76] Hörster-Philipps, *Joseph Wirth*, 628–9 and 650–60. See also Procès-verbal d'audition der Schweizerischen Bundesanwaltschaft, Dr. Kindt-Kiefer, 8 August 1947, BAR, E 4320 (B), 17.

[77] Summarised in an internal Caritas report of 1963: F. Klein and M. Vorgrimler, Die Christliche Nothilfe (CHN) und der Deutsche Caritasverband (DCV). Ihre Zusammenarbeit in der Zeit von 1946–1963, Freiburg ca. 1963, Archiv des Deutschen Caritasverbandes (henceforth: ADCV), 371.4 B8.

[78] Hörster-Philipps, *Joseph Wirth*, 659.

[79] See also Geneva Circle, 12 June 1950, KADOC, Archief CEPESS, 3.1.11.

[80] Cf. Finanzminister Schäffer an Präsidenten des Deutschen Bundestages, 5 May 1950, betr. Anfrage Nr. 66 der Abgeordneten Dr. Dr. Höpker-Aschoff, Dr. Schäfer und der Fraktion der FDP betr. erlassene Kaffeesteuer, photocopy of Bundestag proceedings in ADCV, 371.4 B8.

In a letter to the SKVP politician Philipp Etter – a federal councillor or member of the Swiss government – written in 1959, Kindt-Kiefer claimed that he had used CHN funds to the tune of 'only' 20,000 francs for the Geneva Circle.[81] According to Stegerwald, the sum was nearer 200,000 francs, however.[82] Kindt-Kiefer's activities were only one element with the specific purpose of facilitating Franco-German exchanges in Adenauer's elaborate strategy after 1948 to procure financial support for the CDU legally or illegally from business circles or any other sources. As Frank Bösch has demonstrated, this dubious funding policy was mainly intended to compensate for the mass membership of the SPD with an estimated fee income six times higher than the CDU and with international support from British and American sources.[83] Adenauer instigated this strategy and spent much time cultivating useful business contacts. He also made sure, however, that he knew nothing officially – especially nothing about the illegal activities of minions like Kindt-Kiefer whom the Chancellor dropped abruptly in 1955 over his attempt to intervene in the Saar conflict during the referendum campaign there.

In early July 1947, Kindt-Kiefer met with Bruno Dörpinghaus, the secretary-general of the newly formed Arbeitsgemeinschaft of the CDU and CSU at national level.[84] Shortly afterwards, Koutzine reported back to Bidault that he would come to Paris in August and introduce him to Rudolf von Moers, who had assisted Adenauer and Dörpinghaus with establishing contacts abroad.[85] In mid-September 1947 Kindt-Kiefer invited Dörpinghaus to a meeting of French and German Christian democrats in Switzerland to take place in October.[86] Dörpinghaus circulated the invitation to three leading Christian democrats: Adenauer, Kaiser and Erich Köhler from the CDU in Hesse.[87] At a meeting in Königstein in early February 1947, Adenauer had successfully averted the formation of a CDU foreign policy commission with Kaiser as its possible chairman.[88] Still, intra-party battles were continuing to rage in the autumn of 1947 over the eventual national leadership of the CDU as well as its socio-economic and foreign policy orientation.

---

[81] Kindt-Kiefer to Etter, 27 June 1959, BAR, E 4320 (B), 17.
[82] According to Klein/Vorgrimler, Die Christliche Nothilfe, ADCV, 371.4 B8, 20.
[83] Bösch, *Die Adenauer-CDU*, 196–7.   [84] Aktennotiz Dörpinghaus, 3 July 1947, ACDP, 01-009-017.
[85] Koutzine to Falaize [Bidault], 19 July 1947, AN 457, AP 59.
[86] Kindt-Kiefer to Dörpinghaus, 13 September 1947, ACDP, 01-009-017.
[87] Dörpinghaus to Adenauer, Köhler and Kaiser, 15 September 1947, ACDP, 01-009-017.
[88] Hans-Peter Schwarz, *Adenauer. Der Aufstieg: 1876–1952* (Stuttgart: DVA, 1986), 530–2.

It appears that Adenauer did not want to engage in Franco-German contact before having secured full control over his party's foreign policy. In the end, only Dörpinghaus went to St Niklausen after the meeting was rescheduled for November because of visa problems. There, he, von Moers and Kindt-Kiefer met with a French delegation of three led by Pierre Pflimlin, who was about to enter the new French government of Robert Schuman as minister for agriculture. It also comprised Koutzine and Jean Morin, the director of Bidault's ministerial cabinet and a close personal advisor.[89] Substantial policy issues were only touched on superficially, although Dörpinghaus went away from the meeting with the impression that the MRP representatives were not going to make cooperation dependent on CDU acceptance of the economic integration of the Saar with France, which would have been impossible for domestic political reasons.[90] Upon his return from Switzerland, however, Dörpinghaus was reproached by Adenauer for having gone at all without guidance from the CDU leadership.[91] Nevertheless, Dörpinghaus' report combined with his own experience of the NEI congress in Luxembourg in February 1948 convinced Adenauer that he now had to engage personally in developing Franco-German cooperation at the informal party level.

According to Dörpinghaus' recollection decades later he was contacted by phone in February 1948 about whether Adenauer – as well as Müller from the CSU[92] – could participate in the next meeting. Apparently, Dörpinghaus replied that he would provided that Bidault also came. According to the CDU secretary-general, the next meeting on 21–2 March 1948 did take place with both politicians present.[93] Although there is no protocol or summary of this meeting, Dörpinghaus's version has been adopted uncritically by historians.[94] Adenauer did, however, take part in the next meeting on 29 June 1948, at which Bidault definitely was not present.[95] After the following meeting in October 1948, in which Bidault did participate, moreover, he reported back to the CDU executive

[89] ACDP, 01-009-017; Bruno Dörpinghaus, 'Die Genfer Sitzungen – Erste Zusammenkünfte führender christlich-demokratischer Politiker im Nachkriegseuropa', in Dieter Blumenwitz *et al.* (eds.), *Konrad Adenauer und seine Zeit. Politik und Persönlichkeit des ersten Bundeskanzlers* (Stuttgart: DVA, 1976), 544.
[90] Ibid.   [91] Adenauer to Dörpinghaus, 8 December 1947, ACDP, 01-009-017.
[92] Aktiennotiz Dörpinghaus für Dr. Josef Müller vom 1.3.1948, ACDP, 01-009-017.
[93] Dörpinghaus, 'Die Genfer Sitzungen', 545–50.
[94] See, for example, Bacharan-Gressel, 'Les Organisations', 50; Chenaux, *Une Europe Vaticane?*, 130.
[95] Geneva Circle, 29 June 1948, ACDP 01-009–017; Compte rendu d'une rencontre à Genève entre des personnalités politiques allemandes appartenant à la Commission des Affaires Étrangeres de la C. D. U. et des personnalités françaises par Barthélémy Ott, Conseiller de la République, AN 457, AP 59.

in the British zone about his 'first meeting' with the MRP politician.[96] It is more likely therefore, that Adenauer was first scrutinised at the meetings in March[97] and June 1948 by other MRP politicians before he was able to meet with Bidault after he had been replaced by Schuman as foreign minister in late July 1948. Confirming this version of events, Morin recounted in an interview in the 1950s that he came away from the early meetings with the distinct impression that Adenauer was 'pro-French' and would be a suitable interlocutor for Bidault.[98]

The Geneva Circle meetings took place regularly every three to four months from mid-1948. From October 1948, they also included politicians from the other western European NEI parties. Until the meeting on 10 June 1949 inclusive, Adenauer and Bidault regularly took part. After Adenauer's election as chancellor, which facilitated Christian democratic cooperation at the intergovernmental level, the meetings were still attended by prominent Christian democrats. On 21 November 1949, for example, von Brentano – the CDU/CSU parliamentary party leader – and Finance Minister Fritz Schäffer were there and – for the MRP – its secretary-general, André Colin, Maurice Schumann and Bichet. The meetings usually took place in Koutzine's private flat. Until 1949, CDU party newspapers sometimes reported Adenauer's participation in CHN/ ICHN meetings to explain his absence from Germany.[99] In June 1950, Rosenberg warned that Agence France Press had reported three times about international meetings in Geneva, although only in a very general way.[100] Nonetheless, the Geneva Circle successfully retained its confidential character. When the cantonal police started an investigation in the spring of 1951 to find out the purpose of the meetings, they even failed to extract the spelling of the participants' names from the staff of the hotel Beau Rivage, where Koutzine was a much better customer than the police, let alone finding out their political functions abroad.[101]

[96] Zonenausschusssitzung CDU britische Zone 28/29.10.1948, Königswinter, printed in *Konrad Adenauer und die CDU*, 718.
[97] Koutzine to Falaize, 23 February 1948, AN 457, AP 59; Adenauer to Kindt-Kiefer, 27 March 1948, Adenauer, *Briefe 1947–1949* (Berlin: Siedler, 1984), 192–3, with no information on the French participants; Adenauer to Kindt-Kiefer, 30 March 1948, ibid., 195, where he refers only to information received from Morin at Geneva, which is also indicative of Bidault's absence.
[98] Georgette Elgey, *La République des illusions 1945–1951* (Paris: Fayard, 1965), 384. This is also the conclusion in Schwarz, *Adenauer. Der Aufstieg*, 559.
[99] See, for example, 'Dr. Adenauer in der Schweiz', *Allgemeine Kölnische Rundschau*, 22 December 1948.
[100] Geneva Circle, 12 June 1950, KADOC, Archief CEPESS, 3.1.11.
[101] Inspektor Marchesi [Polizeikorps, Politische Abteilung, Kanton Genf] an den Leiter der Politischen Abteilung, 5 April 1951, BAR, E 4320 (B), 102.

Christian democratic networking after 1945 extended beyond the formalised cooperation in the NEI and the confidential meetings of the Geneva Circle with their partially overlapping membership, however. Directly and indirectly affiliated organisations played a role, too, such as the NEI's youth organisation and the parties' study centres and foundations that began to develop contacts. A younger generation of future leaders organised themselves and were given access to high-level transnational networking early on. The list of younger participants at the NEI congress in Luxembourg in February 1948, who did not yet officially represent their parties, included at least three prominent names: the Belgian Leo Tindemans, who was twenty-six and later became secretary-general of the European Union of Christian Democrats (EUCD) 1965–74, the first president of the EPP 1976–85 and Belgian prime minister 1974–7; Giulio Andreotti, who was twenty-nine, already a member of the Italian parliament, held ministerial posts from 1954 onwards and was prime minister seven times during 1972–92;[102] and Hans-August Lücker from the CSU, who was thirty-two, first became a Member of the European Parliament (MEP) in 1958 and was leader of the CD Group 1969–75. Other party forums for exchanges included the national congresses, which were regularly attended by delegations from sister parties after World War II.[103]

The European Movement also brought Christian democrats together. Although there is no hard evidence, Poher has recalled that Schuman and Adenauer met for the first time after World War II at its congress at The Hague in May 1948, in which both definitely took part.[104] National parliamentary commissions also organised foreign contacts. Thus, Pezet directed a study trip of a Senate commission to Germany in the spring of 1949 which included meetings with von Brentano, Arnold and other CDU politicians.[105] Importantly, leading Christian democrats also utilised direct private contacts. This is especially true of Adenauer and Schuman, who was not well networked within either the MRP or the NEI, but nevertheless needed close

---

[102] Andreotti had already attended the first meeting at Luzerne in 1947. See Giulio Andreotti, *Visti da vicino* (Milan: Rizzoli, 1982), 142.

[103] See, for example, Rosenberg to Escher, 30 May 1949, BAR, CVP-Archiv JII.181, 2348 about the lasting impression left by Schuman's discourse on the need for Franco-German reconciliation at the MRP congress in 1949.

[104] Poher, *Trois fois président*, 92. See also Robert Rochefort, *Robert Schuman* (Paris: Éditions du Cerf, 1968), 233.

[105] Ernest Pezet to Roger Massip, 10 May 1958, AHC, Fonds Ernest Pezet, P.E. 16, Dossier 9: Commission d'information et d'enquête sénatoriale en Allemagne. Origines du Plan Schuman et de la C.E.C.A., and the annex Extraits du Rapport politique de M. Ernest Pezet, Président de la Commission Senatoriale d'Information en Allemagne, 25 avril – 4 mai 1949.

personal contacts with German leaders to implement his policy of reconciliation and integration as French foreign minister from 1948 to 1952.

Bizarrely in view of the importance of their relationship, it is impossible on the basis of the available evidence to reconstruct when Adenauer and Schuman actually met for the first time. Because of his personal background and policy preferences, Schuman was eyed with suspicion in France as possibly being too germanophile. The Communist leader Jacques Duclos once denounced Schuman, who had to serve in a minor administrative post in the German army in Alsace-Lorraine during World War I, as 'the German officer' in the Assemblée Nationale.[106] As a consequence, Schuman had an interest in playing down their familiarity with each other for the purposes of French politics.[107] If Maurice Schumann really suggested an early meeting between Adenauer and Schuman at the NEI congress in Luxembourg in early 1948, as he recalled decades later,[108] Adenauer would not have told the MRP leader, who remained more attached to Gaullist policy goals for longer than many other leading MRP politicians, that he knew his colleague already. Some authors have argued that it is a myth that Adenauer and Schuman became acquainted in the interwar period.[109] Based on his recollections of conversations with him before his death in 1963, Lücker on the other hand has made far-reaching claims about a close friendship even going back to a first meeting in Düsseldorf in 1912.[110] There is no hard evidence for most of his assertions, however, while others are obviously false. This is true of an alleged meeting at a SIPDIC congress 'in Bierville' in the autumn of 1925, for example, which confuses Catholic party cooperation and Sangnier's peace movement.[111] More credible, but also without evidence, Lücker has also claimed that Adenauer and Schuman met privately for the first time after World War II in Bad Kreuznach in March 1947.[112]

---

[106] Cited in Rochefort, *Robert Schuman*, 177; see also Hüser, *Frankreichs 'doppelte Deutschlandpolitik'*, 286. Charles de Gaulle also said about Schuman that 'he is a German, a good German, but a German'. Cited in Bossuat, *Les Fondateurs*, 150.

[107] Cf. Konrad Adenauer, *Erinnerungen 1945–1953* (Stuttgart: DVA, 1965), 296; Robert Schuman, *Pour l'Europe* (Paris: Nagel, 1963) even gives 1949 as the year of their first meeting, which is obviously incorrect.

[108] Maurice Schumann, 'Regards sur le MRP', *France Forum* 316 (1997), 38–9, adopted in Bruno Béthouart, 'La France, Robert Schuman et l'Europe', *Historisch-Politische Mitteilungen* 7 (1999), 209.

[109] Roth, 'Robert Schuman', 129.

[110] Hans August Lücker and Jean Seitlinger, *Robert Schuman und die Einigung Europas* (Luxembourg, Bonn: Éditions Saint-Paul / Bouvier, 2000), 16.

[111] Ibid., 30, 80 and 97.

[112] Ibid., 60. Such a meeting could have been brokered by Aloys Ruppel, director of the Gutenberg Museum in Mainz, who knew Schuman from before 1918, when he headed the archives of the

Nevertheless, it is highly likely that Adenauer and Schuman did know each other from before World War II, but perhaps more superficially. Thus, Schuman definitely participated in the small SIPDIC congress in Cologne in 1932 which Adenauer chaired. In view of Adenauer's intense interest in relations with France, Schuman's fluent German as well as the common bond of membership in the same Catholic student fraternity in Bonn, they should at least have met and talked then, if not on other occasions, too. Supporting evidence comes from a press communiqué that the CDU issued after a private meeting between Adenauer and Schuman in Bassenheim in the French zone in October 1948, that both politicians had been 'on friendly terms since before 1933' – information that, given Adenauer's tight control over information policy, must have come from him directly.[113] Moreover, when Adenauer reported this meeting internally to the CDU executive in the British zone, he referred to Schuman as 'an old acquaintance'.[114] After Bassenheim, the two politicians began to exchange letters.

Franco-German relations were at the top of the political agendas not only of Adenauer and Schuman, but of the networking Christian democrats more generally. Crucially, in their transnational contacts and communication they quickly arrived at a common version of the recent European past and in particular, of Germany's role in it, that was compatible with the inclusion of the emerging western German state into new forms of European integration. Müller from the Bavarian CSU and Lewandowski from the ÖVP later recalled that some Dutch Catholics in particular raised the issue of the recognition of a collective national guilt for German war crimes as a possible precondition for the full inclusion of the CDU/CSU in transnational cooperation in advance of the NEI congress in Luxembourg in early 1948.[115] Adenauer rejected the idea of collective guilt

Lorraine region in Metz. Although Ruppel exchanged letters with Schuman and saw him after 1945, however, their correspondence includes no reference to a possible meeting between Schuman and Adenauer. See Mainzer Stadtarchiv (henceforth: StA Mz), 80/17. In a meeting with Hans Schäffer in early June 1950, however, Adenauer recalled a first postwar meeting with Schuman 'in 1946 or 1947'. See Tagebuch Hans Schäffer, 3 June 1950, printed as 'Konrad Adenauer und der Schuman-Plan. Ein Quellenzeugnis', in Klaus Schwabe (ed.), *Die Anfänge des Schuman-Plans 1950/51 / The Beginnings of the Schuman-Plan* (Baden-Baden: Nomos, 1988), 133.

[113] Der französische Aussenminister Robert Schuman, Presseerklärung CDU, Bonn, 12 October 1948, Stiftung Bundeskanzler Adenauer Haus (henceforth: SBKAH), I/02.02.

[114] Zonenausschuß CDU britische Zone, 28./29.10.1948, printed in *Konrad Adenauer und die CDU*, 718.

[115] Müller, *Bis zur letzten Konsequenz*, 360–1; Rudolf Lewandowski, 'Der Traum von Europa', *Rheinischer Merkur*, 15 June 1973. See also written interview with Müller, n.d. [post-Luxembourg], ACSP, Nachlass Josef Müller. See also Jac Bosmans, 'Das Ringen um Europa. Die Christdemokraten der Niederlande und Deutschlands in den "Nouvelles Équipes Internationales" (1947–1965)', in Jac Bosmans (ed.), *Europagedanke, Europabewegung und Europapolitik in den Niederlanden und Deutschland seit dem Ersten Weltkrieg* (Münster: LIT, 1996), 140.

in his improvised speech, emphasising the role of Christians in the resistance against national socialism.[116] At this stage, his defensive attitude derived more from a political reflex than a real political need to rebuff the idea of collective guilt, however. At Luxembourg, the Christian democrats actually agreed with ease on a confessional variation of the at that time popular conception of the two Germanies: the guilty Protestant-Prussian east which was lost for Western civilisation, and the Catholic-Roman west, which could, and actually deserved to be, rehabilitated and integrated into the new Europe.

The French philosopher Émile Caro first spoke of what he perceived as the two Germanies in 1872: the Germany of Prussian militarism and the Germany of Goethe and Kant. The particular Catholic *topos* of the two Germanies dated back to the interwar period, however. Sangnier, for example, argued after 1918 that a Catholic-influenced Germany interested in reconciliation opposed a militant Prussian-dominated Germany intent on revenge.[117] In his report for the NEI congress in Luxembourg,[118] the KVP trade unionist Serrarens claimed that the Germany west of the river Elbe, broadly speaking, had been first under the civilising influence of the Roman Empire, then of the Carolingian Empire and, later, of democratic emancipatory ideas. Up to a point, the historic free cities like Hamburg and Frankfurt shared this same tradition. The idea of a better western Germany culminated in a new romantic vision of the extended Catholic Rhineland not as a contested border region between two countries – France and Germany – with historic nationalist claims, but the emotional hotbed of reconciliation in a de-nationalised Europe. In Luxembourg, Adenauer heaped praise on 'the Rhenish people' who – contrary to the eastern German provinces – had always been filled with the spirit of liberty, citing the fact that the National Socialists recorded their worst result in the last elections during the Weimar Republic in the very predominantly Catholic constituency of Cologne-Aachen.[119] In the same vein, the Swiss SKVP deputy Karl Wick conjured up the image of the European region between

---

[116] No verbatim notes were taken, but see the converging reports of it in Konrad Adenauer, Ansprache, NEI-Kongreß, Luxembourg, 30.1.-1.2.1948, rekonstruiert von Hans August Lücker nach Erinnerungen und zeitgenössischen Quellen, Mitteilung Lückers an das ACDP, Oktober 1981, ACDP 09-002-011/2; 'Die Luxemburger Tagung. Adenauer als Gast der christlichen Parteien Westeuropas', *Die Welt*, 3 February 1948; 'Christlich-demokratische Internationale?', *Rheinischer Merkur*, 7 February 1948.
[117] Vecchio, *Alla ricerca*, 292.
[118] P. J. S. Serrarens, Le problème allemand, son aspect politique, NEI, Le problème allemand, session de Luxembourg 30–31 janvier et 1er février 1948, BAR, CVP-Archiv JII.181, 2350.
[119] 'Christlich-demokratische Internationale?', *Rheinischer Merkur*, 7 February 1948.

the Loire and the Rhine as 'a mediator between Germany and France' – reconstituting a kind of democratic Carolingian Europe from its former Lotharingian centre.[120]

In contrast, Serrarens argued in his report, the alienation of the German East from civilised Europe began with Luther and the reformation, which destroyed its unity. The fight of the Protestants against the Catholic Church later culminated in Bismarck establishing Prussian hegemony over Catholic Austria in 1866 and in the Prussian-liberal *Kulturkampf* in the 1870s. 'Central Europe is Europe's central problem,' Serrarens put it, and this problem had arisen as a result of what he called the 'Prussification of Germany' leading straight to national socialism and World War II – and, crucially, greater support for both nationalism and Marxism as derivatives of Protestant-influenced materialism in Soviet-occupied eastern Germany after 1945. In his report on 'spiritual and cultural aspects' of the German question, the Luxembourger Pierre Frieden – drawing upon all available cultural prejudices and actual experiences during the occupation – supplemented Serrarens' analysis with an amateurish psychological study of the archetypical Protestant-Prussian German: he was exhibitionist, expressing his views in deafening tones. He had an overpowering desire to play an important role. 'He likes to be, and to feel, very important.' On top of everything came a dangerous romanticism and idealism which could easily be abused by evil political leaders like Hitler.[121]

Variations of this cliché-ridden interpretation of the origins of national socialism as a Prussian-Protestant phenomenon were widespread among Catholic western German intellectual elites after 1945.[122] As Maria Mitchell has shown, many Catholic CDU/CSU politicians held such views.[123] Crucially, however, the Manichean view of two Germanies united the transnationally networked Christian democrats in western Europe. The historical evidence clearly had to be twisted somewhat to make the black-and-white interpretation of the recent German past appear credible. After

---

[120] Die deutsche Frage, Exposé zuhänden der Konferenz christlicher Politiker, Luxemburg, 30./31. Januar, 1. Februar 1948, Nationalrat Dr. Karl Wick, BAR, CVP-Archiv JII.181, 2662.

[121] Pierre Frieden, Le problème allemand, son aspect spirituel et culturel, NEI, Le problème allemand, session de Luxembourg 30–31 janvier et 1er février 1948, BAR, CVP-Archiv JII.181, 2350. This idea was also shared by Catholic intellectual circles in Germany, who were nevertheless opposed to the CDU/CSU's interconfessional character. See also Marie-Emmanuelle Reytier, 'Die deutschen Katholiken und der Gedanke der europäischen Einigung 1945–1949. Wende oder Kontinuität?', *Jahrbuch für europäische Geschichte* 3 (2002), 171; Heinz Gollwitzer, *Europabild und Europagedanke* (Munich: Beck, 1951), 174–201 and 246–61.

[122] Reytier, 'Die deutschen Katholiken'.

[123] Maria Mitchell, 'Materialism and Secularism: CDU Politicians and National Socialism 1945–1949', *Journal of Modern History* 67 (1995), 278–308.

all, fascism first succeeded in Catholic Italy. National socialism had deeper roots in some regions of the former Catholic Habsburg Empire, especially German-speaking Bohemia, although it was enriched with racist ideology. Adolf Hitler came from Braunau in Catholic Upper Austria and was largely politically socialised in Vienna, where he lived from 1907 to 1913. At the same time, Prussia remained a fortress of the Weimar Republic until 1932 under the leadership of the SPD – the only party at that stage with fully democratic credentials.

Another facet of the Catholic interpretation of national socialism further facilitated the moral rehabilitation of the western Germans, the inclusion of the CDU/CSU in party cooperation and of the new western German state in European integration: the diffusion of the question of guilt through its Europeanisation. Frieden suggested that there were indeed specifically German aspects of the success of national socialism, especially the romantic disposition of mainly Protestant elites which made them susceptible to the national socialist ideological salvation messages. At the same time, fascism 'developed not only in Germany, but in Europe as a whole'.[124] As Wick argued, national socialism was 'more the expression of an international *Zeitgeist* than of a national *Volksgeist*'. In his view, it was 'the Teuton expression of a deep societal crisis just as bolshevism is its Russian-Asian expression'.[125] Ultimately, both political regimes could only succeed in an unjust and morally corrupt modern world. This was a world that in the eyes of the Christian democrats had largely emerged in the nineteenth century under the influence of the materialist ideology of liberalism with its individualist creed and interest in capitalist exploitation resulting in a loss of religious faith and values and creating a moral vacuum. In fact, Wick even spoke of a 'European collective guilt' – the guilt largely, of the other, non-Catholic Europe. Rather conveniently, this consensual Christian democratic view of recent European history not only absolved the western Germans from confronting their past, but also Catholic Europe from discussing its crucial role in the evolution and stabilisation of fascist, clerical and collaborationist regimes until 1945.

At the height of the Cold War in 1948–9, the Catholic idea of the two Germanies and the two Europes made the deepening division of Germany into a democratic west and a communist Soviet-controlled east almost

---

[124] Pierre Frieden, Le problème allemand, son aspect spirituel et culturel, NEI, Le problème allemand, session de Luxembourg 30–31 janvier et 1er février 1948, BAR, CVP-Archiv JII.181, 2350.

[125] Die deutsche Frage, Exposé zuhänden der Konferenz christlicher Politiker, Luxemburg, 30./31. Januar, 1. Februar 1948, Nationalrat Dr. Karl Wick, BAR, CVP-Archiv JII.181, 2662.

seem like a blessing, as only it appeared to allow a Christian democratic reconstruction of the amputated Federal Republic. The division of Europe was its inevitable and acceptable consequence despite the exclusion of Catholic countries like Poland. It assisted the Christian democrats in becoming the hegemonic political force in continental western Europe as the main bulwark against Soviet communism, and also made it easier to overcome the Franco-German antagonism. In western Germany, these objectives could only be pursued in cooperation with the CDU/CSU. Although it was an inter-confessional party, its leadership, members and voters were predominately Catholics with a new dominance of western and southern German traditions of political Catholicism compared to the interwar Centre Party. Finance Minister Schäffer also emphasised this in Geneva in November 1949.[126] In contrast, the SPD had a much stronger following among Protestants and in northern Germany. The CDU/CSU was also in favour of a federal state which was fully compatible with its sister parties' preference for a decentralised Germany, whereas the SPD shared the British Labour Party's dream of the centralised welfare state. Under the strong influence of Adenauer, moreover, the CDU/CSU pursued much more moderate policies than the SPD on contested issues like the future of the Saar and German representation on the International Ruhr Authority. Adenauer's unequivocal preference for Western integration over exploring possible options for German unification was contested within the CDU/CSU, not only by Kaiser, but also Brüning, who returned from his exile in the US, and Müller, who supported intra-German talks in 1948, for example. These internal divisions were also obvious to the French participants in the early meetings of the Geneva Circle.[127] They, as well as the other sister parties in western Europe, worked hard to support Adenauer by investing him with the authority of a highly respected transnational interlocutor and future statesman. This in turn assisted him in his internal fight for his foreign policy concept and in the conflict with the SPD.

While Adenauer used both the idea of two Germanies and this external support strategically, especially against Kaiser,[128] his policy preferences were long-standing and stable, largely going back to the interwar period.

[126] Geneva Circle, 21 November 1949, ACDP, 01-009-017.
[127] Compte rendu d'une rencontre à Genève entre des personnalités politiques allemandes appartenant à la Commission des Affaires Étrangères de la C.D.U. et des personnalités françaises, par Barthélémy Ott, Conseiller de la République, AN 457, AP 59.
[128] See also Wilfried Loth, 'German Conceptions of Europe during the Escalation of the East-West Conflict, 1945–1949', in Becker and Knipping (eds.), *Power in Europe?*, 527.

In conversations with American secret service officers in 1945 he already espoused the idea of two Germanies, one influenced by Roman culture, the other Prussian-dominated.[129] In November 1948 he also told Robert Murphy, the political advisor to Lucius D. Clay, the military governor in the US zone, that the mentality of the western Germans was more suitable for a policy of reconciliation with France than that of the eastern Germans, where Marxism and nationalism had a stronger hold over the population.[130] As his close advisor Herbert Blankenhorn recalled later, Adenauer was 'a real western German who felt himself to be part of the Rhenish-Western cultural space'.[131] Werner Weidenfeld has also pointed out that Prussia for Adenauer stood for militarism and materialism and a dangerous adoration of the state.[132] He certainly regarded its dissolution by the Allies in 1945 as a healthy by-product of World War II. Most importantly in the eyes of the transnationally networked Christian democrats, however, Adenauer accepted the division of Germany. Contradicting Müller, he insisted in the Geneva Circle in June 1948, for example, that 'we have two separate Germanies of a totally different kind ... This is a fact which cannot be changed.'[133] In these circumstances, moreover, his primary foreign policy objective was Franco-German rapprochement in an integrated western Europe. As Koutzine summarised it in an analysis for Bidault in 1951: 'Chancellor Adenauer aims at the creation of a European federation. His entire foreign policy is essentially based on this objective. He considers the Franco-German entente as the cornerstone of his grand design which can only be realised in a wider western European context. Chancellor Adenauer thus sacrifices deliberately the question of German unity. He believes that the integration of western Germany is more important than the restoration of the unity of the former Reich.'[134]

For tactical reasons, Adenauer never formulated his policy so clearly in public as Koutzine did in his internal analysis. To legitimise his refusal to negotiate or even just contemplate unification involving concessions to the Soviet Union during 1947–8 and over the Stalin notes in 1952, Adenauer mostly drew upon the 'magnet theory' that the integration of the Federal

---

[129] Schwarz, *Adenauer. Der Aufstieg*, 447.
[130] Murphy to Bohlen, 24 November 1948, cited in ibid., 562–3.
[131] Herbert Blankenhorn, *Verständnis und Verständigung. Blätter eines politischen Tagebuchs 1949 bis 1979* (Frankfurt/Main: Propyläen, 1980), 43.
[132] Werner Weidenfeld, *Konrad Adenauer und Europa. Die geistigen Grundlagen der westeuropäischen Integrationspolitik des ersten Bundeskanzlers* (Bonn: Europa Union-Verlag, 1976), 42–51 and 192–200. See also Doering-Manteuffel, 'Rheinischer Katholik', 239.
[133] Geneva Circle, 29 June 1948, ACDP, 01-009-017.
[134] Koutzine, La Tactique du Chancelier Adenauer, AN 457, AP 59.

Republic into the Western world would somehow extricate the German
East from Soviet control sooner or later, eventually leading to reunification. He also made tactical concessions to nationalist sentiment such as
during the conflict with Schuman over the Saar Conventions in early 1950.
Despite all camouflage, however, the task to implement his foreign policy
concept seemed daunting in the beginning. The more Adenauer was
attacked domestically, however, the more he became everyone's darling
among the western European Christian democrats. Even leading
Protestants within the CDU such as Hermann Ehlers, who supported
Adenauer's Western orientation, had a stronger preference for reunifica-
tion and retained contacts in eastern Germany.[135] From 1949, the liberal
FDP, whose national-liberal wing was particularly keen to exploit any
opening for reunification, were unreliable fellows in the national coalition
government. Reinhold Maier, the liberal minister-president of Baden-
Württemberg, claimed with some justification in 1953 that many
Catholics 'welcomed' no progress over reunification. One year before the
FDP left the coalition government with the CDU in Northrhine-
Westphalia and at the national level, one of their leaflets from 1955 alleged
that 'for the CDU reunification starts with the separation of the Saar region
and ends with writing off the Protestant Germans in the Soviet zone'.[136]

Yet most important – and most motivating for transnational Christian
democracy – was SPD policy under Kurt Schumacher, who had survived
the concentration camp to become the party's uncontested postwar leader.
Although there were other tendencies within the party more favourable to
Adenauer's policy of Western integration, Schumacher had a very strong
national orientation and continued to think in terms of balance of power,
which would allow Germany to play a mediating role in Europe. He was
not opposed to European integration as such, but concerned that it would
make reunification impossible. Using nationalist rhetoric, he also insisted
much more categorically than Adenauer on Germany's formal equality
from the start, leading his party into unified opposition to the initially
associate membership of the Federal Republic in the Council of Europe in
June 1950.[137] Even under Schumacher's successor, Erich Ollenhauer, the
SPD retained its 'habit of seeing things in purely German terms', as

[135] Bösch, *Die Adenauer-CDU*, 122.   [136] Ibid., 121.
[137] Cf. Detlef Rogosch, 'Sozialdemokratie zwischen nationaler Orientierung und Westintegration
1945–1957', in Mareike König and Matthias Schulz (eds.), *Die Bundesrepublik Deutschland und
die europäische Einigung 1949–2000. Politische Akteure, gesellschaftliche Kräfte und internationale
Erfahrungen* (Stuttgart: Franz Steiner, 2004), 287–310.

William Paterson has put it.[138] At least as important as Schumacher's unfocused policy on European integration was his political style which deterred socialist sister parties, especially the French SFIO, severely limiting the SPD's potential to use transnational networks to advance its policy objectives. His nationalist campaign culminated in his interruption in the Bundestag debate about German participation in the International Ruhr Authority in November 1949 when he called Adenauer 'Chancellor of the Allies'. André François-Poncet, French ambassador to the German Reich in the 1930s and High Commissioner from 1949 to 1953, felt that he was dealing with 'a Hitler from the Left'.[139] Paradoxically, Schumacher, who was persecuted by the National Socialists and was leading the only political party that had stood up for the Weimar Republic in voting against the so-called Enabling Law in March 1933, appeared to represent everything that Frieden believed had facilitated the rise of national socialism: his nationalist rhetoric was aggressive and loud, and he had an idealised vision of a unified Germany and its mediating role in Europe. The more Schumacher and the SPD seemed to incarnate the Christian democrats' imagined German East, the more the Christian democrats and even many continental European socialists saw Adenauer as the only hope for the German West in an integrated Europe embedded in larger Western structures. He was firm, but calm and quiet, reserved, but witty, and his claim that his primary allegiance was European, not German, was sincere and credible.[140]

Such an integrated Europe had to have a strong economic dimension. As Hanns Jürgen Küsters has pointed out in relation to Adenauer, however, for the Christian democrats the economic content 'was instrumental for the solution of political problems'.[141] A general common market was the ultimate objective for most Christian democrats. The economic resolution of the NEI congress in The Hague in September 1948 still refrained from making concrete proposals for economic integration. In their public message for 1949 the NEI stipulated, however, that the Benelux customs union of the Low Countries that was under construction at the time should be seen as an exemplary step on the road to the 'reconstruction of the

---

[138] William E. Paterson, *The SPD and European Integration* (Farnborough: Saxon House, 1974), 130.

[139] Cited in Poidevin, *Robert Schuman*, 216.

[140] As in his improvised speech in Luxembourg. Cf. Hans August Lücker, Mitteilung an das ACDP, October 1981, Konrad Adenauer und die Tagung der NEI (heute EUCD) Anfang 1948 in Luxemburg, ACDP, 09-002-011/2.

[141] Hanns Jürgen Küsters, 'Konrad Adenauer und die Idee einer wirtschaftlichen Verflechtung mit Frankreich', in Andreas Wilkens (ed.), *Die deutsch-französischen Wirtschaftsbeziehungen 1945–1960 / Les Relations économiques franco-allemandes 1945–1960* (Sigmaringen: Jan Thorbecke, 1997), 67.

European economy as a whole'.[142] In the Geneva Circle, Bidault amongst others, pushed hard for economic integration. Western Europe should be 'very progressive' in the economic field, but more prudent as regards direct political integration, which was a more sensitive issue domestically.[143] When the Brussels Pact between France, Britain and the Benelux countries was formed in 1948, Bidault linked his proposal for a European assembly of national parliamentarians to the objective of creating a customs and economic union.[144] Later on, many Christian democrats saw the Schuman Plan of May 1950 as 'the prototype for the common European market', as the MRP politician Alfred Coste-Floret, who was to become NEI secretary-general from 1955 to 1960, put it.[145] Whether this aim could best be realised as a result of further vertical integration of economic sectors like transport and agriculture, for example, or by the direct progression to a horizontal customs union was highly contested in the first half of the 1950s. For the transnationally networked Christian democrats this was never a clear dogmatic alternative, however, but depended largely on the political feasibility of the various proposals.

The Christian democrats never intervened directly through the NEI or the Geneva Circle in the negotiation and implementation of economic treaty clauses, either in the context of the ECSC during 1950–1 or the EEC during 1955–7. This was the task of national governments and ministries – largely controlled by them – in inter-state negotiations with input from domestic political actors. Nevertheless, they had three broad objectives and conditions in the early stages of economic integration. The first concerned the full inclusion of the German economy in economic reconstruction.[146] The pragmatic reason for this demand lay in the traditional interdependence especially of the Benelux economies with the German economy which Lamalle had already emphasised in his report on economic aspects of the German question at the NEI congress in Luxembourg. Whatever the French security concerns, the German economy was needed for revitalising

---

[142] Botschaft der NEI für 1949, ÖstA, Archiv der Republik (henceforth: AdR), BKA/AA, II–pol, Int.14, Zl.80.755–pol/49.

[143] Geneva Circle, 21 October 1948, Aktennotiz Felix Hurdes für Leopold Figl und Karl Gruber, IfZG Innsbruck, Karl Gruber Archiv, Karton 41.

[144] See also Barthélemy Ott, *Georges Bidault. L'indomptable* (Annonay: Imprimerie du Vivarais, 1975), 86.

[145] Cited in Gérard Bossuat, 'La Vraie Nature de la politique européenne de la France (1950–1957)', in Gilbert Trausch (ed.), *Die Europäische Integration vom Schuman-Plan bis zu den Verträgen von Rom / The European Integration from the Schuman-Plan to the Treaties of Rome* (Baden-Baden: Nomos, 1993), 207. For other examples see Bichet in the Geneva Circle, 11 December 1950, ACDP, 01-009-017; Nicolas Margue in the NEI executive committee, Paris, 4 November 1950, ACDP, 09-002-002.

[146] See also Résolution adoptée par la Conférence des Nouvelles Équipes Internationales tenue à Luxembourg du 29 janvier au 1er février 1948, ACDP, 09-002-011/2.

the western European economy as a whole, both as an importer of agricultural products and a provider of finished industrial goods. The full integration of the German economy had another, political dimension, however. The use of 'negative methods' as in the Versailles Treaty would make the Germans susceptible to the temptations of what Lamalle called the 'oriental barbarism' of Soviet communism, with potentially terrible economic and security effects on western Europe.[147] The allegiance of the western Germans had to be acquired not just with promises of freedom, but of more bread and butter and long-term prosperity.

The second core objective was to enhance western Europe's security more generally. This was to be achieved through rising welfare from economic integration, which would limit the appeal of the communist ideology and parties elsewhere, as in France and Italy, for example. This was a recurring theme in discussions in the Geneva Circle. In March 1949, for example, Gortais for the MRP and Lina Morino for the DC – the two political parties most concerned about the domestic communist challenge – urged the Christian democrats to proceed quickly with economic integration to prevent the Soviet Union from exploiting western Europe's economic crisis for its purposes.[148] The third objective was that such economic integration would be market-based, but would require a strong social dimension. Neo-liberals like Ludwig Erhard, the German economics minister from 1949, who probably only joined the CDU officially in 1963, were a small minority in Christian democracy after 1945. Despite strong variations in socio-economic policy preferences within and among the NEI parties, the dominant credo was that Europe needed a distinctive third way societal model between liberal capitalism and Soviet communism – not nationalisation, although such a policy option could make sense in specific cases, but Europeanisation with interventionist policies with redistributional dimensions to structure markets. As Gortais argued in the Geneva Circle in June 1949, the integrated Europe needed to overcome the economic and social conservatism of the interwar period and develop a common European economic strategy.[149] Naturally, such a strategy would have to cater for the special needs of core electoral constituencies of the Christian democrats, especially the middle classes and farmers.

---

[147] Désiré Lamalle, Le problème allemand, son aspect économique, NEI, Le problème allemand, session de Luxembourg 30–31 janvier et 1er février 1948, BAR, CVP-Archiv JII.181, 2350.
[148] Geneva Circle, 8 March 1949, ACDP, 01-009-017.
[149] Geneva Circle, 10 June 1949, ACDP, 01-009-017.

The more concrete focus of transnational Christian democracy in the first few years after World War II, however, was its concern with one sector, coal and steel. Arguably, the main French objective after 1945 was to secure access to, and control of, this German sector, with the dual aim of replacing German exports in third countries and preventing the future use of Germany's heavy industry base for renewed aggression against its neighbours.[150] Alan S. Milward has argued that the Schuman Plan proposing the integration of the coal and steel industries of the six founding member states of the ECSC 'was invented to safeguard the Monnet Plan' for domestic French economic modernisation, which missed its targets during 1949–50.[151] This might be true for the actual plan as it was developed by Monnet and a small group of 'pro-European' officials in the French Planning Commissariat and the Quai d'Orsay. The link with the modernisation plan was circumstantial, however. The same holds for the French dissatisfaction with the limited policy competences of the International Ruhr Authority and Adenauer's interest in German equality.[152] These factors only provided additional incentives for going ahead with the integration of coal and steel, which was a highly interdependent sector, as Wendy Asbeek-Brusse has demonstrated.[153] As Milward himself has admitted, however, Monnet's concept might have ended up in a binder without the bold decision by Schuman to assume the political responsibility for proposing it to Adenauer and the French government.[154] Yet, he could only take this step with a reasonable chance of success in May 1950 because transnational Christian democracy had discussed this option for a long time and was immediately able to garner strong political support and to construct domestic and transnational alliances with other parties and social groups to make the Schuman Plan a success.

In 1945, Adenauer again brought up his concept from 1923 of introducing some form of joint control over the coal and steel production of the Ruhr in conversations with French officers.[155] He repeatedly came back to this idea in the transnational forums of the NEI and the Geneva Circle. In the context of the economic report on the German question, the

---

[150] Hüser, *Frankreichs 'doppelte Deutschlandpolitik'*, 718.   [151] Milward, *The Reconstruction*, 395.
[152] Ibid., 392–4.
[153] Wendy Asbeek Brusse, *Tariffs, Trade and European Integration, 1947–1957. From Study Group to Common Market* (New York: St. Martin's Press, 1997), 64–7.
[154] Milward, *The Reconstruction*, 396.
[155] Schwarz, *Adenauer. Der Aufstieg*, 457. Regarding his interwar proposal, which he developed against the background of the Rhineland occupation, see ibid., 277–83; Küsters, 'Konrad Adenauer', 63. In greater detail, although with a polemical tinge, Henning Köhler, *Adenauer und die rheinische Republik. Der erste Anlauf 1918–1924* (Opladen: Westdeutscher Verlag, 1986).

integration of basic industries had already been discussed at the Luxembourg congress in early 1948,[156] where Adenauer may have raised the possibility of joint control for the first time in a transnational party forum.[157] When Morin, the director of Bidault's ministerial cabinet, mentioned the formation of a French commission to study options for interlocking French and German coal and steel industries in the Geneva Circle in March 1948, Adenauer immediately suggested to Kindt-Kiefer that this should better be done in cooperation with trustworthy German interlocutors such as his advisor, the banker Robert Pferdmenges.[158] During his meeting with Schuman in Bassenheim in October 1948 and again in a subsequent letter to him, Adenauer once more suggested the 'organic interlocking' of French and German basic industries as a solution for French security and an important step towards Franco-German reconciliation.[159] Following upon Adenauer's public declaration as newly elected chancellor on 20 September 1949 that he would give the highest priority to overcoming the Franco-German conflict,[160] von Brentano urged the other Christian democrats at a meeting of the Geneva Circle in November 1949 to take up Adenauer's idea. This was not to create Franco-German trusts or cartels, as in the case of the interwar steel cartel, which would have been unacceptable for the MRP. Instead, it would be geared towards establishing 'effective French control over the production of German companies'.[161] Finally, in a letter sent to Bidault via Koutzine dated 22 March 1950, Adenauer suggested the integration of the French and German coal, steel and chemical industries as a first concrete step towards close Franco-German relations after the conflicts over the Saar Conventions and the conditions for the membership of the Federal Republic in the Council of Europe.[162] The German chancellor received an encouraging first response from Bidault, who was prime minister at that time.[163] This also explains why Bidault was fully informed of the background to the Schuman Plan, and why he actually supported it when the French government discussed it

[156] Cf. Lewandowski, 'Das Europa', 349. The discussions at Luxembourg were not minuted, however, and only the reports have survived in archives.
[157] Josef Müller, 'Die NEI und die Anfänge der Europäischen Gemeinschaft', in EVP-Fraktion (ed.), *Zur Geschichte*, 35–6.
[158] Adenauer to Kindt-Kiefer, 30 March 1948, *Adenauer. Briefe 1947–1949*, 195.
[159] Schwarz, *Adenauer. Der Aufstieg*, 562.
[160] Helga Haftendorn, *Deutsche Außenpolitik zwischen Selbstbeschränkung und Selbstbehauptung 1945–2000* (Stuttgart, Munich: DVA, 2001), 27.
[161] Geneva Circle, 21 November 1949, ACDP, 01-009-017.
[162] Vorschlag von Bundeskanzler Adenauer, Koutzine to Bidault, 22 March 1950, AN 457, AP 59.
[163] Koutzine to Dörpinghaus, 23 March 1950, ACDP, 01-009-017; Koutzine to Bidault, 22 March 1950, AN 457, AP 59.

on 9 May – this despite the fact that he had some misgivings about the foreseen degree of supranationalism, that he had failed to study Monnet's concept when it was first submitted to his office and that he had not been consulted by Schuman in advance. Schuman probably feared that his main rival in MRP foreign policy-making would react less favourably than he actually did.

Discussions with Christian democratic participation about integration in coal and steel also took place in other private and public forums before May 1950. Thus, Pflimlin and Monnet debated the option of creating a supranational authority for regulating the energy complex during a dinner in London in July 1948, for example.[164] When Pezet was in Germany for a study visit with a commission of the French Senate in April and May 1949, he was struck by the enthusiasm of many of his German interlocutors including von Brentano and Arnold, for example, for integration in the coal and steel sector – lasting impressions that he relayed to Schuman upon his return to Paris.[165] Leading Christian democrats saw such European integration not just as an opportunity for better Franco-German relations, but also as a means to prevent the reconstruction of German heavy industry as a state within the state, which had played such a crucial role in the last years of the Weimar Republic in financing the rise of Hitler and Hugenberg. Integration in coal and steel was also discussed publicly, however. French newspapers ventilated this option during 1948–9, albeit not yet foreseeing the full equality of the Federal Republic.[166] Moreover, the European Movement at its congresses in Brussels and Westminster in February and April 1949 also singled out the coal and steel industries as an especially suitable sector for starting supranational vertical integration, an idea taken up once more during the first session of the Consultative Assembly of the Council of Europe in August 1949, where it was propagated by, among others, André Philip, the federalist SFIO politician.[167]

Adenauer was excited that the French Christian democrats had finally taken up his ideas for sector integration in coal and steel with full German

---

[164] John Gillingham, *Coal, Steel and the Rebirth of Europe, 1945–1955. The Germans and French from Ruhr to Economic Community* (Cambridge: Cambridge University Press, 1991), 160.

[165] Commission d'information et d'enquête sénatoriale en Allemagne. Origines du Plan Schuman et de la C. E. C. A., Pezet to Roger Massip, 10 May 1958, AHC, Fonds Ernest Pezet, P. E. 16, Dossier 9.

[166] Bossuat, *L'Europe des français*, 126.

[167] Pierre Gerbet, 'Les Origines du Plan Schuman: le choix de la méthode communautaire par le governement français', in Raymond Poidevin (ed.), *Histoire des débuts de la construction européenne (mars 1948–mai 1950) / Origins of the European Integration (March 1948–May 1950)* (Baden-Baden: Nomos, 1986), 206.

equality. On the margins of his reply to Schuman, he wrote by hand that this had been his aim for twenty-five years.[168] On 11 May 1950 he wrote to the industrialist Paul Silverberg, with whom he had originally discussed the concept in 1923 that 'our project ... of interlocking French and German coal and steel production has finally made progress'.[169] In his memoirs, the chancellor later recalled how much Schuman's initiative and private letter to him of 8 May 1950 – one day before the submission of the plan to the French government – assisted him in isolating Kaiser and Gustav Heinemann from his own party in his Cabinet in the debate – also on 9 May – about accession to the Council of Europe – a coincidence that allowed him to dispatch with this issue after the difficult first three months of 1950 with the heated German public debate about the French Saar Conventions. This issue had cost the Christian democratic network much time and energy.[170]

Starting European integration in the coal and steel sector for the Christian democrats was a natural policy choice. Its precise institutional form was much less clear. In his analysis of the debate on Europe in France, political scientist Craig Parsons has made a great deal of the importance in his view of a fundamental cleavage cutting across political parties between constitutionalists in favour of a European federation and functionalists advocating economic integration with limited political features.[171] While this might be true for the socialists and Radicals, which split down the middle over the decision on the EDC project in 1954, the Manichaean interpretation of the European debate is misleading for the MRP or, indeed, transnational Christian democracy more generally after 1945.[172] Federalists including von Brentano, Teitgen and de Menthon,[173] for example, were keen to construct a European federal state and played an influential role in the Consultative Assembly of the Council of Europe and in drafting the EPC treaty in the ECSC Ad hoc Assembly during 1952–3. Others like de Schryver were more sceptical. They were either keener on faster economic progress, concerned about the political legitimacy of such an ad hoc transition to a federal Europe, or they feared that the smaller states would become marginalised – the main motive for the Benelux

---

[168] Adenauer to Schuman, 8 May 1950, printed in *Adenauer. Briefe 1949–1951* (Berlin: Siedler, 1985), 208–9.

[169] Adenauer to Silverberg, 11 May 1950, printed in ibid., 209.

[170] Adenauer, *Erinnerungen 1945–1953*, 328.

[171] Craig Parsons, *A Certain Idea of Europe* (Ithaca, N. Y., London: Cornell University Press, 2003), 44.

[172] On the attitudes of the French political parties on 'Europe' see also in comparative perspective Gerbet, 'Les Partis politiques'.

[173] On de Menthon's ideas on Europe see also Ducerf, 'François de Menthon'.

governments for insisting on the inclusion of a Council of Ministers in the ECSC Treaty during 1950–1.[174] Crucially, however, European Christian democracy experienced no significant opposition at all to the delegation of sovereignty to European bodies. It was open throughout to new institutional forms for European integration.

Their affinity for the delegation of sovereignty to new European bodies had confessional and ideological reasons that were specific to transnational Christian democracy. First, the political concept of supranationalism had an intriguing parallel in the quasi-supranational authority of the Pope and the Catholic hierarchy. Despite the postwar rhetoric of secularism and inter-confessionalism, this still seemed the natural order of things not only for stout Catholics like Schuman. Secondly, the widespread discursive cultural rationalisation of integration as the emergence of a kind of democratic Carolingian Empire also made supranationalism appear almost like the natural order of European history destroyed by modern nationalism. Strictly speaking, the historic character of the Carolingian Empire was prenational. In a larger sense, however, it appeared as a supranational cultural and political space which was even more or less identical with the core Europe of the founding member states of the ECSC. The Carolingian tradition was evoked again and again as exemplary for postwar Europe. This medieval order was defended against external enemies of Christendom as the emerging postwar order had to be protected against the Soviet threat. At the NEI congress in Bad Ems in 1951, for example, von Brentano spoke of the common defence of the European *Abendland* in what he presented as a tradition reaching from Charlemagne to the battle of 955 against the heathen Magyars, the 'liberation' of Granada in 1492 and the victory of the multinational army led by the Polish King Johann III Sobiesky against Ottoman troops in 1683, ending their siege of Vienna.[175] Importantly, this was not merely a rhetorical construct to rally the Christian democratic troops behind the EDC project. Instead, it was the widely shared world-view of transnational Christian democracy. In the private venue of the Geneva Circle, for example, Bidault, when reporting his experiences of negotiations with Stalin and Molotov, spoke of 'a new Islam that will never retreat even one step and of which we have to expect

---

[174] On de Schryver's attitudes to institutional questions see also Kwanten, *August-Edmond De Schryver*, 435–9.
[175] Entwurf von Hassel für einen Vortrag für MdB von Brentano bei der NEI-Tagung in Bad Ems, September 1951, Bundesarchiv (henceforth: BA), N 1351, 8a. See also Adenauer's speech at the same congress: Stenogramm der Rede des Herrn Bundeskanzlers anlässlich der NEI-Tagung in Bad Ems am 14. September 1951, 15.30 Uhr, Kursaal, Bad Ems, BA, N 1351, 8a.

everything'.[176] Organising Europe against this 'new Islam' in some partly supranational form – thirdly – was also nicely compatible with the idea – derived from Catholic social teaching – of society structured by the principle of subsidiarity. In a speech at the NEI congress in Tours in 1953, Teitgen elaborated this concept with a suggestion to base Christian democratic policy on European institutions on the encyclical *Quadragesimo anno* of 1931.[177] As the subsidiarity principle was concerned with the allocation of social tasks at different levels, from the family upwards, Christian democrats found it easier to imagine the allocation of political decision-making at more than one – including a new European – level than the majority of collectivist socialists, who were still preoccupied with the idea of a centralised nation-state economic order.

Transnational Christian democracy also shared a general preference for combining the establishment – as in the case of the ECSC High Authority – of what Pezet called a 'para-political' institution run by appointed experts,[178] with a popular parliamentary dimension. As Milward has already observed,[179] Christian democrats were not enthusiastic supporters of the neo-functionalist idea of superior technocratic government by experts acting independently of national political or economic pressures. At their congress in The Hague in September 1948, the NEI passed a political resolution which rather vaguely advocated integration 'of a federal or confederal kind'.[180] As a long-term solution, however, the NEI already envisaged a bicameral system with a chamber of member states and a chamber of deputies that would eventually be directly elected – a constitutional design that the Christian democrats also managed to insert into the EPC Treaty and that has influenced European constitutional debates ever since. Below these general constitutional preferences, however, transnational Christian democracy was unified in its institutional pragmatism. Advocating the necessity of 'the abandonment of national sovereignty in favour of an international exercise of power', Bidault insisted in the Geneva Circle in December 1948, for example, that his party was 'more attached to results

[176] Geneva Circle, 21 October 1948, protocol Felix Hurdes, IfZG Innsbruck, Karl Gruber Archiv, Karton 4. For a balanced assessment of Bidault's European policy see also Georges-Henri Soutou, 'Georges Bidault et la construction européenne 1944–1954', in Berstein, Mayeur and Milza (eds.), *Le MRP*, 197–230.
[177] Henri Teitgen, L'Autorité supranationale et la notion de souveraineté. Aspects politiques, Congrès de Tours, 1–6 septembre 1953, BAR, CVP-Archiv JII.181, 2382.
[178] Geneva Circle, 12 June 1950, KADOC, Archief CEPESS, 3.1.11.
[179] Milward, *The European Rescue*, 227–31.
[180] Entschließung, Politischer Ausschuss, NEI-Kongress, Den Haag, 17.-19.9.1948, ACSP, Nachlass Josef Müller.

than their legal form'.[181] Similarly, as Hans-Peter Schwarz and Raymond Poidevin have shown for Adenauer and Schuman,[182] other leading Christian democrats shared a general preference for integration with supranational features, but mainly had an instrumental approach to using institutional designs in particular political circumstances for achieving their primary policy objectives.

Some of these objectives were nationally specific such as Adenauer's interest in achieving the Federal Republic's equality and full sovereignty through European integration and Schuman's aim of guaranteeing effective French control of Germany's heavy industry. Other pragmatic constitutional considerations largely united transnational Christian democracy. One of these was the desire to offer an idealistic western European youth an attractive vision of their future. According to the Christian democratic diagnosis, the youth felt betrayed by fascism and national socialism after 1945 and were now looking for alternative paths to a better world. In this situation, the proposal to rebuild Europe as a federation in the making was the Christian democratic alternative to the promises of communism.[183] Yet such an offer could only ever be attractive if the new Europe were to look fundamentally different from the old Europe of nationalist conflicts and inter-state negotiations, so that the constitutional form acquired symbolic importance. With this objective in mind, the youth organisations pushed hard within the national parties as well as in their transnational cooperation for supranational institutional designs.[184]

A second pragmatic advantage of supranational institutions and majority voting was that it would deprive domestic interest groups of easy access to political parties and ministries in areas of Europeanised policy-making with a complex institutional set of rules and actors. In the Geneva Circle in July 1950, Pezet drew attention to the pitched battles with domestic protectionist economic interests in the intergovernmental Benelux customs union, which had particular difficulties in agreeing on the agricultural dimension, and in the debate about the plan for a Franco-Italian customs

---

[181] Geneva Circle, 22 December 1948, AN 519, AP10.
[182] Poidevin, *Robert Schuman*, 377; Hans-Peter Schwarz, *Adenauer. Der Staatsmann: 1952–1967* (Stuttgart: DVA, 1991), 147. Gerbet, 'Les Partis politiques', 214.
[183] See, for example, the essay by the Austrian NEI youth representative Rudolf Lewandowski, Il est hors de doute, Thesenpapier zur Kooperation christdemokratischer Jugend in Europa, März 1948, ACDP, 09-002-005/1.
[184] Chenaux, *Une Europe Vaticane?*, 154–7.

union which had failed in the previous year.[185] In the coal and steel sector, both the MRP and the CDU/CSU had to confront well-organised private business interests. These interests, moreover, were actually once again well connected across borders from 1946 onwards.[186] More importantly, they shared a strong preference for the traditional instrument of transnational cartels to which the Christian democrats – and in particular the Christian trade unions – were by now opposed.

Crucially, however, insisting on supranational forms of integration as Schuman did when he proposed his plan and in subsequent talks with the Labour government in London, practically guaranteed the self-exclusion of Britain from core Europe integration. By May 1950, the creation of such a core Europe without Britain had become a central objective of transnational Christian democracy. The historiography of European integration is full of lyrical narratives about the eternal unfulfilled longing of continental Europeans for British 'leadership' after 1945. Milward has claimed, for example, that the French government was aware of the danger that the Schuman Plan 'might mean the end of the Franco-British cooperation in Western Europe', but that this outcome 'was definitely not desired'.[187] Gérard Bossuat has gone one step further in stating categorically that 'nobody ever dreamed of a union without England'.[188] Of the MRP leaders, Bidault has usually been called upon as chief witness for the idea that the pro-British consensus encompassed the entire political spectrum. Thus, Dieter Krüger claims that Bidault was still hoping for British leadership of the integration process in late 1949.[189] Similarly, Parsons suggests that he continued to be opposed to the 'break with Britain' even after the creation of the ECSC.[190] Some anecdotal evidence appears to corroborate this idea such as Alain Poher's recollection in his memoirs that Bidault used to speak of the 'Europe of the Germans' when referring to the triumvirate of Adenauer, Schuman and De Gasperi, who also spoke German fluently.[191]

---

[185] Geneva Circle, 12 June 1950, KADOC, Archief CEPESS, 3.1.11. On the plan for a bilateral Franco-Italian customs union see in greater detail Bruna Bagnato, *Storia di una illusione europea. Il progetto di Unione Doganale italo-francese* (London: Lothian Press, 1995).

[186] Cf. Françoise Berger, 'Les Sidérurgistes français et allemands face à l'Europe: convergences et divergences de conception et d'intérêts 1932–1952', *Journal of European Integration History* 3 (1997), 35–52. See also Matthias Kipping, *Zwischen Kartellen und Konkurrenz. Der Schuman-Plan und die Ursprünge der europäischen Einigung 1944–1952* (Berlin: Duncker & Humblot, 1996).

[187] Milward, *The Reconstruction*, 396.   [188] Bossuat, *L'Europe des français*, 174.

[189] Dieter Krüger, *Sicherheit durch Integration? Die wirtschaftliche und politische Zusammenarbeit Westeuropas 1947 bis 1957/58* (Munich: Oldenbourg, 2003), 176.

[190] Parsons, *A Certain Idea*, 56.   [191] Poher, *Trois fois président*, 68.

Georges-Henri Soutou and Dietmar Hüser first undermined the idea of Bidault as the main protagonist within the MRP and the French government, opposed not only to Schuman as his rival for the foreign ministry, but to his core Europe policies as well.[192] The former was unrelated to the latter, however, as Bidault's role in transnational party cooperation clearly shows. As a politician, Schuman perhaps did run on petrol of low octane rating, as Bidault once quipped, and Bidault on alcohol, as the Lotharingian retorted.[193] However, they shared a Western orientation which required close cooperation between the United States and an integrated western Europe, but not Britain's membership of it. Already in his first meeting with Adenauer in October 1948, Bidault argued that it would be 'difficult to build a Europe with England and equally difficult to build a Europe with which England would agree'.[194] The core question was not Britain's participation, but whether Germany and France would stop their 'quarrel' and agree to construct 'a common Europe' together.[195] After his experiences with British policy over the creation of the Council of Europe, Bidault reached a much more drastic conclusion in the Geneva Circle in June 1949: 'Three kinds of Europe are possible: an English Europe, which means no Europe at all. A Russian Europe, which means Asia. As for a Europe for everyone, the basis for this is a Franco-German rapprochement.'[196] Bidault did not say this merely to please his German interlocutors. In two meetings of the MRP executive in February 1949, for example, he argued similarly that Britain was 'playing with Europe, not playing Europe. It will always be peripheral. No Europe will be possible without Germany, however.' Britain 'will agree to nothing that will bind it afterwards'.[197]

Bidault and other Christian democrats in the transnational network were continuously prodded by Adenauer and his CDU allies to drop Britain, combined with the apparently unconditional offer of close Franco-German collaboration in the construction of core Europe. The choice was clear: either a continental Europe under strong Christian democratic influence and with a German government directed by him or a larger socialist Europe with Britain governed by the Labour Party and the

[192] Soutou, 'Georges Bidault'; Hüser, *Frankreichs 'doppelte Deutschlandpolitik'*.

[193] Poidevin, *Robert Schuman*, 190.

[194] Geneva Circle, 21 October 1948, Aktennotiz Felix Hurdes für Leopold Figl und Karl Gruber, IfZG Innsbruck, Karl Gruber Archiv, Karton 41.

[195] Ibid.   [196] Geneva Circle, 10 June 1949, ACDP, 01-009-017.

[197] Cited in Dalloz, *Georges Bidault*, 295; Du Réau, 'Le MRP', 78. See also Bacharan-Gressel, 'Les Organisations', 52.

German government run by Schumacher. In December 1948, for example, Adenauer warned that, in the case of an SPD victory in the first federal elections, 'the German parliament will come under British influence' and 'Labour Britain and socialist western Germany will dominate the Christian democratic forces'.[198] At the following meeting in March 1949, Adenauer derided British illusions over Soviet intentions and military capabilities. In his view, the English naively believed that the Russians would stop their advance at the Channel. In this critical situation 'the role of France has never been more important: defending and saving Europe'.[199] In June 1949, Adenauer once more drew attention to British assistance for the SPD in the election campaign. In the case of an SPD victory, this close link 'would have repercussions for all of Europe'.[200] As his adjutant Dörpinghaus claimed in the same meeting, 'Europe will be built on an agreement between England and Germany or France and Germany'.[201] In private, Adenauer came back again and again to his deeply held belief in a special historical British role apart from the European continent, which was incompatible with the idea of integration on the basis of equality. In early 1950, for example, when he discussed the Schuman Plan with Hans Schäffer – a state secretary in the German Finance Ministry during 1930–2, who emigrated to Sweden in 1933, where he became a Swedish citizen – he insisted that Britain still wanted 'to divide and rule' Europe.[202]

The consensus on the concept of core Europe with supranational features excluding Britain continued to grow within transnational Christian democracy between 1947 and 1950. It increasingly extended to those Christian democrats who – unlike Adenauer – temporarily favoured greater British engagement in continental European affairs out of fear of Germany. Taviani, who represented De Gasperi in the Geneva Circle and reported back to him, is an excellent example of this process of conversion. Britain initially appeared to him like an appendix of the United States in Europe, and its participation in European integration as a natural consequence of the DC's strongly Atlanticist orientation shortly after the war. His understanding of Britain's relationship with 'Europe' began to change under the influence of both transnational party networking and the experience of British policy until 1949, however. By the time Schuman published Monnet's plan and the Labour government rejected the option of

[198] Geneva Circle, 22 December 1948, AN 519, AP 10.
[199] Geneva Circle, 8 March 1949, ACDP, 01-009-017.
[200] Geneva Circle, 10 June 1949, ACDP, 01-009-017.   [201] Ibid.
[202] Tagebuch Hans Schäffer, 3 June 1950, printed as 'Konrad Adenauer und der Schuman-Plan', 133.

British membership, Taviani was an ardent supporter of a politically integrated core Europe. Encouraging the French participants in the Geneva Circle in December 1950 to move ahead despite domestic political difficulties, he exclaimed: 'France can lead Europe, after the defection of England.'[203] In a revealing passage in a book first published in 1954, Taviani argued that the deeper cultural roots of Britain's detachment from European integration lay in 'its insular mentality, which can never be extinguished'.[204] Similarly, Serrarens – the KVP politician and leader of the European Christian trade unions – no longer shared the allegedly general Dutch preference for British involvement one year before the publication of the Schuman Plan. Supporting Bidault, he insisted in June 1949: 'There is a British tendency to limit Europe to inter-state negotiations, if not to create no Europe at all. If England dominates, nothing will be achieved.'[205] In this atmosphere of increasing hostility towards Britain over what Bichet called 'the English problem',[206] the Belgian World War II emigrants de Schryver and Van Zeeland and a few other politicians at least retained an interest in the eventual British involvement in the integration process. In the first NEI executive meeting after the publication of the Schuman Plan, de Schryver insisted that the creation of core Europe should 'assist' and not destroy 'the entente with England'.[207] His was no longer a warning not to proceed without Britain, however, but only to leave a door open for its possible participation at a later stage. As Pezet argued in the Geneva Circle a few days later, the British could accept facts and might join eventually, but 'we must play the role of the engine'.[208]

The Christian democratic preference for core Europe was strengthened between 1947 and 1950 by the British policy of opposition to supranational forms of integration. The Labour government first insisted on a strictly intergovernmental organisation of the OEEC when it was set up in 1947–8. It then tried to torpedo the French initiative for a Council of Europe with a consultative assembly during 1948–9. It ultimately conceded its formation, but boycotted its further deepening and expansion into meaningful policy-making. At the same time, the British government also opposed incipient regional economic integration as in the case of the abortive French plan for a customs union with Italy in 1949, or with Italy and the Benelux countries,

---

[203] Geneva Circle, 2 October 1950, KADOC, Archief CEPESS, 3.1.11.
[204] Paolo Emilio Taviani, *Solidarietà atlantica e Comunità Europea* (Florence: Le Monnier, 1954), 248.
[205] Geneva Circle, 10 June 1949, ACDP, 01-009-017.
[206] Geneva Circle, 21 November 1949, ACDP, 01-009-017.
[207] NEI executive committee, Brussels, 1–2 July 1950, ACDP, 01-002-002.
[208] Geneva Circle, 12 June 1950, KADOC, Archief CEPESS, 3.1.11.

which might have hampered British trading interests.[209] Milward has explained the British reticence as a rational 'national choice' which essentially resulted from Britain's very different trading patterns and economic interests.[210] Political and cultural factors also account for the British refusal – in the words of the Labour Foreign Minister Ernest Bevin – to be treated as 'just another European country', however. These factors include the perceived incompatibilities between deeply engrained British political traditions – especially the idea of parliamentary sovereignty and the continuity of democratic government during the 1930s and the war – and those of continental Europe; the very different experience of World War II as the only western European power that could claim with some justification to have won it; and the Protestant rationalisation of cultural difference between Britain and a continental Europe that was influenced in different ways by the equally alien traditions of Catholicism and radical republicanism.

With reversed premises, transnational Christian democracy – unlike socialism – also saw such a fundamental cultural divide between continental western Europe and Britain. The decision for an integrated core Europe for them was – in the words of Bichet – 'a cultural choice – a form of civilisation'.[211] Britain might want to join core Europe organisations at some point for pragmatic reasons such as avoiding negative economic effects of self-exclusion, but would it make this cultural choice? The Christian democrats doubted this as much as the vast majority – socialist and conservative – of the British political elite. After all, Britain did not share the traditions of Catholicism and confessional politics. It was not united with continental Europe in the collective experience of the breakdown of democratic structures as well as occupation and collaboration during World War II. It did not share the same obsessive preoccupation with the German question that bound Adenauer and Schuman together. Its connections were more global and it had to deal with many other thorny issues at the same time – from retaining control over its Asian colonies to stabilising the continued international role of sterling.

The cultural barriers seemed even higher than they might actually have been because with the exception of the small Catholic exile, the Christian democrats had little knowledge of Britain and few contacts there. The tiny

---

[209] For an overview see John W. Young, *Britain and European Unity, 1945–1999*, 2nd edn (London: Macmillan, 2000).
[210] Milward, *The Rise and Fall.*
[211] Robert Bichet, *Réflexions et propos d'un vieil homme* (Paris: La Pensée Universelle, 1991), 137.

British inter-party NEI équipe had no influence in British politics. At the same time, neither the Christian democrats nor the British Tories wanted any formal links with each other. Just as most British Conservatives probably knew more about Marx and Engels, who had at least lived in Britain for some time, than about Catholic social teaching and continental Christian democratic party traditions, most Christian democrats had little understanding of British conservatism. As long as transnational Christian democracy was so fully controlled by Catholics as in the early postwar years before the Dutch Protestant parties joined the NEI in 1954 and Protestant CDU/CSU politicians became more active in party cooperation, their incomprehension had a strong confessional dimension. The role of Britain in Europe looked very different from the perspective of a Catholic KVP deputy from the south-eastern Dutch province of Limburg than it did for a Protestant parliamentarian from a trading city in the western Randstaad, for example.

The absence of networking allowed deeply engrained cultural assumptions to come to the fore again shortly after World War II. Thus, Jean-Claude Delbreil has found in his interviews with MRP eyewitnesses that many of them not only recollected their 'strong anti-British reticence', but actually believed that the more recent history of the current EU with Britain as an 'awkward partner',[212] corroborated their preference for an integrated core Europe.[213] Of the remaining survivors from the MRP decision-making elite in the late 1940s and early 1950s, Delbreil found Teitgen, Bichet and Robert Lecourt especially outspoken about their anti-British attitudes. In discussing the Western European Union (WEU) as a solution to German rearmament after the failed EDC, Teitgen argued in the Geneva Circle in January 1955, for example, that 'if the headquarters of European politics are to be moved to London, we know that we have nothing to expect from the British but sabotage'.[214] Over lunch, he and Bidault advocated continuing core Europe integration with the Federal Republic in the economic field, somewhat astonishing their German interlocutor with the idea only ten years after the war that 'the Englishman is our hereditary enemy'.[215]

With Hitler half-forgotten and Joan of Arc back in action against the English, the transnational cooperation of European Christian democrats

---

[212] Stephen George, *An Awkward Partner. Britain and the European Community* (Oxford: Clarendon Press, 1990).
[213] Delbreil, 'Le MRP', 351.
[214] Geneva Circle, 31 January 1955, protocol Karl von Spreti, ACDP, 01-172-31.   [215] Ibid.

fulfilled a number of important functions in the emergence of a partly supranational core Europe without Britain from 1947 to 1951. First, it contributed much to the lasting creation of transnational social trust and political capital. The little trust that the SIPDIC parties managed to build up in the second half of the 1920s largely dissipated during 1930–3 and was then comprehensively destroyed by World War II. Moreover, it was never much more than instrumental trust directed at securing specific interests – especially in the stabilisation or revision of the Versailles Treaty – which were irreconcilable. In contrast, party cooperation in the NEI and the Geneva Circle went much further in creating trust in the form of normative-emotional bonds between the transnationally networked party elites – social trust as a fundamental precondition not only for democratic governance within a nation-state, but also for effective transnational party links and successful intergovernmental negotiations conducted by the same Christian democratic political elites and in many cases, the same politicians. The meetings in the NEI and the Geneva Circle allowed the Christian democrats consistently to communicate their congruent political beliefs and preferences over longer periods. This made their decision-making mutually reliable and calculable despite conflicting domestic pressures from coalition partners, public opinion and economic pressure groups.

Neither the favourable structural conditions of the Cold War, the detached British policy on 'Europe' or their mutual ideological affinity alone explain why the Christian democrats were actually prepared to take great political risks and invest so much political capital in their attempt to achieve core Europe integration in 1950–1. They first needed to overcome their own deeply rooted mistrust and hesitations after 1945. Talking to the US emissaries William Clayton and Averall Harriman, Bidault claimed 'never once' to have 'eaten a German'.[216] His Gaullist public rhetoric shortly after World War II appeared to suggest, however, that he did have at least one German grilled *à point* for dinner every evening. Yet, as Georgette Elgey noted after interviews with eyewitnesses in the 1950s, Bidault – after the first informal contacts – was extremely impressed with Adenauer's calm personality and his preference for Franco-German reconciliation at almost any price including sacrificing the option of German unity, at least in the medium term.[217] Before the French foreign minister

---

[216] Cited in Dalloz, *Georges Bidault*, 189. See also Marc Trachtenberg, *A Constructed Peace. The Making of the European Settlement 1945–1963* (Princeton, N.J.: Princeton University Press, 1999), 72–3 who quotes Bidault as arguing in private in 1945 already that the German threat was a 'convenient myth'.
[217] Elgey, *La République*, 385.

met with Adenauer, Churchill's private proposition to him that he as former leader of the Resistance should take the lead in propagating Franco-German reconciliation and cooperation sounded hollow.[218] Afterwards it began to look much more like practical politics. It was also reassuring for the MRP elite that Adenauer appeared to fear his own countrymen even more than they did, urging them repeatedly to integrate the Germans into stable supranational structures. In one of many conversations, Adenauer warned Teitgen after his election as chancellor, for example, that without knowing its direction, many Germans would still join any column of men marching past their house.[219] His deeply rooted mistrust of his countrymen was well founded: in 1952, according to one opinion poll, 25 per cent of Germans still had a 'good opinion' of Hitler.[220]

Adenauer was initially just as suspicious of French politicians and policies – and especially of Bidault's motives and objectives. As late as July 1948 – at a meeting of the CDU executive committee in the British zone – he identified 'two strands' in French policy': one represented by Bidault, who was 'a more aggressive adversary of Germany', and the other by Schuman, 'a milder adversary'.[221] Adenauer made much within his party of his ability as diplomatic ringmaster to tame these aggressive French cocks. It assisted him in achieving full control over the CDU's foreign policy. At the same time, he was still uncertain whether he could realise his objective of Franco-German reconciliation and core Europe integration with the MRP, and whether the MRP could garner sufficient domestic support for such a policy. After his initial contacts with MRP representatives at the NEI congress in Luxembourg and in the Geneva Circle, however, he came back reassured from his first meeting with Bidault that no fundamental divide existed between a pro-European and a more nationalist wing within the French sister party – especially after the formation of a rival Gaullist party in 1947. Adenauer reported back to Schuman that he had an excellent impression of Bidault, who gave a 'good presentation'.[222] He subsequently found that Bidault in fact largely shared his assessment of international relations, the Soviet Union, Britain's role and the need for Franco-German-led core Europe integration. According to Koutzine, Adenauer and Bidault agreed later at a private meeting in 1958 that their transnational cooperation played a crucial role in the formative

[218] Cf. Jean-Claude Demory, *Georges Bidault 1899–1983. Biographie* (Paris: Éditions Julliard, 1995), 278.
[219] Pierre-Henri Teitgen, '*Faites entrer le témoin suivant*'. *1940–1958: de la Résistance à la Vème République* (Paris: Ouest-France, 1988), 476.
[220] Cited in Judt, *Postwar*, 58.   [221] *Konrad Adenauer und die CDU*, 521.
[222] Adenauer to Schuman, 4 November 1948, *Adenauer. Briefe 1947–1949*, 337.

period of European integration in bringing together their political parties and the core Europe countries.[223]

Whenever the growing transnational trust was shaken by domestic pressures, moreover, the Christian democrats immediately activated their informal network contacts to get their European policies back on track – particularly in the difficult months prior to the Schuman Plan. Schuman's first official visit to the Federal Republic in January 1950 was a domestic political and public relations disaster in Germany and France as it became overshadowed by the anticipated signing of the Saar Conventions. As his MRP interlocutors had repeatedly assured him that the French government would not change the status quo of the Saar region to avoid domestic political problems for Adenauer, the German chancellor temporarily sensed French duplicity. He contacted Koutzine, however,[224] and one meeting in the enlarged Geneva Circle and others during an informal trip by von Brentano to Paris in late March 1950 had a soothing effect.[225] Von Brentano even managed to negotiate an informal CDU–MRP agreement on the conditions for German accession to the Council of Europe. When Schuman officially denied the existence of such an agreement under the influence of domestic protests,[226] and von Brentano angrily suggested to cancel his participation as speaker at the next NEI congress,[227] it was NEI President de Schryver who intervened to calm the nerves and encourage the French and German Christian democrats to concentrate once more on finding a way out of the diplomatic impasse.[228]

Importantly, these party contacts allowed the Christian democrats to freely discuss the various intra-party and other domestic political constraints, which sometimes pulled them in different directions. Thus, Maurice Schumann explained in the Geneva Circle in February 1950 that the Saar Conventions chiefly resulted from the need to adjust the existing legal framework to the forthcoming membership of the Saar in the Council of Europe. Both sides should play down the significance of the Conventions. For the Saar to become a 'bridge' between France and Germany,

[223] Koutzine to Papini, 8 May 1985, cited in Roberto Papini, *The Christian Democrat International* (Lanham: Rowman & Littlefield, 1997), 133. See also the short reference in Georges Bidault, *Noch einmal Rebell. Von einer Résistance in die andere* (Berlin: Propyläen, 1966 [French 1965]), 129.

[224] Koutzine to Bidault, 22 January 1950, AN 457, AP 59. See also Koutzine to Dörpinghaus, 20 January 1950, ACDP, 01-009-017.

[225] Geneva Circle, 13 February 1950, AN 457, AP 59.

[226] On this incident see also Ulrich Lappenküper, *Die deutsch-französischen Beziehungen 1949–1963*, vol. I (Munich: Oldenbourg, 2001), 238.

[227] Von Brentano to de Schryver, 31 March 1950, KADOC, Archief August E. de Schryver, 7.2.4.4.

[228] De Schryver to Adenauer, 4 April 1950, ibid.

Schumann argued, 'we must avoid placing dynamite in it'.[229] According to Raymond Poidevin, Robert Schuman was never certain to what extent Adenauer understood domestic French politics.[230] The same was true for most MRP politicians and their knowledge of German politics. Crucially, however, as a result of their close informal party contacts the leading Christian democrats were much better informed, and could more easily conceive of European policy-making as an emerging supranational political system with multiple sites of decision-making.

Their transnational party cooperation – secondly – also allowed the Christian democrats to coordinate their policy objectives. Embedded in broadly similar ideological traditions, they developed what Markus Jachtenfuchs in his study of the EU's constitutional history has called a shared *gesellschaftliches Deutungssystem*:[231] a social system for interpreting the world as it was evolving in the early Cold War. This convergence of world-views resulting from a mutually reinforcing combination of structural incentives and their transnational communication in turn was a precondition for developing common ideas for the constitutionalisation of core Europe and for preparing concrete European policy-making. The transnational cooperation of the Christian democrats had no direct influence on the negotiation of the ECSC Treaty. It did give their European policies overall direction, however. After the London conference with French participation ended on 7 June 1948 with the recommendation to create a constituent assembly to draw up a constitution for a western German state, which cost Bidault his position as foreign minister, Schuman claimed, 'France has no German policy.'[232] Less than two years later it had a distinctive policy for the control of western Germany through at least partially supranational core Europe integration without Britain which in this particular form was decisively shaped by the MRP and its sister-parties. The shared policy objectives also enhanced the Christian democrats' political commitment to overriding domestic pressures such as in the case of Adenauer and the thorny issue of deconcentration of the steel industry as a precondition for the successful conclusion of the negotiations in early 1951.[233]

---

[229] Geneva Circle, 13 February 1950, AN 457, AP 59.　　[230] Poidevin, *Robert Schuman*, 200.

[231] Jachtenfuchs, *Die Konstruktion Europas*, 262.

[232] Cited in Dreyfus, 'Les Réticences', 121; Poidevin, *Robert Schuman*, 190. For Bidault's self-justification see also René Girault, 'The French Decision-Makers and their Perception of French Power in 1948', in Becker and Knipping (eds.), *Power in Europe?*, 48.

[233] On this issue see also Gillingham, *Coal, Steel*, 266–83.

Thirdly, transnational party cooperation also provided those Christian democrats most in favour of the creation of a supranational core Europe without Britain with mechanisms for socialising individual politicians and sections of party elites into their policy consensus. De Gasperi, for example, initially adhered to a more Atlanticist foreign policy after 1945. As Ralf Magagnoli has pointed out, however, the Italian prime minister became more and more converted to core Europe supranationalism, which he advocated strongly in the EPC debate during 1952–3, as a result of his contacts with Schuman and other Christian democratic leaders.[234] As in the case of Adenauer, the need to cultivate close relations with the United States for De Gasperi was of course more easily compatible with the core Europe concept once the US administration switched its policy during 1949–50 to supporting French leadership of a geographically confined, but more integrated western Europe excluding Britain. At the same time, Bidault's inclusion in the core Europe consensus through the Geneva Circle proved crucial for swinging the French government behind the Schuman Plan in May 1950, when the prime minister supported Schuman in the key ministerial meeting and subsequently in the MRP executive.[235] His policy disagreements with Schuman mainly concerned colonial policy, not Europe.[236]

The Christian democrats also used their networks to marginalise internal opposition to their evolving European policy. Within the CDU, sceptical views and opposition to Adenauer's policy of core Europe integration were mainly articulated by liberal free-traders worried about French protectionism and the impact on global trade liberalisation; Protestant conservatives concerned about the consequences for German unity; and left-Catholic nationalists like Kaiser who also feared that the coal and steel community would be too liberal and not geared enough towards the interests of workers. To free himself as much as possible from these intra-party constraints, Adenauer made transnational networking the exclusive domain of Catholic party elites. He avoided the involvement of CDU politicians like Friedrich Holzapfel – formerly of the nationalist DNVP in the Weimar Republic – until the socialisation of younger

[234] Ralf Magagnoli, *Italien und die Europäische Verteidigungsgemeinschaft. Zwischen europäischem Credo und nationaler Machtpolitik* (Frankfurt/Main: Lang, 1999), 97. Unaware of the long-standing transnational party contacts, he puts too much emphasis on one late meeting with Schuman in 1951.

[235] Dalloz, *Georges Bidault*, 295–307; Soutou, 'Georges Bidault', 214–17. See also Bernard Clappier, 'Die entscheidenden Jahre', in Jacques Santer *et al.* (eds.), *Robert Schuman – Christlicher Demokrat und Europäer. Aktualität eines Vorbilds* (Melle: Ernst Knoth, 1988), 60.

[236] Pierre Letamendia, 'La Place des problèmes européens dans la vie interne du parti sous la IVe République', in Berstein, Mayeur and Milza (eds.), *Le MRP*, 103.

Protestants like Kai-Uwe von Hassel, the EUCD president 1973–81, into the core Europe consensus was guaranteed.[237] Adenauer at first had to tolerate the participation of Kaiser in the Geneva Circle. Rather predictably, his internal rival raised the spectre of a second Rapallo during the Berlin blockade in March 1949 with his enthusiastic evaluation of the opportunities for striking a deal with the Soviet Union. This provoked a sharp comment from Bidault that '[we are] politicians with responsibility. We have to see and discuss the situation as it is'.[238] It also reinforced MRP reliance on close cooperation with Adenauer as the only guarantor of Franco-German reconciliation and core Europe integration. The patterns of transnational networking and policy-making at party level were mirrored in the allocation of ministerial portfolios. When Adenauer formed his first coalition government in 1949, Kaiser was given the ministry for 'all-German questions', which was of more ceremonial than substantive political relevance. At the same time, Adenauer as chancellor retained personal control of foreign relations until 1955, only to cede the foreign ministry to von Brentano, who not only shared the same core Europe ideas but was well networked in western European Christian democracy. While Kaiser quickly became less of an internal threat after 1949, Adenauer not only played a key role in deposing Müller as leader of the CSU in the year of the first Bundestag elections, but also replaced him immediately with Fritz Schäffer in the Geneva Circle. Müller later claimed that Adenauer informed Bichet in writing that nobody would in future be allowed to speak for the CDU/CSU unless specifically authorised by him.[239]

Although the MRP leadership was more heterogeneous than the CDU under Adenauer after 1949, the French party had a monolithic organisation, not much internal debate on major political issues and – like the German sister-parties – grassroots members who were quite deferential towards the top echelons at national level. Once the key foreign policy-makers like Bidault and Schuman were committed to a constructive policy of integration towards western Germany and the core Europe concept, and the new policy was rubber-stamped by the national party congress, the MRP leadership largely had a free hand in conducting European policy. After the defection of some well-known politicians to the rival Gaullist party in 1947–8, the minimal internal dissent was articulated by left-wing politicians like Hamon, who like their German counterparts were not given access to the non-material resources of party cooperation. They

---

[237] See also Schwarz, *Adenauer. Der Aufstieg*, 648–50.
[238] Geneva Circle, 8 March 1949, ACDP, 01-009-017.   [239] Müller, *Bis zur letzten Konsequenz*, 61.

still hoped for domestic political cooperation with the Communists in the search for a third way in socio-economic and foreign policy. This was hardly compatible with the supranational ECSC or the EDC, which were strongly backed by the Americans. Hamon recollected later, however, how the small and shrinking anti-supranationalist Left became aggressively marginalised in the face of a 'frenzied European fury'[240] to the point where some left the MRP to attempt a fresh start as Christian progressives and a few others were expelled for not having supported the EDC Treaty in 1954.

Their transnational cooperation – fourthly – allowed the Christian democrats to identify suitable domestic and transnationally constituted partners for implementing their European policy. After the CVP/PSC won the Belgian elections in June 1950 with a narrow absolute majority, the Christian democrats were the largest parties and in government everywhere in the six ECSC founding member-states. Nonetheless, in view of the residual scepticism within their own parties – as in the case of the CDU – and the need (with the exception of Belgium) to manage coalition governments, the Christian democrats could not impose their core Europe policy. Instead, they needed to engage in entrepreneurial coalition-building to create sufficient domestic support for the Schuman Plan in the core countries – especially France and Germany – to initiate intergovernmental negotiations and later, secure the ratification of a treaty. Thus, de Schryver warned in the Geneva Circle in December 1949 against politicising the European issue too much: 'We have to proceed cautiously so as to avoid the perception that we only desire the triumph of our partisan ideas . . . for our own profit.'[241] In particular, it would be imperative not to antagonise the socialists to the point where they might attempt to thwart Christian democratic policies on Europe. Crucially, however, transnational Christian democracy could afford to split the fragmented continental socialism and concentrate on nurturing its support where it was most needed for domestic political reasons: in France where the centrist 'Third Force' government depended on close cooperation between the MRP and the SFIO.

Even socialists who supported the Schuman Plan were unhappy about some of its aspects.[242] As Christian Pineau – one of the most ardent SFIO supporters of core Europe, who signed the EEC Treaty for France as foreign minister in March 1957 – recalled later, 'it started in a very

[240] Cited in Delbreil, 'Le MRP', 356.   [241] Geneva Circle, 21 November 1949, ACDP, 01-009-017.
[242] On the French political parties and the Schuman Plan see by way of introduction Gerbet, 'Les Origines', 201–3.

Christian democratic manner which . . . put a lot of socialists off'.[243] It once more raised the anticlerical spectre of the Vatican dominating European politics – as Guy Mollet and Jules Moch warned in deliberations of the SFIO executive about the Schuman Plan.[244] At the SPD party congress in Hamburg in 1950, Schumacher similarly denounced the Schuman Plan as 'conservative and clerical' in nature.[245] As Peter Pulzer has put it, 'it was not at all clear to everyone' – especially many socialists – 'whether they were witnessing the birth of a United States of Europe or the resurrection of the Holy Roman Empire'.[246] This fear was accentuated by frequent references by Catholic conservatives in particular to the need to recreate some kind of Christian *Abendland*, and the more widespread idea among Christian democrats like De Gasperi, for example, of core Europe as 'a Christian democratically updated version of a Carolingian res publica christiana'.[247] The socialist fears were also strongly reinforced by similar, although more confessionally motivated, perceptions of the Christian democratic core Europe project among Scandinavian socialists. Moreover, the Schuman Plan would most likely lead to the creation for the first time of a western European organisation without Britain governed by the Labour Party. On 10 May 1950 – one day after Schuman's press conference – the SFIO executive opted for supporting the plan, but pleaded vehemently for British membership of any new organisation. After a heated debate, the federalists André Philip, Salomon Grumbach and others only just managed to avert a decision to make SFIO support conditional on British participation.[248] With socialist Britain outside and the Christian democrats the hegemonic political force inside, many socialists also feared that the Schuman Plan Europe would be too liberal. Market integration and increased competition could lead to declining income levels in the coal and steel sector. Alternatively, industrialists might enrich themselves at the expense of consumers by running informal cartels.[249] On top of these

[243] 'The Testimony of an Eyewitness: Christian Pineau', in Richard Griffiths (ed.), *Socialist Parties and the Question of Europe in the 1950's* (Leiden, New York, Cologne: Brill, 1993), 62.
[244] Capelle, *The MRP*, 18; Loth, *Sozialismus*, 266.
[245] Susanne Miller and Heinrich Potthoff, *A History of German Social Democracy: from 1848 to the Present* (Leamington Spa: Berg, 1986), 168.
[246] Pulzer, 'Nationalism', 23.
[247] In relation to De Gasperi see Giulia Prati, *Italian Foreign Policy, 1947–1951. Alcide De Gasperi and Carlo Sforza between Atlanticism and Europeanism* (Göttingen: Bonn University Press, 2006), 165.
[248] Loth, *Sozialismus*, 266; Lappenküper, *Die deutsch-französischen Beziehungen*, vol. I, 253.
[249] Kevin Featherstone, *Socialist Parties and European Integration. A Comparative History* (Manchester: Manchester University Press, 1988), 340; Rudolf Hrbek, 'The German Social Democratic Party', in Griffiths (ed.), *Socialist Parties*, 68–9; Kurt Klotzbach, 'Die deutsche Sozialdemokratie und der Schuman-Plan', in Schwabe (ed.), *Die Anfänge*, 337.

arguments came the more pronounced germanophobia of some socialists. With Schumacher SPD leader, they had no suitable partner in Germany. They also lacked a reassuring equivalent of the Catholic cultural ration- alisation of the rise of national socialism and the Europeanisation of the guilt question. Thus, the SFIO deputy Francis Leenhardt warned that the Schuman Plan 'would mean German industrial domination, France reduced to a vegetable garden – Hitler's dream come true after his defeat, in short a German Europe!'[250]

Neither the CDU/CSU nor the DC needed socialist parliamentary support for the Schuman Plan or the ECSC Treaty. Socialist opposition actually assisted Adenauer and De Gasperi in their deliberate strategy of domestic polarisation between the Christian democratic-controlled centre- right and what they portrayed as a radical, uncompromising and quint- essentially anti-Western Left. In the German case, internal dissent within the SPD and tacit trade union support for the Schuman Plan weakened Schumacher to the point where he presented no real political danger for Adenauer's European policy during 1950–1. Members of the SPD's so-called mayoral wing around Max Brauer from Hamburg, Ernst Reuter from Berlin and Wilhelm Kaisen from Bremen made their preference for Western integration clear.[251] The social democrat-dominated trade union congress DGB actually decided to support the Schuman Plan while the Bundestag was debating the French proposal, so that Adenauer was able to break the embarrassing news to Schumacher in parliament. The chancellor in fact had good working relations with the moderate DGB leader Hans Böckler, with whom he was acquainted through a regional political net- work from the time when Adenauer was mayor and Böckler a member the City Council of Cologne during the Weimar Republic.[252]

Transnational Christian democracy secured the vital support of SFIO with two crucial policy dimensions of the Schuman Plan. The first was its supranational design. Many socialists like Philip and Mollet were in fact more committed federalists than Schuman or Bidault. In the tradition of

---

[250] Cited in Wilfried Loth, 'The French Socialist Party, 1947–1954', in Griffiths (ed.), *Socialist Parties*, 32.
[251] William Diebold, *The Schuman Plan. A Study in Economic Cooperation 1950–1959* (New York: Praeger, 1959), 96; Hrbek, 'The German', 69.
[252] Schwarz, *Adenauer. Der Aufstieg*, 689. More generally on European-level trade union policy towards European integration see also Maria Eleonora Guasconi, 'The International Confederation of Free Trade Unions' Policy Towards the European Integration Process from 1950 to 1957', in Eric Bussière and Michel Dumoulin (eds.), *Milieux économiques et intégration européenne en Europe occidentale en XXe siècle* (Arras: Artois Presses Université, 1998), 359–70; Patrick Pasture, 'Trade Unions as a Transnational Movement in the European Space 1955–65. Falling Short of Ambitions?', in Kaiser and Starie (eds.), *Transnational European Union*, 109–30.

Briand, the institutional set-up mattered for them at least as much as the policy content. The supranational design was wholly incompatible with their second preference for British involvement, however. SFIO politicians like Mollet were reminded once more of their incoherent preferences when the British Labour government refused to accept Schuman's supranational nexus as a condition for participation in intergovernmental negotiations. On 12 June 1950, finally, the Labour Party issued its policy statement, 'European Unity', which was sharply anti-supranational. This made it much easier for the SFIO to come out strongly in favour of sectoral core Europe integration in July 1950.[253] It also strengthened the position of Paul-Henri Spaak and other Belgian federalists within their party, who eventually managed to persuade thirty-seven socialist parliamentarians to vote for the ECSC Treaty in 1951, with only four No votes and six abstentions in the Chamber of Deputies.[254] In the Netherlands, where PvdA support was crucial for Dutch ECSC membership because of the coalition with the Catholic KVP, the social democrats eventually also resigned themselves to British self-exclusion.[255]

The institutional preferences of the Belgian and Dutch socialists were not clear-cut, and the Benelux governments secured a less supranational design in the inter-state negotiations. Yet the Belgian and Dutch socialists were united with the SFIO in their strong support for the Schuman Plan's second crucial policy dimension that allowed the Christian democrats to garner sufficient domestic political support in all six ECSC founding member states: the rejection of the cartel solution. French and German heavy industry were not opposed to European cooperation in the sector as such, but they were still attracted by the traditional instrument of market regulation through informal or institutionalised agreements on market shares and price levels.[256] With the exception of the relatively marginal Christian trade unions and the few neo-liberals like Erhard, transnational Christian democracy was not strictly opposed to cartels on ideological grounds. In fact, Adenauer, when he first suggested cooperation in the

---

[253] Loth, *Sozialismus*, 267.

[254] Thiery E. Mommens and Luc Minten, 'The Belgian Socialist Party', in Griffiths (ed.), *Socialist Parties*, 144; Michel Dumoulin, 'La Belgique et les débuts du Plan Schuman (mai 1950-février 1952)', in Schwabe (ed.), *Die Anfänge*, 276.

[255] Cf. Wendy Asbeek Brusse, 'The Dutch Socialist Party', in Griffiths (ed.), *Socialist Parties*, 110; Albert Kersten, 'A Welcome Surprise? The Netherlands and the Schuman Plan Negotiations', in Schwabe (ed.), *Die Anfänge*, 303.

[256] Kipping, *Zwischen Kartellen*, 75–80; Andreas Wilkens, 'L'Europe des ententes ou l'Europe de l'intégration? Les industries française et allemande et les débuts de la construction européenne (1948–1952)', in Bussière and Dumoulin (eds.), *Milieux économiques*, 267–83.

coal, steel and chemical industries to Bidault in March 1950, spoke of the need to 'prevent a Franco-German fight over markets'.[257] The societal alliance against the cartel solution was overwhelmingly strong in core Europe by 1950, however. It included much of Christian democracy, all socialist and liberal parties and the trade unions. The steel-finishing industries also desired low prices to keep their products competitive in world markets.[258] Moreover, the American administration insisted on the decartelisation of German heavy industry. It strongly favoured a European anti-cartel policy broadly in line with the established US anti-trust law, and it used formal contacts and informal transatlantic networks to push its preference.[259] In these circumstances, supranational market integration with an anti-cartel thrust not only made it easier for transnational Christian democracy to forge a sufficiently strong societal coalition for their core Europe without Britain based on a close Franco-German partnership; they were also able to impose this policy solution with relative ease on the national industrial interest groups such as the German Bundesverband der deutschen Industrie (BDI) and the French Conseil National du Patronat Français (CNPF) – the Patronat – which were internally divided. This is especially true of Germany. Although Adenauer depended on support from industry for funding his party and its electoral campaigns, the BDI relied even more on Adenauer and the CDU/CSU for guaranteeing private ownership within a market economy integrated in the Western world with ensuing export opportunities.[260]

Transnational Christian democracy also aimed at supporting inter-governmental relations over European integration. This fifth function of party cooperation consisted of informal strategic interventions to secure national governmental policy-making and the conduct of inter-state nego-tiations consistent with the main Christian democratic objectives. National bureaucracies did not necessarily share the same policy goals. Even if they did, they could throw spanners in the wheels of smooth intergovernmental cooperation through their conservative attachment to national policy

---

[257] Vorschlag von Bundeskanzler Adenauer, Koutzine to Bidault, 22 March 1950, AN 457, AP 59.

[258] Cf. Philippe Mioche, 'Le Patronat de la sidérurgie française et le Plan Schuman en 1950–1952: les apparences d'un combat et la réalité d'une mutation', in Schwabe (ed.), *Die Anfänge*, 305–18.

[259] Cf. Kipping, *Zwischen Kartellen*, 156–64. For the general context see also Tony Freyer, *Antitrust and Global Capitalism, 1930–2004* (Cambridge: Cambridge University Press, 2006); David J. Gerber, *Law and Competition in Twentieth Century Europe: Protecting Prometheus* (Oxford: Clarendon Press, 1998).

[260] See also Volker Berghahn, *The Americanisation of West German Industry 1945–1973* (Cambridge: Cambridge University Press, 1986), 243–4; Bührer, *Ruhrstahl*, 91; Gerard Braunthal, *The Federation of German Industry in Politics* (Ithaca, N.Y.: Cornell University Press, 1965), 285–8.

traditions, their attention to administrative detail or their easy accessibility for domestic lobbying. The French state administration in particular was initially a stronghold of resistance to the supranational core Europe of integrated markets.[261] The economic ministries were steeped in the tradition of protectionism and the Quai d'Orsay attached to the Gaullist conception of national power. Within this hostile administrative environment, Monnet built personal networks that helped him to devise his plan and to garner crucial support such as from Bernhard Clappier from the Quai d'Orsay, who submitted it to Schuman.[262] The MRP politician had to overrule strong opposition within his ministry to the supranational concept and the exclusion of Britain. The French ambassador to London, René Massigli, for example, cautioned again and again against any German adventure without full British involvement.[263] Leading officials also leaked confidential information with the aim of preventing undesired policy outcomes. This appears to be true of information on the informal agreement between Teitgen and von Brentano about the conditions for German accession to the Council of Europe in late March 1950 which prompted Schuman's official denial. In such cases, the Christian democrats stepped in to impose solutions on reluctant national administrations and to transfer as much trust as possible from their societal network to intergovernmental relations.

They also streamlined ministerial preferences and behaviour by parachuting reliable Christian democrats into core governmental positions. This happened, for example, when De Gasperi made Taviani – the Italian representative in the Geneva Circle and the NEI – state secretary in the Palazzo Chigi, his foreign policy advisor and chief Italian negotiator of the ECSC and EDC treaties during 1951–3. Taviani's leading role with the backing of the prime minister accelerated the Europeanisation of the Italian foreign ministry and its political orientation.[264] In selected cases, transnational Christian democracy also formed informal alliances with the pro-core Europe advance guard in national ministries bypassing national coalition governments. Although he had no political party affiliation with political Catholicism or postwar Christian democracy, Monnet played a key role in this strategy. When he went to Bonn to explain his plan in greater detail on behalf of Schuman, Monnet left an excellent impression

---

[261] See also Bossuat, 'La Vraie Nature', 206.
[262] Jean Monnet, *Mémoires* (Paris: Fayard, 1976), 342–55.   [263] Cf. Bossuat, 'La Vraie Nature', 206.
[264] Magagnoli, *Italien*, 99. See also in the context of Italian policy towards the West more generally, Guido Formigoni, *La Democrazia cristiana e l'alleanza occidentale, 1943–1953* (Bologna: il Mulino, 1996).

on Adenauer, who had not met with him before. Informal network contacts further encouraged the German chancellor to support Monnet as a reliable European broker who basically shared the Christian democratic interest in Franco-German reconciliation through economic integration with a supranational institutional design. Thus, Hans Schäffer, who knew the senior French official from interwar business contacts, confirmed that Monnet's policy choice was not circumstantial and exclusively geared towards realising particular French interests, but – as in the case of Adenauer – derived from ideas originally developed in the 1920s.

These five core functions of transnational Christian democracy contradict national state-centric explanations of the origins of the ECSC. More recent source-based historical accounts of early European integration have interpreted the creation of the ECSC as the outcome of so-called national interests negotiated by governments in inter-state bargaining. Traditional diplomatic and revisionist economic historical accounts disagree over the driving forces behind the integration process. Yet both tend to prioritise structural pressures and incentives over political leadership; explain integration outcomes with preferences derived from identifiable security or economic interests, not norms and policy ideas; and concentrate exclusively on national policy-making at the expense of its transnational dimension. This dominance of national state-centric accounts has resulted from disillusionment with Lipgens' original normative account of postwar integration as having resulted from ideas developed by national resistance movements.[265] It is also explained by extreme over-reliance on governmental sources by contemporary historians of European diplomacy and of economic policy-making alike. This has blinded them to the crucial agenda-setting role of partly transnationally constituted political forces in western European democracies after 1945, and their shared norms and policy ideas for initiating and driving the integration process forward.

Structural pressures did encourage western European cooperation in some form. This is true of the international relations and economics of integration. The Cold War required western Europe to organise itself within the larger Western world dominated by the United States to guarantee its external security against the Soviet Union and the communist parties as its 'fifth column' in domestic politics. Steeped in a strong tradition of anti-communism, transnational Christian democracy saw this need despite widespread latent cultural distrust of the United States and dislike of its allegedly 'free for all' excessively individualistic socio-economic

---

[265] Lipgens, *A History*.

system. Moreover, as Geir Lundestad has pointed out,[266] US policy to encourage the formation of some kind of 'United States of Europe' and pressure to integrate the emerging western German state on the basis of equality set important framework conditions for European policy-making. At the same time, the historically grown interdependence of the continental western European national economies – especially of Germany and the Benelux – and the extreme fragmentation and national protectionism after 1945 provided incentives for reducing trade barriers, opening up markets and coordinating national reconstruction policies. Yet western Europe could have accommodated these pressures with a policy of German membership of NATO and progressive trade liberalisation in the strictly intergovernmental OEEC Europe. Sectoral integration of the geographically more confined core Europe of the supranational ECSC sprang from a strategic policy choice in an epochal historical moment when different and mutually contradictory options for the integration of Germany and European cooperation were hotly contested.

In such a situation, political elites could exercise entrepreneurial leadership to impose a particular option domestically. Neither in France nor in any of the five other ECSC founding member states did organised socioeconomic interests push strongly for supranational core Europe market integration in coal and steel. Interest groups were internally divided and completely marginal to the initial policy-making process, although they later attempted to influence technical details of the actual treaty during the intergovernmental negotiations. Support for the Schuman Plan also did not promise to yield short-term electoral pay-offs either, especially in France. Thus, domestic political calculations do not account for Schuman's initiative or the strong political support of transnational Christian democracy for it. Similarly, Christian democratic policy-makers were not primarily inspired in their preference formation by economic interests or changing trade statistics. Milward has identified the period 1948–51 as one of significant growth in 'Little Europe' trade and diverging British trade patterns, arguing (without demonstrating a causal link, however) that the 'political settlement between France and Germany was to acknowledge the differences between these paths'.[267] Yet the Christian democrats developed their core Europe concept before the first signs of a continental Europeanisation of trade patterns became visible for

---

[266] Geir Lundestad, *'Empire' by Integration. The United States and European Integration, 1945–1997* (Oxford: Oxford University Press, 1998), 132.
[267] Milward, *The Reconstruction*, 360.

bureaucratic experts. Moreover, Adenauer, Schuman and De Gasperi were neither interested in specific trade implications of integration nor deferential to bureaucratic policy-making by national administrations which is the focus of economic explanations of French and continental European policies.[268]

While Schuman and Monnet agreed on the idea of vertical integration in the coal and steel sector, their support for it was motivated by different concerns. Although the faltering French Modernisation Plan provided an additional incentive for searching for a durable solution for Franco-German relations, Schuman did not support Monnet's project in order to safeguard this plan, but as a starting point for durable Franco-German relations. Adenauer's overriding concern was also to create a new basis for relations with France in a multilateral institutionalised continental Europe. When Hans Schäffer listed a number of tactical advantages of the Schuman Plan in the internal meeting on 3 June 1950 including the depoliticisation of the Saar issue and progress towards the full sovereignty of the Federal Republic, the German Chancellor dismissed them as petty considerations. Ultimately, Adenauer insisted, the Schuman Plan had to be seen in political terms as the unification of two countries disunited for centuries and as the only means to defend western Europe against a military advance by 'the Russians'.[269] Crucially, these core objectives of transnational Christian democracy derived from a shared set of norms and policy ideas with a strong confessional dimension. The Christian democrats attempted to build a Catholic Europe – not in the culture war sense of Vatican rule, as Mollet and Schumacher alleged with their anticlerical rhetoric, but as a decentralised federation in the making based on the principle of subsidiarity and excluding Protestant-socialist Northern Europe in its formative phase. It is this shared set of norms and policy ideas combined with the political hegemony of the Christian democratic Centre-Right in continental western Europe around 1950 that largely account for what the socialist Pineau has rightly recalled as the start of integration 'in a very Christian democratic manner'.

The study of the role of transnational Christian democracy in the formation of ECSC core Europe not only demands bringing ideas back into the explanation of the origins of European integration, however. It also demonstrates that the formation of preferences and European

[268] Esp. ibid.; Frances M. B. Lynch, *France and the International Economy. From Vichy to the Treaty of Rome* (London: Routledge, 1997).
[269] Tagebuch Hans Schäffer, 3 June 1950, printed in 'Konrad Adenauer und der Schuman-Plan', 138.

policy-making did not take place exclusively in national political spheres, but actually had strong transnational dimensions. Parsons has attempted to explain French European policy from an ideational perspective alleging that the formation of the ECSC resulted from strong leadership of an alliance of supranationalists across party divides within the 'Third Force' centrist governments. Yet supranationalism as such was not the core objective for the majority of MRP foreign policy-makers with a few exceptions like de Menthon. Instead, by 1950 this elite had a strong interest in encouraging at least the temporary self-exclusion of Britain from continental European integration to facilitate Franco-German reconciliation through initially economic integration. It used cross-party support for supranationalism including within the SFIO to achieve this strategic objective. Moreover, the MRP foreign policy-making elite secured sufficient domestic and international support for its core Europe concept through its intensive transnational networking at the informal party and governmental levels. These two levels overlapped to a large extent. Parsons' nationally introspective claim that 'France's partners generally preferred broad, weak cooperation' is plainly wrong.[270] Transnational Christian democracy pushed hard for the agenda of institutionally strong and geographically limited European integration. The core Europe project was neither designed by governments nor was its fate decided in France alone. Instead, the ECSC resulted from a transnational political struggle in which the continental European Christian democrats succeeded in imposing their core ideas sufficiently adjusted to garner enough domestic and transnational support for it.

[270] Parsons, *A Certain Idea*, 2.

CHAPTER 7

Deepening integration: the supranational coalition embattled

Tumultuous scenes in the French Assemblée Nationale on 30 August 1954: the Communists and Gaullists get up and sing the 'Marseillaise'. The Republican Paul Reynaud makes a short speech. Never in its history – he claims – has the parliament of the Fourth Republic rejected a treaty without first giving those who concluded it a chance to defend it. The MRP deputies and some Socialists and Republicans now intonate the national anthem. They shout at the Communists and Gaullists, who attempt to join in, that they should sing 'Deutschland über alles'[1] because the creation of a national German army would now be inevitable.[2] This – even by French parliamentary standards – heated political confrontation followed upon the defeat of the European Defence Community (EDC) in the Assemblée Nationale. With a clear majority of 319 against 264 in a procedural vote, the EDC opponents had rejected starting the ratification process for the treaty concluded by the ECSC states on 27 May 1952. At this stage, it was already ratified in the Benelux countries and Germany.[3] Linked to the EDC, and dead with its rejection, was the EPC constitution drafted by the Constitutional Committee of the Ad hoc Assembly in 1952–3. Moreover, the coming into force of the Bonn Conventions of 1952 regarding the full sovereignty of the Federal Republic also hinged on the EDC as the US administration had linked the two issues from the beginning. After the French parliamentary vote, the future of Christian democratic core Europe, established only two years earlier when the ECSC High Authority under its first president, Jean Monnet, began its work in Luxembourg, was in doubt. Having informed the chancellor of the

---

[1] The first verse – exclusively used from 1933–45 – of the *Deutschlandlied*, the German national anthem during the Weimar Republic from 1922, not the national anthem of the Federal Republic of Germany from 1949 ('Einigkeit und Recht und Freiheit', third verse).
[2] 'L'Assemblée nationale a voté la question préalable', *Le Monde*, 1 September 1954.
[3] The only multilateral study of the EDC history, although not based on archival sources, remains Edward Fursdon, *The European Defence Community: A History* (Basingstoke: Macmillan, 1980).

253

outcome of the French vote, Felix von Eckardt, the director of the Federal Press Office in Bonn, noted in his diary, 'I have never seen Adenauer so depressed before.'[4]

Ever since its failure, historians have wondered from when on the EDC no longer had a chance of ratification in the French parliament. Jacques Bariéty, for example, has identified the point of no return as being before the collapse of the centrist Pinay-Schuman government in December 1952. It appeared to result from conflicts over budgetary issues, but 'the real reason' – according to Bariéty – was the coalition's inability to muster a majority for the EDC.[5] In view of the Soviet détente initiatives, which started with the Stalin notes of March 1952 proposing the unification of a neutralised Germany, Wilfried Loth has even asked whether 'there ever existed a chance to find a majority for the EDC in the French parliament'.[6] In retrospect, the attempted direct move from the more limited sectoral ECSC project towards a European army of sorts with a federal two-chamber constitution seems to have been much too ambitious. From this perspective – borrowing a distinction introduced by Stanley Hoffmann[7] – national politicians could more easily legitimise functional economic integration as 'low politics' in the domestic arena. In contrast, defence integration would have affected a core dimension of national sovereignty as 'high politics', provoking much greater public debate and fiercer domestic opposition to the pooling of sovereignty at the European level.

The conditions for defence integration were never more propitious during the Cold War than in the early 1950s, however. The sudden military invasion of South Korea by communist North Korea on 25 June 1950 forced western Europe to focus on its defence, weakened by French and British overseas commitments and limited US troop stationing, and the need for the Federal Republic to make a substantial military contribution to it. When the French government proposed the Pleven Plan in October 1950 to avoid Germany's full immediate integration into NATO as desired by the United States and Britain, the Assemblée Nationale voted 349 to 235

---

[4] Felix von Eckardt, *Ein unordentliches Leben. Lebenserinnerungen* (Düsseldorf: Econ, 1967), 301. See also Konrad Adenauer, *Erinnerungen 1953–1955* (Stuttgart: DVA, 1966), 298.

[5] Jacques Bariéty, 'La Décision de réarmer l'Allemagne, l'échec de la Communauté Européenne de Défense et les accords de Paris du 23 octobre 1954 vus du côté français', *Revue belge de philologie et d'histoire* 71 (1993), 358.

[6] Wilfried Loth, 'Blockbildung und Entspannung. Strukturen des Ost-West-Konflikts 1953–1956', in Bruno Thoß and Hans-Erich Volkmann (eds.), *Zwischen Kaltem Krieg und Entspannung. Sicherheits- und Deutschlandpolitik der Bundesrepublik im Mächtesystem der Jahre 1953–1956* (Boppard: Boldt, 1988), 15.

[7] Hoffmann, 'Obstinate or Obsolete?'.

in favour.[8] The original plan included discriminatory features such as the integration of all future German troops at battalion level, no German high command and initially no German membership of NATO. Although these features were watered down in the intergovernmental negotiations from February 1951 on, however, the French parliament still voted 327 to 287 in favour of the EDC project in February 1952, albeit attaching socialist-inspired conditions, especially concerning the supranational principle and American and British security guarantees. Crucially, the decision against the EDC in August 1954, when 80 MRP deputies voted for, and only 2 against the EDC, but slight majorities of their former Third Force coalition partners, the socialists (53:50) and Radicals (34:33) against,[9] was contingent upon important structural transformations that were outside the control of the Christian democratic network. They concerned in particular, the political rise of the anti-supranationalist Gaullists and the collapse of the MRP vote to 12.6 per cent in the French elections of June 1951, the dissolution of the Third Force party coalition, and the tentative détente after Stalin's death on 5 March 1953. They had nothing to do with public opinion. According to opinion polls, a clear majority of the French favoured the EDC before and after the parliamentary vote. In fact, even a slight majority of Gaullist supporters wanted to see it ratified.[10]

Parsons has convincingly argued the importance of 'disconnected politics of coalition building' in France having 'shifted to bar the way to ratification' of the EDC Treaty.[11] After losses in the 1951 elections, the SFIO went into opposition, making way for centre-right governments until January 1956. The collapse of the centrist coalition, which had ruled since 1944–5, marked the transition from 'heterodox Third Force to a right-left cleavage'.[12] Unlike in the cases of Germany and Italy, where right-wing dissent over European integration was largely controlled within the governing Christian democratic people's parties, the new centre-right coalitions in France from January 1953 comprised the Gaullists. At the same time, the SFIO leadership could no longer contain internal opposition to the EDC with compromises and pay-offs in other policy areas within the centrist coalition framework. When the party executive imposed a kind of three-line whip to support the EDC after the national SFIO congress in May 1954, the internal rebellion had assumed such proportions

---

[8] Wilfried Loth, *Der Weg nach Europa. Geschichte der europäischen Integration 1939–1957*, 3rd edn (Göttingen: Vandenhoeck & Ruprecht, 1996), 94.
[9] Cf. Fursdon, *The European*, 297; Gerbet, 'Les Partis politiques', 82–5.
[10] Cf. Letamendia, 'La Place', 111.   [11] Parsons, *A Certain Idea*, 74.   [12] Ibid., 77.

that threats would not have been credible.[13] Sanctions against dissenters from the official pro-EDC line – as in the case of the MRP, which actually expelled four members including the left-Catholic Hamon[14] – would have destroyed the party.

Moreover, the dissent among the socialists and Radicals would have been more limited, and also easier to control, had Stalin only lived a few years longer. Instead, geopolitical motives combined with domestic issues formed an explosive mix in the run-up to the vote in the Assemblée Nationale.[15] Stalin's détente initiatives in 1952, and his death in the following year, actually strengthened the resolve of transnational Christian democracy to proceed with core Europe integration. The MRP executive roundly defeated a motion by Hamon in favour of negotiating over the Stalin notes and postponing the ratification of the EDC Treaty.[16] The Soviet proposal raised the spectre of a united neutralised Germany run by the social democrat Schumacher, who Teitgen called a 'national socialist' in a conversation with Otto Lenz, the state-secretary in the German chancellery.[17] When Bidault replaced Schuman as foreign minister in January 1953 in a move to assuage the Gaullists, he sent Koutzine to Bonn to inform Adenauer that he would 'continue the established policy [on Europe]'. Based on Koutzine's report, the chancellor notified the members of the CDU executive four days later that France would definitely ratify the EDC Treaty in the spring.[18] Adenauer in turn categorically rejected negotiations with the Soviet Union over German unification. He argued that the Soviet proposals were merely a tactical ploy to prevent the ratification of the EDC and more generally, undermine his policy of western integration as well as the cohesion of the Atlantic Alliance.

---

[13] The vote at the national congress was 1969 to 1215 in favour of the EDC. Loth, *Sozialismus*, 290. See also Loth, 'The French Socialist Party', 41, for early dissent against the official pro-EDC party line in February 1952.

[14] Cf. Danièle Zéraffa-Dray, 'Le Mouvement républicain populaire et la Communauté européenne de défense 1950–1954', in Berstein, Mayeur and Milza (eds.), *Le MRP*, 193.

[15] For a more exclusively geopolitical interpretation see also William I. Hitchcock, 'France, the Western Alliance, and the Origins of the Schuman Plan, 1948–1950', *Diplomatic History* 21 (1997), 603–30.

[16] Geneva Circle, 16 June 1952, AN 519, AP 10.

[17] Ibid. See also *Im Zentrum der Macht. Das Tagebuch von Staatssekretär Lenz 1951–1953* (Düsseldorf: Droste, 1989), 366.

[18] *Im Zentrum der Macht*, 535 and 539. Teitgen even continued to be optimistic about the ratification of the EDC well into 1954, informing Adenauer accordingly, who appears to have hoped that a large pro-EDC vote among the independent and agricultural French deputies could still swing the vote. Cf. Arnuf Baring (ed.), *Sehr verehrter Herr Bundeskanzler! Heinrich von Brentano im Briefwechsel mit Konrad Adenauer 1949–1964* (Hamburg: Hoffmann und Campe, 1974), 137; Schwarz, *Adenauer. Der Staatsmann*, 124.

Stalin's death had a different influence on the centre-left in French politics, however.[19] Even the most anticlerical socialists would have preferred an integrated Europe run by the Pope from Rome over one controlled by Stalin from Moscow. Stalin's legacy of the repression of the 'kulak' farmers, the GULAG concentration camps, the purges in the Red Army in the late 1930s and the ruthless imposition of communist rule in east-central Europe after 1944–5 served as a strong deterrent to sacrificing European integration for vague notions of détente. Many socialists and Radicals thought, however, that it could be worthwhile to negotiate with Stalin's successors, not least to alleviate France of its heaviest international burdens, especially the continuing war against the communist Viet Minh in French Indochina, which was effectively lost after the defeat at Dien Bien Phu in May 1954. The Radical prime minister, Pierre Mendès-France, did not force the demise of the EDC in August 1954 as a *quid pro quo* for the Soviet agreement to the – formally temporary – division of Vietnam in the Geneva Accords in the previous month. This is what Teitgen insinuated in the Geneva Circle in January 1955, for example,[20] and Adenauer also believed.[21] In the changed international circumstances, German rearmament seemed less urgent and could still be achieved with an alternative solution, however. Moreover, for someone like Mendès-France, the EDC's supranational principle could not be reconciled with his strong preference for close Franco-British relations.[22]

What the sympathising British Catholic newspaper *The Tablet* called the French MRP's 'Schumania' – its Catholic-inspired preference for supranational core Europe integration[23] – thus came under attack from many sides for a variety of reasons culminating in the vote of August 1954: the Gaullists because of their dislike of supranational solutions; the communists who fought core Europe integration as an American-inspired capitalist plot; many socialists and Radicals who thought that it was too supranational, not supranational enough, blocking détente with the Soviet Union, or too Christian democratic in nature; and the military

---

[19] See also Pierre Guillen, 'The Role of the Soviet Union as a Factor in the French Debates on the European Defence Community', *Journal of European Integration History* 2 (1996), 71–83.

[20] Geneva Circle, 31 January 1955, ACDP, 01-172-31.

[21] Schwarz, *Adenauer. Der Staatsmann*, 136. Instead, see Georges-Henri Soutou, 'La France, l'Allemagne et les accords de Paris', *Relations Internationales* 52 (1987), 451–70.

[22] Cf. Elisabeth Du Réau, 'Pierre Mendès France, la création de l'Union européenne occidentale (UEO) et son devenir', in René Girault (ed.), *Pierre Mendès France et le rôle de la France dans le monde* (Grenoble: Presses universitaires de Grenoble, 1991), 33.

[23] 'Christian Democrats Meet', *The Tablet*, 18 August 1954.

establishment demanding additional US and British security guarantees and freedom over the development of a national nuclear force de frappe. The EDC's common arms procurement policy and integrated command structure seemed to exclude the option of an independent French nuclear deterrent.[24] In these increasingly difficult circumstances, the MRP had to fight on too many fronts simultaneously. It lost its controlling influence over French European policy, which had facilitated the implementation of the Schuman Plan so much during 1950–1. In June 1954, when Mendès-France became prime minister, the Christian democrats even went into opposition for the first time during the Fourth Republic, which minimised their ability to influence the fate of the EDC.

Throughout this period of perpetual crisis in the core Europe project, transnational Christian democracy remained a predominantly informal network despite repeated attempts to increase its organisational cohesion. Adenauer made such an attempt in the run-up to the NEI congress in the German spa Bad Ems in September 1951. During his visit to Rome in June, he agreed to closer bilateral relations between the CDU and the DC. Both parties supported the creation of a 'Christian International', tentatively agreed a name change to reflect the desired greater ideological orientation, and discussed the option of transferring the NEI secretariat to one of the smaller ECSC member-states.[25] In his speech in Bad Ems, Adenauer embedded his plea for greater organisational cohesion in a familiar anti-communist discourse about Soviet 'pan-slavist expansion policy'. In view of this threat, European integration was 'the only means to rescue the European *Abendland*', and party integration one crucial dimension of this process.[26] Adenauer's advisor Blankenhorn regarded supranational party integration as potentially contributing to the necessary 'reform of bourgeois parties' in general. As the CDU itself was increasingly criticised within the NEI for not engaging more fully in party cooperation, Blankenhorn noted in his diary on the way to a meeting of the executive committee in Brussels that the Christian democrats would have to activate, educate and train their rank-and-file membership much better instead of

---

[24] Cf. Georges-Henri Soutou, 'La Politique nucléaire de Pierre Mendès-France', *Relations Internationales* 59 (1989), 113–30; Pierre Guillen, 'Les Chefs militaires français, le réarmement de l'Allemagne et la CED', *Revue d'histoire de la deuxième guerre mondiale* 33 (1983), 3–33. See also, in a long-term bilateral perspective beginning in 1954, Georges-Henri Soutou, *L'Alliance incertaine. Les rapports politico-stratégiques franco-allemands 1954–1996* (Paris: Fayard, 1996).

[25] CDU Bundesvorstandssitzung, 3 July 1951, *Adenauer: 'Es mußte alles neu gemacht werden.' Die Protokolle des CDU-Bundesvorstandes 1950–1953* (Stuttgart: Klett-Cotta, 1986). 48.

[26] Konrad Adenauer, Ansprache, NEI congress, Bad Ems, 14–16 September 1951, BA, N 1351, 8a.

using 'organisational patterns from the nineteenth century' and treating politics as essentially limited to election campaigns.[27]

Critical observers of transnational Christian democracy also pointed out the growing need to conceptualise the legitimacy of supranational governance with a parliamentary dimension, albeit in the form of the ECSC Parliamentary Assembly with delegates from the six national parliaments and initially only consultative functions. Commenting on the NEI congress in Swiss Fribourg in 1952, the liberal daily newspaper *Neue Zürcher Zeitung* emphasised the important role of political parties in fostering trans-regional networks and creating allegiance in processes of national integration as in Switzerland, thus building societal bridges for developing a common 'state conscience' as a 'political act'.[28] The German Christian democratic weekly *Rheinischer Merkur* also pleaded for greater organisational cohesion that would go significantly beyond the exchange of views among politicians from different parties at the NEI congresses. Party integration would in future be crucial not only for coordinating common European policy-making, but also for making party elites understand the degree to which domestic decisions were increasingly becoming interdependent with European and national policy developments elsewhere in the Community.[29] More concretely, Klaus Bölling, who was later government spokesman for the social democratic chancellor Helmut Schmidt from 1974 to 1981, commented in the West Berlin *Tagesspiegel* that the NEI were too heterogeneous. Its congresses included too many 'European holiday-makers'. Bichet, for example, had 'a healthy appetite but not much to say'. One of the younger foreign delegates in Bad Ems, Bölling observed scathingly, even asked Adenauer for an autograph. The chancellor wanted NEI reform, but 'once again', Bölling wrote, 'the French are the retarding element'.[30]

Substantial organisational reform proved so difficult to achieve not least because national politicians were constantly preoccupied with more pressing short-term intra-party, domestic and intergovernmental issues. As Blankenhorn admitted, Adenauer wanted the NEI to change, but the CDU under his leadership had not invested enough resources before the congress in Bad Ems to prepare actual reform proposals and to create a

---

[27] Herbert Blankenhorn, Tagebuch, 31 August 1951, BA, N 1351, 7a.
[28] 'Probleme der übernationalen Willensbildung. Zum Kongreß der "Nouvelles Équipes Internationales"', *Neue Zürcher Zeitung*, 21 August 1952.
[29] 'Christliche Internationale', *Rheinischer Merkur*, 14 September 1951.
[30] Klaus Bölling, 'Eine christliche Internationale? Konferenz der "Nouvelles Équipes Internationales"', *Tagesspiegel*, 19 September 1951.

sufficiently strong coalition for it within the Christian democratic network. The trip to Brussels by Blankenhorn to discuss Adenauer's ideas with the NEI president, de Schryver, who urged caution in view of the MRP's reticence, yielded no results.[31] The DC agreed with Adenauer's agenda, but preoccupied with factional infighting, did nothing to promote actual reforms. Thus, the NEI's basic organisational structure with national équipes and French and Belgian participation by individual politicians, not the parties, remained unchanged until the creation of the EEC in 1957–8. The formation of the EEC led to an upgrading of the NEI Bureau. From 1957 onwards, it comprised the NEI president, the secretary-general and six, not four, vice-presidents, to guarantee the representation of all six ECSC/EEC parties and the Swiss and Austrians.[32] The Bureau was also formally charged with decision-making between the occasional meetings of the executive committee, now called Comité Directeur, and it always met before this larger committee to streamline NEI decision-making. The main purpose of this reform was to create a forum for debate among the parties of western Europe, without the presence of the exile équipes from eastern Europe. By this time, their own central European regional organisation was located in New York, and they received strong support from American organisations including the CIA. As Karl-Josef Hahn, a German-speaking political refugee from Czechoslovakia after its occupation by Nazi Germany who was responsible for the Dutch KVP's external relations, wrote in a letter to Rosenberg, 'their close link with the Americans is clearly a problem for us'.[33]

Continued opposition to NEI membership within the MRP remained the main barrier to more effective organisational integration and the creation of a European-level political party. When, in 1958, the Italian representatives once more urged that such a European party of sorts ought to be formed, de Schryver still believed that it was impractical and useless to try.[34] Yet, he was increasingly isolated within his own party, the CVP/PSC. A younger generation of transnationally networked politicians including Tindemans, worked with the party leader, Théo Lefèvre, to develop a very strongly federalist European programme and to support greater party integration. This group imposed CVP/PSC membership in the NEI on de Schryver in 1958 when the party formally joined. When de Schryver was

---

[31] CDU-Bundesvorstand, 6 September 1951, *Adenauer: 'Es mußte alles neu gemacht werden'*, 66.
[32] NEI, Procès-verbal de la réunion du Comité Directeur tenue à Paris, le 2 février 1957, BAR, CVP-Archiv JII.181, 2358.
[33] Hahn to Rosenberg, 24 February 1958, BAR, CVP-Archiv JII.181, 2359.
[34] Kwanten, *August-Edmond de Schryver*, 488.

appointed minister for the Congo in 1959 to manage its transition to independence, Lefèvre succeeded him as NEI president in April 1960 before becoming Belgian prime minister in 1961. At this stage, shortly after the creation of the EEC, the MRP opponents of NEI membership were completely isolated. Even they began to realise that the MRP in continued electoral decline was in danger of missing out on greater transnational resources for resisting the Gaullist onslaught after the transition to the Fifth Republic in 1958, and for influencing European policy-making effectively.

Until the eventual integration of the MRP in the NEI in 1964, and the party's subsequent dissolution to make way for a reorganisation of French centrist politics, the other NEI parties combined conducted a war of attrition against it over organisational reform. They never considered proceeding without the MRP, however. France was crucial for the integration project. Moreover, the Christian democrats had no viable alternative for cooperation with other French parties. De Gaulle's extreme anti-supranationalist rhetoric and his party's image as more right-wing put the Christian democrats off. With the exception of small minorities within the CDU/CSU and the DC, cooperation with the Gaullists instead of the MRP was out of the question. This was highlighted once more at a press conference on 15 May 1962 when the French president ridiculed the Community idea with his condescending attack on soulless Brussels bureaucrats who thought and spoke (the artificial language) Volapük, provoking the withdrawal of the MRP members from the French government. Christian democrats throughout the EEC regarded this as a frontal assault on what was an integral part of their common belief system, and united behind their MRP partners.

The Christian democrats were no longer prepared to accept MRP dominance over party cooperation, however. They fired one of several warning shots when Bichet announced his retirement as NEI secretary-general at the start of 1955 and attempted to apply the hereditary principle to his succession.[35] Bichet proposed the young, but inexperienced, Philippe Farine, who had lost his parliamentary seat in 1951. The other Bureau members rejected his proposal outright, however. On the recommendation of Schuman, the honorary president of the French NEI équipe, they eventually elected Alfred Coste-Floret, a member of the Assemblée Nationale with good knowledge of Franco-German relations and

---

[35] Comité Directeur, 19 February 1955, ACDP, 09-002-003.

European policy issues.[36] The MRP succeeded in filling the post of secretary-general one more time. In 1960, however, they only managed to do so by putting forward a Lotharingian, Jean Seitlinger, who spoke perfect German and was better able than either Coste-Floret, who did have German, or Bichet, who did not, to act as cultural broker in party relations. Moreover, as their repeated attempts to fundamentally overhaul the NEI structure failed until 1964–5, the Christian democrats started initiatives to compensate for the lack of formal integration. They included the enlargement of the NEI to integrate the two Dutch Protestant parties, the decentralisation of NEI activities and the start of party cooperation at the level of secretary-generals outside of the NEI framework.

The Protestant enlargement of the NEI was first discussed at the annual congress in Bad Ems in September 1951 after a public appeal from Christian-Protestant politicians from within the German CDU and from the Swiss and Dutch confessional Protestant parties for greater inter-confessional cooperation.[37] As part of his strategy to transform the CDU into a more truly inter-confessional people's party, Adenauer was keen to integrate the younger generation of Protestant CDU supporters of his policy of western integration into the Christian democratic network. Moreover, while the Swiss confessional Protestant party was small, and Switzerland detached from the core Europe integration process, the Dutch Anti-Revolutionary Party (ARP) and the more conservative-evangelical Christian-Historical Union (CHU) were still latent sources of anti-Catholic resentment against ECSC core Europe. When the ARP replaced the Liberals in the broad coalition government dominated by the Catholics and the social democrats in 1952, the KVP invited it and the CHU in the following year to join the NEI équipe. Opposition to such a rapprochement within the two Protestant parties once more drew upon the image of a 'Vatican Europe' which had also influenced Dutch party discourses about European integration after 1945. Characteristically, one Protestant clergyman in the CHU warned that the Dutch Protestants were now 'going to take part in the "Papal quest for power"'.[38] As in the case of the CDU/CSU, however, the new enthusiasm of a younger generation of Protestant leaders for the originally Catholic-inspired core Europe project helped bridge the confessional divide. When the two parties joined the Dutch

[36] NEI, Communiqué de Presse, no date, ACDP, 09-002-006; NEI, Comité Directeur, 2 April 1955, ACDP, 09-002-003. See also Bichet, *La Democratie chrétienne*, 248.
[37] NEI Executive Committee, Bad Ems, 14 September 1951, ACDP, 09-002-002.
[38] Rutger Simon Zwart, *'Gods wil in Nederland': christelijke ideologieën en de vorming van het CDA (1880–1980)* (Kampen: Kok, 1996), 199.

équipe in 1954, W. P. Berghuis, the ARP leader 1956–68, quickly played an active role in the NEI. The participation of the ARP and CHU in the Dutch équipe was to be followed by their merger with the KVP, first in a party federation in 1973 and then in the new unitary Christian Democratic Appeal (CDA) formed in 1980. It was also the first step in the evolving CDU/CSU's strategy to transform the NEI into a broadly based inter-confessional European level people's party in its own image.

According to the NEI statutes, the Dutch équipe was autonomous in deciding its internal composition. In contrast, the other Christian democratic parties needed French cooperation for the decentralisation of NEI activities. In June 1953, Bichet unwittingly provided them with an opportunity to use their financial leverage to realise in outlines this second objective of their strategy to compensate for the lack of formal NEI integration. Bichet submitted a paper to the NEI executive proposing a massive increase in the budget to employ several staff to fulfil the organisation's 'supranational mission': develop a common political doctrine and programme, liaise with the CD Group in the ECSC Assembly, and coordinate relations with international bodies as diverse as the UN, NATO and Pax Christi.[39] One idea was to create on a permanent basis the post of a paid deputy secretary-general. One year before, the Benelux parties – on the initiative of the KVP – had first proposed to attach someone to the NEI secretariat in Paris to enhance cooperation between it and their party organisations.[40] When Bichet submitted his proposal, they were paying, from their own resources, the KVP member and freelance journalist W. J. Schuijt for an initial trial period of eight months.

The other NEI parties eventually agreed to a budget increase in 1954 to fund Schuijt's role in the secretariat.[41] When he was elected to the Dutch Tweede Kammer in 1956, however, an acrimonious debate ensued about whether he could continue in his NEI post, and the Bureau subsequently failed to replace him.[42] Konrad Kraske, the CDU's deputy secretary-general, first suggested that his compatriot Hans Albrecht Schwarz-Liebermann,

---

[39] Robert Bichet, Notiz zur Verstärkung des Internationalen Sekretariats, 25 June 1953, KADOC, Archief August E. de Schryver, 7.2.6.9.

[40] Houben to de Schryver, 18 August 1952; de Schryver to Lamalle, 3 April 1953, both in KADOC, Archief August E. de Schryver, 7.2.6.9.

[41] NEI, Note sur les résultats de 'l'expérience 1954' du Secrétariat élargi, no date, BAR, CVP-Archiv JII.181, 2353.

[42] Coste-Floret to de Schryver, 20 November 1956, ACDP, 09-002-006; Rosenberg to Van de Poel, 28 November 1956, KDC, Archief KVP, 1192; Schuijt to Comité Directeur, 3 December 1956, ACDP, 09-002-007; NEI, Procès-verbal du Comité Directeur réuni à Namur (Belgique) le 8 décembre 1956, BAR, CVP-Archiv JII.181, 2358.

who became deputy director of the Political Committee of NATO in 1957, could combine the NEI role with his new post. This solution proved to be impossible for legal and political reasons in early 1958, however.[43] The NEI took until 1960 to appoint the Italian Arnaldo Ferragni instead. The other NEI parties rejected Bichet's master-plan for building his own little empire in Paris, however. Instead, Rosenberg proposed for the Germans, Swiss and Austrians in December 1953 that the CDU should be responsible for cooperation with the German-language équipes via a small centre attached to its party headquarters in Bonn,[44] not the NEI secretariat in Paris, which was decided by the NEI executive in February 1954.[45] Kraske was charged by the CDU secretary-general, Bruno Heck, with coordinating the liaison with the NEI secretariat.[46] In June 1954, Kraske sent a paper to Bichet outlining the Bonn office's responsibilities as agreed with the ÖVP and the SKVP, such as coordinating cooperation among the three parties, and between them and the NEI secretariat, as well as translating NEI documents into German.[47] When approached by Coste-Floret in the following year, however, who wanted to be updated about recent institutional changes, Kraske had to admit that his virtual office within the CDU headquarters was not very active. It was only a 'technical office', he explained, and should remain so to avoid the danger of 'linguistically, but later perhaps also politically oriented' camps developing within an increasingly fragmented NEI.[48]

Whereas the strategy of decentralisation to compensate for MRP control over the secretariat was only partially successful, the other NEI parties also forged links among their secretary-generals, who met regularly from 1954 – an initiative first discussed in the Geneva Circle in 1949–50.[49] The CVP/PSC and the MRP participated in these meetings from the beginning, but Jacques Mallet for the MRP initially insisted that they would have to

[43] Kraske to Coste-Floret, 6 January 1958, ACDP, 09-002-008.
[44] Martin Rosenberg, Memorandum zur Intensivierung der Tätigkeit der NEI und einer entsprechenden Verstärkung des Sekretariats, Bern, 23 December 1953, ACDP, 01-085-051/2, developing the initial ÖVP criticism in Stellungnahme der ÖVP zum Reorganisationsplan der NEI, Vienna, 25 September 1953, BAR, CVP-Archiv JII.181, 2351. See also Maleta to Rosenberg, 24 November 1953, Heck to Rosenberg, 3 February 1954, both in BAR, CVP-Archiv JII.181, 2351; Maleta to Bichet, 14 January 1954, Heck to Bichet, 3 February 1954, both in ACDP, 09-002-006.
[45] Comité Directeur, 13 February 1954, BAR, CVP-Archiv JII.181, 2358; see also NEI, Note sur les résultats de 'l'expérience 1954' du Secrétariat élargi, no date, BAR, CVP-Archiv JII.181, 2353.
[46] Heck to Bichet, 18 March 1954, BAR, CVP-Archiv JII.181, 2351.
[47] Kraske to Bichet, 12 May 1954, ACDP, 09-002-091.
[48] Kraske to Coste-Floret, 5 May 1955, ACDP, 09-002-091.
[49] Geneva Circle, 21 November 1949, ACDP 01-009-017; Geneva Circle, 12 June 1950, KADOC, Archief CEPESS, 3.1.11.

be kept completely separate from the NEI.[50] After his election as NEI secretary-general, however, Coste-Floret travelled to Bonn and negotiated his inclusion into this forum as NEI secretary-general, a formula to which the French équipe eventually gave its blessing.[51] At this stage in the mid-1950s, transnational Christian democracy became more and more interested in using the existing network not only for influencing European policy-making, but also for transferring political ideas and practices across borders for use in the domestic political context. The national parties were keen on developing effective strategies for recruiting members, for political communication such as utilising television, and for election campaigns. Thus, the CDU wanted to acquire a mass membership, which the Italian and Belgian parties already had, not least to be better able to compete logistically and financially with the social democrats. The CSV from Luxembourg, on the other hand, was mainly interested in campaigning strategies and techniques after its election losses in 1952.[52] Its secretary-general, Pierre Grégoire, borrowed extensively and successfully from the CDU experience, especially in the run-up to the Bundestag election of 1953, which was discussed at meetings of the secretary-generals during 1953–5.[53] The Christian democrats also exchanged ideas about the use of applied sociological methods for analysing the composition of the electorate and changing mass opinion, to target voters more specifically and with finely tuned political messages.

The closer cooperation between the party headquarters and the effective transformation of the NEI Bureau into a decision-making forum for the EEC parties with self-restrained Austrian and Swiss participation also allowed the Geneva Circle to become absorbed into the reformed NEI structures. Koutzine and the French participants had always argued that only the Geneva Circle provided a suitable forum for open informal discussion among representatives of the western European parties. This was no longer the case, however. Moreover, the primary rationale for creating the Geneva Circle – to foster Franco-German high level contacts – also fell away. Cooperation between the CDU/CSU and the MRP was smooth. Governmental relations between Germany and France

---

[50] Konferenz der Generalsekretäre, 31 May 1954, ACDP, 09-002-078/1; Rosenberg to de Schryver, 4 June 1954, BAR, CVP-Archiv JII.181, 2403.
[51] Konferenz Generalsekretäre 14 May 1955, ACDP, 09-002-078/1. See also Chenaux, *Une Europe Vaticane?*, 265.
[52] Cf. Schroen, 'Die Christlich-Soziale Volkspartei Luxemburgs'.
[53] See, for example, CDU-Bundesgeschäftsstelle, Der Wahlkampf der CDU zu den Bundestagswahlen 1953. Bericht zur Vorlage bei der Konferenz der Generalsekretäre, 11.–12.12.1955, no date [December 1955]; Konferenz der Generalsekretäre, Brussels, 11–12 December 1955, ACDP, 09-002-078/1.

also became ever closer even with changing coalition governments in Paris, especially after the last remaining bilateral issue – the Saar question – was resolved in 1955–6. Increasingly, Franco-German rapprochement at elite level was also reflected in, and facilitated by, changing popular attitudes. For the first time in 1957, only 15 per cent of French people stated that they had a 'bad opinion' of the Germans, compared to 19 per cent stating they had a bad opinion of the British, and more trusted Germany than Britain.[54]

At a trilateral meeting in January 1952, the Benelux parties agreed that the Geneva Circle was no longer useful to them, as it was mainly a bilateral forum for Franco-German contacts.[55] The Belgians and Luxembourgers no longer took part after this meeting, although the Dutch did until October 1953. In 1952, the MRP, the CDU/CSU and the DC insisted that its informal character still made the Geneva Circle special, however.[56] Although party leaders no longer took part in the Geneva Circle, they were at least informed of the proceedings. Joseph Fontanet reported in March 1952, for example, that Bidault, Robert Schuman and Maurice Schumann regularly received detailed reports.[57] Nonetheless, the Swiss and Austrians also became increasingly concerned about the essentially bilateral character of the meetings. In March 1953, when the Italians took part for the last time, Rosenberg queried whether their continued engagement brought any benefits for the political parties from the smaller non-ECSC states, and he no longer participated.[58] The Austrian ÖVP decided in November 1953 in conjunction with the decentralisation plan for NEI activities to end its involvement.[59] Only politicians from the MRP and the CDU/CSU continued to meet before the Dutch and Belgians appeared once more for the last meeting to discuss the Saar question in October 1955.[60]

Until its demise, the Geneva Circle nonetheless remained important for informal Christian democratic networking. Those who supported a further deepening of core Europe continued to use the existing contacts to

---

[54] Bossuat, *L'Europe des français*, 406.
[55] Meeting of representatives of the KVP, CVP/PSC and CSV, 25 January 1952, KADOC, Archief CEPESS, 3.1.11.
[56] Koutzine to Houben, 3 April 1952, KADOC, Archief August E. de Schryver, 7.2.7.2.
[57] Geneva Circle, 24 March 1952, KADOC, Archief CEPESS, 3.1.11.
[58] Geneva Circle, 2 March 1953, Archiv des Karl von Vogelsang-Instituts (henceforth: AKVI), Karton NEI, a) b).
[59] Maleta to Rosenberg, 24 November 1953, BAR, CVP-Archiv JII.181, 2351; Maleta to Koutzine, 8 July 1954, AKVI, Karton NEI, c) e).
[60] Geneva Circle, 10 October 1955, BA, N 1239, 165.

marginalise dissent within their parties. When Koutzine met with Adenauer's advisors Blankenhorn and Lenz to discuss Franco-German issues after Bidault's appointment as foreign minister in January 1953, for example, he also met with Kaiser, the deputy CDU leader. Koutzine returned from the meeting warning Bidault that Kaiser and other nationalists in German politics were 'ready to make any concession to Moscow at the expense of the Allies, and any concession to the Allies at the expense of the Russians' to achieve German unification in some form. Koutzine also informed Bidault that Kaiser had criticised the French approach towards Germany as fully in line 'with the traditional objectives of French policy since Richelieu', and that when he subsequently related this experience to Lenz, Adenauer's advisor 'raised his arms towards the sky in a gesture which was very telling'.[61] In 1948, Adenauer wrote to Schuman about the positive impression he had of Bidault. By 1953, trust within the Franco-German Christian democratic network reached a level where even advisors like Koutzine and Lenz had greater confidence in each other, and habitually expressed it in their contacts, than in less enthusiastically pro-integration members of their own national parties.

Their informal networking was most successful when the Christian democrats discussed policy objectives and informed each other of their likely positions on thorny bilateral and European issues. This was the case, for example, when they met on 10 October 1955 to debate the likely rejection of the Saar statute in the forthcoming referendum. After the French demands immediately after World War II for an annexation of the Saar region, which was inhabited by German-speakers only, and its subsequent economic integration into France in 1947, the Europeanisation option was the last line in the diplomatic defence, especially of the by now well-established French economic interests in the region. At the same time, Adenauer agreeing to the Europeanisation of the Saar region came at the price of sharp attacks on him from within his party, his coalition partners and the opposition. He publicly had to support a solution agreed only to stabilise the Franco-German partnership, but which was not very credible in the circumstances of the Saar region. All the while, other leading CDU politicians campaigned against it, and for the reintegration of the Saar region into Germany, together with their recently legalised sister party in the region. Crucially, the leading MRP politicians Schuman, Teitgen and Pflimlin recognised in the Geneva Circle that French postwar policy had

---

[61] Koutzine to Falaize [Bidault], 30 January 1953, AN 457, AP 59.

created this political mess.[62] When the Dutch KVP politician Sassen suggested that the pro-French government of Prime Minister Johannes Hoffmann from the Christian People's Party could resign, and the referendum be postponed to achieve a better outcome at a later stage, the other participants rejected this idea outright. Schuman and Pflimlin insisted that they would accept a negative vote. Schuman even added a 'mea culpa': he would regard such an outcome as partly his own fault because French European policy had never succeeded in making the Europeanisation option credible for the citizens of the Saar region, especially after the demise of the EDC/EPC in the previous year. Although the MRP politicians gave no guarantee that they would support the reintegration of the Saar region into Germany, all participants clearly accepted this outcome, and the discussion moved on to the theme of European economic integration.[63]

As in the period before the creation of the ECSC, the informal Christian democratic network supported and stabilised governmental relations and multilateral bargaining. On one occasion – in the bilateral Franco-German context – it tried to completely bypass the French coalition government and the professional diplomats in the Quai d'Orsay, however, and failed. This happened when the tense bilateral governmental bargaining over the Saar issue reached an impasse in April 1954 after Adenauer's support in principle for the Europeanisation option at a meeting with Foreign Minister Bidault on 9 March. Adenauer tried to activate his Geneva Circle contacts to achieve a more favourable outcome than he expected from continued official talks with André François-Poncet, the French ambassador to Bonn. Replacing Bidault, who took part in the Indochina Conference in Geneva, Deputy Prime Minister Teitgen met with Adenauer on the margins of the ministerial meeting of the Council of Europe on 19–20 May 1954. Although Adenauer and Teitgen involved the Dutch socialist Marinus van der Goes van Naters, who had developed the Europeanisation idea in the Council of Europe, and the Belgian socialist foreign minister, Paul-Henri Spaak, they knew each other very well from the Geneva Circle. Moreover, many of Adenauer's close allies within the

---

[62] Geneva Circle, 10 October 1955, BA, N 1239, 165. For the French debate about the Saar referendum and the Europeanisation option see also Judith Hüser, 'Frankreich und die Abstimmung vom 23. Oktober 1955: innen- und außenpolitische Problemstellungen zur Lösung der Saarfrage', in Rainer Hudemann (ed.), *Die Saar 1945–1955: ein Problem der europäischen Geschichte*, 2nd edn (Munich: Oldenbourg, 1995), 359–79.

[63] See also Lewandowski, 'Das Europa', 353. According to this source, the meeting took place on 8 October 1955.

CDU like von Brentano and Lenz, for example, had close relations with Teitgen, whom they trusted as a particularly strong supporter of close Franco-German relations within a federal Europe. In fact, Teitgen did make a number of important concessions in the talks. According to the informal agreement, the Europeanisation of the Saar region would develop in three clearly defined steps, involve 'analogous' economic relations with Germany as well as France, and come with the crucial proviso that its status could change as a result of a future peace treaty with Germany.[64] A German foreign ministry official passed on the results of the talks to his US and British counterparts, however, forcing the German chancellor to apologise officially to Teitgen and the French government.[65] The minutes were also leaked to the public – possibly by van Naters and Spaak, as Adenauer thought.[66] It immediately became clear that Teitgen's policy was not fully in line with that of Schumann, the state-secretary in the Quai d'Orsay, who was considered the most 'Gaullist' European in the MRP at the time, and the most 'European' Gaullist when he switched his allegiance to de Gaulle's Union pour la Défense de la République, formed in 1968, before acting as foreign minister from 1969 to 1973. Moreover, many French opponents of the EDC seized upon Teitgen's concessions in the informal accord to undermine its prospects of ratification, and those of a quick resolution of the Saar issue. Hard-line nationalist diplomats in the Quai d'Orsay also launched vicious attacks on Teitgen for his alleged leniency.[67] When the Laniel-Bidault government collapsed shortly afterwards, the informal agreement brokered by the Christian democratic network became defunct. Clearly, informal negotiations between party leaders could only succeed if the participants – like Adenauer – had sufficient authority to turn the results into government policy. In the fragmented French coalition politics before the EDC vote, however, the MRP was no longer able to do so.

Alongside the formalised NEI and the informal network contacts that originally evolved around the Geneva Circle, but increasingly proliferated, transnational Christian democracy also developed a significant

---

[64] Lappenküper, *Die deutsch-französischen Beziehungen*, vol. I, 392–448 for a detailed description of the intergovernmental negotiations over the Saar issue during 1953–4. See also Teitgen, *Faites*, 510.

[65] Adenauer to Teitgen, 25 May 1954, printed in *Adenauer. Briefe 1953–1955* (Berlin: Siedler, 1995), 104. See also Adenauer's explanation in the Cabinet on 25 May 1954, in *Die Kabinettsprotokolle der Bundesregierung*, vol. VII: *1954* (Boppard: Boldt, 1993), 219–21.

[66] *Le Monde*, 27 May 1954; see also Schwarz, *Adenauer. Der Staatsmann*, 134; Capelle, *The MRP*, 128.

[67] See Lapppenküper, *Die deutsch-französischen Beziehungen*, vol. I, 445. Lenz also sometimes experienced similar attempts by German diplomats to boycott contacts and negotiations over the Saar question and other issues at the party level, to retain control over foreign policy-making. See *Im Zentrum der Macht*, 431 and 523.

parliamentary dimension during the 1950s. From September 1952, the ECSC Assembly provided a second, much more important focal point for party cooperation than the Consultative Assembly of the Council of Europe. With the composition of the delegations determined by national parliaments, and the resulting exclusion of the French and Italian communists, the Christian democrats had 41 members compared to 27 socialists, 14 liberals and 5 unaffiliated in the Ad hoc Assembly. This was the Parliamentary Assembly of the ECSC enlarged for the anticipated EDC ratification by three members each from the three larger member-states. The Christian democrats immediately formed one group headed by the Belgian Sassen. Mainly as a result of the initial boycott by eight German social democrats, moreover, the Christian democrats even had an absolute majority in the Constitutional Committee that drafted the EPC during 1952–3, with 14 members compared to only 5 socialists, 6 liberals and 1 unaffiliated.

Their transnational cooperation in the Parliamentary Assembly of the ECSC and – from 1958 – the EEC became more important for the Christian democrats than its formal powers would suggest. These were largely limited to oversight functions and the right to oust the High Authority with a two-thirds majority, which was of symbolic value only as long as the clear majority of the Assembly and the High Authority treated each other as institutional allies in the battle for deeper integration. Yet, their hegemonic role in the Assembly allowed the Christian democrats to behave like a European-level 'government party', as Ernst B. Haas first observed,[68] promising added public visibility and electoral benefits. Unlike the NEI, the CD Group also received European level state funding. Its more abundant financial resources induced the practice – begun in 1957 and also applied by other political groups – of cross-subsidising the NEI.[69] This practice of dubious legality was expanded and continued until the EU statute for European political parties was passed in 2004. It gave the CD Group growing leverage over transnational party cooperation and allowed it to play an influential role in later reform debates. The composition of the CD Group overlapped to a large degree with the NEI and informal networks. The German delegation included von Brentano, Lenz and Kiesinger, for example, and the French, Teitgen, de Menthon and Poher.[70] The CD Group thus had a high degree of cohesion from the

---

[68] Haas, *The Uniting of Europe*, 436.
[69] Procès-verbal de la réunion du Bureau [of the CD Group in the ECSC Assembly] qui a eu lieu le 17 mai 1957, Strasbourg, ACDP, 09-001-001/1.
[70] See also Jean-Jacques Baumgartner, 'La C.D.U. et les autres partis démocrates-chrétiens', in Alfred Grosser (ed.), *Les Rélations internationales de l'Allemagne occidentale* (Paris: Colin, 1956), 143.

outset. At the same time, it could not be dominated by the MRP, as the NEI was from its inception. The MRP had only 4 delegates, but the Dutch Catholic and Protestant parties combined 6, the CDU/CSU 8 and the DC even 14. With the growing electoral strength of the CDU/CSU, which achieved an absolute majority in the German elections in 1957, the German and Italian parties became by far the most influential national delegations in the CD Group, whereas it took them until the mid-1960s to exercise similar influence over the European-level party organisation.

With the proliferating network contacts, including this parliamentary dimension, transnational Christian democracy could activate various channels to advance core Europe integration. One possible step would have been to promote horizontal integration in an industrial customs union as first discussed at the intergovernmental level in the Customs Union Study Group in 1947. The North Korean attack on South Korea disrupted the debate about functional economic integration with political objectives, however. French, British and Belgian troops were already stationed in colonies like French Indochina. At the same time, the Soviet Union was building up a heavily armed East German police force of 70,000 men. In these circumstances, moving more US, British and other NATO troops to the Korean war theatre in the summer of 1950 aggravated the security void in western Europe. Its defence was only guaranteed by the American nuclear deterrent. This situation was not reassuring for the Europeans, especially the Germans. If the Soviet Union were to invade western Europe regardless, it would be massively destroyed in the course of its own defence. When the US and Britain first formally demanded German rearmament in the NATO context in early September 1950, Foreign Minister Schuman initially played for time. After several drafts were prepared by Monnet and his advisors, the French government finally agreed a plan for the creation of a European army with German contingents as an alternative option, which Prime Minister René Pleven made public on 24 October 1950.

The French government was able to develop its proposal for a European solution drawing upon similar suggestions made by leading European politicians. In March 1950, Churchill first publicly aired the idea of a European army.[71] On 11 August 1950, the Consultative Assembly of the Council of Europe passed a resolution for the creation of a European army by eighty-nine votes against five with twenty-nine abstentions by the

---

[71] Fursdon, *The European*, 75. See also Anthony Nutting, *Europe Will Not Wait. A Warning and a Way Out* (London: Hollis & Carter, 1960), 77.

German, British and Scandinavian socialists.[72] Adenauer formally offered a German contribution to the defence of western Europe in a memorandum submitted to the US, British and French governments on 29 August 1950.[73] This followed upon interviews with a Lotharingian newspaper and the *Cleveland Plain Dealer* in November and early December of 1949 – long before the outbreak of the Korean War – when he first suggested the setting up of German units within a European army. The idea was subsequently taken up, and discussed publicly, by – among others – the French socialist Léon Blum and the former commander of US troops in Germany, General Lucius Clay.[74] German rearmament was still a red rag for many in the autumn of 1950, however, especially in France. Within the French government, the socialist defence minister, Jules Moch, who had lost two sons in World War II, was opposed, as was the socialist president, Vincent Auriol. In contrast, the MRP leadership, although initially unenthusiastic about what they regarded as an inevitable, but politically premature move to defence integration, was united and supportive. In fact, the Christian democratic network had regularly discussed the issue of German rearmament since the meeting of the Geneva Circle in December 1948 – one year before Adenauer first seriously raised the topic in public.

Encountering Bidault only for the second time, Adenauer launched the idea of German rearmament at this meeting. The CDU leader insisted that 'Germany does not desire to become remilitarised', which was in line with public opinion in the western zones of occupation. Yet, he continued, 'one needs 25 German divisions with American equipment to face the Russians'.[75] Adenauer made it clear that he was not thinking of a German national army or German soldiers integrated in the US army. Instead, he advocated the creation of a European army as a safeguard against a renewed 'German militarism'. The Belgian CVP/PSC secretary-general, Robert Houben excitedly said that he had not so far heard anyone discuss the question of German rearmament 'from the perspective of the defence of Europe'. Bidault fully shared Adenauer's perception of the Soviet ideological and strategic military threat. At this point, however, he was still concerned that it would be premature to discuss German rearmament publicly. It would provoke violent reactions among the French and

---

[72] Marie-Thérèse Bitsch, *Histoire de la construction européenne* (Paris: Editions Complexe, 1996), 84.
[73] On the deliberations within the German government prior to this offer involving Adenauer and selected close foreign policy and military advisors see also Birgit Ramscheid, *Herbert Blankenhorn (1904–1991). Adenauers außenpolitischer Berater* (Düsseldorf: Droste, 2006), 152–67.
[74] Schwarz, *Adenauer. Der Staatsmann*, 735; Loth, *Der Weg nach Europa*, 92.
[75] Geneva Circle, 22 December 1948, AN 519, AP 10.

Benelux publics in particular. 'For the time being,' he concluded, 'the only guarantee is the Stars and Stripes flying in Berlin and some other points to make the Russians think.'[76] At the next meeting of the Geneva Circle on 8 March 1949, however, Bidault insisted that the Christian democrats collectively had to oppose 'a new Munich policy' of appeasement towards the Soviet Union. The formation of the Brussels Pact in 1948 combining France, Britain and the Benelux countries was merely a 'gesture' without military significance. 'The defence of France and of the free Europe appears to us to be closely linked', he added.[77] Although the issue of German rearmament was not discussed explicitly, Adenauer once more drew upon his vivid description of the Soviet threat, and vague allusions to the possibility of a Soviet-US understanding at the expense of western Europe, to suggest the need for stronger western European conventional defence.[78] At the next meeting, on 10 June 1949, the CDU leader again warned against 'the instability of public opinion in the United States, which might one day accept an understanding with the Soviet Union at the expense of Europe. We must not have another Godesberg and Munich.' Adenauer also argued that 'Soviet western expansion is not a consequence of communism, but the historical tradition of Russia'. To resist this threat, western Europe collectively would have to be well armed.[79]

During 1949–50, the Christian democrats were largely preoccupied with the creation of the Federal Republic and the first German elections, from which the CDU/CSU emerged as the largest political party, with Franco-German reconciliation and the preparation of the Schuman Plan. When the Geneva Circle met for the first time after the outbreak of the Korean War on 2 October 1950, however, the participants shared core preferences for German rearmament. As Taviani summarised, transnational Christian democracy agreed its desirability and the need to organise the common defence of western Europe on the river Elbe.[80] They also wanted the setting up of German troops within a future European army. Speaking for Adenauer, Blankenhorn reiterated that the German government did not demand a national army. The MRP and the French government should propose the European solution because 'a French initiative would accelerate the process. It would be a great pity if this initiative [for a European army] did not come from Paris.' Blankenhorn set two important conditions: first, and most importantly, that the integration of German troops

---

[76] Ibid.   [77] Geneva Circle, 8 March 1949, ACDP, 01-009-017.   [78] Ibid.
[79] Geneva Circle, 10 June 1949, ACDP, 01-009-017.
[80] Geneva Circle, 2 October 1950, KADOC, Archief CEPESS, 3.1.11.

would have to be 'on the basis of equality'; and secondly, that national contingents should be set up and integrated at the level of divisions, as only this would make military sense. Throughout the discussions about German rearmament from 1950 to 1952, the CDU/CSU politicians returned again and again to the principle of equality as in the Schuman Plan, which they regarded as essential for securing a majority for the future EDC Treaty in the German parliament, and for enhancing its domestic legitimacy.[81] At an abstract level, the MRP leadership accepted the principle. It clashed with the requirement to create a working consensus within the French govern-ment for proposing a European army in the first place, however. One crucial aspect of the evolving official French proposal made public by Pleven three weeks later was precisely its implicit discriminatory features. For some in the Third Force government they were an indispensable element of the coalition bargain. Moreover, Moch, who later voted against the EDC in 1954, also favoured the inclusion of German troops – and only German troops – at battalion level only, to strengthen their control within the European army by officers of different national origin. Representing Bidault in the Geneva Circle, the MRP secretary-general, André Colin, and Barthélémy Ott were torn between the necessities of transnational policy coordination at political party level and the domestic requirements of French coalition politics. Unable to anticipate the adverse shifts in the structural conditions for European integration policy-making in the period 1951–4, they hoped that time – and further progress in Franco-German reconciliation – would somehow dissolve the obvious contradiction.

Unlike the Schuman Plan for sectoral economic integration, the Pleven Plan was overshadowed from the beginning by two main problems. The first of these was that in the particular form it took, and its timing, it did not originate from transnational core Europe policy deliberations, but was induced externally. As the MRP deputy Marc Schérer said in the Geneva Circle on 11 December 1950, 'fear is [currently] the principal engine [driving the integration process]'.[82] The MRP was only able to create a tentative consensus within the coalition government under the impres-sion of the acute Soviet threat in Korea. Taviani argued that 'without the Korean War, your project would have been fine' at a later stage of the integration process. The discriminatory features were unacceptable to the Germans, however, and incompatible with the supranational principle. 'If we have to die together,' De Gasperi's confidant added, 'we cannot make any differences.' Carl Schröter, the deputy CDU/CSU parliamentary party

---

[81] See, for example, Geneva Circle, 11 December 1950, ACDP 01-009-017.   [82] Ibid.

leader in the German Bundestag, once more insisted that 'we absolutely need equality of rights'. Even the Belgians, who were close to the MRP on most other issues, supported this demand. The new CVP/PSC leader, Lefèvre, criticised the Pleven Plan as 'not very realistic', especially the vague idea that German equality would come 'some months or years' after the creation of a European army.[83]

Not only was the Pleven Plan a negative integration choice under the impression of the Soviet threat and the possible creation of a German army within NATO, but – as Taviani put it – it also looked 'more like the policy of the [French] socialists'.[84] The participation of the Federal Republic in the functional economic integration in coal and steel did not create the same opposition within French politics as its rearmament so shortly after the war. The MRP was able to control the Schuman Plan initiative and the subsequent intergovernmental negotiations once the socialist SFIO opted for it after the Labour Party categorically rejected British participation. In contrast, defence integration split the French socialists so deeply from the beginning that the MRP had to accept provisions in the original proposal which would clearly be unacceptable in intergovernmental negotiations, to appease the SFIO and to get the policy off the ground in the first place. The problem was, Sassen stated soberly, that 'without the French socialists, we will get neither brigades nor divisions nor the production of tanks'. The MRP politicians also continuously emphasised that parliamentary ratification of the EDC Treaty without most of the originally envisaged discriminatory features would be impossible without majority SFIO support, and that it would therefore be crucial to allow the French socialists to retain a stake in defence integration. This was difficult for the CDU/CSU and the DC to swallow. As Teitgen emphasised once more in the Geneva Circle in June 1952, however, 'if we leave the [French] socialists outside of the coalition, they will become a much greater danger to the idea of European integration'.[85]

The Christian democrats were capable of controlling the limited dissent within their own parties in the period 1950–4, for example from a small number of Protestant pacifists in the CDU like Gustav Heinemann, president of the German Protestant synod and interior minister in Adenauer's government, who resigned and left the party over the issue of rearmament in October 1950. Its extremely divisive nature induced core Europe governments – especially the French – to assert control over the EDC negotiations, however – this with the primary aim of securing the

---

[83] Ibid.   [84] Ibid.   [85] Geneva Circle, 16 June 1952, AKVI, Karton NEI, a) b).

internal stability of the governing coalition. At the same time, national bureaucrats and military experts successfully influenced the ministerial policy-making especially of defence ministries during the intergovernmental negotiations. This actually made it more difficult for Christian democratic leaders to exercise overall political control than in the case of the ECSC, where the economic ministries shared a broad preference for functional integration, the sectoral business interests were split and the trade unions generally supportive. As a result, the Christian democratic network mainly concentrated during the EDC negotiations and afterwards on exchanging information on these domestic constraints and how they might affect governmental negotiating positions and the parliamentary ratification process.

Soviet diplomatic initiatives to prevent the integration of the Federal Republic into western defence structures, and how they might affect German policy, was one important topic in the discussions in the Geneva Circle and the NEI. One year before the Stalin notes of March 1952, for example, Lefèvre queried what the Germans would do if Stalin were to offer a conference of the Four Powers to discuss the reunification of a neutralised Germany within the borders of 1938.[86] He believed that German agreement to such a solution would be 'suicide', but this form of suicide could nevertheless appeal to the German public. Schröter insisted that 'neutralism is impossible'. He thought that an offer involving border changes in the east was extremely unlikely. In this case, a minority within the CDU would probably advocate negotiations with a view to public opinion. Internally, however, Adenauer 'has brutally rejected this option'.[87] At the next meeting, on 23 April 1951, Blankenhorn, who like most Christian democrats equated neutrality under international law with ideological 'neutralism', warned that only fast progress on integration and moving the western defence from the Rhine to the Elbe to encompass the Federal Republic would provide sufficient protection against Soviet temptations.[88] Under the impression of heavy CDU/CSU losses in regional elections in the federal states of Hesse, Bavaria and Württemberg-Baden in 1950, Schröter warned that Adenauer would have to show real results of his western integration policy to win the national elections in 1953, or the influence of Schumacher, who favoured a united Germany as mediator between East and West, would grow.[89] With the CDU improving once

---

[86] Geneva Circle, 26 February 1951, AN 519, AP 10.   [87] Ibid.
[88] Geneva Circle, 23 April 1951, KADOC, Archief CEPESS, 3.1.11.
[89] Geneva Circle, 16 October 1951, ACDP, 01-009-017.

more in opinion polls, Lenz confirmed in the Geneva Circle on 16 June 1952 that Adenauer would continue to oppose negotiations with the Russians, as Soviet offers were exclusively directed 'against western integration'. Public opinion was no longer such a problem, he argued, as most West Germans shared a dispassionate view of German unity. In fact, 55 per cent no longer believed that it would happen in the foreseeable future.[90]

At the same time, the Christian democrats from Germany, Italy and the Benelux countries increasingly worried about the EDC's ratification prospects in the Assemblée Nationale. Fontanet admitted in the Geneva Circle on 2 March 1953 that Gaullist support for the new centre-right government of René Mayer was conditional on an 'appeasement formula' for the EDC which was based on 'a kind of misunderstanding'. In parliament, the political parties had informally agreed a temporary 'truce' over the EDC, and it was important not to proceed too quickly.[91] Three months later, Teitgen elaborated the problems caused for the MRP and the pro-EDC camp in the Assmblée Nationale by Soviet 'détente propaganda', which united 'neutralists, nationalists and communists'. Moreover, the French feared that the SPD could come to power in the German elections in September, creating more uncertainty. If, however, the German voters were to endorse Adenauer and his policies, Teitgen predicted overly optimistically, 'the EDC would be ratified with 400 votes the next day'.[92] Yet, when the CDU/CSU succeeded in increasing its share of the vote, Teitgen observed that the French EDC opponents construed the election result as a plebiscite for Adenauer, 'not democracy', and abused it for their purposes. In these circumstances, everything depended for the EDC ratification on the renewed participation of the socialists in the French government.[93]

Although the very strong MRP support did not suffice to pass the EDC Treaty, the French Christian democrats were in a pivotal position in the ratification process for the Western European Union (WEU), the strictly intergovernmental replacement solution for German rearmament with British membership negotiated and signed by Mendès-France on 23 October 1954. On 23 December 1954, 61 of the 85 MRP deputies

---

[90]   Geneva Circle, 16 June 1952, AKVI, Karton NEI, a) b).
[91]   Geneva Circle, 2 March 1953, AKVI, Karton NEI, a) b).
[92]   Geneva Circle. 29 June 1953. See also *Im Zentrum der Macht*, 666.
[93]   Geneva Circle, 19 October 1953, AKVI, Karton NEI, c) e).

opted against German rearmament in this particular form, and all others abstained, in the first vote on the inclusion of the Federal Republic in the Brussels Pact, which the Assemblée Nationale actually rejected by 281 to 259 votes. The MRP leadership saw no political merit in the combined WEU/NATO solution. At a public gathering of the German Europa Union, for example, Schuman called the WEU 'a mere London façade in the English style, with some Parisian decorations'. It would mean 'abandoning forever a European solution to which we remain attached over and above all other concerns'.[94] In the debate in the Assemblée Nationale, Teitgen denounced the WEU/NATO solution as the creation of 'a German army with an American commander and British control'.[95] It was the precise opposite of the EDC/EPC: strictly inter-governmental, not supranational, Atlantic, not continental European, and with a dominant British role as in the OEEC and the Council of Europe in the late 1940s. On the merit of the WEU Treaty, and because they expected electoral benefits from it in a political situation where public opinion was more pro-EDC than the Assemblée Nationale, the MRP parliamentary party wanted to bring the WEU Treaty down – and with it, the government headed by the pro-British Mendès-France, who became a hate figure for the Christian democrats when he tacitly supported the second-rate funeral for what they regarded as their EDC policy.

The mistrust between Mendès-France and the MRP was mutual. Ostensibly to enhance the ratification prospects of the EDC Treaty, the French prime minister tried to negotiate a far-reaching interpretative protocol with the other ECSC governments in Brussels from 19 to 22 August 1954. It would have watered down its supranationality and effectively eliminated the provisions of article 38, on which the EPC was based and which also included the perspective of a common market. This formula was totally unacceptable to the MRP. As Mendès-France recalled later,[96] his impression during the preparatory discussions at inter-governmental level was that the MRP leaders were putting the Christian democrats in the other five ECSC countries under severe pressure to reject any further modifications to the EDC after they had already conceded the so-called additional protocols of February 1953 concerning the non-inclusion in the EDC of the French

[94] Cited in Poidevin, *Robert Schuman*, 381.
[95] 'Les Adversaires des accords de Paris ont poursuivi leur offensive à l'Assemblée', *Le Monde*, 24 December 1954.
[96] Pierre Mendès France, *Choisir. Conversations avec Jean Bothorel* (Paris: Stock, 1974), 74.

colonial army.[97] When the EDC failed in the French parliament, even the British foreign minister, Anthony Eden, who had no access to the Christian democratic network in continental Europe, recognised the crucial importance of MRP support for a replacement solution. When Taviani in his capacity as Italian defence minister came to London to discuss alternative options, Eden asked him whether he and other Christian democratic leaders could 'exercise influence on the French MRP' to support an inter-governmental organisation with British membership to achieve German rearmament.[98]

Without the ratification of the Paris Treaties, not only the rearmament of Germany, but also its sovereignty and an effective conventional defence of western Europe would have been jeopardised. Although they strongly supported the EDC and secured its ratification in four parliaments by the time of the French vote, the Christian democrats from the other five ECSC states desperately wanted the WEU/NATO option to succeed as the only 'realistic alternative', as Taviani described it to Eden.[99] Between the negotiation of the Paris Treaties in early October 1954 and the French parliamentary ratification, transnational Christian democracy thus invested substantial resources in making sure that their common security preferences would override the MRP's domestic political incentives for bringing down the WEU/NATO solution. On 5 October 1954, von Brentano wrote to Teitgen warning him not to use the ratification of the future treaties for taking revenge on Mendès-France: 'I want to tell you plainly that I would consider a negative vote by the Assemblée Nationale a catastrophe.'[100] Directly after the signing of the Paris Treaties, Adenauer dispatched Kiesinger to Paris to canvass MRP leaders to ease their ratification, as well as encouraging other NEI parties to lobby for it bilaterally.[101] As Blankenhorn recalls in his memoirs, the CDU leadership expected after these consultations that the MRP would 'give the treaties its unified support'.[102] When news reached Bonn of the MRP's role in the defeat of the French government in the first vote in the ratification process, Adenauer was stunned. The following day, Christmas Eve, he wrote a

---

[97] In fact, Teitgen suggested to von Brentano during a meeting in Paris in July 1954 that the German government could perhaps consider minor concessions not requiring treaty changes, to allow Mendès-France to save his face and to enhance the ratification prospects in France. See von Brentano to Adenauer, 13 July 1954, cited in Baring (ed.), *Sehr veehrter Herr Bundeskanzler!*, 139. On the additional protocols as 'interpretative texts' see also Fursdon, *The European*, 207.

[98] 'Dibattito / débat / discussion', in: Enrico Serra (ed.), *Il rilancio dell'Europa e i trattati di Roma / The Relaunching of Europe and the Treaties of Rome* (Baden-Baden: Nomos, 1989), 161.

[99] Ibid. [100] Cited in Baring, *Sehr veehrter Herr Bundeskanzler!*, 142. [101] Ibid., 142.

[102] Blankenhorn, *Verständnis*, 203.

personal letter to Schuman saying that the negative vote 'troubles me in the extreme'. The demise of the WEU/NATO replacement solution, following upon the EDC failure, 'could lead the German people to turn away from the idea of reconciliation and cooperation between France and Germany and of European unification'. Adenauer pleaded with Schuman that he and other members of the MRP parliamentary party should not allow their final decision to become overshadowed by their 'fully justified personal sentiments [against Mendès-France]'.[103] The Christian democrats quickly activated other communication channels, too. Gerd Brands, who was von Brentano's right-hand man in his function as president of the Ad hoc Assembly, called the CVP/PSC leader Lefèvre on Christmas Eve. He met with him in Brussels the following morning, asking him in the name of Adenauer and von Brentano to urge the MRP leaders to rescue the treaties. Lefèvre, who was also a member of the Ad hoc Assembly, promptly left for Paris for informal consultations before the ratification process conti-nued.[104] No record of these talks exists, but as Bichet recalls in his memoirs, Adenauer's personal letter to Schuman and these direct contacts made all the difference in converting enough MRP deputies to vote for, instead of abstaining, in the subsequent votes until 30 December.[105] Pflimlin recalls in his memoirs that, in eventually voting for the WEU/NATO solution, they defied Lecourt, the parliamentary party leader. A convinced European federalist, who would be president of the European Court of Justice from 1967 to 1976, Lecourt was keen to ensure that the MRP voted cohesively against the WEU/NATO solution to strengthen its federalist identity and to bring down the Mendès-France government.[106]

One month after this WEU/NATO ratification ordeal, the Christian democrats met in the Geneva Circle. Teitgen solved the voting riddle for his interlocutors, explaining that the MRP 'delegated 15 votes to pass the WEU Treaty'. Most of the fifteen MRP politicians who eventually voted for the WEU solution were long-time participants in transnational Christian democratic networking including Schuman, Bidault, Teitgen, Pflimlin, Bichet and others. Teitgen also emphasised that, in the internal discussions within the parliamentary party, the only argument in favour of passing the WEU Treaty was 'Chancellor Adenauer'. The MRP was

---

[103] Adenauer to Schuman, 24 December 1954, printed in *Adenauer Briefe 1953–55*, 203–4.
[104] Brands to von Brentano, 28 December 1954, cited in Baring, *Sehr verehrter Herr Bundeskanzler!*, 413, footnote 117. See also von Brentano to Lefèvre, 20 January 1955, ibid., to thank him for his intervention.
[105] Bichet, *La Démocratie chrétienne*, 316. See also Letamendia, 'La Place', 107.
[106] Pierre Pflimlin, *Mémoires d'un européen de la IVe à la Ve République* (Paris: Fayard, 1991), 81.

convinced that the WEU was 'very bad', but it would nevertheless also provide enough 'votes under the table' for the treaty in the Senate, the second chamber, to avoid any last-minute problems.[107] Splitting their vote in this way to allow a treaty to pass, to which they were fundamentally opposed, the MRP leaders put their transnational allegiances above domestic calculations of party advantage. Their decision reflected the strength of cross-border political integration and the accumulation of substantial social and political trust during the eight years of intensive Christian democratic networking since 1947. Hans-Peter Schwarz has argued that the negative EDC vote demonstrated that Adenauer relied too much on party cooperation with the MRP to advance his integration policy. When the MRP no longer controlled the foreign ministry, and was even out of power from June 1954, the chancellor had no strategy for close collaboration with the Mendès-France government.[108] Yet Adenauer, as well as transnational Christian democracy as a whole, and the Radical French prime minister had wholly incompatible political ideas and objectives for European integration. The interpretative protocol for the EDC would have completely changed its nature. It can only be argued with hindsight that even a severely mutilated EDC might still have developed institutional dynamics that could later have led to further integration and more supranational decision-making mechanisms. Crucially, however, it was only Adenauer's investments in party cooperation and his own willingness to override domestic electoral concerns on more than one occasion, such as over the Saar issue, that at least got him, and European Christian democracy, the WEU to enable German rearmament to take place and enhance the security of western Europe.

The EDC's failure and the WEU/NATO replacement solution only strengthened transnational Christian democracy's resolve to defend, and extend in the economic sphere, their supranational ECSC core Europe. As Schuman claimed in October 1954, 'we have lost a battle, but we can still win the war.'[109] Until the Schuman Plan, the predominant approach that transnational Christian democracy had to institutional questions was pragmatic support for supranationalism in some form to advance specific causes – especially binding Germany into structures that would prevent unilateral action. Thereafter, their partly confessionally motivated predisposition turned into a hard-core programmatic preference for

---

[107] Geneva Circle, 31 January 1955, ACDP, 01-172-31. See already Schuman to Adenauer, 17 January 1955, *Adenauer. Briefe 1953–1955*, 508, footnote 3.
[108] Schwarz, *Adenauer. Der Staatsmann*, 134.   [109] Cited in Poidevin, *Robert Schuman*, 381.

European policy-making. As long as it was limited to the sectoral ECSC, supranationalism was insufficiently embedded in European institutions and could have been reversed in further integration. Initially, the Benelux governments – including many Christian democrats – still favoured the retention of a national veto in the Council of Ministers. As the young Belgian CVP student representative Wilfried Martens, who later became Belgian prime minister from 1979 to 1992 and European People's Party (EPP) president in 1990, observed at the NEI congress in Tours in 1953, these countries traditionally regarded national sovereignty as 'a means to protect the small against the large'.[110] At the same time, as some of its opponents argued, the EPC's ambitious supranational set-up was one important reason for the EDC's failure in France. When the EDC was replaced by the WEU, and Mendès-France made clear that he would not extend the appointment of Monnet as president of the ECSC High Authority, who personified the Community Europe, it appeared more doubtful than ever at the end of 1954 that the supranational principle would prevail in future integration.

With its partly supranational institutional design, the ECSC immediately became the reference point for transnational Christian democracy even before the treaty was concluded. After prior consultation with Adenauer, Blankenhorn proposed in the Geneva Circle on 2 October 1950 that the future EDC's institutional structure should be 'analogous with the Schuman Plan'.[111] Such a European solution without the resurrection of a German national army would not only ease French support for German rearmament, it was hoped, but would also simultaneously advance the cause of supranational integration at the same time. Although there were obvious problems with the Pleven Plan, such as its discriminatory features and lack of any precision on political control, the Christian democrats were convinced, and largely remained so until the demise of the EDC, that the intergovernmental alternative of the integration of a German national army into NATO would be hazardous. When the Dutch L. G. A. Schlichting hinted in the Geneva Circle in June 1953 that non-supranational options would be available, if the ratification of the EDC were to fail, Teitgen developed the apocalyptic scenario that any such alternative would mean 'the end of German democracy'. Blankenhorn concurred that 'this is very much Adenauer's view, too'. From this

---

[110] Aussprache zur Souveränitätsfrage in der europäischen Integration, NEI-Kongreß, Tours, 4.–6.9.1953, Zusammenfassung des NEI-Sekretariats, ACDP, 09-002-014.
[111] Geneva Circle, 2 October 1950, KADOC, Archief CEPESS, 3.1.11.

perspective, the supranational principle also had important functional advantages, as Teitgen explained. 'The day when French and German soldiers work together side by side in the same army, the rest will follow.'[112]

During the first half of the 1950s, the Christian democrats discussed extensively and refined supranationalism as a constitutional concept for core Europe to rationalise their political approach. The institutional form of integration played an important role in all speeches and debates at NEI congresses and in informal network contacts.[113] The 1953 NEI congress was entirely devoted to the supranational principle. It followed upon the drafting of the European Political Community (EPC), which was essentially a Christian democratic project from the beginning. Although Schuman was sceptical whether full-blown federal integration could succeed so quickly after the start of limited sectoral economic integration, he first proposed the creation of a political authority for the future EDC on 20 September 1951.[114] De Gasperi took this up and together with Taviani, succeeded in getting article 38 inserted into the EDC Treaty during the negotiations in late December 1951.[115] It charged the future EDC Assembly with submitting proposals for a political community within six months of its constitution. After the EDC Treaty was signed in Paris on 27 May 1952, de Schryver immediately called a meeting of the Geneva Circle for 16 June 1952.[116] At this meeting, Teitgen outlined his tentative ideas for a constitution with a rotating prime minister of a future European Union, four ministers for foreign relations, defence, the Schuman Plan and finance, and a bicameral parliamentary system similar to the US Congress.[117] The participants were stunned by this far-reaching proposal, but enthusiastic about the MRP initiative. Schuman and Teitgen also invoked the established cross-party federalist advocacy coalition with socialists like Spaak, who proposed these ideas to De Gasperi in Rome on the same day. Two days later, Teitgen and Spaak met in Paris to devise a cross-party strategy

---

[112] Geneva Circle, 29 June 1953, AN 457, AP 59.

[113] See, for example, Kai-Uwe von Hassel, Die Integration Europas, Entwurf für einen Vortrag von Heinrich von Brentano bei der NEI-Tagung in Bad Ems, September 1951, BA, N 1351, 8a.

[114] Cf. Hanns Jürgen Küsters, 'Zwischen Vormarsch und Schlaganfall. Das Projekt der Europäischen Politischen Gemeinschaft und die Haltung der Bundesrepublik Deutschland (1951–1954)', in Trausch (ed.), *Die Europäische Integration*, 261.

[115] On De Gasperi and the EDC/EPC see also Antonio Varsori, 'Alcide De Gasperi and the European Project', in Paul-F. Smets (ed.), *Les Pères de l'Europe: 50 ans après. Perspectives sur l'engagement européen* (Brussels: Bruylant, 2001), 105–22.

[116] De Schryver to members of the Geneva Circle, 6 June 1952, KADOC, Archief August E. de Schryver, 7.2.7.4.

[117] Geneva Circle, 16 June 1952, AKVI, Karton NEI, a) b).

for the work of the future EDC Assembly.[118] On 30 June, Schuman issued internal guidance for French foreign policy to support the formation of a 'solid core of permanent institutions without which the unity to which we aspire, would dissolve'.[119] When De Gasperi and Schuman succeeded at the first meeting of the ECSC Council of Ministers on 10 September 1952 in accelerating the whole process and constituting the ECSC Assembly as the Ad hoc Assembly, the Christian democrats as by far the largest political group had the federalist von Brentano elected to its presidency.

The CD Group immediately began to play an influential role within transnational Christian democracy in advancing supranationalism as an integration concept. From the beginning, the ECSC Assembly, like the Parliamentary Assembly of the EEC from 1958, was heavily weighted in a federalist direction, which the delegates set in concrete by continuously self-selecting strongly pro-integration members from national parliaments.[120] The Christian democrats were especially strongly united behind deeper integration and the long-term goal of European federation. As in the case of the NEI and informal network contacts, national party members who dissented from this hegemonic position, such as Kaiser in the CDU and Hamon in the MRP, had no access to parliamentary cooperation. This in turn strengthened the ideological cohesion of transnational Christian democracy, which invested considerable resources in defending and advancing the supranational principle – both in the context of the EDC and of the plans for further sectoral economic integration and a common market.

Von Brentano and Teitgen, two participants of the Geneva Circle with a shared professional background as lawyers, together played a crucial role in drafting the EPC in the Constitutional Committee of the Ad hoc Assembly. The Christian democrats also voted en bloc for the EPC in the Assembly when it was passed with fifty votes for and five abstentions. The absence of thirty-one delegates, of whom fifteen were known to be opposed to the federalist EPC, indicated, however, that support for it in this form was more fragile, especially in France. The EPC foresaw a bicameral system with two parliamentary chambers, one consisting of national parliamentarians and the other directly elected. The Christian democratic network never expected that this federalist constitution would be adopted wholesale by the member-states. In negotiations later in 1953,

---

[118] Cf. Chenaux, *Une Europe Vaticane?*, 169.   [119] Cf. Krüger, *Sicherheit durch Integration?*, 286.
[120] On the ECSC Parliamentary Assembly, see also John Fitzmaurice, *The Party Groups in the European Parliament* (Farnborough: Saxon House, 1975), chapter 2.

the governments restricted the federalist scope, most importantly by replacing the chamber of national parliamentarians with a Council of Ministers as in the ECSC and in the EEC later. This does not reflect, however, that federalist motivations were marginal in the policy process and that the democratic form necessarily followed the specific functions allocated to the institutions, as Berthold Rittberger has suggested.[121] Rather, transnational Christian democracy and the cross-party federalist alliance had a much greater majority in the Ad hoc Assembly than in intergovernmental settings, where they had to make intra-party and coalitional concessions. Whereas the Belgian Christian democrats followed a much more federalist line in the NEI, the Geneva Circle and in the Ad hoc Assembly, for example, the more Atlanticist Van Zeeland was still foreign minister.[122] In France, moreover, the MRP had to cooperate with several coalition partners, among them the Gaullists, and agree a common negotiating position. The EPC nevertheless fulfilled an important function as a federalist goalpost. Legitimising a strong parliamentary dimension of integration, it made it more difficult for less federalist-minded coalition governments to retreat towards a much more inter-governmental solution. Crucially, the inter-governmental negotiations did not touch the foreseen direct election of the future EP, which would be included in the EEC Treaty as an objective, but not implemented until 1979.

Although the EPC failed together with the EDC, its demise actually strengthened the supranational cause in two ways. The supranational principle became decoupled from the politically charged defence integration. Moreover, its constitutional integrity had suffered from the Pleven Plan's original discriminatory features. Although watered down during the negotiations, the Federal Republic would still not have been allowed to become a member of NATO, although it could have asked for joint Council meetings between the EDC and NATO. Teitgen played this down and insisted in the Geneva Circle in June 1952 that the creation of the EDC would 'logically lead to' Germany's NATO membership,[123] but this was for the future. Even a temporary inequality of rights in the EDC could not be reconciled with the federal principle, however.

---

[121] Berthold Rittberger, '"No Integration without Representation!?" European Integration, Parliamentary Democracy, and Two Forgotten Communities', *Journal of European Public Policy* 13 (2006), 1211–29; see also in a long-term perspective, by the same author, *Building Europe's Parliament. Democratic Representation beyond the Nation-State* (Oxford: Oxford University Press, 2005).

[122] On Van Zeeland's European preferences and policies see also Vincent Dujardin and Michel Dumoulin, *Paul Van Zeeland 1893–1973* (Brussels: Éditions Racine, 1997).

[123] Geneva Circle, 16 June 1952, AKVI, Karton NEI, a) b).

The failure of the EDC allowed transnational Christian democracy to shift the integration process back to the economic sphere, where it would arouse less antagonism and bring more practical benefits, especially facilitating European-level decision-making and constraining the influence of domestic interest groups on national policy-making. All the while, the Christian democrats continued to invest substantial resources in advocating supranationalism. At their congress about European economic integration in September 1954, the NEI once more emphasised their dual support for a strong supranational authority in combination with a directly elected parliament – as in the EPC – to strengthen the popular legitimacy of integration. During the inter-governmental deliberations in the Spaak Committee, the NEI congress discussed the two proposals for further sectoral and horizontal economic integration in September 1955. In his speech, the Dutch economics minister, Jelle Zijlstra, once more emphasised the need for a supranational organ as a core element of the institutional set-up of future organisations.[124] The subsequent debate again highlighted that the Christian democrats strongly supported the retention of the supranational principle including a directly elected parliament. As Franz-Josef Strauß, at that time CSU minister for nuclear policy before becoming defence minister 1956–62, finance minister 1966–9 and minister-president of Bavaria 1978–88, warned in crass terms, the alternative was 'federation or the demise of European culture' resulting from a process of renationalisation.[125]

The experience of the EDC failure also strengthened the Christian democratic resolve to retain for the time being the effective nexus – established with the creation of the ECSC – between the supranational principle and geographically limited core Europe integration. The Christian democrats were sceptical about, or hostile to the WEU, not least because of the leading British role combined with its strictly inter-governmental institutional structure. In the Geneva Circle on 31 January 1955, Teitgen insisted that the WEU Treaty could not be 'a point of departure for European policy. If the headquarters of European policy-making are relocated to London, we can expect nothing from England but sabotage.' Bidault added, 'I cannot imagine how we can conduct European policy with the British leading.' The CDU politicians von Spreti and Lenz agreed. They suggested that as in the case of the Schuman Plan, the

---

[124] Jelle Zijlstra, Die Europäische Integration, Bericht, NEI-Kongress, Salzburg, 16.–19.9.1955, BAR, CVP-Archiv JII.181, 2382.
[125] Aussprache [German contributions], NEI-Kongress, Salzburg, 16.–17.9.1955, ACDP, 09-002-017. See already the year before, Zusammenfassung der Aussprache, NEI-Kongress, Brügge, 10.–12.9.1954, AN 519, AP 9.

Christian democratic network should develop its own initiatives for deeper economic integration, propose them to Britain, and if opposed, implement them among the six ECSC states.[126] That the British government would reject them was practically certain, not only because of Britain's long-standing preference for intergovernmental solutions as in the WEU. More importantly, integration in a continental European industrial customs union with common external tariffs would have destroyed the Commonwealth preference system. Established as a combination of bilateral treaties at Ottawa in 1932, this preference system not only had real economic significance for Britain, as it still conducted 50 per cent of its trade with Commonwealth countries and its colonies by the mid-1950s, but also great cultural and symbolic political value, especially for the Empire wing of the ruling Conservative Party.[127]

Christian democracy's advocacy of horizontal economic integration was strengthened not just by the failure of the EDC, but also the unsuccessful attempt at agricultural sector integration. On 12 June 1950, Pflimlin, French minister of agriculture 1947–9 and again 1950–1, had proposed in the name of the MRP parliamentary party in the Assemblée Nationale a plan for European market regulations for particular commodities, with a High Authority with decision-making powers. The French cabinet formally adopted his ideas on 5 September 1950. At the same time, René Charpentier, another MRP deputy and future vice-president of the French Agricultural Commission from 1951–8, launched the initiative in the Council of Europe on 8 August 1950, where he would head the commission that discussed the so-called Green Pool project.[128] Unlike the Schuman Plan, however, this French initiative was addressed to all member-states of the Council of Europe and not combined with a supranational *junktim*. Preliminary inter-governmental discussions eventually led to four conferences on European agricultural policy, which brought no results, however. The British government only participated in these conferences to steer them away from supranational solutions. It had no interest in increased imports from continental Europe as long as the free import of agricultural products from Commonwealth countries was the *quid pro quo* for Britain's preferences for its own industrial exports to those markets. In 1954, the

[126] Geneva Circle, 31 January 1955, ACDP, 01-172-31.
[127] On the British reaction to the proposals for further economic integration see in greater detail Wolfram Kaiser, *Using Europe, Abusing the Europeans. Britain and European Integration 1945–63* (Basingstoke: Macmillan, 1999), chapter 2; Milward, *The Rise and Fall*, chapter 7.
[128] See also Gerbet, 'Les Partis politiques', 79.

Green Pool talks were transferred to the OEEC and abandoned in the following year.[129]

Although the Christian democrats played a crucial role in advancing the Schuman Plan and the Green Pool project, both initiatives differed fundamentally, which largely explains why the former succeeded, but not the latter. Whereas the Christian democratic network meticulously debated and prepared the proposal for integration in coal and steel, although it was officially presented by the French government, it never even discussed sectoral integration in agriculture before April 1951, almost one year after Pflimlin's parliamentary initiative. Rather than reflecting a strong prior consensus among transnational Christian democracy as in the case of the Schuman Plan, the Pflimlin initiative was dominated by national French bureaucratic policy-making and the demands of the domestic farmers' lobby and the peasant parties, which in turn influenced the MRP's tactics.[130] In 1948, the French government first decided to prioritise increasing agricultural exports to overcome the dollar shortage, but it had no multilateral strategy to achieve this objective. In 1951, French production reached pre-war levels, with growing surpluses of wheat, butter, sugar and other commodities.[131] The peasant parties voted for the ECSC in the expectation of forthcoming benefits from the Green Pool. What they wanted were specific deals for commodities with French surplus production for European export markets, however, not wholesale integration in an agricultural customs union, for which the Dutch socialist Sicco Mansholt lobbied at this time.[132] The farming vote was crucial for the MRP, however. In the early 1950s, 15 per cent of its members and 25 per cent of its voters were farmers.[133] Especially after the MRP's electoral slump in 1951, and an increased share of the vote for the peasant parties, the Christian democrats felt the need to keep the talks in the larger Council of Europe and OEEC framework. The inclusion of Britain alongside Germany as the two main European importers of foodstuffs appeared to promise greater economic

---

[129] See in much greater detail Guido Thiemeyer, *Vom 'Pool Vert' zur Europäischen Wirtschaftsgemeinschaft. Europäische Integration, Kalter Krieg und die Anfänge der Europäischen Agrarpolitik 1950–1957* (Munich: Oldenbourg, 1999).

[130] On its origins see also Richard T. Griffiths and Fernando Guirao, 'The First Proposals for a European Agricultural Community: the Pflimlin and Mansholt Plans', in Richard Griffiths and Brian Girvin (eds.), *The Green Pool and the Origins of the Common Agricultural Policy* (Bloomsbury: Lothian Press, 1995), 1–19.

[131] Cf. Krüger, *Sicherheit durch Integration?*, 236.

[132] See in greater detail Guido Thiemeyer, 'Sicco Mansholt and European Supranationalism', in Wilfried Loth (ed.), *La Gouvernance supranationale dans la construction européene* (Brussels: Bruylant, 2005), 39–53.

[133] Callot, *Le Mouvement Républicain Populaire*, 226–30.

benefits for French farmers. These tactics required, however, that the MRP shed its supranational ambitions without a realistic chance of actually getting British governments to agree to any scheme at all. Instead of extending the cohesive ECSC core Europe, therefore, the Green Pool initiative dissipated in the wider western Europe. As Pflimlin, who strongly supported the supranational core Europe, conceded in his memoirs, his original choice under ministerial and interest group pressure to launch the idea in the Council of Europe was 'a terrible tactical blunder'.[134] It was only the customs union proposal that allowed the idea to become resuscitated as a *quid pro quo* in the negotiations during 1956–7 for French agreement to the industrial customs union – this time in the form of Mansholt's concept of an agricultural customs union, but with common policies for a large number of commodities as developed by the EEC in the Common Agricultural Policy (CAP) during the 1960s.

When the Christian democrats began to discuss the Green Pool proposal, it immediately became clear that they could easily reach a consensus on the main objectives of agricultural policy integration. The first was that it would have to come about within the kind of supranational framework established by the ECSC as an institutional role model. In the Geneva Circle on 23 April 1951, Fontanet insisted that bilateral treaties or intergovernmental agreements provided no long-term solution.[135] Secondly, as Pflimlin also soon realised, the supranational option in turn required agricultural integration within the ECSC core Europe. Such limited core Europe integration was also the only policy acceptable to the powerful Bauernverband, the German interest group that organised up to 90 per cent of farmers, of which some 70 per cent voted CDU/CSU, and all except 10 per cent, for smaller coalition parties.[136] Thirdly, despite the more liberal preferences of the more efficient Dutch farmers,[137] the Christian democrats could easily agree that their predominantly market-oriented economic policy preferences were not applicable to agricultural policy with its intended social functions such as controlling migration to cities and retaining 'healthy' rural living conditions and family farming. Any

---

[134] Pierre Pflimlin, *Itinéraires d'un européen. Entretiens avec Jean-Louis English et Daniel Riot* (Strasbourg: La Nuée Bleue, 1989), 110.

[135] Geneva Circle, 23 April 1951, KADOC, Archief CEPESS, 3.1.11. On bilateral Franco-German negotiations see also Lynch, *France*, 146–68.

[136] Cf. Werner Bührer, 'Agricultural Pressure Groups and International Politics. The German Example', in Griffiths and Girvin (eds.), *The Green Pool*, 79.

[137] On Dutch policy-making on the Green Pool and the CAP see also Richard T. Griffiths, 'The Common Market', in Richard T. Griffiths (ed.), *The Netherlands and the Integration of Europe 1945–1957* (Amsterdam: NEHA, 1990), 185.

common agricultural policy would therefore be highly interventionist and protectionist. When the Geneva Circle discussed the future external policy of some kind of common market for agriculture on 2 July 1951, Charpentier insisted that all American imports would have to be replaced by European production and could be redirected to Asian markets. Even the Dutch KVP politician A. E. Th. Koolen agreed that 'one has to start with protection'.[138] As long as strong economic growth and rising income levels appeared to allow consumers to shoulder the costs of European agricultural protectionism in the form of prices way above world market levels, internal dissent as from the Economics Minister Erhard was easily contained or not even articulated. Based on these shared objectives, the Christian democrats in close cooperation with protectionist agricultural ministries and the national and European-level farmers' lobby played a crucial role in the evolution of the CAP in the 1960s. Thus, they served the interests of one of their core electoral constituencies, the farmers, at the expense of the politically badly organised consumers.

The combined demise of the EDC and the Green Pool finally led transnational Christian democracy to concentrate on the objective of industrial market integration from 1954 to 1956. Although the Christian democrats now promoted such horizontal economic integration in a much more focused way, they could draw upon policy deliberations about this issue that had taken place within and between the parties since 1948. Facilitated by strong economic growth and rapidly falling unemployment across the ECSC from about 1951, Christian democratic discourses about horizontal economic integration were increasingly characterised by greater reliance on market forces and toned-down demands for European-level state intervention. These demands originally derived from the stronger Christian social influence on party programmes in the immediate postwar period as well as anxieties – especially in France – about increased competition in a customs union, especially from German producers. In part reflecting the state-centred French economic policy tradition and the more recent development of *planification* as a national reconstruction strategy, the MRP initially advocated European-level legislation to harmonise wages and social security provisions and, effectively, production costs. At the governmental level, the harmonisation agenda was mainly pushed by French governments in 1951–2 and again in the Val Duchesse negotiations in 1956–7. At this stage, however, it was a special concern of the governing

---

[138] Geneva Circle, 2 July 1951, ACDP, 01-009-017.

socialist SFIO, whose demands proved unrealistic in view of stiff resistance, especially from the German government.

The MRP executive first discussed western European market integration in November 1948, when Teitgen argued that it was crucial to use the German industrial potential effectively for European reconstruction. In February 1949, the MRP executive resolved to support 'all plans of economic integration which facilitate the increase in the living standards of Europeans'. The MRP leaders were opposed to simple liberalisation of trade as in the form of the reduction and eventual abolition of quantitative restrictions within the OEEC. It preferred institutionalised integration with supranational dimensions and economic policy coordination and harmonisation at the European level.[139] Until its congress in Sorrent in April 1950, this originally more interventionist MRP line also influenced NEI policy-making and public statements, which still propagated an agenda of economic 'rights' and European-level social policy in conjunction with demands for market integration.[140] Subsequently, however, French and Italian left-Catholics were allowed to speak on Christian social ideas and domestic socio-economic policy-making, but the more liberal, market-oriented Christian democrats exercised tight control in the field of European economic integration policy – in their transnational network as at the national level, for example in the case of the CDU/CSU with the rapid programmatic shift during 1947–9 towards Erhard's concept of social market economy.

Brentano's report on 'European economic policy' for the NEI congress in Sorrent, which may in part have been drafted in the economics ministry, already reflected Erhard's ordo-liberal economic philosophy.[141] Starting from a positive evaluation of market integration in the late nineteenth century, the leader of the CDU parliamentary party demanded to base the future 'European economic community' on the international division and specialisation of labour combined with the free movement of people, goods and capital to create growth and jobs and increase living standards across western Europe. Christian democracy should continue to defend private property as the cornerstone of the European economic system and 'help overcome *étatisme*'. State intervention – von Brentano argued – only led to an inefficient national-level allocation of resources favouring protectionist

[139] See Pierre Guillen, 'Le MRP et l'union économique de l'Europe 1947-mai 1950', in Berstein, Mayeur and Milza (eds.), *Le MRP*, 132–9.
[140] Résolution economique, NEI congress, Sorrent, 12–14 April 1950, ACDP, 09-002-011/4.
[141] Heinrich von Brentano, Europäische Wirtschaftspolitik aus christlicher und demokratischer Überzeugung, Sprechzettel, NEI congress, Sorrent, 12–14 April 1950, ACDP, 09-002-011/4.

interests at the expense of the common good. The emerging transnational Christian democratic preference for market-based horizontal integration, which was reflected in the resolution of the NEI congress in Tours in 1953 calling for the creation of an 'economic community',[142] increasingly encompassed the MRP leadership, too. In the Geneva Circle on 19 October 1953, Teitgen said that he would very much 'welcome the creation of a common market', which he saw as the only suitable policy framework for rejuvenating the French economy.[143] The MRP would first have to win the socialist SFIO over to horizontal market integration, however, to stand a realistic chance of overcoming protectionist lobbying, especially from the Patronat. The deeply entrenched resistance to liberalisation among polit- ically influential French interest groups threatened to block any progress on the road to a common market. As Margaretha Klompé, the Dutch KVP politician, put it in the Geneva Circle: 'From this point of view, I fear the French much more than the Germans.'[144]

The Christian democratic network further advanced the agenda of market integration at the NEI congress in Bruges in September 1954, which was entirely devoted to this theme. In the summer, the national party headquarters responded to a detailed questionnaire about the next objectives and best methods of further economic integration prepared by Robert Houben from the Belgian CVP/PSC.[145] He summarised the results in his report on European economic policy.[146] At this stage, all parties supported horizontal economic integration in an industrial customs union, the complete abolition of quantitative restrictions, freedom of movement, goods and capital, convertibility of currencies and a broadly liberal foreign trade policy. Crucially, the French équipes emphasised that, although it would also support further sector integration, 'the moment has come to progress towards global integration'.[147] Compared to the more strictly ordo-liberal German objectives set out in the CDU response, the MRP developed a set of ideas for the common market which could provide a

---

[142] Karl Josef Hahn, (ed.), *La Démocratie chrétienne dans le monde. Résolutions et déclarations des organisations internationales démocrates chrétiennes de 1947 à 1973* (Rome: Union Mondiale Démocrate Chrétienne, 1973), 110.

[143] Geneva Circle, 19 October 1953, AKVI, Karton NEI, c) e).

[144] Geneva Circle, 29 June 1953, AN 457, AP 59.

[145] For the German and French answers Antwort der CDU and Questionnaire, réponse française, both in KADOC, Archief Robert Houben, 246.2/3.

[146] Die Sozial- und Wirtschaftspolitik der christlichen Demokraten im Europa von morgen, NEI congress, Bruges, 10–12 September 1954, ACDP, 09-002-016.

[147] Antwort der CDU and Questionnaire, réponse française, both in KADOC, Archief Robert Houben, 246.2/3.

suitable basis for a compromise in inter-governmental negotiations between this German position and French demands under socialist influence for greater state intervention and harmonisation of social policies: transition periods for tariff reductions, joint investments to mitigate adjustment problems such as temporarily increased regional unemployment, and a collective approach towards the economic development of European – especially French – 'overseas [colonial] territories'. In its *Manifesto of Bruges*, the NEI parties publicly demanded the creation of a 'European economic space' with 'the complete freedom of exchange and circulation of citizens and ideas, the liberalisation of the exchange of goods, services and capital' which would lead to welfare gains for all.[148] It would have to be embedded in an institutional structure with supranational features and – drawing upon the EPC draft constitution – a directly elected EP. Only two weeks after the death of the EDC and four after De Gasperi's, the Christian democrats staged their demand for horizontal economic integration with a torchlight procession in honour of the former Italian prime minister, one of the 'founding fathers' of core Europe in the incipient Christian democratic integration mythology.[149]

While Monnet and Spaak came out publicly in favour of further sector integration after the ratification of the WEU/NATO solution, the Christian democrats continued to push strongly for the common market. In February 1955, they decided once more to focus on economic integration at the next NEI congress in mid-September 1955.[150] This congress took place only ten days after the intermediate meeting of ECSC foreign ministers at Nordwijk on 6 September to evaluate the ongoing inter-governmental deliberations in the Spaak Committee about sectoral integration in nuclear energy and a common market. While the left-Catholic Fanfani presented a lofty report on institutional integration, the NEI charged Zijlstra with preparing the economic report. Although the Protestant ARP economics minister supported the domestic neo-corporatist institutional design of concerted policy-making between government, business and trade unions in the Netherlands, he favoured liberal market integration at the European level like Klompé, who – speaking for the KVP – demanded a new start in economic integration immediately after the EDC's failure,[151] and the

---

[148] Manifeste du Bruges, NEI congress, Bruges, 10–12 September 1954, KADOC, Archief Robert Houben, 246.2/3.
[149] 'Für supranationale Integration', *Rheinischer Merkur*, 17 September 1954.
[150] NEI Executive Committee, Paris, 19 February 1955, ACDP 09-002-003.
[151] Cf. Anjo G. Harryvan and Albert E. Kersten, 'The Netherlands, Benelux and the Rélance Européenne 1954–1955', in Serra (ed.), *Il rilancio*, 128.

non-party foreign minister in the coalition government, Willem Beyen. In his report, Zijlstra set out the objective of 'complete liberalisation of trade and capital transactions between European states' which would result in the formation of a 'functioning economic unit'. This in turn would allow Europe to become more competitive and to profit from the international division of labour. The common market would require a European-level cartel policy to create a level playing field. Increased competition would lead to the relocation of production, but without catastrophic consequences for any sectors or regions, especially in the prevailing conditions of strong growth throughout the ECSC. Zijlstra drastically rejected as 'nonsense' the idea that liberalisation required prior harmonisation of production costs. Instead, national governments would have to finely tune domestic economic and fiscal policies in the process of integration to help national economies adjust to the competitive pressures within the common market.[152] At the next NEI congress in Luxembourg in May 1956, the Christian democrats once more reaffirmed 'the urgent need to create a common European market'. Effectively adopting Zijlstra's view, although retaining the ambiguous, but meaningless term 'harmonisation', they underlined 'the need for sufficient transition periods and of harmonisation not in advance but concurrently with legislation'.[153] They also demanded the adoption of the Spaak Report of April 1956 as the basis for inter-governmental negotiations, which the ECSC foreign ministers decided only a few days later, at their meeting in Venice.[154]

The Christian democrats no longer had the same direct control over the subsequent Val Duchesse negotiations leading up to the signing of the Treaties of Rome on 25 March 1957 as in the case of the ECSC from 1950–1. In Belgium, a socialist-liberal coalition came to power after marginal CVP-PSC losses in national elections in 1954. In France, the centre-left *Front républicain* narrowly won the elections of January 1956, allowing the SFIO leader, Guy Mollet – still an opponent of core Europe integration without Britain in 1950 – to become prime minister. Nonetheless, the determined collective push by transnational Christian democracy for horizontal economic integration in the form of a common market with

---

[152] Jelle Zijlstra, Die europäische Integration, Bericht, NEI congress, Salzburg, 16–17 September 1955, BAR, CVP-Archiv JII.181, 2383; Aussprache [deutschsprachige Beiträge], NEI congress, Salzburg, 16–17 September 1955, ACDP, 09-002-017.

[153] Résolution, NEI congress, Luxembourg, 25–27 May 1956, ACDP, 09-002-018.

[154] See also the reports 'Stellungnahme der europäischen christlichen Demokraten zu den aktuellen Integrations- und Gewerkschaftsfragen Europas', *Luxemburger Wort*, 26 May 1956; 'Der N.E.I.-Kongress erfolgreich abgeschlossen', *Luxemburger Wort*, 28 May 1956.

clear supranational features from 1954 to 1956 strongly influenced the course of integration, once more highlighting the need for a radical reconceptualisation of the origins of European Union. Firstly, societal political actors played a crucial role in shaping governmental preferences for formal inter-state negotiations and facilitating compromise solutions. Secondly, the transnational networks of pro-integration political actors like the Christian democratic parties in turn influenced their internal policy formulation and decision-making with major repercussions for inter-state relations and negotiations. Thirdly, their policy objectives were to a large extent informed by *long durée* collective and partially unifying experiences across national borders. They developed, discussed and agreed their guiding ideas in deliberation and negotiation in formal cooperation structures like the NEI and more informal network contacts.

Christian democratic party cooperation until 1957 underlines, first of all, the continuities in European integration across the ill-fated EDC project. State-centric diplomatic historical accounts of the origins of the EEC and Euratom as the result of intergovernmental bargaining of national preferences have uncritically adopted the contemporary rhetoric that it amounted to a *relance européenne*: the 'relaunch' of European integration in the economic sphere. After all, after the demise of the EDC it took the Benelux governments until May 1955 to submit their memorandum for combined sectoral and horizontal integration,[155] and the German government until May 1955 to develop their own plan, reinforcing the proposal for a common market.[156] Seen from this perspective, the chances of these projects being realised were slim at the outset, and the French government was only finally converted by the simultaneous experience of the debacle of the joint military intervention with Britain and Israel in Suez and the Soviet crushing of the Hungarian uprising in November 1956. In contrast, Milward and others have argued that underneath the public agitation about the EDC, governmental planning for economic integration continued throughout the period 1952–4, not just in the context of the Green Pool discussions, but also in the form of the Beyen Plan for tariff reductions submitted by the Dutch government in the OEEC in 1952, for example.[157] As Richard Griffiths has shown, Dutch postwar policy was characterised by a 'relentless ... search for a multilateral trade agreement'.[158] Agricultural

[155] Harryvan and Kersten, 'The Netherlands', 146–56.
[156] Cf. Hanns Jürgen Küsters, 'The Federal Republic of Germany and the EEC-Treaty', in Serra (ed.), *Il rilancio*, 497.
[157] Milward, *The European Rescue*, 173–96.   [158] Griffiths, 'The Common Market', 183.

policy integration in the regional Benelux was frequently disrupted by acrimonious conflicts with the more protectionist Belgian government and agricultural lobby. The larger Green Pool plan came to nothing, and the British government prevented any OEEC discussion of industrial tariff reductions with the argument that tariff issues could only be dealt with in the GATT. Societal political actors continued to debate further sectoral and horizontal economic integration throughout the first half of the 1950s even more intensely than national bureaucracies, however. Milward has found no evidence of a Dutch government interest in French customs union schemes before 1952.[159] While this applies to the official French proposal of 1949 for a Franco-Italian scheme including the Benelux countries, but excluding western Germany,[160] the KVP played a full role in discussions about a western European customs union in the Christian democratic network from 1948 to 1952. While French governments afraid of domestic protectionist pressures curbed attempts to link the plan for a common market intimately with the EDC/EPC, the MRP members as part of the CD Group in the Ad hoc Assembly strongly worked for precisely this solution when devising the draft constitution. When the ECSC governments found the energy to concentrate once more on plans for deepening integration after the settlement of the WEU/NATO solution in the autumn of 1954, they could draw upon a range of clearly defined policy options developed by societal political actors. They included transnational Christian democracy, but also the socialist federalist network around Spaak, which mainly advocated further sector integration, and the Jean Monnet Action Committee, formally founded in 1955, which played a crucial role in converting the German social democrats to the core Europe project, so that they eventually voted for the ratification of the Treaties of Rome in July 1957.[161]

Moreover, most state-centric diplomatic and economic historical accounts of the origins of the EEC overestimate the cohesion of governmental policy-making. National governments operated within the more pluralistic postwar parliamentary democracies characterised by complex coalition politics. They depended on purposeful individual and collective political actors and their ability to control party policy-making, build advocacy coalitions and garner cross-party support to develop coherent

---

[159] Milward, *The European Rescue*, 173.
[160] Cf. Pierre Guillen, 'Le Projet d'union économique entre la France, l'Italie et le Benelux', in Poidevin (ed.), *Histoire des débuts*, 143–64.
[161] Cf. Monnet, *Mémoires*, 477; François Duchêne, *Jean Monnet. The First Statesman of Interdependence* (New York, London: W. W. Norton, 1994), 286–7.

policy objectives for inter-governmental negotiations and assess the viability of possible compromise solutions domestically and in other member states. In the German case, for example, Adenauer continued to ally himself closely with other transnationally networked core Europe supporters like the new foreign minister, von Brentano,[162] to overrule more orthodox ordo-liberal objections within his own party to a core Europe industrial customs union. Economics Minister Erhard feared that this could develop protectionist features under French influence and prove detrimental to his overriding aim of global trade liberalisation.[163] Tired of acrimonious intra- and inter-ministerial debates and drawing upon his constitutional competence to issue policy guidelines, the chancellor decreed in a circular letter of 19 January 1956 that all ministries would in future have to demonstrate a 'clear, positive attitude to European integration' including full support for a common market among the ECSC states with 'common institutions' – in Erhard's words, an 'integration command',[164] which even risked the future of the coalition with the liberal FDP.

The case of Dutch European policy similarly points to the great importance of political leadership in fragmented coalition politics for realising integration objectives. Dutch policy has usually been explained with allegedly shared national 'interests': a strong preference for trade liberalisation, a pronounced scepticism towards supranational integration and an all-pervasive pro-British and Atlantic orientation. Dutch politics of integration policy was more complex, however.[165] The confessional NEI parties were united behind the common market proposal and colluded with Beyen and the social democratic prime minister Willem Drees to advance horizontal economic integration, whereas many social democrats like Mansholt actually favoured further sector integration. This coalitional majority was crucial for inserting the common market into the Benelux memorandum of April 1955. It also allied the Dutch government closely to the Christian democratic-controlled governments from Germany, Italy and Luxembourg in insisting on the issue linkage between the common market and Euratom during 1956 – two topics that the French government

---

[162] On von Brentano's strong support for the Messina initiative see also Hans von der Groeben's recollections in *Deutschland und Europa in einem unruhigen Jahrhundert. Erlebnisse und Betrachtungen* (Baden-Baden: Nomos, 1995), 279–292.
[163] For the personal and policy conflicts between Adenauer and Erhard see also Daniel Koerfer, *Kampf ums Kanzleramt. Erhard und Adenauer* (Stuttgart: DVA, 1987).
[164] Cited in Schwarz, *Adenauer. Der Staatsmann*, 288–9.
[165] See in outlines Harryvan and Kersten, 'The Netherlands', 128.

attempted several times to decouple.[166] At the same time, the Catholic KVP – unlike Drees, who preferred multilateral trade treaties, and the somewhat more sceptical Protestant parties – favoured a supranational institutional design. They now saw the future European Commission as a bulwark against the domination of the Community by the larger member states, especially France and Germany, and worked with socialist federalists to overturn the earlier Dutch preference in the ECSC negotiations for a strong Council of Ministers. Paradoxically, as the combination of the common market with supranational institutions could only be realised without Britain, and was already firmly institutionalised in the ECSC, the minority Catholic KVP as the culturally most 'continental' political party even achieved a deepening of core Europe in collusion with Christian democrats, some liberals and socialist federalists from other ECSC countries.

State-centric interpretations of intergovernmental negotiations also fail to take account of the overlapping identities of state and non-state actors in European policy-making. When Christian democrats lost direct influence on national policy-making as in the case of the MRP in 1954, they relied more on transnational resources of party cooperation, which is also why Schuman and Bidault once more attended NEI congresses and participated in the Geneva Circle in person in 1955. More importantly, however, the Christian democrats in government never made a clear distinction between their party roles and state functions. After the creation of the Federal Republic in 1949, the party contacts at the highest level of political leaders in the Geneva Circle were largely replaced with formally intergovernmental contacts by the same politicians like Adenauer and Bidault as prime ministers at the time of the Schuman Plan declaration in May 1950. They wore two hats at the same time in the bilateral and multilateral intergovernmental forums – party and government – Adenauer even as combined CDU leader and chancellor. As the Christian democrats largely controlled most national governments in the ECSC member states for most of the time until the signing of the Treaties of Rome, party policy-making translated quite smoothly into governmental action after taking account of the complex coalition politics. Political parties guaranteed an organic link not only between the domestic and European levels of policy-making, but also between societal political actors and state actors.

Their transnational networking in turn played a crucial role in developing common policy objectives such as the common market, and

---

[166] Hanns Jürgen Küsters, *Fondements de la Communauté Économique Européenne* (Luxembourg: Office des publications officielles des Communautés Européennes, 1990 [German 1982]), 148.

embedding them securely in binding European and domestic policy commitments that could override other party interests or countervailing domestic interest-group pressures. In the important case of the MRP, the party leadership moved progressively towards support for horizontal economic integration in the transnational Christian democratic network between 1950 and 1954. It committed itself fully to this overriding objective at the NEI congress in Bruges in September 1954, deliberately narrowing down its European policy options. The MRP subsequently supported the Euratom and common market projects in the election campaign in December 1955 and during the formation of the new French government in January 1956. At that time, however, important domestic electoral constituencies were still not fully behind the plan for a common market. The agricultural interest groups only came out in favour of the Spaak Report as a basis for intergovernmental negotiations in the summer of 1956. The business representatives in the French Economic Council actually rejected the report in July. The CNPF under the leadership of Georges Villiers stopped short of condemning the common market plan, but attached partially unrealistic conditions such as the harmonisation of labour costs.[167] As the domestic opposition weakened, however, the MRP formally adopted the common market plan as official party policy in the spring of 1956.[168] Although the party leaders did not dare suggest this publicly, they actually supported the issue linkage established by the Christian democrats in four national governments at Venice in late May 1956, and upheld during the negotiations, between horizontal economic integration and Mollet's main interest in Euratom. They provided important parliamentary and political support for Mollet to agree to this condition for obtaining sectoral integration in nuclear energy.

The strong transnational policy consensus also facilitated the parliamentary ratification of the Treaties of Rome, especially in the crucial case of France. The constitutional need or the political choice of using referendums to legitimise European treaty changes has further complicated constitutional adaptation in the enlarged EU. This became abundantly clear for the first time when a slight majority of Danes rejected the Maastricht Treaty in 1992 only to pass it one year later after Denmark was granted an 'opt-out' for monetary union. It became clear again, and more drastically, when the French and Dutch rejected the Constitutional Treaty in

---

[167] Summarised in Parsons, *A Certain Idea*, 107–9.

[168] Jean-Paul Brunet, 'Le MRP et la construction européenne 1955–1957', in Berstein, Mayeur and Milza (eds.), *Le MRP*, 242.

referendums in 2005. In the absence of a stable government majority and a stronger consensus on core Europe integration, however, the French Fourth Republic parliament in particular was not going to rubber-stamp the creation of a customs union. The MRP played a crucial role as a facilitator in the post-EDC domestic politics of integration.[169] It did so with strong support from its voters, for whom the salience of the European issue was much higher than for any other French party. In an opinion poll in September 1955, for example, 75 per cent of MRP supporters expressed the view that further European integration was 'indispensable' or at least 'very useful'.[170] Thus, in February 1955, the party made its support for the new government of Prime Minister Edgar Faure dependent on his backing of further European integration, which secured French participation in the Messina conference and the Spaak Committee. After the elections, on 12 January 1956, the MRP executive appealed to all republican parties to prioritise the plans for Euratom and a common market – this not least with the aim of finally reintegrating the socialists into what Parsons has called the 'society of Europeans'.[171] Putting its European vocation above other strategic or specific policy preferences, the Christian democrats then colluded with pro-Community groups to induce President René Coty, an independent republican supporter of core Europe, not to appoint their arch-enemy Mendès-France, but the pro-Community socialists Mollet as prime minister and Christian Pineau as foreign minister.[172] Mollet had already supported the creation of a common market in the preceding election campaign.[173] Sixty-four MRP deputies actually voted for the new government while nine abstained. Converted to the core Europe pro-gramme and interested in economic integration as a framework for revital-ising the French economy, Mollet in turn addressed the MRP in his first government statement proposing a new broad cross-party coalition for further European integration. Only the formation and continued stability of the Mollet government and of this advocacy coalition across the government–opposition divide eventually guaranteed the ratification of the Rome Treaties with full MRP support by 342 to 239 votes in July 1957.[174]

As in the case of the ECSC, moreover, the role of transnational Christian democracy in the formation of the EEC once more reveals the limited explanatory value of rational choice accounts that explain preferences and bargaining outcomes with domestically derived 'national interests'. Liberal

---

[169] Ibid.   [170] Cited in Letamendia, 'La Place', 111.   [171] Parsons, *A Certain Idea*, 91.
[172] See also 'The Testimony of an Eyewitness', 59.
[173] *Le Monde*, 28 December 1955, quoted in Bossuat, *L'Europe des français*, 293.   [174] Ibid., 358.

inter-governmentalist theoretical explanations emphasising the influence of well-organised domestic economic interests on the framing of govern-mental preferences collapse in the light of the evidence from the European policy debate between the Messina Conference and the signing of the Treaties of Rome. Both the German BDI and the French CNPF were initially opposed to the core Europe customs union, although for diametri-cally opposed reasons. The BDI leadership was close to Erhard. As the political influence of heavy industry declined throughout the first half of the 1950s, the BDI increasingly supported global trade liberalisation and was fearful of the possible detrimental effects of the small customs union on German trade with third countries in the future European Free Trade Association (EFTA), which took a comparable share of German exports. In contrast, the CNPF's position reflected widespread fears of intense German competition in the common market among small- and medium-sized companies and larger businesses in especially protected sectors. At the same time, the farmers' organisations in both countries had yet to be convinced of the advantages of an agricultural customs union, as long as the outlines of common European-level subsidy policies were so unclear. After all, the EEC Treaty only provided in very general terms for the later introduction of such policies. In these circumstances, the pro-Community political parties had to exercise entrepreneurial leadership to overcome resistance from organised interest groups.

Milward's source-based explanation of the origins of European Union as the intended 'rescue of the nation-state' also fails to conceptualise convinc-ingly the transnational and domestic politics of integration. Bureaucrats in economic ministries took a keen professional interest in trade statistics. These showed, for example, as Milward has rightly pointed out, that French trade with the ECSC partners grew fast from 15.4 per cent to 25.8 per cent of all foreign trade between 1951 and 1956.[175] At best, however, such trade convergence eventually facilitated decision-making by allowing export businesses and allied trade unions to acquire a stake in further economic integration, thus reducing domestic protectionist opposition to such a policy, which nevertheless remained substantial in France in the period 1955–7. No convincing evidence exists of governmental decision-making, let alone political party policy formulation, as opposed to the bureaucratic evaluation of policy options, however, that pro-Community leaders in the Christian democratic and other political parties were moti-vated by trade statistics and predictions about the sectoral and regional

[175] Milward, *The European Rescue*, 169.

economic effects of horizontal economic integration. Throughout the period from the Schuman Plan to the Val Duchesse negotiations, the Christian democratic network discussed core Europe integration as a political project, with overriding political objectives such as Franco-German reconciliation. They certainly expected economic benefits from their policy preference – especially for two of their most important electoral constituencies, the middle class and farmers. Although they could rely on a strong permissive consensus among their voters in favour of further integration, however, the Christian democrats first had to convince organised interest groups of these economic benefits.

The Christian democrats' ideational motivation for these political objectives continued to be embedded in their shared, predominately Catholic experience of confessional and regional identities and opposition to the overbearing centralised liberal and socialist nation-state and its perversion in the totalitarian *Machtstaat* of interwar Europe. For the Christian democrats, European integration was not a means of rescuing this type of nation-state, but for the first time of creating in their own image a tamed Europeanised nation-state embedded in a supranational constitutional system. This vision also informed their continued support for supranational forms of integration, which was actually more ideologically coherent by the mid-1950s than at the time of the Schuman Plan. As they discussed options for further economic integration during 1954–5, the Christian democrats were united behind the aim of strengthening the existing partly supranational core Europe. They at least partially succeeded with the insertion of the federalist objective in the preamble to the EEC Treaty of 'ever-closer union', the introduction of majority voting in the Council of Ministers from stage two of the integration process at the start of 1966, the sole right of initiative for the European Commission, and the provision for the future direct election of the Parliamentary Assembly. All NEI parties from the ECSC states supported this type of institutional framework as a continuation of the principles established in the ECSC Treaty. They were not the only political force to do so. As the Dutch example demonstrates, where the KVP was initially the only political party to advocate the direct election of the EP, transnational Christian democracy continued to act as an advance guard for supranational core Europe, however. Parsons' nationally introspective claim in his study of French European policy-making, that 'on their own, France's partners preferred an OEEC/WEU Europe in 1955', is plainly wrong.[176] Instead, the Christian democrats managed to

[176] Parsons, *A Certain Idea*, 102.

reconstruct the ECSC advocacy coalition with many liberals and socialists, who became increasingly coopted into the core Europe policy consensus even in countries like Germany and Italy.

Thus, the EEC marked the deepening of a core Europe aimed at economic market-based integration with limited state intervention and the potential for a protectionist policy to serve the interests of farmers, as well as some European level neo-corporatist coordination with business and trade unions in the consultative Economic and Social Committee. This was economic integration with overriding political objectives, however, and an institutional structure to secure these objectives with the Commission, the Court of Justice and the EP, which in the eyes of the Christian democrats could in future provide European level policy-making with parliamentary legitimacy. The Christian democrats had to strike compromises with socialist parties, which the MRP continued to preach for French politics, where this strategy was finally vindicated after the election of the Mollet government. Their concessions remained limited, however. Paradoxically, the ordo-liberal influence was in some ways greater than that of European socialism as it became embedded in the evolution of competition policy in the 1960s. On the whole, negative market integration initially prevailed over attempts to create European level socio-economic policies. The EEC Treaty provided few openings for social engineering with the exception of agricultural policy, where it largely served the interests of an important electoral constituency of Christian democratic parties. In this sense, the origins of the European Union were predominantly Christian democratic, secured by the political parties through their intra-party and domestic political manœuvring, their transnational cooperation and their governmental coordination.

CHAPTER 8

Informal politics: from Rome to Maastricht

When the European Commission was set up and began to work in Brussels at the start of 1958, transnational Christian democracy was still in a pivotal political position in core Europe. Its political hegemony appeared to be secure. At the end of 1958, the Christian democrats were the sole or dominant government party in Germany, Italy, Belgium and Luxembourg. Excluding the social democratic PvdA, the Dutch confessional parties formed a minority government in December 1958 before enlarging the coalition to include the Liberals in May 1959. The MRP at least played a minor role in the governments of the Fifth Republic after Pierre Pflimlin, its new party leader since 1956, resigned as the last prime minister of the Fourth Republic after only two weeks at the end of May 1958. In the EP, moreover, the Christian democrats formed by far the largest group, with 66 of 142 members. During the 1960s, five of six EP presidents were Christian democrats.

At the same time, transnational Christian democracy's European policy preferences were well embedded in the EEC Treaty. Its initial geographical limitation promised to allow the further deepening of the integration process without British interference for many years. Although the EEC Treaty articles concerning the two core supranational policy areas, the future CAP and competition policy were quite generally phrased, Christian democratic-controlled member-state governments could steer the policy deliberations and decision-making in the Council of Ministers in close collaboration with the Commission, which had the sole right of initiative. After all, it was headed until 1967 by its federalist-minded German Christian democratic president, Walter Hallstein.[1] It also included socialist federalists like Mansholt from the long-standing cross-party advocacy coalition for a supranational Europe.

---

[1] On Hallstein see the contributions in Wilfried Loth, William Wallace and Wolfgang Wessels (eds.), *Walter Hallstein – the Forgotten European?* (Basingstoke: Macmillan, 1998).

Moreover, transnational Christian democracy very successfully mobilised other societal networks with broadly converging preferences. They included the farming lobby. As well as using the traditional national route for influencing policy-making, it increasingly operated transnationally, within the Committee of Professional Agricultural Organisations (COPA), formed in 1958.[2] These organisations had excellent links with national agricultural ministries. Farming interests were also deeply embedded within the Christian democratic parties and national and European parliamentary groups. The CDU/CSU, for example, continued to have very close links with the highly protectionist Bauernverband.[3] A political representative of these farming interests, Hans-August Lücker from the Bavarian CSU, was even leader of the CD Group in the EP 1969–75. Similarly, the design of an EEC-level competition policy in the 1960s also saw the emergence of a Christian democratic-centred advocacy coalition with strong support from the German and Dutch Christian democratic-led governments. The German Commissioner for Competition Policy, Hans von der Groeben, fostered the formation of a closely knit expert network of mostly ordo-liberal competition lawyers and economists, to help shape this new policy field. A CDU member, he had been a career civil servant in the German Ministry of Economics before joining the Commission in 1958. In 1955–6, von der Groeben had already drafted, together with Pierre Uri, the Spaak Report outlining possible solutions for a western European common market.[4]

Yet western European Christian democracy entered a structural crisis in the 1960s. Between the setting up of the EEC and its first enlargement in 1972–3, electoral support for Christian democratic parties declined everywhere in western Europe. In Germany, the CDU/CSU lost only marginally in national elections. When the social-liberal coalition under the leadership of the social democratic Chancellor Willy Brandt formed in 1969, however, the CDU/CSU was forced into opposition and, in 1972, came only second for the first time in a national election. Support for the Italian DC also declined continuously, if only marginally, but it managed to stay in power due to the continued exclusion of the communists from

---

[2] On the influence of the farmers' lobby, although not its transnational dimension, see Ann-Christina Lauring Knudsen, *Defining the Policies of the Common Agricultural Policy. A Historical Study*, PhD (Florence: European University Institute, 2001).

[3] In comparison with business interest groups see, for the first five years of the EEC, Wolfram Kaiser, 'Quo vadis, Europa? Die deutsche Wirtschaft und der Gemeinsame Markt 1958–1963', in Rudolf Hrbek and Volker Schwarz (eds.), *40 Jahre Römische Verträge: Der deutsche Beitrag* (Baden-Baden: Nomos, 1998), 206–10.

[4] See also his recollection in Groeben, *Deutschland und Europa*.

government formation. The French MRP dissolved in 1967 after its disastrous showing in the national elections in November 1962, when it gained only 5.3 per cent of the vote. Most MRP members joined the new Centre Démocrate under the leadership of Jean Lecanuet. In the increasingly polarised political system of the Fifth Republic opposing the Gaullists on the Right and the socialists and communists on the Left, the Christian democrats now cooperated with the remaining Radicals and Independents. Especially marked was the electoral decline of the Christian democrats in Belgium and the Netherlands, where they nonetheless remained central to government formation. The Belgian CVP/PSC plummeted from 46.5 per cent in 1958 to just 31.7 per cent in 1968. Electoral support for the KVP declined from 31.6 per cent in 1959, when it still succeeded at organising approximately 90 per cent of Dutch Catholics, to just 17.7 per cent in 1972. The two Protestant confessional parties also shrank. The united CDA gained 35.3 per cent in elections in 1989, but its support eventually collapsed to only 22.2 per cent in 1994. The Christian democratic parties outside the EEC did not fare better. The Austrian ÖVP was able to form a single-party government 1966–70, but its electoral support dwindled rapidly thereafter and it only re-entered a coalition government as the junior partner of the socialists in 1986.

The structural crisis of Christian democratic parties resulted from a number of factors.[5] The most important of these was the increasingly rapid secularisation of western European society. In Belgium, for example, this process was eventually reflected in the fast decline of religious practice, with levels of church attendance falling by almost 2 per cent annually after 1968. The process of secularisation eroded the up to then cohesive, well-organised Catholic milieux and weakened their societal organisations. The social influence of the Catholic Church, which traditionally advised its flock to support 'Christian' parties, also declined. As a consequence, those Christian democratic parties – like the CVP/PSC and the KVP, ARP and CHU – with the most confessional character also lost the most votes, while support for the CDU/CSU and the DC as centre-right people's parties held up better. At the same time, western European social democrats transformed themselves from traditional class-based parties into more broadly oriented catch-all parties. This was reflected in the German SPD's Bad Godesberg programme of 1959, for example, which finally shed Marxist rhetoric of class interests and nationalisation. As the parties of the Left also moderated their traditional anti-clericalism, they became

---

[5] For an intelligent discussion of the reasons for this structural crisis see also Conway, 'Introduction'.

more attractive for Catholic workers and in particular the new white–collar middle class. At the same time, liberal parties attacked the Christian democrats with varying combinations of more neo-liberal socio-economic and libertarian cultural policy profiles. Their electoral success in the Benelux countries largely came at the expense of the Christian democrats. Belgium also saw renewed sharp tensions between the Flemish and Walloon communities. As in the 1930s, the rise of organised nationalism in Flanders, where the Volksunie gained 16.9 per cent of the vote in 1968, further eroded electoral support for the CVP there.

More generally, western Europe experienced fundamental social change in the 1960s, which shook all tenets of the postwar Christian democratic ideology and policy profile. The youth and student movement culminating in the unrests of 1968 rejected traditional 'bourgeois' values like religion and family which were at the heart of the Christian democratic belief system. In a Europe which had, as a result of the postwar 'economic miracle' become more and more affluent, and where young academics did not have to worry about their career prospects in their march through state institutions, many protests were also directed against the allegedly all-pervasive and perverse materialism of the capitalist 'system' – a system that was closely associated with the Christian democratic parties even where they had a more centre-left socio-economic policy profile, and despite those parties' own robust scepticism – embedded in Catholic social teaching – regarding what they saw as excessively individualistic US-style capitalism. In this new left-wing perspective, the EEC institutions did not provide a new focus for youth idealism, as Adenauer and others had hoped after 1945. Instead, as they seemed to be almost exclusively concerned with market integration and economic liberalisation, they were often seen and portrayed as the supranational embodiment of rampant capitalism.

The more radical revolutionary slogans inspired by the likes of the Cubans Fidel Castro and Ernesto (Che) Guevara enjoyed little societal support outside self-contained university circles. Still, socio-economic policy discourses within the EEC and its member-states were less and less concerned with reconstruction and economic growth. Instead, they became increasingly dominated by proposals for more fiscal redistribution and Keynesian demand management, especially after the short economic downturn of 1966–7. The Christian democratic parties had played an important pro-active role in the extension of the welfare state after 1945: at the European level, with their interventionist policies for coal and steel as well as agriculture, and at the national level, with lavish pension reforms as in Germany in 1957 as well as a whole range of other social policy measures.

They remained fundamentally attached to the concept of subsidiarity, however, which limited the scope of state intervention in the economy and society. Their primary focus was still on private ownership and enterprise in the economy and the idea that society should evolve around the family and autonomous societal groups and professional bodies. As much as they sometimes tried, the Christian democrats could not overtake the socialists on the Left. At the same time, their anti-communism was no longer a significant vote winner, in the period of détente between the Cuban Missile Crisis in 1962 and the Soviet invasion of Afghanistan in 1979.

Christian democratic core Europe was also challenged on two fronts in the 1960s: by de Gaulle and the applications for EEC membership by Britain, Denmark, Ireland and Norway from 1961–2. When he became president of the Fifth Republic, de Gaulle did not attempt to destroy the EEC, as many Christian democrats initially feared. The industrial customs union proved a useful economic framework for his policy of controlled liberalisation including the introduction of convertibility of the French franc at the end of 1958. Moreover, French companies actually did well out of the new opportunities offered by the emerging western European market. At the same time, the EEC customs union for agricultural products combined with common policies for particular commodities promised major gains for French farmers. In January 1962, the French government succeeded in negotiating a first set of such common policies which it had linked in the negotiations in the Council of Ministers to the smooth transition to stage two of tariff reductions in the industrial customs union.[6]

De Gaulle remained adamantly opposed to the deepening of the integration process within the supranational EEC Treaty framework, however. Instead, he suggested inter-governmental cooperation in foreign policy in 1961. His proposal led to the Fouchet negotiations which were aborted in April 1962 when the Dutch and Belgian governments refused to continue talks without British participation and EEC accession.[7] In 1965, when the Hallstein Commission submitted an over-ambitious and ill-timed proposal for the introduction of Community own resources and limited budgetary powers of the EP, the French government abstained for six months from deliberations in the Council of Ministers. Political scientist Andrew Moravscik has argued from his rigid theoretical rational choice

---

[6] Gisela Hendriks, 'The Creation of the Common Agricultural Policy', in Anne Deighton and Alan S. Milward (eds.), *Widening, Deepening and Acceleration: The European Economic Community 1957–1963* (Baden-Baden: Nomos, 1999), 139–50.

[7] Cf. Georges-Henri Soutou, 'Le Général de Gaulle et le plan Fouchet d'Union Politique Européenne: un projet stratégique', in Deighton and Milward (eds.), *Widening, Deepening and Acceleration*, 55–71.

perspective, which emphasises the importance of domestically derived economic interests for inter-governmental bargaining, that de Gaulle's overriding concern and motivation for starting the so-called Empty Chair crisis was French agriculture.[8] The Commission budgetary proposal would actually have been advantageous for France, however. Although the other five EEC governments were also critical of the style and parts of the content of the Commission's proposal, they temporarily colluded with it to put pressure on the French government. This in turn confirmed de Gaulle's worst fears, strengthening his obsessive opposition to supranational forms of integration and his commitment not to allow the transition to majority voting in the Council in line with the EEC Treaty at the start of 1966.[9]

Not only was de Gaulle's strictly inter-governmental approach diametrically opposed to the supranational preferences of transnational Christian democracy, but his foreign policy of establishing western Europe as a third force in global politics under French leadership also ran counter to their policy of close transatlantic defence cooperation in NATO. His demand in 1959 to establish a directorate of the United States, Britain and France in NATO appalled all EEC partners. The Fouchet Plan was also clearly directed against what de Gaulle perceived with some justification as the hegemony of the 'Anglo-Saxons' in NATO. In January 1963, the French president rejected the British EEC application at a press conference, arguing that the country was not sufficiently 'European' and that its accession would 'drown Europe in the Atlantic'.[10] Finally, in 1966, de Gaulle took France out of the integrated military command, although not out of NATO. Cultural ambivalence towards the United States was endemic

---

[8] Andrew Moravcsik, 'De Gaulle Between Grain and Grandeur: The Political Economy of French EC Policy 1958–1970 (Part 1)', *Journal of Cold War Studies* 2:2 (2000), 3–43; '(Part 2)' in the subsequent issue in this volume, *Journal of Cold War Studies* 2:3 (2000), 4–68. The weak source basis and manipulative use of sources by Moravcsik to support his theory-driven argument are exposed in R. H. Lieshout, M. L. L. Segers and A. M. van der Vleuten, 'De Gaulle, Moravcsik and *The Choice for Europe*. Soft Sources, Weak Evidence', *Journal of Cold War Studies* 6 (2004), 89–139.

[9] For the complex interplay of these different factors before and during the crises see in particular, Ludlow, *The European Community*, chapters 3 and 4, and several contributions to Jean-Marie Palayret, Helen Wallace and Pascaline Winand (eds.), *Visions, Votes, and Vetoes. The Empty Chair Crisis and the Luxembourg Compromise Forty Years On* (Brussels: Lang, 2006). On Hallstein's policy in 1965 see also Matthias Schönwald, 'Walter Hallstein and the "Empty Chair" Crisis 1965/66', in Wilfried Loth (ed.), *Crises and Compromises: The European Project 1963–1969* (Baden-Baden: Nomos, 2001), 157–71.

[10] Printed in English translation as document 30 in A. G. Harryvan and Jan van der Harst (eds.), *Documents on European Union* (Basingstoke: Macmillan, 1997), 132–6. As the culmination of complex negotiations see Piers Ludlow, *Dealing with Britain. The Six and the First UK Application to the EEC* (Cambridge: Cambridge University Press, 1997).

within transnational Christian democracy and the desire for a more equal European role in the Atlantic Alliance strong.[11] Yet Christian democratic leaders conceived of the European role as based chiefly on the common EEC trade policy and future patterns of foreign policy cooperation which would allow the smaller member-states a voice and some influence. In view of the Soviet threat they were also adamant that EEC member-states had to invest significant material and ideational resources to keep US troops in Europe at a time of relative American economic decline and imperial overstretch in the 1960s.[12]

Paradoxically, de Gaulle's policies actually conjured up the second threat to the Christian democratic core Europe: the premature enlargement of the EEC. His aggressively unilateral foreign policy induced strong pressure by the newly elected Kennedy administration on the British government in the first half of 1961 to enter the EEC. American governments had supported supranational European integration from the formation of the ECSC in 1950–1 and the creation of the EEC in 1957–8 to the British challenge to core Europe in the form of the European Free Trade Association (EFTA) of the so-called 'outer Seven' set up in 1959–60.[13] Kennedy became much more adamant that Britain would have to join the EEC, however, when de Gaulle threatened to transform it into more of a rival than a partner of the US within the western world. As I have shown elsewhere,[14] the transatlantic motivation to retain a British world role of sorts by aligning its European policy with this strong US preference moved the Conservative government of Prime Minister Harold Macmillan to apply for membership of the EEC so early after its creation, in August 1961. Compared to this overriding objective, economic motives were diffuse and marginal in the decision-making process. At the same time, de Gaulle's inter-governmental preferences made it easy for Macmillan to play down the far-reaching supranational constitutional implications of

---

[11] On the European Christian democrats and the United States see also in greater detail Wolfram Kaiser, 'Trigger-happy Protestant Materialists? The European Christian Democrats and the United States', in Marc Trachtenberg (ed.), *Between Empire and Alliance. America and Europe during the Cold War* (Lanham: Rowman & Littlefield Publishers, 2003), 63–82.

[12] As was reflected, for example, in the so-called burden-sharing debate and German policy to partly offset US foreign currency 'support' costs of troop stationing. See Hubert Zimmermann, *Money and Security. Troops and Monetary Policy in Germany's Relations to the United States and the United Kingdom, 1950–1971* (Cambridge: Cambridge University Press, 2002).

[13] For an overview full of insights on US policy towards Europe, but misleading regarding domestic European motives for integration, see Lundestad, *'Empire' by Integration*.

[14] Kaiser, *Using Europe*, chapter 6.

EEC membership which allowed him to bring the majority of his party behind the new policy.

De Gaulle came to power to prevent a military coup over the war in Algeria, not because of Europe. Yet his inter-governmental agenda for the EEC made its institutional deepening and expansion into new policy areas impossible. Combined with a somewhat more US-friendly foreign policy of another Fourth Republic government, such deepening in turn could have delayed Britain's application and led to its accession under stricter conditions which would have suited transnational Christian democracy's preferences better than when it actually happened in 1972–3. De Gaulle's aggressively unilateral foreign policy instead endeared Britain and its EEC membership more to transnational Christian democracy than it would normally have done, especially in view of the two larger British parties' general preference for inter-governmental cooperation and their deep internal divisions over 'Europe', which rendered the Labour governments during 1974–9 incapable of developing coherent policies or exercising any leadership within the Community. As it was, the British membership applications of 1961 and 1967 not only entailed another one by Denmark, which was mainly interested in its participation in the CAP, but also the Republic of Ireland, which was even neutral, and the similarly peripheral Norway.[15] When the two former countries joined together with Britain in 1973, the Christian democrats were not only confronted with more complex institutional decision-making and policy preference structures, but they also lost their original hegemonic political position. Without natural allies in Protestant Northern Europe with its conservative parties, they were reduced to the second-largest group in the EP when the British Labour MPs ended their boycott in 1975. The Christian democrats now had 53 MEPs to the socialists' 66. In 1973, moreover, the Commission temporarily included just two Christian democrats out of the new total of thirteen. The enlargement of the European Communities (EC), as they were called after the institutional merger of the ECSC, the EEC and Euratom in 1967, appeared inevitable and economically and politically in some ways desirable in the 1960s. Yet it threatened the postwar foundations of core Europe and the Christian democratic influence within it.

Their structural crisis and the Gaullist impasse in European integration, which prevented the further deepening of their core Europe, fostered an

---

[15] On the European policies of those western European countries that joined the EC/EU between 1973 and 1995 see, in comparative perspective, Wolfram Kaiser and Jürgen Elvert (eds.), *European Union Enlargement. A Comparative History* (London: Routledge, 2004).

almost obsessive preoccupation of transnational Christian democracy with modernising party ideology and policy ideas to acquire an image more in tune with rapidly changing societal norms and preferences – the political party equivalent of the cultural opening of the Catholic Church during the Second Vatican Council of 1962–5. Confronted with the recurring demand in domestic politics to define more clearly the nature of the (Christian) 'C' in its party name, which Adenauer preferred to ignore, Heck from the CDU suggested in June 1958, for example, that the NEI should aim to 'develop a common theory of Christian politics'.[16] Not least for this purpose, the NEI created the Centre International Démocrate-Chrétien d'Études et de Documentation in Rome in 1960–1, which also cooperated with Latin American and eastern European exile parties under the umbrella of the newly created Christian Democratic World Union.[17] Under the leadership of the excellently networked Dutchman Hahn it was supposed to make a major contribution to reviving policy debate among Christian democrats, who were increasingly worn out by the pleasant burden of almost permanent government responsibility. Hahn and his collaborators also participated in the intensifying cooperation of national party study centres like CEPESS in Belgium and what became the Konrad Adenauer Foundation in Germany.[18] At the same time, the NEI congresses were increasingly geared towards topical themes such as Christian democracy and the Third World in Paris in 1960, the doctrinal basis of Christian democratic political action in Lucerne in 1961, and social policy in Vienna in 1962.

Compared to the immediate postwar period, when they were still an important forum for the networking of party elites, these NEI congresses were much less relevant for transnational party cooperation by the early 1960s, however. In an article in the Austrian Catholic journal *Die Furche*, Friedrich Abendroth, a sympathetic observer of the NEI congress in Vienna in 1962, called it 'the most disappointing [in ten years] … The entire form of this congress belongs to the past, to the time of the ceremonial meetings of party functionaries with a welcome speech, the report of the President and an extended private function … This experience does not augur well for the future.'[19] The institutional set-up for transnational party cooperation seemed as outdated as some Christian

---

[16] Vorschlag von Dr. Heck, 12 June 1958, BAR, CVP-Archiv, JII.181, 2359.
[17] Cf. Papini, *The Christian Democrat International*, chapter 4.
[18] See also Irving, *The Christian Democratic Parties*, 246.
[19] Friedrich Abendroth, 'Unter dem Mittagsdämon', *Die Furche*, 30 June 1962.

democratic policies. At the same time, the MRP, which increasingly looked like a spent force in French and European politics, still controlled the NEI organisation with its secretariat in Paris. Moreover, its Belgian president, Lefèvre, failed to exercise crucial leadership in modernising the institutional forms of party cooperation, which the German, Italian and Belgian parties in particular expected from him when he was elected in 1960. Lefèvre had played an active role in the Christian democratic network in the 1950s. When he became Belgian prime minister in 1961, however, he got bogged down in the complex domestic politics of controlling rising social tensions, especially in the coal and steel sector, and managing decentralisation in response to nationalist Flemish demands. He was only finally persuaded to relinquish his NEI post in 1965, when the CDU/CSU and the DC colluded with the young Tindemans from the Belgian CVP to make him secretary-general and search for an Italian president.

The CD Group in the EP exercised the greatest pressure in the 1960s to modernise the NEI. Under the leadership of Poher until 1966, the MEPs became very dissatisfied with the lack of coordination between them and the NEI. National faultlines were less important for the CD Group.[20] The analysis of voting patterns in the EP in this period shows the socialists as the most cohesive group. Yet the differences among the Christian democrats continued to relate to socio-economic policy issues, not integration. The CD Group had a very cohesive agenda for deepening the integration process. It had a growing interest in extra-parliamentary support for its activities from an effective European-level party organisation, not least to legitimise this political agenda in the face of the dual challenge from Gaullism and the possible EEC enlargement. Most importantly, the CD Group demanded an EEC dimension of party cooperation within the NEI, which at this time still included the Austrian and Swiss parties as well as representatives from the eastern European exile. Poher concluded already at the CD Group's Bureau meeting in November 1959 that 'the NEI formula is outdated' and 'serves no useful purpose in its current form'.[21] The CD Group gained limited administrative influence over the NEI when the Italian Arnaldo Ferragni was appointed deputy secretary-general to both organisations in 1960.[22] Its ultimate aim remained, however, to

---

[20] Cf. Geoffrey Pridham and Pippa Pridham, *Transnational Party Cooperation and European Integration. The Process towards Direct Elections* (London: George Allen & Unwin, 1981), 43.

[21] Procès-verbal de la réunion du Bureau du Groupe démocrate-chrétien, Strasbourg, 26 November 1959, ACDP, 09-001-001/1.

[22] Procès-verbal de la réunion du Bureau du Groupe démocrate-chrétien, Strasbourg, 13 May 1960, ACDP, 09-001-001/1.

create a transnational party organisation with identical membership as the CD Group and more integrated with it.

After acrimonious internal debate, the NEI were eventually transformed into the European Union of Christian Democrats (EUCD) at the congress in Taormina in December 1965, at the height of the Empty Chair crisis in the EEC.[23] The organisational changes were relatively modest, however. As a rule, the NEI now included parties, not groups of individual politicians. Moreover, the leaders of the CD Groups in the EP and in the Consultative Assembly of the Council of Europe as well as two more MEPs were represented in the reorganised EUCD leadership. Christian democratic commissioners also had a right to attend meetings, and often – like Hallstein – did so. This cooperation facilitated the coordination of policy debates and initiatives. It could potentially provide the besieged Commission with enhanced political legitimacy in its defence of the supranational principle. The EUCD also organised fewer congresses. Instead, it set up a number of mixed working groups with the CD Group in the EP. Weekend workshops to discuss ideology and concrete EC-level policy issues also became a regular feature. The election of Mariano Rumor as the new EUCD president reflected the DC's numerical strength in the CD Group, but also an increased Italian interest in playing a more pro-active role in party cooperation. The crucial issue of a separate organisational structure for the EC parties remained unresolved, however.

Institutional incentives for upgrading EC-level party cooperation became much stronger after the EC summit of The Hague at the beginning of December 1969. After de Gaulle's resignation over a failed referendum in April 1969, it appeared to herald a more dynamic phase of European integration. As the new Gaullist president, Georges Pompidou, desired British membership, not least as a precaution against Brandt's German *Ostpolitik*, EC enlargement seemed a foregone conclusion with the predictable effect of strengthening European socialism relative to Christian democracy in the Council of Ministers, the Commission and the EP. At the same time, the EC prime ministers and the French president agreed at The Hague to start new policy initiatives in economic and monetary union and foreign policy cooperation, which initially led to the Werner and Davignon reports of 1970. While the former set out a plan for achieving fixed exchange rates by 1980, the latter promised to add a political dimension to the

---

[23] For the organisational changes see also Papini, *The Christian Democrat International*, 86; Karl Josef Hahn (in cooperation with Friedrich Fugmann) (eds.), *Die Christliche Demokratie in Europa* (Rome: EUCD, 1979), 295–7.

existing foreign trade and development policy dimensions of the EC's external relations. At the same time, de Gaulle's resignation at least raised the prospect of moderate Gaullists and other centre-right leaders like Valéry Giscard d'Estaing lifting the implicit French government veto against the direct election of the EP, which might also acquire new decision-making powers.

The Christian democrats anticipated that such far-reaching combined deepening and widening of the Community would create an advocacy void at European level, which would provide transnationally organised political actors like political parties with exciting new opportunities for influencing the political process. To capitalise on these new opportunities, the EUCD created an informal permanent conference of the EC parties as early as 1970 which became institutionalised two years later in the Political Committee of the EUCD. The Dutch MEP Tjerk Westenterp was the first to suggest going beyond this initial step and creating a European political party, a proposal first discussed in the EUCD Bureau in October 1970.[24] It was supported by many party representatives including, for example, Jacques Santer, later prime minister of Luxembourg and president of the European Commission, who demanded a 'relaunch' of transnational Christian democracy.[25] When after EC enlargement the French, British and Danish governments finally agreed to direct elections for the EP, albeit without granting it new powers, the Christian democrats from the EC member-states formed the EPP in 1976. Two years later, they agreed a framework programme for the EP elections in 1979, which clearly articulated their federalist goals for Europe, but otherwise remained quite vague.[26]

The creation of the EPP forced Christian democratic parties from outside the EC as well as conservative parties to contemplate the future of their own role in party networks. The Austrian ÖVP first initiated talks between Christian democratic and conservative parties at the highest level in the mid-1960s. They were primarily designed to support Chancellor Josef Klaus's attempt to negotiate a privileged Austrian EEC association short of full membership which, he was planning to argue, would be compatible with the 1955 neutrality law.[27] When this initiative failed in 1967, not least

---

[24] Procès-verbal de la réunion du bureau [EUCD], 24–25 October 1970, ACDP, 09-004-055.
[25] Ibid.
[26] See also Eberhard Grabitz *et al.*, *Direktwahl und Demokratisierung – eine Funktionenbilanz des Europäischen Parlaments nach der ersten Wahlperiode* (Bonn: Europa-Union-Verlag, 1988), 557.
[27] On this Austrian policy of 'going it alone' see Michael Gehler, *Der lange Weg nach Europa. Österreich vom Ende der Monarchie bis zur EU. Darstellung* (Innsbruck: Studienverlag, 2002), chapter 7. For an

316   *Christian Democracy and the Origins of European Union*

due to Italian opposition in view of a bombing campaign of German nationalists in South Tyrol, the British Conservatives under their new leader Edward Heath organised several so-called inter-party conferences, especially meetings with representatives from the German CDU/CSU. Heath, as well as his successor as Tory leader from 1975, Margaret Thatcher, saw the German parties as natural partners. They played an influential role in a leading EC member-state and integrated Protestant-conservative and neo-liberal with Catholic political traditions. As leader of the opposition, Thatcher was keen to establish close links with the CDU/CSU and other continental European centre-right people's parties. When she met the CDU secretary-general, Heiner Geißler, at the beginning of November 1977, Thatcher insisted that the Conservatives 'as a pro-European party will have to demonstrate to their supporters and enemies that they are not isolated, but work closely with like-minded parties from other EC countries'.[28]

The CDU/CSU was also interested in fostering relations with conservative parties such as the British Tories. Helmut Kohl, elected CDU leader in 1973 and later German chancellor 1982–98, aimed in the long run at transforming the EPP into a European-level people's party in the image of the CDU/CSU which could compete successfully with the socialists. This would require the integration of Christian democratic and conservative political traditions and parties, however. Although it was chiefly promoted by the Bavarian CSU under its leader Franz Josef Strauß, the CDU thus helped pave the way for the creation of the European Democratic Union (EDU) of EC and non-EC Christian democratic and conservative parties in 1978.[29] The Italian and Benelux Christian democrats did not even send observers to its founding congress, however. At this stage, so shortly before the first direct EP elections, they attacked the CDU/CSU for cooperating with some political parties like the Irish Fianna Fáil in the EDU with which EPP parties competed in domestic politics, and for diluting the EPP's more centrist identity. The relationship between Christian democratic and conservative parties in the enlarged EC thus remained unresolved for the time

introduction to Austrian European policy since 1945 in English see Michael Gehler and Wolfram Kaiser, 'A Study in Ambivalence: Austria and European Integration 1945–95', *Contemporary European History* 6 (1997), 75–99.

[28] Henning Wegener, Besuch des Generalsekretärs bei der Konservativen Partei Großbritanniens am 3./4. November 1977, Bonn, 9 November 1977, ACDP, 01-641-011/4.

[29] Cf. Franz Horner, *Konservative und christdemokratische Parteien in Europa. Geschichte, Programmatik, Strukturen* (Vienna, Munich: Verlag Herold, 1981), 76–9; Andreas Khol and Alexis Wintoniak, 'Die Europäische Demokratische Union (EDU)', in Veen (ed.), *Christlich-demokratische und konservative Parteien*, 405–58.

being.[30] The CDU/CSU strategy eventually proved successful, however. The two German parties and their associated political foundations played a key role in the enlargement of the EPP, especially towards Scandinavia and eastern Europe after 1990. After the collapse and break-up of the DC in 1994, Silvio Berlusconi's Forza Italia joined the EPP in 1999. In 2002, the by now largely Europeanised Gaullist Rassemblement pour la République followed suit.[31]

Keith Middlemas has called the period from 1973–83 the 'stagnant decade' in European integration.[32] It was only stagnant from a state-centric institutional perspective, however. Compared to the ambitions of the summit of The Hague to combine EC enlargement with its institutional adaptation and new common policies for external relations and monetary policy, actual progress towards these objectives was limited. Institutional reform was restricted to the regular organisation of European Council meetings from 1974, which only became legally integrated into the Community in the Single European Act (SEA), and the direct elections of the EP. The scope of European Political Cooperation also remained limited, and monetary policy coordination faltered before the European Monetary System was finally introduced in 1979. Yet the period until the 'solemn declaration' on EC Unity at the European Council in Stuttgart in June 1983, which initiated the completion of the Single European Market, also provided many incentives for transnational societal actors like political parties, businesses and trade unions to intensify their formal and informal activities. During the economic stagnation after the oil crisis of 1973, societal actors could develop new policy ideas to promote institutional deepening and socio-economic reforms, for example. In upgrading their links, when they set up the EPP, transnational Christian democrats could build on three decades of networking, not least within the context of the NEI/EUCD as organisations that were not limited to, but clearly centred on, the EEC core Europe. Unlike the socialists, whose EC cooperation remained a subordinate part of the global SI until 1974, when they founded the Confederation of Socialist Parties of the European Community, which

---

[30] Discussed in a long-term perspective, but with emphasis on more recent developments, in Karl Magnus Johansson, *Transnational Party Alliances. Analysing the Hard-Won Alliance between Conservatives and Christian Democrats in the European Parliament* (Lund: Lund University Press, 1997).

[31] Cf. Pascal Delwit, 'Démocraties chrétiennes et conservatismes: convergences subies ou volontaires?', in Pascal Delwit (ed.), *Démocraties chrétiennes et conservatismes en Europe. Une nouvelle convergence?* (Brussels: Editions de l'Université de Bruxelles, 2003), 18–19.

[32] Keith Middlemas, *Orchestrating Europe. The Informal Politics of the European Union 1973–95* (London: Fontana, 1995), 73.

was much less integrated than the EPP, the Christian democrats had a cohesive political agenda for further European integration.

The former NEI secretary-general Coste-Floret once tersely stated in an interview that 'today we have the EPP because we had the NEI before'.[33] The same is true for the present-day EU. It would not exist, or at least not in its current constitutional form, as it was essentially shaped by the Maastricht Treaty of 1992 with its introduction of the institutional pillar structure, co-decision rights for the EP and monetary union, without the creation of the ECSC/EEC core Europe in the 1950s. Historical institutionalism has acknowledged the crucial importance of initial institutional and policy decisions for closing off alternative options and defining corridors for later choices.[34] The formation of the supranational core Europe promoted by transnational Christian democracy excluded in the future the preferred British option of inter-governmental cooperation limited to fostering freer trade. When EFTA was set up, its members did not conceive of it as an alternative to the EEC any more. When the Macmillan government suggested some form of preferential trade arrangement between the two blocs in 1960, all six EEC governments and the Hallstein Commission were united in dismissing this option as not only incompatible with the GATT, but also involving the danger of drowning 'Europe' not in the Atlantic, but the North Sea. Further protecting the original bargains of 1950–1 and 1957–8, the Community quickly defined willingness to join it as a full member as an absolute precondition for the status of association according to article 238 of the EEC Treaty as a preliminary step towards accession. The negotiations with Britain during 1961–3 also demonstrated that new member-states could negotiate transition periods, but would have to accept wholesale the existing legal-institutional and policy arrangements – the so-called *acquis communautaire*.[35] The barriers to reversing core elements of the original institutional and policy choices were as high in the emerging political system in the 1960s as they are in the constitutionally even more complex present-day EU.

[33] Cited in Delbreil, 'Le MRP', 325.
[34] Paul Pierson, 'The Path to European Integration: A Historical Institutional Analysis', *Comparative Political Studies* 29 (1996), 123–63. See also Paul Pierson, *Politics in Time. History, Institutions, and Social Analysis* (Princeton, N.J.: Princeton University Press, 2004).
[35] On its institutional significance see from an empirical historical perspective, Morten Rasmussen, 'State Power and the acquis communautaire in the European Community of the early 1970s – an Institutional Analysis', in Jan van der Harst (ed.), *Beyond the Customs Union: The European Community's Quest for Completion, Deepening and Enlargement, 1969–1975* (Baden-Baden: Nomos, forthcoming).

The supranational institutions also contributed to protecting and extending the original bargains. Adhering to a rational choice conceptualisation of institutional delegation and oversight, Mark Pollack has at least ascribed supranational institutions like the Commission the ability to develop their own political agendas derived – in this perspective – from their institutional self-interest in enhancing their own and the EU's powers.[36] Historical institutionalism has gone further, arguing that the ability of member-state governments to control the exercise of powers delegated to supranational institutions is not impressive. Pierson has pointed out three important 'gaps' that weaken member-state control of the integration process, for example. The first of these consists of the restricted time horizon of decision-makers in member-state governments, who constantly have one eye on the next elections. The second are possible unanticipated consequences of original decisions resulting from the extreme complexity of policy-making in the EU. The third set of 'gaps' derives from shifts in the preferences of changing member-state governments, which can undermine the intentions behind the original policy design.[37]

While this theoretical conceptualisation of supranational institutional politics goes some way towards making social scientists more sensitive towards the crucial importance of change over time for understanding present-day EU politics, it still places too much emphasis on formal institutions like member-state governments and the European Commission, explaining their preferences and strategies as rational choices derived from domestic interest group pressures and institutional self-interest, for example. As I have argued from a contemporary historical perspective in this book, however, analysing the origins of European Union requires most of all a sophisticated understanding of how human actors like the Christian democrats with their particular cognitive structures and historically embedded individual and collective identities, norms and policy ideas shaped the original institutional and policy bargains of the ECSC/EEC core Europe. Although its political hegemony dissipated after 1957–8, transnational Christian democracy remained a very important collective political actor after the institutionalisation of core Europe and continued to shape the Community's formal and informal institutions.

---

[36] Mark A. Pollack, *The Engines of European Integration – Delegation, Agency, and Agenda Setting in the EU* (Oxford: Oxford University Press, 2003).
[37] Pierson, 'The Path to European Integration'.

Its roles and influence between the treaties of Rome and Maastricht and beyond should not be measured by applying the same criteria for the analysis of political parties as have been used for national political systems, however. One year before the first direct elections of the EP in 1979, David Marquand enquired whether the EC still was – in the words of de Gaulle – a 'Europe des patries' or already a 'Europe of parties'.[38] Marquand assumed that the EC was somewhere on a continuum from the Europe of fatherlands to a European party democracy. The EC was, and still is, neither one nor the other ideal type, however, just as it was not, and still is not, a traditional international organisation or a European federal state. Up to a point, political parties increasingly do perform traditional functions within the EU as in national political systems. They have increased their organisational strength, which is reflected in the greater voting cohesion of the enlarged EPP in the EP across the EU enlargements from 1973 to 2004, but the EPP still has no centralised decision-making procedures. It has begun to seek office and successfully insisted in 2004 on the appointment of a Portuguese EPP politician, Manuel Barroso, as Commission president, for the first time on the grounds that it was the largest group in the EP, but it still cannot participate in forming a European government which depends on parliamentary support. Partisan ideological and policy competition has increased in the EP. On the other hand, declining voter participation in European elections since 1979 has cast doubt over the electoral legitimacy of EU-level political parties in the eyes of many citizens.[39] At the same time, the transnational Christian democratic network may have played other important roles specific to the European level. They include, first, its contribution to socialising younger generations and new member parties from accession states into established policy ideas and preferences and behavioural patterns, and, second, its role in the coordinated defence especially of its constitutional ideas and preferences, utilising different institutional channels.

The Christian democratic network facilitated transnational entrepreneurial leadership by individual outstanding politicians like Schuman and Adenauer and later Kohl, for example, with the potential to socialise other Christian democrats into their emerging core Europe consensus. The French MRP politicians Poher and Pflimlin have emphasised, for example, how their close personal cooperation with Schuman both in the national

---

[38] David Marquand, 'Towards a Europe of the Parties', *The Political Quarterly* 49 (1978), 425–45.
[39] See also Amie Kreppel, *The European Parliament and the Supranational Party System* (Cambridge: Cambridge University Press, 2002); Simon Hix and Christopher Lord, *Political Parties in the European Union* (Basingstoke: Macmillan, 1997).

context and in the EP influenced their thinking on 'Europe'.[40] Such socialisation had a strong transnational dimension as well. Lücker from the Bavarian CSU was so impressed by Schuman during their discussions about European issues in the EP and shortly before his death in 1963 that he has constructed a Catholic coalition for the beatification of the former French foreign minister. In confessional terms, this would require the recognition by the Vatican of his contribution to Franco-German reconciliation and European integration as a 'miracle'.[41] More than one generation separated Schuman, born in 1886, and Lücker, born in 1915. Kohl, who was born in 1930, is forty-four years younger than Schuman. Yet he has emphasised in his memoirs the profound influence of his first encounter with the French foreign minister at a transnational Christian democratic youth event in 1950 and of his experience, when a young history student, of Hallstein as a law professor in Frankfurt.[42] Kohl has also recalled the importance of long-standing network contacts for his dominant role in the creation of the EPP and the deepening of European integration during his time as German chancellor. He first met with Tindemans at a congress in Konstanz as early as September 1950, for example. Both had developed excellent working relations by the time Kohl supported Tindemans in his quest for the EPP presidency and the Flemish politician the CDU leader in his attempt to strengthen the bonds between Christian democratic and conservative parties in Europe in the 1970s.[43]

These party leaders' political strategies were not only informed by their converging guiding ideas for the postwar European order, but they and others succeeded by their emotive appeal as much as by rational arguments at assimilating large sections of the younger generation of Christian democrats into their supranational policy consensus. This in turn allowed the second and third generation including Poher, Tindemans and Kohl to pursue broadly the same objectives using similar mechanisms of marginalising internal dissent, conserving the 'party of Europe' image and concerting their integrationist policies in their transnational networks. Adjusting to the subsequent EC enlargements, these networks also appear to have influenced the Europeanisation of political parties in accession states. Although it has so far only been systematically explored for the Spanish socialists,[44] the EPP and its allied political foundations seem to

---

[40] Poher, *Trois fois président*, 53; Pflimlin, *Mémoires*, 329–32.
[41] Interview with Hans August Lücker, 22 March 2004.
[42] Helmut Kohl, *Erinnerungen 1930–1982* (Munich: Droemer, 2004), 25.   [43] Ibid., 75.
[44] Cf. Pilar Ortuño Anaya, *European Socialists and Spain: the Transition to Democracy* (Basingstoke: Palgrave, 2002).

have played a similarly important pro-active role in the transformation of the originally Francoist Alianza Popular founded in 1976 and renamed Partido Popular in 1989, into a mainstream centre-right party which was eventually accepted by the EPP in 1992. Political parties in accession states clearly need to be receptive to such socialisation. The case of the British Conservatives demonstrates its limits when domestic traditions and interests strongly pull in the opposite direction.[45] Catholic Tories like Chris Patten and more centrist conservatives have been more predisposed towards closer cooperation with the EPP, or even membership of it, whereas the majority of the members and party leadership have recently become so aggressively nationalistic that the new Tory leader, David Cameron, even threatened in 2005 to stop the long-established parliamentary cooperation with the EPP.[46]

Enlarging the EPP membership and increasing its numerical strength and influence in the EP, the transnational Christian democracy of the postwar period has transformed itself into more of a centre-right people's party type network. In the light of this transformation and the dominance of neo-liberal socio-economic policy ideas compared to the greater influence of social Catholicism after 1945, Martin Conway has argued that 'the age of Christian democracy in Europe has ended'.[47] At least up until the Constitutional Treaty signed in Rome on 29 October 2004, the EPP network has quite successfully continued to defend and extend core tenets of the Christian democratic European legacy, however, contributing a great deal to Prime Minister Thatcher's incredibly self-referential amazement about the 'quintessentially un-English outlook displayed by the Community'.[48] Over time, the EPP network has used a number of different strategies to defend and advance especially its constitutional preferences for the EU. One of the weaker instruments has been public advocacy. In a resolution after a meeting of party leaders on 22 February 1960, for example, the NEI parties clearly articulated in the face of the creation of EFTA their strong preference for the 'political unity of the Six' as the 'driving force of European unity'.[49] Three years later, after de Gaulle's veto against British EEC accession, they also reaffirmed their commitment to European policies

[45] For some interesting insights see Nick J. Crowson, *The Conservative Party and European Integration since 1945* (London: Routledge, 2007), 191–6.
[46] http://news.bbc.co.uk/1/hi/uk_politics/4507516.stm. Accessed 31 January 2007.
[47] Conway, 'The Age', 43.
[48] Margaret Thatcher, *The Downing Street Years* (London: Harper Collins, 1993), 81.
[49] Konferenz der Parteivorsitzenden, Paris, 22 February 1960, ACDP, 09-002-033/1.

that would be compatible with the US security interests and guarantee for western Europe. At the very least, such collective public policy commitments facilitated the reining in of deviant preferences and behaviour within the member parties such as Erhard's admiration for EFTA and his support for a trade deal between the two blocs or minority Gaullist support especially in the Bavarian CSU and the DC for 'third force' foreign policy concepts.

More importantly, the EPP network has consistently enshrined federalist objectives in its and its member parties' programmes as well as EP policy statements on constitutional questions. Even when it was not the largest group, the EPP always secured the chairmanship of the Political Committee for itself to facilitate this task. In the 1960s the Christian democrats initiated the parliamentary report by the CDU politician Hans Furler, the EP president 1960–2 and vice-president 1962–73, which advocated the direct election of the EP and granting it substantial powers. In 1975, Alfred Bertrand from the Belgian PSC, the chairman of the CD Group, coordinated the EP's recommendations for the Tindemans Report of 1976. Charged by the European Council in Paris in December 1974 with preparing such a report on EC reform, the Belgian prime minister from the CVP largely adopted these proposals shaped to a great extent by the Christian democratic network which he co-led in his party role – with the overriding objective 'to remain faithful to the objectives of the founding fathers'.[50]

Members of the EPP network have also consistently prioritised their European commitments to influence intra-party politics and inter-governmental negotiations. As Philip Gassert has shown, for example, transnationally networked Europeanists in the CDU played a crucial role in bringing down Chancellor Erhard in 1966 to replace him with Kiesinger, who had extensive experience in transnational party cooperation and prioritised mending strained relations with France.[51] In January 1966, the Christian democratic-led EEC governments yielded not one constitutional iota to de Gaulle's demands to scrap majority voting, making it abundantly clear that the institutional treaty provisions would remain unchanged. Aside from reining in the Commission in its quest to become a European government, which all EEC governments regarded as misguided or at least premature, the Luxembourg compromise was not a compromise,

[50] Leo Tindemans, *De Memoires. Gedreven door een overtuiging* (Tielt: Lannoo, 2002), 311.
[51] Philipp Gassert, 'Personalities and the Politics of European Integration: Kurt Georg Kiesinger and the Departure of Walter Hallstein, 1966/67', in Loth (ed.), *Crises and Compromises*, 267.

but in the main a face-saving exercise for the French president. Taking recourse to a purely informal national 'veto' quickly fell into disrepute. From the 1980s onwards, moreover, the regular meetings of EPP party leaders and prime ministers before sessions of the European Council have played a key role in defining policy options and coordinating negotiating strategies. Thus, Karl Magnus Johansson has demonstrated for both inter-governmental conferences leading to the SEA and the Maastricht Treaty that this advance coordination combined with the Franco-German coop-eration between Kohl and the socialist president, François Mitterrand, greatly facilitated the total isolation of Thatcher in the debates as a precondition for achieving institutional reform.[52] According to the British prime minister's own recollections in her memoirs, cut off from these continental European party networks, she felt bulldozed into funda-mental reforms such as the extension of majority voting in the Single European Act (SEA) and co-decision rights for the EP and more majority voting in the Maastricht Treaty.[53]

The influence of transnational Christian democracy has also extended into the supranational institutions to secure the original constitutional bargains. One strategy has been to appoint federalist or integrationist politicians like Hallstein and Santer to the European Commission. Paradoxically, even de Gaulle once unwittingly played a crucial role in securing Christian democratic constitutional objectives. In 1962, he appointed the lawyer and leading MRP politician Lecourt to the European Court of Justice (ECJ), thus removing him from domestic French politics before the elections of November 1962. Before presiding over the ECJ from 1967 to 1976, the hard-core Christian democratic federalist Lecourt played a crucial role in shifting the balance within the ECJ towards a strongly supranational jurisdiction. Under his influence, the two landmark decisions Van Gend en Loos of 1963 and Costa versus E.N.E.L. of 1964 declared for the first time the direct effect of Community law and its supremacy over national law.[54] In some cases, the transnational Christian democratic network has even extended its influence beyond the parties proper. From the perspective of Kohl and the EPP network, the French socialist Jacques Delors was the ideal choice for Commission

[52] Karl Magnus Johansson, 'Party Elites in Multilevel Europe: The Christian Democrats and the Single European Act', *Party Politics* 8 (2002), 423–39; 'Another road to Maastricht: the Christian Democrat Coalition and the Quest for European Union', *Journal of Common Market Studies* 40 (2002), 871–93.
[53] Thatcher, *The Downing Street Years*, 549–50.
[54] The politics of the ECJ's jurisdiction in the 1960s is the topic of research conducted by Morten Rasmussen at the University of Copenhagen. I would like to thank him for this piece of information.

president when the succession to Gaston Thorn was discussed at the Fontainebleau summit in 1984. He was an MEP from 1979 to 1981 before becoming French economic and finance minister. Crucially, Delors was a Catholic and European federalist with a 'pronounced Christian democratic profile'.[55] Coming from the Christian trade union movement, he was actually a member of the MRP for eight months in 1945 before joining the left-Catholic JR in 1954.[56] Like another left-Catholic, Robert Buron from the MRP, he eventually joined the socialists, but only in 1974. Delors could combine conversing in Catholic political language of federalism, subsidiarity and a Europe of the Regions originally derived from personalism[57] with working with the initially more sceptical Mitterrand to advance the integration process. His fiscal prudence even endeared him temporarily to Thatcher, who could not make sense out of these convoluted continental European intellectual and party traditions. Subsequently, Kohl also promoted Delors to the chairmanship of the so-called Delors Committee in 1988 to discuss monetary union – a decision with the foregone conclusion desired by Kohl that this committee would recommend the adoption of a clear timetable for the transition to a common currency and the creation of a European Central Bank to control monetary policy.

As these examples of EPP network activities demonstrate, Christian democracy continued to play an important role in European integration after the signing of the Rome Treaties. They did so not primarily as political parties that pass resolutions at national- and European-level congresses. Instead, the EPP network, as the Christian democratic network after 1945, has defined policy agendas, promoted policy solutions, built advocacy coalitions for them and facilitated the entrepreneurial leadership by networked party politicians who, unlike many political scientists, have never made a clear distinction between their overlapping party and governmental roles. In this and other ways, transnational Christian democracy has helped to link the emerging European political society with national and supranational politics and national polities with supranational institutions and policy-making in the complex informal politics of the present-day EU. European Union was shaped in crucial ways by political networks, especially transnational Christian democracy.

[55] Laurent Ducerf, 'Die christliche Demokratie in Frankreich seit 1945. Eine historiographische Bilanz', *Historisch-politische Mitteilungen* 2 (1995), 313.

[56] Jacques Delors, *Mémoires* (Paris: Plon, 2004), 15 and 167.

[57] For the intellectual origins of this concept see Udine Ruge, *Die Erfindung des 'Europa der Regionen'. Kritische Ideengeschichte eines konservativen Konzepts* (Frankfurt/Main, New York: Campus, 2003).

Bibliography

UNPUBLISHED SOURCES

Archiv des Deutschen Caritasverbandes (ADCV), Freiburg i.B., Germany
  F. Klein / M. Vorgrimler, Die Christliche Nothilfe (CHN) und der Deutsche
  Caritasverband (DCV). Ihre Zusammenarbeit in der Zeit von 1946–1963,
  371.4 B 8
Archiv für christlich-demokratische Politik (ACDP), St Augustin, Germany
  CD/EVP-Fraktion im Europäischen Parlament 09-001
  Europäische Union Christlicher Demokraten 09-004
  Europäische Volkspartei 09-007
  Nachlass Hans Broermann 01-396
  Nachlass Bruno Dörpinghaus 01-009
  Nachlass Kai-Uwe von Hassel 01-157
  Nachlass Bruno Heck 01-022
  Nachlass Fritz Hellwig 01-083
  Nachlass Egon A. Klepsch 01-641
  Nachlass Heinrich Krone 01-028
  Nachlass Otto Lenz 01-172
  Nachlass Georg Strickrodt 01-085
  Nouvelles Équipes Internationales 09-002
Archiv für christlich-soziale Politik (ACSP), Munich, Germany
  Nachlass Josef Müller
Archiv des Karl von Vogelsang-Instituts (AKVI), Vienna, Austria
  Karton NEI
  Nachlass Rudolf Lewandowski
  ÖVP-Bundesparteileitung (BLP), Konvolut BMf Unterricht [Hurdes], Mappe
  NEI
  ÖVP-Bundesparteileitung (BLP), Karton 333, Büro Generalsekretär [Hurdes]
  1949
Archiv der Kommission für Zeitgeschichte (AFZG), Bonn, Germany
  Nachlasssplitter Joseph Joos
Archives of the Catholic University of America (ACUA), Washington, United
  States

National Catholic Welfare Conference (NCWC/USCC), Executive Department
Archives d'État, République et Canton de Genève, Geneva, Switzerland
  Archives de la Police des Étrangers, Dossier Victor Koutzine (224´443)
Archives d'Histoire Contemporaine (AHC), Fondations Nationales des Sciences Politiques, Centre d'Histoire de l'Europe du vingtième siècle, Paris, France
  Fonds Ernest Pezet
Archives Nationales (AN), Paris, France
  Papiers Robert Bichet 519 AP 9–10
  Papiers Georges Bidault 457 AP 59, 70, 73–74
Archivio Storico Istituto Luigi Sturzo (ASILS), Rome, Italy
  Fondo Luigi Sturzo
Bundesarchiv (BAR), Bern, Switzerland
  CVP-Archiv JII.181
  E 4264, 620/629
  E 4320 (B), 17/96/102/107
Bundesarchiv (BA), Koblenz, Germany
  Nachlass Herbert Blankenhorn N 1351
  Nachlass Jakob Kaiser N 1018
  Nachlass Heinrich von Brentano N 1239
Churchill Archives Centre (CAC), Churchill College, Cambridge, England
  Dilke – Crawford – Roskill Collection
  Private Papers of Sir Edward Louis Spears
Fondation Jean Monnet pour l'Europe, Lausanne, Switzerland
  Fonds Robert Schuman
Historisches Archiv der Stadt Köln (HAStK), Cologne, Germany
  Nachlass Christine Teusch NL 1187
  Nachlass Wilhelm Marx NL 1070
Institut für Zeitgeschichte (IfZG Innsbruck), University of Innsbruck, Austria
  Karl Gruber Archiv, Kartons 3–4, 6, 14, 22
Institut für Zeitgeschichte (IfZG Vienna), Universität Wien, Vienna, Austria
  Nachlass Felix Hurdes NL 48
  Nachlass Lois Weinberger NL 42
Katholiek Documentatie Centrum (KDC), Nijmegen, Netherlands
  Archief P. J. M. Aalberse
  Archief C. M. J. F. Goseling
  Archief KVP
  Archief W. H. Nolens
  Archief van de R. K. Staatspartij
Katholiek Documentatie- en Onderzoekscentrum (KADOC), Leuven, Belgium
  Archief Alfred Bertrand
  Archief CEPESS
  Archief CVP-Nationaal
  Archief M. Dewulf
  Archief Hendrik Heyman

Archief Robert Houben
Archief August E. de Schryver
Archief Léo Tindemans
Archivalia Theo Lefèvre (Bewaargeving W. Dewachter)
Landesarchiv Nordrhein-Westfalen (LAV NRW), Hauptstaatsarchiv Düsseldorf
  (HAS), Germany
  Nachlass Josef Hofmann RWN 210
Mainzer Stadtarchiv (StA Mz), Mainz, Germany
  Nachlass Aloys Ruppel 80/17
Nationaal Archief (NA), The Hague, Netherlands
  Archief H. K. J. Beernink
  Archief Dr. W. P. Berghuis (Collectie 405)
  Archief M. A. M. Klompé
  Archief van de Christelijk-Historische Unie
  Collectie J. A. Veraart
National Archives (NA USA), College Park/MD, United States
  Selected files
Österreischiches Staatsarchiv (ÖStA), Allgemeines Verwaltungsarchiv (AVA),
  Vienna, Austria
  Nachlass Richard Schmitz
Österreichisches Staatsarchiv (ÖStA), Archiv der Republik (AdR), Vienna,
  Austria
  Bestand Bundeskanzleramt/Auswärtige Angelegenheiten, II-pol, Liasse
  'International'
Stiftung Bundeskanzler Adenauer Haus (SBKAH), Rhöndorf/Bad Honnef,
  Germany
  Korrespondenz mit Heinrich von Brentano
  Korrespondenz mit Bruno Dörpinghaus
Westminster Diocesan Archives, London, England
  Cardinal Hinsley Papers

PUBLISHED SOURCES AND MEMOIRS

Adenauer. Briefe 1945–1947, Berlin: Siedler, 1983.
Adenauer. Briefe 1947–1949, Berlin: Siedler, 1984.
Adenauer. Briefe 1949–1951, Berlin: Siedler, 1985.
Adenauer. Briefe 1951–1953, Berlin: Siedler, 1987.
Adenauer. Briefe 1953–1955, Berlin: Siedler, 1995.
Adenauer im Dritten Reich, Berlin: Siedler, 1991.
Adenauer: 'Es mußte alles neu gemacht werden.' Die Protokolle des CDU-Bundesvorstandes 1950–1953, Stuttgart: Klett-Cotta, 1986.
Adenauer, Konrad, *Erinnerungen 1945–1953*, Stuttgart: DVA, 1965.
  Erinnerungen 1953–1955, Stuttgart: DVA, 1966.
  Erinnerungen 1955–1959, Stuttgart: DVA, 1967.
  Erinnerungen 1959–1963. Fragmente, Stuttgart: DVA, 1968.

Andreotti, Giulio, *Visti da vicino*, Milan: Rizzoli, 1982.

Atholl, Katharine, *Searchlight on Spain*, London: Allen Lane, 1938.

The Tragedy of Warsaw and Its Documentation, London: J. Murray, 1944.

Working Partnership. Being the Lives of John George, 8th Duke of Atholl and of His Wife Katharine Marjory Ramsay, London: Arthur Barker, 1958.

Baring, Arnulf (ed.), *Sehr verehrter Herr Bundeskanzler! Heinrich von Brentano im Briefwechsel mit Konrad Adenauer 1949–1964*, Hamburg: Hoffmann und Campe, 1974.

Barzel, Rainer, *Ein gewagtes Leben. Erinnerungen*, Stuttgart, Leipzig: Hohenheim, 2001.

Geschichten aus der Politik. Persönliches aus meinem Archiv, Frankfurt: Ullstein, 1987.

Baur, Hugo, *Mein politischer Lebenslauf*, Konstanz: Oberbadische Verlagsanstalt, 1929.

Bichet, Robert, *La Démocratie chrétienne en France. Le Mouvement Républicain Populaire*, Besançon: Jacques et Demontrond, 1980.

Réflexions et propos d'un vieil homme, Paris: La Pensée Universelle, 1991.

Bidault, Georges, *Noch einmal Rebell. Von einer Résistance in die andere*, Berlin: Propyläen, 1966 [French 1965].

Blankenhorn, Herbert, *Verständnis und Verständigung. Blätter eines politischen Tagebuchs 1949 bis 1979*, Frankfurt/Main: Propyläen, 1980.

Brüning, Heinrich, *Briefe und Gespräche 1934–1945*, ed. Claire Nix, Stuttgart: DVA, 1974.

Memoiren 1918–1934, Stuttgart: DVA, 1970.

Bulletin du Secrétariat International des Partis Démocratiques d'Inspiration Chrétienne, 10 vols. (1928–31).

Carter, Barbara Barclay, *Italy Speaks, with a Preface by Luigi Sturzo*, London: Victor Gollancz, 1947.

Clappier, Bernard, 'Die entscheidenden Jahre', in Jacques Santer *et al.* (eds.), *Robert Schuman – Christlicher Demokrat und Europäer. Aktualität eines Vorbilds* (Melle: Ernst Knoth, 1988), 57–65.

Delors, Jacques, *Mémoires*, Paris: Plon, 2004.

Devant la crise mondiale. Manifeste de catholiques européens séjournant en Amérique, New York: Éditions de la Maison française, 1942.

'Dibattito / débat / discussion', in Enrico Serra (ed.), *Il rilancio dell'Europa e i trattati di Roma / The Relaunching of Europe and the Treaties of Rome*, Baden-Baden: Nomos, 1989, 159–91.

Die Kabinettsprotokolle der Bundesregierung, vol. VII: *1954* (Boppard: Boldt, 1993).

Die Protokolle der Reichstagsfraktion der Deutschen Zentrumspartei 1920–1925, Mainz: Matthias-Grünewald-Verlag, 1981.

Die Protokolle der Reichstagsfraktion und des Fraktionsvorstands der Deutschen Zentrumspartei 1926–1933, Mainz: Matthias-Grünewald-Verlag, 1969.

Dörpinghaus, Bruno, 'Die Genfer Sitzungen – Erste Zusammenkünfte führender christlich-demokratischer Politiker im Nachkriegseuropa', in Dieter Blumenwitz *et al.* (eds.), *Konrad Adenauer und seine Zeit.*

Politik und Persönlichkeit des ersten Bundeskanzlers, Stuttgart: DVA, 1976, 538–65.

Eckardt, Felix von, *Ein unordentliches Leben. Lebenserinnerungen*, Düsseldorf: Econ, 1967.

Erzberger, Matthias, *Erlebnisse im Weltkrieg*, Stuttgart, Berlin: DVA, 1920.

Ferrari, Francesco Luigi, *Lettere e documenti inediti*, 2 vols., Rome: Edizioni S. I. A. S., 1986.

'L'Organisation internationale de la démocratie populaire', *Politique* 5 (1931), 319–30.

Gehler, Michael and Wolfram Kaiser (eds.), *Transnationale Parteienkooperation der europäischen Christdemokraten. Dokumente 1945–1965 / Coopération trans-nationale des démocrates-chrétiens en Europe. Documents 1945–1965*, Munich: K. G. Saur, 2004.

Germain, Maurice [Maurice Lemesle], *Les Chrétiens à la recherche de l'Europe. Essai romancé. Préface de M. Champetier de Ribes*, Paris: Editions Spes, 1931.

Groeben, Hans von der, *Deutschland und Europa in einem unruhigen Jahrhundert. Erlebnisse und Betrachtungen*, Baden-Baden: Nomos, 1995.

Hahn, Karl Josef, *Standplaats Europa. Memoires van een christen-democraat*, Weesp: De Haan, 1984.

(ed.), *La Démocratie chrétienne dans le monde. Résolutions et déclarations des organisations internationales démocrates chrétiennes de 1947 à 1973*, Rome: Union Mondiale Démocrate Chrétienne, 1973.

Harryvan, A. G. and Jan van der Harst (eds.), *Documents on European Union*, Basingstoke: Macmillan, 1997.

Hofmann, Josef, *Journalist in Republik, Diktatur und Besatzungszeit. Erinnerungen 1916–1947*, Mainz: Matthias-Grünewald-Verlag, 1977.

Im Zentrum der Macht. Das Tagebuch von Staatssekretär Lenz 1951–1953, Düsseldorf: Droste, 1989.

Isacker, Philip van, *Tussen Staat en Volk. Nagelaten Memoires*, Antwerp: Uitgeverij Sheed & Ward N. V., 1953.

Joos, Joseph, *Am Räderwerk der Zeit. Erinnerungen aus der katholischen und sozialen Bewegung*, Augsburg: Verlag Winfried-Werk, 1951.

So sah ich sie: Menschen und Geschehnisse, Augsburg: Verlag Winfried-Werk, 1958.

'Was erwartet Deutschland von Frankreich', *Deutsch-Französische Rundschau* 3 (1930), 984–94.

Kasulaitis, Algirdas J., *Lithuanian Christian Democracy*, Chicago: Leo XIII Fund, 1976.

Kohl, Helmut, *Erinnerungen 1930–1982*, Munich: Droemer, 2004.

'Konrad Adenauer und der Schuman-Plan. Ein Quellenzeugnis', in Schwabe (ed.), *Die Anfänge*, 131–40.

Konrad Adenauer und die CDU der britischen Besatzungszone 1946–1949. Dokumente zur Gründungsgeschichte der CDU Deutschlands, Bonn: Eichholz-Verlag, 1975.

'L'Affaire Joos', *Politique*, 14 April 1931, 369–71.

'La IVe Conférence internationale des partis démocratiques d'inspiration chréti-enne (21–22 juillet 1928)', *Politique*, 15 August 1928, 761–2.

'La VIe Conférence des partis démocrates-populaires (24 au 28 juillet)', *Politique*, 15 August 1930, 760–4.

'La Troisième Conférence internationale des partis démocrates d'inspiration chrétienne (9–10 juillet 1927)', *Politique*, 15 August 1927, 754–7.

Lewandowski, Rudolf, 'Das Europa der christlichen Demokratie', in Andreas Khol, Robert Prantner and Alfred Stirnemann (eds.), *Um Parlament und Partei. Alfred Maleta zum 70. Geburtstag*, Graz, Vienna, Cologne: Styria, 1976, 345–59.

'Der Traum von Europa. Die Christlich-Demokratische Internationale: Ihr Ursprung und ihre Entwicklung', in EVP-Fraktion (ed.), *Zur Geschichte*, 65–73.

Lipgens, Walter (ed.), *Documents on the History of European Integration*, vol. I: *Continental Plans for European Union 1939–1945*, Berlin – New York: Walter de Gruyter, 1985.

(ed.), *Documents on the History of European Integration*, vol. II: *Plans for European Union in Great Britain and in Exile 1939–1945*, Berlin, New York: Walter de Gruyter, 1986.

(ed.), *Europa-Förderationspläne der Widerstandsbewegungen 1940–1945*, Munich: Oldenbourg, 1968.

Lipgens, Walter and Wilfried Loth (eds.), *Documents on the History of European Integration*, vol. IV: *Transnational Organizations of Political Parties and Pressure Groups in the Struggle for European Union, 1945–1950*, Berlin, New York: Walter de Gruyter, 1991.

'Manifestes de Paix', *Politique*, 5 January 1931, 184–6.

Maritain, Jacques, *Messages 1941–1944*, Paris: P. Hartmann, 1944.

Mendès France, Pierre, *Choisir. Conversations avec Jean Bothorel*, Paris: Stock, 1974.

Monnet, Jean, *Mémoires*, Paris: Fayard, 1976.

Müller, Josef, *Bis zur letzten Konsequenz. Ein Leben für Frieden und Freiheit*, Munich: Süddeutscher Verlag, 1975.

Nutting, Anthony, *Europe Will Not Wait. A Warning and a Way Out*, London: Hollis & Carter, 1960.

Onaindía, Alberto de, *Capítulos de mi vida II: Experiencias del exilio*, Buenos Aires: Editorial Vasca Ekin S. R. L., 1974.

People and Freedom Group (ed.), *For Democracy*, London: Burns Oates, 1939.

Pezet, Ernest, *Chrétiens au service de la Cité: de Léon XIII au Sillon et au M. R. P. 1891–1965*, Paris: Nouvelles Éditions Latines, 1965.

Pflimlin, Pierre, *Itinéraires d'un européen. Entretiens avec Jean-Louis English et Daniel Riot*, Strasbourg: La Nuée Bleue, 1989.

Mémoires d'un européen de la IVe à la Ve République, Paris: Fayard, 1991.

Poher, Alain, *Trois fois président. Mémoires* (Paris: Plon, 1993).

Poschinger, Heinrich von (ed.), *Fürst Bismarck und die Parlamentarier*, vol. III: *1879–1890*, Breslau: Trewendt, 1896.

Schreiber, Georg, *Deutschland und Österreich. Deutsche Begegnungen mit Österreichs Wissenschaft und Kultur. Erinnerungen aus den letzten Jahrzehnten*, Cologne, Graz: Böhlau, 1956.

Schryver, August de, *Oorlogsdagboeken 1940–1942*, Tielt: Lannoo, 1998.

Schuman, Robert, *Pour l'Europe*, Paris: Nagel, 1963.

Schumann, Maurice, 'Regards sur le MRP', *France Forum* 316 (1997), 38–9.

Serrarens, P. J. S., *25 Jahre Christliche Gewerkschafts-Internationale*, Utrecht: Huis van den Arbeid, 1946.

Shuster, George N., *The Ground I Walked on. Reflections of a College President*, Notre Dame, Ind.: Notre Dame University Press, 1961.

Sieniewicz, Konrad, 'Die Beteiligung der Christlichen Demokraten aus Mitteleuropa', in EVP-Fraktion (ed.), *Zur Geschichte*, 43–8.

Sonnenschein, Carl, 'Italienisches Reisetagebuch', *Hochland* 18 (1921), 536–57.

Spiecker, Karl [Carl], *Germany – from Defeat to Defeat*, with a Preface by Professor R. W. Seton-Watson, London: MacDonald & Co., 1945.

Steed, Henry Wickham, 'Foreground and Background', *Fortnightly Review* 146 (1939), 361–70.

Our War Aims, London: Secker and Warburg, 1939.

The Hapsburg Monarchy, London: Constable and Company, 1913.

Sturzo, Luigi, 'Democracy, Authority, and Liberty', in People and Freedom Group (ed.), *For Democracy*, 95–116.

Italien und der Faschismus, Cologne: Im Gilde-Verlag, 1926 [English 1926].

'Italy after Mussolini', *Foreign Affairs* 21 (1943), 412–26.

Italy and Fascism, London: Faber and Gnyer, 1926.

La mia battaglia da New York, Milan: Garzanti, 1949.

Miscellanea Londinese. Volume primo (anni 1925–1930), Bologna: Zanichelli, 1965.

Miscellanea Londinese. Volume secondo (anni 1931–1933), Bologna: Zanichelli, 1967.

Miscellanea Londinese. Volume terzo (anni 1934–1936), Bologna: Zanichelli, 1970.

Miscellanea Londinese. Volume quarto (anni 1937–1940), Bologna: Zanichelli, 1974.

Nationalism and Internationalism, New York: Roy Publishers, 1946.

Scritti inediti, vol. II: *1924–1940*, ed. Franco Rizzi, Rome: Cinque lune, 1975.

Scritti inediti, vol. III: *1940–1946*, ed. Francesco Malgeri, Rome: Cinque lune, 1976.

Scritti storico-politici (1929–1949), Rome: Zanichelli, 1984, 73–85.

'Vorgeschichte und Programm der italienischen Volkspartei', *Abendland. Deutsche Monatshefte für europäische Kultur, Politik und Wirtschaft* 1 (1926), 237–41.

Taviani, Paolo Emilio, *I giorni di Trieste. Diario 1953–1954*, Bologna: il Mulino, 1998.

Solidarietà atlantica e Comunità Europea, Florence: Le Monnier, 1954.

Teitgen, Pierre-Henri, *'Faites entrer le témoin suivant'. 1940–1958: de la Résistance à la Vème République*, Paris: Ouest-France, 1988.

Terrenoire, Louis, 'Corporatism and Democracy', in People and Freedom Group (ed.), *For Democracy*, 185–209.

Thatcher, Margaret, *The Downing Street Years*, London: Harper Collins, 1993.
'The Testimony of an Eyewitness: Christian Pineau', in Griffiths (ed.), *Socialist Parties*, 57–62.
Tindemans, Leo, *De Memoires. Gedreven door een overtuiging*, Tielt: Lannoo, 2002.
Veraart, J. A., 'Internationaal werk in Londen. Fragmenten uit mijn dagboek, 1940–1945', *Katholiek Cultureel Tijdschrift* 3 (1946–7), 56–63.

BOOKS

Adamthwaite, Anthony, *Grandeur and Misery: France's Bid for Power in Europe 1914–1940*, London: Arnold, 1995.
Aldrich, Richard, *The Hidden Hand. Britain, America and the Cold War Intelligence*, London: John Murray, 2001.
Altermatt, Urs, *Der Weg der Schweizer Katholiken ins Ghetto. Die Entstehungsgeschichte der nationalen Volksorganisationen im Schweizer Katholizismus 1848–1919*, Zurich: Benzinger, 1972.
    Katholizismus und Moderne. Zur Sozial- und Mentalitätsgeschichte der Schweizer Katholiken im 19. und 20. Jahrhundert, Zurich: Benzinger, 1989.
Anderson, Margaret L., *Windthorst. A Political Biography*, Oxford: Clarendon Press, 1981.
Asbeek Brusse, Wendy, *Tariffs, Trade and European Integration, 1947–1957. From Study Group to Common Market*, New York: St Martin's Press, 1997.
Bagnato, Bruna, *Storia di una illusione europea. Il progetto di Unione Doganale italo-francese*, London: Lothian Press, 1995.
Ball, Stuart, *The Conservative Party and British Politics 1902–1951*, Harlow: Longman, 1995.
Bariéty, Jacques, *Les Relations franco-allemandes après la première guerre mondiale*, Paris: Pedone, 1977.
Bariéty Jacques and Antoine Fleury (eds.), *Mouvements et initiatives de paix dans la politique internationale*, Bern: Lang, 1987.
Becker, Jean-Jacques and Serge Berstein, *Victoire et frustrations 1914–1929*, Paris: Éditions du Seuil, 1990.
Becker, Josef and Franz Knipping (eds.), *Power in Europe? Great Britain, France, Italy and Germany in a Postwar World, 1945–1950*, Berlin, New York: Walter de Gruyter, 1986.
Beke, Wouter, *De Christelijke Volkspartij tussen 1945 en 1968: breuklijnen en pacificatiemechanismen in een catch-allpartij*, Leuven: Leuven University Press, 2004.
Belitz, Ina, *Befreundung mit dem Fremden: Die Deutsch-Französische Gesellschaft in den deutsch-französischen Kultur- und Gesellschaftsbeziehungen der Locarno-Ära. Programme und Protagonisten der transnationalen Verständigung zwischen Pragmatismus und Idealismus*, Frankfurt/Main: Lang, 1997.

Bell, David S. and Christopher Lord (eds.), *Transnational Parties in the European Union*, Aldershot: Ashgate, 1998.

Berghahn, Volker, *America and the Intellectual Cold Wars in Europe. Shepard Stone between Philanthropy, Academy, and Diplomacy*, Princeton, N.J.: Princeton University Press, 2002.

The Americanisation of West German Industry 1945–1973, Cambridge: Cambridge University Press, 1986.

Berstein, Serge, Jean-Marie Mayeur and Pierre Milza (eds.), *Le MRP et la construction européenne*, Paris: Editions Complexe, 1993.

Besier, Gerhard and Francesca Piombo, *Der Heilige Stuhl und Hitler-Deutschland: die Faszination des Totalitären*, Munich: DVA, 2004.

Biographisches Handbuch der deutschsprachigen Emigration nach 1933, 2 vols., Munich, New York: K.G. Saur, 1980.

Bitsch, Marie-Thérèse, *Histoire de la construction européenne*, Paris: Editions Complexe, 1996.

Blackbourn, David, *Marpingen. Apparitions of the Virgin Mary in Bismarckian Germany*, Oxford: Clarendon Press, 1993.

Blantz, Thomas E., *George N. Shuster: On the Side of Truth*, Notre Dame, Ind.: University of Notre Dame Press, 1993.

Blaschke, Olaf, *Katholizismus und Antisemitismus im deutschen Kaiserreich*, Göttingen: Vandenhoeck & Ruprecht, 1997.

Religion im Kaiserreich. Milieus, Mentalitäten, Krisen, Gütersloh: Kaiser, 1996.

Bohn, Jutta, *Das Verhältnis zwischen katholischer Kirche und faschistischem Staat in Italien und die Rezeption in deutschen Zentrumskreisen*, Frankfurt/Main: Lang, 1992.

Bornewasser, Johannes A., *Katholieke Volkspartij, 1945–1980*, vol. I: *Herkomst en groei (tot 1963)*, Nijmegen: Valkhof Pers, 1995.

Bösch, Frank, *Die Adenauer-CDU. Gründung, Aufstieg und Krise einer Erfolgspartei 1945–1969*, Stuttgart, Munich: DVA, 2001.

Bosmans, Jac, *Romme: biografie 1896–1946*, Utrecht: Uitgev. Het Spectrum, 1991.

Bossuat, Gérard, *Les Fondateurs de l'Europe*, Paris: Éditions Belin, 1994.

L'Europe des français 1943–1959. La IVe République aux sources de l'Europe communautaire, Paris: Publications de la Sorbonne, 1996.

Boyer, John, *Culture and Political Crisis in Vienna. Christian Socialism in Power, 1897–1918*, Chicago, Ill.: Chicago University Press, 1995.

Braunthal, Gerard, *The Federation of German Industry in Politics*, Ithaca, N.Y.: Cornell University Press, 1965.

Braunthal, Julius, *Geschichte der Internationale*, 2 vols., Hanover: Dietz, 1961–3.

Brinkley, Alan, *Voices of Protest. Huey Long, Father Coughlin, and the Great Depression*, New York: Alfred Knopf, 1982.

Brown, Dorothy M. and Elizabeth McKeown, *The Poor Belong to Us. Catholic Charities and American Welfare*, Cambridge, Mass: Harvard University Press, 1997.

Buchanan, Tom, *Britain and the Spanish Civil War*, Cambridge: Cambridge University Press, 1997.

The Spanish Civil War and the British Labour Movement, Cambridge: Cambridge University Press, 1991.

Buchanan, Tom and Martin Conway (eds.), *Political Catholicism in Europe, 1918–1965*, Oxford: Clarendon Press, 1996.

Buchstab, Günter (ed.), *Christliche Demokraten gegen Hitler. Aus Verfolgung und Widerstand zur Union*, Freiburg: Herder, 2004.

Bührer, Werner, *Ruhrstahl und Europa. Die Wirtschaftsvereinigung Eisen- und Stahlindustrie und die Anfänge der europäischen Integration 1945–1952*, Munich: Oldenbourg, 1986.

Bussière, Eric and Dumoulin, Michel (eds.), *Milieux économiques et intégration européenne en Europe occidentale en XXe siècle*, Arras: Artois Presses Université, 1998.

Cabaud, Charles, *Joseph Fontanet. Frontenex 1921 – Paris 1980*, Paris: Éditions France-Empire, 1990.

Callot, Émile-François, *Le Mouvement Républicain Populaire. Origine, structure, doctrine, programme et action politique*, Paris: Marcel Rivière, 1978.

Campanini, Giorgio (ed.), *Francesco Luigi Ferrari a cinquant' anni dalla morte*, Rome: Edizioni di Storia e Letteratura, 1983.

Canavero, Alfredo and Jean-Dominique Durand (eds.), *Il fattore religioso nell'integrazione europea*, Milan: Edizioni Unicopli, 1999.

Capelle, Russell B., *The MRP and French Foreign Policy*, New York: Frederick A. Praeger, 1963.

Caron, Jeanne, *Le Sillon et la démocratie chrétienne, 1894–1910*, Paris: Plon, 1967.

Carpenter, Ronald H., *Father Charles E. Coughlin. Surrogate Spokesman for the Disaffected*, Westport, Conn.: Greenwood Press, 1998.

Chadwick, Owen, *A History of the Popes, 1830–1914*, Oxford: Clarendon Press, 1998.

Chafe, William H. (ed.), *The Achievement of American Liberalism: The New Deal and Its Legacies*, New York: Columbia University Press, 2003.

Chenaux, Philippe, *Une Europe Vaticane? Entre le Plan Marshall et les Traités de Rome*, Brussels: Éditions Ciaco, 1990.

Cholvy, Gérard (ed.), *L'Europe: ses dimensions religieuses*, Montpellier: Carrefour, 1998.

Clark, Christopher and Wolfram Kaiser (eds.), *Culture Wars. Secular–Catholic Conflict in Nineteenth-Century Europe*, Cambridge: Cambridge University Press, 2003.

Cointet, Michèle, *La France à Londres: renaissance d'un état (1940–1943)*, Brussels: Éditions Complexes, 1980.

Conway, Martin, *Catholic Politics in Europe 1918–1945*, London: Routledge, 1997.
Collaboration in Belgium. Léon Degrelle and the Rexist Movement 1940–1944, New Haven, Conn.: Yale University Press, 1991.

Conway, Martin and José Gotovitch (eds.), *Europe in Exile. European Refugee Communities in Britain 1939–1945*, Oxford, New York: Berghahn, 2001

Coupland, Philip M., *Britannia, Europa and Christendom. British Christians and European Integration*, Basingstoke: Palgrave, 2006.

Coutouvidis, John and Jaime Reynolds, *Poland 1939–47*, Leicester: Leicester University Press, 1986.

Craveri, Piero, *De Gasperi*, Bologna: il Mulino, 2006.

Crowson, Nick J., *The Conservative Party and European Integration since 1945*, London: Routledge, 2007.

Dalloz, Jacques, *Georges Bidault. Biographie politique*, Paris: L'Harmattan, 1992.

Deighton, Anne and Alan S. Milward (eds.), *Widening, Deepening and Acceleration: The European Economic Community 1957–1963*, Baden-Baden: Nomos, 1999.

De Jong, Louis, *Het Koninkrijk der Nederlanden in de Tweede Wereldoorlog*, vol. III: *Mei '40*, The Hague: Martinus Nijhoff, 1970.

Het Koninkrijk der Nederlanden in de Tweede Wereldoorlog, vol. IX/2: *Londen*, The Hague: Martinus Nijhoff, 1979.

Delbreil, Jean-Claude, *Centrisme et démocratie-chrétienne en France. Le Parti Démocrate Populaire des origines au M.R.P. (1919–1944)*, Paris: Publications de la Sorbonne, 1990.

Les Catholiques français et les tentatives de rapprochement franco-allemand (1920–1933), Metz: S.M.E.I., 1972.

Delzell, Charles F., *Mussolini's Enemies. The Italian Anti-Fascist Resistance*, Princeton, N.J.: Princeton University Press, 1961.

Demory, Jean-Claude, *Georges Bidault 1899–1983. Biographie*, Paris: Éditions Julliard, 1995.

De Rosa, Gabriele, *Da Luigi Sturzo ad Aldo Moro*, Brescia: Morcelliana, 1988.

Luigi Sturzo, Turin: Unione Tipografico – Editrice Torinese, 1977.

Rufo Ruffo della Scaletta e Luigi Sturzo (con lettere e documenti inediti tratti dall'archivio Ruffo della Scaletta), Rome: Edizioni di Storia e Letteratura, 1961.

(ed.), *Luigi Sturzo e la democrazia europea*, Rome: Editori Laterza, 1990.

Deutsch, Karl W., *Political Community and the North Atlantic Area: International Organization in the Light of Historical Experience*, New York: Greenwood Press, 1969 [1957].

The Analysis of International Relations, Englewood Cliffs: Prentice Hall, 1968.

Devuyst, Youri, *The European Union at the Crossroads. The EU's Institutional Evolution from the Schuman Plan to the European Convention*, Brussels: Lang, 2nd edn, 2003.

Diebold, William, *The Schuman Plan. A Study in Economic Cooperation 1950–1959*, New York: Praeger, 1959.

Di Lalla, Manlio, *Storia della Democrazia Cristiana*, 3 vols., Turin: Marietti, 1979–1982.

Dolan, Jay P., *In Search of an American Catholicism. A History of Religion and Culture in Tension*, Oxford: Oxford University Press, 2002.

The American Catholic Experience: A History from Colonial Times to the Present, Garden City: Doubleday, 1985.

Duchêne, François, *Jean Monnet. The First Statesman of Interdependence*, New York, London: W.W. Norton, 1994.

Dujardin, Vincent and Michel Dumoulin, *Paul Van Zeeland 1893–1973*, Brussels: Éditions Racine, 1997.

Dumoulin, Michel (ed.), *Wartime Plans for Postwar Europe*, Brussels: Bruylant, 1995.

Dumoulin, Michel and Anne-Myriam Dutrieue, *La Ligue Européenne de Coopération Économique (1946–1981). Un groupe d'étude et de pression dans la construction européenne*, Bern: Lang, 1993.

Durand, Jean-Dominique, *L'Europe de la démocratie chrétienne*, Paris: Editions Complexe, 1995.

(ed.), *Les Semaines sociales de France. Cent ans d'engagement social des catholiques français 1904–2004*, Paris: Parole et Silence, 2006.

Duroselle, Jean-Baptiste, *Les Relations franco-allemandes de 1918 à 1950*, vol. II, Paris: Centre de Documentation Universitaire, 1967.

Duverger, Maurice, *Les Partis politiques*, 5th edn, Paris: Colin, 1964.

Eldin, Grégoire *et al.*, *L'Europe de Robert Schuman*, Paris: Presses de l'Université de Paris-Sorbonne, 2001.

Elgey, Georgette, *La République des illusions 1945–1951*, Paris: Fayard, 1965.

Elvert, Jürgen, *Mitteleuropa! Deutsche Pläne zur europäischen Neuordnung (1918–1945)*, Stuttgart: Steiner, 1999.

Evans, Ellen L., *The Cross and the Ballot: Catholic Political Parties in Germany, Switzerland, Austria, Belgium and the Netherlands, 1785–1985*, Boston, Mass.: Humanities Press, 1999.

Evans, Richard, *The Coming of the Third Reich*, London: Allen Lane, 2003.

EVP-Fraktion des Europäischen Parlaments (ed.), *Zur Geschichte der christlich-demokratischen Bewegung in Europa*, Melle: Ernst Knoth, 1990.

Featherstone, Kevin, *Socialist Parties and European Integration. A Comparative History*, Manchester: Manchester University Press, 1988.

Finke, Roger and Rodney Stark, *The Churching of America, 1776–1990: The Winners and Losers in our Religious Economy*, New Brunswick, N.J.: Rutgers University Press, 1992.

Fitzmaurice, John, *The Party Groups in the European Parliament*, Farnborough: Saxon House, 1975.

Fleury, Antoine and Lubor Jílek (eds.), *Le Plan Briand d'Union fédérale européenne. Perspectives nationales et transnationales, avec documents*, Bern: Lang, 1998.

Foerster, Rolf Hellmut, *Die Idee Europa 1300–1946*, Munich: dtv, 1963.

Fogarty, Michael P., *Christian Democracy in Western Europe 1820–1953*, London: Routledge & Kegan Paul, 1957.

Formigoni, Guido, *La Democrazia cristiana e l'alleanza occidentale, 1943–1953*, Bologna: il Mulino, 1996.

Forster, Bernhard, *Adam Stegerwald (1874–1945). Christlich-nationaler Gewerkschafter, Zentrumspolitiker, Mitbegründer der Unionsparteien*, Düsseldorf: Droste, 2003.

Freyer, Tony, *Antitrust and Global Capitalism, 1930–2004*, Cambridge: Cambridge University Press, 2006.

Friese, Elisabeth, *Helene Wessel (1898–1969). Von der Zentrumspartei zur Sozialdemokratie*, Essen: Klartext Verlag, 1993.

Fursdon, Edward, *The European Defence Community: A History*, Basingstoke: Macmillan, 1980.

Gassert, Philipp, *Kurt Georg Kiesinger 1904–1988. Kanzler zwischen den Zeiten*, Munich: DVA, 2006.

Gehler, Michael, *Der lange Weg nach Europa. Österreich vom Ende der Monarchie bis zur EU. Darstellung*, Innsbruck: Studienverlag, 2002.

Gehler, Michael and Wolfram Kaiser (eds.), *Christian Democracy in Europe since 1945*, London: Routledge, 2004.

George, Stephen, *An Awkward Partner. Britain and the European Community* (Oxford: Clarendon Press, 1990).

Gerber, David J., *Law and Competition in Twentieth Century Europe: Protecting Prometheus*, Oxford: Clarendon Press, 1998.

Gillingham, John, *Coal, Steel and the Rebirth of Europe, 1945–1955. The Germans and French from Ruhr Conflict to Economic Community*, Cambridge: Cambridge University Press, 1991.

   European Integration 1950–2003. Superstate or New Market Economy?, Cambridge: Cambridge University Press, 2003.

Gillman, Peter and Leni Gillman, *Collar the Lot! How Britain Interned and Expelled Its Wartime Refugees*, London: Quartet Books, 1980.

Giovagnoli, Agostino, *Il partito italiano: la democrazia cristiana dal 1942 al 1994*, Rome: Laterza, 1996.

Girault, René (ed.), *Pierre Mendès France et le rôle de la France dans le monde*, Grenoble: Presses universitaires de Grenoble, 1991.

Goldner, Franz, *Die österreichische Emigration 1938–1945*, Vienna, Munich: Herold, 1972.

Gollwitzer, Heinz, *Europabild und Europagedanke*, Munich: Beck, 1951.

Gorguet, Ilde, *Les Mouvements pacifistes et la réconciliation franco-allemande dans les années vingt (1919–1931)*, Bern: Lang, 1999.

Grabitz, Eberhard et al., *Direktwahl und Demokratisierung – eine Funktionenbilanz des Europäischen Parlaments nach der ersten Wahlperiode*, Bonn: Europa-Union-Verlag, 1988.

Gresch, Norbert, *Transnationale Parteienzusammenarbeit in der EG*, Baden-Baden: Nomos, 1978.

Greschat, Martin and Wilfried Loth (eds.), *Die Christen und die Entstehung der Europäischen Gemeinschaft*, Stuttgart: Kohlhammer, 1994.

Griffiths, Richard T. (ed.), *Socialist Parties and the Question of Europe in the 1950's*, Leiden, New York, Cologne: Brill, 1993.

   (ed.) *The Netherlands and the Integration of Europe 1945–1957*, Amsterdam: NEHA, 1990.

Griffiths, Richard T. and Brian Girvin (eds.), *The Green Pool and the Origins of the Common Agricultural Policy*, Bloomsbury: Lothian Press, 1995.

Gualerzi, Giorgio, *La politica estera dei popolari*, Rome: Cinque lune, 1959.

Haas, Ernst B., *The Uniting of Europe. Political, Social, and Economic Forces 1950–57*, Notre Dame, Ind.: University of Notre Dame Press, 2004 [1958].

Haftendorn, Helga, *Deutsche Außenpolitik zwischen Selbstbeschränkung und Selbstbehauptung 1945–2000*, Stuttgart, Munich: DVA, 2001.

Hagspiel, Hermann, *Verständigung zwischen Deutschland und Frankreich. Die deutsch-französische Außenpolitik der zwanziger Jahre im innenpolitischen Kräftefeld beider Länder*, Bonn: Ludwig Röhrscheid, 1987.

Hahn, Karl Josef (in cooperation with Friedrich Fugmann) (eds.), *Die Christliche Demokratie in Europa*, Rome: EUCD, 1979.

Halsey, William M., *The Survival of American Innocence: Catholicism in an Era of Disillusionment, 1920–1940*, Notre Dame, Ind.: University of Notre Dame Press, 1980.

Hanisch, Ernst, *Der lange Schatten des Staates. Österreichische Gesellschaftsgeschichte im 20. Jahrhundert*, Vienna: Ueberreuter, 1994.

Hans-Seidel-Stiftung (ed.), *Josef Müller, der erste Vorsitzende der CSU. Politik für eine neue Zeit*, Grünwald: Atwerb-Verlag, 1998.

Harris, Ruth, *Lourdes. Body and Spirit in the Secular Age*, London: Allen Lane, 1999.

Hastings, Adrian, *The Construction of Nationhood. Ethnicity, Religion and Nationalism*, Cambridge: Cambridge University Press, 1997.

Hazareesingh, Sudhir, *Political Traditions in Modern France*, Oxford: Oxford University Press, 1994.

Hehl, Ulrich von, *Wilhelm Marx 1863–1946. Eine politische Biographie*, Mainz: Matthias-Grünewald-Verlag, 1987.

Hehl, Ulrich von and Friedrich Kronenberg (eds.), *Zeitzeichen: 150 Jahre Deutsche Katholikentage 1848–1998*, Paderborn: Schöningh, 1999.

Heitzer, Horstwalter, *Der Volksverein für das katholische Deutschland im Kaiserreich 1890–1918*, Mainz: Matthias-Grünewald-Verlag, 1979.

 Die CDU in der britischen Zone 1945–1949. Gründung, Organisation, Programm und Politik, Düsseldorf: Droste, 1988.

Herbst, Ludolf, *Option für den Westen. Vom Marshallplan bis zum deutsch-französischen Vertrag*, Munich: dtv, 1989.

Herbst, Ludolf, Werner Bührer and Hanno Sowade (eds.), *Vom Marshallplan zur EWG. Die Eingliederung der Bundesrepublik Deutschland in die westliche Welt*, Munich: Oldenbourg, 1990.

Herman, Valentine and Juliet Lodge, *The European Parliament and the European Community*, London: Macmillan, 1978.

Hetherington, S.J., *Katharine Atholl 1874–1960. Against the Tide*, Aberdeen: Aberdeen University Press, 1989.

Hettler, Friedrich Hermann, *Josef Müller ('Ochsensepp'). Mann des Widerstandes und erster CSU-Vorsitzender*, Munich: Kommissionsverlag UNI-Druck, 1991.

Heumos, Peter, *Die Emigration aus der Tschechoslowakei nach Westeuropa und dem Nahen Osten 1938–1945*, Munich: Oldenbourg Verlag, 1989.

Hirschfeld, Gerhard (ed.), *Exil in Großbritannien. Zur Emigration aus dem natio- nalsozialistischen Deutschland*, Stuttgart: Klett-Cotta, 1983.

Hitchcock, William I., *The Struggle for Europe. A History of the Continent since 1945*, London: Profile Books, 2003.

Hix, Simon and Christopher Lord, *Political Parties in the European Union*, Basingstoke: Macmillan, 1997.

Hochgeschwender, Michael, *Freiheit in der Offensive? Der Kongreß für Kulturelle Freiheit und die Deutschen*, Munich: Oldenbourg, 1998.

Hodel, Markus, *Die Schweizerische Konservative Volkspartei 1918–1929. Die goldenen Jahre des politischen Katholizismus*, Fribourg: Universitätsverlag, 1994.

Höfling, Beate, *Katholische Friedensbewegung zwischen zwei Weltkriegen. Der 'Friedensbund Deutscher Katholiken' 1917–1933*, Waldkirch: Waldkircher Verlagsgesellschaft, 1979.

Horne, John N. and Alan Kramer, *German Atrocities, 1914: A History of Denial*, New Haven, Conn.: Yale University Press, 2001.

Horner, Franz, *Konservative und christdemokratische Parteien in Europa. Geschichte, Programmatik, Strukturen*, Vienna, Munich: Verlag Herold, 1981.

Hörster-Philipps, Ulrike, *Joseph Wirth 1879–1956. Eine politische Biographie*, Paderborn: Schöningh, 1998.

Hürten, Heinz, *Spiegel der Kirche – Spiegel der Gesellschaft? Katholikentage im Wandel der Welt*, Paderborn: Schöningh, 1998.

Hüser, Dietmar, *Frankreichs 'doppelte Deutschlandpolitik'. Dynamik aus der Defensive – Planen, Entscheiden, Umsetzen in gesellschaftlichen und wirtschaftlichen, innen- und außenpolitischen Krisenzeiten 1944–1950*, Berlin: Duncker & Humblot, 1996.

Irving, R. E. M., *The Christian Democratic Parties of Western Europe*, London: George Allen & Unwin, 1979.

Jachtenfuchs, Markus, *Die Konstruktion Europas. Verfassungsideen und institutionelle Entwicklung*, Baden-Baden: Nomos, 2002.

Jackson, Angela, *British Women and the Spanish Civil War*, London, New York: Routledge, 2002.

Jansen, Thomas, *Die Entstehung einer Europäischen Partei. Vorgeschichte, Gründung und Entwicklung der EVP*, Bonn: Europa Union Verlag, 1996.

Jeismann, Michael, *Das Vaterland der Feinde: Studien zum nationalen Feindbegriff und Selbstverständnis in Deutschland und Frankreich 1792–1918*, Stuttgart: Klett-Cotta 1992.

Johansson, Karl Magnus, *Transnational Party Alliances. Analysing the Hard-Won Alliance between Conservatives and Christian Democrats in the European Parliament*, Lund: Lund University Press, 1997.

Johansson, Karl Magnus and Peter Zervakis (eds.), *European Political Parties between Cooperation and Integration*, Baden-Baden: Nomos, 2002.

Johnson, Gaynor (ed.), *Locarno Revisited. European Diplomacy 1920–1929*, London: Routledge, 2004.

Joll, James, *The Second International, 1889–1914*, 2nd edn, London: Routledge, 1974.

Judt, Tony, *Postwar. A History of Europe since 1945*, London: Heinemann, 2005.

Jungnickel, Rudolf, *Kabale am Rhein. Der Kanzler und sein Monsignore*, Weimar: Wartburg Verlag, 1994.

Junker, Detlef, *Die Deutsche Zentrumspartei und Hitler 1932/33. Ein Beitrag zur Problematik des politischen Katholizismus in Deutschland*, Stuttgart: Ernst Klett, 1969.

Kaiser, Wolfram, *Using Europe, Abusing the Europeans. Britain and European Integration 1945–63*, Basingstoke: Macmillan, Basingstoke 1999.

Kaiser, Wolfram and Jürgen Elvert (eds.), *European Union Enlargement. A Comparative History*, London: Routledge, 2004.

Kaiser, Wolfram, Brigitte Leucht and Morten Rasmussen (eds.), *Origins of a European Polity: Supranational and Transnational European Integration 1950–72* (forthcoming).

Kaiser, Wolfram and Peter Starie (eds.), *Transnational European Union. Towards a Common Political Space*, London: Routledge, 2005.

Kaiser, Wolfram and Helmut Wohnout (eds.), *Political Catholicism in Europe 1918–1945*, London: Routledge, 2004.

Kalyvas, Stathis N., *The Rise of Christian Democracy in Europe*, Ithaca, N.Y.: Cornell University Press, 1996.

Kanawada, Leo V., *Franklin D. Roosevelt's Diplomacy and American Catholics, Italians, and Jews*, Epping: Bowker, 1982.

Karnofski, Eva-Rose, *Parteienbünde vor der Europa-Wahl 1979. Integration durch gemeinsame Wahlaussagen?*, Bonn: Europa Union Verlag, 1982.

Keating, Joan, *Roman Catholics, Christian Democracy and the British Labour Movement 1910–1960*, PhD, Manchester: University of Manchester, 1992.

Keller, Thomas, *Deutsch-französische Dritte-Weg-Diskurse. Personalistische Intellektuellendebatten in der Zwischenkriegszeit*, Munich: Fink, 2001.

Keßler, Richard, *Heinrich Held als Parlamentarier. Eine Teilbiographie 1868–1924*, Berlin: Duncker & Humblot, 1971.

Kipping, Matthias, *Zwischen Kartellen und Konkurrenz. Der Schuman-Plan und die Ursprünge der europäischen Einigung 1944–1952*, Berlin: Duncker & Humblot, 1996.

Kleinmann, Hans-Otto, *Geschichte der CDU 1945–1982*, Stuttgart: DVA, 1993.

Klemperer, Klemens von, *Ignaz Seipel. Christian Statesman in a Time of Crisis*, Princeton, N.J.: Princeton University Press, 1972.

Knipping, Franz, *Deutschland, Frankreich und das Ende der Locarno-Ära 1928–1931*, Munich: Oldenbourg, 1987.

Rom, 25. März 1957. Die Einigung Europas, Munich: dtv, 2004.

Knudsen, Ann-Christina Lauring, *Defining the Policies of the Common Agricultural Policy. A Historical Study*, PhD, Florence: European University Institute, 2001.

Koerfer, Daniel, *Kampf ums Kanzleramt. Erhard und Adenauer*, Stuttgart: DVA, 1987.

Köhler, Henning, *Adenauer. Eine politische Biographie*, Berlin: *Propyläen*, 1994.

Adenauer und die rheinische Republik. Der erste Anlauf 1918–1924, Opladen: Westdeutscher Verlag, 1986.

König, Mareike and Matthias Schulz (eds.), *Die Bundesrepublik Deutschland und die europäische Einigung 1949–2000*, Stuttgart: Steiner, 2004.

Krebber, Werner (ed.), *Den Menschen Recht verschaffen. Carl Sonnenschein: Person und Werk*, Würzburg: Echter, 1996.

Kreppel, Amie, *The European Parliament and the Supranational Party System*, Cambridge: Cambridge University Press, 2002.

Kriechbaumer, Robert (ed.), *Anspruch und Realität: zur Geschichte der ÖVP seit 1945*, Vienna, Cologne, Weimar: Böhlau, 1995.

Krüger, Dieter, *Sicherheit durch Integration? Die wirtschaftliche und politische Zusammenarbeit Westeuropas 1947 bis 1957/58*, Munich: Oldenbourg, 2003.

Krüger, Peter, *Das unberechenbare Europa. Epochen des Integrationsprozesses vom späten 18. Jahrhundert bis zur Europäischen Union*, Stuttgart: Kohlhammer, 2006.

Die Außenpolitik der Republik von Weimar, Darmstadt: Wissenschaftliche Buchgesellschaft, 1985.

Krüger, Peter, and Ernst Weisenfeld (eds.), *Eine ungewöhnliche Geschichte. Deutschland–Frankreich seit 1870*, Bonn: Europa Union Verlag, 1988.

Krumeich, Gerd and Joachim Schröder (eds.), *Der Schatten des Weltkriegs. Die Ruhrbesetzung 1923*, Essen: Klartext, 2004.

Kselman, Thomas and Joseph A. Buttigieg (eds.), *European Christian Democracy. Historical Legacies and Comparative Perspectives*, Notre Dame, Ind.: University of Notre Dame Press, 2003.

Küppers, Heinrich, *Joseph Wirth. Parlamentarier, Minister und Kanzler der Weimarer Republik*, Stuttgart: Steiner, 1997.

Küsters, Hanns Jürgen, *Fondements de la Communauté Économique Européenne*, Luxembourg: Office des publications officielles des Communautés Européennes, 1990 [German 1982].

Kwanten, Godfried, *August-Edmond De Schryver 1898–1991. Politieke biografie van een gentleman-staatsman*, Leuven: Leuven University Press, 2001.

Lamberts, Emiel (ed.), *Christian Democracy in the European Union [1945/1995]*, Leuven: Leuven University Press, 1997.

(ed.), *The Black International / L'Internationale noire 1870–1878*, Leuven: Leuven University Press, 2002.

Lambrecht, Rudolf, *Deutsche und französische Katholiken, 1914–1933. Auseinandersetzungen, Standpunkte, Meinungen, Kontakte*, PhD, Münster: Westfälische Wilhelms-Universität, 1967.

Lappenküper, Ulrich, *Die deutsch-französischen Beziehungen 1949–1963*, 2 vols., Munich: Oldenbourg, 2001.

Latour, Francis, *La Papauté et les problèmes de la paix pendant la Première Guerre Mondiale*, Paris: L'Harmattan, 1996.

Legoll, Paul, *Konrad Adenauer et l'idée d'unification européenne, janvier 1948 – mai 1950*, Bern: Lang, 1989.

Letamendia, Pierre, *Le Mouvement Républicain Populaire. Histoire d'un grand parti français*, Paris: Beauchesne, 1995.

Lipgens, Walter, *A History of European Integration*, vol. I: *1945–1947*, Oxford: Clarendon Press, 1982 [German 1977].

Lipset, Seymour and Stein Rokkan, *Party Systems and Voter Alignment: Cross-national Perspectives*, New York: Free Press, 1967.

Lodge, Juliet and Valentine Herman, *Direct Elections to the European Parliament. A Community Perspective*, London: Macmillan, 1982.

Lönne, Karl-Egon, *Politischer Katholizismus im 19. und 20. Jahrhundert*, Frankfurt/Main: Suhrkamp, 1986.

Loth, Wilfried (ed.), *Crises and Compromises: The European Project 1963–1969*, Baden-Baden: Nomos, 2001.

Der Weg nach Europa. Geschichte der europäischen Integration 1939–1957, 3rd edn, Göttingen: Vandenhoeck & Ruprecht, 1996.

Entwürfe einer Europäischen Verfassung. Eine historische Bilanz, Bonn: Europa Union Verlag, 2002.

Katholiken im Kaiserreich. Der politische Katholizismus in der Krise des wilhelminischen Deutschlands, Düsseldorf: Droste, 1984.

Sozialismus und Internationalismus. Die französischen Sozialisten und die Nachkriegsordnung Europas 1940–1950, Stuttgart: DVA, 1977.

Loth, Wilfried, William Wallace and Wolfgang Wessels (eds.), *Walter Hallstein – the Forgotten European?*, Basingstoke: Macmillan, 1998.

Lücker, Hans August and Karl Josef Hahn, *Christliche Demokraten bauen Europa*, Bonn: Europa Union Verlag, 1987.

Lücker, Hans August and Jean Seitlinger, *Robert Schuman und die Einigung Europas*, Luxembourg, Bonn: Éditions Saint-Paul / Bouvier, 2000.

Ludlow, Piers, *Dealing with Britain. The Six and the First UK Application to the EEC*, Cambridge: Cambridge University Press, 1997.

The European Community and the Crises of the 1960s. Negotiating the Gaullist Challenge, London: Routledge, 2006.

Lundestad, Geir, *'Empire' by Integration. The United States and European Integration, 1945–1997*, Oxford: Oxford University Press, 1998.

Luther, Kurt Richard and Ferdinand Müller-Rommel (eds.), *Political Parties in the New Europe. Political and Analytical Challenges*, Oxford: Oxford University Press, 2002.

Lynch, Frances M. B., *France and the International Economy. From Vichy to the Treaty of Rome*, London: Routledge, 1997.

Magagnoli, Ralf, *Italien und die Europäische Verteidigungsgemeinschaft. Zwischen europäischem Credo und nationaler Machtpolitik*, Frankfurt/Main: Lang, 1999.

Maier, Charles S., *Recasting Bourgeois Europe: Stabilization in France, Germany and Italy in the Decade after World War I*, Princeton, N.J.: Princeton University Press, 1975.

Maimann, Helene, *Politik im Wartesaal. Österreichische Exilpolitik in Großbritannien 1938–1945*, Vienna, Cologne, Graz: Böhlau, 1975.

Malgeri, Francesco, *Chiesa, cattolici e democrazia. Da Sturzo a De Gasperi*, Brescia: Morcelliana, 1990.

Luigi Sturzo, Milan: Edizioni Paoline, 1993.

Marcus, Sheldon, *Father Coughlin. The Tumultuous Life of the Priest of the Little Flower*, Boston, Toronto: Little, Brown and Company, 1973.

Martin, Benjamin F., *Count Albert de Mun. Paladin of the Third Republic*, Chapel Hill, N.C.: University of North Carolina Press, 1978.

Martina, Giacomo, *Pio IX*, vol. III: *1867–1878*, Rome: University Gregoriana, 1990.

Mayeur, Jean-Marie, *Des partis catholiques à la démocratie chrétienne, XIXe–XXe siècles*, Paris: Colin, 1980.

Mayne, Richard and John Pinder, *Federal Union: The Pioneers. A History of Federal Union*, Basingstoke: Macmillan, 1990.

McGreevy, John T., *Catholicism and American Freedom. A History*, New York: W.W. Norton & Company, 2003.

Michel, Henri, *Histoire de la France libre*, 3rd edn, Paris: Presses Universitaires de France, 1972.

Middlemas, Keith, *Orchestrating Europe. The Informal Politics of the European Union 1973–95*, London: Fontana, 1995.

Miller, Susanne and Heinrich Potthoff, *A History of German Social Democracy: from 1848 to the Present*, Leamington Spa: Berg, 1986.

Milward, Alan S., *The European Rescue of the Nation-State*, London: Routledge, 1992.

The Reconstruction of Western Europe 1945–51, London: Methuen, 1984.

The Rise and Fall of a National Strategy 1945–1963, London: Frank Cass, 2002.

Milward, Alan S. *et al.*, *The Frontier of National Sovereignty. History and Theory 1945–1992*, London: Routledge, 1993.

Misner, Paul, *Social Catholicism in Europe: From the Onset of Industrialization to the First World War*, New York: Crossroad, 1991.

Mittag, Jürgen (ed.), *Politische Parteien und europäische Integration. Entwicklung und Perspektiven transnationaler Parteienkooperation in Europa*, Essen: Klartext, 2006.

Mittendorfer, Rudolf, *Robert Schuman – Architekt des neuen Europa*, Hildesheim, Zurich, New York: Georg Olms, 1983.

Molony, John, *The Worker Question: A New Historical Perspective on Rerum Novarum*, Dublin: Gill and Macmillan, 1991.

Moravcsik, Andrew, *The Choice for Europe. Social Purpose and State Power from Messina to Maastricht*, London: UCL Press, 1998.

Morris, Charles R., *American Catholic. The Saints and Sinners Who Built America's Most Powerful Church*, New York: Times Books, 1997.

Morsey, Rudolf, *Der Untergang des politischen Katholizismus. Die Zentrumspartei zwischen christlichem Selbstverständnis und 'Nationaler Erhebung' 1932/33*, Stuttgart, Zurich: Belser, 1977.

Die Deutsche Zentrumspartei 1917–1923, Düsseldorf: Droste, 1966.

(ed.), *Zeitgeschichte in Lebensbildern. Aus dem deutschen Katholizismus des 19. und 20. Jahrhunderts*, 3 vols., Mainz: Matthias-Grünewald-Verlag, 1973–9.

Müller, Guido, *Europäische Gesellschaftsbeziehungen nach dem Ersten Weltkrieg. Das Deutsch-Französische Studienkomitee und der Europäische Kulturbund*, Munich: Oldenbourg, 2005.

Niedermayer, Oskar, *Europäische Parteien? Zur grenzüberschreitenden Interaktion politischer Parteien im Rahmen der Europäischen Gemeinschaft*, Frankfurt, New York: Campus, 1983.

Niedhart, Gottfried, *Die Aussenpolitik der Weimarer Republik*, Munich: Oldenbourg, Munich 1999.

Nipperdey, Thomas, *Religion im Umbruch*, Munich: Beck, 1988.

Ortuño Anaya, Pilar, *European Socialists and Spain: the Transition to Democracy*, Basingstoke: Palgrave, 2002.

Ott, Barthélémy, *Georges Bidault. L'indomptable*, Annonay: Imprimerie du Vivarais, 1975.

Oudenhove, Guy van, *The Political Parties in the European Parliament*, Leyden: Sijthoff, 1965.

Palayret, Jean-Marie, Helen Wallace and Pascaline Winand (eds.), *Visions, Votes, and Vetoes. The Empty Chair Crisis and the Luxembourg Compromise Forty Years On*, Brussels: Lang, 2006.

Papini, Roberto, *Le Courage de la démocratie*, Paris: Desclée de Brouwer, 2003 [Italian 1995].

The Christian Democrat International, Lanham: Rowman & Littlefield, 1997.

Parsons, Craig, *A Certain Idea of Europe*, Ithaca, London: Cornell University Press, 2003.

Pasture, Patrick, *Histoire du syndicalisme chrétien international. La difficile recherche d'une troisième voie*, Paris: L'Harmattan, 1999.

Paterson, William E., *The SPD and European Integration*, Farnborough: Saxon House, 1974.

Pauley, Bruce F., *From Prejudice to Persecution: A History of Austrian Antisemitism*, Chapel Hill: University of North Carolina Press, 1992.

Pegg, Carl H., *Evolution of the European Idea, 1914–1932*, Chapel Hill: University of North Carolina Press, 1983.

Pennera, Christian, *Robert Schuman. La jeunesse et les débuts politiques d'un grand européen, de 1886 à 1924*, Sarreguemines: Éditions Pierron, 1985.

Pierson, Paul, *Politics in Time. History, Institutions, and Social Analysis*, Princeton, N.J.: Princeton University Press, 2004.

Piva, Francesco and Francesco Malgeri, *Vita di Luigi Sturzo*, Rome: Cinque lune, 1972.

Poidevin, Raymond (ed.), *Histoire des débuts de la construction européenne (mars 1948–mai 1950) / Origins of the European Integration (March 1948–May 1950)*, Baden-Baden: Nomos, 1986.

Robert Schuman, homme d'État 1886–1963, Paris: Imprimerie nationale, 1986.

Pollack, Mark A., *The Engines of European Integration – Delegation, Agency, and Agenda Setting in the EU*, Oxford: Oxford University Press, 2003.

Portelli, Hugues and Thomas Jansen (eds.), *La Démocratie chrétienne. Force internationale*, Nanterre: Institut Politique Internationale et Européenne, Université de Paris X-Nanterre, 1986.

Pouthier, Jean-Luc, *Les Catholiques sociaux et les démocrates chrétiens français devant l'Italie fasciste, 1922–1935*, PhD, Paris: Institut d'Études Politiques, 1981.

Prati, Giulia, *Italian Foreign Policy, 1947–1951. Alcide De Gasperi and Carlo Sforza between Atlanticism and Europeanism*, Göttingen: Bonn University Press, 2006.

Preda, Daniela, *Alcide De Gasperi federalista europeo*, Bologna: il Mulino, 2004.

Prégardier, Elisabeth, *Engagiert. Drei Frauen aus dem Ruhrgebiet*, Annweiler: Plöger, 2003.

Prégardier, Elisabeth and Anne Mohr (eds.), *Helene Weber (1881–1962). Ernte eines Lebens, Weg einer Politikerin*, Annweiler: Plöger, 1991.

Pridham, Geoffrey and Pippa Pridham, *Towards Transnational Parties in the European Community*, London: Policy Studies Institute, 1979.

    Transnational Party Co-operation and European Integration. The Process towards Direct Elections, London: George Allen & Unwin, 1981.

Radkau, Joachim, *Die deutsche Emigration in den USA. Ihr Einfluß auf die amerikanische Europapolitik 1933–1945*, Düsseldorf: Bertelsmann, 1971.

Ramscheid, Birgit, *Herbert Blankenhorn (1904–1991). Adenauers außenpolitischer Berater*, Düsseldorf: Droste, 2006.

Rittberger, Berthold, *Building Europe's Parliament: Democratic Representation beyond the Nation-State*, Oxford: Oxford University Press, 2005.

Rochefort, Robert, *Robert Schuman*, Paris: Éditions du Cerf, 1968.

Röder, Werner, *Die deutschen sozialistischen Exilgruppen in Großbritannien. Ein Beitrag zur Geschichte des Widerstandes gegen den Nationalsozialismus*, 2nd edn, Bonn-Bad Godesberg: Verlag Neue Gesellschaft, 1973.

Rohe, Karl, *Wahlen und Wählertraditionen in Deutschland. Kulturelle Grundlagen deutscher Parteien und Parteiensysteme im 19. und 20. Jahrhundert*, Frankfurt/ Main: Suhrkamp, 1992.

Rossini, Giuseppe, *Il movimento cattolico nel periodo fascista (momenti e problemi)*, Rome: Cinque lune, 1966.

Ruge, Udine, *Die Erfindung des 'Europa der Regionen'. Kritische Ideengeschichte eines konservativen Konzepts*, Frankfurt/Main, New York: Campus, 2003.

Ruppert, Karsten, *Im Dienst am Staat von Weimar. Das Zentrum als regierende Partei in der Weimarer Demokratie 1923–1930*, Düsseldorf: Droste, 1992.

Sassoon, Donald, *One Hundred Years of Socialism. The West European Left in the Twentieth Century*, London, New York: I.B. Tauris, 1996.

Saunders, Frances Stonor, *Who Paid the Piper? The CIA and the Cultural Cold War*, London: Granta Books, 1999.

Schatz, Klaus, *Vaticanum I, 1869–1870*, 2 vols., Paderborn: Schöningh, 1992.

Schepens, Luc, *De Belgen in Groot-Brittannië 1940–1944. Feiten en Getuigenissen*, Nijmegen: Uitgeverij B. Gottmer, 1980.

Schildt, Axel, *Zwischen Abendland und Amerika. Studien zur westdeutschen Ideenlandschaft der 50er Jahre*, Munich: Oldenbourg, 1999.

Schlie, Ulrich, *Kein Friede mit Deutschland. Die geheimen Gespräche im Zweiten Weltkrieg 1939–1941*, Munich, Berlin: Langen Müller, 1994.

Schmiermann, Sjef, *Prof. Dr. J. A. Veraart (1886–1955). Aspecten van het politieke leven van een recalcitrant katholiek democraat*, PhD, Nijmegen: University of Nijmegen, 1988.

Schreiner, Reinhard, *Bidault, der MRP und die französische Deutschlandpolitik, 1944–1948*, Frankfurt/Main: Lang, 1985.

Schulze, Hagen, *Otto Braun oder Preußens demokratische Sendung*, Frankfurt, Berlin, Vienna: Propyläen, 1981.

Schuster, Peter, *Henry Wickham Steed und die Habsburgermonarchie*, Vienna, Cologne, Weimar: Böhlau, 1970.

Schwabe, Klaus (ed.), *Die Anfänge des Schuman-Plans 1950/51 / The Beginnings of the Schuman-Plan*, Baden-Baden: Nomos, 1988.

Schwarz, Hans-Peter, *Adenauer. Der Aufstieg: 1876–1952*, Stuttgart: DVA, 1986.

Adenauer. Der Staatsmann: 1952–1967, Stuttgart: DVA, 1991.

Scoppola, Pietro, *La Chiesa e il fascismo. Documenti e interpretazioni*, Bari: Laterza, 1971.

Seibt, Ferdinand, Hans Lemberg and Helmut Slapnicka (eds.), *Biographisches Lexikon zur Geschichte der Böhmischen Länder*, vol. III, Munich: Oldenbourg, 1991.

Serra, Enrico (ed.), *Il rilancio dell'Europa e i trattati di Roma / The Relaunching of Europe and the Treaties of Rome*, Baden-Baden: Nomos, 1989.

Sorgenfrei, Helmut, *Die geistesgeschichtlichen Hintergründe der Sozialenzyklika 'Rerum Novarum'*, Heidelberg: Kerle, 1970.

Soutou, Georges-Henri, *L'Alliance incertaine. Les rapports politico-stratégiques franco-allemands 1954–1996*, Paris: Fayard, 1996.

Spael, Wilhelm, *Das katholische Deutschland im 20. Jahrhundert. Seine Pionier- und Krisenzeiten 1890–1945*, Würzburg: Echter, 1964.

Stirk, M.L. and Peter M.R. Stirk (eds.), *Making the New Europe. European Unity and the Second World War*, London: Pinter, 1990.

Stirk, Peter M. R. (ed.), *European Unity in Context. The Interwar Period*, London: Pinter, 1989.

Suppan, Arnold, *Jugoslawien und Österreich 1918–1938. Bilaterale Außenpolitik im europäischen Umfeld*, Vienna, Munich: Verlag für Geschichte und Politik, 1996.

Thiemeyer, Guido, *Vom 'Pool Vert' zur Europäischen Wirtschaftsgemeinschaft. Europäische Integration, Kalter Krieg und die Anfänge der Europäischen Agrarpolitik 1950–1957*, Munich: Oldenbourg, 1999.

Thrasolt, Ernst, *Dr. Carl Sonnenschein. Der Mensch und sein Werk*, Munich: Verlag Jos. Kösel & Friedr. Pustet, 1930.

Trachtenberg, Marc, *A Constructed Peace. The Making of the European Settlement 1945–1963*, Princeton, N.J.: Princeton University Press, 1999.

Trapl, Miloš, *Political Catholicism and the Czechoslovak People's Party in Czechoslovakia 1918–1938*, Boulder/Colo.: Social Science Monographs, 1995.

Trausch, Gilbert (ed.), *Die Europäische Integration vom Schuman-Plan bis zu den Verträgen von Rom / The European Integration from the Schuman-Plan to the Treaties of Rome*, Baden-Baden: Nomos, 1993.

Uertz, Rudolf, *Christentum und Sozialismus in der frühen CDU. Grundlage und Wirkungen der christlich-sozialen Ideen 1945–1949*, Stuttgart: DVA, 1981.

Universalità e cultura nel pensiero dei Luigi Sturzo. Atti del Convegno Internazionale di Studio Roma, Istituto Luigi Sturzo 28, 29, 30 ottobre 1999, Soveria Mannelli: Rubbettino, 2001.

Van Allen, Rodger, *The Commonweal and American Catholicism. The Magazine, the Movement, the Meaning*, Philadelphia: Fortress Press, 1974.

Vaussard, Maurice, *Histoire de la démocratie chrétienne*, vol. I: *France – Belgique – Italie*, Paris: Éditions du Seuil, 1956.

Vecchio, Giorgio, *Alla ricerca del partito. Cultura politica ed esperienze dei cattolici italiani nel primo Novecento*, Brescia: Morcelliana, 1987.

La democrazia cristiana in Europa (1891–1963), Milan: Marsia, 1979.

Veen, Hans-Joachim (ed.), *Christlich-demokratische und konservative Parteien in Westeuropa*, vol. V, Paderborn: Schöningh, 2000.

Velaers, Jan and Herman Van Goethem, *Leopold III. De koning, het land, de oorlog*, Tielt: Lannoo, 1994.

Vilar, Sergio, *Historia del anti-franquismo 1939–1975*, Barcelona: Plaza & Janes, 1984.

Wachtling, Oswald, *Joseph Joos: Journalist, Arbeiterführer, Zentrumspolitiker. Politische Biographie 1878–1933*, Mainz: Matthias-Grünewald-Verlag, 1974.

Weber, Eugen, *Action Française. Royalism and Reaction in Twentieth-Century France*, Stanford, Calif.: Stanford University Press, 1962.

Weidenfeld, Werner, *Konrad Adenauer und Europa. Die geistigen Grundlagen der westeuropäischen Integrationspolitik des ersten Bundeskanzlers*, Bonn: Europa Union-Verlag, 1976.

Weymar, Paul, *Konrad Adenauer. Die autorisierte Biographie*, Munich: Kindler Verlag, 1955.

Whyte, John H., *Catholics in Western Democracies. A Study in Political Behaviour*, Dublin: Gill and Macmillan, 1981.

Wohnout, Helmut, *Regierungsdiktatur oder Ständeparlament? Gesetzgebung im autoritären Österreich*, Vienna: Böhlau, 1993.

Young, John W., *Britain and European Unity, 1945–1999*, 2nd edn, London: Macmillan, 2000.

Zéraffa-Dray, Danièle, *Histoire de la France: d'une République à l'autre 1918–1958*, Paris: Hachette, 1992.

Ziegerhofer-Prettenthaler, Anita, *Botschafter Europas. Richard Nikolaus Coudenhove-Kalergi und die Paneuropa-Bewegung in den zwanziger und dreißiger Jahren*, Vienna: Böhlau, 2004.

Zimmermann, Hubert, *Money and Security. Troops and Monetary Policy in Germany's Relations to the United States and the United Kingdom, 1950–1971*, Cambridge: Cambridge University Press, 2002.

Zwart, Rutger Simon, *'Gods wil in Nederland': christelijke ideologieën en de vorming van het CDA (1880–1980)*, Kampen: Kok, 1996.

ARTICLES

Altermatt, Urs, 'Die Christlichdemokratische Volkspartei der Schweiz 1945–1999', in Veen (ed.), *Christlich-demokratische und konservative Parteien*, 35–115.

Anderson, Margaret L., 'Voter, Junker, *Landrat*, Priest. The Old Authorities and the New Franchise in Imperial Germany', *American Historical Review* 98 (1993), 1448–74.

Antonetti, Nicola di, 'Sturzo e il modello della rappresentanza organica', in De Rosa (ed.), *Luigi Sturzo e la democrazia europea*, 202–20.

Asbeek Brusse, Wendy, 'The Dutch Socialist Party', in Griffiths (ed.), *Socialist Parties*, 106–34.

Auerbach, Hellmuth, 'Die europäische Wende der französischen Deutschlandpolitik 1947/48', in Herbst, Bührer and Sowade (eds.), *Vom Marshallplan zur EWG*, 577–91.

Bacharan-Gressel, Nicole, 'Les Organisations et les associations pro-européennes', in Berstein, Mayeur and Milza (eds.), *Le MRP*, 41–66.

Badel, Laurence, 'Le Quai d'Orsay, les associations privées et l'Europe (1925–1932)', in René Girault and Gérard Bossuat (eds.), *Europe brisée, Europe retrouvée. Nouvelles réflexions sur l'unité européenne au XXe siècle*, Paris: Publications de la Sorbonne, 1994, 109–31.

Ball, Stuart, 'The Politics of Appeasement: the Fall of the Duchess of Atholl and the Kinross and West Perth By-election, December 1938', *The Scottish Historical Review* 64 (1990), 49–83.

Ballof, J. Dominica, 'Christine Teusch (1888–1968)', in Morsey (ed.), *Zeitgeschichte in Lebensbildern*, vol. II, 202–13.

Bariéty, Jacques, 'La Décision de réarmer l'Allemagne, l'échec de la Communauté Européenne de Défense et les accords de Paris du 23 octobre 1954 vus du côté français', *Revue belge de philologie et d'histoire* 71 (1993), 354–83.

'Le "Pacte Briand-Kellogg de renonciation à la guerre" de 1928', in Bariéty and Fleury (eds.), *Mouvements*, 355–67.

Baumgartner, Jean-Jacques, 'La C. D. U. et les autres partis démocrates-chrétiens', in Alfred Grosser (ed.), *Les Relations internationales de l'Allemagne occidentale*, Paris: Colin, 1956, 137–52.

Becker, Winfried, 'The Emergence and Development of Christian Democratic Parties in Western Europe', in Lamberts (ed.), *Christian Democracy*, 109–20.

Bell, Philip M. H., 'British Plans for European Union 1939–45. II: Other Contributions 1939–41', in Lipgens (ed.), *Plans for European Union*, 156–204.

Benz, Hartmut, 'Der Peterspfennig im Pontifikat Pius IX. Initiativen zur Unterstützung des Papsttums (1859–1878)', *Römische Quartalschrift* 90 (1995), 90–109.

Berger, Françoise, 'Les Sidérurgistes français et allemands face à l'Europe: convergences et divergences de conception et d'intérêts 1932–1952', *Journal of European Integration History* 3 (1997), 35–52.

Berger, Stefan, 'Internationalismus als Lippenbekenntnis? Überlegungen zur Kooperation sozialdemokratischer Parteien in der Zwischenkriegszeit', in Mittag (ed.), *Politische Parteien*, 197–214.

Berstein, Serge, 'French Power as Seen by the Political Parties after World War II', in Becker and Knipping (eds.), *Power in Europe?*, 163–83.

Béthouart, Bruno, 'La France, Robert Schuman et l'Europe', *Historisch-Politische Mitteilungen* 7 (1999), 197–217.

Binder, Dieter A., '"Rescuing the Christian Occident" and "Europe in Us": The People's Party in Austria', in Gehler and Kaiser (eds.), *Christian Democracy*, 139–54.

Bluhm, Gesa, 'Vertrauensarbeit. Deutsch-französische Beziehungen nach 1945', in Ute Frevert (ed.), *Vertrauen. Historische Annäherungen*, Göttingen: Vandenhoeck & Ruprecht, 2003, 365–93.

Bock, Hans-Manfred, 'Kulturelle Eliten in den deutsch-französischen Gesellschaftsbeziehungen der Zwischenkriegszeit', in Rainer Hudemann and Georges-Henri Soutou (eds.), *Eliten in Deutschland und Frankreich im 19. und 20. Jahrhundert. Strukturen und Beziehungen*, vol. I, Munich: Oldenbourg, 1994, 73–91.

Börzel, Tanja, 'What's So Special about Policy Networks? An Exploration of the Concept and Its Usefulness in Studying European Governance', *European Integration online Papers* (EIoP) 1–16 (1997): http://eiop.or.at/eiop/texte/ 1997-016a.htm. Accessed 1 February 2007.

Bosmans, Jac, 'Das Ringen um Europa. Die Christdemokraten der Niederlande und Deutschlands in den "Nouvelles Équipes Internationales" (1947–1965)', in Jac Bosmans (ed.), *Europagedanke, Europabewegung und Europapolitik in den Niederlanden und Deutschland seit dem Ersten Weltkrieg*, Münster: LIT, 1996, 123–48.

'The Primacy of Domestic Politics: Christian Democracy in the Netherlands', in Gehler and Kaiser (eds.), *Christian Democracy*, 54–66.

Bossuat, Gérard, 'La Vraie Nature de la politique européenne de la France (1950–1957)', in Trausch (ed.), *Die Europäische Integration*, 191–230.

Boyer, John W., 'Catholics, Christians and the Challenges of Democracy: The Heritage of the Nineteenth Century', in Kaiser and Wohnout (eds.), *Political Catholicism*, 7–45.

Brandes, Detlef, 'Confederation Plans in Eastern Europe during World War II', in Dumoulin (ed.), *Wartime Plans*, 83–94.

Brelie-Lewien, Doris von der, 'Abendland und Sozialismus. Zur Kontinuität politisch-kultureller Denkhaltungen im Katholizismus von der Weimarer Republik zur frühen Nachkriegszeit', in Detlef Lehnert and Klaus Megerle (eds.), *Politische Teilkulturen zwischen Integration und Polarisierung. Zur politischen Kultur der Weimarer Republik*, Opladen: Westdeutscher Verlag, 1990, 188–218.

Brunet, Jean-Paul, 'Le MRP et la construction européenne 1955–1957', in Berstein, Mayeur and Milza (eds.), *Le MRP*, 233–49.

Buchanan, Tom, 'Great Britain', in Buchanan and Conway (eds.), *Political Catholicism*, 248–74.

Bührer, Werner, 'Agricultural Pressure Groups and International Politics. The German Example', in Griffiths and Girvin (eds.), *The Green Pool*, 77–90.

Burgess, Michael, 'Political Catholicism, European Unity and the Rise of Christian Democracy', in Stirk and Stirk (eds.), *Making the New Europe*, 142–55.

Chenaux, Philippe, 'Bijdrage tot de internationale christen-democratie', in Wilfried Dewachter *et al.* (eds.), *Tussen staat en maatschapsij 1945–1995. Christen-democratie in België*, Tielt: Lannoo, 251–61.

'Der Vatikan und die Entstehung der Europäischen Gemeinschaft', in Greschat and Loth (eds.), *Die Christen*, 97–124.

'Les Démocrates-chrétiens au niveau de l'Union Européenne', in Lamberts (ed.), *Christian Democracy*, 449–58.

'L'Europe des Catholiques: principes et projets', in Dumoulin (ed.), *Wartime Plans*, 199–213.

'Occidente, Cristianità, Europa. Un studio semantico', in Canavero and Durand (eds.), *Il fattore religioso*, 41–53.

Clark, Christopher, 'The New Catholicism and the European Culture Wars', in Clark and Kaiser (eds.), *Culture Wars*, 11–46.

Conway, Martin, 'Belgium', in Buchanan and Conway (eds.), *Political Catholicism*, 187–218.

'Catholic Politics or Christian Democracy? The Evolution of Inter-War Political Catholicism', in Kaiser and Wohnout (eds.), *Political Catholicism*, 235–51.

'Introduction', in Buchanan and Conway (eds.), *Political Catholicism*, 1–33.

'Legacies of Exile: The Exile Governments in London during World War II and the Politics of Postwar Europe', in Conway and Gotovitch (eds.), *Europe in Exile*, 255–74.

'The Age of Christian Democracy. The Frontiers of Success and Failure', in Kselman and Buttigieg (eds.), *European Christian Democracy*, 2003, 43–67.

'The Rise and Fall of Western Europe's Democratic Age 1945–1973', *Contemporary European History* 13 (2004), 67–88.

Dechert, Charles, 'The Christian Democrat "International"', *Orbis. A Quarterly Journal of World Affairs*, 11 (1967), 106–27.

Delbreil, Jean-Claude, 'Christian Democracy and Centrism: The Popular Democratic Party in France', in Kaiser and Wohnout (eds.), *Political Catholicism*, 116–35.

'Le MRP et la construction européenne: résultats, interprétation et conclusion d'une enquête écrite et orale', in Berstein, Mayeur and Milza (eds.), *Le MRP*, 309–63.

Delwit, Pascal, 'Démocraties chrétiennes et conservatismes: convergences subies ou volontaires?', in Pascal Delwit (ed.), *Démocraties chrétiennes et conservatismes en Europe. Une nouvelle convergence?*, Brussels: Éditions de l'Université de Bruxelles, 2003, 7–24.

De Rosa, Gabriele, 'I problemi dell'organizzazione internazionale del pensiero di Luigi Sturzo', in De Rosa (ed.), *Luigi Sturzo e la democrazia europea*, 5–25.

Doering-Manteuffel, Anselm, 'Rheinischer Katholik im Kalten Krieg. Das "christliche Europa" in der Weltsicht Konrad Adenauers', in Greschat and Loth (eds.), *Die Christen*, 237–46.

Donald, Moira, 'Workers of the World Unite? Exploring the Enigma of the Second International', in Martin H. Geyer and Johannes Paulmann (eds.),

The Mechanics of Internationalism, Oxford: Oxford University Press, 2001, 177–203

Dreyfus, François-Georges, 'Les Réticences du MRP face à l'Europe 1944–1948', in Berstein, Mayeur and Milza (eds.), *Le MRP*, 115–30.

Ducerf, Laurent, 'Die christliche Demokratie in Frankreich seit 1945. Eine histor-iographische Bilanz', *Historisch-politische Mitteilungen* 2 (1995), 313–23.

'François de Menthon, un démocrate chrétien au service de l'Europe (1948–1958)', in *La Savoie dans l'Europe*, Moûtiers-Tarentaise: Mémoires et documents de l'Academie de la Val d'Isère, 2002, 295–316.

Dumoulin, Michel, 'La Belgique et le Plan Briand: l'annonce de réformes de structures au plan européen', in Fleury and Jílek (eds.), *Le Plan Briand*, 93–102.

'La Belgique et les débuts du Plan Schuman (mai 1950–février 1952)', in Schwabe (ed.), *Die Anfänge*, 271–84.

'The Socio-economic Impact of Christian Democracy in Western Europe', in Lamberts (ed.), *Christian Democracy*, 369–74.

Durand, Jean-Dominique, 'Les Rapports entre le MRP et la démocratie chréti-enne italienne 1945–1955', in Berstein, Mayeur and Milza (eds.), *Le MRP*, 251–72.

Du Réau, Elisabeth, 'Du Plan Schuman au Plan Pleven. La France, la construction europénne et l'insertion de l'Allemagne fédérale dans le système occidental (1948–1950)', in Saki Dockrill *et al.* (eds.), *L'Europe de l'Est et de l'Ouest dans la Guerre froide 1948–1953*, Paris: Presses de l'Université de Paris-Sorbonne, 2002, 185–98.

'Le MRP et la naissance du Conseil de l'Europe', in Berstein, Mayeur and Milza (eds.), *Le MRP*, 67–85.

'Pierre Mendès France, la création de l'Union européenne occidentale (UEO) et son devenir', in Girault (ed.), *Pierre Mendès France*, 25–38.

Düwell, Kurt, 'Karl Arnold. Überzeugter Föderalist zwischen gesamtdeutschen Zielen und europäischen Visionen', in Präsident des Landtags Nordrhein-Westfalen (ed.), *Karl Arnold: Nordrhein-Westfalens Ministerpräsident 1947–1956*, Düsseldorf: Landtag Nordrhein-Westfalen, 2001, 91–112.

Ebertz, Michael N., 'Herrschaft in der Kirche. Hierarchie, Tradition und Charisma im 19. Jahrhundert', in Kurt Gabriel and Franz-Xaver Kaufmann (eds.), *Zur Soziologie des Katholizismus*, Mainz: Matthias-Grünewald-Verlag, 1980, 89–111.

Elvert, Jürgen, 'A Microcosm of Society or the Key to a Majority in the Reichstag? The Centre Party in Germany,' in Kaiser and Wohnout (eds.), *Political Catholicism*, 46–64.

'Heinrich von Brentano. Vordenker einer Konstitutionalisierung Europas', in Roland Koch (ed.), *Heinrich von Brentano. Ein Wegbereiter der europäischen Integration*, Munich: Oldenbourg, 2004, 159–81.

Farrell-Vinay, Giovanna, 'Sturzo e l'Inghilterra', in *Universalità*, 181–223.

Fazekas, Csaba, 'Collaborating with Horthy: Political Catholicism and Christian Political Organizations in Hungary', in Kaiser and Wohnout (eds.), *Political Catholicism*, 195–216.

Fetzer, Thomas, 'Zivilgesellschaftliche Organisationen in Europa nach 1945: Katalysatoren für die Herausbildung transnationaler Identitäten?', in Hartmut Kaelble *et al.* (eds.), *Transnationale Öffentlichkeiten und Identitäten im 20. Jahrhundert*, Frankfurt, New York: Campus, 2002, 355–92.

Flint, James, '"Must God Go Fascist?" English Catholic Opinion and the Spanish Civil War', *Church History* 56 (1987), 364–74.

Forgacs, David, 'Sturzo e la cultura politica inglese', in De Rosa (ed.), *Luigi Sturzo e la democrazia europea*, 342–7.

Frank, Robert, 'The Meanings of Europe in French National Discourse: A French Europe or an Europeanized France?', in Mikael af Malmborg and Bo Stråth (eds), *The Meaning of Europe*, Oxford, New York: Berg, 2002, 311–26.

Gallagher, Tom, 'Portugal', in Buchanan and Conway (eds.), *Political Catholicism*, 129–55.

Gassert, Philipp, 'Personalities and the Politics of European Integration: Kurt Georg Kiesinger and the Departure of Walter Hallstein, 1966/67', in Loth (ed.), *Crises and Compromises*, 265–84.

'"Wir müssen bewahren, was wir geschaffen haben, auch über eine kritische Zeit hinweg" – Kurt Georg Kiesinger, Frankreich und das europäische Projekt', in König and Schulz (eds.), *Die Bundesrepublik Deutschland*, 147–66.

Gehler, Michael, '"Politisch unabhängig", aber "ideologisch eindeutig europäisch". Die ÖVP, die Vereinigung christlicher Volksparteien (NEI) und die Anfänge der europäischen Integration 1947–1960', in Michael Gehler and Rolf Steininger (eds.), *Österreich und die europäische Integration 1945–1993. Aspekte einer wechselvollen Entwicklung*, Vienna, Cologne, Weimar: Böhlau, 1993, 291–326.

Gehler, Michael and Wolfram Kaiser, 'A Study in Ambivalence: Austria and European Integration 1945–95', *Contemporary European History* 6 (1997), 75–99.

'Transnationalism and Early European integration: The NEI and the Geneva Circle 1947–57', *The Historical Journal* 44 (2001), 773–98.

Gerard, Emmanuel, 'Religion, Class and Language: The Catholic Party in Belgium', in Kaiser and Wohnout (eds.), *Political Catholicism*, 94–115.

'Uit de voorgeschiedenis van het ACW: het einde van de Volksbond en de oprichting van het Democratisch Blok (1918–1921)', *De Gids op Maatschappelijk Gebied* 69 (1978), 501–30.

Gerbet, Pierre, 'Les Origines du Plan Schuman: le choix de la méthode communautaire par le gouvernement français', in Poidevin (ed.), *Histoire des débuts*, 199–222.

'Les Partis politiques et les Communautés européenes sous la Quatrième République', in Joël Rideau *et al.* (eds.), *La France et les Communautés européenes*, Paris: Fondations Nationales de Sciences Politiques, 1975, 77–99.

Geyer, Michael, 'Germany, or, The Twentieth Century as History', *South Atlantic Quarterly* 96 (1997), 663–702.

Girault, René, 'On the Power of Old and New Europe', in Ennio di Nolfo (ed.), *Power in Europe? vol. II: Great Britain, France, Germany and Italy and the*

Origins of the EEC, 1952–1957, Berlin, New York: Walter de Gruyter, 1992, 553–61.

'The French Decision-Makers and their Perception of French Power in 1948', in Becker and Knipping (eds.), *Power in Europe?*, 47–65.

Gisch, Heribert, 'Die europäischen Christdemokraten (NEI)', in Wilfried Loth (ed.), *Die Anfänge der europäischen Integration 1945–1950*, Bonn: Europa Union Verlag, 229–36.

Glees, Anthony, 'Das deutsche politische Exil in London 1939–1945', in Hirschfeld (ed.), *Exil in Großbritannien*, 62–79.

Gotovitch, José, 'Views of Belgian Exiles on the Postwar Order in Europe', in Lipgens (ed.), *Plans for European Union*, 414–50.

Griffiths, Richard T., 'Creating a High Cost Club: The Green Pool Negotiations: 1953–1955', in Griffiths and Girvin (eds.), *The Green Pool*, 21–50.

'The Common Market', in Griffiths (ed.), *The Netherlands*, 183–208.

'The Schuman Plan', in Griffiths (ed.), *The Netherlands*, 113–35.

Griffiths, Richard T. and Fernando Guirao, 'The First Proposals for a European Agricultural Community: the Pflimlin and Mansholt Plans', in Griffiths and Girvin (eds.), *The Green Pool*, 1–19.

Grosbois, Thierry and Yves Stelandre, 'Belgian Decision-Makers and European Unity, 1945–63', in Anne Deighton (ed.), *Building Postwar Europe. National Decision-Makers and European Institutions, 1948–63*, Basingstoke: Macmillan, 1995, 127–40.

Gross, Feliks, 'Views of East European Transnational Groups on the Postwar Order in Europe', in Lipgens (ed.), *Plans for European Union*, 754–85.

Guasconi, Maria Eleonora, 'The International Confederation of Free Trade Unions' Policy Towards the European Integration Process from 1950 to 1957', in Bussière and Dumoulin (eds.), *Milieux économiques*, 359–70.

Guillen, Pierre, 'Le MRP et l'union économique de l'Europe 1947–mai 1950', in Berstein, Mayeur and Milza (eds.), *Le MRP*, 131–47.

'Le Projet d'union économique entre la France, l'Italie et le Benelux', in Poidevin (ed.), *Histoire des débuts*, 143–64.

'Les Chefs militaires français, le réarmement de l'Allemagne et la CED', *Revue d'histoire de la deuxième guerre mondiale* 33 (1983), 3–33.

'Mendès France et l'Allemagne', in Girault (ed.), *Pierre Mendès France*, 39–54.

'Plans by Exiles from France', in Lipgens (ed.), *Plans for European Union*, 279–352.

'The Role of the Soviet Union as a Factor in the French Debates on the European Defence Community', *Journal of European Integration History* 2 (1996), 71–83.

Guiotto, Maddalena, 'Luigi Sturzo e il mondo politico e intellettuale della Germania di Weimar', in *Universalità*, 443–65.

Haas, Peter M., 'Introduction: Epistemic Communities and International Policy Co-ordination', *International Organization* 46 (1992), 1–35.

Hagspiel, Hermann, 'Die Auffassung und die Benützung von Konzepten der "Neuen Diplomatie" in der deutsch-französischen Verständigungspolitik (1924–1928)', in Bariéty and Fleury (eds.), *Mouvements*, 337–53.

Hanschmidt, Alwin, 'Anläufe zu internationaler Kooperation radikaler und liberaler Parteien Europas 1919–1923', *Francia* 16 (1989), 35–48.

'Eine christlich-demokratische "Internationale" zwischen den Weltkriegen. Das "Secrétariat International des Partis Démocratiques d'Inspiration Chrétienne" in Paris', in Winfried Becker and Rudolf Morsey (eds.), *Christliche Demokratie in Europa. Grundlagen und Entwicklungen seit dem 19. Jahrhundert*, Cologne, Vienna: Böhlau, 1988, 153–88.

Harryvan, Anjo G. and Albert E. Kersten, 'The Netherlands, Benelux and the Rélance Européenne 1954–1955', in Serra (ed.), *Il rilancio*, 125–57.

Hartmann, Jürgen, 'Strukturprobleme christdemokratischer Parteien in Europa', *Zeitschrift für Politik* 25 (1978), 175–93.

Haushefer, Heinz, 'Die internationale Organisation der Bauernparteien', in Heinz Gollwitzer (ed.), *Europäische Bauernparteien im 20. Jahrhundert*, Stuttgart: Fischer, 1977, 668–90.

Häussermann, Ekkhard, 'Konrad Adenauer und die Presse vor 1933', in Hugo Stehkämper (ed.), *Konrad Adenauer. Oberbürgermeister von Köln*, Cologne: Rheinland-Verlag, 1976, 207–47.

Heard-Lauréote, Karen, 'Transnational Networks. Informal Governance in the European Political Space', in Kaiser and Starie (eds.), *Transnational European Union*, 36–60.

Hendriks, Gisela, 'The Creation of the Common Agricultural Policy', in Deighton and Milward (eds.), *Widening, Deepening and Acceleration*, 139–50.

Henzler, Christoph, Josef Müller contra Fritz Schäffer – Das Ringen um die Parteiführung 1945–1948', in Hanns Seidel-Stiftung (ed.), *Josef Müller. Der erste Vorsitzende der CSU*, Grünwald: Atwerb-Verlag, 1998, 95–121.

Hirst, Paul, 'Democracy and Governance', in Jon Pierre (ed.), *Debating Governance*, Oxford: Oxford University Press, 2000, 13–35.

Hitchcock, William I., 'France, the Western Alliance, and the Origins of the Schuman Plan, 1948–1950', *Diplomatic History* 21 (1997), 603–30.

Hochgeschwender, Michael, 'A Battle of Ideas: The Congress for Cultural Freedom (CCF) in Britain, Italy, France, and West Germany', in Dominik Geppert (ed.), *The Postwar Challenge. Cultural, Social and Political Change in Western Europe, 1945–58*, Oxford: Oxford University Press, 2003, 319–38.

Hoffmann, Stanley, 'Obstinate or Obsolete? The Fate of the Nation State and the Case of Western Europe', *Daedalus* 95 (1966), 862–915.

'Paradoxes of the French Political Community', in Stanley Hoffmann *et al.*, *In Search of France*, 2nd edn, Cambridge, Mass.: Harvard University Press, 1967 [1963], 1–117.

Holl, Karl, 'Europapolitik im Vorfeld der deutschen Regierungspolitik. Zur Tätigkeit proeuropäischer Organisationen in der Weimarer Republik', *Historische Zeitschrift* 219 (1974), 33–94.

Hollstein, Jürgen, 'Zur Geschichte christlich-demokratischer Zusammenarbeit in Europa: Die "Nouvelles Équipes Internationales" (NEI)', *Libertas* 23 (1989), 82–117.

Hrbek, Rudolf, 'The German Social Democratic Party', in Griffiths (ed.), *Socialist Parties*, 63–77.

Hüser, Judith, 'Frankreich und die Abstimmung vom 23. Oktober 1955: innen- und außenpolitische Problemstellungen zur Lösung der Saarfrage', in Rainer Hudemann (ed.), *Die Saar 1945–1955: ein Problem der europäischen Geschichte*, 2nd edn, Munich: Oldenbourg, 1995, 359–79.

Ignesti, Guiseppe, 'Momenti del popolarismo in esilio', in Pietro Scoppola and Francesco Traniello (eds.), *I cattolici tra fascismo e democrazia*, Bologna: il Mulino, 1975, 75–183.

Jansen, Thomas, 'Die Europäische Volkspartei (EVP) 1976–1995', in Veen (ed.), *Christlich-demokratische und konservative Parteien*, 459–540.

'The Dilemma for Christian Democracy. Historical Identity and/or Political Expediency: Opening the Door to Conservatism', in Lamberts (ed.), *Christian Democracy*, 459–72.

'The Integration of the Conservatives into the European People's Party', in Bell and Lord (eds.), *Transnational Parties*, 102–16.

Johansson, Karl Magnus, 'Another Road to Maastricht: the Christian Democrat Coalition and the Quest for European Union', *Journal of Common Market Studies* 40 (2002), 871–93.

'European People's Party', in Johansson and Zervakis (eds.), *European Political Parties*, 51–80.

'Party Elites in Multilevel Europe: The Christian Democrats and the Single European Act', *Party Politics* 8 (2002), 423–39.

'The Transnationalization of Party Politics', in Bell and Lord (eds.), *Transnational Parties*, 28–50.

Johansson, Karl Magnus and Peter Zervakis, 'Historical-Institutional Framework', in Johansson and Zervakis (eds.), *European Political Parties*, 11–23.

Jones, Erik, 'Comment on Conway', *Contemporary European History* 13 (2004), 89–95.

Kaiser, Wolfram, 'Christian Democracy in Twentieth-century Europe', *Journal of Contemporary History* 39 (2004), 127–138.

'"Clericalism – That Is Our Enemy!" European Anticlericalism and the Culture Wars', in Clark and Kaiser (eds.), *Culture Wars*, 47–76.

'Cooperation of European Catholic Politicians in Exile in Britain and the United States during World War II', *Journal of Contemporary History* 35 (2000), 439–65.

'From State to Society? The Historiography of European Integration', in Michelle Cini and Angela K. Bourne (eds.), *Palgrave Advances in European Union Studies*, Basingstoke: Palgrave, 2006, 190–208.

'Transnational Western Europe since 1945: Integration as Political Society Formation', in Kaiser and Starie (eds.), *Transnational European Union*, 17–35.

'Trigger-happy Protestant Materialists? The European Christian Democrats and the United States', in Marc Trachtenberg (ed.), *Between Empire and*

Alliance. America and Europe during the Cold War, Lanham: Rowman & Littlefield Publishers, 2003, 63–82.

'Quo vadis, Europa? Die deutsche Wirtschaft und der Gemeinsame Markt 1958–1963', in Rudolf Hrbek and Volker Schwarz (eds.), *40 Jahre Römische Verträge: Der deutsche Beitrag*, Baden-Baden: Nomos, 1998, 206–10.

'"Überzeugter Katholik und CDU-Wähler": Zur Historiographie der Integrationsgeschichte am Beispiel Walter Lipgens', *Journal of European Integration History* 8 (2002), 119–28.

Keating, Joan, 'Looking to Europe: Roman Catholics and Christian Democracy in 1930s Britain', *European History Quarterly* 26 (1996), 57–79.

'The British Experience: Christian Democrats without a Party', in David Hanley (ed.), *Christian Democracy in Europe. A Comparative Perspective*, London: Pinter, 1994, 168–81.

Keller, Thomas, 'Katholische Europakonzeptionen in den deutsch-französischen Beziehungen', in Hans Manfred Bock, Reinhart Meyer-Kalkus and Michel Trebitsch (eds.), *Entre Locarno et Vichy. Les relations culturelles franco-allemandes dans les années 1930*, vol. I, Paris: CNRS Éditions, 1993, 219–39.

Kersten, Albert, 'A Welcome Surprise? The Netherlands and the Schuman Plan Negotiations', in Schwabe (ed.), *Die Anfänge*, 285–304.

Kettenacker, Lothar, 'Der Einfluß der deutschen Emigranten auf die britische Kriegszielpolitik', in Hirschfeld (ed.), *Exil in Großbritannien*, 80–105.

Khol, Andreas and Alexis Wintoniak, 'Die Europäische Demokratische Union (EDU)', in Veen (ed.), *Christlich-demokratische und konservative Parteien*, 407–58.

Klemann, Hein A. M., 'The Dutch Reaction to the Briand Plan', in Fleury and Jílek (eds.), *Le Plan Briand*, 149–69.

Klotzbach, Kurt, 'Die deutsche Sozialdemokratie und der Schuman-Plan', in Schwabe (ed.), *Die Anfänge*, 333–44.

Knudsen, Ann-Christina Lauring, 'Creating the Common Agricultural Policy. Story of Cereals Prices', in Loth (ed.), *Crises and Compromises*, 131–54.

Kohler[-Koch], Beate und Barbara Myrzik, 'Transnational Party Links', in Roger Morgan and Stefano Silvestri (eds.), *Moderates and Conservatives in Western Europe. Political Parties, the European Community and the Atlantic Alliance*, London: Heinemann, 1982, 193–223.

Kohler-Koch, Beate and Berthold Rittberger, 'Review Article: The "Governance Turn" in EU Studies', *Journal of Common Market Studies* 44 (2006), 27–49.

Krüger, Peter, 'Briand, Stresemann und der Völkerbund. Männer, Mächte, Institutionen – und das Schicksal', in Knipping and Weisenfeld (eds.), *Eine ungewöhnliche Geschichte*, 85–100.

'Der abgebrochene Dialog: die deutschen Reaktionen auf die Europavorstellungen Briands 1929', in Fleury and Jílek (eds.), *Le Plan Briand*, 289–306.

Kuk, Leszek, 'A Powerful Catholic Church, Unstable State and Authoritarian Political Regime: The Christian Democratic Party in Poland', in Kaiser and Wohnout (eds.), *Political Catholicism*, 150–71.

Küsters, Hanns Jürgen, 'Der Streit um Kompetenzen und Konzeptionen deutscher Europapolitik 1949–1958', in Herbst, Bührer and Sowade (eds.), *Vom Marshallplan zur EWG*, 335–74.

'Die Verhandlungen über das institutionelle System zur Gründung der Europäischen Gemeinschaft für Kohle und Stahl', in Schwabe (ed.), *Die Anfänge*, 73–102.

'Konrad Adenauer und die Idee einer wirtschaftlichen Verflechtung mit Frankreich', in Andreas Wilkens (ed.), *Die deutsch-französischen Wirtschaftsbeziehungen 1945–1960 / Les Relations économiques franco-allemandes 1945–1960*, Sigmaringen: Jan Thorbecke, 1997, 63–84.

'The Federal Republic of Germany and the EEC-Treaty', in Serra (ed.), *Il rilancio*, 495–524.

'Zwischen Vormarsch und Schlaganfall. Das Projekt der Europäischen Politischen Gemeinschaft und die Haltung der Bundesrepublik Deutschland (1951–1954)', in Trausch (ed.), *Die Europäische Integration*, 259–93.

Lamberts, Emiel, 'Christian Democracy in the European Union (1945–1995)', in Lamberts (ed.), *Christian Democracy*, 473–81.

'Conclusion. The Black International and Its Influence on European Catholicism (1870–1878)', in Lamberts (ed.), *The Black International*, 465–80.

'Introduction', in Lamberts (ed.), *The Black International*, 7–12.

'L'Internationale noire. Une organisation secrète au service du Sainte-Siège', in Lamberts (ed.), *The Black International*, 15–101.

'The Influence of Christian Democracy on Political Structures in Western Europe', in Lamberts (ed.), *Christian Democracy*, 282–92.

'The Zenith of Christian Democracy: The Christelijke Volkspartij/Parti Social Chrétien in Belgium', in Gehler and Kaiser (eds.), *Christian Democracy*, 67–84.

Landuyt, Ariane, 'Ideas of Italian Exiles on the Postwar Order in Europe', in Lipgens (ed.), *Plans for European Union*, 491–554.

Lappenküper, Ulrich, 'Der Schuman-Plan', *Vierteljahrshefte für Zeitgeschichte* 42 (1994), 403–45.

Latour, Francis, 'La Voix de Benoît XV contre le "suicide de l'Europe" pendant la Grande Guerre', in Cholvy (ed.), *L'Europe*, 19–32.

Laurent, Pierre-Henri, 'Reality not Rhetoric: Belgian-Dutch Diplomacy in Wartime London, 1940–44', in Stirk and Stirk (eds.), *Making the New Europe*, 133–41.

Letamendia, Pierre, 'La Place des problèmes européens dans la vie interne du parti sous la IVe République', in Berstein, Mayeur and Milza (eds.), *Le MRP*, 103–12.

Lieshout, R. H., M. L. L. Segers and A. M. van der Vleuten, 'De Gaulle, Moravcsik and *The Choice for Europe*. Soft Sources, Weak Evidence', *Journal of Cold War Studies* 6 (2004), 89–139.

Lipgens, Walter, 'Der Zusammenschluß Westeuropas. Leitlinien für den historischen Unterricht', *Geschichte in Wissenschaft und Unterricht* 34 (1983), 345–72.

'Plans of Other Transnational Groups for European Union', in Lipgens (ed.), *Plans for European Union*, 786–824.

'Transnational Contacts', in Lipgens (ed.), *Continental Plans for European Union*, 659–97.

'Views of Churches and other Christian Groups on the Postwar International Order', in Lipgens (ed.), *Plans for European Union*, 699–753.

Lönne, Karl-Egon, 'Germany', in Buchanan and Conway (eds.), *Political Catholicism*, 156–86.

Lord, Christopher, 'Introduction', in Bell and Lord (eds.), *Transnational Parties*, 1–9.

Loth, Wilfried, 'Adenauer's Final Western Choice, 1955–58', in Wilfried Loth (ed.), *Europe, Cold War and Coexistence 1953–1965*, London: Frank Cass, 2004, 23–33.

'Blockbildung und Entspannung. Strukturen des Ost-West-Konflikts 1953–1956', in Bruno Thoß and Hans-Erich Volkmann (eds.), *Zwischen Kaltem Krieg und Entspannung. Sicherheits- und Deutschlandpolitik der Bundesrepublik im Mächtesystem der Jahre 1953–1956*, Boppard: Boldt, 1988, 9–23.

'Deutsche Europa-Konzeptionen in der Gründungsphase der EWG', in Serra (ed.), *Il rilancio*, 585–602.

'Die Résistance und die Pläne zu europäischer Einigung 1940–1947', in Dumoulin (ed.), *Wartime Plans*, 47–56.

'German Conceptions of Europe during the Escalation of the East-West Conflict, 1945–1949', in Becker and Knipping (eds.), *Power in Europe?*, 517–36.

'The French Socialist Party, 1947–1954', in Griffiths (ed.), *Socialist Parties*, 25–42.

'Von der "Dritten Kraft" zur Westintegration. Deutsche Europa-Projekte in der Nachkriegszeit, in Franz Knipping and Klaus-Jürgen Müller (eds.), *Aus der Ohnmacht zur Bündnismacht. Das Machtproblem in der Bundesrepublik Deutschland 1945–1960*, Paderborn: Schöningh, 1995, 57–83.

'Walter Lipgens (1925–1984)', in Heinz Duchardt *et al.* (eds.), *Europa-Historiker. Ein biographisches Handbuch*, vol. I, Göttingen: Vandenhoeck & Ruprecht, 2006, 317–36.

Loughlin, John, 'French Personalist and Federalist Movements in the Interwar Period', in Stirk (ed.), *European Unity*, 188–200.

Lucardie, Paul, 'From Family Father to DJ: Christian Democratic Parties and Civil Society in Western Europe', in Lamberts (ed.), *Christian Democracy*, 210–21.

Luykx, Paul, 'The Netherlands', in Buchanan and Conway (eds.), *Political Catholicism*, 219–47.

Luykx, Theo, 'De rol van August De Schryver in het politieke leven tot en met de Tweede Wereldoorlog', in *Veertig jaar Belgische politiek. Liber amicorum aangeboden aan Minister van Staat A.E. De Schryver ter gelegenheid van zijn 70ste verjaardag*, Antwerp, Utrecht: Standaard, 1968, 121–211.

McMillan, James F., 'France', in Buchanan and Conway (eds.), *Political Catholicism*, 34–68.

Maimann, Helene, 'Views of Austrian Exiles on the Future of Europe', in Lipgens (ed.), *Plans for European Union*, 629–50.

Malgeri, Francesco, 'Alle origini del Partito Popolare Europeo', *Storia e Politica* 18 (1979), 285–310.

'Il popolarismo e la crisi della democrazia italiana: gli anni dell'esilio', in Campanini (ed.), *Francesco Luigi Ferrari*, 105–27.

'Sturzo e la democrazia cristiana nel Secondo Dopoguerra', in De Rosa (ed.), *Luigi Sturzo e la democrazia europea*, 166–82.

'Sturzo e la Spagna negli anni Trenta', in *Universalità*, 403–23.

Mans, G. M. V., 'Ideas of Netherlands Exiles on the Postwar International Order', in Lipgens (ed.), *Plans for European Union*, 451–75.

Marquand, David, 'Towards a Europe of the Parties', *The Political Quarterly* 49 (1978), 425–45.

Martin, Benjamin F., 'The Creation of the Action Libérale Populaire. An Example of Party Formation in Third Republic France', *French Historical Studies* 9 (1975–6), 660–89.

Masala, Carlo, 'Born for Government: The Democrazia Cristiana in Italy', in Gehler and Kaiser (eds.), *Christian Democracy*, 101–17.

Mayeur, Jean-Marie, 'La Démocratie d'inspiration chrétienne en France', in Lamberts (ed.), *Christian Democracy*, 79–92.

'Les Élites catholiques en France et en Allemagne de la fin du XIXème siècle à la fin de la deuxième guerre mondiale', in Louis Dupeux, Rainer Hudemann and Franz Knipping (eds.), *Eliten in Deutschland und Frankreich im 19. und 20. Jahrhundert. Strukturen und Beziehungen*, vol. II, Munich: Oldenbourg, 1996, 185–92.

McMillan, James F., 'France', in Buchanan and Conway (eds.), *Political Catholicism*, 34–68.

Melandri, Pierre and Maurice Vaïsse, 'France: From Powerlessness to the Search of Influence', in Becker and Knipping (eds.), *Power in Europe?*, 461–73.

Milward, Alan S., 'Conclusions: The Value of History', in Milward *et al.*, *The Frontier*, 182–201.

Milward, Alan S. and Vibeke Sørensen, 'Interdependence or Integration? A National Choice', in Milward *et al.*, *The Frontier*, 1–32.

Mioche, Philippe, 'Le Patronat de la sidérurgie française et le Plan Schuman en 1950–1952: les apparences d'un combat et la réalité d'une mutation', in Schwabe (ed.), *Die Anfänge*, 305–18.

Mitchell, Maria, 'Materialism and Secularism: CDU Politicians and National Socialism 1945–1949', *Journal of Modern History* 67 (1995), 278–308.

Mittag, Jürgen and Helga Grebing, 'Im Spannungsfeld von nationalstaatlicher Politik und internationaler Weltanschauung. Annäherung an die europäische Parteienkooperation vor dem Ersten Weltkrieg', in Mittag (ed.), *Politische Parteien*, 165–95.

Mommens, Thiery E. and Luc Minten, 'The Belgian Socialist Party', in Griffiths (ed.), *Socialist Parties*, 140–61.

Moravcsik, Andrew, 'De Gaulle Between Grain and Grandeur: The Political Economy of French EC Policy 1958–1970 (Part 1)', *Journal of Cold War Studies* 2 (2000), 3–43.

'De Gaulle Between Grain and Grandeur: The Political Economy of French EC Policy 1958–1970 (Part 2)', *Journal of Cold War Studies* 2 (2000), 4–68.

Morelli, Anne, 'Don Sturzo face à la guerre d'Espagne et spécialement au problème de la Catalogne et du Pays Basque', *Sociologia* 24 (1990), 15–37.

'Francesco Luigi Ferrari au sein du monde universitaire, journalistique et politique belge', in Campanini (ed.), *Francesco Luigi Ferrari*, 451–70.

Morsey, Rudolf, 'Helene Weber (1881–1962)', in Morsey (ed.), *Zeitgeschichte in Lebensbildern*, vol. III, 223–34.

Müller, Guido, 'Anticipated Exile of Catholic Democrats: The Secrétariat International des Partis Démocratiques d'Inspiration Chrétienne', in Kaiser and Wohnout (eds.), *Political Catholicism*, 252–64.

'"Außenpolitik ohne Eigenschaften?" Der russische Faktor in der deutsch-französischen Annäherung 1922/23–1932', in Ilja Mieck and Pierre Guillen (eds.), *Deutschland – Frankreich – Russland. Begegnungen und Konfrontationen*, Munich: Oldenbourg, 2000, 181–213.

'France and Germany after the Great War. Business Men, Intellectuals and Artists in Non-Governmental European Networks', in Jessica C.E. Gienow-Hecht and Frank Schumacher (eds.), *Culture and International History*, New York: Berghahn, 2003, 97–114.

'Gesellschaftsgeschichte und internationale Beziehungen: die deutsch-französische Verständigung nach dem Ersten Weltkrieg', in Guido Müller (ed.), *Deutschland und der Westen. Internationale Beziehungen im 20. Jahrhundert*, Stuttgart: Steiner, 1998, 49–64.

Müller, Guido und Vanessa Plichta, 'Zwischen Rhein und Donau. Abendländisches Denken zwischen deutsch-französischen Verständigungsinitiativen und konservativ-katholischen Integrationsmodellen 1923–1957', *Journal of European Integration History* 5 (1999), 17–47.

Müller, Josef, 'Die NEI und die Anfänge der Europäischen Gemeinschaft', in EVP-Fraktion (ed.), *Zur Geschichte*, 35–6.

Overesch, Manfred, 'Senior West German Politicians and their Perception of the German Situation in Europe 1945–1949', in Becker and Knipping (eds.), *Power in Europe?*, 117–34.

Papini, Roberto, 'Les Débuts des Nouvelles Équipes Internationales', in Portelli and Jansen (eds.), *La Démocratie chrétienne*, 31–40.

Pasture, Patrick, 'The Fist of the Dwarf. Formation, Organisation and Representation of the Christian Trade Unions as a European Pressure Group (1945–1958)', *Journal of European Integration History* 1 (1995), 5–26.

'Trade Unions as a Transnational Movement in the European Space 1955–65. Falling Short of Ambitions?', in Kaiser and Starie (eds.), *Transnational European Union*, 109–30.

Pelinka, Anton, 'European Christian Democracy in Comparison', in Gehler and Kaiser (eds.), *Christian Democracy*, 193–206.

Peterson, John C., 'Policy Networks', in Antje Wiener and Thomas Diez (eds.), *European Integration Theory*, Oxford: Oxford University Press, 2003, 117–35.

Pierson, Paul, 'The Path to European Integration: A Historical Institutional Analysis', *Comparative Political Studies* 29 (1996), 123–63.

Pinder, John, 'Federalism in Britain and Italy: Radicals and the English Liberal Tradition', in Stirk (ed.), *European Unity*, 201–23.

Pollard, Sidney, 'Italy', in Buchanan and Conway (eds.), *Political Catholicism*, 69–96.

Pridham, Geoffrey and Pippa Pridham, 'Transnational Parties in the European Community. II: The Development of European Party Federations', in Stanley Henig (ed.), *Political Parties in the European Community*, London: George Allen & Unwin, 1979, 278–98.

Pulzer, Peter, 'Nationalism and Internationalism in European Christian Democracy', in Gehler and Kaiser (eds.), *Christian Democracy*, 10–24.

Rasmussen, Morten, 'State Power and the acquis communautaire in the European Community of the early 1970s – an Institutional Analysis', in Jan van der Harst (ed.), *Beyond the Customs Union: The European Community's Quest for Completion, Deepening and Enlargement, 1969–1975*, Baden-Baden: Nomos, forthcoming.

Reytier, Marie-Emmanuelle, 'Die deutschen Katholiken und der Gedanke der europäischen Einigung 1945–1949. Wende oder Kontinuität?', *Jahrbuch für europäische Geschichte* 3 (2002), 163–84.

'L'Allemagne: les *Katholikentage*', in Durand (ed.), *Les Semaines*, 359–75.

Rittberger, Berthold, '"No Integration without Representation" European Integration, Parliamentary Democracy, and Two Forgotten Communities', *Journal of European Public Policy* 13 (2006), 1211–29.

Roes, Jan, 'A Historical Detour: The Roman Catholic State Party in the Netherlands', in Kaiser and Wohnout (eds.), *Political Catholicism*, 80–93.

Rölli-Alkemper, Lukas, 'Catholics between Emancipation and Integration: The Conservative People's Party in Switzerland', in Kaiser and Wohnout (eds.), *Political Catholicism*, 65–79.

Rogosch, Detlef, 'Sozialdemokratie zwischen nationaler Orientierung und Westintegration 1945–1957', in König and Schulz (eds.), *Die Bundesrepublik Deutschland*, 287–310.

Ross, Ronald J., 'Catholic Plight in the Kaiserreich: A Reappraisal', in Jack R. Dukes and Joachim Remak (eds.), *Another Germany. A Reconsideration of the Imperial Era*, Boulder, Colo.: Westview Press, 1988, 73–94.

Roth, François, 'Robert Schuman: du catholique lorrain à l'homme d'état européen, 1886–1963', in Cholvy (ed.), *L'Europe*, 113–35.

Schieder, Wolfgang, 'Kirche und Revolution. Sozialgeschichtliche Aspekte der Trierer Wallfahrt von 1844', *Archiv für Sozialgeschichte* 14 (1974), 419–54.

Schmiermann, Sjef, 'Prof. Dr. J. A. Veraart (1886–1955). Een recalcitrant katholiek democraat', *Jaarboek van het Katholiek Documentatie Centrum* 20 (1990), 122–42.

Schönwald, Matthias, 'Walter Hallstein and the "Empty Chair" Crisis 1965/66', in Loth (ed.), *Crises and Compromises*, 157–71.

Schreiner, Reinhard, 'La Politique européenne de la CDU relative à la France et au MRP des années 1945–1966', in Mayeur and Milza (eds.), *Le MRP*, 273–90.

Schroen, Michael, 'Die Christlich-Soziale Volkspartei Luxemburgs (CSV)', in Veen (ed.), *Christlich-demokratische und konservative Parteien*, 335–404.

Schwarz, Hans-Peter, 'Adenauer und Europa', *Vierteljahrshefte für Zeitgeschichte* 27 (1979), 471–523.

'Die Europäische Integration als Aufgabe der Zeitgeschichtsforschung', *Vierteljahrshefte für Zeitgeschichte* 31 (1983), 555–72.

'Die Strassburger Anfänge multilateraler Integrations-Historiographie', in Poidevin (ed.), *Histoire des débuts*, 447–57.

Seyfert, Michael, '"His Majesty's Most Loyal Internees": Die Internierung und Deportation deutscher und österreichischer Flüchtlinge als "enemy aliens". Historische, kulturelle und literarische Aspekte', in Hirschfeld (ed.), *Exil in Großbritannien*, 155–82.

Soutou, Georges-Henri, 'Deutschland, Frankreich und das System von Versailles. Strategien und Winkelzüge der Nachkriegs-Diplomatie', in Knipping and Weisenfeld (eds.), *Eine ungewöhnliche Geschichte*, 73–84.

'Georges Bidault et la construction européenne 1944–1954', in Berstein, Mayeur and Milza (eds.), *Le MRP*, 197–230.

'La France, l'Allemagne et les accords de Paris', *Relations Internationales* 52 (1987), 451–470.

'La Politique nucléaire de Pierre Mendès-France', *Relations Internationales* 59 (1989), 113–30.

'Le Général de Gaulle et le plan Fouchet d'Union Politique Européenne: un projet stratégique', in Deighton and Milward (eds.), *Widening, Deepening and Acceleration*, 55–71.

Suppan, Arnold, 'Catholic People's Parties in East Central Europe: The Bohemian Lands and Slovakia', in Kaiser and Wohnout (eds.), *Political Catholicism*, 217–34.

Terrenoire, Louis, 'Corporatism and Democracy', in People and Freedom Group (ed.), *For Democracy*, 185–209.

Thiemeyer, Guido, 'Sicco Mansholt and European Supranationalism', in Wilfried Loth (ed.), *La Gouvernance supranationale dans la construction européene*, Brussels: Bruylant, 2005, 39–53.

Trebitsch, Michel and Hans Manfred Bock, 'L'Image du voisin: opinion et rencontres', in Robert Frank, Laurent Gerrereau and Hans Joachim Neyer (eds.), *La Course au moderne. France et Allemagne dans l'Europe des années vingt, 1919–1933*, Paris: Musée d'histoire contemporaine de la Bibliothèque de documentation internationale contemporaine, 1992, 28–31.

Trinchese, Stefano, 'L'internazionale democratico-cristiana attraverso la corrispondenza di F. L. Ferrari', in *Universalità*, 339–58.

Uhlig, Ralph, 'Internationalismus in den zwanziger Jahren. Die Interparlamentarische Union', *Historische Mitteilungen der Ranke-Gesellschaft* 4 (1991), 89–100.

Varsori, Antonio, 'Alcide De Gasperi and the European Project', in Paul-F. Smets (ed.), *Les Pères de l'Europe: 50 ans après. Perspectives sur l'engagement européen*, Brussels : Bruylant, 2001, 105–22.

Verstraelen, Jules, 'Die internationale christliche Arbeiterbewegung', in S. Herman Scholl (ed.), *Katholische Arbeiterbewegung in Westeuropa*, Bonn: Eichholz-Verlag, 1966, 419–41.

Viaene, Vincent, 'A Brilliant Failure. Wladimir Czacki, the Legacy of the Geneva Committee and the Origins of Vatican Press Policy from Pius IX to Leo XIII', in Lamberts (ed.), *The Black International*, 231–56.

'The Roman Question. Catholic Mobilisation and Papal Diplomacy during the Pontificate of Pius IX (1846–1878)', in Lamberts (ed.), *The Black International*, 135–77.

Vincent, Mary, 'Spain', in Buchanan and Conway (eds.), *Political Catholicism*, 97–128.

Vogt, Martin, 'Die deutsche Haltung zum Briand-Plan im Sommer 1930: Hintergründe und politisches Umfeld der Europapolitik des Kabinetts Brüning', in Fleury and Jílek (eds.), *Le Plan Briand*, 307–29.

Voigt, Klaus, 'Ideas of German Exiles on the Postwar Order in Europe', in Lipgens (ed.), *Plans for European Union*, 555–628.

Weber, Christoph, 'Ultramontanismus als katholischer Fundamentalismus', in Wilfried Loth (ed.), *Deutscher Katholizismus im Umbruch zur Moderne*, Stuttgart: Kohlhammer, 1991, 20–45.

Welle, Klaus, 'Die Reform der Europäischen Volkspartei 1995–1999', in Veen (ed.), *Christlich-demokratische und konservative Parteien*, 541–66.

Wendt, Bernd-Jürgen, 'Europe between Power and Powerlessness', in Becker and Knipping (eds.), *Power in Europe?*, 539–53.

Werner, Michael and Bénédicte Zimmermann, 'Vergleich, Transfer, Verflechtung: der Ansatz der histoire croisée und die Herausforderung des Transnationalen', *Geschichte und Gesellschaft* 28 (2002), 607–36.

Wilkens, Andreas, 'L'Europe des ententes ou l'Europe de l'intégration? Les industries française et allemande et les débuts de la construction européenne (1948–1952)', in Bussière and Dumoulin (eds.), *Milieux économiques*, 267–83.

Wohnout, Helmut, 'Middle-class Governmental Party and Secular Arm of the Catholic Church: The Christian Socials in Austria', in Kaiser and Wohnout (eds.), *Political Catholicism*, 172–94.

Wurm, Clemens, 'Deutsche Frankreichpolitik und deutsch-französische Beziehungen in der Weimarer Republik 1923/24–1929: Politik, Kultur, Wirtschaft', in Klaus Schwabe and Francesca Schinzinger (eds.), *Deutschland und der Westen im 19. und 20. Jahrhundert*, vol. II: *Deutschland und Westeuropa*, Stuttgart: Franz Steiner, 1994, 137–157.

'Early European Integration as a Research Field: Perspectives, Debates, Problems', in Clemens Wurm (ed.), *Western Europe and Germany. The Beginnings of European Integration 1945–1960*, Oxford, Washington: Berg, 1995, 9–26.

Zamojski, Jan E., 'The Social History of Polish Exile (1939–1945). The Exile State and the Clandestine State: Society, Problems and Reflections', in Conway and Gotovitch (eds.), *Europe in Exile*, 183–211.

Zeender, John K., 'German Catholics and the Concept of an Inter-confessional Party 1900–1922', *Journal of Central European Affairs* 23 (1964), 425–39.

Zéraffa-Dray, Danièle, 'Le Mouvement républicain populaire et la Communauté européene de défense 1950–1954', in Berstein, Mayeur and Milza (eds.), *Le MRP*, 181–95.

Zwart, Rutger S., 'Christian Democracy and Political Order in the Netherlands', in Lamberts (ed.), *Christian Democracy*, 242–53.

Index

Schryver, August-Edmond de
attitudes to Britain 234
election as NEI president (1949) 202
exile 124, 126
and federalism 227
and ICDU 160
meeting with Soyeur (1946) 196
and NEI reform 204
and politicising European issue 243
Schuijt, W. J. 263
Schumacher, Kurt 220, 244
Schuman Plan 224
Schuman, Robert
and economic integration 117
entrepreneurial leadership 9
first meeting with Adenauer 212
as foreign minister 165
Lorraine as 'petite patrie' 190
official visit to Germany (1950) 239
PDP member 97
possible beatification 321
proposal for political authority for EDC 283
and Saar referendum 267
Schuman Plan 224
SIPDIC congress (1932) 107
and Vatican support for European
integration 181
on WEU 278
Schumann, Maurice 126, 160, 206, 211, 213, 239
Schwarz-Liebermann, Hans Albrecht 263
Second International 29
Sécretariat International des Partis
Démocratiques d'Inspiration Chrétienne
and Briand Plan (1929) 104
collective learning process 117
and corporatism 98
creation 86
and dissolution of PPI 100
and economic integration 117
and European economic cooperation 106
and family policy 98
and fascism 99
German boycott of SIPDIC congress (1931) 110
ideological cohesion 116
peace initiative (1938) 112
peace resolution (1926) 100
peace resolution (1931) 102
resolution for European 'common market'
(1932) 107
secularisation 306
Segers, Paul W. 65, 107
Seipel, Ignaz 41
Seitlinger, Jean 262
Semaines sociales (France) 19
Serrarens, P. J. S. 64, 90, 187, 194, 215, 234

Sforza, Carlo 122
Shuster, George N. 134, 143
Sieniewicz, Konrad 194
Sillon 26
Silverberg, Paul 227
Simon, Paul 88, 91, 97, 103, 107
Simondet, Henri 89, 102
Single European Act (1987) 317
Slovene People's Party 53, 59
social Catholicism 30
socialisation 241, 306, 321
Socialist International 198
social market economy 177
social partnership (Austria) 171
Sonnenschein, Carl 65, 77
Soyeur, Jules 193, 196, 201
Spaak, Paul-Henri 246, 268, 283
Spaak Report (1956) 294
Spears, Edward Louis 141
Spiecker, Carl 124, 162, 176, 200
Šrámek, Jan 145, 160
Steed, Henry Wickham 121, 140, 151
Stegerwald, Adam 25, 47, 64, 94
Stegerwald, Aloys 208
Stocky, Julius 102, 107, 108, 110
Strauß, Franz-Josef 286, 316
Sturzo, Luigi 34, 162
assessment of Franz von Papen 57
and Badoglio government 154
and British democracy 150
and British representation in SIPDIC 113
criticism of SIPDIC and anti-Semitic
persecutions in Germany 114
exile in Britain 121
formation of ICDU 144
manifesto *Devant la Crise Mondiale*
(1942) 149
meeting with Bidault (1946) 193
opposition to Austrian SIPDIC participation 113
participation in first SIPDIC congress 86
and postwar Germany 159
preparation of transnational party links 72
proposal for resolution for liberty (1928) 100
and Prussia 156
reform proposal for SIPDIC (1935) 114
SIPDIC and fascism 99
and SIPDIC peace resolution (1931) 103
and territorial disputes 156
visit to Paris (1925) 85
subsidiarity principle 170, 229, 308
Swiss Conservative People's Party 50, 165, 204
Syllabus errorum 14

Tariff Truce Conference (1930) 105
Taviani, Paolo Emilio 202, 233, 248, 273, 274

NEW STUDIES IN EUROPEAN HISTORY

Books in the series

Royalty and Diplomacy in Europe, 1890–1914
RODERICK R. MCLEAN

Catholic Revival in the Age of the Baroque
Religious Identity in Southwest Germany, 1550–1750
MARC R. FORSTER

Helmuth von Moltke and the Origins of the First World War
ANNIKA MOMBAUER

Peter the Great
The Struggle for Power, 1671–1725
PAUL BUSHKOVITCH

Fatherlands
State Building and Nationhood in Nineteenth-Century Germany
ABIGAIL GREEN

The French Second Empire
An Anatomy of Political Power
ROGER PRICE

Origins of the French Welfare State
The Struggle for Social Reform in France, 1914–1947
PAUL V. DUTTON

Ordinary Prussians
Brandenburg Junkers and Villagers, 1500–1840
WILLIAM W. HAGEN

Liberty and Locality in Revolutionary France
Six Villages Compared
PETER JONES

Vienna and Versailles
The Courts of Europe's Dynastic Rivals, 1550–1780
JEROEN DUINDAM

From *Reich* to State
The Rhineland in the Revolutionary Age, 1780–1830
MICHAEL ROWE

Re-Writing the French Revolutionary Tradition
ROBERT ALEXANDER

Provincial Power and Absolute Monarchy
JULIAN SWANN

People and Politics in France, 1848–1870
ROGER PRICE

Nobles and Nation in Central Europe
WILLIAM D. GODSEY, JR.

The Russian Roots of Nazism
White Emigrés and the Making of National Socialism, 1917–1945
MICHAEL KELLOGG

Technology and the Culture of Modernity in Britain and Germany, 1890–1945
BERNHARD RIEGER

The World Hitler Never Made
Alternate History and the Memory of Nazism
GAVRIEL ROSENFELD

Madness, Religion and the State in Early Modern Europe
A Bavarian Beacon
DAVID LEDERER

Facism's Mediterranean Empire: Italian Occupation During the Second
World War
DAVIDE RODOGNO

Family, Power and Community in Early Modern Spain
The Citizens of Granada, 1570–1739
JAMES CASEY

Popular Culture and the Public Sphere in the Rhineland, 1800–1850
JAMES M. BROPHY

Politics and the People in Revolutionary Russia
A Provincial History
SARAH BADCOCK

Carnal Commerce in Counter-Reformation Rome
TESSA STOREY

Christian Democracy and the Origins of European Union
WOLFRAM KAISER